HERVÉ RYSSEN

PLANETARIAN HOPES

OMNIA VERITAS.

Hervé Ryssen

Hervé Ryssen (France) is a historian and an exhaustive researcher of the Jewish intellectual world. He is the author of twelve books and several video documentaries on the Jewish question. In 2005, he published *Planetarian Hopes,* a book in which he demonstrates the religious origins of the globalist project. *Psychoanalysis of Judaism,* published in 2006, shows how intellectual Judaism displays all the symptoms of hysterical pathology. There is no "divine choice", but the manifestation of a disorder that has its origins in the practice of incest. Freud had patiently studied this question on the basis of what he observed in his own community.

France is home to one of the largest Jewish communities in the Diaspora, with a very intense cultural and intellectual life. Hervé Ryssen has been able to develop his extensive work on the basis of numerous historical and contemporary sources, both international and French.

Planetarian Hopes

Les espérances planétariennes, Levallois-Perret, *Baskerville, 2005.*

Translated and published by Omnia Veritas Limited

⊘MNIA VERITAS®

www.omnia-veritas.com

© Omnia Veritas Limited - Hervé Ryssen - 2023

Nota bene: All footnote references cited by the author in this book come from books consulted in three municipal libraries in Paris between 2003 and 2005.

The idea of a world without borders and of a finally unified humanity is certainly not new. What is new at the beginning of the third millennium is that, for the first time in their history, Westerners have the feeling that the whole of humanity has embarked on this path. The fall of the Berlin Wall in 1989 and the collapse of the Soviet bloc were undoubtedly important factors in this realisation of world unification and the acceleration of the process at the end of the 20th century. Indeed, it was during these subsequent years that what has been called "mundialisation or globalisation[1] " became the subject of recurrent debate. The triumph of democracy over communism seemed to have opened the door to a new era, to a "New World Order", and to prepare all nations for an inevitable planetarian merger.

The bipolar world, which had characterised the short 20th century (1914–1991), was temporarily giving way to a world dominated by the American "superpower", but above all democracy seemed to impose itself on all continents and offer humanity the guarantee of a better world, to such an extent that some already spoke of "The End of History": consumer society and trade would replace the imperialisms and the war instinct which had hitherto marked the destiny of humanity. In a renewed spirit of cooperation, nations would draw closer together and soon merge into a world republic, the only guarantor of universal peace.

However, the "End of History", as predicted in 1992 with the triumph of democracy, no longer seemed to be on the agenda after the fall of the two World Trade Center towers on 11 September 2001. But instead of halting the forward march of the democratic ideal, it seemed, on the contrary, that this spectacular event precipitated the course of history even further. The machine went haywire, and the Western

---

[1]The two terms are practically equivalent. In the French-speaking world the term "globalisation" is the more common one (Translator's note, hereafter).

democracies took advantage of the trauma to extend their influence and impose their will with renewed vigour. The United States imposed itself on the world through its diplomacy, its armed forces, its continuous hidden manoeuvres that invariably resulted in "great democratic revolutions" in poor countries, with red T-shirts for the crowd and global media triumph for the lucky winner, while European nations were rapidly dissolving into a large and increasingly multi-ethnic whole, with vague contours that prefigured what the world of tomorrow should be: without races and without borders.

The Westerners, who are pushing for the adoption of a democratic regime in all countries of the world, also insist on the absolute necessity of respect for minorities and the reception of refugees, to such an extent that democracy can only be conceived as a "multicultural, multi-ethnic and multiracial" whole. The planned fusion of the world's nations, as we can see, involves the establishment of "plural" societies within the framework of parliamentary democracy. The two concepts are now inseparable. This seems to be the assembly plan of these grandiose globalisation projects which, once again, are products of Western thought and will.

Yesterday's world, which we called "bipolar", was already primarily a Western vision. Many countries in Asia, Africa and South America had been affected by our ideological struggles and had had to position themselves on the side of Moscow or Washington, even though the vast majority of these populations had preserved their ancestral ways of life and had lived in a traditional way throughout the century, without having to choose between the Marxist system and the market economy. After the Second World War, it became customary to lump these countries together under the generic term "third world", in the sense of "third world[2]". And it was precisely this third world that was little concerned with the ideological disputes generated by Western thought. So let us avoid the sin of Westernism.

Is the concept of "globalisation" more justified today? The term is first and foremost an economic phenomenon. Certainly, the multiplication of economic exchanges, the development of a global financial capitalism, the relocation of companies and the emergence of new communication and information technologies have brought the economies of the world closer together and accentuated their

---

[2]The term changed its meaning and was later used to designate poor countries, which at the time were commonly referred to as "underdeveloped countries". In the 1990s, the more "politically correct" term "developing countries" or "countries of the South" was preferred.

interdependence. From this economic perspective, one can rightly speak of "globalisation". This seems to be the continuation of a long process that began in the 16th century, after the discovery of new continents, and continued with the westernisation of the world until the 19th century with the colonisation of Africa and Asia, but also with the settlement of North America and Oceania. The globalisation of ideas (Darwin, socialism, liberalism) had completed Europe's hegemony over the world before 1914, a hegemony that it would largely lose after two wars that had also become globalised.

However, we should not believe that the evolution of the world's economies towards greater unity is a regular, continuous and inevitably unstoppable process. Economists agree that the world is no more open today than it was before the First World War. In 1991, the relative level of capital exports was lower than in 1915[3]. As for multinationals, most are still dependent on their national roots. Global firms are still counted on the fingers of one hand. For George Soros—the famous international speculator—the emergence of a truly global capitalism took place in the 1970s. In 1973, the oil-producing countries, grouped in OPEC (Organisation of Petroleum Exporting Countries), increased the price per barrel for the first time: "Oil exporters enjoyed sudden and large surpluses while oil-importing countries had to finance large deficits. The responsibility for recycling the funds fell to commercial banks with the behind-the-scenes encouragement of Western governments. Eurodollars were invented and large offshore markets developed[4]."

But the diffuse sense of globalisation is still much more recent. In the mid-1990s, Europeans began to feel confusedly that the whole world had entered an accelerated phase of global unification. The numerous relocations of companies to low-wage labour-intensive countries and the resulting job losses regularly fuelled the debate. Moreover, we could add that the popularisation of air travel, the development of tourism and migratory flows reinforced the idea that the world had become a "global village". But truth be told, this is only an image, for while it is true that the peasants of yesteryear crossed their villages with their carts or on the back of a donkey two or three times a day, it must be admitted that only a tiny minority of human beings on this earth now frequent international airports on a regular basis. The

---

[3]Elie Cohen, *Mondialisation et souveraineté*, Le Débat, November-December 1997, p. 24-27.
[4]A financial market that develops outside its country of origin. George Soros, *La crisis del capitalismo global; La sociedad abierta en peligro*, Editorial Debate, Madrid, 1999, p. 139, 140.

vast majority of humanity is still anchored in its civilisational area, even in its own hometown. The possibilities offered to us by internet technology have therefore not brought us new friends on the other side of the planet. The "global village" in question, far from being a reality, is a perspective, a mobilising utopia, and this is precisely the ideological dimension that characterises the Western world of our time.

The economic globalisation we have been hearing so much about for a decade is not the primary factor in this planetarian consciousness in the project phase. Globalisation', as the English-speakers say, is not just the economic phenomenon of which we take note, but a quiet yearning to fuse the peoples of the earth into a single mould, to abolish borders and to establish a world government. Our whole philosophy leads us down this path: liberals call for trade liberalisation and the adoption by all the peoples of the world of the democratic system and the "open society", while their "opponents", called "alter-globalists", campaign for the opening of borders to all the world's migrants and for giving ever more power to international bodies, supposedly capable of solving major global problems such as the management of ecological challenges, "unequal trade" between the "North" and the "South", hunger and poverty in the world. It is from this planetarian perspective that we see this plural, multi-ethnic and multicultural society being built up before our eyes, which is the necessary and compulsory step towards the great universal fraternity desired by Western ideologists. This is the only way to gradually dissolve the entrenched traditional societies which are the main obstacles to this project. Through the democratic game of elections, any nationalist reaction is prevented by the growing weight of the various minorities in relation to the former majority. By promoting miscegenation, the ethnic bases of the indigenous peoples are undermined and their identity reflexes cancelled out. On the other hand, immigration—legal or illegal—has the inestimable advantage for employers of constituting an inexhaustible pool of cheap labour. As we can see, the plural society is in this respect incomparably more effective than Soviet society, which showed its limits after seventy years of communist experience, when its philosophical principles were originally precisely the same as those that underpin liberal society today, namely respect for the human person and planetarian fraternity.

The construction of plural societies in Europe is undeniably the most important phenomenon of the end of the 20th century, if not of the whole of European history in the last 3000 years. The fact that the peoples of the West have been the only ones to have embarked on this path is entirely symptomatic of the progress of the planetarian idea in

Western minds in recent decades. The world in which we live today in the big French cities is no longer the same as it was twenty years ago: the multi-ethnic society is taking shape before our eyes in an astonishing way, without any real connection with recent economic mutations. Japan, for example, whose economy is just as globalised as ours, has not been engulfed by this ideological maelstrom. This is because it is not a natural phenomenon, but corresponds to the realisation of a political objective that is very characteristic of Western thinking.

These planetarian hopes, which have so deeply penetrated the minds of Westerners, did not suddenly appear with the fall of the Berlin Wall and the victory of the democracies, although they certainly spurred them on vigorously. An intellectual like Jean-François Revel, who in 1983 could still predict the disappearance of our democracies, "short and precarious parentheses on the surface of history" and the "probable, not to say ineluctable" victory of communism, can make us smile in retrospect, in view of the dazzling evolution of the world in just a few years. It is true that his pessimism could be explained by the situation at the time: the stagnation of the Afghan resistance against the USSR, the resurgence of repression in Poland and the complacency of Western governments[5]. Ten years later, in *The End of History and the Last Man*, an essay published in 1992 and widely translated around the world, Francis Fukuyama announced the triumph of liberal democracies from a "globalist perspective[6] ", as it appeared on the cover, and nothing less than "the end of History". Noting the victory of democratic regimes almost everywhere in the world, this American author wrote: "If human societies, over the centuries, evolve towards or converge on a single form of socio-political organisation, such as liberal democracy, if there appear to be no viable alternatives to liberal democracy, and if people living in liberal democracies express no radical dissatisfaction with their lives, we can say that the dialogue has reached a final and definitive conclusion. The historicist philosopher will be forced to accept the superiority and finality of the liberal democracy that he

---

[5]Jean-François Revel, *Comment les démocraties finissent*, Grasset, 1983.
[6]For our part, we prefer to use the term "planetarian", not for the sake of neologism, which is always tricky to handle, especially in the title of a work, but because the word "mundialist" seems to us to have an ideological aspect. Its use has changed over the last few years: the radical left, which called itself mundialist until 1998-99, then claimed to be anti-globalist, then "alter-globalist" since 2003. The "anti-globalisation" banner was then retained by nationalists, and the very term "mundialist" sometimes seems to have an insulting connotation, at least in France.

himself proclaims[7]." According to Fukuyama, the liberal state must be "universal", although the author means by this no more than the recognition granted by each state to all its citizens, without discrimination of any kind. Nowhere in his essay did he evoke the aspiration for a world state, a world government, although it was understood that international institutions would be in charge of the destinies of humanity. He simply noted that "these same economic forces now encourage the breaking down of national barriers through the creation of a single, integrated world market", but he did not consider the possibility of the destruction of nations and the disappearance of states. Only aggressive nationalism will have to disappear with the victory of the liberal model: "The fact that the political neutralisation of nationalism may not occur in the present or the next generation does not mean that it will not take place[8]."

This ideal of universal peace that accompanies the democratic creed, just as it accompanied the communist creed, nevertheless raises some questions, for "human beings will rebel against this idea. That is to say, they will rebel at the prospect of becoming undifferentiated members of the universal and homogeneous state, each one similar to the others wherever he goes on the planet." This was the only passage in his voluminous 461-page book where the eventuality of a world state was evoked, and it was immediately followed by common-sense considerations of the "tedium" that such a New World Order[9] would generate. The new citizens of the world would indeed feel that a life of mere consumerism is ultimately very "boring"; "they will want to have ideals to live and die for, and they will want to risk their lives, even if the international system of states has succeeded in abolishing the possibility of war." The students of May 1968, for example, "had no rational reason to rebel, for they were for the most part spoiled children of one of the freest and most prosperous societies on the planet." For, "this is the contradiction that liberal democracy has not yet resolved[10]." Francis Fukuyama's essay was ultimately quite prudent; some

---

[7]Francis Fukuyama, *El fin de la Historia y el último hombre*, Planeta, Barcelona, 1992, p. 199, 200.

[8]Francis Fukuyama, *El fin de la Historia y el último hombre*, Planeta, Barcelona, 1992, p. 373.

[9]The expression "New World Order" comes from US President George Bush Senior, who uttered it with particular intonation in his televised address as he prepared to bomb Saddam Hussein's Iraq in 1991. The New World Order was supposed to succeed the era of East-West confrontation after the collapse of the communist system.

[10]Francis Fukuyama, *El fin de la Historia y el último hombre*, Planeta, Barcelona, 1992, p. 419, 438.

intellectuals, as we shall see below, are moving much more boldly in this planetarian perspective.

In any case, these concepts are nothing new; they continue, in a new form, the ideas already expounded by the Enlightenment philosophy of the 18th century. Tocqueville already announced in 1848, inspired by "a constant concern and a single thought: the irresistible and universal advent of Democracy in the world[11]." Before him, Kant, the solitary philosopher, already considered in 1784 that "a cosmopolitan state of public state security should be established so that [the states] do not destroy each other". The Konigsberg philosopher furthermore harboured "the hope that, after several revolutions of restructuring, there will finally come into being that which Nature harbours as its supreme intention: a universal cosmopolitan state within which all the original dispositions of the human species will develop[12]." However, the men of the 18th century were too full of racial prejudices to envisage the plural, multi-ethnic and multicultural society as our planetarian philosophers understand it. The truth is that the anthropology of Buffon, Maupertuis, Diderot, d'Alembert or Voltaire will forever remain a taboo subject on which it is better not to dwell if we want to keep these great ancestors in the sacred pantheon of democracy.

On the other hand, while the term "Humanity" was in vogue in the philosophy of the Age of Enlightenment, references to the Nation were also very recurrent, and the two terms almost always went together. Dedication to humanity and the fatherland" was part of the phraseology of the time. Moreover, the term "humanity" probably had a narrower meaning than it does today, and in everyday language its meaning often did not go much beyond that of "the people". Of course, the philosophers of that time were not yet thinking concretely about the great universal intermingling and the "global village". We know to what extent the men of the French Revolution were rabid patriots as well as humanists. Babeuf, ancestor of socialism and fervent "defender of the fatherland", declared: "Only disinterested friends of humanity and the fatherland can found a true republic." Although the philosophy behind their struggle was humanist, the soldiers of the Year II of the Revolution did not care about universal brotherhood, and were more concerned with destroying the "tyrannical" regimes of Europe than with the idea of merging peoples. The "Declaration of the Rights of Man and of the Citizen" illustrates this perfectly, for it includes the term "citizen" in

---

[11]Alexis de Tocqueville, *Democracy in America, Warning to the twelfth edition.*
[12]Immanuel Kant, *Idea for a Universal History in a Cosmopolitan Key*, 1784, Universidad Nacional Autónoma de México, 2006, p. 54, 60.

addition to the undifferentiated "man": in other words, it was understood that all Frenchmen were now equal in law, for it was above all in this sense that "universal" was understood. Thus, in the new republic, foreigners were closely watched.

Francis Fukuyama's idea of an "End of History" was not new either. Hegel had already defined history as the unstoppable progression of man towards the highest heights of rationalism and freedom. This process, according to him, had a logical end point in the modern liberal state that had appeared after the American declaration of independence in 1776 and the French Revolution. Marx also shared this belief in the possibility of an end of history.

For the Marxists, social classes would also disappear as inevitably as they had once been formed, and the state itself would disappear at the same time. Friedrich Engels said: "Society, reorganising production in a new way on the basis of a free association of equal producers, will send the whole state machine to its rightful place: to the museum of antiquities, next to the spinning wheel and the bronze axe[13]." Even with this, a transitional phase of dictatorship was indispensable: the proletariat will seize state power and transform the means of production "provisionally" into state property. The capitalist state machine, the capitalist police, capitalist functionaryism, capitalist bureaucracy will be replaced by the power machine of the proletariat, but without the class antagonisms; thus the proletarian state will naturally extinguish itself.

In contrast to other forms of 19th century socialism, Marx's socialism had a strong universal vocation. According to him, the historical process was dragging capitalism towards globalisation and was in any case tending towards the establishment of a world market in which frontiers would be erased and national differences would disappear. The proletarians could then consider themselves as abstract, unbound individuals, which would make possible the great leap into the classless paradise of communist society. This universalised proletariat, without nationality, would then become a kind of universal nation, built on the ruins of the old nations and particularisms.

Indeed, contemporary planetarian messianism first appeared with Marxism. Bukharin's words on the Bolshevik revolution of 1917 are quite eloquent in this respect: "The new era is born. The era of the dissolution of capitalism, of its internal decomposition, of the communist revolution of the proletariat (...) It will bend the rule of

[13]Friedrich Engels, *The Origin of the Family, Private Property and the State (IX Barbarism and Civilisation)*, 1884

capital, make wars impossible, erase the frontiers between states, transform the whole world into a community working for itself, unite and liberate the peoples[14]." These were the "Guidelines of the Communist International" drafted by Bukharin himself, though the reader will have noticed the strange similarities with the words of the liberal thinkers. Only their economic ideas differentiate them: the former thought that collectivisation would liberate the proletariat from the exploitation of the bourgeoisie, while the latter realised the utter failure of collectivised society. For the rest, one can only note with astonishment the extent to which Marxist aims are similar to those of today's planetarian thinkers, even to the extent of their belief in the ineluctability of unification and the end of history. The world is inevitably evolving towards the realisation of its destiny: the process of final unification that nothing in the world can prevent. This is a recurrent idea in the planetarian discourse, and we will see that this immovable belief is strongly linked to a religious faith.

The conjunction of views is also easily explained by the fact that they all drew their worldview from the same source—the philosophy of the Enlightenment—which constitutes the obligatory reference for Marxist thinkers and above all for liberals[15]. It simply had to be updated, adapted to current realities. In the 19th century, with the industrial revolution, it had become a little dusty and no longer seemed at all able to arouse the enthusiasm of either the working masses, who had suffered above all from liberal bourgeois society, or the European youth, who had carried out their revolutions of national liberation in Europe in the course of the century, and who now aspired to overthrow the "vile bourgeoisie". Marxism would thus take over from universal fraternity at the same time as social equality, while the democratic spirit went astray in patriotism, leading to the outbreak of the First World War.

But let us not be too harsh on that patriotism. Indeed, it is a patriotism for which much can be forgiven, and our intellectuals today still feel a certain benevolence for the revanchist enthusiasm of the French in 1914, because it was thanks to the blood of one million four hundred thousand Frenchmen, "killed for France", that the Prussian,

---

[14] Ernst Nolte, *La guerra civil europea, 1917-1945*, Fondo de cultura económica, Mexico, 2001, p. 112, 113.

[15] Indeed, both Marxism and the classical and neoclassical economic school (the liberals) drink from the source of the Enlightenment and its abstract, idealistic and universal conception of man. They raise the egoistic and materialistic *homoeconomicus* with a cosmopolitan vocation to an irreducible category. This powerful current, which still dominates today, was opposed by German Romanticism and the German historicist school of economics in the 19th century. (NdT).

Austrian, Russian and Ottoman monarchies could be overthrown, and democratic regimes could be established all over Europe. The fall of the monarchies and empires was the real celebration of the democrats of that era. With hindsight, the Alsace-Lorraine question was only a very minor issue in the midst of the immense transformations brought about by the European conflict. The militarism of the French Republic of 1914 is therefore still remembered and celebrated by planetarian thinkers, for it was first and foremost a militarism capable of imposing universal ideas on those who had not yet integrated them.

In fact, this is exactly what the historian Michel Winock told us, who conceptualised the patriotic idea in a planetarian sense, making the distinction between "open nationalism, coming from the optimistic philosophy of the Enlightenment and the reminiscences of the Revolution (for example, in Michelet[16], but also in General De Gaulle), and closed nationalism, based on a pessimistic vision of historical evolution and the idea of decadence." Open nationalism, Winock explained, is "the child of a young, expansive and missionary nation, marked by faith in the progress and fraternity of peoples." It is the nationalism of "a nation permeated by a civilising mission, generous, hospitable, in solidarity with other nations in formation, defender of the oppressed, and which raises the banner of freedom and independence for all the peoples of the world." On the contrary, closed nationalism is a "fenced-in, frightened and exclusivist nationalism that defines the nation by excluding intruders: Jews, immigrants, revolutionaries." This nationalism is "a collective paranoia, fuelled by obsessions of decadence and plotting". This nationalism is invariably pessimistic: "France is threatened with death, undermined from within by its parliamentary institutions, by economic and social transformations, a country where the "hand of the Jew" is always denounced, the degradation of the old society, the ruin of the family and de-Christianisation. It is a "deadly nationalism"[17].

The wars of the Revolution and of the Napoleonic Empire are thus justified, since they had the merit of spreading the ideas of the Enlightenment and of destroying the old aristocratic nations of Europe during that first assault. The First World War, for its part, made it possible to definitively liquidate the double Catholic monarchy of

---

[16] One of the great French historians of the 19th century, although he has been rather controversial in contemporary historiography since the end of the 20th century. Liberal and anti-clerical, he was an outspoken supporter of the Republic.

[17] Michel Winock, *Nationalisme, antisémitisme et fascisme en France*, Points Seuil, 1990, p. 7, 22, 38.

Austria-Hungary, to overthrow the Kaiser and establish a republic in Germany, and above all to overthrow Tsar Nicholas II, who still refused to grant citizenship to the Jews of Russia. It is in this sense that one can be a patriot and a warmonger. One can thus applaud the patriotic enthusiasm of the French soldiers who marched in good faith to the massacre to regain Alsace-Moselle, not because one approves of their imbecilic chauvinism, but because they were expected to fight for the great democratic ideals. Their chauvinism will be condemned once the war is over, without any consideration for their wounds and their sacrifice.

It is in this sense that some media and cultural personalities understand it today, such as Jean-François Kahn, the press director of a major weekly newspaper, when he declared: "For my part, I am as rabidly patriotic as reason allows", adding on the following page of his book, *The French are formidable*: "It is, indeed, "formidable" to be French insofar as that concept takes on the extensive sense of the term that History gives it, and not the very limited significance that obtuse nationalists and stateless reactionaries (who are often the same) confer on it[18]." In the same vein, we have Jean Daniel, the head of another great progressive daily, and his declaration of patriotic faith when he noted: "Breakfast with Azoulay [the famous "Jewish banker" and adviser to Morocco's King Hassan II]: This Jew is a Moroccan patriot as much or more as I am a French patriot. Almost. In other words, the bond of Judaism is very, very relative when there is neither persecution, nor coercion, nor religious consciousness[19]."

The same patriotism of circumstance oozes from a communist-inspired writer like Guy Konopnicki, who had celebrated the victory of the French national football team in the 1998 World Cup. Clearly, it was not the France of the homeland that Guy Konopnicki appreciated in the victory of the French football team, towards which he had already expressed his contempt, but the triumph of the mixed-race *Black-Blanc-Beur* France[20]. It was then that he was overcome with intense patriotic

---

[18] Jean-François Kahn, *Les Français sont formidables*, Balland, 1987, p. 24-25. We will refrain from commenting here on this curious amalgam between "obtuse nationalists" and "stateless reactionaries". The reader will naturally understand it after becoming familiar with planetary thinking in the course of reading this book.

[19] Jean Daniel, *Soleils d'hiver, Carnets 1998-2000*, Grasset, Poche, 2000, p. 122 [Jean Daniel was the founder of *Le Nouvel Observateur*, member of the Board of Directors of Agence France-Presse (AFP) and winner of the Prince of Asturias Prize for Communication and Humanities in 2004].

[20] Black-White-Maghrebi: This is an expression coined by the French media and cultural sphere (NdT).

fervour, snatching the tricolour flag from Jean-Marie Le Pen's hands and singing the *Marseillaise* loudly. So that, a few years later, we will hear him, with great sincerity, desolate at having heard the national anthem booed by the immigrant youth he had praised so much. On 6 October 2001, 70,000 spectators of North African origin whistled the *Marseillaise* during a France-Algeria match at the *Stade de France in* the presence of the President of the Republic. For Guy Konopnicki, this represented the collapse of his ideal of a multi-ethnic France, of the mixed-race France so desired by the *intelligentsia*: "I am dismayed when the *Marseillaise* I sang in the middle of a crowd of North Africans, when Zidane and all the others brought us such a beautiful victory, is booed. France is precisely that country where, despite the difficulties and racism, we all live together without distinction of any kind[21]." It is clear, then, that it is not France that he loves, but the embryo of a miniature universal republic that it represents.

Long before them, the famous German poet Heinrich Heine, abhorred by the nationalists on the other side of the Rhine, expressed his love for the republican France that had welcomed him. In 1830, after the abdication of Charles X—whom he called "that royal madman"—he was enthusiastic about the French revolutionary movement and old General Lafayette: "It is already sixty years since he returned from America, since he brought us the declaration of the rights of man, those ten commandments of the new religion"; "Lafayette … the tricolour flag … the Marseillaise … I am as if intoxicated. Bold hopes rise from my heart[22]." When one knows Heinrich Heine's views and his contempt for European cultures, it is clear here too that his love and admiration were not so much for France as for the universal republic it embodied. As for his "audacious hopes", we bet he was referring to a new little military tour to subdue Europe with blood and fire and blow off a few crowned heads. It is in that sense that one can declare oneself "rabidly patriotic".

The planetarian intellectuals, full of generous ideas of pacifism and tolerance, are at the forefront of patriotism and aggressive militarism as soon as a democratic "just cause" is involved. In this case, they play the bugle without complexes and become propagandists for the armed forces. Thus, French soldiers were "formidable" in 1792, 1914 and 1940, when it was a question of going to the front to destroy non-democratic political regimes. Equally "formidable" are the Soviet troops or the Serbian partisans who fought against the Nazis; as were

---

[21] Guy Konopnicki, *La Faute des Juifs*, Balland, 2002, p. 26.
[22] Heinrich Heine, *De l'Allemagne*, 1835, Gallimard, 1998, p. 291.

the Iraqi patriots who rallied behind Saddam Hussein and whom the West generously supported in their war against the mullahs' regime in neighbouring Iran in the 1980s. On the other hand, French soldiers during the Algerian war are infamous torturers. This is what Guy Konopnicki wanted to tell us at all costs: "At that time, the young Jews of Paris took a radical stand against French colonialism and its army of torturers[23]." The Serb soldiers who rejected the Bosnian or Kosovar Muslims were also assimilated to "bloodthirsty beasts" responsible for immense "mass graves". They will therefore be bombed by the US air force in 1999 in a new operation "Just Cause". As for Saddam Hussein's Iraqi soldiers in 1991 and 2003, they are now nothing more than pawns in the service of tyranny, who can be vitriolised without a second thought. Thus, patriotism will be exalted when it corresponds to the interests of planetarian politics. When the cause seems just, then the flag is torn from the hands of Western patriots, singing at the top of their lungs their national anthem in order to drag them into the conflict. Progressive intellectuals, always ready to mobilise in the name of pacifism and universal brotherhood, to sign all petitions in favour of human rights, then enter into a warmongering frenzy that invariably invades the press and all the media.

This attitude is the direct result of the warrior messianism of Enlightenment philosophy. It is these liberal ideas that gave rise to national liberation movements throughout the 19th century, against what used to be called "tyrannies", i.e. monarchical regimes. German, Hungarian and Polish liberals sang the Marseillaise in 1830 and 1848, exalting good old-fashioned republican patriotism. The identity of the people was no longer embodied in the person of the crowned monarch, but in the whole nation and the people in arms under the baton of the new republican regime, which already foreshadowed the great collective massacres of the 20th century.

However, the advent of the reign of the bourgeoisie and the horrible injustices of triumphant capitalism were to arouse the suspicion and hostility of the working-class world towards liberal ideas. Never, indeed, have humble people suffered so much as during that period, which will forever remain one of the most horrible periods in history for the humble and destitute. Under those conditions, socialism was legitimate. But the socialism that would finally prevail was not that of Proudhon, Blanqui or Sorel[24], that Gallic socialism steeped in the

---

[23] Guy Konopnicki, *La Faute des Juifs*, Balland, 2002, p. 20.
[24] Great alternative historical figures of French socialism, anarchism and syndicalism (NdT).

terroir, rooted in history and traditions, but that of Karl Marx. From then until the inter-war period, Marxism would keep the flame of pacifism and the universal spirit inherited from the Age of Enlightenment burning: "Workers of all countries, unite!". The liberals, for their part, kept the flame of the warrior and patriotic spirit of the great ancestors, always ready to die for a "Just cause[25]". The planetarian idea, as we can see, was at the time both the habit of militant pacifism and the habit of warlike patriotism. This idea was already at that time the "system", and the opposition to the "system".

At the beginning of the 20th century, the concepts of pacifism and universal brotherhood were still largely absorbed by the socialist galaxy, within which Marxist theories were to assert themselves. But Marxism was above all strong in Germany. At that time, France hardly knew Marxism in a denatured form (Jaurès was spiritually closer to Michelet than to Marx); English Fabian socialism was not Marxist at all, and in the United States this doctrine was the concern of only a handful of Jewish immigrants from Eastern Europe. Marxism would not truly cross the Rhine to the West until after 1917.

The anarchist current maintained a certain vigour in its Italian, French, Russian and especially Spanish strongholds. But this libertarian socialism was very similar to Marxist principles in terms of the universalism of ideas: the eradication of religion, borders and nations; the establishment of a globalised society remained the ultimate goal that would finally ensure universal peace.

However, there still existed within the socialist movement currents which retained a "race" instinct—a term very much in vogue at the time—where anti-Semitism was not entirely absent. In France, hatred of the Republic and all its ideological arsenal was evidently largely generated by the shameless exploitation of the workers and the violent repressions they had suffered at the hands of the guardians of the democratic order. The workers remembered the 30,000 of their dead during the repression of the Commune in 1871. On many occasions, under Ferry or Clemenceau, the Republic had not hesitated to fire on the poor in order to guarantee bourgeois order, which explained some resentments. On 1 May 1908, on the Place de la Bourse in Paris, the revolutionary proletariat hung and booed the effigy of Mariana the "Riflewoman"." It is the most significant act in our history since 14 July", Charles Maurras would say[26] in *La Action française* of 4 August

---

[25] "Just Cause" was the name given to a US bombing operation over Panama in 1990.

[26] Charles Maurras (1868–1952): Important intellectual of the 20th century. He was the

1908. In fact, Georges Sorel's syndicalists and the "reactionaries" converged after analysing their common opposition to bourgeois hypocrisy and noting the similarity of their conclusions. In 1911, as a result of the convergence of these two currents, the Proudhon circle was born. The 1914 war put an end to this experiment, and the Sorelian tendency of socialism was then marginalised in France, although this combination of nationalism and socialism remained an ideological matrix of primary importance, for it was from this fusion that Mussolini formulated his conception of fascism after drawing inspiration from the French example.

The second great doctrinal transformation of that period took place in 1916. In that year, Lenin published his most important theoretical contribution to Marxism, *Imperialism, the Highest Stage of Capitalism.* As the capitalist contradictions enunciated by Marx were, at the turn of the century, about to be disproved both by the course of history and by Bernstein's conclusions about the improvement of the workers' living conditions, Lenin produced a theoretical effort pointing out a new set of contradictions on the basis of contemporary data. *Imperialism* was to become for the modern epoch the equivalent of Marx's *Manifesto* of 1848. Lenin's stroke of genius consisted in adapting Marxist theory to the situation of the backward countries. For Marx, it was in fact in European industrial societies that the internal and fatal contradictions of capitalism were to appear. Lenin globalised these contradictions: the rivalry of the European powers for the division of the world through colonisation, he said, could only end in a war between imperialist rivals at loggerheads, and out of this apocalypse would come the world socialist revolution. Thus Leninist theory shifted the driving force of revolution from internal class struggle to war between nations. The antagonism between the exploiting nations of Europe and the colonised peoples legitimised the struggle of the world proletariat for their liberation. The theory explained why revolution could take so long in advanced societies: the profits of the imperialists allowed them to create a labour aristocracy at the head of the labour movement which reneged on its base. The isolated Marxists of backward Russia could therefore seize power. Russia, the weak link of capitalism, thus logically became the centre of the world revolution.

The Bolshevik revolution of October 1917[27] was to raise great hopes throughout the world. In 1918, after four years of war, Russian

---

ideologue of the nationalist, monarchist, anti-parliamentary and anti-Semitic *L'Action Française* (NdT).

[27] End of October in the Julian calendar in Russia; beginning of November 1917 in the

communism once again represented the hopes of the European pacifists who had been cruelly disappointed in 1914 to see helplessly the adhesion of the masses to patriotism in all the countries of Europe. The victors in Russia, the Bolsheviks, who still had to fight some internal resistance, wanted peace at all costs in order to consolidate their revolution. On 23 November 1917, they asked for an armistice. On 3 March, they signed the peace of Brest-Litovsk, ceding to Germany vast territories from the Ukraine to the Baltic countries and abandoning without hesitation the Western allies. From their point of view, this was not a betrayal, since the war was for them a war between capitalist states in which they had no interest. Moreover, on December 7, 1917, they appealed to all the peoples of the East, inviting countries like India, Egypt, and all colonised peoples to free themselves from the yoke of imperialism, thus further weakening the positions of the British and French. This is why Marxism at that time represented the planetarian pacifist ideal and the liberation of the oppressed. The Third Workers' International, the Communist International, was expected to succeed where the socialist Second International had failed miserably in 1914.

The construction of Soviet society in Russia was to put revolutionary ideals to a severe test. Anarchists all over the world would quickly become disillusioned after the crushing of Makhno's Ukrainian supporters and the bloody repression of Kronsdadt in 1921. They would also be seriously mistreated by the Reds during the Spanish civil war, despite representing a much larger militant mass. However, the vast majority of progressive intellectuals in the West remained fascinated by the Bolshevik revolution, regardless of the excesses it had brought about, and the bulk of the rank and file remained devoted to the cause and defence of the USSR at least until the end of the Second World War and the destruction of National Socialism, and even beyond in terms of fidelity to Marxist principles.

All pacifists were not Marxists in 1918, but those who professed such ideas were labelled as such by their opponents. The physicist Albert Einstein, for example, was after the First World War one of those personalities at the forefront of calling for world disarmament in his lectures. Although the hatred of German nationalists crystallised in him, it was not so much because he was the apostle of disarmament as because he was the propagandist of globalism, because for Einstein universal peace could only be guaranteed by the establishment of a world government. In a defeated Germany, torn apart by civil war and in which the communists played the leading role, Einstein was

Gregorian calendar in the West, with a time lag of 13 days.

inevitably exposed to the accusations and threats of those who saw him as a traitor and a Bolshevik. That is to say that his pacifist ideas were assimilated to Marxism at that time. Although less dogmatic in his struggle for peace, the great Viennese writer Stefan Zweig had the same difficulties in Austria.

Undoubtedly, the Bolshevik revolution had shaken many spirits in the West, and aroused murderous hatreds everywhere. To this sacralisation of Marxist doctrine elevated almost to the rank of theology," wrote Pascal Bruckner, "democratic thinkers replied with a praise of moderation designed to curb the outbursts of history. It was the greatness of a Karl Popper, an Isaiah Berlin, a Raymond Aron to stand up and try to demobilise revolutionary hopes that claimed total freedom in order to expand absolute terror[28]."

Another Viennese, the philosopher Karl Popper, had indeed been seduced by Bolshevism in his youth, although he had quickly turned away from it to become the champion of liberal democracy. Like Albert Einstein, Joseph Roth and Stefan Zweig, Karl Popper, himself a Jew, had gone into exile after Adolf Hitler came to power. He took refuge in London, where in 1945 he published his famous book *The Open Society and its Enemies*[29], in which he criticised Marxism and totalitarian systems. This book was to become one of the obligatory references for liberal thinkers and would inspire another philosopher much better known for his international speculative activities.

Indeed, the billionaire George Soros has always recognised Karl Popper as his teacher and mentor and has made himself the apostle of the "open society", encouraging and promoting it worldwide through his foundation. Karl Popper's spiritual heir is not content with just thinking about concepts: he spends billions to spread democratic ideals, especially in the former Eastern Bloc countries and in Central Europe, where he is originally from. But as he himself said, his action had already begun before the fall of the Berlin Wall: "In 1979, when I had earned more money than I could possibly need, I set up a foundation called the Open Society Fund, whose objectives I defined as helping to open up closed societies, helping to make open societies more viable and fostering a critical way of thinking. Through the foundation, I became deeply involved in the disintegration of the Soviet system[30]." These are obviously statements that could lead us a long way in

---

[28] Pascal Bruckner, *La Mélancolie démocratique*, Éditions du Seuil, 1990, p. 150.

[29] Karl Popper, *The open Society and its enemies*, London, 1945.

[30] George Soros, *La crisis del capitalismo global; La sociedad abierta en peligro*. Editorial Debate, Madrid, 1999, p. 12.

interpreting the fall of the communist regime: did it die because of its own weaknesses, or was it helped to die?

It is clear that planetarian aspirations could have been frustrated by the development of the communist countries, which were supposed to build a fraternal society for the proletarians and above all to finally achieve world unification. These disappointments would gradually alienate Western intellectuals from international communism, at least from the Soviet version.

One of the main breaking points was undoubtedly the Soviet policy towards the State of Israel. Created in 1948, the state was immediately recognised by the Soviet Union, which hoped to make it a strong ally in the Middle East. But the Israeli Jews gained greater financial support in the United States, so they quickly privileged their relations with that country. Moscow then abruptly changed its policy and supported Arab demands, which put many Marxist intellectuals in a Cornelian dilemma: how to reconcile their support for the workers' homeland with their love for Israel? Many turned away from the Soviet Union for good at this time, all the more so as the radicalisation of the USSR's anti-Zionist line took an anti-Semitic turn that became more pronounced in 1951. The defence of the *refuseniks*—those Russian Jews whom the Soviet regime prevented from emigrating to Israel—and respect for human rights in the USSR was then the main focus of the struggle of all these new human rights activists. Many Jews used these new provisions of the Soviet state as a pretext to embark on a sudden and very particular anti-communism, which was all the more virulent because it allowed them to disavow a system in which some Jews had played a very important and compromising role for thirty years.

On this point, the testimony of the great Russian writer Aleksandr Solzhenitsyn is of paramount importance for us[31]. He rightly pointed out that neither the organised famine, nor the bloody repressions, nor the millions of deaths in the gulags during the terrible period of the 1920s and 1930s in the USSR, had affected the support of progressive Western intellectuals for the Bolshevik regime. During the Second World War, the Soviet troops, galvanised by the film-maker Eisenstein and the poet Ilya Ehrenbourg, according to the above logic of "modulable patriotism", were applauded by the entire Western *intelligentsia*, as well as being amply supplied in arms, aircraft and military and transport equipment of all kinds by the democratic United States. It was only when the German armies were destroyed, largely thanks to the blood shed by the Russians, and after the Soviet Union

---

[31] Alexandre Soljénitsyne, *Deux siècles ensemble*, Fayard, 2003.

supported the Arab states, that these intellectuals began to turn their backs on the communist regime. This tendency became even more pronounced when the Jews of the USSR were removed from the main leadership positions from 1951 onwards. The struggle for the rights of the *refuseniks* then became the great planetarian cause and benefited from all the media power of the West. The ideology of human rights seemed to have been invoked solely to defend the Jews removed from power in the USSR. But tens of millions of Soviets who would also have chosen exile had no choice but to suffer in silence.

Nevertheless, socialist ideas continued for a long time to exert a formidable power of attraction through the various currents of Marxism, which, while criticising the USSR, kept intact the planetarian hopes of communism. The May 1968 revolt testifies to the predominance of this ideology in the universities of the West at that time. The USSR was now only a model for the old "Stalinists" in the Communist Party, but the revolutionary myth persisted through Trotskyism, Maoism, anarchism, and more generally in all the emancipation struggles of the Third World. They all continued to believe in that universal messianism nourished by the intellectual productions of the "Frankfurt School", represented by Herbert Marcuse, Max Horckheimer, Theodor Wiesengrund Adorno, Jürgen Habermas, who were the standard-bearers of the rebels alongside Marx, Lenin and Mao. The time had not yet come to look back on the undisputed successes of liberal democracy in achieving planetarian goals and to put aside the ideals of youth. For the students of May 1968, the enemy to beat was still international capitalism, which invariably had the face of European civilisation, guilty of having given birth to capitalism and the oppression not only of European proletarians, but also, and above all, of workers all over the world. So the struggle of the Viet Minh was supported in the same way as the Algerian FLN fellagas had been supported. Here again, it was not a question of betrayal but of a liberating struggle against capitalist oppression. Soon, the revolutionary myth, with its proletariat and its European working classes who had to lead the socialist revolution, would be replaced by the masses of the third world who populated the countries of the South and who would sooner or later increasingly populate the rich countries.

The time had indeed come to find a replacement working class. Western societies underwent a major economic mutation characterised by a strong increase in the tertiary sector to the detriment of the industrial sector. With the transition to a post-industrial economy, the number of workers began to decline. This evolution of society and the general enrichment that accompanied this economic and social mutation did not in any way affect the struggle of the progressives, whose planetarian convictions were reaffirmed with even greater vigour. Their hopes then shifted to all the "oppressed minorities": immigrants in the first place, victims of colonisation, but also all categories of people who might feel oppressed or offended by bourgeois society and the domination of the "white heterosexual male". Added to this were also the demands of feminists and all sexual minorities, which, together with the struggle of the peoples of the Third World, were to fuel the idea that the European proletariat could be replaced, especially as the immigrants were to constitute the great reserve of new revolutionaries, or at least the new voters[32].

The poorest people obviously suffered the impact of competition from this new piecework workforce, imported by the big employers who were counting on this reservoir to exert downward pressure on wages. The closures and relocations of companies that multiplied, with all the problems arising from the coexistence of communities in the once working-class suburbs, hit the most disadvantaged indigenous workers first. They were indeed the first to suffer from this new form of society invented by the ideologues and supported by big business. In fact, the influx of foreign labour from the Maghreb and sub-Saharan Africa and the massive immigration of the 1980s–1990s had considerably transformed their social environment. A French film from the 1950s, 1960s, 1970s and even the 1980s showed an autochthonous European society. In twenty years, French society has undergone a profound demographic mutation, a phenomenon of such magnitude that it is incontrovertible that a global society is taking shape.

The working-class suburbs of the 1960s had become veritable urban ghettos from which the minority "little whites[33]" wanted to escape. If we take a cold, far-sighted look at the evolution of the Western world, we realise that, after a century of social struggles, the only tangible result of local communism in France is to have transformed its communes into third world cities, in a surprising conjunction of views with the employers.

---

[32] This post-Marxist *"widening of the battlefield"* can be understood by reading a book of the contemporary left, especially in the Spanish-speaking world: *Hegemony and Socialist Strategy. Hacia una radicalización de la democracia* (1987), Ediciones Siglo XXI, Madrid, 2015, by Ernesto Laclau and Chantal Mouffe (NdT).

[33] Les *"petits blancs"* is a derogatory expression used by some to refer to French natives and white Europeans, highlighting their supposed faint-heartedness. The African word babtou, verlan de toubab, has also become popular.

Feeling betrayed by their supposed defenders, abandoned by their intellectuals in favour of immigrants and minorities of all kinds, the "little whites" have rightfully taken refuge in the arms of the "populists". According to Marx's *Communist Party Manifesto*, "the workers have no fatherland"; unless, of course, that is all they have. In the discourse of the progressives, the "proletarians" were now contemptuously called the *"beaufs* [yokels][34]", i.e. the backward native French, attached to their despicable traditions and incapable of understanding the immense progress represented by the plural society. If, in the 19th century, Marxism translated into the defence of the working class world, the end of the 20th century revealed in broad daylight the importance of universalism, which was inherent to its cause and to its project of a world society, a world state and a world government.

The planetarian ideal and the will to build the plural society have finally prevailed over the anti-capitalist creed. The shift came about naturally because in the minds of all Marxists, capitalism is, consciously or not, assimilated to an arrogant and imperialist white race. The Marxist "vulgate" has long held the idea that the white man is guilty of almost all the evils of the earth. He is largely responsible for the worst crimes and atrocities committed in history, from the massacre of the American Indians to the genocide of the Jews to all the horrors of colonisation and slavery. Their whole history is an unspeakable horror, and all their traditions are not worth the noblest customs of an African tribe. And to make matters worse, the white man has created this desperate consumer society in which we are currently mired up to our necks. This is what Marxism teaches from its various chairs. It is thus easier to understand why European youth is so prone to loathe all the generations that preceded it. Nowhere else in the world is there this fascination for the multi-ethnic society, this love for the open society, but also this aversion and indifference for their own traditions and their own peoples, which they hope to see die out as quickly as possible. This enterprise of deep guilt could not have borne any other fruit. When the advocates of globalisation call loud and clear for the abolition of borders, not only for goods but also for all people, they know full well that migratory flows will go in one direction and will be directed towards the countries of the North. Whether consciously or not, they

---

[34] The *"beaufs"*, from *"beau-frère"*, literally the "brother-in-laws", but not in the Spanish sense of "cuñadismo", but in the sense of the conservative-minded, narrow-minded, prejudiced and intolerant average citizen, often parodied and mocked by the cultural sphere of entertainment. (NdT).

want their own species to disappear. This is because the French, and also many Europeans, are convinced that their old traditions, bequeathed to them by the past, are barriers to universal love between all the inhabitants of the planet. What they are no longer able to see is that the will to build a plural society to replace traditional societies is specifically European and Western, and that nowhere else in the world are the borders of their territory opened, their past, their religion and their old customs rejected in the name of a very hypothetical universal peace.

This being the case, it must be admitted that today's immigration is not a natural phenomenon but the product of a universalist ideology working towards the disappearance of nations, which corresponds to both Marxist and liberal aspirations. The planetarian minds will explain that this evolution is inevitable, that the inhabitants of poor countries will try in every way and by every means to reach the rich countries and that it is totally illusory to put wires on the borders as long as the problem of malnutrition in Africa is not solved. Political will is combined here with the humanitarian credo to tie the hands of Westerners in the name of human rights and democracy. But the truth is that the Europeans' inability to resolve the issue of migratory flows is mainly due to ideological considerations rather than to actual material impossibilities. With much more precarious means, the countries of the South regularly allow themselves to expel tens of thousands of foreigners from their territories in a few days when they deem it necessary: In September 2003, Djibouti expelled 80,000 Somalis and Ethiopians (15% of the population) who had entered the country illegally; in 1998, Ethiopia unceremoniously expelled 50,000 Eritreans; in 1996, Gabon got rid of 80,000 illegal immigrants and Libya of 330,000; in 1983, Nigeria got rid of 1.5 million undesirables, and then repeated this in 1985 without provoking the epidermal reactions of the Western media.

Numerous other examples could be cited, but to show that border control depends only on political will it is enough to point to the cases of the late Soviet Union or China, or any other country that does not make "human rights" its only reference system, but is also based on the legitimate right of all peoples on this earth to exist on a given territory according to their own rules, laws and customs. For that, after all, is the fundamental diversity that is the richness of the world. As we can see, immigration in the West today is not inevitable, and its "inevitable" character corresponds to a disguised political discourse, hidden under the mask of "tolerance" and the ideology of human rights.

The current militants and sympathisers of Marxism, defenders of the poor and the humble, do not see the contradiction in encouraging mass immigration, in total agreement with big business, when this, whether legal or clandestine, clearly exerts a downward pressure on the wages of the most disadvantaged French workers and destroys the old popular culture. Marxism has had the practical result of eradicating the identity consciousness of Westerners, who are so uprooted that they come to consider it "reactionary" to defend Breton culture, but indispensable to rescue at all costs an Indian tribe in Amazonia. Moreover, they will feel more at home in an immigrant neighbourhood than in a French neighbourhood because they have acquired the conviction that these immigrants are not intruders, but the legitimate representatives of the world proletariat, the only one capable of liberating the world from capitalist society, assimilated, more or less consciously, to the oppressive and conquering white race. In the name of diversity, the plural society is preached, without realising that all traditions, whatever they may be, crumble in the Western consumer society, finally ending up in the kind of American society that it abhors and pretends to fight.

Another striking paradox, quite similar, will also be observed, which makes us suspect that the idea of blaming the European world, especially through a biased historiography, is not a natural phenomenon, but is undoubtedly the aim of certain intellectuals who have decided to destroy the ancient civilisation.

We know that Marxism is opposed to the control of religions, of all religions, considered as "the opium of the people", because they only serve to make the proletarians forget their condition as men exploited by capitalism and to legitimise the domination of the propertied class. But we can observe how the struggle of the Marxists and the supporters of secularism is directed more strongly, almost exclusively, against Catholicism than against Protestantism, not to speak of Judaism and Islam. And yet Protestantism is a religion much closer to market realities. It is Protestants who think that commercial success is the sign of predestination, of divine election, not Catholicism. It is the Anglo-Saxon Puritan Protestants who consciously massacred the North American Indians, because they identified themselves with the Old Testament and with the Jewish people by slaughtering the natives to the last one, believing themselves to be the new chosen people taking possession of the land of Canaan. It was also Puritan Protestantism that presented religion in the most austere and "backward" way: it was the English Puritans who banned dancing, theatre and racing, not the

Catholics. Their frugality, self-discipline, honesty and aversion to the simplest pleasures constituted a kind of secular asceticism that should logically have repelled the militant Marxists, whose one of the slogans of May' 68 was "enjoyment without limits". But in spite of this, it is Catholicism which crystallises in it the Marxist hatred of religion. There must therefore be a hidden external element added to the anti-capitalist vulgate. There is a contradiction which can only be explained by a religious hatred present in Marxism, but which we also see in many cultural products of our western democratic society.

We can also see how in the West no criticism is raised against Hinduism, one of the few great religions that is not based on a doctrine of universal equality. On the contrary, Hindu doctrine divides people into a rigid caste system that defines the rights, privileges and lifestyles of each caste. It sanctifies the poverty and social immobility of the lower castes, promising them the possibility of higher reincarnation in later lives. In that respect, this religion should come under stronger attack from the doctrinaires of Marxism, as should Islam and Judaism, for that matter. But, again, this is not the case, and only Catholicism is the target of the usual mockery.

These obvious contradictions confirm us in our view that anti-Catholicism is not only a reaction by the champions of freedom against "moral order"; it is not only a progressive partisanship against "obscurantism", but the manifestation of a religious hatred that goes back long before the 19th century and the social struggles. These relentless attacks on traditional European society are not the exclusive attribute of Marxism, for we perceive the same theme of blaming spreading widely throughout the democratic system, in which the media occupy a position of real power, so that it is difficult to distinguish the influence of Marxism from that of liberal thought. This is because both policies are rooted in the same ground fertilised by cosmopolitanism. Here we have an important element that goes a long way towards blurring the traditional political divide between "right" and "left".

Globalisation is thus not so much an economic phenomenon as the culmination of a very precise ideological and political will to unify the world in one way or another. In this perspective, the collapse of the communist bloc in 1991 was a very important step. Freed from the Soviet ballast, militant Marxism has since emerged, mainly in the West, as the vector of cosmopolitan ideas and the spearhead of a pluralistic society. Whereas in its former Soviet version it took a more archaic, reactionary and militaristic form, today it is presented as a force for progress, benefiting from the complicity of almost all the major media and state subsidies. Far from having been defeated and crushed by the failure of the Soviet experience, Western Marxism has, on the contrary, been totally liberated. It has since embarked on a frenzied globalist, or "alter-globalist" propaganda, making a world society without borders and without discrimination of any kind the ultimate goal of its political project.

The geostrategic challenges and the antagonism between Moscow and Washington actually concealed the extraordinary ideological similarities between Marxist thought and the democratic ideal. It is indeed illuminating to note how these two ideologies share the same aspirations: both tend in their principles towards the unification of the world, the abolition of borders, the establishment of a world government and the creation of a new man. But in this, as in almost everything else, the Soviet model was a resounding failure. After the fall of the Berlin Wall, the experiment had to be taken stock of. Undoubtedly, capitalist democracy had succeeded where communism had failed. The ongoing construction of the multi-ethnic plural society and the outline of a world government was the work of democracies. Moreover, communism had failed in its historic task of building a classless society, respecting human rights and diverse communities. Instead, the Soviet Union had become a kind of barricaded camp, where freedom was guarded, life was quite difficult, and it was in any case impossible to leave, except for the Jews, who benefited from the support of Western countries. It was clear that the realisation of planetarian hopes would be the work of democracy and not the fruit of the Soviet experience.

Long ago, most intellectuals in the West, moulded with ideas of egalitarian society and messianic hopes, had already accepted the end of the homeland of socialism as the ideal for the workers of the world. The main Marxist parishes had long since taken the measure of the failure of sovietism and effected its mutation. They had reoriented their struggle in a planetarian sense, mobilising their troops for humanitarian causes rather than against the capitalist mode of production: the equality of citizens, the "fight against discrimination", the struggle against racism in the West and for the recognition of national or sexual minorities, activism for the abolition of borders, as well as for the defence of the environment within a planetarian ecological vision, took on an unprecedented upsurge. All the messianic hopes of Marxism seemed to be quickly accommodated by liberal democracy, while maintaining the revolutionary credo to mobilise the mass-generated idealists of a desperate consumer society.

The novelist Mario Vargas Llosa[35] expressed this sentiment very well with regard to the evolution of the planetarian ideal: "One of the ideals of our youth—the disappearance of borders, the integration of the countries of the world in a system of exchange beneficial to all—is now tending to become a reality. But contrary to what we thought, it was not the socialist revolution that brought about this internationalisation, but its bête noire: capitalism and the market. However, this is the most beautiful progress in modern history because it lays the foundations of a new civilisation on a planetarian scale which is organised around political democracy, the predominance of civil society, economic freedom and human rights[36]."

The intellectual Michel Winock had found himself in the position of recognising the same evidence, albeit somewhat obsessed by a recurring theme that seems to trouble many intellectuals: "Real socialism, as it was built in the East of our continent, has turned out to be another closed society where Jews, like other minorities, are looking for their place. Only the "open society" can offer the opportunity for a true pluralist democracy capable of integrating the Jews without forcing them to alienate their own being, their collective memory, their double solidarity (French and Jewish)[37]."

For these intellectuals, whose predecessors and ideological fathers had given birth to such monstrosities, the demise of the very troublesome Soviet regime had been an infinite relief. But instead of acknowledging their mistakes and pronouncing a mea culpa, Western intellectuals in the 1990s took advantage of that time of change to throw themselves without further ado into the other cosmopolitan project promoted by the democratic society. Working within democracy was much more effective. In literature, the press and the cinema, we witnessed an unbridled acceleration of planetarian ideas, as if the tragic mistakes of the previous era had to be forgotten as quickly as possible and the crimes of communism exorcised. There was no repentance, no apology for the millions of deaths in the Gulag[38], the deportations, the

---

[35] Multi-award-winning writer and defeated candidate in the 1990s presidential elections in Peru.

[36] In Alain Finkielkraut, *La Humanidad perdida*, Anagrama, Barcelona, 1998, p. 144-145.

[37] Michel Winock, *Nationalisme, antisémitisme et fascisme en France*, Points Seuil, 1990, p. 223.

[38] Gulag: General Directorate of Correctional Labour Camps and Colonies. It was the branch of the NKVD that ran the penal system of forced labour camps in the Soviet

famines and the murders perpetrated in the name of the communist ideal and the great brotherhood of peoples by those who had been its most ardent propagandists.

In the West, this historic event did not ultimately have a major impact. Society continued to evolve without major changes apart from the agitation of the planetarian intellectuals who then redoubled their efforts to promote their ideal. The aim was to forget their mistake as soon as possible, to rethink the egalitarian society, to "invent", as they called it, new utopias. The planetarian ideologues, animated by a millenarian enthusiasm, seemed to have found the messiah in the rubble of the Berlin Wall, and were convinced that the fraternal world would finally become a reality.

This new philosophy, which sings the praises of the unity of mankind and plural democracy as a substitute for communist discourse, has really taken off in the 1990s. The flowering of planetarian intellectual production, which really took hold through Marxism in its cultural versions in May 1968, is now continuing in an even more ecstatic way with democratic intellectuals, more or less imbued with cultural Marxism, but freed from all the heavy economic considerations that weighed heavily on Marxist-Leninist works[39]. On the other hand, their contempt for old European culture and old civilisation remains intact. This is because the intellectuals of the 1990s are the same ones who had fostered the spirit of May 1968. From this affiliation, the planetarian intellectuals intend to pursue the realisation of planetarian hopes in a different way.

Ready-made, ready-to-use concepts such as "the Earth belongs to everyone" are therefore very fashionable, and not only in school playgrounds. We like to call ourselves "citizens of the world": it is less old-fashioned than being vulgarly Galician or Andalusian and does not give rise to terrible accusations. According to the canons decided by UNESCO, a beautiful 12th century church will be declared "world heritage of humanity", which is perfectly in line with what the philosopher Lévy told us when he declared: "When we hear Japanese people playing a score by Beethoven or Chinese people singing an opera by Verdi, we should not imagine that they have been seduced by

---

Union. See Aleksandr Solzhenitsyn, *Archipelago Gulag*, Tusquets, 2015. (NdT).

[39] Typically, what was scientific and rigorous in the materialist analysis of Socialism, with regard to the economic and social conditions of the European proletariat, was progressively replaced by the degenerate by-products of the progressive left of the system such as anti-fascism, anti-racism, environmentalism, etc. (NdT).

"Western" music. This music is not "Western", it is universal[40]." We are far from this idea of globalisation as synonymous with mere economic evolution. Obviously, these reflexes have been created by a tireless and permanent awareness campaign that has been invading our television screens for decades.

The Soviet system was in fact an anomaly, for it did not correspond at all to the generous ideas that had enthused millions of people, ideas on which the built-up regime was supposed to have been based. With the end of that system, it can be said that in a way we are back to normal. With the annoying Siberian burden lifted from its shoulders, the communist idea can once again play its role correctly, in accordance with its principles: to be the sting of democracy within liberal democracy itself in order to achieve a universal pluralistic society. Indeed, it is by remaining in active opposition that Marxism is really effective. It is in opposition that it can render its best service, for it allows it to keep the opponents of the liberal system in a planetarian perspective. In a way, it is the safety valve of a hopeless liberal system, purely materialistic and fatally engendering radical oppositions. These are recuperated by the communist ideal and reheated in the globalist broth. Without it, the opponents of bourgeois democracy and consumer society would inevitably join the identity and ethnic reaction movements, which the cosmopolitan system does not want for anything in the world. The scenario unfolding before our eyes is therefore the one imagined by Georges Orwell in his famous fictional novel *1984*, in which the head of the underground opposition, the famous and elusive Goldstein, was nothing more than an agent of the system whose mission was to channel the opposition. Communism has thus regained the role it should never have ceased to have: that of a mobilising utopia within democracy. Sovietism is dead; perhaps it has even been murdered. But the communist ideal has been carefully preserved, recycled within liberal democracy, accommodated and subsidised within institutions. This is how the planetarian spiral works: on the one hand, the system, on the other, a false and fictitious opposition. The two forces are absolutely complementary and indispensable to each other.

Today, the conjunction of the planetarian ideals of Marxists and Western democrats is no longer hindered by the geostrategic conflict between Moscow and Washington. The West can finally give free rein to its instincts for planetarian domination, embodied victoriously in the democratic model it seeks to impose on all the peoples of the planet. As in the time of the glorious French Revolution, the "war against tyrants"

[40] Pierre Lévy, *World philosophy*, Odile Jacob, 2000, p. 150.

has been declared. But this time, the struggle is on a global scale, and it is the United States that has immediately led the liberating armies once the dismantled USSR was no longer in a position to oppose these grandiose designs. The first Gulf War against Iraq in 1991 was followed by the bombing of Serbia in 1999, and, after the attacks of 11 September 2001, by the invasion of Afghanistan, and by a second Gulf War that ended with the occupation of Iraq.

Much has been said about those "neo-conservatives" who gravitated around US President George W. Bush Junior and determined his warmongering policy. These former Trotskyists who had mutated into fervent democrats in the 1980s, during the era of President Reagan, were now ready to declare all the wars necessary to impose the democratic ideal throughout the world. But it must be said, at the risk of misunderstanding the evolution of the world, that the geopolitical interest of the State of Israel was at stake in the Gulf War, and that most of the neo-conservatives in the US administration were themselves heavily influenced by Zionism and convinced that an Iraqi power that might one day threaten the Hebrew State had to be destroyed[41].

In fact, the US wars in Iraq undeniably benefited from the support of most of the international Jewish community. Again, as in the case of the wars against Serbia and Afghanistan, cosmopolitan intellectuals were among the most ardent warmongering lobbyists, for the simple reason that these wars corresponded to globalist objectives: NATO's bombing of Serbia had the effect of encouraging the spread of Islam in the Balkans, thus fulfilling the globalist goal of promoting the multi-ethnic societies that must accompany the establishment of democracy. As General Wesley Clark, NATO's commander-in-chief in Europe at the time of the events, unabashedly put it, "There must no longer be a place in Europe for ethnically homogeneous societies."

The invasion of Afghanistan by US troops was a response to the 9/11 attacks and the need to combat anti-Semitism in the world spread by Islam. We thus saw how the democratic system encouraged Islam within Western states with a view to establishing a pluralistic society, but how it fought it hard on the international scene insofar as it opposed the interests of Israel and Western states, especially in the Middle East.

These wars correspond perfectly to the project of building a global empire, which can only be imposed on the ruins of traditional societies

---

[41]John J. Mearsheimer- Stephen M. Walt: *The Israel Lobby and American Foreign Policy*, Harvard University, 2006. Israel's geopolitics is often confused with its religious eschatology. Evidently, on the other hand, the US military-industrial and energy complex participates in and benefits from this foreign policy. (NdT)

and national freedoms. In this perspective, the media system obviously represents the cornerstone of the planetarian hopes, since it is through continuous "awareness-raising" campaigns that these ideas will progressively impose themselves in the minds of Westerners. However, it seems that our fellow citizens are beginning to experience a more or less diffuse feeling of mistrust towards an over-repeated soothing political discourse that makes the abolition of borders the sesame of paradise on earth.

In this respect, the rejection of the European constitution by French voters in the referendum of May 2005 was perhaps a sign of an awareness of the imminent danger that seems to lurk beneath the noblest and most generous ideas[42]. For, in the minds of their better-informed supporters, the European constitution and the formation of a European government prefigure the realisation of much larger projects.

The idea of a universal peace that would guarantee us a Europe without borders is often an argument that seduces Westerners, but this time it seems that our compatriots preferred their tribal freedom to all the illusions of globalisation. Faced with the promises of "Peace" and "Prosperity" (the famous Social Europe so often touted by our politicians), the French preferred to politely refuse, like those who ignore a slightly deceitful peddler who insists too much on selling his miracle remedy. We will see below that, in the mouths of some experts, the words "tolerance" and "human rights" can be used as powerful anaesthetics, and that behind honeyed speeches, polite manners and fine promises, unspeakable intentions can be hidden.

---

[42]The referendum on the Treaty establishing a Constitution for Europe was held in France on 29 May 2005, to consult citizens on whether France wanted to ratify the EU Constitution. The result was a victory for the No with 55% of voters against and a turnout of 69%. Nicolas Sarkozy then manoeuvred to approve the treaty by having it voted through the parliamentary chambers, thus perpetuating the ultimate anti-constitutionality. (NdT).

PART ONE

COSMOPOLITAN THINKING

osmopolitan thinking is now the dominant way of thinking throughout the West. It is an individual's way of seeing and understanding the world through the prism of humanity, and no longer through what is close to him and what makes up his identity: his family, his language, his work, his region and his nation. Contrary to the other countries of the world, the cosmopolitan Western individual defines himself as a "citizen of the world". He was born on earth, in a family he did not choose, and he expresses himself in a language he believes has been imposed on him. He believes that people all over the world have a common origin—which has been confirmed by scientists—and that their vocation is to merge into a single people and thus annul their differences and prepare for universal and eternal peace on Earth. Ideally, moreover, all languages should disappear and humanity should speak only one language so that people can understand and communicate with each other. The management of human affairs would evidently be handed over to a world government, whose wisdom and good judgment would surely reflect the hopes of humanity. This is the mental universe of the average European cosmopolitan man. However, these deep convictions are not without some paradoxes. Although he desires a plural, multi-ethnic and multicultural society, this desire is reserved for the West, for as far as the countries of the South are concerned, he declares himself a militant for the right of soil and blood and a fervent defender of the Indians of Chiapas or the Eskimos threatened by modernity. He says he is ready to help his fellow humans in the far reaches of Africa or Amazonia, victims of some climatic cataclysm, but close to him, in the neighbouring farms in the interior of his country, hundreds of peasants commit suicide every year in the general indifference. A member of a trade union, he defends social rights against the bosses, but he is also a defender of the rights of immigrants, and in general of freedom of movement, without realising something obvious: that mass immigration, legal or illegal, puts downward pressure on wages and employment conditions. The accomplished cosmopolitan man also often feels a visceral hostility towards religions, all religions. But in fact, the religion he most abhors of all is invariably the Catholic religion. Liberal and hedonistic, it would have been logical for him to reject Islam or Protestant rigorism, but he nevertheless reserves his staunchest vindictiveness for Catholicism. Here too there is no logical explanation. All these contradictions can be explained by the extraordinary influence of the media system and the pressure of conformity. In all the media, on television, in the cinema, on all the radios and in all the subsidised press, the same message is repeated: the untiring apology for democracy and civic equality, a stiff discourse made up of the usual clichés and ready-to-use phrases. We will then understand that the "defence of the values of the republic" involves greater "vigilance" against "any form of discrimination", that "democracy" guarantees the "equality" of all citizens, that "racism" is not an opinion but a crime, and that social cohesion involves the reduction of the social divide and greater solidarity among all. In a system where only the government would deliver its slogans through loudspeakers in the streets, squares and markets, citizens would not easily accept the propaganda of their leaders. But in a country where the entire media and cultural system in unison serves as an intermediary of "citizen awareness", no escape seems possible, if such an idea can still cross our minds. A film at the cinema, a best-selling novel, a popular programme on television, a political commentary on a radio station: all lead us again and again to the worship of the democratic values of Western mercantile society. An opponent, disgusted by the capitalism or liberalism around him, could commit himself to the defence of the oppressed, but not everyone. If one thinks like a globalist, the only true oppressed can only be those in the South, across the oceans. In all cases, the Western citizen's way of thinking invariably revolves around the planet instead of connecting with what used to be the real strength of the great civilisations: history, respect for lineage and tradition. Modern Western civilisation rests on an essential principle that is dual: it generates both power and opposition to that power. Western globalism is represented by both mercantile liberalism and its opposition in the Marxist tradition. In both cases, the idealisation of a unified world and a plural society is at the heart of all aspirations.

From then on, in our democracies, citizens can say anything, express anything: absolutely anything. And this freedom is all the more appreciable because it operates in a closed mode, in the vacuum of the planetarian spiral. The ideological safety barrier marked by the spirit of "human rights" guards against anyone coming too close to the danger zone and falling into the nauseating swamp of "intolerance" and "hatred". A few metres in that direction and you can already feel a tension that prevents you from going any further. If you persist in approaching the border, despite all the warning signs, you risk your professional and social life through ideological electrocution. It is therefore totally impossible to lean over the railing to observe a strange world. Any thought, any cultural product must necessarily pass through the sieve of the media system and must receive the authorisation of the high priests. And this is precisely the closed world that provides "warmth and joie de vivre for the whole family inside the house."

1. One Earth for humanity

The desire to unify the world and abolish borders is part of an ideological process that tends to view humanity's destiny from a planetarian angle. Since we no longer think in terms of nation or tribe, we must rise a little higher and rethink the great human epic from a cosmic point of view. Indeed, seen from space, national borders have disappeared from the face of the earth. It is a powerful argument of the planetarian ideology. On the other hand, the demonstration of a common origin of humanity is a way of advocating future unification. Nations and peoples, which until then made up the diversity of the earth, would only be a parenthesis in the history of mankind. The question then arises whether it is scientific discoveries that support the planetarian idea, or whether it is the planetarian idea that generates some scientific discoveries.

The Cosmos Gypsies

The ideological process tending towards the elimination of national borders and the unification of the world finds overwhelming justification if one looks at the planet from space. And how can one fail to have such a natural view of the world, no matter how little one bothers to look at things from higher up: there are no longer any visible borders, except for seas and mountains, and the differences between human beings become imperceptible. From this point of view, one can indeed speak of a "global village". Indeed, if we look at our small world from space, the planetarian idea becomes majestic, and the unification of the Earth becomes evident. Seen from the cosmos, the idea of a unified Earth seems very natural.

This is what a section of the Western intelligentsia, fascinated by the idea of a unified world where universal peace would reign, explains. Edgar Morin[43] is one of those French intellectuals who view the evolution of today's world with optimism and who is enthusiastic about

---

[43]Edgar Morin (Paris, 1921), born Edgar Nahum, is a centenarian French philosopher and sociologist of Sephardic origin. He is a prolific and award-winning author, widely translated into English.

the great transformations that European societies are undergoing. The acceleration of the globalisation process at the end of the second millennium is not only a divine surprise, but also the long-awaited advent of a new world that will revolutionise customs and free minds from all the old national traditions and prejudices. From his point of view, "in the cosmos we must place our planet and our destiny, our meditations, our ideas, our aspirations, our fears and our wills." In reality, we are only "tiny humans, on the tiny film of life that surrounds the tiny planet lost in the gigantic universe[44]."

The scientific discoveries of the 20th century have made it possible to situate humanity's destiny in the infinite universe, so this new dimension invites us to reconsider humanity from a broader point of view, from the perspective of its universal collective destiny, far removed from petty national disputes. "In the 1960s, when a prodigious cosmic evolution took shape, previously unimaginable strangeness appeared in today's universe: quasars (1963), pulsars (1968), black holes later, and astrophysicists' calculations suggest that we only know about 10% of matter, the remaining 90% still being invisible to our detection instruments (...). Here we are in a marginal galaxy, the Milky Way, which appeared 8 billion years after the birth of the world." It is impossible to continue thinking in terms of nations and tribes after such considerations. Seen from the cosmos, human conflicts seem laughable. They must disappear once and for all to make way for the conquest of the universe.

It is this space view of the planet that has inspired so many Hollywood-produced science-fiction film screenwriters. American cinema has contributed mightily to imbuing Western minds with this weightless view of the world. The enemy is no longer any terrestrial power, but an extraterrestrial force against which all Humans must ally themselves. Thus, wars against extraterrestrial or extrahuman powers go on and on, from *Star Wars* to *Independence Day*, via the *Matrix, Star Trek, Alien* or *Depredator*. These fictions instil in people's minds the image of humanity united against an external danger, and reinforce the idea that all human beings should unite under the same banner. If St. Paul said that there was no longer "neither Jew nor Greek", Hollywood cinema seems to tell us today: "There are no more whites, no more yellows, no more blacks. There are only Humans fighting against the empire of Evil."

---

[44]Edgar Morin and Anne-Brigitte Kern, *Terre-Patrie*, 1993, Editorial Kairós, Barcelona, 2005, p. 49–50, 74

One might respond that perhaps we should think about coming down to earth, and take a closer look at the realities. But the planetarian project ignores realities in favour of the idea of an intergalactic destiny of humanity. Thus, the turbulence and damage generated by human conflicts resulting from the application of this ideology will be seen as transitory evils that will gradually subside. If the idea is beautiful, then much will be forgiven to those who apply its principles." A planet as a homeland? Yes, that is our rootedness in the cosmos[45] ", concluded Edgar Morin. We will be the "Sinhalese of the Cosmos".

Lucy, the grandmother of humanity

Anthropologists strongly support the planetarian idea by establishing that the entire population of humankind would have common ancestors, especially the one nicknamed "the grandmother of humankind". Lucy—that's her name—would have lived in the African Great Lakes region three million years ago. Her skeleton, found in 1974, was that of an australopithecine, probably female, less than twenty years old. Yves Coppens, Donald Johanson and Maurice Taïeb, co-directors of the mission that discovered Lucy, were at the origin of this fantastic discovery. This triumvirate could be proud of having carried out this scientific project, the purpose of which went beyond mere expert discussions. Thanks to them, humanity was one, and men were all brothers. This discovery would make a whole generation of teenagers marvel and willingly declare themselves "Africans", waiting to declare themselves "Chinese" or "Malaysians" after the next oldest skeleton was found[46]." Lucy remains incontestably that ancestor of humanity", Yves Coppens asserted, adding: "After all, a founding Lucy of a tropical, African, coloured, matriarchal humanity is not the worst image we could find for the humanity of the origins[47]." We will see later what role the idea of matriarchy plays in planetarian thinking.

The interpretation of this discovery, and especially the publicity it received, made Lucy the symbol of the common origin of all human

---

[45] Edgar Morin and Anne-Brigitte Kern, *Tierra-Patria*, 1993, Editorial Kairós, Barcelona, 2005, p. 47, 48, 223, 224.

[46] *Le Figaro* of 7 March 2005 reported that an Australopithecus skeleton about 2.8 million years old had been found some sixty kilometres from where Lucy had been found. In the end, Lucy was only 2.2 million years old, so humanity would have been 800,000 years younger than the 1999 estimate, before suddenly ageing again by 600,000 years. No one was fazed by this.

[47] Yves Coppens, *La rodilla de Lucy, los primeros pasos hacia la humanidad*, Tusquets, Barcelona, 2005, p. 149.

beings. The idea was obviously taken up and used by many intellectuals. The philosopher Pierre Lévy, for example, explained that, thanks to the discovery of Lucy's skeleton in Africa, we now know that "our most direct ancestors all lived in the same geographical area", that of the African Great Lakes." From that almost mythical starting point, humanity begins to separate on its own, it disperses[48]."

The great political upheavals of the 20th century can therefore be interpreted as the vicissitudes of the crisis of unification, as "the upheavals of societies and cultures inherited from the divergence phase", as explained by Professor Langaney, geneticist and director of the biological anthropology laboratory of the Natural History Museum: "All people today, i.e. some six billion individuals, are descended from a single, small prehistoric population—some thirty to fifty thousand people, living at least a hundred thousand years ago. We are therefore in all likelihood the descendants of tens of thousands of Palaeolithic hunters living in an area limited to Africa and the Middle East[49]." According to Edgar Morin, "the *homo sapiens* diaspora, which began thirteen hundred centuries ago, spread across Africa and Eurasia, crossed the Bering Strait a hundred thousand years ago[50]".

However, this common origin is not so obvious a priori. In *La Humanité perdue[51]*, Alain Finkielkraut addressed the issue from the very first page of his book: "The idea that all the peoples of the world form a single humanity is certainly not consubstantial to the human race. Indeed, what has long distinguished humans from other animal species is precisely that they did not recognise one another."

Indeed, Claude Lévi-Strauss confirmed, as he was quoted on the subject: "The notion of humanity, which encompasses, without distinction of race or civilisation, all forms of the human species, is of very late appearance and of limited expansion... For large fractions of the human species, and for tens of millennia, this notion seems to have been totally absent." The question remains the same: "the difficult question of knowing how to contribute, from where we are and to the extent of our possibilities, to making the world a habitable place for those beings all alike and all different who make up humanity[52]."

[48] Pierre Lévy, *World philosophy*, Odile Jacob, 2000, p. 16-19.
[49] Interview with André Langaney, *L'Histoire* magazine, no. 214, October 1997.
[50] Edgar Morin and Anne-Brigitte Kern, *Tierra-Patria*, 1993, Editorial Kairós, Barcelona, 2005, p. 65.
[51] Alain Finkielkraut, *L'Humanité perdue*, Le Seuil, 1996.
[52] Alain Finkielkraut, *La Humanidad perdida*, Anagrama, Barcelona, 1998, p. 13, 14, 130." *All equal, all different*" was the title of a 1994 "campaign against intolerance", financed by the Council of Europe. The presentation brochure featured a young

One human race

Another important step in planetarian thinking came in February 2001, with the simultaneous publication in two Anglo-Saxon journals, *Nature* and *Science*, of scientific analyses of the sequencing of the human genome. These showed that the human genome was made up of 30,000 genes and, above all, that the genetic heritage was almost identical in all human beings. Immediately, in France, the minister of scientific research Roger-Gérard Schwartzenberg, and with him almost all Parisian journalists, claimed that these results confirmed that "races do not exist."

In the *Courrier de l'UNESCO* (United Nations Educational, Scientific and Cultural Organisation) of September 2001, one could read several analyses supporting this approach: "The human genome has finally been decoded. The completion of this project invalidates the myth of race. Research by geneticists concludes that we are all descended from a single common ancestor, born in Africa. Most genetic variations are similarly distributed in all human populations."

"Indeed, scientists claim that, in all our genetic material, only 0.012% corresponds to variations resulting from differences between "races". Scientific research therefore demonstrates that almost all of our genetic heritage is common to all humans, thus invalidating the idea that some populations are genetically more intelligent or advanced than others[53]." It was indeed necessary for science to intervene in this sensitive area of knowledge, as the most backward populations always have some difficulty in realising this.

Let us recall that "the fight against racism is enshrined in UNESCO's Constitution", and that it denounces "ignorance and prejudice, the dogma of the inequality of races and men"." For half a century, the organisation has been attacking the roots of evil. This dimension is present in the education programmes that the international organisation helps to develop, as well as in the lectures given by many professors who have been appointed to UNESCO chairs in universities in developing countries.

UNESCO is also combating racism through the exact sciences. Its 55-member International Bioethics Committee (IBC) (scientists, lawyers, economists, demographers, anthropologists, philosophers, nutritionists, etc.) drew up a Universal Declaration on the Human Genome and Human Rights (UDBHR), adopted in 1997." Two decades

---

European woman in the arms of a young African man on the cover.
[53] *Le Courier de l'UNESCO*, septembre 2001, p. 23

after the UNESCO declaration on race and racial prejudice (1978), this first international text on bioethics definitively invalidates the pseudo-scientific foundations of racism."

Since the Convention on the Prevention and Suppression of the Crime of Genocide (1948), the UN has adopted a series of conventions and declarations, proclaimed an international year of mobilisation against racism (2001), organised three Decades of struggle against racism (1973–1982, 1983–1992, 1994–2003), as well as two world conferences on the same subject in Geneva (1978 and 1983).

The World Conference "Against Racism, Racial Discrimination, Xenophobia and Intolerance" which took place in September 2001 in Durban, South Africa, was part of the United Nations' efforts to combat this scourge. The internationally renowned geneticist Axel Kahn, who was also one of the organisers of the event, made an outstanding speech: "The surprise of recent scientific findings is that man has no more genes than the donkey or the ox, and even less than the toad … All men actually have a great genetic homogeneity, as their common ancestor is very young compared to the evolution of life; he lived more than 200 000 years ago in Africa. All continents seem to have been populated from a population whose groups would have left Africa 70 000 years ago. Skin colour, which plays such an important role in racist prejudice, does not so much reflect genetic divergence as a phenomenon of progressive tanning of the epidermis as one moves northwards towards the equator. There is on average more diversity within individuals of a particular ethnicity than, between two different ethnicities, be they apparently as different as Scandinavian or Melanesian populations."

Axel Kahn continued: "This scientific demonstration, though indispensable, may be insufficient. Everyone can see how the worst excesses of racism are very well adapted to the non-existence of human races… All in all, modern biology and genetics do nothing to confirm racist prejudices. But it would be a contradiction in terms to try to base an anti-racist commitment on science. There is no scientific definition of human dignity; it is a philosophical concept. Thus, the anti-racist struggle for the recognition of the equal dignity of all people is first and foremost of a moral nature and reflects a deep conviction that is not exclusive to the scientist." In other words, the fact that races do not exist is not a reason to stop fighting racism.

This is what the great Professor André Langaney told us: "Race, in the common sense of the word, is essentially an ethological, or rather a perceptive concept, which results from the observation of a difference and the emotional context which provokes this observation, i.e.

according to the prejudices or reactions of the subject. Under these conditions, the race that provokes racism no longer has much to do with those that anthropologists wanted to define, but rather physical differences are, among many others, one of the possible causes of what would be better called "*otrism*" rather than racism. The criteria that lead to racism are often more cultural, linguistic or behavioural than physical[54]." Therefore, except for cultural, linguistic, behavioural and physical differences, all men are absolutely alike in all respects.

Ecology: catastrophic scenario

The unification of the world is in fact a necessity for the survival of our planet. The great ecological challenges require without further delay a world authority capable of imposing on everyone the implementation of an effective policy to protect our environment and to solve the great planetarian problems. The most alarmist reports urge us to abdicate our sovereignty in favour of a world government:

It is only a beginning," warned sociologist Edgar Morin. The deterioration of the biosphere is continuing, desertification and tropical deforestation are accelerating, biological diversity is diminishing." For the next thirty years, the most pessimistic scientists "see an irreversible continuation of the generalised degradation of the biosphere, with the modification of climates, the increase in temperature and evapotranspiration, the rise in sea level (from 30 to 140 centimetres), the extension of drought zones, all this with a probable demography of 10 billion human beings."

But even if "optimists believe that the biosphere possesses within itself the potential for self-regeneration and immune defence that will enable it to safeguard itself", the author warned that "in any case, the duty of caution applies." The best way to solve these problems is to manage them on a global scale.

Ecological issues therefore require the formation of international institutions, even a world government." In any case, Edgar Morin stressed, nation-states, including the large polyethnic nation-states, are already too small for the great inter- and transnational problems: the problems of the economy, of development, of techno-industrial civilisation, of the homogenisation of lifestyles and lifestyles, of

---

[54] André Langaney, *Les Hommes, passé, présent, conditionnel*, Armand Colin, 1988.

ecology, of drugs; these are planetarian problems that exceed national competencies[55]."

Like anthropology and genetics, ecology also feeds the mill of the great planetarian idea. This evidence need not be insisted upon, and one is surprised that Hollywood films have not yet dealt with the subject in their productions. The heatwave of summer 2003, for example, could be a good catastrophic scenario, just like the tsunami of 26 December 2004, when the whole planet, or almost[56], had felt solidarity and mobilised, in a great show of fraternity, to help the unfortunate victims.

Emerging from the planetarian iron age

Since its beginnings, humanity has progressed rather slowly before it became aware of its universal human nature. It is only since the 16th century of our era, with the discoveries of other continents, that we have been able to realise the finiteness of the terrestrial universe. That chapter could be considered as year zero of the "planetarian era".

This process of unification is taking place today, in front of our very eyes, straddling two millennia." Our terrestrial family tree and our earthly identity card can be known today, at last, at the end of the fifth century of the planetarian era," said Edgar Morin. At the dawn of the 21st century, "after millennia of confinement in the repetitive cycle of traditional civilisations", we are entering a new world." The human species now appears to us as humanity. From now on, humanity and the planet can reveal themselves in their unity, not only physical and biospheric, but also historical: that of the planetarian era. Migrations and crossbreeding, producers of new societies, polycultural seem to announce the common homeland for all humans[57]."

The "pursuit of hominisation" should enable us to emerge from the "planetarian iron age". We must not look backwards, on the contrary, we must look forwards. Our task, according to Edgar Morin, is to "reform Western civilisation", "federate the Earth" and "bring about the era of planetarian citizenship." We must therefore "consider planetarian citizenship, which would give and guarantee earthly rights to all[58]."

---

[55] Edgar Morin and Anne-Brigitte Kern, *Tierra-Patria*, 1993, Editorial Kairós, Barcelona, 2005, p. 81, 82, 86.

[56] We will see later that priorities were not the same for everyone.

[57] Edgar Morin and Anne-Brigitte Kern, *Tierra-Patria*, 1993, Editorial Kairós, Barcelona, 2005, p. 74, 223, 43.

[58] Edgar Morin and Anne-Brigitte Kern, *Tierra-Patria*, 1993, Editorial Kairós, Barcelona, 2005, p. 136, 142, 143.

At the beginning of the third millennium, the challenge is therefore crucial: "to save humanity, to co-pilot the biosphere, to civilise the Earth". Will Humans succeed in deflecting the gigantic meteorite that threatens to pulverise our planet, as predicted by Hollywood's doomsday scripts? "The task is immense and uncertain," Edgar Morin replied, but he insisted once again: "It would require a planetarian citizenship, a planetarian civic consciousness, a planetarian intellectual and scientific opinion, a planetarian political opinion ... a planetarian public opinion[59]."

What then are the "regenerative ways"? How to civilise in depth? How to get out of the prehistory of the human mind? How to get out of our civilised barbarism[60]? "Certainly, Wolfgang Amadeus Mozart, Michelangelo or Leonardo da Vinci, the palace of Versailles or the cathedral of Chartres are but specks of dust compared to the bright future that is finally opening up before us. Edgar's legitimate questions and anxieties could be answered more naturally from the vantage point he has already envisaged: in the cosmos. Problems are easily solved from there, and the time will soon come when interplanetarian travel will be within the reach of all budgets. The philosopher will then be able to embark on one of these journeys and appease his tormented soul.

In *The Melancholy of Democracy*, Pascal Bruckner explained at the very beginning of his book that "the planet has reached an unprecedented stage in its adventure; the unification of the globe on a technical and material level is about to become so politically. The very idea of universal peace is ceasing to be a dream of utopians and is becoming a reality in fact. All that we have suffered under the name of history has been nothing more than upheavals and convulsions to reach this glorious stage[61]."

"Imagine: the whole planet hooked up to gas and voting in parliamentary elections, armies dismantled, the rich distributing their goods to the poor, men treating women as equals, murderers becoming nurses, Jesus, Moses, Mohammed cancelling humanity's moral debt, the globe once again an annex of Eden: are we ready for that? ... We live in a turning point where all political and military barriers have been lifted, where the world of possibilities seems immense. The ability to make this planet a slightly better and more rational place is within our

---

[59] Edgar Morin and Anne-Brigitte Kern, *Tierra-Patria*, 1993, Editorial Kairós, Barcelona, 2005, p. 226, 229, 144.
[60] Edgar Morin, *El Método 6, Ética; chapter: Las vías regeneradoras*, Ediciones Cátedra-Anaya, Madrid, 2006, p. 187.
[61] Pascal Bruckner, *La Mélancolie démocratique*, Éditions du Seuil, 1990, p. 13.

grasp. It is even possible to dream of a gigantic insurrection for democracy in the South and a global plan of action to end misery[62]."

For Albert Jacquard, another planetarian philosopher, the success of this gigantic operation of world unification necessarily depended on the establishment of democratic societies. But here we are also confronted with the major problem already identified by Edgar Morin: how to unify the planet without standardising and thus impoverishing the ethnic and cultural diversity that make up the richness of the Earth?

We must call for the establishment of an "ethical democracy, which is much more delicate than a managerial democracy. It will be necessary to define rules of behaviour respected by all, on the basis of the diversity of the imperatives expressed by each. This objective presupposes a general agreement on the common core accepted by all peoples, while preserving their specificities, their diversities and all cultures. This common core must emerge from a reflection on the meaning we give to our life project, and, first of all, a reflection on the point of convergence of this project, which is the same for all[63]."

How did we not think of this before? In fact, the problem is almost solved. It is enough for Western intellectuals, philosophers and sociologists to reflect and invent new ideological norms and products in order to chart our destiny. The inevitable cannot be avoided. Historical evolution confirms that humanity is heading towards these great spaces. The 18th century was the century of triumphant philosophy, the 19th century of triumphant industry and the 20th century of triumphant economics." From now on, we must choose what the 21st century will be: the triumph of barbarism or the triumph of humanity[64] ", Albert Jacquard assured us. If the poets join the sociologists, then the cause of the Good can only triumph.

---

[62] Pascal Bruckner, *La Mélancolie démocratique*, Éditions du Seuil, 1990, p. 165.

[63] Albert Jacquard, *A Toi qui n'es pas encore né(e)*, Calmann-Lévy, 2000, p. 87.

[64] Albert Jacquard, *Pequeña filosofía para no filósofos*, Debolsillo, Random House Mondadori, Barcelona, 2003, p. 220.

2. The planetarian ideal

The planetarian discourse has never been so omnipresent as since the fall of the communist bloc. Whereas before, these ideas were mainly disseminated by the May 68 movement and Marxism in general, they are now championed by a generation of formerly Marxist intellectuals who have joined the cause of liberal democracy and the market economy. In France, Jacques Attali is obviously one of the most emblematic examples, both for the profusion of his literary output and for the influence of his ideas and the eminent functions he occupied within the French state apparatus. Edgar Morin, Alain Finkielkraut, Albert Jacquard, Guy Sorman, Marek Halter, Bernard-Henri Lévy, André Glucksmann, Alain Minc and Pascal Bruckner are the main representatives of the cosmopolitan thinking that is so influential in France today. Fervent democrats, their thinking is also imbued with the same planetarian ideals as Marxism. On this level, there is no detectable difference. They all aspire to world government, the abolition of borders and the intermingling of peoples and civilisations, at least within the West. For his part, the very famous and influential philosopher Jacques Derrida, who died during the summer of 2004, had remained faithful to his Marxist convictions until his last day, but his thinking fitted in perfectly with that of his democratic colleagues. In fact, they are all marked by the influence of Freudo-Marxism.

Through Wilhelm Reich, Herbert Marcuse and the student leader Daniel Cohn-Bendit, the Freudo-Marxist current had a considerable influence on the events of May '68. The boundary between Marxism and democratic ideology is blurred, shifting and permeable. Albert Einstein, for example, bordered on both. Jacques Attali, who was the main advisor to socialist president François Mitterrand in the 1980s and one of the main propagandists of the planetarian idea, has a way of thinking that also mixes cultural Freudo-Marxism and economic liberalism. The man was also later director of the European Bank for Reconstruction and Development.

The question is whether liberal ideology would have moved towards the planetarian ideal without the help of Marxist ideas. Certainly, the idea of globalisation was already present in the philosophy of the Enlightenment, but in small doses, for no one then thought of merging nations. On the other hand, Marxist thought developed this theme extensively, symbolised by the famous internationalist slogan: "Workers of all countries, unite! Since the fall of the Berlin Wall in 1989, liberal ideology has regained the initiative in the planetarian escalation. But this time it is no longer enough to establish world government; it is also necessary to encourage the great universal miscegenation and uprooting. Marxism had not gone that far. The two currents are nowadays very much intertwined, so that it is not at all easy to distinguish in planetarian thinking what is specifically Marxist or liberal.

Citizens of the world

When young people declare themselves in good faith to be "citizens of the world" in school playgrounds, one might rightly think that their convictions are not the fruit of deep reflection on their status, but simply the result of media "awareness-raising" campaigns. In television debates or in books, through film, press and radio, and now also the internet, the concept of global citizenship is relentlessly hammered home, so that it is necessary to forge one's own personal culture to try to get off the beaten track and to understand the dominant discourse and decipher the coded messages.

The famous French sociologist Albert Jacquard is one of those intellectuals who have a decidedly planetarian vision of the world. He was not born in a modest village in the Auvergne or Brittany: "I was born on a planet with two billion inhabitants[65] ", he said in his dictionary. He too dreams of harmony, universal brotherhood and peace for the human race. The happiest man is not the reticent one who withdraws into his family, his friends and his village, but the one who opens up to all the cultures of the world and seeks to connect with people from other continents:

"Every human being whom I exclude from the ties I weave is a source from which I deprive myself. The dream, then, is to exclude no one." In this perspective, one must declare oneself a "citizen of the world" as the American Gary Davis did in 1947, tearing up his passport to show his desire to see all borders disappear. At the time, the minister Georges Bidault had stated that "borders are the scars of history". Now,

---

[65] Albert Jacquard, *Pequeña filosofía para no filósofos*, Debolsillo, Random House Mondadori, Barcelona, 2003, p. 1.

Albert Jacquard judiciously and opportunely added: "Scars are formed in order to disappear."

A "community of Mediterranean peoples" would he a first step towards the unification of the world." A Mediterranean cultural community must be built[66] "he insisted in another of his books. Indeed, the idea is recurrent in his works. It would be, he explained, "an exercise that would enable us to better organise the community of all nations[67]."

The very prolific essayist Jacques Attali was obviously going further in this direction. His *Dictionary of the 21st century* shows that he is a great visionary and a prodigious creator of ideas. The future of humanity holds no secrets for this prophet[68]. Globalisation will continue, accelerate and impose itself thanks to international institutions: "A consciousness of world unity will be awakened, thanks to which international organisations will find the means for their tasks; the UN will disseminate rules and enforce duties; a world police force will be installed in lawless areas; the IMF, charged with collecting and distributing a world tax on international transactions, will regulate the financial markets, which will no longer be places and agents of panic but will be at the service of reducing injustice."

This is the ideal scenario, a goal to be achieved or at least a step towards the establishment of a world government, although he warned us that "a thousand setbacks will come to muddy the course of this calm river." While we await the advent of this better world, Attali invited us to develop the good habits recommended to bring us a little closer to the earthly paradise that is within our reach: "What should be done to avoid the worst is easy to say: put science and technology at the service of justice; take advantage of their immense potential to eliminate poverty everywhere, break down hierarchical systems and rethink democracy: encourage diversity, share wealth, promote health and education, eliminate arms expenditure, replant the forests, develop clean energy, open up to the culture of others, encourage all kinds of mixing, learn to think globally[69]."

---

[66] Albert Jacquard, *A Toi qui n'es pas encore né(e)*, Calmann-Lévy, 2000, p. 151.

[67] Albert Jacquard, *Pequeña filosofía para no filósofos*, Debolsillo, Random House Mondadori, Barcelona, 2003, p. 73, 162, 76.

[68] Jacques Attali is a personality who over the years has become more visible to the Spanish and Spanish-speaking public. Many of his works have been translated into Spanish. One of his books that seems to us to be the most recommendable in relation to what we are dealing with here is: *Breve historia del futuro*, Ediciones Paidós Ibérica, Barcelona, 2007. This work was published after Hervé Ryssen's *Las Esperanzas planetarianas* (Baskerville, 2005) (NdT).

[69] Jacques Attali, *Dictionary of the 21st century*, Paidós Ibérica Pocket, Barcelona,

In this new form of civilisation, the "hyperclass" will be the ruling class. It will be composed "of mobile and transparent elites who will drag the whole of society with them towards the utopia of fraternity. It will bring together several tens of millions of individuals. They will be the guarantors of freedom, citizens' rights, the market economy, liberalism and the democratic spirit. They will cultivate and develop a keen awareness of the planetarian challenges."

Of course, these prophecies reflect nothing more than personal intentions and convictions. But they have the merit of being clearly stated by a man who played an important role in France at the end of the 20th century.

Among the planetarian thinkers at the beginning of this millennium, there is one whose enthusiasm surpasses that of Jacques Attali. Pierre Lévy's book, *World Philosophy*, is an ode to planetarian unification declaimed in a prophetic tone bordering on a divinatory trance. From the beginning to the end of the book, the oracle speaks to us: "From now on, the great adventure of the world is no longer limited to countries, nations, religions or any other *ism*. The great adventure is the adventure of humanity, the adventure of the most intelligent species in the known universe. This species is not fully civilised. It has not yet become fully conscious that it forms a single intelligent society. But the unification of humanity is being made, now. After so many efforts, the unification of humanity has finally arrived[70]." We must understand this speech: Beethoven, Molière, Botticeli and Van Gogh are nothing but leagues compared to what will be produced by the finally unified humanity that is taking shape.

For us, the humans of the year 2000, "our compatriots are everywhere on Earth. We are the first generation of people to exist on a global scale," he continued." The end of the 20th century marks a decisive and irreversible threshold in the process of planetarian unification of the human species." The world in which you have lived until now is dying. Don't fight, don't fight any more. Let yourselves go, let yourselves be guided. Your limbs are heavy, very heavy. Let yourselves be lulled to sleep by this beneficent lethargy...

"Let us realise that East and West are promised to marry, and that they will benefit each other. Only then will humanity be one with itself." Look at the Jews: a tip of the East in the West, a drop of the West in the East"; "Humanity is a great carpet of shining pearls where luminous

---

2007, p. 16, 18.
[70] Pierre Lévy, *World philosophy*, Odile Jacob, 2000, p. 12.

forms circulate[71] "; "We are the sons and daughters of all poets. All human efforts to expand our consciousness converge in an oosphere that henceforth lives within us because it is the objectification of the collective consciousness and intelligence of humanity." Let go, let do ... You are now fast asleep." We have no enemies: we are a shower of diamonds where the light of the worlds sparkles[72]."

Michel Serres certainly does not have the lyrical talent of Lévy; in fact, he lags far behind. His way of expressing himself is extremely confused, which is surprising for a scientist who sits in the French Academy. We will therefore limit ourselves to quoting a few short sentences, for his prose is very stony and almost unintelligible. However, here and there, one can perceive that the writer is imbued with the same planetarian zeal when he criticises, for example, the "antiquated absurdities that are the borders between nations[73]."

"Without land or tribe, we are citizens of the world and brothers of men", he wrote. Unfortunately, many passages in his books are simply unreadable, even totally incoherent, such as this one we have chosen, among others: "The family root abandons blood in favour of adoption and an extension of the family, henceforth a directive choice, towards humanity in general. All men have the right to feel at home everywhere and at home with everyone. The West came to leave the local and to bring in gestation the universal[74]." Under the pen of an academic, such phrases are quite unique. An amusing detail caught our attention: Michel Serres' face looks strikingly similar to that of the Italian writer Alberto Moravia, who also professes beautiful and noble planetarian ideas. The same plumage, the same ramage, as the good Monsieur de La Fontaine would say[75].

"Man is finally human because he is finally universal... Man is no longer vernacular, he is planetarian", enthused the great philosopher Alain Finkielkraut, who announced to us:

"The end of the cloistered existence: as generalised communication and connection have erased—miraculous lifting—the wrinkles that borders had carved on the face of humanity, the suffered belonging disappears in favour of the chosen relationship: all the dead are available from now on; "Happiness if I feel like it", everyone can

---

[71] Pierre Lévy, *World philosophy*, Odile Jacob, 2000, p. 153-156.

[72] Pierre Lévy, *World philosophie*, Odile Jacob, 2000, p. 174-176, 184

[73] Michel Serres, *L'Incandescent*, Le Pommier, 2003, p. 113.

[74] Michel Serres, *L'Incandescent*, Le Pommier, 2003, p. 222.

[75] Jean de La Fontaine was a 17th century French poet and fabulist. His fables are a classic of literature that French schoolchildren used to learn (NdT).

christen their child with any name on Earth, plug themselves in, without leaving their room, to any entertainment, access live catastrophes, explore the most distant cultures lying on the sofa, burst without warning into all the memorable places, go, without leaving home, to window shop in the antipodes and navigate at will through the data banks of the great world amalgam that traditions have become[76]." Finkielkraut was probably revealing his own aspirations rather than reality here, but his thinking illuminates the path that contemporary political philosophy is pointing us in the right direction.

Alain Finkielkraut was, however, well aware that this revolutionary spirit that tends to "wipe out the past" and "create a new man" had already been put into practice in the Soviet Union under Lenin and Stalin. At the time, "the USSR embodied this apotheosis in the face of exclusivist homelands". It represented "the fatherland of humanity" and made "the division of humanity into compatriots and foreigners obsolete[77]." Marxism had attracted to itself all the ardent spirits of egalitarian messianism, and left no room for any other idea of planetarian unification than its own. But it must be recognised that today the ideological affiliation with Marxism is no longer really positive, after the collapse of that system and the horrors we know. It is therefore necessary to look for ideological references and kinship in other intellectuals.

Julien Benda was perhaps the only non-Marxist representative of the planetarian spirit during the inter-war period in France. Alain Finkielkraut and Bernard-Henri Lévy both refer to him for their ideological references. In *The Betrayal of the Intellectuals*, wrote Finkielkraut, Julien Benda exalted the "Enlightenment against Romanticism; defence of the universal against the glorification of the particular; affirmation of the freedom of the spirit against the rootedness of man in the soil of his homeland, of the spirit in tradition, of action in customs, and of thought in language[78]." It is in the work of this

---

[76] Alain Finkielkraut, *La Humanidad perdida*, Anagrama, Barcelona, 1998, p. 145, 146, 147.

[77] Alain Finkielkraut, *La Humanidad perdida*, Anagrama, Barcelona, 1998, p. 58, 59." Homeland without roots, however, nation without nature, territory whose natives are not indigenous because, in this bastion of the new era, institution has prevailed over origin, the human spirit has defeated the spirit of the place. This victory renders the division of humanity into compatriots and foreigners obsolete. No one is a foreigner, no face is rejected or evicted in a landscape that no longer expresses itself in geographical but in technical terms... The humanism present in the name of the USSR will continue to inspire political combat and intellectual work for a long time to come. The same will be true of thought in general..."

[78] Alain Finkielkraut, *La Humanidad perdida*, Anagrama, Barcelona, 1998, p. 64, 65.

renowned intellectual, "the great priest of the Spirit[79] ", that we must look for the elements that will support the new civilisation. In the *Address to the European Nation*, which he wrote in 1932, he presented himself as the only non-Marxist thinker to proclaim a globalist discourse which would not come into vogue until the end of the century: "Intellectuals of all countries, you must be those who proclaim to your nations that they are perpetually in the camp of evil, by the mere fact of being nations". Plotinus blushed to have a body. You must be those who blush to have a nation." The style reminds us a little of the professorship, but at least the lesson has the merit of being clear.

The abolition of borders and the intermingling of peoples is an ideal to be achieved, but an open society will only be viable if race instincts and local particularisms are annihilated. Pure races must be crossed in order to dissolve feelings of identity, which could give rise to nationalist resurgence. The languages themselves must even disappear in favour of a common language. This was the visionary ambition of a man called Ludwig Lazarus Zamenhof. He was a young student of the cultivated Polish bourgeoisie who had devoted himself at an early age to working on the development of a language understood by all, based on the common roots of the most common languages of the world. His work culminated in the publication of his fundamental work in 1887, which presented the Esperanto language[80]: *Fundamentals of Esperanto*. Zamenhof explained his motivations: "Men are equal: they are creatures of the same species. They all have one heart, one brain, vital organs, needs and ideals; the difference of languages is the essence of difference and mutual hostility between peoples. Only language and nationality differentiate them... If I had not been a ghetto Jew, the idea of uniting humanity would never have occurred to me, or I would not have been so obstinately obsessed with it throughout my life. No one can feel the unhappiness of human division more than a ghetto Jew. No one can feel the need for a humanly neutral and anational language as strongly as a Jew who has been forced to pray to God in a dead language, while receiving his education and instruction in the language of a people who reject him and who have fellow sufferers all over the world with whom he cannot understand... My Jewishness was

---

[79] Alain Finkielkraut, *Le Mécontemporain*, Gallimard, 1991, p. 16.
[80] Esperanto's vocabulary comes mainly from Western European languages, while its syntax and morphology show Slavic influences and strong resemblances to isolating and agglutinative languages such as Chinese or Japanese. (NdT).

the main reason why, from my earliest childhood, I devoted myself to an essential idea and dream: the dream of uniting mankind[81]."

World government

The aspirations to establish a world government find their primary justifications in the yearning for universal peace. In this sense, Julien Benda was a pioneer who expressed some of the inter-war globalist aspirations very well. In the conclusion of his book *The Betrayal of the Intellectuals*, he also considered the fusion of peoples with characteristic prophetic enthusiasm: "The will to present oneself as distinct would be transferred from the nation to the species, proudly standing up against everything that is not itself. In reality, such a movement exists: there is, above classes and nations, a will of the species to make itself loved by things, and when a human being flies in a few hours from one end of the earth to the other, the whole human race shudders with pride and adores itself as if it were distinct in the midst of creation." ... It may sometimes be thought that such a movement will assert itself more and more, and that in this way inter-human wars will be extinguished; a "universal brotherhood" will thus be arrived at, but that, far from signifying the abolition of the spirit of the nation with its prides and appetites, it will on the contrary be its supreme form, the nation calling itself Man and the enemy calling himself God. And from then on, unified in an immense army, in an immense factory, knowing nothing but heroisms, disciplines, inventions, casting off all free and disinterested activity, satisfied to place the good beyond the real world and no longer having for god but itself and its appetites, humanity will achieve great things, I mean a truly great mastery over the matter around it, a truly joyful consciousness of its power and its greatness[82]." After anthropology, genetics and planetarian ecology, pacifism also militates for the great cause of world unification. After the Second World War, Julien Benda became a travelling companion of the Communist Party. His generous ideas did not prevent him from justifying the crushing of the 1956 Hungarian uprising and the trials following the repression.

The very famous scientist Albert Einstein was one of the first, perhaps the first, contemporary personages to call explicitly for the

---

[81] Letter from Louis Lazarus Zamenhof of 21 February 1905 to the French Esperantist Michaux.

[82] Julien Benda, *La Traición de los intelectuales*, Ediciones Ercilla, Santiago de Chile, 1951, p. 187, 188.

establishment of a world government. Perhaps this is one of the reasons why he is so much adulated, for we shall see later in this book that his scientific aura has recently been somewhat tarnished. After the war, in November 1945, he published an article in the *Atlantic Monthly* magazine: "Since the United States and Great Britain have the secret of the atomic bomb and the Soviet Union does not, they should invite the Soviet Union to prepare and submit the first draft of a constitution for world government ... After the three great powers have drafted a constitution and adopted it, the smaller nations should be invited to join the world government ... The power of this world government would embrace all military affairs, and it would have to have only one more power; that of being able to interfere in countries where a minority is oppressing the majority, thus creating the kind of instability which leads to war. Conditions such as those that currently exist in Argentina and Spain should be addressed. The concept of non-intervention must be done away with, as doing away with it is part of peacekeeping."

And Einstein added with some aplomb: "While it is true that the Soviet Union is ruled by a minority, I do not consider that internal conditions are in themselves a threat to world peace[83]." In an article published in January 1946 in the *Survey Graphic, he* further wrote, "Mankind's desire for peace can only be realised by the creation of a world government."

The sociologist Edgar Morin also wanted the establishment of a world government. However, he denied that he wanted to promote paternalism or racism towards the populations of the South. For, in his view, these grandiose achievements must be the task of the West, since that is where the technological development and the power to impose these prospects on the rest of humanity are to be found. The happiness of earthlings necessarily passes through a phase in which the peoples of the South must, by hook or by crook, accept the idea of universal democracy. Such projects undoubtedly justify a "right to interfere":

"The human association to which we aspire could not (as we have already said elsewhere[*]): "be based on the hegemonic model of the white, adult, technical, western man; it must, on the contrary, reveal and awaken the feminine, youthful, senile, multi-ethnic, multicultural, civilisational ferments...". [84]"," explained Edgar Morin. It is therefore

---

[83] *Atlantic Monthly, Boston, November 1945, and November 1947,* in *Ideas and Opinions by Albert Einstein,* Crown Publishers, Inc. New York, 1954, p. 119.
[84] Edgar Morin and Anne-Brigitte Kern, *Terre-Patrie,* 1993, Editorial Kairós, Barcelona, 2005, *p.* 144-145, *Edgar Morin, M. Piatelli-Pamarini, *L'Unité de l'homme,* Editions Seuil, Points Essais, 1978 p. 350-355. 350-355

not a question of promoting white male domination, but simply of using its technologies and military might to destroy authoritarian regimes and ensure the global triumph of democracy. The West will in a sense be the laboratory in which the multicultural experiment will unfold, while at the same time being the guardian of the New World Order." There is above all the immaturity of nation-states, of minds, of consciences, that is to say fundamentally the immaturity of humanity to realise itself. We cannot hide from ourselves the enormous obstacles that stand in the way of the emergence of a world-society. The unifying progression of globalisation gives rise to national, ethnic and religious resistances that produce a growing balkanisation of the planet, and the elimination of these resistances would mean, under current conditions, an implacable domination[85] ", warned Edgar Morin.

In his *Dictionnaire du XXIème siècle*, Jacques Attali also took up the idea of the right to interfere: "In a globalised and connected world, everyone will have an interest in ensuring that their neighbour does not fall into barbarism. This is the beginning of democracy without borders." According to him, the New World Order should be able, if necessary, to exercise "ruthless domination", as Edgar Morin suggested with some reluctance. The "international institutions", he said, would see their powers grow considerably: "The prevention of conflicts and wars will require a planetarian authority to take stock of threats, to alert financial institutions, to supervise sanctions in case of violations." A universal peace organisation will be discussed in the first place during talks to establish a world government." There will be less talk of a right to interfere than of a "duty to interfere"." Globalisation" will eventually be completed: "After the establishment of European continental institutions, perhaps the urgent need for a world government will appear."

All nomads

In the words of one of his tour de force, Jacques Attali is a "prodigious creator of ideas". The world government to which he

---

[85] Edgar Morin, *El Método 6, Ética; chapter: Ética planetaria*, Ediciones Cátedra-Anaya, Madrid, 2006, p. 185." There is the possibility of a planetary public opinion: through the media, there are flashes of planetary solidarity with the Romanian orphans, the Cambodian refugees... The possibilities of becoming aware of the common destiny increase with the dangers; they are fed by the damoclean threats of nuclear weapons, the degradation of the biosphere, the global degradation also, of the anthroposphere by heroin and AIDS." Edgar Morin, *Tierra-Patria*, Editorial Kairós, Barcelona, 2005, p. 162.

aspires is not only the guarantor of universal peace; it is also the symbol of a new form of civilisation. The old world is dying. That world, where from the cradle we had a roof over our heads, a family, a religion and a whole culture in which to develop our lives, is on the verge of extinction. And so much the better, Jacques Attali assured us, because then uncertainty, fear and hesitation can stimulate our creativity. Life must be "reinvented". People must show creativity in order to forge their destiny. The emerging world civilisation will offer a "greater fluidity and circulation of knowledge". The "Civilego" will be "the civilisation of civilisations. The "Civilego" will organise the harmony of all races, will make them tolerant of each other, will encourage them to be generators of new differences. The Civilego will create new tribes of nomads, bearers of regional solidarities."

"Nomad" and "Nomadism" are indeed key terms in Jacques Attali's thinking; most of his books always revolve at some point around this idea." Civilisations," wrote Attali, "which became sedentary ten thousand years ago, will soon be rebuilt one after the other on the basis of nomadism. The history of nomadism shows that its tribes can give rise to exceptional artists, specialists in light, portable works: music, jewellery, statuettes, paintings, oral literature, and so on. Contrary to legend, there is no being more peaceful than the nomad. Everyone will have to be light, free, hospitable, vigilant, connected and fraternal."

Of course, this is not to mention the hundreds of thousands of Asian or Indian workers used as cheap, exploitable piecework in Israel, Arabia and the Gulf Emirates. It is about the vision of the world developed by Jacques Attali, i.e. a generalised nomadism that will mainly affect European and Western peoples. Western societies may not yet be ready for the generalisation of this way of life, but the issue will be resolved quickly: "A very specific law will have to be invented, different from sedentary law, because without law, there is no nomadism. In fact, the first nomadic object was the Law itself, a word received in the desert in the form of stone tablets carried in the Tabernacle, a sacred object par excellence." Jerusalem, holy city among all, is not already "an international city at the forefront of multiple loyalties and democracy without frontiers? "Ways of life will be completely transformed. Everything will have to be renewed in the world to come. Music", for example, will indeed reflect new ways of living: "urban nomads will create new instruments for an instantaneous, collective music, accessible to all, breaking the barriers of learning, mixing distant cultures; a mélange of instruments and harmonies." As you will understand, the idea of métissage is an obsession for Jacques Attali.

In *Lost Humanity*, Alain Finkielkraut also developed the idea of this exclusive humanity, accustomed to airports and always on the move around the globe: "Modern man can be proud of the progress he has made: a tourist of himself and a tourist of the other, he wanders, like the world, through an immense amusement park, through an endless museum where identity and difference are offered equally to his discretionary gaze. Tourism, in other words, is not merely the itinerant way in which sedentary contemporaries occupy their free time, it is the state towards which humanity is heading, and this state, when it comes to the balance sheet, stands as the supreme value. Destination tourism, moreover, has the status of a Sovereign Good." All tourists, tourists forever"! So reads the final formula of emancipation and fraternity[86]." All that remains is to explain this great project to the little Vietnamese.

For Pierre Lévy, the major point of divergence with Jacques Attali's views was whether we are heading towards the state of "nomads" or whether the term "mobile" would be more appropriate. Lévy was categorical on this point: "We are no longer sedentary, we are mobile. Not nomadic, since nomads had neither fields nor cities. Mobile: moving from one city to another, from one neighbourhood to another in the global megalopolis ... We are American Buddhists, Indian computer scientists, Arab ecologists, Japanese pianists, doctors without borders[87]. We no longer cling to a profession, a nation or a common identity. We change our diet, our job, our religion. We move from one life to another, we continually invent our hobbies and our lives. We are unstable, in our family life as well as in our professional life. We marry people from other cultures and other religions. We are not unfaithful or disloyal, we are mobile... We have to invent more and more things. We enter the future that we invent by travelling our planet." Of course, not all French people will identify with this image of the new humanity. For it is the "hyperclass" that was described here, and not the sedentary yokels who will always be out of date. We Europeans are still too selfish and steeped in crude prejudices." The distinction we make between our own countrymen and "foreigners" is as absurd as a discrimination between people born on Monday and people born on Friday. A human being is no more Jewish, American or Chinese than a year is really odd or even," explained Lévy.

[86] Alain Finkielkraut, *La Humanidad perdida*, Anagrama, Barcelona, 1998, p. 150, 151.
[87] In May 1968, a slogan proclaimed: "We are all German Jews".

"The idea of nationhood has become a dead end … borders are the still-standing ruins of a bygone world. They serve only to harbour criminals." Humans must be "allowed to move without borders"; all humans, probably even gangsters and criminals. Our duty is to "welcome the marginalised of globalisation, instead of accusing this or that scapegoat, or giving alms from a distance, without wanting to feel them close to us… The world is knocking at our door. That world also wants to go sightseeing, to connect to networks, like us. It wants to consume like us … You are a human being. Welcome to planet Earth!"

The abolition of borders and freedom of immigration are the last revolutions to be carried out," continued Lévy gallantly. We are making great strides towards the proclamation of a world confederation. Imagine the world festival that will be[88]! "The Bolsheviks of 1917 could not have been more enthusiastic.

Improvising your identity

New fraternities will emerge, explained Jacques Attali in *Europe(s)*. Traditional identities will be blurred: "We will have to learn to build nations without borders by authorising membership of several communities, multiple voting rights, multiple loyalties. Borders will no longer separate those who have rights and those who do not… New technologies could allow the creation of specific groups, invent solidarity, think of the world as a network rather than in a hierarchical way, discover or draw new borders." Over the corpse of old identities will emerge the feeling of "multi-belonging": "everyone will have the right to belong to several hitherto antagonistic tribes, to be ambiguous, to be situated at the confines of two worlds. They will borrow elements from different cultures and use them to improvise their own from the scraps of the others." We do not yet know what the suicide rate will be, but it is above all important to adapt to it and to accept this revolution because the process is irreversible." If France is Christian, Atlantic and European, it is also Muslim, Mediterranean and African. Its future lies, like that of any great power, in the multiplicity of its belonging, in the resolute acceptance of its ambiguities[89]."

The great writer Marek Halter agreed with Jacques Attali in his concept of identity, based on "multi-belonging" and "multiple loyalties". This former communist militant found in the planetarian

---

[88] Pierre Lévy, *World philosophy*, Odile Jacob, 2000, p. 42.
[89] Jacques Attali, *Europe(s)*, Fayard, 1994, p. 198.

ideal a new version of intellectual and spiritual fulfilment, like many of his former comrades. In his book *One Man, One Cry, he* revealed some of his motivations as a writer: "Even before reading Herbert Marcuse's *One-Dimensional Man, I* had been suspicious of men of order because they were defined by a single function in society. They thus became easy prey for all dictatorships. Let a man define himself exclusively as German, French or Polish, and it is enough to appeal to his patriotism to make him march in step. Each additional cultural or religious dimension that is added makes man more complex and more difficult to manipulate. Freer too. So, I am French, Polish, Russian, Argentinian, painter, writer, and also Jewish. I am Jewish not only because my parents were Jewish, not only out of a spirit of fidelity to the rites of my ancestors, but because I chose to be so. And I decided to do so because that choice confirmed my freedom[90]." The Jewish identity of the writer appears here as an appendix, as something superfluous, without much importance, although it completes this multiple identity quite well. What Marek Halter was trying to tell us is that being Jewish, for a Jew, in the end represents only a tiny part of himself, a thin layer on the surface of the complexity and richness of the human being.

Multicultural society

In Jacques Attali's prophetic visions, European nations have become multicultural and multiracial. France will obviously take on a "Fraternity" project. It will deal with the Muslim question, within the strict framework of republican secularism. Several Muslims will be ministers. French society could be a beacon for new cultures, a laboratory of fraternal and creative civility." Great Britain will be a "juxtaposition of indifferent communities from the five continents, the first European civil society." Germany, for its part, will have to face the ageing of its population. It will therefore have to "open up to immigration to compensate for the current demographic deficit. The share of the naturalised foreign population should in fact reach a third of the total population, and half of that of the cities," he wrote with foresight. Another solution would be to encourage the German birth rate, but Jacques Attali did not envisage this, since only a multiracial society would guarantee the realisation of planetarian projects.

Canada will be the "laboratory of utopia, a formidable land of multiculturalism and democracy without borders, where everyone will

---

[90] Marek Halter, *Un Homme, un cri*, Robert Laffont, Paris, 1991, p. 22.

simultaneously be a member of several once mutually exclusive collectivities." Brazil will be "the best prototype of the "Lego culture" that is advertised as universal: a showcase of fragments of civilisation that everyone will be able to assemble as they wish". Ultimately, the only industrial nation that did not deserve the esteem of our intellectual was Japan, a society that was undoubtedly too homogeneous and impervious to cosmopolitan ideas. According to him, Japan is "a democracy still shallow and largely controlled by corrupt clans. Japan can only avoid decline by opening itself to the ideas, cultures and enterprises of other Western elites[91]."

Michel Wieviorka, one of our greatest sociologists of today, also took up the idea that in "the new era" we are entering "we invent and will invent our identities more and more often[92]." He drew on the theses of the father of cultural relativism, Franz Boas, who explained the hybrid and changing character of cultures. He also quoted the famous American sociologist Nathan Glazer (*We are all multiculturalist now*, Cambridge, Harvard University Press, 1997)." The point is clear, said Wieviorka, it is a matter of recognising the cultural diversity of our societies and the plurality of claims that this implies[93]." Today, it is simply a matter of fighting against "the undervaluing or marginalisation that constantly affects groups whose members are victims of discrimination (in employment, access to education, housing, etc.) but also disadvantaged from the outset in their social life because of their national origin, their religion, their physical attributes, their gender and sexual preferences, etc." Indeed, this is the problem of all multicultural and egalitarian societies that the Western way of life seeks to impose by levelling the world. According to him, some minorities can be considered as the great victims of the white western society. These are the so-called "primary minorities": "The Aborigines of Australia, the Maoris of New Zealand and the Indians of the three Americas received the modernity full on. Those who embody these peoples today, he wrote, constitute a remnant of history. They represent, without a doubt,

[91] Jacques Attali, *Dictionnaire du XXIᵉ siècle*, Fayard, Paris, 1998." The countries bordering the Mediterranean will organise themselves into a common market whose institutions will be installed in Jerusalem, which will become the capital of two states and three religions. Western, technical, capitalist and democratic civilisation will give way to a civilisation of assembly, a Lego civilisation (which I propose to call civiLego), whose ideal and vocation will be the reconstruction of the harmony of the world through the tolerance of its opposites and the infinite intermingling of its values." Jacques Attali, *Dictionary of the 21st century*, Paidós Ibérica Pocket, Barcelona, 2007, p. 15–16.
[92] Michel Wieviorka, *La Différence*, Balland, 2001, p. 1.
[93] Michel Wieviorka, *La Différence*, Balland, 2001, p. 83.

what remains when everything has been destroyed by the violence of conquest—with all the devastating consequences it entails, such as disease, alcoholism, self-destructive behaviour of individuals (suicides) or of group norms (violence on children, vandalism within the community)."

"These groups, Michel Wieviorka added, are sometimes reticent about multiculturalist policies that tend to put them on the same level as immigrant minorities. Primary minorities are also affected by modernity, but "paradoxically," Wieviorka argued, "their greatest chances of survival and development lie not in the communal resistance that encloses them without saving them, but in an openness to the world of late modernity, to the reinvention of cultural forms that do not isolate the past but revalue it by betting on the great characteristic of our time: the recognition of differences within and thanks to democracy[94]." This is a rather paradoxical view, Wieviorka said." This is a rather paradoxical view.

So it is said that the last tribe of the equatorial forest will not escape the vigilance of our modern thinkers. The obsession with miscegenation is undoubtedly characteristic of planetarian thinking. Note also the frequent use of the concept of "invention", as if everything bequeathed by past generations must necessarily be discarded.

Hybridisation and crossbreeding

Obviously, it is somewhat contradictory to claim to enrich through diversity when the whole theory promotes homogenisation and standardisation through mixing and blending.

Hence the paradox: cultures must be preserved and opened up at the same time… We must defend cultural singularities while promoting hybridisation and miscegenation, we must link the safeguarding of identities and the propagation of a mestizo or cosmopolitan universality, which tends to destroy these identities"." Such are the torments of the cosmopolitan spirit. Cosmopolitan?

"That is why we take the word cosmopolitan to mean (literally) citizen of the world and (concretely) child of the Earth, and not abstract individuals who have lost all their roots. We desire the development of networks in the planetarian fabric. We preach miscegenation, in the

---

[94] Michel Wieviorka, *La Différence*, Balland, 2001, p. 112.

conditions in which it is symbiosis and not the taking of substance from one civilisation by another[95]."

So let it be understood: Edgar Morin's idea is not to encourage a prolific and dominant people to spread by absorbing and making a numerically inferior people disappear through intermarriage, but to promote, in a way, a miscegenation that would weaken a dominant people, nullifying its specificity, while keeping the dominated people intact, like a bottle of pure ink to be used to wisely dose the different mixtures.

The Italian writer Primo Levi was also an advocate of a mixed-race society, at least for European societies. He was the author of numerous novels and essays translated into all languages and studied even in schools and institutes all over the world. In an anthology entitled *Asymmetry and Life,* in the chapter *Racial Intolerance, he* made himself the champion of miscegenation: "The more distant the areas of origin, the more favourable the crossbreeding, as natural selection shows not only in animals, but also in plants." To make the idea more easily acceptable without the risk of offending the populations, we must start from the postulate that we are already mixed races, and rely, if necessary, on the reinforcement of the genetic proofs of the experts: "the Indo-European race is not pure, as nothing proves it[96]." In fact, there are hardly any differences between the human races." In fact, despite the efforts of all anthropologists, no serious anthropological study has succeeded in demonstrating a difference in value between human races after eliminating non-racial, i.e. cultural, factors." Races do not exist, so the question is settled. From this point on, all hopes are permitted. The disappearance of frontiers will lead to the mixing of the world's populations and widespread interbreeding. It is in this sense that we can expect the definitive disappearance of conflicts and wars. The triumphant humanity will in a way be a victory of the human being over his animal condition: "I think that racial prejudice is something very unhuman. I think it is pre-human, that it precedes man, that it belongs to the animal world rather than to the human world. I think it is a prejudice of a savage type, of ferocious beasts."

In his book entitled *France and immigration; from 1900 to the present day,* published in 2004, the demographer Gérard Noiriel sought to show that the French population was the product of a great mix. To do this, the author opted for an original thematic rather than

---

[95] Edgar Morin and Anne-Brigitte Kern, *Tierra-Patria,* 1993, Editorial Kairós, Barcelona, 2005, p. 145, 149.
[96] Primo Lévi, *L'Asymétrie et la vie,* Robert Laffont, 2002, p. 200.

chronological plot in four parts: *Leaving, Making a place for oneself, Integrating, Cultivating differences.* This presentation makes it possible to mix in the same chapters all the peoples who arrived in succession, and thus attenuate the differences between the Poles and the animist and Muslim populations of Africa who have recently landed. There is no difference. There is no difference.

The mestizo society is the model also proposed by the talented essayist Guy Sorman in *The World is my Tribe.*" France should continue on its unique path, that of the mixing of cultures rather than the exclusion of the other". France—the country of human rights—represents the ideal model of any nation for all authors who know how to value and appreciate "a mixed-race world that is becoming more and more mixed[97]." The phenomenon of globalisation, which in the end is nothing other than the Americanisation of the world, is fortunately leading humanity towards this destiny.

But Guy Sorman's apology for miscegenation carries with it some rather unique contradictions. His wanderings around the world took him to Argentina, where the Jewish community is large. In the population, he observed the descendants of Spaniards and Italians." Finally, the Jews arrived. They brought their obsessions and complexities in their suitcases." Although Guy Sorman did not elaborate on the subject, he did, however, reveal it in his discourse and his perception of humanity and peoples when he denounced, for example, the racism of the Argentinians: "The Argentine people—as obsessed by the purity of blood in this new Spain as in the old—thought they were the only white tribe in Latin America (in fact there are few Indians and mestizos, except on the margins); to this day they boast of their whiteness, as if it were a virtue[98]." Guy Sorman therefore seemed to suspect some latent racism in the Argentine population simply because of this "whiteness". Agreed; however, it might surprise us that it was precisely in Argentina that Jews decided to settle en masse, and not in the neighbouring, indeed more mixed-race, countries. Another obvious contradiction appeared in the writer's interest in Israel, for attachment to this homeland, founded on irreducible ethno-religious foundations, is not at all compatible, in principle, with an apology for miscegenation and the establishment of the universal society of which he is an apologist. Unless, of course, this humanist discourse is merely a product for export, like the internationalism and communist pacifism that was once aimed at Western countries for the cause of the Soviet Union." As a Frenchman

---

[97] Guy Sorman, *Le Monde est ma tribu*, Fayard, 1997, p. 399.
[98] Guy Sorman, *The World is My Tribe*, Editorial Andrés Bello, Barcelona, 1998, p. 46.

of Jewish origin, but a Volterian and secular Frenchman, I cannot but be anxious about Israel, so far away and yet so close[99] ", he simply told us.

Another classic theme of the planetarian idea appears in his work: that of the futility of any opposition, as if the destiny of humanity had already been mapped out by superior forces, whether sectarian or religious. The great migrations of the peoples of the South towards the North, for example, are ineluctable; it is therefore useless to want to oppose these movements: "In this respect, it will be proposed to McMundo to manage the Great Migration instead of prohibiting it, since such a prohibition is useless[100] ", he wrote. It will therefore be completely useless to try to oppose what is already programmed. This idea of ineluctability is recurrent in the planetarian discourse, as it was in the Marxist discourse that predicted the coming victory of the proletariat and the disappearance of social classes.

Citizen consumerism

The advent of a world without borders will come about through the transformation of entrenched citizens into planetarian consumers. The consumer society and democratic regimes will overcome the last shocks of identity crises that we are probably currently experiencing. Alain Finkielkraut explained it perfectly: "Consumption puts nationalist warmongering out of action." The philosopher thus described the ineffable joys of the consumer society, and its remarkable usefulness in uprooting the identity of individuals:

"Postmodern man is grateful to technology for having broken his points of rootedness. He is not a nomad but a tourist who sees the world and wanders through the great tents of humanity. He is a tourist with a sweet tooth who appreciates India and its basmati rice or Central Europe and its apple strudel. From this position of tourist altruism, of shopping-gallery xenophilia, he condemns en bloc, under the name of fundamentalism, nationalism or tribalism, all that remains or is left of love of country in the post-totalitarian world." Thus, "anti-racism becomes a modality of consumer society, and consumption, even if it is seasoned with foreign flavours, a variety of anti-racism[101]." These are

---

[99] Guy Sorman, *The World is My Tribe*, Editorial Andrés Bello, Barcelona, 1998, p. 337.
[100] Guy Sorman, *Le Monde est ma tribu*, Fayard, 1997, p. 181.
[101] This is the peculiar conclusion of a book on the philosophy of Charles Péguy [French philosopher, poet and essayist, considered one of the leading modern Catholic writers]: Alain Finkielkraut, *Le Mécontemporain*, Gallimard, 1991. It should be noted that

the guidelines that will form the fabric of the new human society of the future, the one that will finally guarantee universal peace and happiness for all human beings. Although we can already see the insolent and sardonic denigrators of this "supermarket philosophy" coming from afar.

The media essayist Pascal Bruckner developed a similar analysis, although it was more the fruit of his political hopes than of his observation of the world: "We must recognise that consumerism and the entertainment industry are an extraordinary collective creation without equivalent in history. For the first time, men and women have erased the barriers of class, race and sex, and have merged into a single crowd ready to be stunned, to enjoy themselves without thinking of anything else... Shopping, distraction, mental wandering through virtual spaces produce a gloom, stultifying perhaps, but so soft, so gentle, that it blends for us with the brightest light[102]." This is one of the few slightly eloquent passages in Pascal Bruckner's books, which, to tell the truth, are always like warm soup on a bitterly cold night in the mountains.

For Jacques Attali, democracy naturally remains the obligatory setting for the establishment of the open society, but it will have to evolve to adapt to the needs defined by the New World Order: "By intensifying the free movement of goods, capital, ideas and people, the market will break down the borders that democracy needs to define the territory where the right to vote is exercised and where the Republic is institutionalised. International law, under pressure from business, will force states to standardise their fiscal and social law at the lowest possible level, creating a world adapted to nomads, whereas until then democracy had been conceived to serve sedentary people... The market will extend to areas currently forbidden or unthinkable: education, health, justice, police, citizenship, air, water, blood, organ transplants, all will have a price." But let us not think that Attali rejects Marxism because of these economic considerations. On the contrary, liberal globalisation owes a great debt to the Marxist ideology that had historically preceded it in its desire to build a universal society. Liberal globalisation has taken over and is achieving point by point what Marxism had failed to achieve. Jacques Attali was lucid in this respect: "Marxism will be recognised as one of the most relevant forms of analysis and forecasting of the evolution of human societies." Certainly,

---

whatever the subject of his books, the conclusion is invariably an appeal to universalism.

[102] Pascal Bruckner, *La tentación de la inocencia*, Anagrama, 1996, Barcelona, p. 71. Luminous images and "resplendent" forms already appeared in Lévy's prose.

Marxism is still very useful today in channelling in a planetarian sense the spirit of rebellion that inevitably pervades a liberal society that only offers its young people to wander in shopping centres.

Pierre Lévy is undeniably the most enthusiastic of the planetarian intellectuals, the most outlandish too: "What neither the great religions, nor public instruction, nor the universal declaration of human rights, nor simple common sense had succeeded in constructing—the concrete unity of humanity—is materialising through commerce [103]... The movement of intellectual, cultural and spiritual unification of humanity would be incomprehensible, incomplete, incoherent and merely impossible if it did not come coupled to and sustained by the global unification movement of the capitalist market and the growth of a gigantic interconnected, interdependent and planetarian technological macrocosm which has tentatively culminated in cyberspace..."

"We don't really know anymore when we work and when we don't work. We will be in business all the time. All kinds of business ... Even wage earners, who are demanding more and more remuneration in shares, will become individual entrepreneurs, moving from one employer to another, managing their careers as a small business ... The practice of commerce will become more and more universal, the more oil there is in the engine of business, the less friction (violence, power, lies, crime) there will be in society and the greater the increase in general wealth. For everyone will work cooperatively and competitively to produce more "value"... The game is to invent new games with symbols. Many individual speculative bubbles will burst, but the speculative bubble of the world economy and finance will never burst. On the contrary, it will increase continuously... There will be no difference between thinking and business. Money will reward ideas that will enable the most fabulous future, the future we will decide to buy[104]." In this New World Order, "there are no more "families", no more "nations" that stick together. We divorce, emigrate, change region or company... So let's consume to drive human development instead of looking for an identity[105]."

"Cyberspace is currently at the epicentre of the self-creative loop of humanity's collective intelligence," Lévy continued." The process of deprogramming and opening up of the human spirit will take several decades before it takes place, but it is ineluctable. It is up to us to delay

---

[103] Pierre Lévy, *World philosophy*, Odile Jacob, 2000, p. 61.
[104] Pierre Lévy, *World philosophy*, Odile Jacob, 2000, p. 100.
[105] Pierre Lévy, *World philosophie*, Odile Jacob, 2000, p. 83, 132

it as little as possible[106]." In the Marxist schema, it was the "classless society" that was to be "ineluctable". This analogy may leave us somewhat circumspect, considering the "collateral damage" that always seems to accompany such prophecies.

Matriarchal society

According to Jacques Attali, the world to come will not only be a world of ethnic and political recomposition. The transformations will have to extend to all aspects of social life, right down to the restructuring of the family unit. Let us not deceive ourselves: their prophetic visions are not merely an extension of the current orientations of the future society to which the planetarian ideologues aspire. According to the intellectuals of this current, traditions have for centuries been a hindrance that prevented human beings from evolving. Religions, and especially the Catholic religion, kept Europeans in a kind of backwardness. It is now a matter of undoing the old tinsel of European societies and forgetting the reactionary concept of family and all that is inherited at "birth". (cf. *Dictionary of the 21st century*):

"Every human being will become a being without father or mother, without antecedents, without roots or posterity, an absolute nomad." The revolution must extend as far as possible. Traditional "marriage" must give way to new forms of partnership: "Everyone will have the right to form several couples simultaneously. Polygamy and polyandry will be the norm." Men and women will at last be free to live their sexuality to the full and to satisfy their "erotic" desires: "It will be lawful to have, by means of a *"clonimage"*, all the sexual relations forbidden to a human being. Even relations with *clonimago* minors will be authorised, as long as it can be assured that it does not require or imply the participation of a real child. Onanism and nomadism. Onanomadism[107]." (sic)

And what did Jacques Attali think of nature, the birds or the sea? The sea? It will be "declared the common property of mankind. An international marine police will have to be set up to ensure that the rights of future generations are respected." This is the planetarian obsession; a tireless propaganda for the unification of humanity and the destruction of the old civilisation; it is a permanent tension towards the

---

[106] Pierre Lévy, *World philosophie*, Odile Jacob, 2000, p. 53, 120, 123
[107] Jacques Attali, *Dictionnaire du XXIe siècle*, Fayard, Paris, 1998.

realisation of this project, with an underlying mystical and religious dimension.

Although Jacques Attali has moved towards liberalism in his approach to the economy, he remains undoubtedly a Marxist in all matters relating to social phenomena, for his thinking on sexual and family restructuring is undeniably heir to that of Wilhelm Reich and Herbert Marcuse.

The father of the concept of sexual revolution is the theorist Wilhelm Reich, who first synthesised the ideas of Sigmund Freud and Karl Marx: "Sex-economic sociology," he wrote in 1933 in his *Mass Psychology of Fascism*, "was born of the effort to harmonise Freud's depth psychology with Marx's economic doctrine: "Psychoanalysis is the mother and sociology the father" of what Reich called "the sexual economy"[108]."

If Marxism proclaimed the division of human society into antagonistic classes, Freud, for his part, divided human individuality in which he believed he could discern several layers: a very old, broad layer, the "Ego", the domain of the unconscious which knows neither good nor evil, nor morality, nor any other value of any kind except "the pleasure principle". Under the influence of the outside world, a derived layer appears, the "I", which in turn gives birth, thanks to the action of social factors, to the "Overself".

Freud proposed a Marxist analogy to account for the role of the different layers of the psyche that were created under the influence of civilisation and the sexuality that governs the infrastructure of the "Id". Freud wrote thus in 1930 in *The Unrest in Culture*: "We already know that culture obeys the rule of economic psychic necessity, for it is obliged to take away from sexuality a large part of the psychic energy which it needs for its own consumption. In doing so, it adopts a behaviour towards sexuality identical to that of a people or a social class that has succeeded in subjecting another to its exploitation[109]." Sexuality, which at the level of the "It" has as its sole objective the pleasure of the different parts of the body, must be subjected to the reproductive function and is therefore concentrated exclusively in the

---

[108] Wilhelm Reich, *La Psychologie de masse du fascisme*, 1933, 1969, 1972 pour la traduction française, Éditions Payot, 1998, p. 20. And for the Spanish translation: Wilhelm Reich, *Psicología de masas del fascismo*, EspaPdf (es.scribd.com), p. 69, 70.
[109] Sigmund Freud, *The Malaise in Culture, Part IV, Collected Works*, EpubLibre, Trans. Luis López Ballesteros y de Torres, 2001, p. 4085. (In French this writing by Freud, *Das Unbehagen in der Kulturs*, is translated by *Le Malaise dans la civilisation*).

genital area. Unconsciously, the organism retains the memory of an ideal state where the "pleasure principle" (the classless society that has disappeared) had absolute dominance, and thus seeks to free itself from the state of slavery in which it is enslaved. But the "I" and the "Overself" create the notion of morality and qualify these attempts at liberation as "perversion" or "amoral acts". In a civilisation built on these foundations, work brings no pleasure; it becomes a source of unhappiness and pain.

Wilhelm Reich drew on many of Freud's discoveries, especially with regard to infantile sexuality. For him, it was a matter of liberating individuals from the oppression of reproductive sexuality so that a "pre-genital sexual organisation" could be reborn. To do this, it was necessary to attack what forms the framework of this sexuality, namely the authoritarian patriarchal family cell, which is also the matrix of capitalism, fascism and reactionary religious sentiment.

According to him, in the past, child and youth sexuality was "positively valued in the original matriarchal labour democracy". The matriarchal sexual organisation, whose "foundation was the absence of private ownership of the means of social production", was dominant. In that type of ideal society, women took care of their offspring alone, while men were kept out of the family nucleus. The transition to the patriarchal society, Reich explained, was made by "the transfer of power and wealth from the democratic *gens* to the authoritarian family of the chieftain"." In this way, sexual repression became an essential component of the division of society into classes[110]."

Today, Reich wrote, children's sexuality "is subjected to systematic repression" through the educational measures of the authoritarian family cell. This "moral inhibition of the genital sexuality of the infant makes him fearful, timid, submissive, obedient, in short, 'good' and 'docile' in the authoritarian sense; since from now on every vital and free impulse is charged with a strong dose of anguish, this limitation paralyses the rebellious forces in man and reduces his capacity for thought and criticism." In short, the main function of the patriarchal family cell is to make the child adapt to the authoritarian order.

"As the first stage of this adaptation, the child goes through the miniature authoritarian state of the family, whose structures he has to accept in order to be able to integrate into the general social order later on." If one wants to destroy the idea of the nation, one must logically

---

[110] Wilhelm Reich, *Mass Psychology of Fascism*, (1933), EspaPdf (en.scribd.com), p. 398, 391, 402, 403

also destroy the traditional family, since the authoritarian family is the reproductive cell of reactionary thinking, which in turn restricts individuals by repressing children's sexuality.

In European societies, this repression causes "sexuality to follow various paths of substitute satisfaction". So that "natural aggression is elevated to a brutal sadism, which is an essential part of the mass psychology of war staged by a few to satisfy imperialist interests." Reich explained the rise of Adolf Hitler's National Socialism as follows: "His [Hitler's] propaganda was able to take root because of the authoritarian and freedom-fearing structure of men." For "Fascism is ideologically the reaction of an agonised society, both sexually and economically, against the painful but determined tendencies of revolutionary thought towards sexual and economic freedom, a freedom which inspires reactionaries with mortal fear at the mere thought of it[111]." For these reactionaries liberation was synonymous with chaos and sexual depravity.

"Natural sexual life endangers the persistence of sexual institutions when the economic declassification of the petty bourgeoisie begins. Since the petty bourgeoisie is the main pillar of the authoritarian order, its "decency" and "preservation" from the influences of "infra humanity" is of fundamental importance; for if the petty bourgeoisie were to lose its moralistic position in sexual matters to the same extent as its intermediate economic position between the industrial working class and the big bourgeoisie, this would surely constitute the most serious threat to the existence of dictatorships ... That is why in times of crisis the dictatorial power always reinforces the propaganda in favour of "decency" and the "consolidation of marriage and the family[112]"."

Women and children are the victims of this patriarchal organisation. In order to achieve the permanence of "the institution of the authoritarian family, more is needed than the economic dependence of women and children on their husbands and fathers. For the oppressed, this dependence is only bearable on condition that the consciousness of women and children as sexual beings is eliminated as much as possible. The woman must not appear as a sexual being, but only as a reproducer. The idealisation of motherhood, its divinisation, so contradictory to the actual brutal treatment of the mothers of the

---

[111] Wilhelm Reich, *Mass Psychology of Fascism*, (1933), EspaPdf (en.scribd.com), p. 195, 196, 201, 229, 299
[112] Wilhelm Reich, *Mass Psychology of Fascism*, (1933), EspaPdf (en.scribd.com), p. 423–425

working people, serve essentially as a means of preventing the emergence of sexual consciousness in women, of preventing the breaking down of imposed sexual repression and the succumbing to sexual anguish and sexual guilt. The acceptance and recognition of women as sexual beings would mean the collapse of the whole authoritarian ideology." It is therefore "a question of abolishing the reactionary equalisation of sexuality and reproduction." Woman must become the enemy of the authoritarian white male." Anti-sexual moral inhibition prevents the conservative woman from becoming aware of her social situation and binds her to the Church as strongly as it makes her fear "sexual Bolshevism"." Wilhelm Reich concluded that "the result is conservatism, fear of freedom, even a reactionary mentality."

Thus, "the ideology of the "fate of the large family" does not only obey the interests of aggressive imperialism, but essentially the intention to overshadow the sexual function of women in relation to their procreative function[113]." Divorce and all deviations likely to break up the family and free women and children from the intolerable oppression exercised by the white male should therefore be encouraged and supported: "The simple pairing of the era of natural labour democracy, which allowed for separation at all times, has been transformed into the permanent monogamous marriage of patriarchy." Monogamous and permanent marriage became the basic institution of patriarchal society, and remains so today. To secure these marriages, natural genital aspirations had to be progressively restricted and devalued." The patriarchal and authoritarian sexual order "becomes the original basis of authoritarian ideology, stripping women, children and young people of their sexual freedom, turning sexuality into a commodity and placing sexual interests at the service of economic domination." For men, brutal sexuality was to replace "natural, orgiastic sensuality"; and so penetrated "the idea on the part of women that the sexual act must have for them something dishonourable about it."

What is true, Reich argued, is that 'the idea of the "decadence of civilisation" is the perception of the irruption of natural sexuality. And it is felt as "decadence" precisely because it constitutes a threat to the way of life based on compulsive morality. Objectively, the only thing that succumbs is the system of sexual dictatorship, which preserved coercive moral instances in individuals in the interests of authoritarian marriage and the family"." In the light of patriarchal demands, the

---

[113] Wilhelm Reich, *Mass Psychology of Fascism*, (1933), EspaPdf (en.scribd.com), p. 451–452, 198, 200, 453

chaste sensuality of matriarchy appears as the lascivious unleashing of tenebrous powers[114]."

"This [patriarchal] idea is no less reactionary when it is advocated by communists". Indeed, Reich observed, "it soon became apparent that the Communist organisations not only left this decisive ground unused, but even agreed with the Church in their condemnation and inhibition of youth sexuality." The situation in the USSR had changed markedly on this issue, for "until about 1928 the Soviet Union was dominated by marriage by pairing. The institution of marriage, in the sense of the authoritarian and mystical conception, had been abolished[115]."

To a reactionary Russian author who denounced "the systematic destruction of conjugal family life" in the Soviet Union and the plans of the Bolshevik regime to "encourage immoral debauchery of all kinds", Reich calmly replied: "From the Christian point of view, sexual life in the Soviet Union was, in fact, immoral." And when the same author also criticised "unnatural relations between brothers and sisters, and between parents and children", Wilhelm Reich laconically noted in parentheses: "This refers to the decriminalisation of incest in the Soviet Union." Indeed, incest is a recurring theme in cosmopolitan ideology.

Wilhelm Reich not only intended to work for the destruction of the European family cell, but also wanted to provide the ideological materials to dismantle the harmfulness of Christianity and the Church, stressing also "the necessity of a relentless struggle against mysticism" [Reich used this word to refer to everything that has to do with religion]: "We have already pointed out that nationalist sentiment is a direct continuation of authoritarian family sentiment. But also mystical feeling is a source of nationalist ideology. Therefore, patriarchal family attitudes and mystical attitudes are the basic psychological elements of the fascist and imperialist nationalism of the masses[116]".

"In the same way that patriarchal domination invokes God and actually refers to real paternal authority, when the child says "God" he is actually invoking the real father. Of course, in the structure of the

---

[114] Wilhelm Reich, *Mass Psychology of Fascism*, (1933), EspaPdf (en.scribd.com), p. 404, 395, 396, 406, 397

[115] Wilhelm Reich, *Mass Psychology of Fascism*, (1933), EspaPdf (en.scribd.com), p. 510, 535. When Wilhelm Reich wrote these lines, Hitler had not yet come to power. Just as Einstein had become a militarist and warmonger from February 1933, Reich would become a natalist so that the USSR could triumph over Germany during the war.

[116] Wilhelm Reich, *Mass Psychology of Fascism*, (1933), EspaPdf (en.scribd.com), p. 533–535, 701, 536

child sexual arousal, the idea of father and the idea of God constitute a unity[117]."

Here again, "sexual economy" is the best weapon to fight against "mysticism", against the power of the Church and to demystify "the legend of Jesus"." Natural sexuality is the mortal enemy of mystical religion", he wrote, because faith in God can only be the fruit of sexual repression. For Reich, indeed, there is the possibility that "faith and the fear of God are an energetic sexual excitement that has changed its goal and content ... Religious man denies his sexuality through the mystification of excitement... Of course, he believes that this force comes from "God". In reality, his longing for and for God is the longing that comes from his arousal of sexual pre-pleasure and that cries out for its satisfaction. Redemption is and cannot be but the redemption of unbearable physical tensions, which can be pleasurable only as long as they can be mixed with a fantasised unification with God, i.e. with gratification and relief." Reich's conclusion after this clinical analysis was unappealable: "A clear sexual consciousness and the natural ordering of sexual life must mortally wound mystical feelings of all kinds[118]."

The new society, freed from the burden of the patriarchal family, the church and the authoritarian state, can take shape through a healthy education of the youth. These young people are oppressed, but they do not know it. It will therefore be a matter of encouraging rebellion against the authoritarian white male: "Young people, especially young women, grasp their social responsibility much more quickly, effectively and willingly when we make them understand it by making them aware of their sexual oppression. It only depends on the correct formulation of the sexual question and on showing its relation to the general social situation."

For Wilhelm Reich, "the totalitarian-dictatorial degeneration of Soviet democracy as early as 1929 was based on the fact that the sexual revolution in the USSR had not only been slowed down, but even purposely eliminated." And on the contrary, according to him "we can predict genuinely democratic social trends whenever we meet with an understanding and vital-positive attitude of the decisive social institutions towards the sexual life of children and young people"." Educators are obliged to educate themselves in the field of sexual

[117] Wilhelm Reich, *Mass Psychology of Fascism*, (1933), EspaPdf (en.scribd.com), p. 605
[118] Wilhelm Reich, *Mass Psychology of Fascism*, (1933), EspaPdf (en.scribd.com), p. 661, 700, 617, 602, 594

economy"." What must be achieved is the elimination of all obstacles to freedom[119]." We recognise here an outline of the famous slogan of May '68: "Let's touch without limits[120]!"

Herbert Marcuse was one of the spiritual masters of the May '68 movement. This Marxist philosopher had worked during his lifetime on the synthesis of Freudianism and socialist conceptions after Reich's work. His conception of the socialist revolution represented an important milestone in the history of the development of post-war Marxist ideology, for he foresaw that the revolution would not be the work of the proletariat, whose influence was beginning to wane in post-industrial society, but of minorities generated en masse by the new consumer society: immigrants, homosexuals, feminists, the marginalised, degraded students, etc.[121] Marcuse has since exerted a powerful influence on Western youth.

Freud was both sceptical and pessimistic, since for him suffering and mental illness were the inevitable price to be paid for civilisation. Marcuse, for his part, tried to modify this view and prophesied a future liberation. Capitalist society is repressive, he said. It is an enormous burden on the psyche of individuals. A non-repressive society would be based on the liberation of instincts freed from the control of repressive reason. This liberation would manifest itself "by an activation of all the erotic zones, and thus by the rebirth of pre-genital polymorphous sexuality [infantile sexuality] and by the decline of genital supremacy." The whole body will become an instrument of pleasure." This transformation of the value and scope of libidinal relations would lead to the disintegration of institutions, and especially of the patriarchal monogamous family."

Protest against the repressive order of procreative sexuality can take different forms: homosexuality is one of them, for example. This is what Sigmund Freud already introduced in 1929 in *Malaise in Culture*: "Man too is an animal of undoubtedly bisexual disposition. The individual is equivalent to the fusion of two symmetrical halves, one of which would be, in the opinion of some researchers, purely masculine, the other purely feminine. But it could also be that each half

---

[119] Wilhelm Reich, *Mass Psychology of Fascism*, (1933), EspaPdf (en.scribd.com), p. 752, 831–833, 1320, 1331
[120] *Jouissons sans entrave!* (NdT)
[121] Herbert Marcuse, *Eros and Civilization. A philosophical inquiry into Freud*, Boston, 1955.

is primitively hermaphroditic[122]." Incitement to homosexuality can be observed in all media since the 1990s. We note here, for example, that in 2001, French television channels broadcast 570 programmes dealing with homosexuality (compared to 551 in 2000). It is not a question of reporting or accompanying a societal phenomenon, but of promoting it. Another example among a thousand: Tina Kieffer, the director of the women's magazine *Marie-Claire,* was not indirectly inciting homosexuality when she asked "if the other sex is still needed", or when she stated: "It's true, the barriers are blown up and men get together more easily. And so do women. This evolution of customs comes at a time when assisted procreation is available."

The liberation of sexual instincts found fertile ground in the 1960s, in what was called the "psychedelic revolution", i.e. the massive use of drugs in the young population. Even the provocative idea of dirt found its justification in the theory according to which the Ego and the Overself would repress the olfactory instincts. Don't the ruling classes associate the idea of "waste" with the lower classes considered as "the dregs of society"? These ideas still serve as a theoretical foundation for revolutionary art. The repressive or stifling culture must be destroyed. Experiments in painting, sculpture and literature, in which the idea of "waste" serves as a revolutionary endorsement, must be considered as alternative means of dynamiting "bourgeois culture" and opening the way to a new world.

The feminist movement is obviously heir to this Freudo-Marxist ideology. The great Marxist philosopher of deconstruction Jacques Derrida recalled the background of the "women's liberation" movement: "On 26 August 1970, a group of women who had called themselves the "Emma Goldman Brigade" walked down Fifth Avenue in New York with many more feminists chanting: "Emma said it in 1910/ Now we say it too"." As an anarchist feminist," wrote Derrida[123], "Emma Goldman called for the restructuring of society as a whole", i.e. social revolution and the blowing up of the European family cell. Goldman was an activist whose aspirations went beyond revolt against

---

[122] Sigmund Freud, *The Malaise in Culture, Part IV, Collected Works,* EpubLibre, Trans. Luis López Ballesteros y de Torres, 2001, footnote, p. 6936." Science sees in this circumstance the sign of a bisexuality, as if the individual were not male or female, but always both, only alternately one more than the other. You are then invited to familiarise yourselves with the idea that the portions of the mixture of masculine and feminine in the individual are subject to great oscillations." in Sigmund Freud, *Lesson XXXIII. Femininity, Collected Works,* EpubLibre, Trans. Luis López Ballesteros y de Torres, 2001, p. 4249.

[123] Jacques Derrida, *Points de suspensions, Entretiens,* Éditions Galiliée, 1992, p. 98.

inequalities against women. In France, the feminist movement has since been shaped by personalities such as Gisèle Halimi or Elisabeth Badinter, for example, who also claim the legacy of Emma Goldman and Louise Weiss. Once again, Judaism is at the forefront of the liberation movement.

The influence of Wilhelm Reich and Herbert Marcuse was decisive in the thinking of May 1968. In 1975, Daniel Cohn-Bendit, who was one of the main leaders of the Paris movement and is now an environmentalist MEP, published a book entitled *Le grand Bazaar (The Big Bazar), in which he* recounted his experiences as an educator in a Frankfurt kindergarten: "It had happened to me several times that some children had opened my fly and started to tickle me. I reacted differently depending on the circumstances, but their desire was a problem for me. I would ask them: Why don't you play together, why did you choose me and not the other boys? But if they insisted, I caressed them in spite of everything". Another passage reads: "I needed to be unconditionally accepted by them. I wanted the children to love me, and I did everything to make them depend on me[124]."

The work of the great Italian writer Alberto Moravia is totally imbued with this "Freudo-Marxist" thinking." The Marx-Freud marriage disproves the worldview of the Renaissance, the Machiavellian separation of morality and politics. It is precisely this marriage that forms the background to my novels. For example, in "*Agostino*", innocence is understood as ignorance of sex and social class, and the discovery of evil is made through the discovery of sex and social classes. In any case, I think that in Italy Catholic moralism is still quite strong. It has its roots in the Counter-Reformation, which was a popular and petty bourgeois, reactionary and intolerant movement[125]."

In order to familiarise oneself with Marxist phraseology, one can read with great interest the famous philosopher Jürgen Habermas, who was also part of the so-called Frankfurt School, together with Marcuse, Horckeimer and Wiesenthal Adorno. In *The Reconstruction of Historical Materialism*, we can read in the preface that Habermas—take air—"thematises socio-historical evolution as a phylogenetic parallel to the ontogenesis of psycho-individual cognitive development, built on the model of genetic psychology."

---

[124] Daniel Cohn-Bendit, *Le grand Bazar*, Belfond, 1975. Daniel Cohn-Bendit openly recounted these experiences in the cultural television programme *Apostrophes* on 23 April 1982. The sequence can still be viewed on internet video platforms (NdT).
[125] Albert Moravia, in Géo, N° 76, Juin 1985.

If after such a fine analysis you are still on the warpath, you can continue your research and discover that Habermas took up Wilhelm Reich's critique of the patriarchal structure of the authoritarian and oppressive family. He sought the origins of its emergence: "It is humans, and not hominids, who are the first to transcend that social structure which arose in the vertebrate order: the one-dimensional hierarchy in which each animal is transitively accorded one status and one status only. It is this status system that, among chimpanzees and baboons, governs the rather aggressive relationships between males, the sexual relationships between males and females, and the social relationships between adults and young. A family-type relationship exists only between the mother and her children or between siblings... Even hominid societies, transformed by social work, do not know the family structure[126]."

We have here a model of a matriarchal society. Habermas again raises a question that seems to concern the representatives of cosmopolitan thought: "Incest between mother and adolescent son is not allowed, although there is no similar limitation to incest between father and daughter, because the role of father does not exist." The role of father is evidently less important in matriarchal societies where polygamy prevails. We have already seen how Jacques Attali promoted this model in his *Dictionnaire du XXIème siècle*. What is more striking and disturbing is to read in another book by Jacques Attali that this social structure was the norm among the Jews of ancient times: "Polygamy is and will remain for a long time, in fact, the practice admitted by the Hebrews, as it is for all the peoples of the region[127]."

It is also strange to come across here the question of incest, a theme so prevalent in Judaism. We know that the rabbis excused the daughters of Loth. According to them, by sleeping carnally with their father, they had sacrificed themselves for the good of humanity. Another revealing passage in the Old Testament told how Amon, son of David, had raped his sister Tamar: "Where would I go with my dishonour? And you would be one of the wicked of Israel. See, speak to the king, who will surely not refuse to give me to you." But he would not listen to her, and being stronger than she, he ravished her and lay down with her[128]."

---

[126] Jürgen Habermas, *The Reconstruction of Historical Materialism*, Taurus Ediciones, Madrid, 1986–1992, p. 136.
[127] Jacques Attali, *Los judíos, el mundo y el dinero*, Fondo de cultura económica, 2005, Buenos Aires, p. 24.
[128] *Historical Books, Second Book of Samuel (II Samuel, 13)*. (NdT).

We know that the Talmud forbids Jewish mothers to sleep with their children from the age of nine years and one day. According to that holy book, the same prohibition applies to the father when the daughter is over three years and one day old. According to the Talmud, a Jewish widow may never have dogs, so if we see a lady walking her dog in the street, she is not a Jewish widow, although she may well have a dog. Let us remember in this respect that the Talmud was conceived in the East and was inspired by Eastern customs. Léon Blum himself, former president of the Council of the Fourth Republic, wrote: "I have never been able to understand what is so repulsive about incest. It is considered a crime in our society, and, without wishing to go into the reasons why incest is tolerated or prescribed in other societies, I simply note that it is natural and frequent to love one's brother or sister with love[129]." Nobel laureate Thomas Mann, in his novel *Blood of Welsungos*, described how a young Jewish girl offered herself to her brother on the eve of her wedding to a goy[130]. Serge Gainsbourg's controversial song with his daughter Charlotte entitled *Lemon Incest* is also well known.

Another interesting phenomenon to note is the links between Judaism and the divorce law that began to dynamite the "patriarchal" family cell. The initiator of divorce law in France was Alfred Naquet. A chemist, lecturer, deputy and senator, he was also the author in 1882 of a book entitled *Religion, Property, Family*, in which he called for the community of property and women: "Marriage is a fundamentally tyrannical institution and an infringement on the freedom of man, the cause of the degeneration of the human species: concubinage or free union is preferable, without the intervention of authority, without religious consecration and legal recognition." So we see that Wilhelm Reich had predecessors.

During one of the sessions of the Chamber of Deputies on 19 July 1884, a Catholic speaker, Monsignor Freppel, had taken the floor: "The movement which is leading us to the adoption of the law of divorce is, in the true and literal sense of the word, a Semitic movement, a movement which began with Mr. Crémieux and ended with Mr. Naquet." Indeed, it was the former rabbi of Brussels, Astruc, who drafted the provisions of the law. In fact, for all these questions, one can consult the rabbinical code *Even HaEzer*. According to tractate *Kethuboth*, one may repudiate a woman without returning her widow's pension in these cases: if she gives forbidden food to her husband; if

---

[129] Léon Blum, *Du Mariage*, 1937, p. 82.
[130] Goy, (plural, goyim). A Jewish term to refer to non-Jews, Gentiles.

she deceives him about her menstruation periods; if she does not fulfil her *Halachic* duty131; if she walks outside the house with her head uncovered; if she runs out into the street. Abba Saul added; if she insults her husband's parents in his presence. Rabbi Tarfon said: if she is loud. Samuel understands this to mean when she raises her voice at home and her neighbours hear her voice. According to Rab, however, it is only the woman who is heard from another room during their conjugal relations. All in all, it seems that, with the divorce law, democracy was somehow catching up with Jewish law; and it could be that the Soviet Union's incest law had the same advantage.

In the same vein, one might even suspect that the law on the abolition of the death penalty in 1981, whose prime mover was the socialist justice minister Robert Badinter, also responded to religious imperatives. Indeed, it is strictly forbidden for goyim to touch the corpse of a Jew. That is why, for example, numerous Israeli rescue teams had travelled to Thailand after the tsunami that had killed nearly 300,000 people in Southeast Asia, many of whom were tourists. The Europeans had sent numerous rescue teams to the site, while the Hebrew state had given priority to finding Jewish bodies. Indeed, under no circumstances were they to be handled by unclean hands, nor were they to be buried with the goyim.

It could also be that psychoanalysis is completely permeated by Hebraic themes, but this matter would also require a separate study[132]. Let us simply say that psychoanalysts have done no more than replace the role that priests had in the past in the villages by means of confession. But with the small difference that confession was free of charge and that psychoanalysts insist on charging their patients onerous fees to ensure the success of the therapy.

To conclude this Freudian chapter, let us look at an example of the advantages of psychoanalytic introspection: a television programme recently dealt with malaise and depression in our societies at the beginning of the 21st century. We were presented with various group methods to combat these ills and to feel better about oneself. One was based on dancing, looking and body contact, in which everyone smiled and seemed fully satisfied with these sessions in which they freed their bodies through contact with others. A second method was led by a psychiatrist: about fifteen individuals were gathered together, sitting in a circle in a large room in the consulting room where gym mats had

---

[131] Prescriptions of Jewish Law.

[132] On Judaism and psychoanalysis, see Hervé Ryssen, *Psychoanalysis of Judaism* (NdT).

been placed. Each participant had to free themselves by bringing their emotional frustrations to the surface under the gaze of the others." It has to be like a storm bursting in the sky," said the psychiatrist. So some people courageously displayed, in front of millions of television viewers, their family conflicts, their inner problems, shaken by spasms, eyes bathed in tears and mouths twisted in pain. The contrast between the two methods was truly shocking.

Having observed the strange similarities between religious and ethnic precepts on the one hand, and political positions on the other, one may legitimately wonder whether it is not the totality of Freudo-Marxist theories that should be analysed from the point of view of Hebraic religion. This would certainly be a way forward to try to explain more deeply the origins of socialist thought and the genesis of the planetarian ideal in general. In any case, these concepts transcend political oppositions that seem increasingly fictitious in today's Western democratic systems.

3. The Planetarian Method

The unification of the globe requires a continuous and patient work of educating the masses, always attracted by the old demons of nationalism. Westerners must learn tolerance and openness to the "Other", for the construction of a plural, multi-ethnic and multicultural society is the only way to achieve global empire, synonymous with the empire of peace. It is therefore a matter of raising awareness of the issues of human equality and global solidarity among the population by all means. In this respect, the "media tsunami" operation in January 2005, on the occasion of the tidal wave in Asia, was an exceptional success. Indeed, one contributor out of two in France had made a donation for the Asian victims, who were now preferred to their own compatriots.

The old identity reflexes must no longer be produced, and everything must be set in motion to blame nationalist reactions, the residue of a tribalism of other times. Europeans, and white men in general, must be convinced that they are largely responsible for humanity's ills. They are responsible for climate change, for the war in Iraq, for the vile exploitation of the countries of the South and for hunger in Africa. Their entire history is a succession of monstrosities: from the Inquisition to Auschwitz, from religious wars to the genocide of the Indians, from African colonisation to the Algerian war. Blaming Europeans is indeed the only way to annihilate their identity reflexes. In this way, they will be much more willing to accept the construction of a plural society on their soil. European construction is part of this worldview, for by abolishing the old nations in favour of a political entity with unclear contours, feelings of ethnic resistance are further diluted. The United States is in this sense the model to follow, and indeed many former Marxist intellectuals today take up the defence of democratic America precisely for this reason. They are thus the intellectual bulwarks of transnational high finance, whose main interest is evidently to promote throughout the world the building of democratic societies in which men of all colours, undifferentiated and equal, will gather to worship the consumer society and enjoy with frenzied enthusiasm all the goods and trinkets generated by the matrix, like ants swarming by the thousands around a few drops of deliciously sweet insecticide. Thus, there are no more races, no more religions, no more borders, no more anything that can stand in the way of the consumerist ideal and the designs of international high finance. The media system makes us understand this in the most playful and amusing way possible, but sometimes also with the severity of a schoolteacher.

A great disdain for the sedentary

The disregard of ancestral traditions and deep-rooted cultures is a full-fledged chapter of the planetarian philosophy. Rootedness, lineage, the spirit of heredity, the religion of the fathers, are a burden, an obstacle to the progress of humanity that must be removed as soon as possible.

Naturally, belief in the virtues of rootlessness and nomadism is a common denominator of planetarian intellectuals. The famous philosopher Emmanuel Lévinas expressed this idea clearly in his essay *Difficult Freedom*. Undoubtedly, the greatest backwardness ever was that of the pagan civilisations of antiquity: "Paganism is the local spirit: nationalism in all that is cruel and ruthless, that is to say, immediate, naive and unconscious. The tree grows and reserves all the sap of the earth. A rooted humanity ... is a forest humanity, a pre-human humanity". The polytheistic European religions were therefore based on savage beliefs: this barbarism had to be replaced by a religion of the Book, and a religion of love and universal brotherhood had to penetrate these blond barbarians: "If Europe had been spiritually uprooted by Christianity, the damage would not be so great... But was not Europe's misfortune due to the fact that Christianity had not uprooted it sufficiently? "Evidently, it was the genius of the Semitic Bedouins that brought Europe out of its lethargy: "The advent of the Scriptures is not the subordination of the spirit to a letter, but the substitution of the letter for the soil. The spirit is free in the letter and chained at the root. It is in the arid soil of the desert where nothing is fixed, that the true spirit descended in a text to realise itself universally[133]."

In reality, everything created so far by Europeans has never allowed them to take flight. From the Parthenon to the Vatican, from Michelangelo to Renoir, from Cervantes to Dostoyevsky, from Bach to Wagner, European civilisation has always remained somewhat mediocre. This is because our rootedness in the past and our traditions made us underdeveloped compared to what the nomadic genius could

---

[133] Emmanuel Levinas, *Difficult Freedom, Essays on Judaism*. Ediciones Lilmod, Buenos Aires, 2004, p. 165, 164.

have brought us: "Freedom from sedentary forms of existence is perhaps the human way of being in the world. For Judaism, the world becomes intelligible in the face of a human face and not as it is for a great contemporary philosopher, who summarises an important aspect of the West in terms of houses, temples and bridges... He puts rooted values in second place and institutes other forms of fidelity and responsibility. Man, after all, is not a tree and humanity is not a jungle. More humane forms, since they imply a conscious commitment; freer, since they allow us to glimpse horizons wider than those of the home village and a humane society[134]."

"Faith in the liberation of man is linked to the crumbling of sedentary civilisations, to the decay of the heaviness of the past, to the fading of local colours, to the fissures that crack all the armatostes and obtuse things linked to human particularisms. You have to be underdeveloped to claim them as your raison d'être and fight on their behalf to have a place in the modern world[135]." This was the message that Emmanuel Levinas, one of the greatest philosophers of 20th century Judaism, had for us.

"Truth is no longer necessarily bound by tradition: it has the same value for all those who are no longer blinded by tradition", responded Alain Finkielkraut. It is the bonds of the past that prevent us from seeing the radiant future before us. Let us throw overboard all that cumbersome mythology, all those old religions and traditions of other times: "A hierarchical universe opens up before the steady gaze that has abolished the realm of the great origin stories[136]."

Alain Finkielkraut particularly insisted on this idea: if you deny your roots, if you deny your homeland, if you deny even your ancestors and relatives, then you have a chance to save yourselves: "Evil, in other words, is born of homelands and patronymics. Evil is the dead taking

---

[134] Emmanuel Levinas, *Difficult Freedom, Essays on Judaism*. Ediciones Lilmod, Buenos Aires, 2004, p. 112, 113.
"The Jewish community is, on the contrary, a community that locates eternity in its very nature. Its being is not based on a land, nor on a language, nor on a legislation subject to renewals and revolutions. Its land is "holy" and a term of nostalgia, its language is sacred and unspoken. His Law is holy and not a temporary legislation, formulated for the political control of time. But the Jew is born a Jew and trusts in the eternal life whose certainty he experiences through the carnal ties that bind him to his ancestors and his descendants." Emmanuel Levinas, *"Between Two Worlds" (The Way of Franz Rosensweig)*, Lecture delivered on 27 September 1959 at the Second Colloquium of French-speaking Jewish Intellectuals, organised by the French Section of the World Jewish Congress, in *Difficult Freedom, Essays on Judaism*, p. 217.
[135] Emmanuel Lévinas, *Difficile liberté*, Albin Michel, 1963, 1995 edition, p. 299.
[136] Alain Finkielkraut, *La Humanidad perdida*, Anagrama, Barcelona, 1998, p. 16, 17.

over the living and is the dictatorship exercised by surnames over given names. Evil is the spirit that, instead of taking flight, falls crushed by its own weight and becomes flesh[137]." Post-modern man will not be vulgarly tied to the past." He ceases to trace the traces of the past within himself as in others." His title of glory, "is to be cosmopolitan, and to declare war on the provincial spirit[138]."

Edgar Morin was saying something similar when he lamented "the great delays and paralysis due to localisms and provincialisms." Millions of people still live in a backward universe: "The curse-laden taboos that were the immune defences of archaic cultures and dogmatic religions have become obstacles to communication, understanding and creation in the planetarian age[139]." Certainly, there is still a long way to go to the completion of that new world, that "planetarian confederation" to which we aspire.

We read in George Steiner the same atavistic distrust of nations: "The nation feeds on lies by empirical necessity", he wrote." The locus of truth is always extraterritorial; its dissemination becomes clandestine through the barbed wire fences and watchtowers of national dogma[140]."

Pierre Lévy was perhaps more pedagogical in his apology for "planetarian citizenship": "I understand, and I share the nostalgia for the world where it was enough to follow the path of the ancestors for everything to go well, the world where every act of daily life was the calm fulfilment of a ritual. A world where the gods dwelt. That beautiful and orderly world … that world that no longer exists. But we must leave that nostalgia behind because it easily becomes a source of suffering and horrified rejection of the real movement of the world as it goes … We must become the artists of our own lives. Our roots will have to be transformed into rhizomes that grow horizontally in all directions … We will have to find a deeper, more universal identity than the one that was proposed to us by the culture where we were born." Do not be afraid now, relax, my words bring you comfort, your muscles relax, you feel a great warmth gently invading you…" We must understand that identity cultures are dead ends. By locking ourselves into identity cultures, we separate ourselves from those who are different … Identity

---

[137] Alain Finkielkraut, *La Humanidad perdida*, Anagrama, Barcelona, 1998, p. 149.

[138] Alain Finkielkraut, *Le Mécontemporain*, Gallimard, 1991, p. 174-177.

[139] Edgar Morin and Anne-Brigitte Kern, *Tierra-Patria*, 1993, Editorial Kairós, Barcelona, 2005, p. 148. American Protestantism seems in this respect much more adaptable than Catholicism and, above all, than Islam today.

[140] George Steiner, *Pasión intacta. El texto, tierra de nuestro hogar*, Ediciones Siruela, Madrid, 1997, p. 422, 420.

cultures divide us. They oppose us. We risk being locked into fear and hatred[141]."

In *The New Middle Ages*, Alain Minc was moralising about the rise of the extreme right, without concealing a certain contempt for the slightly backward natives who did not yet understand the great destiny of humanity. He severely criticised the "pusillanimous temptation" of the French." There are two possible uses for the income provided by our unitary and centralised nation-state. Either to shut oneself up under its protective wing, to huddle like the inhabitants of the Middle Ages in the keep of their castle, to ignore as much as possible what is going on outside it, and to take up our old isolationist and protectionist cant. Or feel stronger in the face of the storm, see the opportunity to be more present in the world, want to be combative and innovative, try to influence the course of events. These are not two new temptations for France: it has always oscillated between parochial reflex and universalism."

The French villages and peasants are in any case doomed to disappear, sooner or later, thus purging that whole swathe of the population which is typically French and old-fashioned; in any case, not sufficiently "cosmopolitan". This peasant population, which has always refused to open up to the world and to welcome foreigners, has always taken refuge in its churches in the meanest way. Today, we are living in an era of positive mixing. The French must move on, open up more to the world: "If they persist in their former vision of the world and persist in believing that we are living through a brief period of adaptation and that everything will return to normality, to the traditional order, then they will be condemned. The fainthearted, the protectionists, the reactionary supporters of the nation-state, the anxious, the xenophobes will have won the day and France will make the worst use of the possibilities offered by the new world disorder[142]." For this new world disorder is a gift to us, we must believe it; it is a real opportunity for France.

But while sedentary people are invited to "make a clean sweep of the past", to forget their ancestral traditions and to reject anything that might link them to their community of origin, "Memory" remains of paramount importance, but only for nomads. Jacques Attali, in his *Dictionnaire*, said that memory is "the identity and the baggage of the nomad, his luxury and his weapon when precariousness and amnesia become generalised." Therefore, what is valid for some is not valid for

---

[141] Pierre Lévy, *World philosophie*, Odile Jacob, 2000, p. 145-147.

[142] Alain Minc, *Le Nouveau Moyen-Age*, Gallimard, 1993, p. 246-247.

others. The aim is to dissolve sedentary societies and favour a nomadic world without borders, which will open the way to happiness and universal peace.

The same spirit of uprootedness was expressed by the great Austrian novelist Elfriede Jelinek. After she was awarded the Nobel Prize for literature in 2004, she wanted to clarify her thoughts in an interview reported in the communist daily *L'Humanité*. The novelist, "born to a Czech socialist Jewish father who died prematurely in a psychiatric hospital", wanted to distance herself from the image of today's reactionary and conservative Austria, from "its everyday life of insipid operettas, with its sanctimonious nature worship, its two outmoded television channels, its musical folklore played on loop, its good-natured apolitism, its affected cordiality." Of that nauseating Austria, he denounced "behind the resentments, the old nostalgia for Empire, the deep-rootedness of the soil and the land, the distrust of foreigners, the power of a backward Catholicism and its alliance with the persistence of Nazi ideology". "My Nobel Prize is not to be regarded as a flower in Austria's buttonhole[143]". From Austria, clearly not.

The great poet Heinrich Heine was also in his time very insolent towards Germany: Heine contributed the symbolic sum of five cents for the construction of a statue of Arminius, the victor of the Roman legions, when he launched a subscription for the construction of the statue. That contempt, which has never been forgotten by the Germans, must be placed alongside all the acts and words that denote the unfathomable contempt of cosmopolitan spirits for all that is alien to them.

Bernard-Henri Lévy also revolted against "the cult of ethnicities, of popular microcultures, of restored collective identities": "fascism is not only the martial music of the devotees of the nation-state: it can also speak a dialect, dance a few jacks, march to the sound of bagpipes… Faced with all this, faced with so much stupidity, I sometimes almost feel like singing the hymn of the one and eternal France. Faced with a Corsican in arms or a Breton disguised as a Druid, I am almost tempted to side with the staunch supporters of the country's territorial cohesion. In fact, what keeps me from doing so is that they are all the same. Whether they are infra, supra or simply nationalists, deep down they all think the same way, which disgusts me." Patriots of all kinds and their antiquarian paraphernalia[144] "disgust him greatly. They are nothing more than the expression of a "tense and pusillanimous self-absorption

---

[143] *L'Humanité* of 8 October 2004.
[144] Bernard-Henri Lévy, *L'Idéologie française*, Grasset, 1981, p. 212-216.

in the poorest identities". We shall see later in this book how the Bolsheviks put their contempt for Russian traditions into practice.

In 1985, Pierre Bergé, the wealthy socialist owner of Yves Saint-Laurent, financed the launch of *Globe* magazine. The first issue dotted the i's and crossed the t's: "Obviously, we are resolutely cosmopolitan. Evidently, everything that smells of the terroir, the jotas, the bagpipes, the traditional or patriotic is alien to us, even odious", wrote BHL with delight[145]. The two creative editors of the project were Georges-Marc-Benamou, a close collaborator of President Mitterrand, and Bernard-Henri Lévy, who incidentally declared to the daily *Le Monde*: "You can write it, I consider myself to be the best writer, the most talented essayist of my generation[146]."

Guy Konopnicki, an author who had remained close to communist ideas, said the same as the democratic intellectuals on this subject. In one of his essays entitled *La France du tiercé*, the writer seemed to have nothing but contempt for the country that had welcomed him: "Even the lousiest of Broadway revues will always surpass the pitiful spectacle of folk dances with souks," he wrote amiably. This did not prevent him from declaring afterwards: "As an immigrant, I am more French than the French." All his books revolve around recurring themes: working-class racism, Judaism, the typically French French, and France: "a holy trinity: Mary-Church-Prosbyrince." (*Les Filières noires*)." The hatreds and grudges of the little Gaul" make him retch; "it would be better to wring the little Gaul's neck and straighten out the clear French genius. Political modernity demands it. We must put an end once and for all to this France and get out of this hexagonal cloister[147]."

On the other hand, and we always come up against the same paradox, this mundialist is obsessed with the disappearance of the Yiddish language[148]. His book, *Le Mur des fédérés* (The *Wall of the Federated*), had a Yiddish subtitle, *Der Rote Yid* (*The Red Jew*). And when he writes a detective novel, he titles it *Pas de Kaddish pour Sylberstein (No Kaddish for Sylberstein)*. It should be noted that the editor-in-chief of his publishing house was Bernard-Henri Lévy.

---

[145] BHL, an acronym for the ubiquitous media philosopher Bernard-Henri Lévy.

[146] *Le Monde*, 21 March 1985. Bernard-Henri Lévy's great talent was also evident on one occasion in Spain, when he was invited by the Spanish television programme *La Clave on* 10 November 1979 to debate with Santiago Carrillo and Roger Garaudy, among others. (NdT).

[147] France's geography forms a hexagon. France is often referred to as a hexagon.

[148] Central European Judeo-German language.

France of the bastards

Of all the planetarian authors, Bernard-Henri Lévy is undoubtedly one of the most vehement and virulent critics of traditional society. In any case, he is the intellectual who uses the harshest terms to lash out against the France of the bell towers and the terroir, and all the adversaries of the open society. This philosopher is also one of the richest men in France, with a personal fortune estimated at 150 million euros, inherited from the timber trading company his father had created in Morocco. But the man also runs several financial companies. Like Jacques Attali or Alain Minc, the socialist and liberal philosophers are nowadays business kings and television stars who know how to seduce the public[149].

In his book *The French Ideology*, Bernard-Henri Lévy denounced the responsibilities of French intellectuals, whose reactionary ideas had inevitably led the country into the Vichy regime and collaboration with Nazi Germany. Socialist writers fared no better than patriotic and nationalist thinkers, who in turn attacked "plutocracy" and the Republic. In fact, at the beginning of the 20th century, we witnessed in France an ideological rapprochement between the two "anti-system" currents—socialist and nationalist—which might well have brought down the Republic had the 1914 war not broken out. The most radical revolutionary socialist circles were at that time very open to certain themes which today would be described as "extreme right", while on the other side, in the monarchists of Action Française, we find Charles Maurras dreaming of a "socialism freed of its democratic and cosmopolitan component." A proletarian right and a socialist-revolutionary movement would converge to give birth to a new political movement known as "Fascism".

On the extreme left, Georges Sorel, author of *Reflections on Violence*, was the intellectual of revolutionary syndicalism. For him, the

---

[149] BHL was part of the new generation of intellectuals of the 1970s known as *"Les Nouveaux Philosophes"*. From the 1980s onwards, Lévy was involved in numerous international causes, with an intense media militancy all over the world. His wanderings took him to Pakistan to support the Afghan Mujahedin, Bosnia-Herzegovina to help the Bosnian Muslims against the Serbs, Georgia during the war in South Ossetia, Israel during the 2008 Gaza war, Libya to support the Libyan revolution against Muammar Kadafi, Iraqi Kurdistan where he met the Peshmerga fighting against Daheeh, in Kiev after the Euromaidan coup d'état of 2013, etc. In 2017 he was awarded an *honorary* doctorate by Bar Ilan University for "more than 40 years of influential contribution to the Jewish people and their nation". He was awarded the same title by Tel Aviv and Jerusalem Universities in 2002 and 2008, respectively. (NdT).

trade unions were the key to the device, the weapon that would serve to overthrow the plutocratic regime by means of a general strike and insurrection. His socialism was too deep-rooted for Bernard-Henri Lévy, for he had set himself the goal of purging society of international finance and the merchant spirit. Words like "people", "blood" and "traditions" were still part of the vocabulary of these revolutionaries for whom plutocratic democracy, not "fascism", was the main enemy. And this is precisely what frightened our cosmopolitan philosopher. At that time, there was no cordon sanitaire around the extreme right. The exchange of ideas was still possible between political adversaries. So much so that Sorel, in his *Posthumous Considerations*, praised both Edward Drumont, the author of *Jewish France,* and Charles Maurras, whom he described as a "true leader" immunised against "the democratic virus". On the same political spectrum, in Gustave Hervé's daily *La Guerre sociale,* one could read that Jaurès' newspaper *L'Humanité* was financed by the Rothschilds and "entirely devoted to serving their dark aims". This was the atmosphere in which many anarchists and socialists moved and in which the CGT (Confédération Générale du Travail) was born. The cult of effort, the struggle against liberal values, against democratic beliefs, against the philosophy of the Enlightenment and the "imposture of human rights": this was the line of conduct followed by the French socialists before 1914.

Georges Sorel and Charles Maurras were then the two great emblematic figures of the French reaction against the regime. The convergence of the two revolutionary currents would take place in Paris in December 1911. The Proudhon circle was born. For the first time in the history of Europe, men of the Left and the Right were to present a joint discourse in which criticism of plutocracy, hatred of cosmopolitanism, contempt for decadent intellectualism and anti-Semitism were expressed. The socialist-revolutionary vocabulary of the time could grate on the ears of our modern planetarian intellectuals: "There are two nobilities, said Edward Berth, Sorel's disciple: that of the sword and that of work." We need "the awakening of force and blood against gold" to bring about "a definitive defeat of plutocracy" (*Cahiers du Cercle Proudhon,* September 1912). For three years, the Proudhon Circle would work to hasten the "awakening of force and blood" and the advent of a "peasant, warrior and Gallic socialism." At that time, patriots all over the world were looking to France, while Germany was still the homeland of Marxism and "scientific socialism". France was undoubtedly the home of fascism and national socialism, the country where the dialogue between nationalists and communists was freely established.

The experience was short-lived and was barely making its way through intellectual circles when the war of 1914 broke out and interrupted it for good." But the monsters were on the loose," wrote BHL; "the foul beast was born[150]".

Georges Valois would later found *Le Faisceau*, the party where this doctrinal synthesis would be maintained, and Berth would join the Communist Party in 1920. Drieu La Rochelle, Lucien Rebatet, Marcel Deat and many others would never forget that experience. Mussolini would recognise that French socialism had been the source of inspiration for Italian fascism. In 1926, he declared: "To whom I owe most is Georges Sorel". Sorel recognised in Italian fascism the incarnation of his socialism, although he also applauded the experience of October 1917. Indeed, Sorel had in spite of everything "a strange tendency to claim Marxism, where Maurras saw at best only a Jewish doctrine."

During the inter-war period, Bernard-Henri Lévy detected a general mood rather than an ideological collusion between socialism and nationalism. He perceived in communist literature the same unhealthy discourse as in extreme right-wing literature, discourses that exalted "race", a term that had been in vogue since the mid-19th century. The cult of the body had a pagan resonance that could only disgust the intellectual wary of displays of force. While the ideology of the Vichy regime exalted the youth and encouraged them to "regenerate their strength in the open air, in a healthy fraternity", the communists were doing the same ten years earlier when they exalted the body and the physical vigour of the people. The daily *L'Humanité* had welcomed the return of the communist delegation which had gone to admire on the Moscow sports grounds a "youth happy to live", "proud of their robust bodies", which "brim with health" and "give the formidable impression of their country's strength." Bernard-Henri Lévy rejected this enthusiasm of the time, and expressed his instinctive revulsion at "this fantasy of an athletic people, rooted as much in their bodies as in their land, their race and their nation."

The intellectual and political world of the inter-war period disgusted him to the core. Although the extreme right did not have a monopoly on abjection: the entire French intelligentsia seemed to have prepared for the arrival of Marshal Pétain and the Holocaust. Marshal Pétain was of course the "truly most repugnant" character. He revealed,

---

[150] Bernard-Henri Lévy, *L'Idéologie française*, Grasset, 1981, p. 149.

through his "singular delirium", "the insane extent of his project". The extreme right-wing intellectuals deserved only contempt: "The infamous joy of the Brasillachs, Céline, Drieu who applaud the collapse of democracy" can only turn one's stomach." They all relished in the abjection of the new order[151]."

It should never be forgotten that the atmosphere that prevailed in France after the defeat of the French armies was only possible because it had been prepared years earlier by French intellectuals, whose cowardice was pathetic. Germany bore less responsibility for French abjection than is generally believed," said Lévy, "[152]". There was "no other case like it in the whole of defeated Europe, no other nation than France to claim so calmly its titles to infamy[153]."

Péguy, Fabre-Luce, Maurras, "attest to our antiquity in abjection". These people represented "the France of the bastards", "the great purulent wound" of the intellectual world. Maurice Barrés, the "prince of youth", became, under Lévy's pen, "the prince of abjection, Barrés the anti-Semite, the furious madman and *boulangist*[154]". Péguy was a "fool", and when he spoke of the "French race" he inspired only "violent disgust". The handsome Marquis de Morès did not leave him a good memory either, judging by what he found "in some of the pamphlets written by his stupid brain". Maurras, "flailing impatiently", "catches some young dog tantrums"; Léon Daudet was an intellectual with a "sick brain"; Jean Giono, "whose philosophy can be summed up in this one conviction that it is better to live by crawling than to risk dying on one's feet", was no better than Thierry Maulnier and his friends of the Young Right who exalted "a community moulded by old obsessions." As for Céline, he was simply "the champion of scum, the champion of filth[155]."

---

[151] Bernard-Henri Lévy, *L'Idéologie française*, Grasset, 1981, p. 48.

[152] Bernard-Henri Lévy, *L'Idéologie française*, Grasset, 1981, p. 56.

[153] Bernard-Henri Lévy, *L'Idéologie française*, Grasset, 1981, p. 60.

[154] Georges Ernest Jean Marie Boulanger was a French military officer and politician who played a leading role in the early years of the French Third Republic. He became very popular with the French public because of his populist, chauvinist and revanchist speeches in a society still traumatised by the loss of Alsace and Lorraine after the Franco-Prussian War of 1870.

[155] Bernard-Henri Lévy, *L'Idéologie française*, Grasset, 1981, p. 113, 235, 260, 146, 205, 210, 22. [Louis Ferdinand Céline, despite his polemical and extremely harsh anti-Semitic pamphlets, is considered one of the most influential writers of the 20th century, as he developed a new style of writing with oral characteristics that modernised both French and world literature. After Marcel Proust, he is the most translated and popular author of 20th century French literature; his most famous novel is *Journey to the End of the Night*].

All of them allowed Marshal Pétain to come to power." Yes, it is that man, swore Lévy, it is all those men who, for the first time in our modern history, perpetrated the absolute crime of legalising racism and xenophobia. It was within their ranks that the French-style final solution was thought out and planned. It is these ordinary brains, steeped in humanism and classical culture, full of patriotic decorum and conformity, that gave birth, for four years, to the French version, so profoundly French, of the abjection of the century[156]." We see here an immense contempt for the indigenous people. In reality, "racism and xenophobia" had been present in all European and world legislation for centuries, in the sense that a citizen had rights that a foreigner did not have. If the Jews had obtained citizenship in 1790 in France, they had to wait until 1870 for the Algerian departments. In reality, the "absolute crime" of which Lévy spoke referred to the loss of French citizenship in 1940.

The French communists and socialists of the last century were no less responsible for "French abjection". In 1940, after the defeat of Nazi Germany, the French communists asked the German authorities for the right to publish their newspapers. They published *"The Appeal to the People of Paris"*, in which the editors proposed to "indict all those who had pushed France into war and deceived the people of France"." At this level of madness, it is no longer enough to say that the communists shared the same language or the same theme with Vichy: they compete for this theme, deny their authorship of the regime and pretend to take over the discourse and the legacy themselves[157]." In short, for Lévy, it can be said that the communists and the fascists engaged "in a fierce competition for the appropriation and control of the evil of the environment" in "a repugnant mimetic rivalry."

In fact, socialist adherents were to swell the Marshal's ranks with unexpected recruits: Gaston Bergery, founder in 1933 of the anti-fascist Common Front; Frossard, a veteran of socialism; Spinasse, former minister of Léon Blum; Marcel Déat, minister in 1936; Lagardelle, heir to Georges Sorel and revolutionary syndicalism; Yvetot, one of the most worthy survivors of the workers' struggles at the beginning of the century; Charles Dhooges, an anarchist. All would join the side of Marshal Pétain's national revolution.

Socialism in the French tradition spread all the filth: "Finally, and to make matters worse, there is a purely racial dimension, incredibly modern, of which it is no exaggeration to say that it was in the socialist

[156] Bernard-Henri Lévy, *L'Idéologie française*, Grasset, 1981, p. 68.
[157] Bernard-Henri Lévy, *L'Idéologie française*, Grasset, 1981, p. 86.

ranks that it first reached its maximum intensity[158]." Indeed, there exists in 19th century French socialism the "idea that the Jew is less odious, as was hitherto believed, for having killed Christ, than for having invented him" and that it is "at the origin of that modern leprosy which is Christianity: that tendency, inaugurated by Voltaire, continued by Blanqui, and culminating in the books of Gustave Tridon, Blanquist and Communard who, as early as 1865, amalgamates in the same abhorrent "Semitism" those evil geniuses of the earth which are Catholicism and Judaism". The "bestial racism which pervades the thought of Proudhon", the "coarsest left-wing extremist literature, that of Sorel, Malon, Chirac, Toussenel" are to be totally discarded. We must "forget this socialism," Lévy asserted, "with the same energy and determination as Marxist, Leninist or Stalinist socialism", as well as Jules Guesde, this "chauvinist, xenophobic patriot, and for a time close to *Boulangism*[159]." Xenophobia also permeated the texts of Vaillant-Couturier, who sang of the "hard virtues of militants 'deeply rooted in the soil' and whose surnames 'have the flavour of our homeland'". The Communist Party of the 1930s had perfectly integrated the notions of "strong country" or "numerous race". During the Lyssenko controversy in France, did Aragon not proclaim himself the champion of the countryside against "decadent, degenerate, cosmopolitan and anti-national art"? It is this notion of terroir and rootedness that most repulsed Bernard-Henri Lévy, and not socialism itself." There is the repressed stinker. The racism, the xenophobia, the moña and the stupidity. Work, family, homeland and deep France[160]." That was "the delirium that sprang from the soil and from the national brains".

The only intellectual figure who was spared was Julien Benda, the internationalist who was not subservient to Marxism and who inspired the Paris of 1968, and his "magnificent "we are all German Jews", thrown like a slap in the face of the other France, that of the cretins and scoundrels who preferred to shout "Cohn-Bendit to Dachau".

Bernard-Henri Lévy's indignation was therefore not limited to the extremes of the French political chessboard. He was repulsed by everything that was deeply rooted and typically French. Even Mounier and his friends at *Esprit* magazine, far removed from any racist or anti-Semitic sentiments, displeased him. In January 1941, the magazine had praised folklore and folk dances, where those fortunate enough to "retain the cellular memory of their ethnic background" excelled. BHL

---

[158] Bernard-Henri Lévy, *L'Idéologie française*, Grasset, 1981, p. 129.
[159] Bernard-Henri Lévy, *L'Idéologie française*, Grasset, 1981, p. 166 (see note 155).
[160] Bernard-Henri Lévy, *L'Idéologie française*, Grasset, 1981, p. 181.

was furiously angry at Mounier: Was it not Mounier himself, in 1940, who gave as an example in France "the vitality" and "imagination" that "Hitlerism has infused into Germany[161] "? All national traditions provoke his sarcasm and contempt. He mocks all French authors who exalt lineage and ancestors: Gustave Thibon is a "hard-working but mediocre theorist, slightly pasty and a spokesman for our homeland and good French common sense"; Mistral, poet and singer of Provence, "was the only personage, except Joan of Arc, to whom Marshal Pétain did the honour of addressing a brief but complete Message". The point is clear: anything that is not cosmopolitan is good for the rubbish. The old French traditions, the spirit of the people, identity solidarity, etc., all these things, for the planetarian intellectual minds, must be erased once and for all.

Systematic blaming

The planetarian idea has no hold on peoples who are strongly imbued with their identity and who live in the midst of more numerous peoples. The industrial and rich nations, on the other hand, are more sensitive to all kinds of reproaches about their past and the domination they may have once exercised. Obviously, the criticism is directed against the dominant peoples, not against the dominated peoples. But for several decades in the West, this criticism has been directed exclusively against Westerners. It would be pure masochism if the victims were themselves responsible for these harsh criticisms that are constantly undermining the pride of the European peoples. This is not always the case. There are countless books on the subject; "awareness-raising" is omnipresent and continues through the press, publishing houses, television and cinema. We will therefore limit our research to a few recent and emblematic examples of this enterprise of permanent accusation.

In a 2004 book with the evocative title The Western Crime, Viviane Forrester (née Dreyfus) tried, after many others before her, to denounce the ignominy of Europeans. Her cowardice in the face of the ordeal of the German Jews was clearly criminal: "In the 1930s," she wrote, "what was already known about the record of Nazi crimes and what was reported in the press should have been enough to provoke the unrestrained, uncompromising and determined opposition of the democratic nations... But true to their genius for inaction when it came

---

[161] Bernard-Henri Lévy, L'Idéologie française, Grasset, 1981, p. 212, 32

to the Jews, so opportunely decimated, the leaders of the two great powers finally pooled their science of passivity." We should realise here that the Europeans should feel guilty for not having wanted to return immediately to the massacre, as soon as Hitler came to power in 1933.

This complicity of the West in the crimes of the Second World War was also evidenced by its inaction during the Warsaw ghetto uprising." The only response," wrote Viviane Forrester, "was silence, mean-spirited and cunning inaction, the lucid and calculated, racist obstruction of the rest of the West."

"Millions of Jews were suffocated in the gas chambers, but no one threatened the Germans with reprisals—there was no threat to gas their cities[162]." All Europeans are guilty, therefore, and not only the Germans. On this point, it is worth noting that neither Churchill's memoirs, nor those of General de Gaulle, nor those of Roosevelt mention the gas chambers during the war. This is probably because these people were cowards.

But it doesn't matter, because the main point is to show that Westerners were guilty of turning a blind eye to what was happening in Europe during the war. France, which "no longer wished to welcome Jews from Germany", was pilloried: "The terror was not to see these men, women and children exterminated and tortured, but to see them released as a dangerous influx; "Not in our house! The voices were unanimous[163] ", wrote Viviane Forrester." The general flight, even the consent by omission to Nazi racism, was hidden, forgotten, unnoticed. Western inertia in the face of barbarism and its connivance with anti-Semitism were not remembered, but kept as much as possible in a consensual silence of a voluntarily repressed memory[164]."

Short of being a great historian, Viviane Forrester would undoubtedly have been a wonderful prosecutor near Novosibirsk in 1937.

---

[162] Viviane Forrester, *Le Crime occidental*, Fayard, 2004, p. 15-16, 32-34.
[I would like to recall, before the representatives of so many nations, including some that do not have Jews in their midst, what the years 1933–1945 were for the Jews of Europe. Among the millions of human beings who met misery and death there, the Jews had the unique experience of total helplessness. They knew a condition inferior to that of things, an experience of total passivity, an experience of the Passion. (…) The anti-Semitism of the 20th century, culminating in the extermination of six million European Jews, meant for the Jews the crisis of a world that Christianity had shaped for 20 centuries." Emmanuel Levinas, *Difficult Freedom, Essays on Judaism*. Ediciones Lilmod, Buenos Aires, 2004, p. 100, 189].
[163] Viviane Forrester, *Le Crime occidental*, Fayard, 2004, p. 36.
[164] Viviane Forrester, *Le Crime occidental*, Fayard, 2004, p. 17.

However, we seem to be able to identify in his vindictiveness the source of such partiality. When he wrote, for example: "This was not a particular aggression against a particular community, but an attack against humanity as a whole, against the very concept of humanity[165]." We can safely say that this is a hallmark that we will often see in this book under the pen of other eminent figures.

The ignominy of the Europeans is obviously not limited to the episode of the Second World War. Their entire history testifies to their cruelty and abjectness. Viviane Forrester was particularly insistent on this point: "Spoliation, massacres and genocide of peoples have been perpetrated on other continents for centuries by and for Europeans. All this in good conscience, with the public's approval and admiration of such feats and their gratitude once their taste for possessions has been satiated. All this thanks to the aptitude of Westerners to manage, erase and conceal what makes them uncomfortable, without altering the image of the world they have, or the role they pretend to play? In the name of their supremacy, with an innate sense of arrogance and the certainty of a natural superiority that justifies their universal arrogance, Westerners have given themselves the right to decree, without scruples, and as if it were a matter of course, the non-importance of numerous living beings judged to be annoying and the subhuman nullity of entire populations, even their presumed harmfulness. From then on, spoliating, oppressing, persecuting, murdering without limits these halogenous masses considered unwelcome and often disastrous, became admissible, even necessary, or better still: demandable[166]."

In the back cover of Viviane Forrester's book, we could discover who the real executioners of the Palestinian people were: "Viviane Forrester shows to what extent Israelis and Palestinians are not victims of each other, but victims of a long European history; that of anti-Semitic crimes of which some were prey and the others did not participate." The case is settled: if the Palestinians are persecuted today and slaughtered like rabbits, it is the fault of the arrogant and racist white European man. In any case, Ms. Forrester cannot be accused of writing history lightly and inventing nonsense. Indeed, her work contains an impressive bibliography: some 277 references for a book of 214 pages. We therefore know that we are dealing with a serious book, published by Fayard, a very serious publisher. In this bibliography, we come across, for example, Aleksandr Solzhenitsyn's book on the role of the Jews in the Russian revolution. Since we ourselves have

---

[165] Viviane Forrester, *Le Crime occidental*, Fayard, 2004, p. 42.
[166] Viviane Forrester, *Le Crime occidental*, Fayard, 2004, p. 57, 65.

exhaustively examined that book for the needs of our present study, we can safely say that Viviane Forrester did not use it at all, and that her overblown bibliography therefore does not reflect the quality of her book, although it is nevertheless quite passable for the intended audience. This worldly figure of the Parisian crème de la crème, daughter of the very rich banker and shipowner Edgar Dreyfus, had already made a name for herself in 1996 with her book *The Economic Horror*, which was a great success in the bookshops, proving that the most blatant publicity can make up for any shortcomings. But in the end, the most important thing is that Viviane Forrester perseveres in her work: a few more books and perhaps she will be able to write French properly.

Viviane Forrester was certainly not the first to point out the ignominy of European civilisation. A Marxist author such as Lucien Goldmann, for example, a disciple of the school of the great George Lukacs, could not fail to denounce the imperialism of the European nations and "colonial expansion, with the super-profits[167] "that it generated. This expansion, he said, was "notably analysed in its functions and consequences by Rosa Luxemburg". It has also been analysed more recently by a true historian, Jacques Marseille, who demonstrated in his master thesis, together with several Anglo-Saxon historians, that the French colonial empire was a burden for the metropolis, and that the French state invested heavily and in vain[168]. The current specialist on the subject, the academic Bernard Lugan, explores this in many of his works.

This natural and systematic tendency to cover European civilisation with opprobrium has been extended and insinuated in certain popular literature, of which the writer Bernard Werber is a good representative. He is a successful author: his books, such as *The Ants*, have sold millions of copies all over the world. In another of his books, an unpretentious little science fiction book entitled *Our Human Friends*[169], Werber set the scene for a man and a woman imprisoned in a glass cage, lost somewhere in the cosmos. On a giant screen in the back of the room, images of the Earth are projected on which the two humans are informed, as if they were watching the 9 p.m. news, that in their absence, a Pakistani Muslim dictator has revealed that he possesses a terrifying bomb. He threatens to destroy the entire planet

[167] Lucien Goldmann, *Marxisme et sciences humaines*, Éditions Gallimard, 1970, Poche, p. 317.
[168] Jacques Marseille, *Empire colonial et capitalisme français*, Albin Michel, 1984.
[169] Bernard Werber, *Nos Amis les humains*, Albin Michel, 2003

"if India does not submit to all his demands regarding Kashmir". His ultimatum ends in ten minutes and we are approaching total planetarian destruction. Samantha[170] and Raul, the two humans in space, are petrified: finally the Earth explodes in slow motion on their screen. They now find themselves in the situation of Adam and Eve, the last representatives of the human species who will have to debate the recreation of humanity. But does humanity deserve a second chance? The history of mankind is punctuated by violent invasions," explains Raul. The Indo-Europeans, for example, because they knew the technique of iron, caste organisation and the use of horses, subjugated all the neighbouring peoples for five thousand years, until they imposed their warrior values and their cult of fighting heroes. —Objection," Samantha interrupts. Certainly, at the same time, the Phoenicians, the Hebrews, the Carthaginians created and developed trade, opened emporiums, the silk, tea and spice routes. They did not have powerful armies, but they proposed an alternative to warlike invasion: alliance and trade between peoples. To navigate better, they invented the compass, maps and sailing. Result: the Carthaginians were destroyed by the Romans, the Phoenicians were massacred and the Hebrews were always persecuted."

This instructive dialogue places Bernard Werber among the planetarian authors obsessed with the destruction of sedentary European civilisations and the systematic apology of the Semites and Semitic civilisations. In fact, the themes of guilt and cosmopolitanism often decide the success of a book, and not its literary value, for on that level the books are more often than not palpably mediocre.

In his time, the great Jean-Paul Sartre also held accusatory views against European civilisation. In the foreword to Franz Fanon's famous Third Worldist book, *The Damned of the Earth,* he expressed his feelings as a Marxist intellectual, filled with guilt for the injustices of the world, resolutely taking up the defence of the colonised peoples: "Colonial violence, he said, is not only intended to keep the enslaved man in check, but also to dehumanise him. Nothing will be spared them to liquidate their traditions, to substitute our language for theirs, to destroy their culture without giving them ours; they will be stunned with exhaustion … guns will be pointed at the peasants. If they resist, the soldiers shoot and they are dead men." The hatred of his own culture even made him say: "To kill a European is to kill two birds with one stone, to remove at once an oppressor and an oppressed: only one man

---

[170] Planetary authors often choose "American" names for the characters in their novels: Samantha, Jonathan, Jennifer, Samuel, Steven, etc.

is left dead and one man free; for the first time, the survivor feels under his feet a national soil"." With the death of the last colonist, expelled or assimilated, the minority species disappears, yielding its place to the socialist fraternity… We were men at his expense, he becomes a man at ours. Another man: of better quality."

There is no spirit of betrayal here in reality, since, for the Marxist, the only enemy to be defeated is the capitalist system represented by Western civilisation and the white peoples. The duty of any militant conscious of the shameless exploitation of the wretched peoples of the South by the rich capitalists of the North is to fight to the death to overthrow the power of the bourgeoisie: "In today's Europe, the slightest hint of distraction of thought is criminal complicity with colonialism." All Whites, indiscriminately, are exploiters. Everything that Europe has created, it owes to the hard work of pre-Columbian, African and Asian peoples, and to the plunder of their wealth on every continent: "You know perfectly well that we are exploiters, you know perfectly well that we have taken the gold and the metals, and then the oil from the new continents and brought it all back to the old metropolises. With excellent results, by the way: palaces, cathedrals, industrial capitals; and when crisis came, the colonial markets were there to cushion or avert it." Europe, "that greasy and livid continent "has thus been "showered with riches[171] "In the face of so much evil and injustice, he insisted, "your passivity places you alongside the exploiters."

Jean Daniel, the famous press director, wrote in the magazine *L'Express*: *"The Damned of the Earth* are, of course, all the men of the underdeveloped world, of the third world, all those who have transferred the class struggle of old Europe to an international scale. That book is a relentless, sometimes irritating, always gripping, exceptionally valuable work[172]."

From 1962 to 1966, Jean-Paul Sartre travelled up to twice a year to Moscow, where he was received by Ilya Ehrenburg and Fedine, the two great intellectual guardians of orthodoxy. When he died in 1980, the very bourgeois Raymond Barre, the liberal minister of economy and finance, represented the bereaved government and paid tribute to "the champion of freedom", "the greatest philosopher of the century". The very liberal President of the Republic Valéry Giscard d'Estaing (1974–

---

[171] Gothic cathedrals were almost all built between the 12th and 13th centuries, before the discovery of the Americas and colonisation.

[172] "Irritating" and "annoying" seem to be the main virtues of planetary intellectuals, who are surprised after being rejected by the rest of the population.

1981) delivered his eulogy with these words: "I feel his death as if one of the greatest luminaries of our time were passing away. He responded to the understanding of the tragic future of the human being with an authentic, militant and, despite all categories, uniquely French generosity." Aleksandr Solzhenitsyn, for his part, refused to meet him.

Note that a successor to Giscard d'Estaing, the also very liberal President of the Republic Jacques Chirac, eulogised the Marxist philosopher Jacques Derrida when he died in the summer of 2004. Once again, and as if by habit, liberalism's reverence for militant Marxism was in evidence.

The tendency to cover European civilisation with manure and to blame Europeans was also detected in the Russian writer Vasili Grossman, author of the long novel *Life and Fate*: "This is one of the greatest books of the century," we read on the back cover. Its author, a Russian Jew born in 1905, was for a long time an absolutely orthodox communist writer and journalist. When he began writing this chronicle of the battle of Stalingrad in 1952, he was no longer the same man. He had lived through the outbreak of anti-Semitism in his own country, listened to the trials, analysed Stalinism. Retired by the KGB, disappeared for twenty years, this book has miraculously survived. Hailed as the *"War and Peace"* of the 20th century, this masterpiece recounts the epic of human survival and is the first great cry for Russian liberation". After its publication, *Life and Fate* was awarded the prize for Best Foreign Novel. In its 800 pages, we read this enlightening passage in which the author makes one of his characters say: "What did this doctrine of peace and love [Christianity] bring to mankind? The Byzantine iconoclasm, the tortures of the Inquisition, the struggle against heresies in France, Italy, Flanders, Germany, the struggle between Protestantism and Catholicism, the intrigues of the monastic orders, the struggle between Nikon and Avvakum[173], the crushing yoke to which science and freedom were subjected for centuries, the Christian persecutions of the pagan population of Tasmania, the evildoers who set fire to black villages in Africa. All these caused greater suffering than the crimes of the bandits and criminals who practised evil for evil's sake[174]..."

Reading these lines, one would think that Vasili Grossman could have written the screenplay for the famous film *The Name of the Rose*, instead of Umberto Eco, an adaptation of a book in which medieval

---

[173] Russian patriarch and churchman at the centre of a schism in the Orthodox Church in 1654.

[174] Vasili Grossman, *Life and Destiny*, Galaxia Gutenberg, 2007, Barcelona, p. 303.

Christianity is portrayed as a horrible purulence. All this is not fortuitous. Already at the time, writers like Heinrich Heine professed the same ideas when they evoked the Middle Ages: "The Middle Ages, centuries of superstition and rapine[175]..." Obviously, all these authors are not followers of Catholicism, and even seem to harbour a rather singular hatred of this religion.

A more exhaustive study of world literature would undoubtedly reveal the extent to which this idea is persistent in the contemporary intellectual world. Whether of Marxist or liberal origin, there are countless history textbooks that tend to blame the Europeans. We are thinking here of the works of Henri Rousso, Serge Bernstein, Catherine Coquery-Vidrovitch and Vidal-Naquet, to name but a few authors from the French cultural sphere. But perhaps even more striking for the general public are the cinematographic works, television series and documentaries. We will devote a separate chapter to them.

Wisdom is Eastern

To end racism, the concept of race must first be eradicated. It is in that perspective that action must be taken. In his essay on racism, the writer and sociologist Albert Memmi stated that "we are almost all mongrels[176]." The problem seems to be that many people, especially among Europeans, seem to ignore this, and continue to see themselves as different from the other members of the human species. Fighting this racism is a necessity if we are to achieve this unified and fraternal humanity: by all means." This plague must be exorcised and combated: first within oneself, for anti-racism must first of all be a mental hygiene; then through pedagogy, in schools and universities; and finally through repression, if necessary[177]." Europeans' racism against minorities still seems to be widespread. Whites are still in the majority in Europe and still occupy the best places. However, the waves of immigration at the end of the 20th century have created a multi-ethnic society in thirty years, at least in France, although the majority of immigrants still occupy the lowest positions in society. This situation cannot be scientifically explained by a specifically racial cause, so it is an injustice that must be relentlessly denounced. But combating visible racism would only address part of the problem. Indeed, immigrant populations are not the only ones to suffer from discrimination. Other minorities are

---

[175] Heinrich Heine, *De l'Allemagne*, 1835, Gallimard, 1998, p. 466.

[176] Albert Memmi, *Le Racisme*, Gallimard, 1982, Poche, 1994, p. 27.

[177] Albert Memmi, *Le Racisme*, Gallimard, 1982, Poche, 1994, p. 14.

also victims of European society. All these oppressed minorities must be brought together to join forces against the oppressor.

This is how Albert Memmi systematically associated in his analysis the case of the Blacks and the "colonised" with that of the Jews, and even with that of women, proletarians and homosexuals. They are all victims of a single oppressor. It is therefore a question of joining forces against the only source of racism and of stirring up all the frustrations, all the injustices in order to try to eradicate them. A society made up of ethnic, religious and sexual minorities, all equal, is the best way to eradicate nationalism and extremism once and for all. In democracy, the enemy is invariably the same.

For Albert Memmi, being a "minority" is not simply a demographic notion: "One can be a minority in several ways. In this broad sense, women and the colonised, demographically more numerous than the dominant, are outnumbered by them. Black Americans and Jews are doubly minorities[178]." But the result is the same: oppression. The racist "chooses the most favourable victim, the most resigned, the one who lets himself be beaten without daring to react. It is a very comfortable attitude. The racist instinctively pounces on the oppressed, he turns, in order to exercise his triumph, to men already defeated by history. That is why the foreigner is an easy prey for the racist. The fragility of the foreigner attracts racism, just as weakness attracts sarcasm and contempt." So the European proletarian, "in order to feel greater", despises the foreign worker." In short, everyone seeks to appear dominant and relatively extraordinary in the lower echelon. Racism is a pleasure available to all." It is a "vain, petty and iniquitous compensation."

"While they were colonised, explained Albert Memmi, there was an Arabophobia, which diminishes once they become a relative economic power. At the same time, however, immigrant workers continue to suffer from it: this is because the unhappy remain under the yoke of the Europeans[179]." All this suffering, it must be stressed, does not prevent future immigrants from fighting for a visa.

In 1977, a survey showed that "hostility against Jews and North Africans is mainly on the part of workers and pensioners. But why do French workers think this way? It is because French workers believe that immigrants jeopardise the advantages they have over them. Fear of unemployment, for example, is not unrelated to this hostility. We have

---

[178] Albert Memmi, *Le Racisme*, Gallimard, 1982, Poche, 1994, p. 97.
[179] Albert Memmi, *Le Racisme*, Gallimard, 1982, Poche, 1994, p. 169.

recently seen an extraordinary commotion in a population, all classes confused, in the Paris region, because Muslim immigrants wanted to build a mosque... Now, in this case the Muslims would not have increased their number or changed their nature with the building of the mosque. This confirms that the evil does not come from the victim but from the accuser[180]." Albert Memmi's logic is unstoppable.

Fear of difference characterises the racist. Fear triggers the discriminatory reflex." One must insist on this component of racism: the disorder, the dread of otherness. Somehow, the foreigner is always strange and terrifying. And from dread to hostility, from hostility to aggression, the distance is not great."

"The racist is a man who is afraid; who is afraid of being attacked or who is afraid because he thinks he is attacked, and who attacks in order to exorcise that fear[181]." It is the "aggressive and denigrating fear of women or young people, homosexuals or the elderly" that defines the oppressor, the potential racist. In short, according to Albert Memmi, the oppressor is the white heterosexual male in his prime. For the elderly are too weak and the young are sufficiently malleable and receptive to "awareness-raising" campaigns.

"I lived until the end of my adolescence in North Africa, in an atmosphere of deep suspicion and mutual distrust, to say the least, between communities", explained Albert Memmi[182]. Here in France, "the habit of democracy has fortunately softened reciprocal rejection, which is great progress. But there is still a fearful or ironic contempt for foreigners, an aloofness towards each other, almost no hospitality, a taste for secrecy and an ever-growing chauvinism, which reveal that aggressive fear of others is always latent[183]." The French are clearly unfriendly, but it is nevertheless good to settle in their country.

Planetarian intellectuals are so perfectly convinced of their legitimacy that they tend to think that their opponents are suffering from some madness of the spirit. Albert Memmi gave us an example of that

---

[180] Albert Memmi, *Le Racisme*, Gallimard, 1982, Poche, 1994, p. 121.

[181] Albert Memmi, *Le Racisme*, Gallimard, 1982, Poche, 1994, p. 147-149, 110. Albert Memmi is the inventor of the concept of Heterophobia: "The rejection of others in the name of any difference".

[182] Indeed, numerous testimonies recount the strong animosity of the Muslim and Christian populations against the Jews in North Africa. In his biography, Albert Memmi described his state of mind and that of his peers: "We lived in enthusiastic expectation of new and incredible times, and thought we could already see the precursory signs: the agony of religions, families and nations. We had only rage, contempt and irony for the retards of history who clung to these residues." Albert Memmi, *Portrait d'un juif*, Gallimard, 1962.

[183] Albert Memmi, *Le Racisme*, Gallimard, 1982, Poche, 1994, p. 40.

oddity which is undoubtedly one of the most characteristic features of the cosmopolitan mentality, together with that tireless activism which gives all its acts and speeches that moralising schoolmaster's touch: "Racism is not a disease, but an archaic attitude, common to the species. The psychotherapy of some avowed racists, assuming they consent to it, would not suppress it. A constant and general vigilance is required, an individual and collective effort, which concerns the psychologist, the sociologist as well as the politician. The fight against racism requires continuous pedagogy, from childhood to death[184]."

Albert Memmi reminded us in passing of some wise precepts: "Remember, says the Bible, that you were a foreigner in Egypt", which means that you should take care of the foreigner because you yourself have been a foreigner and may one day be a foreigner again." Obviously, this is a very practical formula to remind the people in whose country one wants to settle. In any case, information and education work is necessary, but to eradicate racism, according to Albert Memmi, "we will have to attack colonisation or the social and political structure of our societies". A real revolution, in short." The universalisation and unification of the Earth, the self-affirmation of the peoples of Africa, Asia and America will perhaps make it laughable to consider others as inferior because of their skin colour or the shape of their nose." To conclude with Albert Memmi, "let us remember that wisdom is oriental[185] ", as he put it so well.

The great and highly regarded ethnologist Claude Lévi-Strauss seemed less explicit on the subject. However, he went on to publish important works, such as the famous *Race and History,* "a classic of anti-racism", published in 1952. It was commissioned by UNESCO. In 1971, he published another work, this time entitled *Race and Culture,* for a UNESCO conference launching an international year of struggle against racism. But his anti-racist commitment did not prevent him from feeling some implicit or explicit antipathies: in *From Near and Far,* he wrote: "colonialism was the greatest sin of the West", thus designating Europeans as guilty in the eyes of history. More explicitly, he wrote in a letter to Raymond Aron in 1967 about Israeli policy: 'I obviously cannot feel the destruction of the redskins as a fresh wound in my side, and react in the opposite direction when it is a question of Palestinian Arabs, even when (as in this case) the brief contacts I have had with the Arab world have inspired me with an inarguable antipathy[186]." Thus,

---

[184] Albert Memmi, *Le Racisme,* Gallimard, 1982, Poche, 1994, p. 160.
[185] Albert Memmi, *Le Racisme,* Gallimard, 1982, Poche, 1994, p. 208, 213.
[186] Claude Lévi-Strauss and Didier Eribon, *De cerca y de lejos,* Alianza Editorial,

the difficulty of getting rid of racism endures, even in the highest spirits." I know myself to be a Jew and the oldness of his blood, as I said some time ago, pleases me", he then wrote without seeming to want to renounce his own identity. Perhaps this is the explanation for some of his aversions.

Open borders

Welcoming the stranger is an essential principle and a necessity for the construction of the "open society". Marek Halter rightly reminded us of the teachings of the Torah: "If a stranger comes to live with you in your country, you shall not oppress him. He shall be to you as one of your own; you shall love him as yourselves, for you were strangers in the land of Egypt."

"We must remind our contemporaries of the wise words of Leviticus[187] ", said Marek Halter. It is somewhat comical to hear an asylum seeker invoke the precepts of his own religion to convince his host to welcome him; and the argument takes on a telling meaning when one knows that the adherents of that religion are among those who are least likely to practice welcoming the stranger and integration. Indeed, at the beginning of the third millennium, foreigners in Israel—assuming that Palestinians are foreigners—are not treated according to biblical precepts.

In his last book, Edgar Morin touched again on this theme, a theme that runs throughout his work: "The planetarian era has given rise to countless migrations from destitute regions to rich nations, and instead of rejection or contempt, the ethics of hospitality asks us to welcome the migrant and adopt him or her into our community[188]." This is obviously the French community to which he now belongs; the discourse is thus perfectly in keeping with his idea of the dissolution of communities and nations.

The great philosopher Jacques Derrida came to the same conclusions on the issue: "I stressed that there was much more room than was claimed to receive more foreigners, and that immigration had not increased, contrary to what was claimed[189]." Indeed, it is the racists

Madrid, 1990, p. 211, 207–208, 214.

[187] Marek Halter, *Un Homme, un cri*, Robert Laffont, Paris, 1991, p. 142.

[188] Edgar Morin, *El Método 6, Ética; chapter: Ética planetaria*, Ediciones Cátedra-Anaya, Madrid, 2006, p. 183.

[189] Jacques Derrida, Élisabeth Roudinesco, *Y mañana, qué...* Fondo de Cultura Económica, Buenos Aires, 2002, p. 71.

who imagine that immigration is increasing, just when all the figures show that it is decreasing.

In *The Democratic Ideal*, Shmuel Trigano also took this perspective. In the subtle style that characterises his writings, the philosopher explained that his "work is part of the democratic project of human liberation. The rediscovery of singularity and identity only make sense if they serve to meet the challenge of living together, recognising man in Man, and ultimately inventing hospitality in human rights"." Inventing" is vital for planetarian thinkers: "inventing" new concepts, "inventing" new products, "inventing" a new society, "inventing" new suffering. The main thing, it has become clear, is to eradicate the old traditions that formed the structure of the old society.

Hospitality' is at the heart of the debate on building the New World Order. But in this matter, any meanness would be an insult to the democratic ideal, as Shmuel Trigano explained: "Hospitality means welcoming guests in one's home in one's own name. This reception is possible because the host who invites them is ready to welcome them into his or her bosom, to open up more than anyone else and give them a place. Everything revolves around the consideration of that place. If this empty place is defined as that of a citizen, i.e. a place offered in the heart of the people by the people, then what comes in addition is the identity which—since it has welcomed the other—also becomes a collective identity. The reception of the other is no longer felt as a lack of identity[190]." The problem of "too much" immigration is therefore a false problem, as long as one decides to "open up more than any other". It was indeed necessary to think about it.

Although the notion of "people" should be defined correctly: "The people is the framework in which identity can be received and individuals can live it and form their personality in it. It carries within it the principle of differentiation, of otherness insofar as it is out of control and is the source of exteriority and heteronomy in the human condition[191]." It could not be clearer. Shmuel Trigano added: "The contemporary need for "community" is a need for hospitality in the cold and empty universe of citizenship that has abandoned the collective spirit and where the experience of the common has been disregarded because of the catastrophes it has generated. Democratic universality, thus achieved in the alliance of identity and hospitality, will be freed from power and the temptation of totality, so that Man can finally be

---

[190] Shmuel Trigano, *L'Idéal démocratique*, Editions Odile Jacob, 1999, p. 337.
[191] Shmuel Trigano, *L'Idéal démocratique*, Editions Odile Jacob, 1999, p. 308.

born in the destiny of mankind[192]." Extraordinary Shmuel, shall we leave it here?

In his *Memoirs (Volume II)*, Nobel laureate Elie Wiesel set himself up as the apostle of refugees and wanderers, albeit with a somewhat maudlin speech: "Why can't man see in every child his own child? What should be our attitude towards the foreigner, the exile, the refugee? ... I take his side. An ethical stance that I claim. The Jew in me adheres to the community of the wanderers, the homeless, the outcasts. On the side of those who seek sanctuary ... Every human being—man, woman or child—is a sanctuary because God resides in him. And no one has the right to violate it. In some countries, refugees are called "illegal". That term is offensive. A human being is never illegal. Their actions may be illegal, but not their essence... Can we hope that, before the end of this century, this century will put an end to these social and political categories? Imagine a human community without refugees, without uprooted people, without exiles: a utopian construction of the spirit? The human sanctuary is a being that dreams of its humanity. Within it, everything is simple: everyone is there thanks to everyone. Let us dream of the day when the whole earth becomes a sanctuary." All this verbiage did not prevent Elie Wiesel from writing a few pages later: "I don't like grandiloquence[193]."

Daniel Cohn-Bendit is not a philosopher. In him, the will to establish a multiracial society is expressed in a more brutal way. In 1987, the former anarchist leader of May '68 was acclaimed in Davos, the world temple of single thinking, mercantile values and globalism. Today he is deputy mayor of the city of Frankfurt am Main in Germany[194].

He at least has the merit of being very clear when he evokes his political thinking. According to him, European integration must replace the old nation states. It is up to the European government to enact a common migration policy: "A European migration law should be in the direction of openness and greater freedom and equality... One could, for example, set a figure of one million entries per year for the whole of the European Union."

"In Frankfurt am Main, he wrote, the resident population is made up of 25% foreigners, and it can be said that Frankfurt would not

---

[192] Shmuel Trigano, *L'Idéal démocratique*, Editions Odile Jacob, 1999, p. 338.

[193] Elie Wiesel, *Memoires (Tome II)*, Éditions du Seuil, 1996, p. 130-132, 148.

[194] Europe's third largest city in terms of financial activities after London and Paris and home to the European Central Bank.

collapse if the percentage of foreigners one day reached one third of the overall population[195]."

The aim is to break once and for all with the burdens of the past. If Europe has so far, over the centuries, only vegetated in comparison with the magnificent development of the peoples of the other continents, it is because it has not been sufficiently open to foreigners: "By rejecting its own foreigners against all reason, Christian Europe was to surrender much of its creative potential into the hands of its adversaries[196]." Of course, the exact opposite can be said elsewhere in the book to justify the long existence of the open society. What is essential is not truth or science; what is essential is discourse and getting the message across by all means: through tiresome advertising, constant repetition, media bombardment, and even lies if necessary. This is how Dani-el-Rojo calmly stated: "The immigration that we have had in the Federal Republic for a few decades is not a new phenomenon, but a long tradition in German history." A "long tradition" that probably dates back to 1992–1993. Although it has to be admitted that "the German naturalisation procedure is an antiquity[197]."

Faced with the ineptitude of the natives to accept planetarian schemes, Cohn-Bendit believes that it is better to precipitate evolution than to do it gently through persuasion: "Since we know that there will always be voices to cry out at the first drop at the flood, it would be sensible—for a certain period of time—rather to increase the scale of allowable capacity for admission." In any case, unredeemed people in their territories have tremendous difficulties in understanding the situation, and react to societal developments in a completely illogical way.

The truth according to Cohn-Bendit is that "there is no cause and effect relationship between the proportion of foreign population and the degree of xenophobia. Xenophobia is important in neighbourhoods with a high foreign population density, but in general, the reasons are indirectly related to the presence of foreigners: most of the time, these are neighbourhoods where the losers and underprivileged of society gather… While the real presence of foreigners in flesh and blood allows for agreements with the Germans, the virtual or imagined presence of a large number of foreigners generates much greater concerns, reservations, even resentment." Explanation: the more foreigners there are in a neighbourhood, the more Germans leave the neighbourhood,

[195] Daniel Cohn-Bendit, *Xénophobies*, Hamburg, 1992, Grasset, 1998, p. 14.
[196] Daniel Cohn-Bendit, *Xénophobies*, Hamburg, 1992, Grasset, 1998, p. 102.
[197] Daniel Cohn-Bendit, *Xénophobies*, Hamburg, 1992, Grasset, 1998, p. 25, 165.

and the less racism there is; which is indeed perfectly logical, and leads Cohn-Bendit to take the reasoning further: "We could deduce that in order to curb xenophobia it would be better to increase, rather than decrease, the number of foreigners[198]". In any case, it is not so necessary to treat backward natives with kid gloves, because most of them are wretches, failures in life, "pusillanimous little Whites": "This hatred for the foreigners around him, both socially and in the hierarchy, is also felt by the individual who has fallen into decline towards himself. He hates foreigners because they try to occupy the social space that he has not been able to climb, that he has not been able to leave[199]."

In his book *Waiting for the Barbarians*, Guy Sorman, in the chapter *Who is German*, quoted the words of Cohn-Bendit, who reiterated his multicultural convictions with formidable aplomb: according to him, a closed border would encourage migratory flows in both directions: "In Germany, as in France, there is nothing better than a closed border for the number of foreigners to increase and transform temporary emigration into permanent settlement[200]." Therefore, the borders should be opened so that immigration decreases.

"In Berlin, Sorman observed, the Turks now form a small original nation whose capital is the Kreuzberg district ..., and it is now overpopulated by Anatolian peasants whose grandchildren, in three generations, have become excellent Berliners who are neither Turks nor Germans, unless they are both at the same time. The government denies them, they say, German nationality."

Let us remember that Turkish immigration is not from a former colony: independent Turkey was an ally of Germany during the First World War, and for a long time maintained close economic ties with the Reich. But it was never a colony, as Algeria was with respect to France. The migration phenomenon in Germany today is just as important, if not more so, which proves, by the way, that the former colonial status is not the cause of today's immigration in Europe as we are wont to believe. The strong presence of a Moroccan community in the Netherlands or Sweden, for example, cannot be explained by the phenomenon of colonisation. It is an eminently political interpretation, which entails an idea of guilt and compensation.

Cohn-Bendit's analysis of racism is always surprising, as surprising as the response of a merchant from the Sentier before a

---

[198] Daniel Cohn-Bendit, *Xénophobies*, Hamburg, 1992, Grasset, 1998, p. 43–45.
[199] Daniel Cohn-Bendit, *Xénophobies*, Hamburg, 1992, Grasset, 1998, p. 156.
[200] Guy Sorman, *Waiting for the Barbarians*, Seix Barral, 1993, Barcelona, p. 31.

court[201]: "In the West, where the settlement of immigrants is strong and long-standing, coexistence is easier. Consequently, it would not be the presence of foreigners that would provoke racism, but their absence: it would be the ghost of the immigrant, rather than the immigrant himself, that would provoke violence." All that remains is to convince the French and Germans that being modern means being multicultural. And "Cohn-Bendit knows how to convince, and multiplies anti-racist campaigns with the support of local television stations, which broadcast *spots* against nationalist jingoism. For example: a world map and the text: "Everywhere in the world outside Germany, we Germans are also foreigners". It is an echo of that "We are all German Jews" of May '68, when the French government of the time tried to expel the student leader to Germany. Cohn-Bendit has a preference for this slogan addressed to foreigners: "Please don't leave us alone with the Germans".

"The boat is far from being full; it is far too empty". The population is ageing, the Germans don't want to have children, they have to be replaced, so welcome refugees, immigrants, all the poor of the world! Germany's new destiny is to welcome them. It is no big deal that Germany is becoming less and less German; on the contrary: the intermingling of the *Deutschtum* will prevent any revival of the Nazi past." Cohn-Bendit therefore proposes American-style quotas[202]."

If we have to insist so much on the construction of the plural society, it is because it is infinitely stimulating: "The contract signed with the multicultural society must prevent us from becoming too homely and comfortable, traditionalist and complacent in our familiar sphere[203]."

The backward Indians who refuse to leave the square are wrong to oppose it, for this evolution is ineluctable: "Whether multicultural society is desirable or not, that question will continue to arouse passions for a long time to come; one way or another, it will continue to exist in every form, and it is useless to ask ourselves whether we want it or

---

[201] An allusion to the traditional Parisian Jewish quarter with a long history of financial scandals (see Hervé Ryssen, *The Jewish Mafia*).
[202] Guy Sorman, *Waiting for the Barbarians*, Seix Barral, 1993, Barcelona, p. 31–32, 47–51." This would be, he says, a way of focusing the public debate on the evaluation of quotas rather than on the principle of immigration itself. This debate on quotas would be concrete and would give rise to interesting coalitions: "We would see the employers' movement expressing itself in favour of immigration for economic reasons, and allying itself with the defenders of human rights and the Greens, in order to increase quotas."
[203] Daniel Cohn-Bendit, *Xénophobies*, Hamburg, 1992, Grasset, 1998, p. 158.

not[204]." There is no point in camouflaging or diabolising the dissatisfaction that multicultural society provokes in the local population, as well as in newcomers. It is an easily conceivable and even inevitable reaction. Be prepared to forget its somewhat surprising character, and things will improve more quickly." In any case, "the democratic state does not have the means to defend itself against immigration. Any hope in this respect is futile. Since the situation is the way it is, it is better to influence it and adjust it, rather than stand idly by and suffer the consequences. We must get used to this relative inconvenience."

Europe's indigenous peoples must get it into their heads that "attempts to blockade are totally illusory in the face of the new world disorder. It is the price of democracy[205]"." The immigration society is now a reality, and no power in the world will be able to reverse it[206]." You read that right: "No power in this world."

In his book *The Egalitarian Machine,* published in 1987, Alain Minc spoke in the same terms of the ineluctability of globalisation, as if it were a matter of prophecies to be fulfilled fatally, as if they were biblical revelations. The chapter entitled *The Ten Commandments* left no room for doubt, stating: "Between a Europe in full demographic decline and the overpopulated countries of the southern Mediterranean, the communicating vessels effect is inevitable. Immigration will be a fatality, a drama or a good thing, depending on how France behaves. Fatal if, incapable of dealing with the situation, we go from excuse to excuse, alternating between half-xenophobic speeches, intolerant practices, and occasionally a little courage: like today, in a way. A drama, if an ageing, timorous, self-absorbed population reacts through exclusion: a sort of South Africa with a human face. A fortunate one, if French society gives itself the opportunity to be flexible, to put the melting pot into practice and to benefit from immigrants the increased dynamism that demography would otherwise forbid it[207]."

The French and Germans must welcome foreigners and show a little more tolerance, for their pettiness sometimes tends to be difficult to bear: "Their *ius soli* [right to land] is still exemplary, but their refugee policy is so parsimonious that it denotes great selfishness[208]." Enough of pettiness and pettiness. There is no need to fear the future, no need

---

[204] Daniel Cohn-Bendit, *Xénophobies*, Hamburg, 1992, Grasset, 1998, p. 26.
[205] Daniel Cohn-Bendit, *Xénophobies*, Hamburg, 1992, Grasset, 1998, p. 170, 160.
[206] Daniel Cohn-Bendit, *Xénophobies*, Hamburg, 1992, Grasset, 1998, p. 51.
[207] Alain Minc, *La Machine égalitaire*, Grasset 1987, p. 264.
[208] Alain Minc, *Le Nouveau Moyen-Age*, Gallimard, 1993, p. 38.

to be timorous. The selfishness of the French, "who are alarmed by a hundred thousand immigrants a year", should take an example from the new German virtues during the war in Yugoslavia. Indeed, Germany has welcomed "with real temperance", "more than five hundred thousand official immigrants per year, of whom two hundred thousand were exiled Yugoslavs, as well as illegals far more numerous than in our country[209]."

The French were thus able to enjoy their bourgeois prosperity, selfish as they are." Preserved until now from the gigantic East-West immigration, thanks to a Germany that serves as a buffer, France has only been confronted with a South-North migration."

However, "the integration machine continues to work"." Faced with migratory changes, the French should congratulate themselves every day on having their right to land: it avoids the friction and friction that Germany is experiencing on its territory, with immigrant communities constantly growing and condemned *ad vitam æternam* to the status of second-class citizens". By a strange paradox, Alain Minc told us, rivalling Cohn-Bendit in boldness, "the right of the soil will make France more homogeneous in the long run than Germany with its right of blood." It is perhaps a paradoxical idea to claim that a country is more homogeneous by settling foreign communities in it. But today's paradox will be tomorrow's prejudice, by dint of repetition, thanks to the tireless propaganda that supports planetarian hopes. It is necessary to "invent" new concepts, to be daring, not to shrink back from anything, even the most enormous prosopopoeias, in order to further bamboozle the backward and astonished natives. Naturally, if the Germans were to adopt "in part the right of the soil, they would set a salutary example."

Ten years later, in *That World to Come*, the very liberal economist Alain Minc still seemed to be motivated by the same obsession: "Immigration, he wrote, is not a misfortune threatening Europe; it is, given its demography, a vital necessity." Clearly, it is out of the question to promote a pro-immigration policy. On the contrary, the opportunity should be seized to interbreed the peoples of Europe. Alain Minc is in no way different from the progressive MEP Cohn-Bendit: "Will the Europeans bear the phenomenon in spite of themselves or will they see it as an opportunity? "Since the phenomenon is inevitable, it is useless to try to oppose it. Moreover, the natives have finally begun to understand it: "Public opinion no longer believes in the nonsense of zero immigration and other fantasies marked by pure xenophobia." In

---

[209] Alain Minc, *Le Nouveau Moyen-Age*, Gallimard, 1993, p. 20.

this new book by Minc, we again come across the same tendency to want to revolutionise, to overturn the mentalities and attitudes of European societies: "Europeans must invent a new model of economic development[210]." Planetarian thinkers never rest. At the core of their being burns a perpetual agitation that generates economic nervousness, stock market frenzy or social revolution, as well as a will to destroy everything that is not the fruit of their messianic imagination or their "invention".

Open Europe

The European idea, as currently conceived by the Brussels-based European Union, is part of the ideological arsenal of globalisation advocates. The introduction of the euro in 2002 was a formidable step towards the unification of the continent, but it was only a step, for Europe must be a stepping stone to global unification. This is exactly the script envisaged by Jacques Attali in his *Dictionary of the 21st century*: "The euro will lead to the creation of a European government at the end of the first quarter of the century. It will even serve as a model, in the second half of the century, for the hypothetical creation of a single world currency."

These are perspectives that are also shared by other planetarian thinkers. Although one should not believe that, in the minds of its creators, the idea of abolishing nations in favour of the European entity will serve to lay the foundations of a powerful empire capable of meeting the challenges of the century. The motivations of a precursor thinker like Julien Benda, quoted by Alain Finkielkraut in *La Humanité perdu*, went in another direction: "The European frontier is only like an illusory immobility in an evolution that cannot be interrupted. With Europe, man, still a prisoner of the sensible, will have taken a great step towards his true destiny", which is none other than that of planetarian unification.

The sociologist Bourdieu was directly affiliated with the thinker Julien Benda when, at a colloquium of intellectuals gathered in Strasbourg in November 1991 during the war in Croatia, he declared: "I would like us to be a kind of European Parliament of Culture. European in the sense that for me it is a stage, a higher degree of universalisation, in the sense that it is already better than being French." In this sense, one could consider, like Benda, that "an impious Europe

---

[210] Alain Minc, *Ce Monde qui vient*, Grasset, 2004, p. 115, 136, 119

will necessarily be less impious than the nation" because "the European will be fatally less attached to Europe than the French to France, than the German to Germany. He will feel more loosely bound in his determination to the soil, in his fidelity to the land." The desire to uproot is undoubtedly the basis of the European project, to which Alain Finkielkraut also fully subscribes, with, however, his little added touch of contempt for the natives: "By becoming European, the Frenchman transcends his native smallness, enlarges his piece of land and occupies a wider, more abstract, more rational, more civilised space than the nation[211]."

At the end of the 20th century, after the collapse of the communist bloc, many intellectuals were excited by the formidable progress of European integration, the penetration of the spirit of globalisation and the accelerated construction of a pluralistic society. Their enthusiasm was not dampened by the war that had broken out in the former Yugoslavia between Serbs, Croats and Bosnians. On the contrary, many of them took up the pen and mobilised with great warlike ardour to defend multi-ethnic Bosnia. Bernard-Henri Lévy and Alain Finkielkraut were at the forefront of the ultra-Belgian freedom fighters who incited the war against Serbia. Their motivations were then the same, as Finkielkraut wrote: "To nations sinful by the very fact of being nations, Bosnia opposed their ontological purity and their multinational innocence. Freed from all lineage, alien to carnal divisions, discord and servitude, its citizens did not have to blush or apologise for their belonging: their name, more than a name, was the emblem of cosmopolitanism; their territory, more than a particular place, was a model of the universal. Being Bosnian was better than being Slovenian, Croatian, Albanian, Macedonian or Serbian[212]."

In Bill Clinton's US administration, the influential men who promoted these principles would a few years later be the same as those who would revolve around President George Bush Jr: same feathers, same branches. War was therefore inevitable, and Serbia was bombed in order to "liberate" Bosnia and Kosovo.

Ultimately, the only way to definitively eradicate national and identity resistance is to make the peoples disappear in the great universal miscegenation, and first and foremost the European peoples who are the most likely to oppose the New World Order: "The mortal danger that the cult of belonging, the segmentation of humanity and the confinement of individuals to their race or culture represent for the

---

[211] Alain Finkielkraut, *La Humanidad perdida*, Anagrama, Barcelona, 1998, p. 136-137.
[212] Alain Finkielkraut, *La Humanidad perdida*, Anagrama, Barcelona, 1998, p. 138.

world can only be definitively avoided by the establishment of multi-ethnic societies[213] ", confirmed Alain Finkielkraut.

Ethnically homogenous nations represent the main obstacle to the establishment of a universal society. This is the essential challenge of our time. After the US bombing of Serbia in 1999, Serbs were persecuted by Kosovo Albanians and had to flee their historical territory. Ultimately, Western intervention had the effect of encouraging the rise of Islam and mafia networks in the area, but always for the sake of building a multicultural Europe.

The planetarian idea is not just a philosophy reserved for the intellectual circles of the Republic. It permeates all the major debates in society and inspires our journalists and politicians. When the *Courrier international* of 2 May 1996 headlined on its front page: "Europe lacks immigrants", its editor, Alexandre Adler, knew that he would be listened to by the political powers that be.

At the same time, Josef Alfred Grinblat, the head of the "Population and Migration" department, pursued an identical policy. In his 1999 report to the UN on the problems posed by Europe's faltering demography and its ageing population, he too advocated "replacement migration". That report envisaged imposing on the European Union no less than a "migration flow of 159 million non-Europeans over the next twenty years". The very liberal Josef Grinblat thus more than satisfied a man of the left like Daniel Cohn-Bendit.

We have also seen numerous other examples of this, such as that of the communist mayor of Bobigny, Bernard Birsinger, who in October 2004 gave a huge plot of land free of charge to the Muslims of his municipality to build a mosque. In the department of Hauts-de-Seine, the liberal mayor of Asnières, Emmanuel Aeschlimann, also did the same by giving land for the construction of a mosque at the beginning of 2005. Prime Minister Nicolas Sarkozy (representative of the "hard" right) laid the foundation stone.

European construction is a springboard for the establishment of a world government. In a very official way, we read in letter No. 8 of the Foundation for Political Innovation published in February 2005 (an institution close to President Jacques Chirac), an article entitled "European Identity? "written by the academic François Ewald, president of the foundation's scientific council: "The question is whether by Europe we mean a great nation delimited in its territory, like

---

[213] Alain Finkielkraut, *La Humanité perdue*, Anagrama, Barcelona, 1998, p. 142. In Alain Finkielkraut, *L'Humanité perdue*, Seuil, 1996, p. 147, for "(…) *it can only be definitively avoided with the establishment of multi-ethnic societies*".

Vidal de la Blache's France in his Hexagon, or an open political construction, freed from the notion of borders, emancipated from all forms of racial, ethnic, religious or civilising identities, destined to expand constantly on the basis of its liberal principles." As the representative of the head of state, Ewald unveiled his grand idea of Europe: "Europe has no identity: it is a promise. It is destined to open up: to Ukraine tomorrow and, why not, the day after tomorrow, to the Maghreb countries. What greater hope can there be for the next century? "

The former Vice-President of the European Commission, the famous Sir Leon Brittan, a great European descended from a persecuted Lithuanian family, advocated the single currency and absolute European integration as early as 1994. Of course, we would be wrong to think that the technocrats in power in Brussels are showing extraordinary political foresight, even though everything seems to have been planned in advance.

Logically, unless a popular backlash slows down the process, Turkey will sooner or later join the European Union, after which it will be Morocco's turn, and then Israel, which already features in European football competitions and Eurovision' contests, for example. All the planetarian spirits are already wholeheartedly committed to Turkey's cause, from the extreme left to the liberal right, and with the support of successive US governments.

Thus, the Socialist MEP Moscovici thought that "Turkey's accession could be a protection against terrorism and a factor in strengthening our security. Turkey's Muslim character would be enriching. Europe must be multicultural and multi-religious. It must be open and recognise various legacies." On the other side of the political chessboard, Lellouche, deputy secretary general of the big right-wing liberal party, was of a similar opinion: "Everything must be done to ensure that the river of Islam flows into the ocean of democracy and human rights214." The metaphor is only valid for the European "Christian club", because in Israel, for example, Islam will always be insoluble. As Jacques Chirac's diplomatic adviser and vice-president of the France-Israel think tank, Lellouche argued that: "to think that Islam is not soluble in democracy is to accept in advance a war of civilisations. The question is whether we will help Islam to reconcile itself with human rights and the market economy, or whether we will let it take refuge in a fundamentalist retreat."

---

[214] *Le Parisien*, 15 September 2004.

The head of the liberal right Nicolas Sarkozy, recently returned from Israel, declared on 21 December 2004 at a meeting of the Circle of Europeans: "The problem is not Turkey, but Europe's identity. If we really want to expand in that region of the world, we must first integrate Israel, whose population, mostly of European origin, shares our values."

Jacques Attali naturally seconded these words and even went further: we must integrate Turkey, he wrote, because "France, due to its past geopolitical choices, is a Muslim nation; Islam is the religion of two million French citizens and of a third of the immigrants in this country." It is necessary to get it into one's head that Europe, like France, is already "a Muslim nation". Obviously, Jacques Attali did not plan to make Europe a land of Islam, but in his vision, Islam and immigration make it possible to dissolve Europe's old national communities, disrupt identity feelings and morally uproot the autochthonous population. Islam is therefore very useful for planetarian projects.

In *Europe(s)*, in 1994, Jacques Attali had already warned: "Europe should no longer accept itself as a Christian club, but as a space without borders, from Ireland to Turkey, from Portugal to Russia, from Albania to Sweden; a space that culturally privileges the nomad over the sedentary, generosity over self-enclosure, tolerance over identity, in short, multi-belonging over exclusion. The recent debates on the right of foreigners to vote, on citizenship and on the right to asylum open the way to these changes215."

Ten years later, the debate on the European constitution is instilling the idea of the merger of states and the creation of a European government. So things have moved very fast since the fall of the Soviet Union, and that is precisely what is stirring people's spirits. Messianic fever seems to have reached its paroxysm. Never before has Europe been inundated with so much planetarian discourse. It is insinuated everywhere through the media: in the press, on the radio, in television reports, in advertising, or in the cinema, where in barely a decade, miscegenation and multiculturalism have become an almost intangible norm. All this is not quite natural. It is in fact a systematic and obsessive will to realise the belief in the messianic message of global unification.

In this perspective, the unification of Europe is an essential step, as envisaged by Jacques Attali in his *Dictionary of the 21st century,* whose text is after all very similar to that of the famous *Protocols of the Elders of Zion,* published at the beginning of the 20th century. Europe will be the springboard for broader projects: 'A Mediterranean Union

---

[215] Jacques Attali, *Europe(s),* Fayard, 1994, p. 196, 198

of the three southern European countries (France, Spain, Italy) with three Maghreb countries (Morocco, Algeria, Tunisia) would be a replacement or even complementary strategy. In the medium term, such a union would have as many inhabitants as the European Union, and would contribute to the political stability of an area that is vital for France. A common market could be set up first, and then go further with a cultural and political union... Of course, the markets of the South would not replace those of Europe—in any case, not for a long time. But the success of a Mediterranean union would prepare for the future opening of the large African markets. The common market between Europe and Africa will be the goal of the next century." It could not be clearer: Turkey's integration is only one stage in the process.

In *The World is My Tribe*, published in 1997, essayist Guy Sorman already supported Turkey's entry into Europe: "Rapprochement with Turkey is urgent, for it would show that it is possible to be Muslim and European."

The great journalist and press director Alexandre Adler was also a militant in this direction. In an article he wrote in *Le Figaro* in October 2004, he showed some consideration for those he was trying to hoodwink: "French public opinion should not be told that Turkey's entry is a minor matter or presents few risks, for this method would only increase the anguish of a very intelligent people216." This contrasts somewhat with the diatribes of Alain Minc and Bernard-Henri Lévy against the backward French. But this insidious flattery was to sell us the goods at a higher profit. Turkey, Adler continued, a country with "free elections, a free press, intellectuals who have nothing to envy ours, admirable universities open to the world" represented an "unexpected opportunity"." Let us now interpret this signal in order to guarantee the future freedom of our continent. Our freedom is clearly at stake. In 1983, Alexandre Adler was one of the signatories of a list supporting dissident communists led by Henri Fiszbin. Today, he openly supports the political positions of the liberal right. His curriculum is finally quite common with that of cosmopolitan thinkers, the vast majority of whom realised that liberal democracy was much more effective than communism for the construction of a society without borders.

Everything seems to be programmed in advance, therefore, unless some resistance stops the machine. In this respect, the victory of the French "No" vote in the referendum of 29 May 2005 is perhaps a

---

[216] In the same vein, we have the book entitled *Les Français sont formidables (The French are formidable)*, by Jean François Kahn, 1987.

warning sign. It highlighted the gulf between the political and intellectual elite and the French people. Indeed, on 1 March 2005, the senators and deputies meeting at the Congress of Versailles had voted with an overwhelming majority (91.71%) in favour of the European constitution and the transition to a federal Europe. Three months later, on 29 May 2005, the electoral roll rejected this constitution with 55% of the votes.

Planetarian wars

Going back a little in history, one can see that a certain filiation towards Turkey was already perceptible in the more "open" spirits of the 19th century. At that time, Balkan Europe was still under the rule of the Ottoman Empire, which used extreme violence to quell the national uprisings of Europeans under its yoke. The annihilation of thousands of Christians without defence aroused the indignation of civilised consciences.

The Serbian uprising of 1875, for example, had been suppressed in a bloodbath by the Turks, and the repression of the Bulgarians the following year had resulted in appalling acts of barbarism. Europe was moved by this, and William Gladstone, a man who had not yet been Prime Minister of the United Kingdom, published his famous work, *The Bulgarian Horrors and the Eastern Question (1876)*, which condemned Turkey and especially Disraeli's pro-Turkish policy. That Jewish Prime Minister—an exception in British political history—also embarked Britain on the war in Afghanistan, which was to cost so much in lives and money, under the everlasting pretext of alleged offences that had never existed. That time too, Gladstone, in 1881, tried strenuously to oppose that disastrous expedition which resulted in the British losing the sympathy of the Afghans. One hundred and twenty-three years later, in 2002, the Afghans were to suffer a new Anglo-Saxon invasion under the leadership of George Bush Jr and his closest advisors, the ultra-Zionist "neo-conservatives"[217]. The attacks of 11 September 2001 in New York could not go unpunished. The Twin Towers in New York, owned by Larry Silverstein, had to be avenged.

---

[217] The neoconservatives are former militants of the extreme left of the 1960s and 1970s who, during the 1980s and 1990s, recycled themselves as ultra-liberal conservatives and occupied various key positions in the world of politics and culture in the United States. For a detailed study, see Mark Gerson's *"The neoconservative vision. From the cold war to the culture wars*, Madison Books, Maryland, USA, 1997. Quoted in note by Israel Shamir, *La otra cara de Israel*, Ediciones Ojeda, Barcelona, 2004, p. 183.

The invasion of Afghanistan in 2002 was followed by the invasion and occupation of Iraq by US troops in 2003. All this despite the fact that Serbia, Iraq and Afghanistan posed no threat to Europe, and if Saddam Hussein's Iraq posed any threat at all, it was only to Israel. These US military interventions were clearly part of the grand planetarian project. The aim was to weaken Islam in the land of Islam, since its adherents seemed so far to be the only ones willing to oppose the proponents of the New World Order with determination. Ideally, all Muslim countries should be subjected to and directly converted to the advantages of market democracy and militant secularism. On the other hand, however, planetarian politics encourages the installation of large Muslim masses in European countries in order to dissolve national communities and suppress the resistance of "ethnically homogeneous" peoples.

Thus Serbia was accused of carrying out a policy of ethnic cleansing on its territories, and deserved to be punished by the "international community". In 1999, it was conscientiously bombed by US aircraft. And as usual, in order to prepare the European population for a new war, huge mass graves of corpses were discovered to support the thesis of a bloodthirsty regime, the people of the West were alarmed by the danger of a "new Hitler" and the tyrant's fearsome armies, even though it was a small, impoverished country. In retrospect, the truth was that these "mass graves" of corpses were mainly military cemeteries. Like the famous mass grave of Timisoara in Romania during the fall of the communist regime, it had to be admitted that the number of victims had to be divided by ten. All this propaganda, this "sensitisation", was aimed at preparing public opinion for a planned war.

During the offensive against Serbia, the US government had been heavily influenced by personalities of ultra-Zionist convictions steeped in Planetarian faith. On 5 December 1996, President Bill Clinton reshuffled his foreign policy cabinet. At the State Department, Madeleine K. Albright replaced Warren Christopher. Albright was actually her former husband's surname, while the "K." referred to the Korbels, a family originally from Czechoslovakia. At the Ministry of Defence, William Perry handed over his portfolio to William S. Cohen. At the head of the CIA, John Deutch was finally preferred to the nominee Anthony Lake[218], although both were members of the *Council on* Foreign Relations (the famous CFR). Lake's former deputy,

---

[218] Anthony Lake was a late convert to Judaism in 2005, before marrying his Jewish wife (NdT).

Samuel R. Berger, now held the strategic post of National Security Adviser.

Thanks to American intervention, the Muslims were able to expel the Serbs from their historic province. The Serb exodus took place gradually, under the pro-consulate of former socialist minister Bernard Kouchner, a delegate of the United Nations. Muslims are now in the majority, having imposed another ethnic cleansing amid general indifference. Six years later, in June 2005, Bernard-Henri Lévy spoke about his political activism during the war in Serbia on a television programme, declaring: "I retched when President Mitterrand declared to me that as long as he was alive, France would never go to war with the Serbs219."

The change of heart of a communist author like Guy Konopnicki was quite symptomatic of the ideological evolution of many Western Jewish intellectuals. He now lamented the "anti-Americanism" that plagued France, from the extreme left to the extreme right: "This lack of humanity is properly repugnant," he wrote. A founding member of SOS-Racisme, he had resigned on 18 January 1991, together with the billionaire Pierre Bergé, to protest against the movement's pacifist positions during the first Gulf War.

He wrote at the time: "For a long time, I was one of those who demonstrated when bombs fell somewhere in the world. This time, I say it without shame, I applauded the deluge of fire that fell on Iraq." An opinion fully shared by the popular singer Patrick Bruel (Benguigui), who also abandoned his militant pacifism to support the action of the most fervent warmongers of the US administration. It is true that Israel's interest was at stake.

Despite this, Konopnicki would not allow himself to be accused by anyone of anti-Muslim racism: "I have campaigned for equal rights for young Arabs in our suburbs, participated in the creation of SOS-Racism, defended the revolt of the Afghans against the Soviet invasion in 1979 and the Muslim fighters under siege in Sarajevo220." But in this new international crisis, the writer could not remain decently indifferent, especially when Jews seemed to be directly threatened. Encouraging Islam in France and fighting it abroad—all this seemed perfectly consistent and in keeping with cosmopolitan ideals.

"Fanaticism struck New York with the destruction of the Twin Towers, just as it had struck Florence and then Berlin with the burning

---

[219] BHL, Saturday 25 June 2005, *Forum* programme on the Franco-German channel *Arte*.
[220] Guy Konopnicki, *La Faute des Juifs*, Balland, 2002, p. 17, 22.

of books and *Kristallnacht* (*Night of Broken Glass*)." Konopnicki dared to denounce what all journalists, without exception, had concealed during those events: "For Osama bin Laden, the destruction of the World Trade Center was a foreshadowing of another destruction of which he was not alone in dreaming, that of the State of Israel. For him, the two towers were a symbolic Israel, a temple of Jewish power221." It had to be said, it must be said. We can now better understand each other's motivations and Konopnicki's relentless fight against the new planetarian enemy: "The totalitarianisms of the 20th century had anti-Semitism in common. The one that is gaining strength at the beginning of the 21st century, however much it dresses up in identitarian garb and presents itself as the expression of forgotten peoples, does not stand out for its originality. Radical Islamism is an ideology of death which, like all other ideologies, arouses anti-Semitism222."

Under these circumstances, the Europeans must be called upon to wage all-out war on Israel's enemies. For the occasion, and once again, Israel's interests will be assimilated to those of the "West", and even more, to those of "civilisation" and the "whole world": "The peace of the world," Konopnicki declared, "is not in the hands of the Israeli government. On the contrary, peace will only be possible, for Israel and for the Palestinians, if the European and American powers are able to confront Islamism and bring it to heel by military, economic and political means223."

Planetarian hopes are fuelled by war between peoples. But the most astonishing thing is that the intellectuals representing this school of thought have managed, with monstrous impudence, to pass themselves off, for decades, as the champions of peace.

This is precisely what another fervent warmonger, Elie Wiesel, who did not hesitate to use grand speeches of peace and love to hasten the war against Iraq in 1991, wanted to tell us: "It is not just a question of helping Kuwait, it is a question of protecting the Arab world." All Westerners must mobilise against the "murderer of Baghdad"." It is imperative to wage war on their war. The destructive force he is using against humanity must be opposed by a greater force if humanity is to survive. For on this depends the security of the civilised world, its right to peace, and not only the future of Israel… Thirst for revenge? No: a thirst for justice. And for peace." The people of Israel are always innocent, so one cannot understand why the Iraqi dictator tried to take

---

[221] Guy Konopnicki, *La Faute des Juifs*, Balland, 2002, p. 128, 69
[222] Guy Konopnicki, *La Faute des Juifs*, Balland, 2002, p. 191.
[223] Guy Konopnicki, *La Faute des Juifs*, Balland, 2002, p. 186.

revenge on that country for US aggression: "Because the Americans and their allies attack Baghdad, Iraq bombs Israel. It is a senseless, criminal, absurd aggression, but coming from Saddam Hussein, this surprises no one224."

Albert Einstein was a great activist in the peace movement during the inter-war period. In the book entitled *Naked Power225*, some of the letters published in it shed light on the great man's motivations. In the spring of 1914, Einstein left Switzerland for Berlin, where he had been appointed director of a scientific institute. At that time he was a pacifist, as he wrote to a friend in December 1914: "The international catastrophe in which we are immersed is a heavy burden for the internationalist that I am". In those years, he corresponded with the French pacifist writer Romain Rolland. He recounted his first meeting with Einstein in 1915 as follows: "Einstein does not expect any renewal of Germany for its own sake. He hopes for a victory for the Allies which will ruin the power of Prussia and the dynasty. Despite his lack of sympathy for England, he prefers her victory to that of Germany because he will know better than to let the world live in peace...". (Note also that Einstein is a Jew, which explains his internationalism and the sarcastic character of his criticism)".

Thus, if we understand Romain Rolland correctly, Einstein was less a pacifist than a patriot, although his patriotism coincided more with the enemies of the German nation, which had nevertheless welcomed him. This was because he identified more with democratic ideals than with Germany. In September 1918, Einstein wrote to another correspondent: "The salvation of Germany lies in my opinion in a rapid and radical process of democratisation modelled on the democratic institutions of the Western powers." His wishes would be fulfilled on 9 November, the day of the proclamation of the republic after Germany's defeat. He wrote at the time: "I am delighted by the turn of events. The German defeat has worked wonders. The university community regards me as a kind of arch-Socialist."

At the end of 1918, he made a speech to the Reichstag as a university representative in which he expressed his sympathy for communist ideas: "The old society in which we were ruled by a power-grabbing class has just crumbled under the weight of its own faults and the liberating blows of the soldiers. The Councils[226] which they have

---

[224] Elie Wiesel, *Memoires (Tome II)*, Éditions du Seuil, 1996, p. 144, 16, 152.
[225] Albert Einstein, *Le Pouvoir nu, Propos sur la guerre et la paix*, Hermann, 1991.
[226] "Councils" is the translation of the Russian term "Soviets".

immediately elected and which will henceforth take decisions in agreement with the Workers' Councils must be recognised for the time being as the organs of the people's will. We owe them, in these difficult days, unconditional obedience and our fervent support." This was a very frank support for the Marxist revolution.

However, Einstein would not persevere in this radical path. On 2 April 1921, he landed in the United States for the first time, accompanied by Chaim Weizmann, the highly influential leader of the Zionist movement. His pacifist activities were then little known in the USA and the aim of that first stay was to raise the necessary funds for the construction of a Hebrew university in Jerusalem, a project that was to prove successful thanks, in particular, to the generosity of a large part of the American medical profession. During his stay, Einstein gave several scientific lectures, thus making himself better known to the American public.

In July 1922, on his return to Germany, he confided to Max Planck: "Several sensible people have advised me to leave Berlin for a while and to avoid any public appearances in Germany. According to them, I would be on the list of those whom the nationalists plan to assassinate." Ten days later, he wrote to another friend: "Since the horrible murder of Rathenau, the city has been in turmoil. Not a day goes by without my being urged to be more careful; I had to absent myself officially and cancel all my lectures. Anti-Semitism is gaining ground." To understand the meaning of these words, it must be remembered that after the war, Germany was engaged in a civil war in which the Bolshevik leaders— of whom numerous Jews such as Rosa Luxemburg and Karl Liebknecht—played a leading role.

In October 1922, Einstein embarked in Marseilles for a trip to the Orient. On the way back, he would pass through Palestine and Spain. On 26 October 1922, he visited Colombo, on the island of Ceylon (Sri Lanka), where he noted in his travelogue about the local people: "Their existence seems to be limited to a gentle life of submissive, but nevertheless serene beings. Seeing these people live, one loses all consideration for the Europeans, who are rather more degenerate and brutal, coarser and greedier." This contempt for European man will in the future be a very noticeable constant in all planetarian literature and audio-visual production.

In 1924, he was re-elected member of the League of Nations Commission for Intellectual Cooperation. In April 1925, he travelled to the Silver Sea. First to Buenos Aires and then to Montevideo, Einstein wrote: "May the devil take these great States and their pride! If I could I would break them all up into tiny countries."

In 1930, he bluntly affirmed his pacifism in a publication: "These men marching in line, radiant, to the sound of an orchestra, inspire me with the deepest contempt. Do they really need a brain? Wouldn't their spinal cord have been more than enough? For me, the army is nothing more than a shameful malformation of our society that should be cured as soon as possible. I would rather suffer a thousand tortures than take part in such a degrading spectacle." At a reception in New York that same year, he gave a speech reaffirming his convictions about "unconditional rejection of war" and "refusal to submit to any form of military service. In countries where conscription exists, the first duty of a pacifist is to refuse it." He remained steadfast in a speech in Lyons in 1931: "I call on all newspapers which boast of supporting pacifist ideals to incite their readers to refuse military service. I appeal to every man and woman, from the most powerful to the humblest, to declare, even before the opening next February in Geneva of the world conference for Disarmament, that they will refuse to take part in any future war or in the preparation of any form of armed struggle."

In those years he shared his convictions with Dr. Freud. The relationship between the two men was at its height in the summer of 1932, when, under the auspices of the International Institute for Intellectual Cooperation, a public debate developed between the two men on the causes of war and its remedies. In that summer, Einstein wrote a letter to Freud in which he said, "International security implies that every nation should, to some extent, get rid of its freedom of action, i.e. its sovereignty[227]."

All this agitation came to an abrupt halt in 1933, after Hitler's rise to power. The new political situation led him to make a U-turn in his positions. He ceased to support the war resistance movement and began to support the rearmament of the Western powers. On 5 May of that year, he wrote in a letter to Paul Langevin: "I am convinced, for my part, that it is still possible to counter the German threat by establishing an economic embargo."

---

[227] "Whoever really wants to abolish war must declare himself resolutely in favour of his own country giving up a part of its sovereignty in favour of international institutions: he must be prepared to make his own country submit, in case of dispute, to the award of an international tribunal." *America and the Disarmament Conference of 1932*, Mein Weltbild, Amsterdam, 1934, in *Ideas and Opinions by Albert Einstein*, Crown Publishers, Inc. New York, 1954, p. 101.

From the outset, he disavowed his past as a pacifist activist to become the champion of the war against Hitler's Germany: "It is still possible to crush those usurpers who have seized power." On 6 June, he wrote to Stephen Wise, the rabbi of the New York Free Synagogue, calling on the American press and media to launch an "awareness" campaign about the war: "The American press must inform the public of the German military threat. It is up to the American press to make the public aware of the disasters that a new war in Europe would bring." The American people at the time were very pacifist and isolationist: they had to be shaken up a little to get them to go to war against Germany.

On 20 July, he also wrote to Queen-Mother Elisabeth of Belgium: "Let me tell you frankly: if I were Belgian, I would not refuse to do my military service today. I would accept it rather willingly because I would have the deep conviction of contributing, through my action, to the safeguarding of civilisation." It is necessary that "Germany should have a united and militarily strong Europe in front of her."

Apparently the Bolshevik dictatorship had not led him to the same considerations. It was therefore not the dictatorial nature of the German regime that provoked his opposition and aroused his new warmongering ardour, but its anti-Semitic nature: "A gang of gangsters has succeeded in seizing power and keeps the rest of the population in a state of terror, systematically indoctrinating the youth[228]."

An "unpublished" note of his from 1935 stated the following: "What really made Hitler the master of Germany was the fierce hatred he always harboured against everything foreign, the special aversion he feels towards an undefended minority, that of the German Jews. Hitler could never endure his intellectual sensibility which regards—and for once I share his opinion—the German race as foreign."

On 9 April 1938, he wrote: "It is no less disturbing and outrageous to witness as a spectator the abolition of the elementary political and individual rights of a part of the population of certain nations, once proud of their cultural heritage... Germany, by inflicting inhuman persecutions on the Jews in her own country or in Austria, has embarked on the path of destruction which I have just described." At the time of writing, the Jews had effectively lost the right to exercise their functions in many liberal professions: these were "inhuman persecutions" which

---

[228] "In 1939, the Gestapo employed 7500 people, against 366 000 for the NKVD in Bolshevik Russia (including gulag personnel)", in *Du Passé faisons table rase, Histoire et mémoire du communisme en Europe*, ouvrage collectif, sous la direction de Stéphane Courtois, Robert Laffont, 2002, p. 209.

foreshadowed the first real persecutions that were to take place a little later, during the Night of Broken Glass on 9 November 1938.

On 25 October, at the height of the war, the *Jewish Council for Russian War Relief* organised a dinner in honour of Einstein. Indisposed for health reasons at his Princeton residence in the United States, Einstein would send a message in which we find these words: "I would like finally to say a few words of capital importance to us Jews. In Russia, the equality of all national and cultural groups that make up the country today is not only evoked in [legal] texts, but is put into practice. That is why it seems to me the most elementary wisdom to want to help Russia as best we can, using all the resources at our disposal." Here is another example that shows that Einstein reasoned first and foremost as a member of the Jewish community. His positions on militarism, pacifism, democracy, Germany or Russia reflected only his specific interests, which could change according to circumstances. Anti-militarist in the 1920s, warmongering with Hitler's rise to power, pro-Soviet from the beginning, he became anti-Soviet when the Jews were removed from power after the Second World War. The millions of victims of Bolshevik power during the interwar period never aroused his compassion at any time.

On 9 June 1944, Einstein was interviewed by the *Free World Magazine* of New York to which he declared: "I see no other solution: either we annihilate the German people or we keep them oppressed. I do not think it is possible either to educate them or to learn them to think and act democratically—at least not in the near future."

After the war, and after Chaim Weizmann, Einstein's old friend and the first president of the State of Israel, died on 9 November 1952, he was offered to become the second president of the Jewish State. But Einstein would turn down the offer because he felt he lacked the skills to lead a state. This was his Zionist view of the new conflict dividing the world: "We [the State of Israel] must adopt a policy of neutrality in the face of the antagonism dividing East and West[229]."

But it is sometimes difficult to distinguish the political activist from the representative of his community, as when he wrote this reflection to Joseph Lewis at the end of 1954, a few months before his death: "You are right in wanting to fight superstition and the power of the priests, for when they are defeated—and I have no doubt that one day we will end up winning—it will seem even more evident to us that

---

[229] Letter from Albert Einstein to Zvi Lurie, member of the Jewish Agency in Israel, 4 January 1955, in Albert Einstein, *Le Pouvoir nu, Propos sur la guerre et la paix*, Hermann, 1991.

man must look to his own heritage for the source of the evils that afflict him, and nowhere else."

During the Second World War, Ilya Ehrenburg was the official propagandist for the USSR and Marshal Stalin in the war against Nazi Germany. In numerous poems and texts, he explicitly called for the extermination of Germans, all Germans, men, women, young and old without distinction, even killing children in their mothers' wombs. Naturally, for the Germans, Ehrenburg was at the top of the list of enemies to be slaughtered. But after the victory, the man naturally became an apostle of peace. This is what his biographer, Lilly Marcou, told us: "This 'nomad of peace' spent most of his life between Moscow and Paris." Witness to the October revolution, the civil war in Spain, the entry of the Germans into Paris", he was "always in the front line". After the war, he was "one of the great figures of the Peace Movement[230]." Having annihilated his enemies, he was indeed always in favour of peace.

The American myth

Populated by uprooted immigrants, the United States obviously represents a powerful symbol in the planetarian imaginary. The French novelist George Perec was naturally fascinated by the American myth when he decided to make a film with Robert Bober about Ellis Island. This island in New York, near the Statue of Liberty, was the centre for the inspection of emigrants between 1892 and 1954.

"It is not known how many millions of Europeans, especially Italians, Russian Jews and Poles, passed through this place, which has since been transformed into a museum." In one of his works entitled *Naci*, Georges Perec wrote: "From 1892 to 1924, nearly sixteen million people passed through Ellis Island, at a rate of five to ten thousand per day. Most of them would only stay for a few hours; two or three percent would be turned away. Ultimately, Ellis Island would be nothing more than a factory for making Americans, after inspection of eyes, pockets, vaccination and disinfection. In 1954, Ellis Island would be closed for good."

The reader can also watch Elia Kazan's beautiful film *America, America*. One of the final scenes strikingly shows that train station where, in a few seconds, an official gave immigrants a new identity by

---

[230] Lilly Marcou, *Ilya Ehrenbourg*, Plon, 1992, p. 11

substituting an incomprehensible surname. However, as beautiful as it is, Elia Kazan's film was still an ode to uprootedness.

Through a sincere and moving testimony, George Perec revealed the essence of his identity and the reason for his nostalgia: "I was born in France, I am French, I have a French name, Georges, an almost French surname: Perec. The difference is tiny: there is no acute accent on the first e in my surname, because Perec is the Polish spelling of Peretz. If I had been born in Poland, I would be called, say, Mordechai Perec, and everyone would know that I am Jewish. But I was not born in Poland, fortunately for me, and I have an almost Breton surname, which everyone spells Perec or Perrec: my surname is not spelt exactly as it is pronounced. To this insignificant contradiction is added the faint but insistent, insidious, inevitable feeling of being somehow foreign in relation to something of myself, of being "different", but not so much different from "others" as different from "my own[231] "."." What I went to Ellis Island to find is the very image of that point of no return, the awareness of that radical rupture ... I seem to have succeeded in occasionally echoing some of those words for me inextricably linked to the very concept of "Jew"; the journey, the waiting, the hope, the uncertainty, the difference, the memory, and those two imprecise, irreparable, unstable and elusive concepts, which incessantly reflect, one in the other, their trembling lights, and which are called "Homeland" and "Promised Land[232]"."

Here at last is a moving and profound testimony that naturally arouses sympathy. We are far removed from the contempt and the political, scientific and moral bluff that we have read elsewhere, where lies, impudence and impudent propaganda are mixed in varying doses.

Be that as it may, the American model has never been very successful in France. It displeases Marxists because of its unbridled economic liberalism and religious faith, and it disgusts nationalists because of the omnipresence of its Zionist lobby, its arrogant financial power, its *melting pot* and its indecent materialism. One might add that its Protestant puritanism is not to everyone's liking either, especially in a country with Catholic and hedonistic roots like France[233]. Nor does its overblown architecture arouse much enthusiasm in the well-born

---

[231] George Perec, *Nací, textos de la memoria y el olvido*. Abada Editores, Madrid, 2006, p. 102-103.

[232] George Perec, *Nací, textos de la memoria y el olvido*. Abada Editores, Madrid, 2006, p. 104–105.

[233] At least until 1914, for several literary accounts suggest that the French lost some of their joie de vivre from then on.

European who appreciates moderation and balance. Its eating habits are also deplorable, its TV series often unbearable, and its inhabitants' optimism, admittedly, has a tendency to exasperate the average Frenchman, who is probably overwhelmed by so much overflowing energy.

Planetarian intellectuals see things differently. Invited to Serge Moati's television programme *Riposte,* the highly influential press director and noted writer Alexandre Adler gave his reasons for appreciating US President George Bush: "He is the most *colour blind* of all US presidents234 ", he said, i.e. the one who chose the most black collaborators among his political advisors and ministers. Indeed, Colin Powell and Condoleezza Rice were the first Blacks to achieve such important positions in the US administration. Alexandre Adler, who was very sensitive to the multiculturalism of the US government, even declared that he wanted to see Colin Powell as President of the United States one day.

But here are some clarifications that will help to understand Alexandre Adler's views: In the United States, in the 1950s, the South Bronx (New York) was home to a great diversity of communities, the Jewish community being the most important, with its synagogue, its mikves235, bakeries and kosher butcher shops236. The Sickser shop had specialised in baby and children's products (pushchairs, baby changing tables and chairs, cots, etc...) Yiddish was spoken, although many customers were Jamaican, black and Italian. The owner then recruited an unemployed 13-year-old black boy who lived in the neighbourhood. Punctual, focused on his work, honest, he was so willing to learn that he worked in the shop until the end of his high school years, gradually working his way up the ladder: unloading trucks, preparing orders, managing the warehouse, and so on. Despite being of Jamaican origin, he learned to speak Yiddish, especially with the Hasidic customers237 who did not speak English. In short, he became the ideal *"Shabbat goy"* (goy employee of Jewish families to perform the essential tasks forbidden on Shabbat). At the age of 17, he entered the City College of New York, where he befriended Jewish students because he knew them well and spoke their dialect.

---

[234] TV programme *Riposte,* presented by Serge Moati, 6 June 2004.

[235] Jewish purification baths.

[236] "Right" or "proper" to be consumed, i.e. it complies with the precepts of the Jewish religion.

[237] Hasidic Judaism is an orthodox and mystical religious movement within Judaism. See *Psychoanalysis of Judaism.*

Throughout his studies (engineering and biology), this knowledge of Judaism was invaluable to him. When he visited Israel years later, he declared to Prime Minister Yitzak Shamir: "*Men kent reden Yiddish*" (We can speak Yiddish). The two men then conversed in Yiddish. His name was: General Colin Powell, US Secretary of Defense238.

Alexandre Adler is a major media figure in France at the beginning of the 21st century. In his youth, at the Ecole Normale Supérieure239, he embraced the communism of his teacher Louis Althusser and quickly joined the Communist Party. In May 1981, he became enthusiastic about the arrival of the Socialists in power. He is currently an occasional adviser to the President of the Republic. After the attacks of 11 September 2001, Adler became even more committed: "I am at war", he declared. Hatred of the United States was, according to him, "the most perverse and pernicious form of self-hatred". He defended George Bush and the United States, unconditionally supported Israel and Ariel Sharon, and campaigned for Turkey's entry into Europe. According to the daily *Libération* (20 June 2004), he is Jewish and German through his parents; his father "insists on eating pork because of his materialistic convictions, but he keeps his head covered! "He has an old Yiddish saying of his mother's: "When they spit in your face, don't say it's raining". Thus, we also saw him appear as a witness in a trial against *France Inter* radio producer Daniel Mermet, a "piece of brute", accused of having complacently allowed an anti-Israeli auditor to express himself on the voicemail of the programme *Là bas si j'y suis*. However, he claimed that he "does not want to gag anyone". He abhors "left-wing scruffs", especially José Bové: "I don't like the Poujade240 who pose as some Mahatma Gandhi, especially when it all ends up being vulgar anti-Judaism."

In short, regardless of the political t-shirts he wore, the only invariable constant in his discourse is his globalist convictions, his support for Israel and his epidermal rejection of anything that is too "typically French", such as the peasant José Bové. Despite belonging to

---

238 Extract from Zev Roth, *Targum Press*, 2000, quoted in *Faits et Documents* of 1 July 2003.

239 The ENS is considered the most prestigious school in France and trains France's scientific research elite. (NdT).

240 Poujade: French politician and trade unionist in the mid-20th century. The term *poujadisme became a* pejorative term, designating a form of corporatism considered to be demagogic. It gradually acquired a meaning close to that of "populism". José Bové is an agricultural politician and trade unionist, a figurehead of the anti-globalisation movement in the 2000s.

the extreme left, the movement's anti-Zionist positions do not endear it to those who place support for Israel above all other considerations.

Economist and media personality Alain Minc was another fervent US supporter. In 1991, he supported the first US offensive against Saddam Hussein's Iraq: "Nuclear proliferation, he said, with a bomb-possessing Iraq would expand unbearably." He justified US hegemony and its preponderance over European diplomacy: "We will soon miss this American guardian that thirty years of Gaullism-Mitterandism taught us to mock, even though we benefit from its protection. With him, order in Europe was not guaranteed; without him, disorder is241."

In *Le Figaro* of 19 November 2004, Guy Sorman also extolled the merits of the United States: "The United States tends or claims to be universal. It promises freedom and equal dignity to all, without discrimination of race or religion; it seeks unprecedented economic prosperity on its territory and expands it beyond its borders. What does it demand in return? A minimum of loyalty, but no servitude. Can they be reproached for exporting democracy without taking into account the diversity of cultures? Same plumage, same branches, Bernard-Henri Lévy declared: "I want to make it clear that I do not consider the *Deep South*, the homeland of the Klu Klux Klan, the country of napalm on Vietnam and of Pinochet's allies, as the indisputable paragon of freedom. What I am saying is that the coarse, brutal and total hatred of America as such is, without a doubt, the hatred of freedom242."

Let us now give the floor to a famous American, the world-renowned writer Norman Mailer. Let us open his recent essay, *Why are we at war?*, to enlighten us, not on the causes of the war being waged by the USA, but on the mentality of the American planetarian intellectuals. We read on the back cover of the book: "Beyond the war in Iraq, what are the secret motives of the Bush administration? Is this formidable military presence in the Middle East destined to be a springboard for US hegemony in the rest of the world? What are the deep roots of American conservatism—its means, its goals, its morality? Norman Mailer offers us a hard-hitting and uncompromising book—in the vein of his famous book published more than thirty years ago, *Why Did We Go to Vietnam?* Mailer thinks America, thinks the world, beyond the religious constraints that shape the thoughts and actions of all. His reflections have sparked heated debates in the United States."

---

[241] Alain Minc, *Le Nouveau Moyen-Age*, Gallimard, 1993, p. 28, 30
[242] Bernard-Henri Lévy, *L'Idéologie française*, Grasset, 1981, p. 280.

The programme was therefore very encouraging, but unfortunately we found the same clichés, the same faults as in our French intellectuals: "We are a Christian nation," he wrote when talking about the United States at war. The preposition "Judeo" in the formula "Judeo-Christian" is nothing but an embellishment."

Indeed, Christians, and Christians alone, are the fierce warmongers, contrary to what anti-Semites may say. Christian conservatives are extremely dangerous individuals: "When the Soviet Union fell, jingoistic conservatives thought this was their chance to take over the world. They thought they were the only ones who knew how to run it. Consequently, their hunger was voracious. They were furious when Clinton was elected. That is one of the reasons they hated him so much. He was thwarting the conquest of the world. From their point of view, back in 1992, it seemed like a no-brainer and possible[243]."

Against the American reactionary right and against the racist Christian Whites who threatened world domination from the American government, Norman Mailer positioned himself as the staunch champion of the oppressed and the champion of the multiracial society: "In the modern world of technology, I don't know whether race or culture is a transcendental question. In the long run, the world tends to be race-less … I don't see immigration as a pressing issue, except in the sense that some white people are so angry about it that they can't think of more important things. They think America is going down the drain. Fine, the country is going down the drain, but in a way that has nothing to do with race or excessive immigration. To take an example, America is losing its way because of television. In advertising, advertisers elevate lies and manipulation to the status of internal values… Bad architecture, invasive marketing, ubiquitous plastic … these lethal forces worry me much more than immigration. I could go on and on about this. Our main problem is not immigration, but American business. They are the force that has succeeded in taking our country away from us[244]." If our democracy is the noblest experiment in the history of civilisation, it may also be the most uniquely vulnerable," concluded Norman Mailer.[245]

The similarities with the words of Daniel Cohn-Bendit or Alain Minc on immigration and plural society are quite striking. We see the same mistrust of the Christian religion, the same contempt for

---

[243] Norman Mailer, *Why are we at war?* Editorial Anagrama, 2003, Barcelona, p. 90.
[244] Norman Mailer, *Why are we at war?* Editorial Anagrama, 2003, Barcelona, p. 98–101.
[245] Norman Mailer, *Why are we at war?* Editorial Anagrama, 2003, Barcelona, p. 121.

indigenous whites who are alarmed to see themselves as a minority, the same readiness to blame others for their own vileness, whether in the programming of war, the desire to "dominate the world" or "lies and manipulation".

The mentality and ideological reflexes of American journalists and intellectuals of planetarian obedience seem perfectly identical to those of our French and European intellectuals. On 17 October 2002, the *Courier International,* a newspaper edited by Alexandre Adler, published a report entitled: *The End of White Society in the USA.* In it, one could read an article that confirmed the opinion of Norman Mailer and Daniel Cohn-Bendit: "I often say that it is not a racial problem in the United States. It's a problem of reasoning," declared Yehudi Webster, professor of sociology at the University of California, Los Angeles, who added: "Most anthropologists agree that the notion of race has no basis in fact."

In the same report, an article by Patrick Goldstein denounced the White domination of Hollywood: "Hollywood also suffers from the fact that its ruling circles too often remain immaculately white." Formulated in this way, it seems clear that white racists dominate the capital of cinema. A third article featured Leon E. Wynter's "fascinating book" entitled *The Skin of America: Popular Culture, Big Business, and the End of White America246.* The writer drew "on all the examples to show that the old racial definitions no longer hold and that American popular culture is increasingly "transracial."

"Multiracial corresponds to a market expectation, not because it is politically correct, but because that is how America wants to see itself, as a unified multiracial society." The author of the article, one Michiko Kakutani, added, however: "This view is simplistic to say the least. Leon Wynter ignores the persistent problems of racism and racial classifications in our country, and the eagerness to prove the central thesis of his book leads him to deny the evidence."

"Denying the evidence' is a reproach that Aleksandr Solzhenitsyn also made to those who refused to acknowledge their responsibility for the crimes of communism. But when Patrick Goldstein pretended to denounce white racism in Hollywood, he was not only denying the evidence, but also accusing others of what he himself felt responsible for. For it is well known that it is not "Whites" who dominate Hollywood, but the Jewish community, whose members sometimes

---

[246] Leon E. Wynter, *American skin: Pop culture, Big Business and the end of White America,* Crown Publishers, New York, 2002.

identify themselves with "Whites" and sometimes with minorities, depending on the circumstances and their exclusive interests.

Hollywood, Jacques Attali told us in *The Jews, the World and Money*, is a Jewish fiefdom: "Today's essential firms are: Universal, Fox, Paramount, Warner Bros, MGM, RCA and CBS are all creations of Jewish immigrants from Eastern Europe"." Adolf Zukor arrived from Hungary in 1890 (...) in 1917 he founded Paramount Pictures, which he put at the service of war propaganda." Carl Laemmle, a native of Laupheim, Württemberg, apprenticed to a tailor, founded Universal Studios in 1912. In 1923, the three Warner brothers, born in Poland, founded Warner Bros. Mayer, born in Minsk, founded Metro. In 1916, Samuel Goldfish founded Goldwyn, which he merged with Metro in 1924. The firm becomes Metro Goldwyn Mayer, "then MGM, which many translate in Yiddish—the language commonly spoken in Hollywood at the time—by Mayer Ganze Mishpoje (the whole Mayer family)"." Goebbels then denounced Hollywood as a *chüdisches Geselschaft*, but neither the American media nor the Jewish producers reacted. When, at a press conference in 1937, Cecil B. De Mille denounced Hollywood as a "jüdisches Geselschaft". De Mille denounces in 1937 "the abuses of Jewish influence on the film industry", John Ford leaves the room slamming the door; but no Jewish producer protests[247]."

Although Dysney was not founded by a Jew, its current president bears the same surname as the famous Bolshevik leader: Eisner." David Sarnoff was born near Minsk in 1891 and emigrated to New York in 1905 (...) he had the idea of combining radio and phonograph. In 1926 he set up the first broadcasting network, then became president of RCA in 1930. In 1939 he launched television, founding NBC." William S. Paley, son of a Russian émigré, launched CBS the same year." Meanwhile, from 1924 to 1938, 150,000 Jews from Germany and Austria managed to enter the United States, despite the very restricted quotas reserved for Jews from the Reich[248]." This is the true nature of "white" dominance in Hollywood.

Moreover, it is perfectly dishonest to denounce the imperialism of Christian Whites as the cause of the war in Iraq when the influence of Jewish circles close to George Bush is well known. The last straw is that these same people then accuse others of "lying and manipulation".

[247] Neal Gabler, *An Empire of Their Own: How the Jews Invented Hollywood*, New York, 1988, quoted in Jacques Attali, *The Jews, the World and Money*, p. 416.
[248] Jacques Attali, *Los judíos, el mundo y el dinero*, Fondo de cultura económica, 2005, Buenos Aires, p. 413-417.

At the time of the US intervention, while Defense Minister Donald Rumsfeld was not Jewish, his deputies were. Paul Wolfowitz was Assistant Secretary of State for Defence; he was appointed in March 2005 as head of the World Bank. Douglas Feith, Deputy Secretary of State for Defence, was in charge of overseeing Turkey's entry into the European Union. Mickael Rubin was in charge of Iran-Iraq affairs. Richard Perle was Dick Cheney's chief of staff, whose deputy on the National Security Council was John Hannah, who in turn had appointed Elliott Abrams to the crucial post of Middle East chief. John Bolton was the Under Secretary of State for Arms Control in Colin Powell's State Department. His deputy was David Wurmser. Among the neo-conservatives in various strategic positions were Ari Fleischer, George Bush's spokesman, Thomas Dine, director of Radio-Liberty, and the fearsome Robert Kagan, doctrinarian of pre-emptive war and inspiration for George Bush's foreign policy.

The "neo-conservative" intellectuals, the current ideologues of American politics, are Jewish intellectuals of the extreme left of the 1960s who were converted to Reaganism in the 1980s[249]. At their head were famous journalists such as Irving Kristol and Norman Podhoretz. The former founded the *Weekly Standard*, which was bought by billionaire Ruppert Murdoch and later run by his son William Kristol. The latter created *Commentary*. Twenty years later, these two newspapers would become the bastions of a violently pro-Israeli right wing.

Let us not forget either that George Tenet, who came from the Israeli intelligence services, was then the director of the CIA, and Marc Grossman the Under-Secretary of State for Defence. These were the "Christians" that Norman Mailer denounced as responsible for the Iraq war.

For the first time, in April 2004, an Anglo-Saxon magazine had issued some criticism of the aims of George Bush's ultra-Zionist entourage. The Canadian magazine *Adbuster*, widely distributed throughout North America, including the USA, devoted a long article to the hawks in the White House entitled *Bush White House Jewish Neo-Conservatives: Why won't anyone say they are Jewish?*

---

[249] Readers can watch the interesting documentary by Adam Curtis, a British writer and documentary filmmaker for the BBC, entitled *The Power of Nightmares* (2004). It exposes the ideological origins of these mostly Jewish-American neo-conservatives and their involvement in US foreign policy in Afghanistan in collusion with radical Islamism, as well as in the subsequent "war on terror" of the "Al Qaeda" organisation. See also note 217.

In France, this information was scarcely reported and only circulated in extreme right-wing and Muslim circles, although a thorough search on the internet gave access to all the information. On 23 May 2004, former US delegate to the Middle East Anthony Zini had also harshly criticised the Bush administration's policies in an interview with NBC, accusing the "mostly Jewish and neo-conservative" administration of having "hijacked US foreign policy to serve their own interests." A few days earlier the same week, Senator Ernest Hollins had accused Bush of having allowed himself to be led into war in order "to pander to Jewish hawks before the presidential election."

Senator John Kerry, Bush's rival, had immediately described these words as "absurd". It should be recalled here that John Kerry himself, George Bush's opponent in the presidential election, was descended from a Jewish family originally from Central Europe. His grandfather, born Fritz Kohn, changed his surname in 1902 while they were still in Czechoslovakia to Frederick Kerry. His brother Cameron had married Kathy Weismann, who was a traditionalist Jew. John Kerry had benefited in France from unprecedented media and publicity coverage for his campaign. Everyone could believe in his victory judging by the complacent media treatment of his candidacy. In France, he would have been elected without a doubt. The problem was that the election was taking place in the United States, and he was soundly defeated by George Bush, much to the surprise of the French public. But no one made much of it, and the incessant flow of news of the democratic regime carried the public's attention away.

The influence of the media, as we can realise, is the cornerstone of the democratic system. The media bloat that ends up suddenly deflating after the event is innumerable. The viewers' attention is immediately demanded by the tinkling of another bell so that the previous tall tale is quickly forgotten. One example in a thousand: the Russian parliamentary elections in December 2003. All the media predicted a landslide result for the democrats, united in the Iabloko party (Apple, another Apple). At the time there was only talk of Iabloko, whose influence was evidently decisive. The rise of Iabloko was irresistible. The president of Iabloko, Grigori Iavlinski—a great Russian-Jewish politician—seemed to have everything to gain and to win a historic victory. Iabloko was finally going to pull Russia out of depression and preserve it from the spectre of nationalism. Iabloko here; Iabloko there. If the elections had taken place in France, Iabloko would undoubtedly have come to power. But the elections took place in Russia, and Iabloko only got 1.5% of the vote. From then on, Iabloko was never heard of again.

Transnational high finance

In the Marxist imagination, high finance can only be at the service of reaction and fascism. The supposed alliance between the two forces is indeed an essential theme to bring together the opponents of the capitalist system. This is what inspired for example a Marxist and libertarian author like Daniel Guérin[250] in his book *Fascism and Big Capital,* published in 1965 and still influencing many anarchist activists. However, it does not require much research to prove that "big capital" is broadly supportive of planetarian hopes. While there are probably old French families with provincial roots to finance reaction, or even the extreme right, the big billionaires always support plural democracy and globalisation. And the difference between a millionaire, the owner of a large estate, and a "nouveau riche" billionaire, is the same as between riding a bicycle and driving a Rolls-Royce.

Samuel Pisar, for example, was one of the major financiers of the socialist party that contributed to François Mitterrand's victory in 1981. He is also a famous writer, author of an international *best-seller, The Blood of Hope.* Like Marek Halter, he was born in Poland, in Bialystok to be precise; like Marek Halter, he and his family saw the Soviet troops arrive after the partition of Poland between Germany and the USSR in 1939. Faced with the advance of German troops on 22 June 1941, the two families were evacuated to the East by the Soviet authorities as a protective measure. After the war, Samuel Pisar emigrated to France, where he made his fortune, although he always maintained close relations with the USSR: "For twenty-five years, I have been travelling through the Soviet Union," he explained. He was one of a group of financiers and international businessmen who kept commercial collaboration between the West and the USSR alive. The first to initiate that collaboration, as early as 1918, was the famous American Armand Hammer, "president of the Western Petroleum Company and a multi-millionaire in his twenties". Samuel Pisar became his friend, with whom he travelled to Moscow in 1972." Now an American citizen, I was also made a Soviet subject as a child." Even so, he still loves "the

---

[250] An anarchist and homosexual doctrinaire born into a bourgeois family. His mother was an Eichtal, a descendant of the Israeli banker and baron, founder of the Free School of Political Science.

France of the rights of man, homeland of the heart of all men of the world[251]."

In his book *The Human Resource,* Pisar recounted some interesting memories that give an insight into his vision of the world. Committed to the socialists who came to power in 1981, Jacques Sttali was also one of his friends. The latter was, in his words, "undoubtedly the most fascinating storehouse of ideas. They call him the President's *"sherpa"*—a reference to the famous guides who are able to venture into the heights of the Himalayas." Samuel Pisar was also closely associated with the socialist ministers Robert Badinter, Laurent Fabius, Pierre Beregovoy—whose suicide will always be a painful memory— as well as the very rich American businessman David Rockefeller.

He knew the world's major stock markets inside out: "There is a guru on Wall Street. He is dedicated to the dollar and dollar lovers. He is the chief economist of the powerful Salomon Brothers, which places the bond issues of most of the governments and multinationals on the planet in the public eye. His name is Henry Kaufman. When he speaks, and he doesn't need many words, the world's stock markets begin to hope or tremble. His forecasts are followed in a second, recorded by banks, interpreted by chancelleries. Fortunes are made and unmade[252]."

His political convictions are in no way contradictory to his financial activities, quite the contrary. His financial cosmopolitanism goes hand in hand with his humanist cosmopolitanism. Like all planetarian intellectuals, his ideas about the world are almost obsessive, as if the man were animated not only by philosophical convictions, but also by an ardent religious faith. And that faith translates here too into a tireless activist proselytising: "The concepts of race, of nation, of ideology, have been shipwrecked forever," he explained." We continue to waste our forces in disputes of other times—of frontiers, of doctrines, of ideologies, of races, of property. On the contrary, we can bring them together to raise ourselves by common effort to higher heights of evolution[253]." He tirelessly shared these reflections with Jean-Jacques Servan-Schreiber, the influential founding editor of *L'Express,* another of his friends." We transform the universe. It is not a question of repairing. It's about inventing[254]." And again, we recognise here the vocabulary so dear to Alain Minc, Jacques Attali, Edgar Morin and Pierre Lévy.

---

[251] Samuel Pisar, *La Ressource humaine,* Jean-Claude Lattès, 1983, p. 148, 34, 18
[252] Samuel Pisar, *La Ressource humaine,* Jean-Claude Lattès, 1983, p. 24, 313.
[253] Samuel Pisar, *La Ressource humaine,* Jean-Claude Lattès, 1983, p. 356, 360.
[254] Samuel Pisar, *La Ressource humaine,* Jean-Claude Lattès, 1983, p. 23.

Among the most influential men on the planet, we also have the famous George Soros, one of the richest men in the world and a symbol of international speculation. When he buys gold mines, the price of the yellow metal rises, and falls when the markets learn that he has sold. It was in 1992, when he reached the height of his glory after one of the most resounding financial coups of the century. Within days, it detected the weakness of the British currency and mobilised some ten billion dollars against sterling. The Bank of England faltered in the face of speculative attacks and finally had to devalue and leave the European Monetary System. Soros then became "the man who broke the Bank of England". In the process, he pocketed more than a billion dollars in one week. However, he positioned himself as an opponent of ultra-liberalism: "If the markets are not regulated quickly, we are going to face catastrophes worse than those of the 1930s."

However, it is not clear how this opponent of ultra-liberalism and George Bush differs from the economists of the neo-liberal Chicago school. Created by Milton Friedman, this school, as Israel Shamir defined it, is "the quasi-scientific expression of the Mammonite tendency that proclaims the superiority of market forces." Hayek, another celebrated economist of this ideology was not at all dissimilar to George Soros' ideals, when he wrote that "the liquidation of state sovereignty is the necessary and logical goal of the liberal programme."

Supposedly an opponent of ultra-liberalism, he is not an opponent of the power of money. George Soros has invested 4 billion dollars in Argentina, and bought a 350,000 hectare property in Patagonia. But the sulphurous reputation of this fearsome market manipulator is not only due to his speculative talents. Besides being a billionaire, George Soros is also a philosopher and philanthropist, and a very mysterious man. Every year he donates 300 million dollars to a network of foundations that help, especially in Eastern Europe and Russia, to promote the "open society". Since the fall of communism in 1989, he has devoted most of his time to his *Open Society Foundation*. The world's largest financier invests half of his income and, by his own admission, 80% of his time in it. He does this not out of kindness of heart or charity—a word he abhors—but to defend the principles of freedom and human rights: "Participatory democracy and the market economy are essential ingredients of an open society, as is a mechanism to regulate markets, in particular financial markets, as well as some arrangements to preserve peace and law and order on a global scale[255]." In this way,

---

[255] George Soros, *La crisis del capitalismo global; La sociedad abierta en peligro.* Editorial Debate, Madrid, 1999, p. 127.

Soros funds cultural and scientific projects, supports writers, artists and "the independent and democratic press" (sic). In 1995, the Soros foundations had fifty offices around the world and employed a thousand people. His foundations teach tolerance and democratic values of the "open society", especially in Central European countries. Perhaps that is why it is the target of virulent attacks, sometimes even hate attacks.

His parents were bourgeois in Budapest. In the spring of 1944, the Nazis entered the Hungarian capital, shattering little George's harmonious world and "opening before him an era of insecurity". Between the Gestapo and the SS, and under false identities, George Soros had to learn to survive. In 1947 he settled in London, a stage in his life that did not prevent him from betraying England in 1992, as we have already seen. My father was an Esperantist," Soros said. It was thanks to the profits he made from publishing a newspaper in Esperanto that he was able to acquire some capital in real estate. He is the only person I know of to have lived off his income. He managed to leave Hungary in 1956 and we met in the United States that year[256]."

Ideologically, George Soros identified with the heritage of the Enlightenment." The Enlightenment has provided the foundation for our ideas about politics and economics; indeed, for our entire worldview. The philosophers of the Enlightenment are no longer read—indeed, they may be unreadable to us—but their ideas have taken root in our way of thinking. The rule of reason, the supremacy of science, the universal brotherhood of man: these were among their main themes[257]"." The Enlightenment offered a set of universal values and its memory lives on even if it seems somewhat faded. Instead of discarding it, we should bring it up to date[258] ", he wrote. But he felt himself above all a tributary of the philosopher Karl Popper, who in his book *The Open Society and its Enemies*, published in 1945, had developed the ideas that he would make his own, to the point of borrowing the name of that book for the name of his foundation." I was greatly influenced by Karl Popper, whose *The Open Society and its Enemies* explained that the Nazi and communist regimes ... had one characteristic in common: they claimed to be in possession of the ultimate truth and imposed their ideas on the world through the use of force."

---

[256] George Soros, *Le Défi de l'argent*, Plon, 1996, p. 43, 47.
[257] George Soros, *La crisis del capitalismo global; La sociedad abierta en peligro*. Editorial Debate, Madrid, 1999, p. 120.
[258] George Soros, *La crisis del capitalismo global; La sociedad abierta en peligro*. Editorial Debate, Madrid, 1999, p. 125.

The role of George Soros and Western billionaires in the collapse of the communist system remains puzzling. On that subject, he stated simply; "In 1979, when I had made more money than I could possibly need, I set up a foundation called the *Open Society Fund*, whose goals I defined as helping to open up closed societies, helping to make open societies more viable, and fostering a critical way of thinking. Through the foundation, I became deeply involved in the disintegration of the Soviet system[259]."

We found an interesting analysis of this by journalist Neil Clark[260] who wrote: "The conventional wisdom, shared by many on the left, is that socialism collapsed in Eastern Europe because of its systemic weaknesses and the failure of the political elite to win popular support. That may be partly true, but Soros' role was crucial. From 1979, he distributed $3 million a year to dissidents such as the Polish Solidarity movement, Charter 77 in Czechoslovakia and Andrei Sakharov in the Soviet Union. In 1984, it founded its first *Open Society Institute* in Hungary and provided millions of dollars to opposition movements and independent media. Ostensibly aimed at building a "civil society", these initiatives were designed to weaken existing political structures and pave the way for the eventual colonisation of Eastern Europe by global capital. Soros now claims, with characteristic immodesty, that he was responsible for the "Americanisation" of Eastern Europe.

The Yugoslavs stubbornly resisted and returned Slobodan Milosevic's unreformed Socialist Party to government. Soros rose to the challenge. Since 1991, his *Open Society Institute* channelled more than $100 million into the coffers of the anti-Milosevic opposition, funding political parties, publishing houses and "independent" media such as Radio B92, the plucky little student radio station of Western mythology, which was actually funded by one of the world's richest men on behalf of the world's most powerful nation." What Soros was inspiring with his "Open Society" was perhaps not so much respect for human rights and fundamental freedoms, but the degree of "openness" of the former communist countries to economic liberalisation and privatisation of state assets at rock-bottom prices." More than a decade after the fall of the Berlin Wall, Soros is the uncrowned king of Eastern Europe. His Central European University, with campuses in Budapest,

---

[259] George Soros, *La crisis del capitalismo global; La sociedad abierta en peligro*. Editorial Debate, Madrid, 1999, p. 11, 12.
[260] *George Soros, NS Profile*, by Neil Clark, The New Statesman, 2 June 2003, quoted in Israel Shamir, *Pardès, Une étude de la Kabbale*, Al Qalam, 2005. Article at https://anarchitext.wordpress.com/2011/04/26/ns-soros/

Warsaw and Prague and exchange programmes in the United States, unabashedly propagates the spirit of neoliberal capitalism and clones the next generation of pro-American political leaders in the region."

Undoubtedly, today's globalisation is more in line with their interests and ideal than the old rigid state system of the former USSR." To stabilise and regulate a truly global economy, some global system of political decision-making is necessary. In a word, we need a global society to support our global economy. A global society does not mean a global state. Abolishing the existence of markets is neither feasible nor desirable; but to the extent that there are collective interests that transcend state borders, the sovereignty of states must be subordinated to international law and international institutions[261]." Soros seemed more measured here than some French planetarian intellectuals, who, as we have seen, aspire to the disappearance of all borders. His convictions are nevertheless globalist:

"The supreme challenge of our time is to establish a universally valid code of conduct for our global society... We therefore need some universally valid rules for the relationship between state and society that safeguard the rights of the individual... Society must mobilise to impose principles on the behaviour of states, and the principles that need to be imposed are the principles of the open society... Democratic states ... should give up some of their sovereignty to establish the rule of international law and find ways to induce other states to do the same. This seems good in principle, but we must beware of unintended consequences. Intervention in the internal affairs of another state is fraught with danger, but non-intervention can be even more damaging[262]." In the same vein as press director Jean François Kahn, who denounced without laughing the tide of "politically correct" ideology in the media, Georges Soros did not hesitate to declare, with delicious cheek, "I realise that I am going against the tide."

When he speaks of "interference", George Soros is not just theorising. In December 2004, elections in Ukraine gave victory to the pro-US president. After the countries of Central and Eastern Europe in the early 1990s, and Georgia a decade later, it was Ukraine's turn to move out of the Russian orbit and into the West after what would be called the "orange revolution", after the colour of the T-shirts worn by its supporters. Here, too, it is not necessary to carry out extensive

---

[261] George Soros, *La crisis del capitalismo global; La sociedad abierta en peligro.* Editorial Debate, Madrid, 1999, p. 28.
[262] George Soros, *La crisis del capitalismo global; La sociedad abierta en peligro.* Editorial Debate, Madrid, 1999, p. 255–256.

research to understand the role of international finance in the triumph of the "open society" in which Madeleine Albright's "Freedom House" was involved, which, let us remember, headed the US State Department in 1999 during the bombing of Serbia.

Two months later, in *Le Figaro* of 24 February 2005, we read that "billionaire philanthropist George Soros has called for Russia to be excluded from the G8 [most industrialised countries], to sanction the rollback of freedoms." It must be said that his tireless activity did not seem to please the Russian and Belarusian authorities, who had banned his foundations on their territories. The only explanation that can be found for this intolerance is obviously the ingratitude of these governments and an incomprehensible anti-Semitism. However, despite this limited and localised opposition, the "billionaire philanthropist" was not discouraged: in March 2005, he launched, in partnership with the World Bank, a programme in favour of the Gypsies (Roma) of Central Europe entitled *Decade for Roma Inclusion*. Like philosophers and filmmakers, the activity of planetarian financiers is tireless, feverish and obsessive. It never stops.

Planetarian cinema

It is often said that, in a democracy, the media constitute the "fourth power" after the executive (the government), the legislative (the Assembly) and the judiciary (the courts). The importance that the audiovisual media have acquired in our everyday world probably belies this order established by jurists and political scientists. The truth is that the media, especially television, play an essential role in brainwashing and shaping the opinions of our contemporaries. There is no need to think about it any further.

On our television screens, cinema is undoubtedly the most popular vehicle for conveying messages to the masses, who are invited to attend to the "hunches" of television programmes and critics who always go for the most humanistic and ideologically charged films.

Planetarian cinema propagates the same message as the philosophy of the same genre: it always tries, in one form or another, to lead the spectator to conceive of a world without borders and to instil tolerance towards the "Other", be it immigrant, homosexual, monstrous, alien, mongoloid or even simply normal. The only individual who has no place in the world to come is the one who defends the culture of his ancestors and his territory. Of course, it is not a question here of denouncing the Amazonian Indians or the African tribes threatened by modernity who do not want to be plundered, but only of dragging through the mud the backward white racists who still reject a plural society.

In the audiovisual world, it is much more difficult to theorise and rationally present to the public all the details of the evolution of the world. The audience does not have to think too much, because they want to relax first and foremost. They must therefore be sensitised to a cause through emotions captured on the screen. To this end, the message will be based above all on human behaviour, the ethnic characteristics of individuals and an atmosphere conducive to detestation or sympathy for the characters. So a character and his behaviour will have to embody an idea: for example, a bad colonist and a good colonised, or a hypocritical, twisted priest and a secular, open and tolerant schoolteacher. Often, the crudest propaganda is even the most effective with the most popular audiences. Thus, Manichean films like Rambo with Sylvester Stalone have done far more damage to communism than intellectual debates in front of television cameras. But more often than not, the message is underlying and contained within the quality of the character. The image lends itself perfectly to an apology for miscegenation and tolerance, a recurring theme in planetarian cinema.

Ethnic mix or diversity in film has become really visible in the West since the 1990s, often as a secondary aspect of the film that audiences were not supposed to pay much attention to. Since then it has been increasingly trivialised[263].

The first films to feature mixed-race couples are so striking that we have had to deal with the subject separately. As far as we know, there was no other film of this genre before that of American director Stanley Kramer, who, in 1967, was probably the first to make an apology for miscegenation in the United States with his film *Guess Who's Coming Tonight*. Kramer imagined a young beauty introducing her husband to her parents. The latter, you guessed it, is a sympathetic, cultured and intelligent black man whose natural charm and kindness overcomes the instinctive and perverse distrust of the American white bourgeoisie. The film garnered ten Oscar nominations. However, film production of this type seemed to dry up in the years that followed, though perhaps more

---

[263] Today's readers know that this phenomenon is now the norm. The big audiovisual production companies and platforms (Netflix, HBO, Disney, etc.) and even the tech giants (Amazon, Apple) have diversified and massified this type of audiovisual production (films and series). The invasive advertising of large companies and corporations is also unanimously multiracial and actively promotes miscegenation in the West. (NdT).

research is needed to be sure. In any case, such scripts and messages regained visibility in the 1990s. In 1995, *The Affair* (USA), Paul Seed portrayed a black American soldier during the Second World War. He suffers the contempt of his comrades: they are very mean and arrogant racist Whites. With his friend, he is sent to the officers' mess kitchen where he meets Maggie, a mother whose husband is at the front. The two are quickly attracted to each other. But their relationship is frowned upon: she is English and white, and he is American and black.

Quentin Tarantino also often accustoms his audience to ethnic diversity: in *Pulp Fiction* (USA, 1993), we witness the murderous ravings of a striking duo, a White and a Black. The gang leader is a Black man; his wife is a completely junkie and emaciated white woman. In *Jackie Brown* (1997), the main character is a Black gunrunner whose wife is a petite blonde who is also totally stoned. In *Reservoir Dogs* (1992), the characters are rabid dogs that devour each other in an impressive final massacre. They are all white and more or less crazy. Director Bob Rafelson also promoted ethnic mixing in For *No Apparent Reason*, released in 2002.

British cinema also experienced this multicultural trend. In *My beautifull laundrette* (UK, 1990), director Stephen Frears served up a cocktail of politically correct clichés: Omar, a young Pakistani, is commissioned by his uncle to revive a run-down laundrette in a London slum. Being very dynamic, he manages to renovate it and get the business up and running again. He hires an old friend, a poor English homosexual thug who becomes his lover. His gang of friends revolt against the fact that one of their own is working for the "Pakis". Evidently, they are very racist and lazy. Fortunately, the Pakis are there to make the economy work and impregnate the English women, as the film shows. Apology of miscegenation and homosexuality, denunciation of racism: the film received the Cesar[264] for the best foreign film, despite being totally soporific. If anyone saw the ending, they could tell us about it. In *Dirty Pretty things* (UK, 2002), the same Stefen Frears, a true planetarian filmmaker, told the story of Okwe, an underground Nigerian who leads a hard life, a taxi driver by day and a hotel security guard by night. One night, he finally discovers a human heart in one of the rooms, a beautiful white woman who will make him love life in England.

French production in this area is exemplary: in 1988, in *Romuald et Juliette*, Coline Serreau showed us an interracial love story. Romuald (Daniel A.) is the young manager of an important company who falls in

---

[264] French Academy Award, equivalent to Spain's Goya Award (NdT).

love with the cleaning lady, a Caribbean mother of five. The script is not credible, but it reflects very well the will to inculcate "tolerance" and "openness" to the other.

In 1989, Gérard Oury offered us *Vanilla-Fresh*: Two secret agents have the mission of blowing up a ship carrying missiles: He is black, an explosives expert and a very nice guy, pseudonym: Vanilla! She is white and a combat swimmer, pseudonym: Strawberry!

In 1993, Mathieu Kassovitz presented the film *Métisse*: Lola is a "splendid Caribbean mulatto" who has two lovers. One is white, Jewish and a rapper, the other black, the son of a diplomat and a law student. One day, Lola summons them to announce that she is pregnant. War breaks out between the two men, but the racism between the Jew and the Negro is not so bad and they quickly make a *ménage à trois*: the Jew, the Muslim Negro and the Christian half-caste." An invigorating comedy that is not afraid of the weight of tradition and the clash of cultures", according to a major weekly in the French press.

Bertrand Blier's film *Un, deux, trois soleil* (France, 1993) is a model of its kind: it tells the dark and ordinary life of Victorine (Annouk Grinberg, the director's wife), originally from the slums. Her mother is crazy, her father is an alcoholic, and her first love has been murdered by a redneck, a *"beauf"*. She calms her violent temperament by meeting Maurice, who gets her twice. The white cop, an imbecile, is married to a black woman who gives birth to little mulatto children. The white teacher only dreams of being ridden by her black and brown pupils. In one scene, Jean-Marielle leaves her door open at night so that little black thieves can enter, inviting them to dinner with these words: "You are lucky for my country. When you grow up, marry a very white Frenchwoman."

In 1997, director Robert Guédiguian presented *Marius et Jeanette*: In Marseille, Jeanette lives alone with her two children she had in two different beds. Her eldest daughter was left to her by a bastard who abandoned her: a stupid white man. The 12-year-old boy is a little African mulatto who studies very well at school. Unfortunately, his father, whom he misses because he was so charming, died on a construction site. Jeanette then meets Marius. He is a big, taciturn big man, a watchman in a disused factory. All the characters in the film are good ordinary people, some of whom make no secret of their communist sympathies. The film naturally won the César for best actress in 1998.

Bernard Stora is the director of the film *Un Dérangement considérable* (1999): "Since his childhood, Laurent Mahaut has devoted all his energy to his life's dream: to be a footballer. If he can become a professional, he will be able to provide for his mother Rosa, and his half-brothers Djamel and Nassim." Bernard Stora also wrote the script for the television film *Une autre vie* (2004): the young Malian Ismael Traoré has come to Marseille to study medicine despite his uncle's arranged marriage. At the hospital, he meets Marta, a beautiful white woman, and neglects his young African wife. For Bernard Stora, the apology of miscegenation seems to be an obsession: while in Emmanuel Roblès' novel, the doctor is a White, Stora has replaced him with a Black to raise public awareness of this theme: a timely television film for "integration week" on France 3. In *La Tresse d'Aminata* (1999), Dominique Baron portrayed a Senegalese teenager adopted as a child by a Breton family. In 2003, director Olivier Lang shot a chapter of the *generalist Doctor Dassin* series, entitled Closely *guarded Secrets*: "Dassin meets an unusual couple who raise his suspicions: a fifty-year-old Frenchman, a sports trainer, and an eighteen-year-old African girl who lives too dependent on her husband."

In *The Man from Another Place* (France, 2004), François Luciani told the story of Pedro, a Caribbean doctor who takes over the vacant medical practice in a small provincial town. It is 1893, and no one has ever seen a coloured man. Evidently, our doctor is very likeable. He is liberal, big, generous, has a good hanger and is brimming with kindness and wisdom. Opposite him, François Luciani shows us distrustful and uneducated Whites who cannot keep up with him. And when the patients scorn his practice, he bursts out: "But who do they think they are, these people in their cold and rainy country? One day, a travelling zoo appears in the village where he sees some brothers of the same breed caged behind a sign saying "cannibals". The Whites, of course, laughed themselves silly, cruelly. His blood boils at such a spectacle, but his anger passes because he has a big heart. In fact, the most beautiful woman in the country already seems to be in love with him. In another scene, our doctor's maid informs us that the factory's boatswain has a habit of brushing all the workers, and when they get pregnant they are fired." He doesn't die of pity, all those people who go to mass on Sundays", the woman concludes. The Catholic religion, of course, is the religion of bastards and hypocrisy. Another scene: an epidemic is spreading in the village; when the courageous doctor realises the seriousness of the situation, he enters the municipal council where the notables are gathered. Of course, the racism of the bad guys prevents him from sitting in the council, but nevertheless, thanks to his natural superiority, he makes himself heard vehemently: "Bravo,

Gentlemen! By dint of greed and stupidity, you have brought about an epidemic of cholera! "But who cares, the important thing is that he has found a tender heart in this ocean of baseness. Undoubtedly, we have with this uplifting film the cosmopolitan stamp. François Luciani comes from a family of Algerian repatriates, as does the director-actor Roger Hanin. Together they have made a beautiful film against intolerance.

In the same vein, the TV series PJ (Policia Judicial) reflected quite well the obsessive desire to sensitise the masses through stories that were always very "politically correct". One episode of this series posed the situation: a suburban suburb. Gunshots are fired by a group of "youths" who listen to the music a bit too loudly. One of the cops—a female cop—is a far-right activist. But later we find out that she has a son she was hiding, a mulatto. The father is a West Indian, a member of the National Front security. This *"capilotractado"* script[265] is by Alain Krief...

In 2004, the filmmaker Eduardo Molinaro offered us *The Hearts of Men*: A medical plane from the Congo flies to Paris with children in need of surgery. A team of French doctors falls under the spell of these adorable children who are the France of the future. In *If I Had Millions*, screenwriter Philippe Niang also seemed to be obsessed with presenting ethnic diversity, as he also repeated in *A Black Baby in a White Basket*. We will see in another chapter that Asian surnames are sometimes misleading.

In 2005, Claude Berri presented *One Stays, One Goes* (with an ethnic cast: Daniel Auteuil, Pierre Arditi, Charlotte Gainsbourg, Nathalie Baye and Miou-Miou)." Two long-time friends, Daniel and Alain, in their fifties, married for fifteen years, are about to meet love. For Daniel, it will be Judith (they always marry within the community), after the son he had with Anne-Marie becomes a quadriplegic following a motorbike accident. Alain, for his part, meets Farida, a young Senegalese woman he has hired as a saleswoman in his African art shop." In 2004, the "typically French" TV series *Plus Belle la vie*[266] was released, in which we are systematically shown young white women with Blacks, while young white men play the role of homosexuals. The scripts are by Olivier Szulzynger.

The Planetarian trademark is also recognisable in the racism that is more or less latent in the screenplays, but always very visible on the screen. The film *The Children of Brazil* (UK, USA, 1978), adapted from

---

[265] Pulled by the hair (*Latin: capilus-tractus*).
[266] 18 seasons in 2022. (NdT).

the novel, tells the story of a Nazi hunter in the 1970s, Ezra Liberman, who uncovers a plot organised by a group of former Nazi émigrés in Paraguay. The horrible Dr. Mengele, a former medical torturer at Auschwitz, is their boss. He lives in a luxurious villa sufficiently isolated from the world to be able to continue his perverse experimental activities on human genetics. He seems to reign over a herd of amorphous, almost enslaved servants: he is the overbearing white man in all his glory. The Nazis appear to be part of the elite of Paraguay's military regime, hosting receptions in sumptuous palaces. They have hatched a mysterious assassination plot, but it is thwarted by the tenacity of vigilante Liberman. The film is by Franklin J. Schaffner.

In *On the Brink of Suspicion* (USA, 1985), an editor of a large Californian newspaper is accused of having savagely murdered his wife in order to receive a huge inheritance. Persuaded of his innocence, a famous lawyer agrees to defend him. However, in the course of the trial, some elements of the case cause her to doubt him, especially the behaviour of a witness who shows all the signs of a dangerous psychopath: he is blond and of Nordic type. He looks dangerous and even assaults the lawyer in the car park. However, he is not the culprit but her own client, the press director who was able to seduce her so perfidiously. He is also a Nordic blond guy, but the lawyer gets the proof of his guilt by chance, after having won the trial and exonerated her client. She then decides to denounce him and publicly confess the prosecutor's ignominy. In a case dating back years, the prosecutor had made a part of the case file disappear that would have prevented another defendant from being sentenced to ten years in prison. The unfortunate person unjustly imprisoned was a Black. Blacks are good, Whites are bad, and the film is by Richard Marquand.

In *Cry Freedom* (UK, 1987), Richard Attenborough transported us to South Africa in the 1970s when the Apartheid regime was imposed on Blacks by Afrikaners. The editor of a liberal newspaper takes up the cause of the Blacks and befriends one of the main leaders, Steve Biko. The latter is murdered in prison by some of the most vile and dastardly Whites. The Blacks, on the other hand, are all touching, dignified and respectable. Their peaceful demonstrations are harshly repressed by a ruthless police force. A film that makes one ashamed to be white, and that is precisely the point.

In the same vein, director Chris Menges made *A World Apart* (UK, 1988), which depicted tensions in South Africa in 1963. White South Africans are naturally racist, and the police are portrayed in the worst possible light: hateful, obtuse and obsessed by an ungraspable enemy.

Menges' work naturally received the Grand Jury Prize at Cannes in 1988. In *Lethal Weapon 2* (1989), Richard Donner also showed white South Africans as ignoble drug dealers.

With *Mississippi Burning* (USA, 1988), Alan Parker was inspired by a true story from the 1960s. The American FBI investigates the disappearance of three young men belonging to a "civic rights" association. They—one Black and two Jews—have been killed by racist Ku Klux Klan members. In this small town in the American South, Whites are cowardly, vile, mean and downright abject. Their women obey meekly but only dream of being separated from such individuals. Milos Forman's film *Ragtime* (USA, 1991) had no other interest than being a moralising film: in 1906 in New York, a black pianist who has bought a car falls victim to the envy and racism of a gang of stupid whites.

In *The Trail of Treason*, Costa-Gavras (USA, 1988) denounced the extreme right-wing militias in the United States. A somewhat provocative and "liberal" radio host is murdered in a car park. He was Jewish, and his killers left graffiti at the scene of the crime: "ZOG" (*Zionist occupation government*). FBI cops investigate an extreme right-wing militia in the Midwest. A beautiful girl is put in charge of infiltrating them. Gary quickly falls in love with her, revealing his psychopathic traits. He insists, for example, that she goes hunting with his friends. It is a rather peculiar hunt as it is a manhunt against a young Black man who is released at night in a forest. The man will naturally be shot down in front of the young woman's eyes. Gary probably intended to impress his new love interest, but she was disgusted by what she witnessed. However, his superiors in the FBI, with whom he is in contact, insist that he continue to infiltrate the far-right network. In fact, a paramilitary camp reveals the importance of the organisation: they have sophisticated weapons and show great determination. Eventually, they will all be arrested. But the fight against the hydra is far from over, as it is known that these networks are supported by powerful figures, prominent politicians who hide their intentions and act underhandedly.

Jonathan Demme's famous film, *The Silence of the Lambs* (USA, 1991), told of the FBI's pursuit of a dangerous psychopath who left behind the corpses of young women who had been atrociously mutilated. The famous "Agent Starling" Clarisse, a young policewoman with a lot of guts, is on the trail of the serial killer. The dangerous moron's name is Billy: he is a tall, blond, blue-eyed man. He lives alone in a seedy house and is holding his next terrified victim hostage in a pit in the basement. Billy loves butterflies and guns. A brief sequence shows us a huge swastika above his bed.

In *The Firm* (USA, 1993), Mitch McDeere (Tom Cruise) is a young graduate who has just been recruited by the Firm, a powerful Memphis law firm. At first he is seduced and fascinated by the perks they offer him, but he gradually realises that the leaders actually work for a Chicago mob gang. All the lawyers presented—a good thirty of them—are white, Catholic and of a Nordic type. They symbolise the most hypocritical and repulsive American elite imaginable. The film is by Sydney Pollack.

In 1993, a comedy entitled *The Addams Family 2: The Tradition Continues* was released. The Adams family is a bit special: it is not clear whether they are witches or vampires, but they certainly worship the devil. They live in an isolated mansion on a hill; they wear black, have black hair and a cadaverous complexion. Their morals are abject; they have a passion for doing evil, though their eccentricity makes them endearing. The two sons are taken to a summer camp with the rest of the little Americans, almost all of whom are blond and make up the imbecilic, cowardly and bigoted majority. Soon the two little black-haired devils are quarantined by the vile herd of little blondes moulded by bourgeois morality. But the little Adams are not going to let themselves be trampled underfoot just like that. They will gather around them the other oppressed individuals of the camp, all the black-haired children unjustly despised by these arrogant blondes. All together, they are going to make a splash at the end-of-holiday show that the parents will be attending. The blondes then get a well-deserved telling off. The bad and ugly ones are actually the good ones, and the bastards are invariably the blondes: the film is by Barry Sonnenfeld.

The Green Mile (USA, 1999) is a film by Frank Darabont. On the death row of an American penitentiary in 1935, there are ignoble prison guards and prisoners full of humanity. All this is entirely plausible. The supernatural powers of the black colossus, accused of the rape and murder of two young girls, are less so. He is good and innocent as a lamb, though unjustly accused. He will be the victim of men, of injustice, and of the cruelty of the psychopathic guardians—the whites.

In *The Believer* (USA, 2001), young neo-Nazis are recruited by a powerful extremist organisation. Dany, their leader, the only smart guy in the gang, is actually a distraught Jew who has disassociated himself from his community. A final scene in the script is implausibly intended to make us believe that these Nazi organisations are supported by the

American big bourgeoisie: the film is by Henry Bean; the script by Mark Jacobson.

The Jury (*Runaway Jury*, USA, 2002) is the story of the manipulation of juries by the gun lobby in the United States. The "bad guys" are manipulative, highly organised and highly effective Nordic Caucasians working for the gun lobby. Espionage, violence, blackmail and manipulation are their speciality; they leave no stone unturned to win the trial, but, fortunately, the bastards are going to lose thanks to the intelligence of the little lawyer Dustin Hoffman: a film by Garry Fleder with a screenplay by David Lieven and Brian Koppelman.

The politically correct spirit is evidently present in Disney's family-friendly cartoon *Pocahontas* (USA, 1995) by Mike Gabriel and Eric Goldberg. Pocahontas, an independent young Indian girl, rejects the husband her father has chosen for her and becomes infatuated with a young English adventurer who is less racist than the others. Eventually, she will give him up to stay with her people. The English are greedy, cruel and nasty, while the Indians are good, wise, noble and respectful. Pocahontas is designed to appeal to everyone: she is dark, sexy, tanned, almond-eyed and has something of the Indian, the Black, the Chinese, the Berber and the Gypsy. She magnificently claims her "planetarian ethnicity[267]".

French cinema is no slouch in this discipline of whipping the majority population. Jean-Jacques Annaud, in *La Victoire en chantantant* (France, 1976), presented a panorama of the French presence in Africa in 1915, where a settler population, exclusively composed of alcoholic cretins, lives in confrontation with Blacks with a great sense of humour.

In 1984, with Train *d'enfer (Train from Hell)*, Roger Hanin made a great militant film. In the 11 January 1985 issue of the independent weekly *Tribune juive*, the magazine's editor, Rabbi Jacques Grunewald, known for his leftist sympathies, commented on Roger Hanin's film as follows: "Atrocious murder on a train: a young Arab is lynched and defenestrated by three tipsy conscripts. From this case, a racist act by three outcasts, Roger Hanin has constructed a film from which he intends to draw a great moral lesson, this time involving the whole of deepest France. It is no longer about three isolated, drunken kids. It's about a real neo-Nazi network involving a whole city, even the whole world." *Tribune juive* added: "Roger Hanin claims that as an Algerian Jew, he has learned since childhood to love Arabs. Apparently, he was

---

[267] The reader can consult the interesting book by Norbert Multeau, *Les Caméras du diable* [*The Devil's Chambers*], Éditions Dualpha, 2001.

not taught to love the French." *Train d'enfer benefited* from the support of the official revenue anticipation agency, chaired by Bernard-Henri Lévy, i.e. it received a subsidy financed by French taxpayers' money.

In *Outside the Law* (*Hors-la-loi*, France, 1984), "fifteen teenagers of various ethnic origins escape from a correctional centre. They break into a village dance and the bar owner, a racist, ends up opening fire on them."

In 1995, in *The Hate* (*La Haine*), Mathieu Kassovitz describes the hatred against French society that torments three young men: an Arab, a Black and a Jew from a suburb. We see again in this film the tendency to assimilate Jews with the most disadvantaged of the population. Mathieu Kassovitz becomes the standard-bearer for a section of immigrants who are reluctant to obey the law and who cry out their hatred of the system. Blacks and Moors thus become the incarnation of the new myth of the rebellious hero, even though they are regularly invited on all the television sets and benefit from the support of the major production companies and record labels. Mathieu Kassovitz returned in 2000 with *The Purple Rivers*: in the glaciers of the Alps, atrociously mutilated corpses are found with their eyes gouged out and their hands cut off. The investigators follow a trail that leads them to the local university, which turns out to be a breeding ground for dangerous neo-Nazis. Again, the film's script is not very credible, although it is amply sufficient for the intended audience.

With *Taxi*, released in 1998, Gérard Pirès had a phenomenal success: Sami Naceri, a madman behind the wheel, manages to defeat a gang of dangerous criminals. They are Germans of the Nordic type, as stupid as they are evil. In *Les Enfants du soleil*, released in 2004, Alexandre Arcady intended to tell us about the plight of the French in Algeria, although his film was more a celebration of the Israeli community. The French "clean-cut, Catholic *pied noir*[268] "as the author puts it, is called Lacombe. Just like "Lucien Lacombe", the simple-minded and dangerous militiaman invented by the writer Patrick Modiano for Louis Malle's film.

In 1999, Alain Berberian gave us his last film, *Six-Pack*: in Paris, a police commissioner is determined to arrest an American serial killer. The man has already murdered and mutilated five women. But he happens to be the cultural attaché of the American embassy and enjoys diplomatic immunity. Everything indicates that the ministry is obstructing the investigation to prevent the arrest of the culprit. In effect, the case is being used by Paris to influence trade negotiations

---

[268] French repatriated from Algeria after independence.

with Washington. The bad guys are played by Nordic European-type men (the police chief, the psychopath) while the good guys (Commissioner Nathan, Inspector Saul) are, once again, played by very dark actors.

In 2004, film director Stéphane Kurc presented *Le Triporteur de Belleville*: in 1940, during the great military debacle of the French troops, Victor Leizer, a young Jew from the Belleville district, has lost his regiment. Together with another lost soldier, they wander through the French countryside deserted by its inhabitants. In the evening, the two companions come across a group of Senegalese on a farm. The leader of the Senegalese turns out to be a professor of French in Dakar. He has been forced to take part in this war far from his homeland. He expresses himself perfectly, in polished language: "Gentlemen, let's stop talking in gibberish!". The good man would rather die with great dignity, beaten by the Germans, than let himself be captured far from his country. Among the millions of soldiers mobilised on the front, Jews and Blacks were undoubtedly in the majority, even if a quick calculation would show that they made up 1 or 2% at most. But when it comes to sensitising French television viewers, anything goes. Naturally, in Stéphane Kurc's script, the bad guys are very bad and the good guys are very good.

We saw another ridiculousness in an episode of *La Crim*, a typically French TV film: a *skinhead* (an imaginary character, a violent, shaven-headed, extreme right-wing individual) is stabbed to death on the outskirts of the city. Everything suggests that the culprit is an Arab, and he is arrested. But the investigation shows that the murderer was the skinhead's father, who could no longer tolerate the fact that his son was a right-wing extremist. Moreover, before his death, he had killed the Arab's brother, who also happened to be a childhood friend. This delirious script came from the pen of Ramsay Lévy.

In the romantic comedy *The Fabulous Fate of Amélie Poulain* (France, 2001), the script and the characters were too French: Serge Kaganski, critic of the magazine *Les Inrockuptibles*, could not stand it and declared in the daily *Libération* of 30 May 2001: "It is a film with a frozen aesthetic that presents above all a retrograde, ethnically clean, nauseating France". This hatred of France and the French seems to be an incurable obsession. If all these directors wanted to drive us to suicide, they would not have done it in any other way. In fact, this "nauseating" France was very well portrayed by François "Truffaut" in *The Last Underground (*1980)*, a* film about the life of a theatre during the German occupation, in which one could perfectly discern French abjection on the one hand, and the genius of humanity on the other. The latter will come to light in the final scene, fervently acclaimed by all the spectators who finally recognise the unique, admirable creative genius incarnated in the person of the little "Lucas Steiner", forced to hide in the basement of the theatre during all that time.

In Alain Berbérian's comedy, *The City of Fear* (La *Cité de la peur*, France, 1994), actor Dominique Farrugia vomited in the face of a bastard in a hilarious scene. And it is much funnier when the mocked people laugh at the one who is mocked to their face. As Dante's verse says: "In the midst of us, the liar laughs at us", or something like that.

The planetarian spirit in filmmaking also manifests itself naturally through a certain anti-Christianity. In his "magnificent and obsessive" film, *Fanny and Alexander* (Sweden, 1982), the brilliant director Ingmar Bergman opposed two characters: a bishop—austere and gloomy—of the Lutheran Church, and a Jew—gentle and charming. The bishop mistreats his adopted children whom he kidnaps in a windowless barn. They are saved by the Jew, who also helps the mother to free herself. The bishop dies atrociously, and the Jew replaces him at the head of the family. Bergman did not intend his fable to have the slightest hint of realism: his Jew, an orthodox who wears a black *yarmukle*, drinks wine in the company of the Swedes at Christmas— something a religious Jew would never do for the world. But that is not the point, you have already understood. Already in 1960, in *The Fire and the Word*, Richard Brooks showed us that behind the face of the good pastor Elmer Gantry could hide the worst scum. His film was naturally awarded an Oscar.

But the model in its genre remains to this day Jean-Jacques Annaud's famous film269, *The Name of the Rose* (France, 1986), whose screenplay is based on the novel by the world-famous Italian writer Umberto Eco: it is a detective story set in a Benedictine monastery in Northern Italy at the beginning of the 14th century. Clichés about the Middle Ages accumulate throughout the film: all the monks are without exception morons, or in one way or another, abnormal. They profit and grow fat off the poor peasants who give them their meagre crops, while surviving in the mud and on the rubbish the monks throw at them. The Catholic Church is a complete perversion: it keeps the spirits in

---

[269] No relation to Marthe Hanau, whose swindle in the 1930s was famous. The reaction of a small saver swindled in that financial scandal has been described in an amusing scene in Henri Vincenot's magnificent book, *La Billebaude*. [Read in Hervé Ryssen, *The Jewish Mafia*].

servitude and in fear of the devil; the monastery keeps under lock and key the Greek books that might destabilise its power. William of Baskerville, the Franciscan monk, masterfully played by Sean Connery, finally manages to unravel the enigma and recover some of these forbidden works, saving them from the flames. It all ends, of course, with the expected climax: torture and the stake. The film was made in collaboration with the expert Jacques Le Goff, a historian of the Marxist school. But if you want a non-Marxist view of the magnificent epoch that was the Middle Ages, you can profitably read Régine Pernoud's little book *Pour en finir avec le moyen âge*, published by Seuil in 1977. No one can ever make us believe that the cathedrals were built with a people of wretched wretches, starving and enslaved. It should also be noted that at no point in the film is it a question of a "rose". It is evidently a title for the cabal's initiates. Indeed, we have discovered that the writer Umberto Eco has just written in 2005 the foreword to a book by Moshe Idel, entitled *Mystiques messianiques*, in which he establishes a link between Hebraic messianism and Marxism: "Many have seen the traces of messianism even in Marx's conception of a transformation of the world thanks to the redemption of the proletarian masses270." We already knew that according to Marx religion was "the opium of the people", but it had to be understood that, in the philosopher's mind, it was above all the Catholic religion.

But let's follow the anti-Catholic spirit in director Constantine Costa-Gavras's acclaimed film *Amen*. Actor Mathieu Kassovitz plays the role of a young Jesuit who, during the Second World War, tries to shake the Vatican out of its immobilism and incite Pope Pius XII to publicly denounce Nazi barbarism. The film's poster showed a swastika and a Catholic cross superimposed on each other. The reviews were evidently complimentary for this "moving and truthful" film.

Suicide Virgins (USA, 1999) is a film by Sofia Coppola: Around 1970, in a small town in Michigan, 13-year-old Cecilia, brought up by her fundamentalist Catholic parents, defenestrated herself. All her sisters commit suicide after her, proving that a Catholic upbringing is not worth that of a good Jewish family: "An intelligent and moving film" said a TV magazine. In Terry Gilliam's film *Brazil* (USA, 1984),

---

270 Moshé Idel, *Mystiques messianiques, de la Kabbale au Hassidisme XIII-XIX siècles*, Calmann-Lévy, 2005. *Messianic Mystics*, Yale University Press, New Haven, London, 1998. [Moshe Idel holds the Chair of Jewish Thought at the Hebrew University of Jerusalem. He is the successor of the great Gershom Scholem (1897–1982), Israeli scholar, philologist and historian, a leading figure in and outside Judaism, unanimously regarded as the world's foremost specialist in Jewish mysticism (see note 543 below)].

we get a brief glimpse of the bad habits of some followers of Catholicism through an older woman who keeps on retreading herself with cosmetic surgeries: a real walking corpse.

One can also cite *Life Imprisonment* (USA, 1994), a popular film in which the prison warden turns out to be both a real bastard and a very pious Christian. The film is by Frank Darabont, whom we have already seen above, thus confirming his planetarian vocation.

Planetarian cinema, like the philosophy implicit in it, aims to destroy roots and traditions. *Dead Poets Club* was made in 1990 with this aim in mind. The film shows us an elite boarding school in the United States, an old and noble institution for the children of high society. There, a professor of letters, Mr. Keating, is going to disrupt the lives of his students and dynamite the dusty old values of these withdrawn Christians. This revolutionary film, even if it doesn't look like it, invites the viewer to reject traditions and norms. The director was Peter Weir.

This is also the message of Robert Mandel's film *Private School*271 *(School Ties*, USA, 1992): David Green is a member of one of the most sought-after prep schools in New England. His intellectual and sporting qualities quickly make him a star at the school. For David, the doors of the best universities open to him and the hope of rising above his humble condition. But in order to be accepted by his wealthy peers, moulded by anti-Semitic prejudices, and to be loved by a young woman from a good family, David has had to hide his Jewishness ... until the day when the truth comes out. It is at that moment that we understand that the Catholic church is made up of repugnant individuals.

Even in an amusing cartoon like *Shrek* (USA, 2001), we see this message of contempt for the old European civilisation. In the Middle Ages, Shrek is a good and lovable ogre who lives in seclusion in the forest. He is the one who confronts the dragon and saves the beautiful princess. The king is an aggressive and ridiculous dwarf, not very representative of European tradition. He intends to marry the princess, but Shrek, who has fallen in love with her, intervenes at the last moment in the cathedral where the ceremony is taking place. The destruction of the cathedral's stained glass windows by the dragon is symbolic. This is what the story by William Strig, author of the novel, and Ted Elliot, the screenwriter, leaves us with.

---

271 No known relation to Ernest Mandel, the Trotskyist leader of the Fourth Workers' International.

On Sunday 3 April 2005, Pope Jean-Paul II died. The television channel TF1 finally decided to deprogramme the American film *Seven*, whose plot follows a kind of Catholic moron who has decided to carry out seven murders symbolising his hatred of the seven deadly sins. The film by cosmopolitan director David Fincher will therefore be shown on another occasion. The same evening, France 2 also decided to change its programming: the film *The Devil's Advocate* (USA, 1997) was postponed so as not to offend susceptible reactionaries. This exceptional deference to the Catholic public probably reflected an apprehension about the possible epidermal reactions of people who had long been humiliated, for we do not see why media decision-makers would be prepared to feel any compassion or gentleness towards highly despised taxpayers.

"Let's wipe the slate clean. If it is not possible to completely erase history before 1789, it can be gradually adulterated a little to accustom the public to accept the cosmopolitan and pluralistic universe of the society of the future. This is the case in *Wild Wild West* (USA, 1999): in 1869 in the United States, renowned scientists have mysteriously disappeared. President Grant then asks agents West and Gordon to solve this enigma. The adventure is a succession of anachronisms and incredible fun, in which director Barry Sonnenfeld had the good idea to cast a black actor as the hero (Will Smith). *The Pact of the Wolves* (France, 2001), tells the story of the Beast of Gévaudan: a mysterious beast ravages the mountains of Gévaudan in 1766, leaving numerous victims behind without anyone being able to identify and kill it. The people are terrified. It was a monster out of hell or a punishment from God, it is not clear. The case takes on a national dimension and threatens the King's authority. The knight Gregory of Fronsac is then sent to the remote region to try to stop the massacre. He is accompanied by the strange and taciturn Mani, an Iroquois Indian from the Mohawk tribe. He has a black belt in kung fu and beats the hell out of the local peasants, who are probably very racist: it's a Christophe Gans film. In Kevin Reynolds' *Robin Hood* (USA, 1991), a Black man brings gunpowder to Europe and accompanies the legendary hero. In 2001, director Peter Brook also had to cast a black actor to play Shakespeare's *Hamlet in the* absence of good white actors. Let's remember the plot: the King of Denmark has just died. His wife, Queen Gertrude, Hamlet's mother, remarries Claudius, her late husband's brother. But the spectre of the King appears before her son to ask him to avenge him, for he has been vilely murdered... Something serious is going on in the kingdom of Denmark. Regarding Shakespeare's play, *The Jew of Venice*, pungently renamed *The Merchant of Venice*, written in 1597, "Peter Brook will say of it: "As long as there is a single anti-Semite in the world, I will never mount it272"." Ethnic diversity is undoubtedly in vogue, also in theatre, as in 2005 on Broadway, Shakespeare's *Julius Caesar* also included a black actor in the role of Brutus. This time it was directed by Daniel Sullivan.

The planetarian ideal manifests itself very successfully in science fiction films. Steven Spielberg, in *E.T., the Extra-Terrestrial* (USA, 1982), teaches us to welcome the other, the alien, which is an absolute good. *Star Trek*, the mythical series where all ethnic minorities are represented, is evidently completely imbued with a planetarian spirit. Some details do not go unnoticed by the initiated who know how to recognise some of the principles of Vulcan society. The screenwriters of the television series are Leonard Nimoy and William Shatner. The bad guys are surprisingly portrayed with Caucasian male features while the good guys form a multi-ethnic humanity.

In *Terminator II* (USA, 1991), the killer cyborg disguised as a cop has the features of a blue-eyed white man with Nordic features, while the computer genius who conceives the microchip destined to revolutionise humanity is a repentant black man willing to destroy the fruits of his labour to save mankind.

Roland Enerich's *Independence Day* (USA, 1996) was a good comedy: a huge flying saucer invades the planetarian sky, releasing numerous smaller ships that hover over the world's major cities. A New York computer scientist deciphers the codes with which the strange travellers communicate. They are not at all friendly, and are preparing to attack Earth. The two heroes who are going to save the planet are a Black man and a Hasidic Jew. There is no need to hide anything, as the audience sees nothing.

In Larry and Andy Wachowski's *The Matrix* (USA, 1999), humans are subjected to a computer programme that dominates their lives and their every thought. They believe they exist, but in reality they are the slaves of the machines. There is only one small focus of human resistance: Sion. The film is full of cabalistic messages: the hero, Neo, is "the chosen one", the mythical liberator of humanity announced by the prophecies who will save "Zion", as revealed by "the Oracle". Humans are represented in the form of a multi-ethnic society, while the

---

272 Jacques Attali, *Los judíos, el mundo y el dinero*, Fondo de cultura económica, 2005, Buenos Aires, p. 254.

matrix, which seeks to dominate the universe, is represented by agents of the system with white male features. The iconic Agent Smith, in his suit and tie, is evidently very evil and malevolent. Once again, the Whites must assume the responsibilities of the real tyrants: for the matrix exists "for real": it produced the film.

In short, we will never get out of this blame game. All this would not be so serious if the scheme were not systematic, but it is clear that the repetition of identical models reveals a precise desire to inculcate a very clear message in the European masses, in which we see that "tolerance" can be likened to a powerful and painless poison that numbs the victim before it kills it. Certainly, it could be objected that most Hollywood stars are still White, but one should not lose sight of the fact that the aim is not to totally destroy White societies, so useful for business prosperity, but to lead them to adopt the plural society in which they will be able to take their rightful place: that is to say, second place. Moreover, these people still represent the vast majority of cinema-goers. We have to be a little gentle with them, and gradually bring them to accept the new planetarian norms. In any case, as Steven Spielberg's popular film *Raiders of the Lost Ark* (USA, 1981) shows so well, the power of Yahweh is so great that it is not even possible to dream of opposing it.

Still, Barry Levinson's comedy *Wag the Dog* (USA, 1997) can be watched with some interest. The White House is in chaos: two weeks before the election, the president is embroiled in a sex scandal. To distract attention, the President's expert advisor (Robert de Niro) launches a rumour about a completely imaginary war. To stage it, he contacts a film producer (Dustin Hoffman). The two of them are going to create a distraction for the public and deceive the whole population with completely false television montages. An amusing film in which we can appreciate how the system is sure enough of its power to denounce itself.

But the planetarian ideal is also very well disseminated through the lyrics of a song and its rhythms. There is no doubt that black music and rhythms have been widely disseminated in the media and attracted a great deal of publicity over the last few decades, especially over the last thirty years or so. We are not judging here the musical quality of the artists or the musical styles. We are simply noting, for example, that rap, which has become so popular lately, is a music that is a priori difficult to access for European ears, and which has only been able to establish itself after constant promotion and bombardment by the entire media system. Nowadays, Europeans are used to it, as with the rest. In fact, human beings get used to everything.

Recall that the record industry is highly concentrated. Edgar Bronfman alone, who ranks among the world's ten biggest fortunes, has acquired the production companies Polygram, Deutsche Gramophon, Decca, Philipps Music Group. As the daily *Libération* admitted (23 May 1998), "these acquisitions will continue to concentrate world record distribution in the hands of a small nucleus of multinationals, to the point of making the market inaccessible to independent labels." The fact that Edgar Bronfman is also the president of the World Jewish Congress is entirely incidental to these economic and musical considerations.

Classical song or "popular music" can also, with its lyrics, be a magnificent support for planetarian ideals. We can cite France Gall, when she sings the songs of Michel Beger, in *"Il jouait du piano debout"*; or Julien Clerc, with *"Mélissa métisse d'Ibiza..."* not forgetting the great Serge Gainsbourg with *"couleur café"*, among many others. Jean Ferrat, originally from Russia, where his father was a jeweller, chose to become a singer to transmit his humanist ideas. In fact, he was very committed to the communist party." Communism, he said, is the hope of the world. Well, okay, sometimes history doesn't move forward at a steady pace. There are advances and setbacks." In *Nuit et brouillard, Potemkine, Les Guerilleros, Les Nomades, Cuba si, Les derniers Tsiganes, A moi l'Afrique, Hospitalité, Bruit des bottes,* etc., he sang of tolerance and the love of humanity. Alain Bashung composed le *"chant des potes"* (*"the song of his colleagues"*) during the great era of SOS Racisme. A defender of the undocumented (illegal immigrants), he declared in February 1997: "Immigration is not the problem. Those who say so do so to hide their lack of imagination." Clémentine Célarié sings very badly, but the important thing is the lyrics of the song: "I made him a mestizo, my son, so that the earth would be united", she sang. He was talking about his son Abraham. Clémentine defends great humanitarian causes, even daring to kiss an HIV-positive man on the mouth on a television set. She asked the TV presenter: "Would you follow me in a chain of kisses on the mouth between homosexuals, heterosexuals, HIV-positive, HIV-negative, all mixed together? "That 2 April 2005, the day of the AIDS *"Sidaction"*, was a memorable one. Poor Clémentine was so confused and embarrassed after being so off-key in her duet with Michel Jonasz. Composer of the *"joueur de blues"*, Michel Jonasz, son of Hungarian communist immigrants, has the good taste to know how to separate his love of music and his passion as an activist; and he does it with a certain talent. Unlike Jean-Jacques Goldman, who prefers to fill his texts with planetarian messages, as in his album *"Entre gris claro y gris oscuro"*, among others273. Charles-Elie Couture also seemed to be tormented by the same obsessions, as was Johnny Clegg, a South African singer nicknamed the "white Zulu" and a militant in favour of the abolition of Apartheid. Eddy Mitchell, for his part, had sung at a gala in support of the army at Christmas 1990 in Iraq. Then there was the committed singer Georges Moustaki, a Greek "from a Jewish family", and Perret, whose song *Lily* still makes the hearts of teenage girls bleed. It was in Eddy Barclay's office that he met his wife Simone Mazaltarim, whom he would later rename Rebecca. At the risk of feeling isolated, the singer Renaud, one of the few true Parisians left, must also be classed among the pan-etharian singers, always ready to rally for humanitarian causes and stand up against injustice and intolerance.

The new ghettos

Of course, the great planetarian revolution may frighten the most timorous. Having barely emerged from communism, should we rush into another globalist utopia? Certainly, communist ideas, however generous they were, had catastrophic consequences and it would be good to be a little cautious before launching humanity on a new race to paradise on earth. At the time, it was also about "wiping out the past" and destroying the old world.

Edgar Morin realised the seriousness of the risks involved: "The dream of the personal flourishing of each of us, of the suppression of all forms of exploitation and domination, of the just distribution of goods, of effective solidarity among all, of generalised happiness, led those who wanted to impose it to use barbaric means that ruined their civilising enterprise. Any decision to suppress conflict and disorder, to establish harmony and transparency, leads to its opposite, and its disastrous consequences are obvious. As the history of the century has shown us, the will to establish salvation on earth has led to the establishment of hell. We must not fall back into the dream of earthly

---

273 *"Entre gris clair et gris foncé"*: let us remember Jacques Attali's words: "everyone will have the right to belong to several tribes that were hitherto antagonistic, to be ambiguous, to place themselves at the confines of two worlds". They seem to be repelled by everything that is frank, clear, with sharp and precise contours, just as the devil fears holy water and vampires fear garlic cloves.

salvation... There is therefore a key problem274 ", he wisely concluded. After having contributed to the destruction of anything resembling tradition, one is obliged to note certain disturbances in the functioning of Western societies which result in a "worldwide unleashing of blind forces, of positive *feedback275*, of suicidal madness ... powers of self-destruction and destruction, latent in every individual and every society ... the deadly attraction of hard drugs, especially heroin, is spreading irresistibly." All this seems very disturbing indeed: "The positive *feedbacks* that lead to *runaway* may eventually produce a mutation. But the forces of control and regulation must prevail. It is therefore a question of slowing down the technical deluge on cultures, civilisation and nature, which threatens cultures, civilisation and nature. It is about slowing down to avoid an explosion or implosion276." In short, we are staying the course, but gently taking our foot off the accelerator pedal.

Like Edgar Morin, Alain Finkielkraut also noted the same difficulties in the birth of this new world society. The disappearance of ancestral religions and traditions and the acceleration of the establishment of the multicultural paradise have brought about a transformation that is perhaps a little brutal for the native Europeans, for, unfortunately, it must be said that "never before have there been so many suicides in France and in Europe." Thus, the birth rate has plummeted and the extraordinary consumption of anxiolytics and antidepressants has skyrocketed.

Jacques Attali's *Dictionary of the 21st Century* also contains some disturbing passages that contrast with the unbridled planetarian enthusiasm of the overall tone of the work. After several considerations on universal "peace", the dictionary entries—in alphabetical order—curiously referred to the words "rebellion", "revolt", "revolution", "risks", "*sorcery*" (*sorcellerie*), "sterility" (*sterilité*). Jacques Attali did not hide from us the difficulties to come. Let the oracle speak: With the challenge of "immigration", "new epidemics will appear, as well as barriers erected to contain foreigners as at the time of the great plague... Many new diseases will be linked to nomadism. It will be the first

---

[274] Edgar Morin and Anne-Brigitte Kern, *Tierra-Patria*, 1993, Editorial Kairós, Barcelona, 2005, p. 136.
[275] Feedback, response or reaction in a system.
[276] Edgar Morin and Anne-Brigitte Kern, *Tierra-Patria*, 1993, Editorial Kairós, Barcelona, 2005, p. 115, 116, 118." We could consider the chaotic and conflictual state of the planetary era as its normal state, its disorders as inevitable ingredients of its complexity, and avoid using the now trivialised and catch-all term crisis." *Earth-Homeland,* p. 112

serious obstacle to oppose it, but also the first embryo of a planetarian police force." The people of yesteryear may be longed for by those who knew them: "The inhabitants of the cities of the North will want to recover the daily life of the villages of the 20th century. They will abandon the large urban agglomerations and try to do all the jobs that can be done remotely in the countryside. They will finance private security in order to live in peace. Residential villages and their surroundings will become protected parks, voluntary camps for the rich" ... or for any other category of citizens who want to escape from the new multi-ethnic paradise. All this is not at all flattering and encouraging, and it is surprising that our intellectuals, aware of all these looming evils, are still willing to go further. After the communist experience, the new planetarian future seems indeed full of threats and dangers of all kinds.

Alain Minc was also fully aware of the model he was proposing when he observed the current evolution of society at the end of the 20th century: "Perhaps the French social fabric is breaking down. Rising unemployment, the emergence of forbidden neighbourhoods in the suburbs, the rise of social exclusion, the depopulation of the countryside, the pressure exerted by insecurity, the fear of the foreigner: these are undeniable realities277"." The crime rate in France has increased fourfold in twenty-five years and armed robbery tenfold. Major crime is gaining ground and petty crime is soaring, all in a climate of hyper-emotionality." The spectre of insecurity has taken shape in recent years: "With neighbourhood crime, insecurity is at the very heart of daily life and threatens it directly. With the riots in the suburbs, the existence of extraterritorial spaces from which an attack on traditional society can emerge is revealed. With the crimes, the growing power of all the mafias becomes evident. Through each of its manifestations, violence demonstrates the extent to which our world is on the defensive against the insidious expansion of all grey zones and, with them, all forms of disorder. Fear of the other, as well as the resurgence of major epidemics278." However, according to Minc, we should not stop at this simple balance sheet, because "compared to other places, France seems to be an oasis." So, if we understand it properly, the work must first of all be done on ourselves.

Bernard-Henri Lévy maintained the same paradoxical discourse. After having denounced all nationalisms, fundamentalisms and populisms in *The Dangerous Purity, he* too admitted that the world to

---

[277] Alain Minc, *Le Nouveau Moyen-Age*, Gallimard, 1993, p. 236.
[278] Alain Minc, *Le Nouveau Moyen-Age*, Gallimard, 1993, p. 98.

come would be chaotic: "I believe that the great metropolises will be increasingly dominated by mafias and ghettos ... I believe in a proliferation of wars, all of them civil wars ... that the United States will start the Civil War again, but in other places and under other forms: Wasps against Latinos; whites against people of colour. I believe there will be as many wars as there are cities, as many wars of secession as there are megalopolises ... I believe that whole states will fall under the actions of the planetarian mafias; and that, if not under their actions, they will fall into their hands279."

The essayist Guy Sorman, in his excellent 1992 work *Waiting for the Barbarians*, also noted the problems associated with a plural society in the making. The chapter *The Judge, the Drug Addict, the Immigrant* perfectly illustrated, as George Soros put it, the "difficult coexistence between the bourgeois and the barbarian". The sentencing of Ozeye, an African heroin dealer, to six years in prison prompted Guy Sorman to make the following observations: "Ozeye's case mobilised several police inspectors for months, who watched him until he fell into the trap; it also mobilised judges, prosecutors, notaries, lawyers, security guards, prison officers. Could not all this time and all this money have been spent on punishing more serious crimes, or on preventing them280? "Are we to understand that a drug dealer selling heroin to teenagers on the street is not in the end something very serious? We see that, like George Soros, a supporter of the liberalisation of drugs, the very liberal Guy Sorman is a spokesman for a certain tolerance." Ozeye and drugs both come from outside, and both represent the irruption of disorder into bourgeois society." The French, who are still too bourgeois in their mentality, will have to get used to modernity and open up to foreign cultures.

The chapter titled *The Black Dutch* established a priori a rather severe diagnosis of the plural society: "80% of crimes and offences committed in Amsterdam are committed by individuals from these minorities: in prisons, one out of two cells is occupied by allochthonous people, when they represent only 5% of the total population281." A sociologist born in Surinam, Philomena Essed, "found that insufficient education or an imperfect command of the language explained 50% of

---

[279] Bernard-Henri Lévy, *La pureza peligrosa*, Espasa Calpe, Madrid, 1996, p. 166-167.
[280] Guy Sorman, *Esperando a los bárbaros*, Seix Barral, 1993, Barcelona, p.8." Los inmigrantes del exterior y los drogados del interior. Is bourgeois society, white and western, under siege by the new barbarians? Is it a real or imaginary threat? "In *Esperando a los bárbaros*, Seix Barral, 1993.
[281] Guy Sorman, *Waiting for the Barbarians*, Seix Barral, 1993, Barcelona, p. 15.

the wage gap or the professional backwardness in relation to the professional backwardness of the population." A Surinamese-born sociologist, Philomena Essed, "found that insufficient education or an imperfect command of the language accounted for 50% of the wage gap or professional backwardness in relation to whites. The other 50% is due to non-objective causes, which can only be explained by racial discrimination ... Minorities should not be integrated, but the Dutch should be self-critical. It is time for them to learn about the weaknesses of their own culture, to accept that they are racist, to recognise all that allogenic cultures could bring them", explained Ms Essed. Guy Sorman pointed out that Philomena Essed, a researcher at the Centre for Racial and Ethnic Studies in Amsterdam, was paid by the tolerant state she denounced, and rightly added that "in a democratic society this is perhaps the most characteristic sign: dissent is subsidised282."

After a trip to Germany, where he had met Daniel Cohn-Bendit, Guy Sorman flew to the United States to get a closer look at "the American tribes". Stanford University was the first stop on his American journey: "Stanford is a reflection of an America that is no longer entirely white: thanks to *affirmative action*, it is the most vigorous of all the universities in the country, and 45% of Stanford students belong to a minority", a percentage that corresponds to their number in the state of California. Sharon Parker, the head of the Office of Multiculturalism, explained that the university funds clubs and demonstrations for the black, Mexican-American and Indian communities." The gay, lesbian and bisexual association felt discriminated against because they didn't have a place to meet, and Sharon Parker got them the old firehouse on campus, which was vacated for them. Whites, as such, are entitled to nothing; the master race must learn humility; their old fraternities have been banned on suspicion that they perpetuated racist traditions." This is positive discrimination. But "there remains one final obstacle in the path of minorities: the diploma. Forty-five per cent of the students admitted belong to minorities, but only 20 per cent get their diploma. And this is because the tests for obtaining the diploma are, so far, the same for all. Should the criteria be diversified at this level as well? Some second-tier universities are already doing so, if only to attract minorities283." Thus, positive discrimination or *"affirmative action"*, in addition to already

---

282 Guy Sorman, *Waiting for the Barbarians*, Seix Barral, 1993, Barcelona, p. 15, 17–18.
283 Guy Sorman, *Waiting for the Barbarians*, Seix Barral, 1993, Barcelona, p. 78, 79, 80

facilitating entry to university, will also make it easier for these minorities, who will in fact soon represent the majority, to obtain a diploma284. Whites who are not satisfied can still migrate elsewhere if they wish: the door is open.

Sorman then visited San Diego: "We are guilty; we must make amends, proclaims Maureen O'Connor, mayor of San Diego, one of California's most prosperous cities. Ms. O'Connor is a Republican, ultra-conservative, but affirmative action, in her view, is not one of the left... How do you teach a white, male foreman not to look a Mexican farmhand in the eye because it's an attack on his culture? How do you make a Laotian-born female firefighter work together with a Filipino, a Mexican and an Irish-born captain when they don't even speak the same language? There is no stereotypical answer; the only solution is to listen. We listen carefully to what minorities can teach us, and it is exciting285," said Maureen O'Connor.

In Boston, Guy Sorman explained to us that all candidates in the competitive exams to join the police "must pass the same exam, but the results are counted on two different lists of suitable candidates: those of the whites and those of the others. The mayor, police chief, and fire chief are required to recruit an equal number of officers from each list" to facilitate the entry of people of colour. In Dallas, the companies that the city council tenders to are primarily "minority" run businesses." The city council has set a goal of reserving 35% of city contracts for *disadvantaged business enterprises* (BDEs). What is a BDE? A business managed or controlled by a representative of a protected minority—Mexican-American, black, Indian—or by a woman? Can an Anglo business owner be a DBE? Yes, if he/she is a woman or disabled286."

This is the "PC" (politically correct) ideology in the United States. Evidently, this feeling of White guilt is not natural. It is the fruit of a long work carried out by Marxist and liberal intellectuals in the second half of the 20th century. These currents of thought have been joined in the United States by an Afrocentrist current, which tends to restore Africa to its place in the cultural evolution of humanity. It is claimed that Cleopatra was black or almost black, that the Egyptian heritage was

284 "The country also passed two other milestones on its way to becoming a majority-minority society in the coming decades: For the first time, the proportion of white people fell below 60%, from 63.7% in 2010 to 57.8% in 2020. And the population under 18 is now majority black, at 52.7 per cent." https://www.washingtonpost.com/dc-md-va/2021/08/12/census-data-race-ethnicity-neighborhoods/, 12 August 2021. (NdT).
285 Guy Sorman, *Waiting for the Barbarians*, Seix Barral, 1993, Barcelona, p. 81.
286Guy Sorman, *Waiting for the Barbarians*, Seix Barral, 1993, Barcelona, p. 84, 86.

transferred to Athens by the Cretans and Phoenicians. The West would therefore owe to the Blacks not only its genetic heritage, since homosapiens originated in Africa, as anthropologists teach us, but also its philosophical and religious heritage287.

The reference work on this subject is that of Professor Martin Bernal." He teaches political science at Cornell in central New York State. He is the guru of Afrocentrism, and his book *Black Athens* is a radical revision of the origins of Western civilisation that has become a cornerstone of the new black education system." Bernal, on the other hand, is White, of English origin, Guy Sorman noted without laughing[288]." My aim is to reduce the intellectual arrogance of Europeans," he says in his conclusion." Once again, we come up against the spirit of revenge and the incandescent hatred that animates the planetarian intellectuals.

Several French intellectuals have contributed, sometimes unwittingly but often decisively, to this controlled demolition of classical culture." From the work of Lévi-Strauss, the idea that there is no hierarchy between cultures: there are neither civilised nor savages"." From this the CP has deduced a generalised cultural relativism. But the real guru of the CP, personally engaged in the battle, is Jacques Derrida. Without reference to Derrida it is difficult to teach literature in the United States. This French philosopher, known in France only to a minority, reigns supreme on the best university campuses in the United States. His method, called 'deconstruction' of the text, emphasises the radical instability of meaning and privileges the reader over the author," wrote Guy Sorman. What a student thinks of an author becomes more important than what the author himself writes.

"Reading Shakespeare is no longer done to understand Shakespeare, but to understand oneself, to raise one's own consciousness and not one's knowledge. The refusal to learn becomes a form of legitimate defence against the oppression of truth and rationality. Truth, in deconstructionist theory, is not truth: it is only a hierarchical discourse, logocentrism or, better, 'phallogocentrism', Derrida writes, of 'the old, dead, white males'... What is left of classical culture when it has been run through the shredder of deconstruction and relativism? Nothing," admits Henry Louis Gates, a leading thinker in the PC movement who heads the Literature department at Harvard.

---

[287]Guy Sorman, *Waiting for the Barbarians*, Seix Barral, 1993, Barcelona, p. 103–106.
[288]Bernal is a historical surname: a certain Bernal was the "Jewish doctor of the expedition of Christopher Columbus" who brought the first tobacco leaves to Europe, wrote Roger Peyrefitte in *Les Juifs*, Éditions Flammarion, 1965, p. 157.

Nothing, but that's not the point. What used to be called culture, values, morals, was nothing more than an ideology imposed by yesterday's masters on the oppressed minorities. Now it is the minorities who speak...". My students," Gates concludes, "all seek out minority origins; when they find 1/32nd Indian blood in them, they go crazy with joy, and even change their names. They are no longer stupidly American, they are multicultural[289]."

Being PC is in fashion. A radical and conformist fashion. You don't need to study hard to be PC; you just need to be in line, that's all. This reminds us of an anecdote of one of our friends whose father had taught him to get good marks in philosophy classes in high school. While one of his classmates complained about the poor grades he was getting despite his efforts, Marcos decided to reveal his secret: it wasn't hard work that allowed him to get good grades, in fact, he didn't hit a mark. He simply knew that that "teacher[290] "was impregnated with PC ideology, so she systematically oriented her dissertations in the planetarian sense, always "insisting on the same thing": "If you say what you think," his father had told him, "she will fuck you up; but if you write what she wants to hear, then you fuck her up! In the oral tests, he never forgot to wear his "Lévis" T-shirt, written in big letters, to win the jury's approval. This was Marcos' secret that enabled him to get his diploma at the great Paris school of political science, a model of French-style PC. As for the other student, he said: "She didn't understand a thing! This is all rather trivial when you are sixteen or seventeen years old, but it is also true that many Western adults find themselves in the same situation.

Guy Sorman added another observation: "Today's professors are the student protesters of 1968". That year, the University of Berkeley, across the bay from San Francisco, "on the slopes of the California hills, one of the most authentic revolutions of the century emerged ... An astonishing cocktail—rich students and leftist professors imported from Europe, like Herbert Marcuse; a hodgepodge of psychoanalysis, sexual freedom, background music, psychedelic drugs and Marxist vulgarity—changed Berkeley from top to bottom, then spread across America, Japan and Europe." Eventually, the revolution became

---

[289]Guy Sorman, *Waiting for the Barbarians*, Seix Barral, 1993, Barcelona, p. 110, 111, 112.

[290]We saw with Albert Memmi and Wilhelm Reich that Western women should also free themselves from the oppression of white men. The feminisation of vocabulary at the end of the 20th century was part of the PC trend in France. But its use remains very marginal due to the reluctance of the population.

institutionalised in Berkeley, and today "almost all of the community activities funded by the State University are controlled by *blacks*, Chicanos or *native Americans*, or by gays, lesbians and bisexuals. The white man still resists, but ultimately his supremacy seems doomed. The fate of the white man seems sealed by demography," wrote Guy Sorman, who summed up perfectly the tangible result of Marxist activism on European civilisation." Twenty-five years later, whites are in the minority. Whites are *sandwiched* between Asians, who do better than whites on admissions questionnaires, and blacks and Latin Americans, who benefit from affirmative action. White students, who, for the most part, come from white schools, are confronted for the first time in their lives with being a minority and being white ... the class struggle has been replaced by a class struggle that is also inevitable: people of colour have replaced the proletariat as the exploited class destined to become dominant[291]."

Yet Guy Sorman did not condemn the plural society, quite the contrary, as these lines written with at least as much aplomb as Daniel Cohn-Bendit attest: "The new fact about immigration in Europe is not so much the number, or its ethnic or religious origin, as the non-integration of the immigrant into companies. Our ancestors were rarely Gauls ... our origins are murky, and that's why we don't want to recognise it... Because we are all multicultural, at least since the Roman invasion. On the other hand, France, which had hundreds of dialects, *patois* and regional languages a century ago, was more multicultural then than it is today[292]." And as for closing borders, let's not even think about it: "Close the borders? It is impossible. What Frenchman would agree to wait two hours at Roissy airport for the police to check the identity of each traveller and the authenticity of each passport? The expulsion of foreigners in an irregular situation is only a theoretical recourse, and for the same reasons: what Frenchman would resign himself to being caught in a police *raid*, in the metro for example, and having to wait for the police to separate the citizens who are in order from those who are not[293]? "The argument is irrefutable.

The French are still too faint-hearted in the face of the modernity of a plural society, all the more so as the evolution of French society in recent years has revealed tensions that were hitherto dormant. The truth forces us to say that numerous depredations are committed every year

---

[291]Guy Sorman, *Waiting for the Barbarians*, Seix Barral, 1993, Barcelona, p.113, 114.
[292]Guy Sorman, *Waiting for the Barbarians*, Seix Barral, 1993, Barcelona, p. 158, 159, 163
[293]Guy Sorman, *Waiting for the Barbarians*, Seix Barral, 1993, Barcelona, p. 194.

against Christian places of worship and cemeteries. For example, about twenty such cases were recorded in five months, between December 2003 and April 2004. Dozens of Christian tombs were desecrated, churches vandalised, stained glass windows destroyed, statues smashed to pieces, without the phenomenon alarming the media. On the contrary, the slightest anti-Semitic graffiti on a letterbox or on a grave in a Jewish cemetery triggered the entire media machine and the displacement of the minister.

But of all the tensions and clashes provoked by the new pluralistic society currently in the making, the demonstration by secondary school students on 8 March 2005 in Paris has remained a symbol and a harbinger for the future. As is often the case, numerous "youths" from the suburbs took advantage of that occasion to loot and attack in the vicinity of the demonstration. This time, the violence was particularly impressive, especially against the students themselves. It was not the events themselves that were important, as attacks on French people by ethnic gangs have been occurring in the suburbs for many years. The most remarkable fact was that for the first time, the mainstream press openly evoked the phenomenon in the wake of the demonstration. This was a historic turning point: for the first time, the media decided to denounce, no longer the racism of the Whites against immigrants (a few tens of assaults per year out of the hundreds of thousands of acts of violence reported), but finally what all French people in the suburbs had known for a long time: the violence of some immigrants against native French people. An association "against anti-white racism" was immediately created ... by Yoni Smadja, who launched a petition supported by Hachomer Hatzaïr and Alain Finkielkraut, who had changed his jacket and was now at the forefront of the "reaction".

On closer examination, however, we saw that the interests defended were always the same, and that the sudden interest shown in the "little white guy" was merely circumstantial. It was quite clear that, in French society today, the Jewish community was beginning to fear the massive presence of Muslim immigrants more and more than the extreme right, which had been covered in mud and rubbish for decades and around which a cordon sanitaire had been deliberately set up. This offensive was also a response to the anti-Zionist "provocations" of the French-Cameroonian comedian Dieudonné, who continued to attack the community with his sarcasm, despite the seventeen lawsuits brought against him by "anti-racist" associations. Down with the Blacks, then[294]!

---

[294]Dieudonné M'Bala M'Bala is a French actor and comedian of Cameroonian origin,

Le *Monde* launched the offensive with an article by Luc Bronner, who entitled his article of 10 March: *The spectre of anti-" white" violence, in* which we read that "the rioters express their hatred for the little French people they attack". Luc Bronner quoted the words of some of them, like Heikel: "I didn't go to the demonstration, I went to take some phones and beat people up. There were small groups running around, rioting. And in the middle, some clowns, the little French people with the faces of victims." With his gang, he claimed to have recovered about fifteen phones using violence. Heikel was one of the 700 to 1000 young people, according to the police, who came mainly from Seine-Saint-Denis and the northern districts of Paris to attack the students during the demonstration. The words of these youths combine economic explanations ("to make easy money"), playful ones ("the pleasure of beating up") and a mixture of racism and social envy ("to take revenge on the Whites"). The same situation was repeated dozens of times: one or two rioters approached a demonstrator and threatened to steal his or her mobile phone, MP3 player or wallet; if the prey resisted, or even accepted, he or she was beaten, thrown to the ground and kicked. Most of the time, other young men, up to ten of them, come along to savage the victim on the ground. In their language, they call the "little whites" "*bolos*"." A *bolos* is a cousin, a victim," explained Heikel, unable to explain, like the others, the origin of the word." It's as if he had "come and take my stuff" written on his forehead." The *skittles* look at the ground because they are afraid, because they are

---

well known and controversial in France. Dieudonné has been characterised by an active political militancy. Although initially aligned with leftist and anti-racist positions, in the early 2000s his positions swung towards views considered "anti-Semitic", giving rise to notable controversies that have intensified over the years. Politically, the comedian has moved closer to the postulates of the National Front in particular, and of the extreme right in general, embracing "negationist" positions. This situation has led to numerous legal problems and the banning of some of his shows by the French government of Emmanuel Valls. In those years at the beginning of the 21st century, he spread in France the American anti-Semitic thesis that Jews had played a fundamental role in the slave trade and their exploitation in the plantations of the American South, an idea that had been adopted and disseminated by Nation of Islam, but which had been refuted as fanciful by prominent figures in the American black world such as the academic Henry Louis Gates. Michel Wieviorka commented that Dieudonné's shows "attract the sympathy of a population that no longer has anything to do with classic anti-Semitism (nationalist, Christian, extreme right), at the risk of combining with it: people of sub-Saharan or North African origin, and sometimes West Indian, can identify with the hatred of those Jews suspected of having participated in their historical misfortune and of not wanting to talk about that past today, which is a fallacious construction". (Source wikipedia). [On the slave trade and other businesses, read Hervé Ryssen, *The Jewish Mafia*, 2008–2022] (NdT).

cowards," said another student." The "little whites" don't know how to fight and they don't run in packs. The risk of attacking them is less great." Other internet sources reported that the students, literally terrified, were astonished by the passivity of the riot police, who just laughed at their misfortunes. It is true that, at the slightest slip on their part, the police are often sanctioned and condemned for actions judged to be racist, which is probably why a certain lack of motivation has taken its toll on them.

This press article was a novelty in the media landscape, as usually the prevailing discourse is constantly denouncing a white, arrogant, petty, mean, sanctimonious, obtuse and racist society that must be replaced by a pluralistic society.

On Sunday, 17 April 2005, a television programme put the spotlight back on these incidents. Daniel Schneidermann had invited sociologist Michel Kokoreff and Yoni Smadja of the Hachomer Hatzaïr association, which had launched the petition against anti-white racism, to his studio. Some journalists, during the investigation, had acknowledged that the aggressors were mostly Blacks. Laurence Ulbrich, from the daily *France Soir*, was the only one who did not admit it publicly ("There were all kinds, there was not just one ethnic group"), while Cyprien Haese, from *e-télé*, *said* that he had "only seen Blacks". As we can see, the testimonies of human beings are often diverse and questionable, today as always.

It can be said that Bernard Stasi's 1984 book, *Immigration, a Fortune for France*, has aged very well, although as Daniel Cohn-Bendit aptly noted: "We must get used to this relative minor inconvenience."

4. Messianism

Messianism is the expectation of the messiah. It is the belief that a messiah will come to establish the kingdom of God on earth. Christians have recognised Jesus Christ as their messiah, but the Jews are still waiting for theirs. For them, the waiting for the messiah is confused with the process of the unification of humanity and the disappearance of national borders. When this happens, the people of Israel will finally be recognised by all as God's chosen people.

Messianic activism

Communism crystallised planetarian hopes for most of the 20th century[295]. However, after the Second World War, commitment to the communist ideal seemed hardly compatible with support for Israel. This was to be a determining factor in precipitating the break with Soviet communism for many planetarian intellectuals. As we have already seen, the USSR had quickly taken sides in favour of the Arab cause as early as 1949 and began to denounce Zionism in all its forms. This was a painful break for many left-wing intellectuals, as Marek Halter explained: "Marcuse, when I met him, was already famous and old. We wrote to each other for the first time in 1967, when the Six Day War in the Middle East had brought the Israeli-Arab conflict to the centre of left-wing disputes and polemics. There were then a few of us who supported the right of the state of Israel to exist and at the same time the Palestinian national claim. In intellectual circles, this seemed contradictory. We were labelled as Zionists and accused of being objectively the lackeys of US imperialism. To cushion the blow, to make ourselves heard, we needed the support of prestigious personalities. We thought of Marcuse. He responded immediately to the letter we wrote to him. As a Jew, faced with the almost hysterical anti-Israelism of the left, especially the extreme left that declared itself close to him, Marcuse felt the same unease as we did: heartbreak and solidarity[296]."

---

[295]Read Hervé Ryssen, *Jewish Fanaticism*.
[296]Marek Halter, *Un Homme, un cri*, Robert Laffont, Paris, 1991, p. 116.

In 1968, Marek Halter met Alain Krivine, the head of the revolutionary Communist League: "As a Jew, I think he understood our struggle and our motivations perfectly; and, despite the ideas he defended, he thought we might be right. Many Jews committed to the extreme left movements told me that they feared for the existence of Israel, adding ironically: "Now that there is no longer any danger to its physical existence, we can be anti-Israeli".

It was exactly what you could read in a book by another communist activist of that time, Guy Konopnicki: In 1967, "I confess, I was twice relieved when Israel went on the offensive. As a communist, because I could condemn imperialist aggression. As a Jew, more secretly, because I could not ignore that an Arab victory would mean a massacre. I have never forgotten those moments, nor who I was then, at a time when I knew nothing of Lacan and the division of the subject. In the room at 120 rue Lafayette, the historic headquarters of the PCF, I was taking the floor with Guy Hernier, as a serving Jew, to denounce the maleficence of Zionism before an assembly of young communist students and youth. It was the seventh day, as in Genesis! There was no longer any danger. But the day before, alas, the day before... On the sixth day, I confessed my relief, even my pride, to another schizophrenic like me at the time, my comrade Alexandre Adler. We celebrated laughing together at that victory of the class enemy[297]! "So the official discourse reflected nothing of the intimate convictions and anxieties of these militants. Do we not see here the same spirit as the Marranos, the Jews of Spain, to whom the Catholic Monarchs had left two options in 1492, conversion or exile? We know that those who had chosen conversion had continued for decades to practice Judaism in secret, and it was precisely for this reason that Spain had established, what many still refer to with horror, the Inquisition, whose mission was to set Catholics on the right path[298].

Support for Israel also shaped the reactions of many intellectuals during the first Gulf War that the Americans and their Western allies declared on Iraq in 1991. After Saddam Hussein's invasion of Kuwait, it was necessary to organise a large Western coalition to force him to retreat, as he threatened Israel and had the nerve to "identify with Nebuchadnezzar", the king of Babylon who had deported the Jews. His

---

[297]Guy Konopnicki, *La Faute des Juifs*, Balland, 2002, p. 121-122.
[298]On the Spanish Holy Inquisition, and many other controversial issues in history, we recommend Jean Sévillia's indispensable book: *Historiquement correct, pour en finir avec le passé unique*, Perrin, 2003. *Historiquement incorrect, pour finir avec le passé unique*, Ed. El Buey mudo, 2005.

downfall in 2003, after the second Gulf War, was scheduled. The "struggle for peace" was once again about bombing and war.

The commitment of intellectuals to great humanitarian causes is never entirely disinterested. The same is true of everything that the planetarian spirit creates and realises. It always has a political meaning, an ideological dimension and an activist zeal. The artist does not work for beauty or out of pure disinterest, but to influence and convince his contemporaries of an idea or an ideal that interests him." I wavered for a long time between painting and writing, Marek Halter acknowledged. Every time I tried to convey an idea or share an indignation through painting, it was a failure." Halter had to find another medium to express his ideas and try to influence world events.

His indignation managed to express itself in a particularly poignant way in relation to the painful chapter of the Second World War. Born into a Polish Jewish family, Marek Halter experienced the torments of exile in his childhood. His family fled first to the USSR when German troops advanced into Poland in 1940, and then in 1941 when they entered the USSR. The German offensive prompted the communist regime to organise the mass evacuation of Jews behind the Ural Mountains to protect them. It was thus in the homeland of socialism that Marek Halter spent most of his childhood. Arriving in Paris after the war, he moved in the circles of the Communist Youth and campaigned for the defence of Israel. In an important book of his bibliography, *The Fool and the Kings*[299], Marek Halter recalled his tireless struggle for peace in the Middle East. We have summarised it here because it is so characteristic of the committed intellectual.

In 1968, he travelled to Israel where he met Golda Meir. On his return to Paris, he founded a magazine. He then left for New York where he forged contacts with Jewish intellectuals who had turned away from the left because of the USSR's anti-Israeli positions, and in the process secured sponsorship for his newspaper. He returned to France via Israel to organise an international conference on peace in the Middle East and the defence of Israel within the left." We went to take the text to the Place des Vosges, to the Russian lady who had mimeographed all our leaflets from May 1968[300]." He then left for East Berlin with Bernard Kouchner (future gauleiter of Bosnia, ndr) to take part in a conference; he passed through Geneva before travelling again to Israel (the trip was

---

[299]Marek Halter, *Le Fou et les rois*, Albin Michel, Poche, 1976.
[300]The collusion between the revolutionaries of May 1968 and the very bourgeois Place des Vosges may seem surprising, but some solidarities—ethnic, religious, messianic—can sometimes overcome social boundaries.

paid for by Jean Daniel of *Le Nouvel Observateur*) and finally returning to Paris. A conference at Harvard University took him to the United States." One hour later, he was on the plane to New York. He then visited Herbert Marcuse in California, passing through Israel before returning to Paris "with the plan we had prepared and the list of personalities we wanted to invite" to an international conference in Rome." A phone call from Tel Aviv brought me back to reality." Among all those calls, there was one from Mendès France[301]: he wanted to see me".

His activism for peace was tireless: "Amsterdam, The Hague, Cologne, Frankfurt, where we set up the Socialist Study Group for Peace in the Middle East, part of the International Committee. Meetings, appointments, etc. We could only measure the usefulness of all these initiatives by what was reported in *Le Monde*, our media sounding board, or in *Le Nouvel Observateur.*" Conferences in Budapest, then in Bologna: "We had to borrow money for the trip from Daniel Jacoby, the Secretary General of the League of Human Rights who was with us." Turin, Rome, Florence, Venice, Paris. He was returning to Beirut: "We didn't go to Damascus. That very night we received a telegram: we were expected in Cairo the next day." I couldn't believe it. In my childhood memories as a Polish boy, Egypt was the country where, as the Easter legend told, the Hebrews had lived in slavery. They had built the pyramids there, before freeing themselves on the banks of the Nile and setting out for the Promised Land." We decided to return to Beirut. Back to Cairo, then to Paris, from where he took off again for Rome with Bernard Kouchner." In May 1972, we were back in Israel." I would return to Paris, take a plane to Geneva, and then return to Paris." The Eliav operation had failed; our meeting in London had been cancelled and the Bologna conference was cancelled. New York: "I have just had a talk with students on the subject: do we have to change man in order to change society, or do we have to change society in order to change man?" Paris, Israel, Paris again, then Buenos Aires: "I have been invited by the Argentine committee for peace in the Middle East" (there is still a lot to do, ndr)." The Argentinians did not hesitate to applaud the ideas I defended. It reassured them. So you could defend Israel and still be a leftist"." On 6 October 1973, I was in New York when I heard the news: war had once again broken out in the Middle East." Trip to Israel: "We passed through Paris where I found my mother ill. We delayed our departure. Sanae was relieved, as if she was afraid to return to Egypt. She flew

---

[301]Mendès-France, former Prime Minister of the 4th French Republic.

immediately to the United States, from where she phoned me later to tell me of her intention to return to Israel."

There it is. These were four years of Marek Halter's fast-paced life. If the question of war and peace in the Middle East were not so serious, one would think of one of those comic films that cinema sometimes produces, where the frenetic atmosphere sets a crazy pace for burlesque adventures. His unstoppable activity was not limited to the four years between the wars in the Middle East (1968–1973) and the struggle for peace. His humanitarian commitment continued. In his book *One Man, One Cry,* we read of the exploits of his boundless militant activity." On 16 November 1979, Andrei Sakharov's wife Elena Bonner phoned me from Moscow. The Olympic Games were to be held in the Soviet Union, and she asked me to organise a campaign for political prisoners[302]." Marek Halter had himself become a specialist in the defence of great humanitarian causes, for two years earlier he had already launched an 'appeal to boycott the football World Cup in Argentina'. It was estimated that "between 80,000 and 100,000 Jews had left Argentina since the military junta took power." It was therefore a question of repeating the same coup with the Olympic Games in the Soviet Union, guilty of preventing Jewish "*refuseniks*" from emigrating to Israel, and thus alerting world public opinion: "We had to take advantage of these games to make a great international demonstration in favour of human rights." We had to protest "against the indignity of a country that claimed the honour of receiving the Olympic message. The Moscow Olympics, like the World Cup in Buenos Aires, finally took place. But our campaign bore fruit: American athletes—at the request of President Jimmy Carter—and West German athletes decided to boycott." (February 1980).

Such is the life of Marek Halter. With such a busy schedule and such a hectic schedule around the world, it seems quite clear to us that the great writer can be considered a member of the "hyperclass" defined by Jacques Attali." Ever since I was old enough to fight, I have been fighting. And the more I fight, the more I am overwhelmed by my impotence[303] ", he confessed. The fight against oppression is in the Jews a legacy of the centuries of atrocious persecution they have suffered. Marek Halter's life is a life of suffering; the struggle for peace in the Middle East is his "cross", his burden for many years: "All suffering is unique for the one who suffers. Telling my life story, making my memory bleed would have served no purpose if it were not to explain

---

[302]Marek Halter, *Un Homme, un cri,* Robert Laffont, Paris, 1991, p. 118.
[303]Marek Halter, *Le Fou et les rois,* Albin Michel, Poche, 1976, p. 47.

my reactions in Israel and Palestine[304]." It is important to understand that the struggle for Israel is the struggle of all humanity: according to the Talmud, "there were six hundred thousand people at the foot of Mount Sinai when Moses gave the Law. Only one third were Jews. The second third belonged to the people of Jethro, chief of a nomadic people and Moses' father-in-law; the third third was composed of Egyptian slaves[305]." This means that God gave the Law not only to the Jewish people, but to all men, including the Goyim slaves, which is great news for us.

The life approach of Nobel Peace Prize laureate Elie Wiesel can be compared to that of Marek Halter. The similarities in the lives and actions of both are quite revealing of a militant attitude that ultimately forms the background of the cosmopolitan personality. Elie Wiesel's *memoirs* are interesting for understanding the great man's motivations and the planetarian mentality in general:

"For thirty years I have been travelling the continents to the point of exhaustion: by dint of speaking at conferences I have reached the point where I can no longer stand the sound of my voice[306]." Like Marek Halter, he travels the globe in all directions to preach peace and universal love, to try to influence the policies of the world's great powers: "We will always be on the same side against the traffickers of hatred. Our signatures are on the many petitions for human rights[307]." And he also added: "I saw myself roaming the Earth, going from city to city, from country to country, like the madman in Rabbi Nahman's tales, reminding men of what they are capable of, for good and for evil, drawing their gaze upon the countless ghosts huddled and lurking around us[308]."

"François Mitterrand's victory was received by me as an act of justice ... the capital is celebrating, especially in the Place de la Bastille. They celebrate the victorious rose. They sing, they dance... In the Pantheon, Roger Hanin conducts the ceremony. The countenance of the newly elected leader, solitary but majestic in front of the crypt of Jean Moulin,[309] is touching. Outside, it is pouring with rain. With his head

---

[304]Marek Halter, *Le Fou et les rois*, Albin Michel, Poche, 1976, p. 85.
[305]Marek Halter, *Un Homme, un cri*, Robert Laffont, Paris, 1991, p. 192.
[306]Elie Wiesel, *Mémoires, tome II*, Éditions du Seuil, 1996, p. 214.
[307]Elie Wiesel, *Mémoires, tome II*, Éditions du Seuil, 1996, p. 47.
[308]Elie Wiesel, *Mémoires, tome II*, Éditions du Seuil, 1996, p. 530.
[309]Jean Moulin (1899–1943) was a French politician and military officer, head of the National Council of the Resistance during the occupation of France by the armies of the Third Reich. Pursued by the Gestapo and the Vichy government, he was eventually

uncovered, the new president listens, immobile, stoic, to the fourth movement of Beethoven's Ninth Symphony conducted by Daniel Barenboim… Once contact between us was established, it turned out to be solid and fruitful. Mitterrand insists on receiving me every time I come to Paris. He repeats this to me[310]."

On the occasion of President Ronald Reagan's visit to Germany in 1985, at the invitation of Chancellor Helmut Kohl and during which he was scheduled to visit the German military cemetery at Bitburg, Elie Wiesel was outraged at what he considered an affront, addressing the American president: ""The Jewish children, Mr President, I saw them, they were thrown into the flames, they were still alive…" Did I succeed in convincing him? The television showed him overwhelmed, his features marked by grief, perhaps by fear too? Did I manage to make him see the suffering he was inflicting on countless victims, their families and friends? … Once the ceremony was over, I was dragged into the garden where he was caught up in the media whirlwind. I would never have believed that there would be so many accredited correspondents at the White House. Questions come from everywhere… Inside, in an elegant room, champagne is served. A Marine officer hands me a sealed envelope. I retreat to a corner to open it. A hastily written note: "I'm in the next office because I've come incognito; I can't show myself; I saw you on the screen a while ago; I'm proud of you." I recognise the handwriting: Jacques Attali." Attali was indeed a good friend, and Elie Wiesel confirmed this: "We see each other every time I am received by President Mitterrand because you have to pass through his office to get into his boss's office … My relationship with him is excellent[311]."

In 1986, Elie Wiesel was awarded the Nobel Prize. After the pomp of the ceremonies in Oslo, he gave lecture after lecture in Stockholm, Copenhagen, Jerusalem and Auschwitz, together with US Secretary of State Henry Kissinger. In Paris, he wrote: "Jacques Chirac presents me with the great red medal. Thanks to Helena Ahrweiler, Rector and Chancellor of the Universities of Paris, and Jacques Sopelza, President of the University of Paris I, I am awarded an honorary doctorate by the Sorbonne… The violinist Ivry Gitlis plays his new composition for us. Helena Ahrweiler is wonderful for her intelligence and erudition[312]."

---

captured, tortured and killed. Considered one of the heroes of the French Resistance, he is buried in the Panthéon in Paris.

[310] Elie Wiesel, *Mémoires, tome II*, Éditions du Seuil, 1996, p. 436.

[311] Elie Wiesel, *Mémoires, tome II*, Éditions du Seuil, 1996, p. 347, 402.

[312] Elie Wiesel, *Mémoires, tome II*, Éditions du Seuil, 1996, p. 415.

In Moscow, during the final period of the Soviet regime, Elie Wiesel seemed to speak as lord and master: 'Taking the floor in January 1990, during a conference on "global survival", he insisted on the role of education through memory. Again, I spoke as a Jew. I called on Mikhail Gorbachev to take a firmer stand against racism and anti-Semitism ... I asked the president of the USSR to open the archives of the infamous trials of the Stalinist era: I told him that we had a right to know how the Yiddish writers Peretz Markish and Der Nister lived through their imprisonment and execution[313]."

However, his initiatives were not always successful: "One intervention left a bitter taste in my mouth. It was the case of Abraham Sarfati. In the early 1980s, Tahar Ben Jelloun asked me to use my contacts in the United States to help this Jewish and communist political prisoner whom the King of Morocco refused to release. I spoke to people around President Jimmy Carter, to senators, to journalist friends; all efforts were in vain[314]."

In post-Soviet Romania, Elie Wiesel was received like a sovereign coming to give his orders: "Aurel Munteanu, Romania's permanent ambassador to the United Nations, escorts us on all our journeys. I express my indignation at the resurgence of anti-Semitism, traditional in his country... Received in a private audience by President Iliescu and his Prime Minister Petru Roman who ask for our help for Romania, especially in economic matters, especially from Washington, I reply that I will not. Why help a regime that tolerates hatred? ... But the starving children," says Petru Roman, "are you forgetting about them? I reply, "Don't make us responsible for their suffering; you are responsible! Make them silence the hatred in your country and the whole world will come to your aid". Still, President Iliescu seemed sincere to me. He ordered that the editors and editorialists of the anti-Semitic weeklies be prosecuted. He also invited me to accompany him to Sighet to show him my hometown[315]."

In 1990 in Oslo, Elie Wiesel organised a colloquium against hatred. The list of participants was impressive: President François Mitterrand, Czech President Vaclav Havel, former US President Jimmy Carter, Nelson Mandela: "To men and women of all origins, of all nations and

---

[313] Elie Wiesel, *Mémoires, tome II*, Éditions du Seuil, 1996, p. 216.

[314] Elie Wiesel, *Mémoires, tome II*, Éditions du Seuil, 1996, p. 120. Abraham Sarfati was the founder of the Moroccan communist party. Tahar Ben Jelloun, who felt close to him, wrote a book entitled *Le Racisme expliqué à ma fille* (*Racism explained to my daughter*).

[315] Elie Wiesel, *Mémoires, tome II*, Éditions du Seuil, 1996, p. 421.

of all confessions, we launch this appeal to unite your efforts to combat the hatred that threatens our humanity[316]..."

"It is strange, Wiesel wrote on the back of a page: the angrier I get, the more annoying I get, the more I voice my demands and discontent, the more I am applauded. I make shocking and hurtful speeches that should prevent the participants from swallowing their food, and yet they applaud and congratulate me ... after dinner. That's right, go figure[317]."

Like his friend Marek Halter, sociologist Edgar Morin put communism on the back burner after the Second World War. In his book *Reliances*, he explained: "Barbaric as it was, Stalinist communism embodied the future, universal peace, fraternity. I was one of those war communists who left the party after the war. I did not see that totalitarianism was shared by the two systems. For us, on the contrary, it was capitalism—what we called the bourgeois democracies—that represented the belly of the foul beast from which came fascism, war, death[318]." Certainly, his heroic commitment to resisting Nazism had given him a certain legitimacy to speak out against communism: "My family comes from the great Sephardic family of the Mediterranean. Morin is the pseudonym I had during the Resistance, albeit by mistake. I had chosen Manin, the character in Malraux's *La Esperanza*, but from the beginning they mistook him for Morin. I kept that pseudonym, I was even tempted to legalise it after the war, to change my surname. But I gave it up. Today, I live in ambiguity. On my papers, it says Nahoum alias Morin, Nahoum-Morin[319]." However, opposition to Soviet communism did not imply a frontal opposition to the supporters of Marxism in France, since the humanist ideas common to all of them made them agree on the essentials.

Unlike Marek Halter or Edgar Morin, the great French philosopher Jacques Derrida remained an orthodox Marxist to the end of his days. Died on 9 October 2004 of a cancer that had been eating away at him for months, he had been nominated for the Nobel Prize before his death. Derrida had begun publishing in the 1960s to become the "pope" of "politically correct" thought in American universities. His work of "deconstruction" is nothing less than an enterprise of scrapping Western metaphysics." There is no future without Marx", he wrote in 1993 in *Spectres of Marx*. On the day of his death, the communist daily *L'Humanité* devoted several pages to the work of this immense

[316]Elie Wiesel, *Mémoires, tome II*, Éditions du Seuil, 1996, p. 503.
[317]Elie Wiesel, *Mémoires, tome II*, Éditions du Seuil, 1996, p. 48.
[318]Edgar Morin, *Reliances*, Éditions de l'Aube, 2000, prefaced by Antoine Spire, p. 31.
[319]Edgar Morin, *Reliances*, Éditions de l'Aube, 2000, p. 25.

philosopher. His great reader and translator, Geoffrey Benington, explained the work and commitment of the philosopher, obsessed all his life with equality and humanism: "From the deconstruction of the text to his commitment in favour of Czech dissidents in 1982 which would lead him to spend two days in prison in Prague, through his fight against racist violence, his defence of the prisoner Mumia Abu-Jamal[320] at the International Parliament of Writers, of which he was vice-president, his support for the strikers of December 1995 and against the expulsion of undocumented immigrants in the name of the concept of hospitality, Jacques Derrida never ceased … to commit himself according to the intellectual modalities and forms that were peculiar to him[321]." In terms of form and style, the philosopher of "deconstruction" undoubtedly had one: his extraordinarily profound thought was rather poorly reflected by a prose that was too heavy. Indeed, the sentences of

---

[320]Mumia Abu-Jamal was an African-American sentenced to death for the murder of several white policemen in the US. Numerous committees in support of his cause were formed throughout the West.

[321] Here is an example of philosophical "deconstruction" applied to the concept of "Hospitality" by Jacques Derrida:

"J.D—(…) I regularly oppose unconditional hospitality, pure hospitality or hospitality of visitation—which consists in letting the visitor, the unexpected newcomer come without asking him for an account, without asking for his passport—to the hospitality of invitation. Pure or unconditional hospitality supposes that the newcomer is not invited where I am still the master in my house and where I control my house, my territory, my language, where he (according to the rules of conditional hospitality, on the contrary) should somehow submit to the rules in use in the place that receives him. Pure hospitality consists in leaving one's home open to the unexpected newcomer, who may be an intruder, even a dangerous intruder, capable of doing harm. This pure or unconditional hospitality is not a political or legal concept. Indeed, for an organised society that has its own laws and wants to retain sovereign control of its territory, its culture, its language, its nation, for a family, for a nation that has an interest in controlling its practice of hospitality, it is indeed necessary to limit and condition hospitality. Sometimes it is possible to do so with the best intentions in the world, because unconditional hospitality can also have perverse effects. However, these two forms of hospitality remain irreducible to each other. This distinction requires reference to the hospitality whose dream and sometimes anguished desire we preserve, that of exposure to (what) arrives. This pure hospitality, without which there is no concept of hospitality, is valid for the crossing of a country's borders, but it also plays a role in everyday life: when someone arrives, when love arrives, for example, we take a risk, we expose ourselves. In order to understand these situations, we have to maintain this horizon without horizon, this limitlessness of unconditional hospitality, always knowing that it is not possible to turn it into a political or legal concept. There is no place for this kind of hospitality in law and politics.

E.R.— In this matter you intervene in a deconstructive way." In Jacques Derrida, Élisabeth Roudinesco, *Y mañana qué...*Fondo de Cultura Económica, Buenos Aires, 2002, p. 69-70. (NdT).

the philosopher of "deconstruction" each had the weight of a sack of cement.

The philosopher Etienne Balibar was also marked for life by the powerful genius he encountered in his youth. Balibar was the author of another article in that homage edition of *L'Humanité*. He wrote: "I remember his arrival at the Ecole Normale Supérieure, where we were preparing to become attachés. He was preceded by his reputation as "the best phenomenologist in France". For us, Derrida was above all the author of the dazzling essay on the origin of Husserl's geometry, in which the question of the historicity of truth was taken away from the debates between sociologism and psychologism. I remember the publication in 1967 of the three manifestos of that new method that would later be called "deconstruction": *The Voice and the Phenomenon, Of Grammatology, Writing and Difference*. We shared the conviction that intellectuals and artists had a role to play in constituting a multiform and multipolar resistance against the control of state or market sovereignties that generate mass violence and feed back on it ... He had just set an example of constructive dialogue by joining forces with "his old enemy Habermas", to dismantle the propaganda machine of endless war against terrorism and rogue states."

Let us recall here that the communists had spoken out against the two US wars in Iraq in 1991 and 2003. It was for them, as the numerous leaflets distributed by them implied, a "racist and imperialist war". The evil Whites continued to want to dominate the planet, as in colonial times. In reality, the US army was multi-ethnic, while Saddam Hussein's troops were composed solely of Arabs. If there was any racism in those tragic events, it must be sought in the US administration, which was indeed quite monochromatic, as we have already seen. But this aspect is completely beyond the comprehension of simple communist militants, as it is for most of the Western masses.

To end this chapter of funeral eulogies for such an eminent personality, all that is missing are the words of a personage which we reproduce below: "In his work, Jacques Derrida tried to find the free gesture that is at the origin of all thought. He shared the same passion for Greek and Jewish thought, philosophy and poetry. A thinker of the universal, Jacques Derrida saw himself as a citizen of the world. He will be remembered as an inventor, a discoverer, an extraordinarily prolific teacher." Just as President Valéry Giscard d'Estaing or Minister Raymond Barre had praised Jean-Paul Sartre in their time, Jacques Chirac[322]—the author of these lines—embodied once again from his

---

[322]Jacques Chirac was still President of the Republic in 2004.

eminent position the fraternal salute of liberalism to militant Marxism. How not to think of George Orwell's novel, *1984*, which describes the methods of totalitarian society: Goldstein the dissident, Goldstein the insubmissive, Goldstein the rebel who embodies clandestine resistance, is received in the presidential office and respectfully greets Big Brother. In this case, we have Big Brother congratulating Goldstein on all his work[323]. In the totalitarian system imagined by Orwell, resistance is in fact nothing more than a fictitious opposition organised by the system itself, which makes it possible to locate and suppress opponents. With the Soviet Union dismantled, cultural Marxism, nested and financed within the democracies, seems to play effectively the role of a meeting place for all dissatisfactions and frustrations.

A remarkable characteristic of Jacques Derrida was that he felt an instinctive distrust of organic communities other than his own: "I have always distrusted the cult of identity, as well as the communitarian, which is so often associated with it. I constantly try to remind myself of the increasingly necessary dissociation between the political and the territorial... I do not hesitate to support, however modestly, causes such as those of feminists, homosexuals, colonised peoples, up to the point where the logic of the claim seems to me potentially perverse or dangerous. Communitarianism or state-nationalism are the most obvious examples of this risk, and therefore of this limit to solidarity[324]."

These statements are very enlightening and entirely symptomatic. This is how many intellectuals supported the immigration of settlers, right up to the day when these immigrants of Muslim origin became aggressive towards the Jewish community. The major ideological shift in planetarian thinking in France can be dated to the year 2000. Indeed, after the second Palestinian Intifada, millions of young Arabs in France began to express very clearly their solidarity with the Palestinian people and their hostility towards the Jews. It was this that caused philosophers like Alain Finkielkraut to take refuge in the skirts of French patriots after having covered them in manure and rubbish, and to support the creation of an association "against anti-white racism". The Jews, who until then had been systematically assimilated to the other oppressed

[323]Read the intriguing work published under the name of J.B.E Goldstein, *Théorie et pratique du collectivisme oligarchique*, original translation published under the title *Теория и практика олигархического коллективизма*. 1948, Vettaz Edition Limited, 2021. (*Theory and practice of oligarchic collectivism*) (NdT).
[324]Jacques Derrida, Élisabeth Roudinesco, *Y mañana qué...* Fondo de Cultura Económica, Buenos Aires, 2002, p. 31.

minorities, to these poor immigrants without defence, as the "League against racism and anti-Semitism" proclaimed, were henceforth to be assimilated to the West and to civilisation. It was then that the values of the Republic and the civic spirit of the French were invoked to combat aggressive Islamism throughout the world. In short, one is reactionary or progressive according to the circumstances, and above all according to the objective interests that invariably correspond to the interests of the planetarian cause and of one's own community. For while one abhors nations and the tribal spirit, encouraging uprootedness, the rejection of traditions and the past, one assiduously cultivates "Memory" and the community spirit for oneself.

Jacques Derrida was born in 1930 in El-Biar into a Jewish family in Algeria. Like the Pole Marek Halter, he seemed to be truly under the influence of an imperious vital need to act through tireless activism in defence of all the causes he believed to be just. In the book of dialogues with the psychologist Elisabeth Roudinesco, his motivations appeared more clearly: "I think I can say that my vigilance was tireless, from the age of 10, with regard to racism and anti-Semitism."

"You say in *The Backstreet* that you didn't want to belong to the Jewish community. You detested the word community, just as today you detest ethnicism, communitarianism, as much as I do. On the other hand, and with regard to this triple identity (Jewish/Maghrebi/French), he speaks of a dissociated identity... Today I find it difficult not to reflect on this question, both in order to deviate from the communitarian temptation and to preserve something—a remnant—of a sort of "feeling of Jewishness"..." Derrida replied: "In me, this "feeling" is obscure, abysmal, above all unstable. Contradictory. (As if a depth of memory authorised me to forget, perhaps to deny the most archaic, to distract myself from the essential. This active, even energetic distraction diverts me to the point that sometimes I also find it inconsistent, accidental, superficial, extrinsic.) Nothing counts for me more than my Jewishness which, however, in so many respects, counts so little in my life. (I know that such statements seem contradictory, even devoid of common sense. But they would only be so in the way of seeing of one who could not say "I", in one piece, but by expelling from himself all otherness, all heterogeneity, all division, even all altercation, all "explanation" with himself. I am not alone with myself, no more than another, I am not one alone. An "I" is not an indivisible atom) ... I have indeed cultivated withdrawal, I even keep myself alert to every Jewish community. But in the face of the slightest sign of anti-Semitism, I do not and will never deny my Jewishness[325]."

This was what he had already declared in 1992 in *Puntos suspensivos*, where he said he felt in his innermost self a "desire for integration into the non-Jewish community, a mixture of painful fascination and distrust, with a nervous vigilance and an exhausting aptitude for perceiving the signs of racism, both in its most discreet configurations and in its noisiest denials[326]." We continually and invariably encounter this obsession in all planetarian intellectuals, whether it is declared and explicit, or underlying and ambiguous.

Shmuel Trigano also followed in that tradition of post-war French intellectuals, whose messianic passions partly explain today's enthusiasm for universalism and the planetarian ideal. After the terrible ordeal of the Holocaust, Trigano explained, "a specifically French-Jewish thought" emerged in Paris in what was called in the 1960s–1970s "the School of Paris", with intellectuals such as Edmond Jabes, Emmanuel Lévinas, Jacques Derrida, Georges Perec and Maurice Blanchot." Only in this place, in France, where the memory and the search for the universal were kept alive, could European Judaism be reborn so quickly after emerging from the darkness of the night." This School aimed to make the spiritual message of Judaism audible in the terms of contemporary thought." The Holocaust forced the Jewish conscience to take responsibility before humanity. The genocide compromised modern man and thus urged Jewish consciousness to produce a response to deficient modernity, a compensation. By securing their uniqueness, Jews were thus the witnesses of the human. The aim was not to erase the specificity of Jewish martyrdom into an abstract universal, but to regard it as the centre of universal human destiny."

Thus, if we understand Shmuel Trigano correctly, the specificity of Jewish thought must become a reference for the whole world. He added in his incomparable style: "All modern men become "Jews" in some way, registering themselves under the sign of the letter, and the Jews become men, but they no longer have a place to dwell in the City as Jews, that is to say under their name of Man[327]." On the contrary, explained Trigano, "in Zionism, it is access to humanity (and no longer to citizenship) that is at stake, the central challenge (since it is this humanity that fundamentally denies anti-Semitism to the Jew,

---

[325]Jacques Derrida, Élisabeth Roudinesco, *Y mañana qué...* Fondo de Cultura Económica, Buenos Aires, 2002, p. 123-125, 207.
[326]Jacques Derrida, *Points de suspensions, Entretiens*, Galilée, 1992, p. 130.
[327]Shmuel Trigano, *L'Idéal démocratique*, Editions Odile Jacob, 1999, p. 101, 115.

dissociating him from his citizenship without accepting him in his Jewishness, which is his form of humanity)." The 338 pages of the book teach us how to correctly handle the various concepts, perhaps a little difficult to grasp for those less familiar with the ideas of this new scholasticism, "the School of Paris".

"All the limits to the post-war restoration of Jewish uniqueness now challenge the Jewish world, which has posed the question of the Jew to Man, to ask the question to itself, and to pose the question of Man to men. The Jewish question is ultimately the question of Man that the Jews pose to men[328]." Shmuel Trigano did not stop there: even "Sartre has not thought of this inversion of his proposal which has become proverbial: "The Jew is a man whom other men regard as a Jew[329]" ... It would be the beginning of a new era", the philosopher concluded brilliantly.

The Jew is humanity, and humanity is the Jew. This was already the opinion of Elie Wiesel, who wrote in his *Memoirs*: "It is so and nothing can be done about it: the enemy of the Jews is the enemy of humanity ... By killing the Jews, the murderers undertook the murder of all humanity ... The Jewish tragedy of Auschwitz has affected all humanity, but it was only after Hiroshima that we have become aware of it. In that sense, one can think today that the whole world has become (metaphorically) Jewish. In other words, there has been a total fusion between the Jewish condition and the human condition[330]."

In his book *The Human Resource*, the financier Samuel Pisar recounted some interesting and evocative memories of his view of the world. The little immigrant from Poland was now a very rich man accustomed to receptions at the Palace of Versailles: "I had already been to Versailles three times to attend three different soirees, each one more beautiful than the last. We had celebrated capitalism, then communism, and finally Zionism. David Rockefeller, owner of the famous Chase Manhattan Bank, a pillar of Wall Street, had reserved the Hall of Mirrors for an extraordinary dinner in honour of his international board of directors. The crème de la crème of world industry and finance were present... David Rockefeller was returning from Moscow where I had accompanied him. There, I saw him participate in an unconventional event: the inauguration of the first branch in the Soviet Union of the Chase Bank, which was opening its offices on Karl-Marx Avenue...

---

[328]Shmuel Trigano, *L'Idéal démocratique*, Editions Odile Jacob, 1999, p. 97, 303.
[329]Quoting Jean-Paul Sartre, *Reflections on the Jewish Question*, Seix Barral, Barcelona, 2005.
[330] Elie Wiesel, *Mémoires, tome II*, Éditions du Seuil, 1996, p. 72, 319, 135.

My third evening at Versailles was that of Baron Guy de Rothschild, reigning prince over Europe's most celebrated industrial and financial empire, who hosted that dinner. The Rothschild reception staff were impeccably dressed and circulated in wigs in the gallery of Les Battles. I savoured the paradox: it was in this warlike atmosphere that I was to deliver the speech introducing the evening's debate on the subject I had christened "The Weapons of Peace". And, by way of example, on the possibilities of coexistence and cooperation between Israel and the Arab world. In front of the magnificent frescoes of the French marshals of history who watched us, I was thinking, as I spoke, of the current marshals, those of Israel: Dayan, Weizmann, Sharon, who themselves worshipped arms and war for the survival of their homeland, the Jewish state[331]."

As we can see, the financiers of socialism sometimes have thoughts far removed from the concerns of their European constituents. As in the case of Guy Konopnicki, we see that beautiful speeches do not necessarily correspond to the thoughts of the speaker. Although he despises the past, Samuel Pisar appreciates and enjoys the rooms of the palace of Versailles; although he works for peace, he is also a militant supporter of Israel and its generals. What transcends these contradictions—and we shall see in another chapter that there are others—is faith; a messianic faith that sustains his planetarian hopes: "As I despise the unspeakable ravages of the past, so I believe in an unlimited future for the intelligence of pacified man. Neither suffering, nor fear, nor horror, have shaken this faith in me. An absolute faith[332]." With this declaration of faith he brought his book to a close.

George Soros is animated by the same messianic faith as Samuel Pisar. For him, life is a struggle. He advocates the triumph of "the universal open society" which must succeed the system that collapsed in the East and which "represented the quintessence of the closed society." This struggle involves continuous campaigns to "sensitise[333] "the population: "We are actively contributing to the training of teachers and the publication of new school textbooks to replace Marxist-Leninist works. We are printing millions of books every year in Russia, and I will continue our efforts to keep alive the great newspapers, i.e. the

---

[331]Samuel Pisar, *La Ressource humaine*, Jean-Claude Lattès, 1983, p. 20-21.
[332]Samuel Pisar, *La Ressource humaine*, Jean-Claude Lattès, 1983, p. 379.
[333]This term is preferable to "propaganda", the latter being perhaps too marked by totalitarian reminiscences.

cultural press which played such a great role in the history of that country[334]."

"Did the fact that you are a Jew have anything to do with your adherence to the open society? When you see how Jews react to persecution, you realise that they tend to look for one or two ways out, always the same ones. Either they transcend their problems by orienting themselves towards something universal, or they identify with their oppressors and try to be like them. I came from an assimilationist family and chose the first way. A third possibility is Zionism, the founding of a nation where Jews are in the majority." George Soros could have explicitly mentioned the communist path in which Jews played such an "eminent" role, but we will see in another chapter how everything seems to indicate that they turned the page and that it is preferable, on this point in history, not to appeal too much to "memory"." I am proud to be a Jew. I believe that Jewish genius exists. Just look at the success of Jews in science, economic life and the arts. It is the result of their efforts to transcend their minority status and achieve something universal. Jewishness is an essential element of my personality and, as I said, I am very proud of it. I am also aware that I carry in me a part of Jewish utopia in my way of thinking. My foundations are linked to that tradition. So, to answer your initial question—do my views have anything to do with my Jewish heritage? —I would say yes, for sure. And I don't see why that would be a problem."

Planetarian expectations seem here to be determined by Jewishness: "As a teenager, I dreamed of being a superman. I have already spoken of my messianic impulses335." And it is indeed this messianic faith that invariably animates the planetarian spirits and leads them to the tireless activism that characterises each of their actions. Having made his fortune, George Soros now has the means to widely influence the course of history: "I am literally fascinated by history, which I have a deep desire to influence." They never stop. In this militant people, all life is conditioned by this absolute faith in the necessity of a planetarian unification to finally see the prophecies come true.

The religious sources of globalism

---

[334]George Soros, *Le Défi de l'argent*, Plon 1996, p. 115.
[335]George Soros, *Le Défi de l'argent*, Plon 1996, p. 186.

The philosophy of the Enlightenment, which had gradually permeated the ruling classes of Ancien Régime society throughout the 18th century, had finally led to the fall of the monarchy and the establishment of the Republic. By proclaiming the equality of all human beings, the French Revolution had laid the political foundations for the first step towards the establishment of a better world. France thus became "the country of human rights": no longer a country inhabited by French people, in a vulgarly tribal manner, but a nation with a universalist vocation whose historic mission would henceforth be to work for universal brotherhood. In these times, France is the modern laboratory where the multicultural, multiethnic and multiracial society must be built; it is an example for all humanity before the general dissolution of all nations; through it the destiny of humanity is realised.

But the 18th century Age of Enlightenment, the French Revolution and the establishment of the Republic, marked by the seal of equality and the anti-religious struggle, represented for the Jews very different things, more than just political changes. This is what the famous philosopher Emmanuel Levinas said in his essay *Difficult Freedom*: "In the Jewish quarters of Eastern Europe, France was the country where prophecies were realised336." In all the countries of Europe where the liberal ideas of the revolution prevailed throughout the 19th century, the governments granted Jews the same rights as Europeans. It was the beginning of the integration of Jewish communities into European society and, for them, the beginning of a prodigious social, financial and political ascent.

We often find in planetarian authors this taste for prophecy, this absolute faith in the accuracy of their analyses, as if they were based on a religious faith. Emmanuel Levinas has been able to shed some light on this question. The ancient prophecies would seem to be the intellectual leaven of our modern philosophers:

"It is indeed possible to group the promises of the prophets into two categories: political and social. The injustice and alienation introduced by the arbitrary dimension of political powers into every human endeavour will disappear; but social injustice, the domination exercised by the rich over the poor, will disappear at the same time as political violence. The Talmudic tradition, represented by Rabbi Chiya ben Abba, speaking in the name of Rabbi Yochanan, sees in the messianic times the simultaneous realisation of all these political and social promises ... As for the future world, it seems to be situated on

---

[336]Emmanuel Lévinas, *Difficile liberté*, Albin Michel, 1963, édition de 1995, p. 330, 334.

another plane. Our text defines it as "the privilege of the one who awaits you". It is, in principle, a personal and intimate order, external to the achievements of history which await a humanity on the way to unite in a collective destiny … There is a contrary opinion on this point, that of Samuel, who states: "Between this world and the messianic age, there is no difference except the end of the 'yoke of nations'—of violence and political oppression". A well-known text, which Maimonides will take up again, trying, for his part, to make a synthesis between Samuel's opinion and that of Rabbi Yochanan337."

The Hebrew prophecies thus promise us the progress of humanity towards a world without frontiers, unified, and parallel to that, the suppression of social inequalities. Peace will reign over the world, abundance will flow from the earth and men will live from the air, free and happy, in perfect equality. Of course, we recognise here the primitive sources of Marxism as well as those which today inspire our planetarian ideology at the beginning of the third millennium and which, through publishing, makes so many of our fellow citizens dream.

Human liberation can only be conceived on a human and global scale. And this idea, as the philosopher Emmanuel Levinas confirmed, "the very idea of a fraternal humanity, united in the same destiny, is a Mosaic revelation[338]." It is through the destruction of the old nations that the divine promises will be fulfilled and that Israel will finally be able to lead the whole of humanity towards happiness and prosperity: "[Our] old texts teach precisely the universalism purified of all particularism of one's own land, of all memory of what has been planted. They teach the human solidarity of a nation united by ideas[339] ", wrote Levinas, who seemed to have forgotten the lesson of the Tower of Babel.

"We have a reputation for believing we are the chosen people and this reputation does a lot of damage to that universalism. The idea of a chosen people should not be regarded as pride. It is not a consciousness of exceptional rights, but of exceptional duties. It is the attribute of moral conscience itself. A conscience that knows it is at the centre of the world and for it the world is not homogeneous: insofar as I am always the only one who can answer the call, I am irreplaceable in taking on responsibilities. The choice is a surplus of obligations for

---

[337]Emmanuel Levinas, *Difficult Freedom, Essays on Judaism*. Ediciones Lilmod, Buenos Aires, 2004, p. 283, 284.
[338]Emmanuel Lévinas, *Difficile liberté*, Albin Michel, 1963, 1995, p. 310.
[339]Emmanuel Levinas, *Difficult Freedom, Essays on Judaism*. Ediciones Lilmod, Buenos Aires, 2004, p. 254.

which the "I" of moral conscience is enunciated 340... The Jews are necessary for the future of a humanity which, knowing that it is saved, has nothing more to hope for. The presence of the Jews reminds conformists of all kinds that all is not well in the best of all worlds. [341]." It is a strange revelation for an intellectual to naively declare that the Jews are on earth to prevent other peoples from living by their own standards.

The discourse is all the more curious when one considers that, paradoxically, the precepts that one tries to instil in others do not seem to apply to the Jewish people: "Israel equals humanity, but humanity contains something of the Inhuman and so Israel refers to Israel, to the Jewish people, to its language, to its books, to its law, to its land." Israel draws its strength from its past and its memory. It is in the clear awareness of existing as a united people, rooted in its traditions and religion, that it can continue to thrive among the nations, without fear of disappearing through assimilation or miscegenation.

This is the explanation of such a paradox: "Contrary to national histories, Israel's past, as an ancient civilisation, is fixed above the nations like a starry sky. We are the living ladder to heaven342... This "setting apart from the nations"—of which the Pentateuch speaks— finds its realisation in the concept of Israel and its particularism. It is a particularism that conditions universality. And it is more precisely a moral category than Israel as a historical fact, even if historical Israel has in fact remained faithful to the concept of Israel and has assigned to itself in morality responsibilities and obligations which it demands of no one, but which sustain the world ... Judaism promises a reconquest, a joy of self-possession in the universal trembling, a radiance of eternity through corruption343." Obviously, corruption refers to the other nations of the world who are asked to forget their past, their traditions and their religion in order to facilitate the advent of the prophecies and thus conform to the laws of the chosen people.

Emmanuel Levinas' words had clear similarities in both substance and form with those of Jacob Kaplan, the Chief Rabbi of the Central Consistory. In *The True Face of Judaism344*, the latter set forth a vision that reflected the same messianic faith in the unification of the world

[340]Emmanuel Levinas, *Difficult Freedom, Essays on Judaism*. Ediciones Lilmod, Buenos Aires, 2004, p. 199.
[341]Emmanuel Lévinas, *Difficile liberté*, Albin Michel, 1963, 1995, p. 261.
[342]Emmanuel Lévinas, *Difficile liberté*, Albin Michel, 1963, 1995, p. 280, 288.
[343]Emmanuel Levinas, *Difficult Freedom, Essays on Judaism*. Ediciones Lilmod, Buenos Aires, 2004, p. 111, 249.
[344]Jacob Kaplan, *Le vrai visage du Judaïsme*, Stock, 1987.

and in universal Peace." Of messianism, he wrote, I remember the most famous passage: "The wolf shall dwell with the lamb, the leopard shall lie down with the kid; the calf, the beast of prey, and the fatling together, and a little child shall lead them. The cow and the bear shall graze, their young shall lie down together; and the lion shall eat straw like the ox. A sucking child shall play over the cobra's den, and a weanling shall stretch out his hand over the viper's den. Nothing evil or vile shall be done in all my holy mountain; for the earth shall be full of devotion to Yahweh, as the waters cover the sea345ᵃ"." It is evidently a picture of the relations that will be established between the nations, happy to maintain union and concord between them," Kaplan added.

To achieve this result, humanity has had a reference text at its disposal since 1948: "For the advent of an era without threat to the human race, we can make use of the universal declaration of the Rights of Man," continued Rabbi Kaplan. It is essentially a work of justice, and since it is based on justice, it is a work of peace. The role played by President René Cassin in the drafting of this declaration is known to all of us [the public of the rue de la Victoire synagogue in Paris, ndlr], but the difficulties he had to deal with in this regard are not known to us all 346... René Cassin himself acknowledged this in a footnote to his lecture in which he stated: "the Talmudists were the first to maintain that the precepts of the Decalogue constituted the recognition of man's rights to life, to property, to religion...". Respect for the Universal Declaration of Human Rights is such an imperative obligation that it implies a duty for all to contribute to all actions aimed at its universal and comprehensive implementation." All humanity must submit. It could be said that "Human Rights" are the privileged tool to achieve the divine promises347.

Regarding the close links between democratic ideas and Judaism, Shmuel Trigano confirmed this by mentioning that medieval Jewish communities were governed by a charter of rights and duties that bound

---

[345]Jacob Kaplan, *Le vrai visage du Judaisme*, Stock, 1987. *Communication à l'académie des sciences morales et politiques, février 1985.*[a: Isaiah, XI, 6–9, Biblia Israelita Nazarena, 2011. On Bibliatodo.com for the English versions of the Bible].

[346]René Cassin was the Secretary General of the Universal Israelite Alliance. In 1945, General de Gaulle appointed him head of the Council of State. His remains rest in the Panthéon, the temple of the great men of the French Republic.

[347]"Judaism can only survive to the extent that it is recognised and propagated by laypeople who, outside of all Judaism, are the promoters of the common life of men", Emmanuel Levinas, *Difficult Freedom, Essays on Judaism*. Ediciones Lilmod, Buenos Aires, 2004 p. 244.

the members to each other: "The Hebraic idea of covenant is thus one of the capital sources of modern democracy348."

As far as social justice is concerned, Jacob Kaplan continued, "the teachings of Judaism are very clear: Israel stands for social equality, not only because it has suffered more than anyone else from injustice and still suffers from it where civilisation has not yet arrived or is in retreat, but because its doctrine, permeated with the love of humanity and the passion for justice, remains, today as of old, the most emotional of protests raised in the name of God and conscience against the abuse of force and the violation of law 349... The world will benefit from stability through the harmony that will be established by the harmony that will be established in the world. The world will benefit from stability because of the harmony that will be established between peoples through respect for justice, and because of that respect, social injustice, malnutrition, misery, slums, selfishness and indifference to the fate of others will disappear. Of course, it will take a long time to achieve this goal. Judaism knows this350."

The unification of nations can only be achieved by the eradication of old prejudices: "For the believing Jew, to abolish racism and prepare for the advent of human brotherhood is to put into practice the biblical doctrine of the unity of mankind351." Unfortunately, it is all too often the case that Judaism is "the target of the enemies of civilisation". This is because "in every age, in every country, Israel, persecuted, martyred, has embodied the principles that were to triumph with the progress of the human spirit. When Nimrod persecuted Abraham, the founder of our religion, guilty for him of not prostrating himself before false gods, which of the two represented civilisation: Nimrod, the cruel and idolatrous tyrant, or Abraham, the peaceful and virtuous shepherd? When in the time of Judas Maccabeus, Antiochus IV Epiphanes wanted to impose on the Jews the frivolous gods and dissolute morals of Greece, with whom did the future of civilisation lie? With the Greeks, light-hearted, mocking, amoral, or with the Jews, serious, sober and dignified352?"

[348]Shmuel Trigano, *L'Idéal démocratique*, Editions Odile Jacob, 1999, p. 88.
[349]*Cahier de la Voix d'Israel*, 1937, in Jacob Kaplan, *Le vrai visage du Judaïsme*, Stock, 1987.
[350]Jacob Kaplan, *Le vrai visage du Judaisme*, Stock, 1987. *Communication à l'académie des sciences morales et politiques, février 1985*.
[351]Jacob Kaplan, *Le vrai visage du Judaïsme*, Stock, 1987. *Sermon delivered at the synagogue rue de la Victoire on 20 April 1967*.
[352]Jacob Kaplan, *Le vrai visage du Judaïsme*, Stock, 1987, chapter "*Racisme et Judaïsme*".

The belief in the superiority of the Jewish people is evident here, but make no mistake: the Jewish people are not racist, they cannot be racist. As Elie Wiesel wrote, "in all lectures in which I address Jewish issues, I emphasise the ethic of Judaism which, by definition, denies racism. A Jew cannot be a racist; a Jew has a duty to combat any system that regards the other as an inferior being. That is why anyone— regardless of colour, origin or social status—can become a Jew: he must simply accept the Law353."

If in the history of the world, no people has been so martyred as the people of God," wrote Rabbi Kaplan, "and if every time civilisation pauses or barbarism rears its head, the members of the Jewish community are the first victims of the reaction, it is because Judaism is in the vanguard of civilisation." In the exhortations of the fifth book of Moses, it is written: "For you are a people consecrated to Yahweh your Elohim: of all the peoples of the earth Yahweh your Elohim has chosen you to be his special people354." Israel is the chosen of the Lord." According to the beautiful image of one of our most celebrated theologians of the Middle Ages, Juda Halevi, the Jewish community is, by God's will, the seed which will germinate future humanity ... So that the ideas of Judaism, strengthened by the power of truth and indestructible by violence, spread throughout the world to become the spiritual food of civilised peoples."

It is therefore clear that, without the Jewish people, the European peoples, as well as the other peoples of the world, are incapable of rising to the level of civilisation. To which the great Rabbi Kaplan added: "No earthly force will impede the evolution of humanity as God intended,

---

[353]Elie Wiesel, *Mémoires, tome II*, Éditions du Seuil, 1996, p. 217. [Note here that although in theory Judaism is open to all, in reality it is extremely difficult for a Goy to be accepted into Judaism. Any rabbi will confirm this to you—or not. But there is also an alternative for goyim to adopt Noachism (https://noahideworldcenter.org/). Emmanuel Levinas explained it this way: "Traditional Jewish thought otherwise provides the framework for conceiving of a universal human society, embracing the righteous of all nations and of all faiths, with whom ultimate intimacy is possible—that which the Talmud formulates, reserving to all the righteous participation in the world to come ... With someone who is not a Jew practising morality, with the Noachide, a Jew can communicate as intimately and religiously as with a Jew. The rabbinic principle that the righteous of all nations share in the world to come does not simply express an eschatological perspective. It affirms the possibility of this ultimate intimacy, beyond the dogmas affirmed by one or the other, the intimacy without reserve. Therein lies our universalism. In the cave where the patriarchs and our mothers rest, the Talmud lays Adam and Eve to rest: it is for all humanity that Judaism came", *Difficult Freedom, Essays on Judaism*, p. 192, 199.
[354]*Deutoronomy VII, 6*, Israelite Nazarene Bible, 2011.

no power of this world will be able to turn us away from the task He has assigned to us. We have an unshakeable certainty, founded both on the biblical promises and on the experience of the remote and recent past. That time will certainly come, called by this voice which, like a cry of invincible hope, has already traversed centuries and millennia, and which will traverse, if necessary, other centuries, other millennia, but which will eventually be heard by all: "In that day Yahweh will be the only One, and His Name will be the only Name355[a]"." Let us recall in passing the words of Daniel Cohn-Bendit: "The immigration society is now a reality, and no power in the world can turn it back356." Such convictions seem to be the underlying motivation of many intellectuals, artists and politicians of our time.

We can now realise to what extent Marxist ideology has to some extent secularised the messianic expectation. In this sense, George Steiner was able to present Marxism from the point of view of biblical prophecy: "Marxism is at bottom an impatient Judaism. The Messiah has taken too long to come, or more precisely, not to come at all. It is up to man to establish the kingdom of justice on this earth, here and now. Love must be exchanged for love, justice for justice, preached Karl Marx in his manuscripts of 1844, in which the phraseology of the Psalms and the prophets is transparently echoed. In the egalitarian programme of communism, there is little left that has not already been relentlessly preached by Amos, when he announced God's anathema against the rich and their abomination of property. Where Marxism triumphed, even and especially in its most brutal forms, it fulfilled that vengeance of the wilderness upon the city so manifest in Amos and the other prophetic and apocalyptic texts of social retribution357." The theme of revenge is indeed recurrent in the mental universe of the supporters of globalism; we shall see the dramatic consequences it had in Bolshevik Russia.

The proximity of George Steiner's thought to that of Levinas or Rabbi Kaplan is still clearly perceptible in the idea he had of the role of Judaism: "So the Jews have thrice called for individual and social perfection, they have been the night watchmen who do not ensure repose, but, on the contrary, awaken man from the sleep of self-esteem and ordinary comfort (Freud woke us even from the innocence of

[355]Jacob Kaplan, *Le vrai visage du Judaisme*, Stock, 1987, Sermon of 22 May 1950. a : *Zechariah, XIV, 9*, Bible Kadosh Israelite Messianic.
[356]Daniel Cohn-Bendit, *Xénophobies*, Hamburg, 1992, Grasset, 1998, p. 51.
[357]George Steiner, *De la Bible à Kafka*, 1996, Bayard, 2002, for the French edition.

sleep[358].)". Again, the same echoes in the words of Daniel Cohn-Bendit when he told us, "The contract signed with the multicultural society must prevent us from becoming too homely and comfortable, traditionalist and complacent in our familiar sphere359."

"It is not the deicidal people whom Christianity persecuted to the limit of extinction during the Middle Ages, it is "the maker of God", the spokesman who has not ceased to remind mankind what it could become, what it must become for man to be truly man ... With the complete physical extinction of all Jews from the face of the earth, the demonstration and proof of the existence of God would collapse, and the Church would lose its raison d'être: the Church would sink360." Once again, the idea that other peoples are somehow underdeveloped is quite clearly expressed. The Jewish people are placed above the other nations who must conform to their principles in order to accede in their turn to the rank of humanity.

We now better understand the ecstatic visions of the philosopher Pierre Levy in *World Philosophie*, a book that is nevertheless intended to be profane and addressed to the general public: "Men and women, rich and poor, atheists and believers, Buddhists and Catholics, people here and people there, why not love each other? That's it! Right now, right now... Let's help the poor, let's help the rich, it makes no difference. We need to learn that there is no social hierarchy, neither above nor below, and that all those distinctions don't matter. This could really contribute to changing society." Indeed, Levy continued, "the idea of social class is a dead end, just like the idea of nationhood361." Doesn't this translate the prophecies exactly?

Alain Finkielkraut was also enthusiastic about the European and Western public's receptiveness and readiness for these new ideas: "The postmodern subject wishes to draw inspiration from that" freedom from the sedentary forms of existence" which, according to Levinas, constitutes the Jewish definition of the human362." Hence "the contemporary enthusiasm for the Jewish theme of exile". Instead of the word "exile", we humbly suggest to Alain Finkielkraut that it might be preferable to use another term, that of "transhumance", for example,

[358]George Steiner, *Pasión intacta. A través de ese espejo, en en enigma*, Ediciones Siruela, Madrid, 1997, p. 447.
[359]Daniel Cohn-Bendit, *Xénophobies*, Hamburg, 1992, Grasset, 1998, p. 158.
[360]George Steiner, *De la Bible à Kafka*, 1996, Bayard, 2002, p. 22, 24.
[361]Pierre Lévy, *World philosophie*, Odile Jacob, 2000, p. 183, 184
[362]Emmanuel Levinas, *Difficult Freedom, Essays on Judaism*. Ediciones Lilmod, Buenos Aires, 2004, p. 112, quoted in Alain Finkielkraut, *Le Mécontemporain*, Gallimard, 1991, p. 177.

since it seems that this double conception of humanity corresponds only to that of a shepherd and his flock.

The development of planetarian thought through the centuries and revolutions would obviously require a full-fledged study, especially through the analysis of religious texts inherited from the Mosaic tradition. In the context of the present study, we can only present one of the most important and essential representatives of this history: Baruch Spinoza, which we can observe through the eyes of the essayist Alain Minc: "Spinoza was the first of a very special genealogy, that of Jewish outcasts, on the margins of their community and sometimes violently opposed to it, all intellectual breakaway intellectuals, all without ancestry, but all at the origin of a dazzling, or sometimes less than honourable, descent. Spinoza, Marx, Freud, Einstein: an astonishing quartet that illustrates the idea, unacceptable to the established authorities of the Jewish community, that Judaism is never more decisive in the course of humanity than when it is installed outside its own walls363."

Like Marx, and many other intellectuals, Spinoza was a Jew in revolt against his own community: "Besides being stupid, the Jews are also wicked ... Their meanness is only comparable to that of the Hebrews whose hatred of foreigners is well known ... They have not excelled other nations in science or piety ... They were not the chosen of God on the basis of true life and high speculations ... If in anything they prevailed over other nations, it was in the prosperity of their business, in that which concerned the security of life, and in the fortune with which they overcame great dangers." The choice of the Jews was therefore only due to their wealth. Indeed, "today, the Jews have absolutely nothing to claim that places them above the nations364"." There is something of Drumont365 in this man", exclaimed Alain Minc. However, Spinoza was not excommunicated in 1656 because he professed a primary anti-Judaism, but because he spread sacrilegious, almost atheistic ideas, and because he attacked all religions. He was a marginal, a dissident, a revolutionary." If excommunication had existed in the Jewish tradition, Marx would have been excommunicated, and

---

[363]Alain Minc, *Spinoza, un roman juif*, Gallimard, 1999, p. 12-13 (see note 348).
[364]Alain Minc, *Spinoza, un roman juif*, Gallimard, 1999, p. 106.
[365]Edward Drumont was an anti-Semitic writer of the late 19th century. He was the author of *The Jewish France* (1886), a book that enjoyed considerable success.

Freud, although a good Jew, would have suffered the same fate. Only Einstein would have been spared366."

He was also a curious character: "All those who came close to Spinoza attested to his difficulty in laughing, even smiling. The taciturn genius, the melancholic philosopher, the nostalgic thinker in search of a submerged past, only laughs in one circumstance: at spiders fighting to the death or when one of them is about to dismember the other ... He only laughs at the sight of insects dismembering with the same precision as the executioners do in the Place de Grève367."

Baruch Spinoza was born in Amsterdam into a Portuguese Jewish family. Holland, explained Alain Minc,—the bourgeois republic of the United Provinces—was "the first free society in the West." In the 17th century, Holland reigned in great religious tolerance and the country had become the official refuge for all the outlaws of the time. But little Holland was also a fearsome trading power. The big business of the Protestant Dutch and Jewish merchants was international trade, which they developed to make the country the leading trading nation in Europe for decades. This economic pre-eminence, as well as the focus of opposition it represented through the spread of the Reformed religion, irritated other powers, especially Louis XIV's France. In 1672, war broke out between the two countries, and France invaded the small republic.

This gave rise to a bizarre episode. In the middle of the war, Spinoza, who had always praised the merits of the Netherlands, crossed the front line into enemy territory at the invitation of Stouppe, the new governor of the city of Utrecht appointed by the Grand Condé, the famous Duke of Enghien and Marshal of France." Later he will be shot for less than that", Alain Minc rightly noted368. This incomprehensible escape remains a mystery in Spinoza's life. Why was he so keen to see Condé, what did he want from him, did he expect a protector?

Stouppe, though a Protestant of Swiss origin, had little regard for the Dutch nation. The Dutch, though adherents of Protestantism, welcomed in their country all religions and all sects: "Roman Catholics, Lutherans, Brownists, Anabaptists, Socianists, Independents, Quakers, Borelists, Armenians, Muscovites, Libertines, Jews, Persians, and a host of inquirers who do not know to which group they belong."

---

366 Alain Minc, *Spinoza, un roman juif*, Gallimard, 1999, p. 10, 12-13.
367 Alain Minc, *Spinoza, un roman juif*, Gallimard, 1999, p. 120-121. [Today's Place du Mairie in Paris. Under the Ancien Régime, the Place de Grève (until 1803) was also used for public executions).
368 Accusations of treason are recurrent.

Therefore, Stouppe concluded, the true God of the Dutch is Mammon, it is money369. Referring to Spinoza, Stouppe wrote: "A few years ago, he wrote a book called *Tractatus theologico-politicus*: the essential aim seems to be to destroy all religions, especially Jewish and Christian, and to open the door to atheism, libertarianism and freedom for all."

"How can we reproach Stouppe for invading a country that is Protestant in name only and whose theological lukewarmness is so great that no one dares to refute Spinoza's demonic ideas370?"

After a long period of silencing of his work, wrote Alain Minc, "Spinoza made his way through the 18th century in a less and less subterranean form, passing the baton a few decades later to Hegel, who was the origin of all that followed371." In the 20th century, "the rediscovery of the political philosopher" paradoxically took place under the auspices of "two branches, one liberal, the other Marxist, Popper and Althusser playing in this case the unexpected role of twins." We find here the germs of Marxism and liberalism, the two strands of globalism amalgamated in their dogmatic origins by the mosaic cement.

Like Marx, Spinoza, though irreligious and rejected by his community, was no less a Jew: "Spinoza is permeated from top to bottom by the ways of thinking and feeling characteristic of the lively Jewish intelligence. I feel, wrote Minc, that I could not feel so close to Spinoza if I myself were not Jewish and if I had not developed in a Jewish environment ... Spinoza is a Jewish intellectual ... For some, Spinoza is the bad novel of a Jew: for others, it is the novel of a bad Jew; undoubtedly, it is a Jewish novel372."

In a science-fiction novel eloquently entitled *He Will Come*, the prolific Jacques Attali conveyed part of the religious and political message of the messianic ideal. In his story, he imagined a child prodigy who could become the Messiah so desired by Israel. In an apocalyptic atmosphere, the boy's father travels to Israel to meet the rabbis.

369One can read with interest Max Weber's famous thesis on the relationship between the capitalist spirit and Calvinist religion (*The Protestant Ethic and the Spirit of Capitalism*, 1920), a book regularly republished; one can also read Werner Sombart's *Les Juifs et la vie économique* (Payot, 1923), a book that is untraceable (except perhaps for the good brother William of Baskerville) and never republished, but just as interesting and instructive. [Since reissued in French in 2012. *Los Judíos y la vida económica,* also published in Spanish by the Universidad Completense de Madrid in 2008].
370Alain Minc, *Spinoza, un roman juif*, Gallimard, 1999, p. 180-182.
371Alain Minc, *Spinoza, un roman juif*, Gallimard, 1999, p. 12.
372Alain Minc, *Spinoza, un roman juif*, Gallimard, 1999, p. 225-227.

The following short excerpts show the permanence of certain themes in Planetarian literature, such as humanism, Africa, the open society, the "tremor", the "ladder", "nomads", "inventing", "saving humanity", war, revenge and incest. Read carefully:

"Jonathan was not even twelve years old. They were about to leave the Ethiopian desert when Mortimer began to wonder at his speech and mannerisms. No doubt he had long been aware of his eldest son's uniqueness ... After fifteen years spent in Africa relieving and healing the victims of barbarism, Mortimer was back as Professor Simmons in London ... A week earlier, two policemen had come to question Mortimer politely about Jonathan and his links with the Open Society. A song of his was then circulating in universities and in some nightclubs that spoke of a volcano, of lava, of the East, of birds' nests and of an earth tremor373."

To understand the true nature of his son, Mortimer then travelled to Jerusalem to consult some wise men inside a crypt. The assembled rabbis, intrigued and curious about the phenomenon, found themselves "exactly under the entrance of what had been the Holy of Holies of the second Temple, right where it had been more than two thousand years ago." One of the rabbis explained: "We are not superior. We are different. We would have liked to be ignored, forgotten in our lands. But we were driven out of it. We became nomads forced to stalk the enemy and invent time. After that, we fell into slavery. When we were set free, God assigned us the mission to save men and to speak in His Name. We did not ask for it. When there is above our heads ... no longer some stones and weeds, but the only place worthy to receive God on this planet, then the world can prepare itself for a perfect time374." It is enough, therefore, to rebuild the Temple on the site of the Great Mosque, as a growing number of orthodox Israeli Jews are actually proposing today." Prayer," he repeats, raising his eyes to his guest's eyes, "is like a great stairway going up to heaven ... Our texts say that 'the heavenly host will rise up with a great tumult', that 'the foundations of the world will be shaken'. The war of the mighty in the heavens will spread throughout the world" ... Our Kabbalah explains that the Envoy will then wear the robes of vengeance, destroy the wicked king, avenge Israel before returning to hide in the garden of Eden375."

Another scene featured this conversation between the rabbis:

373Jacques Attali, *Il viendra*, Fayard, 1994, p. 29.
374Jacques Attali, *Il viendra*, Fayard, 1994, p. 82.
375Jacques Attali, *Il viendra*, Fayard, 1994, p. 192, 227

According to you, even sexual taboos will be abolished," smiled Mortimer. — Absolutely," said Nahman. — Even incest, Mortimer dared to ask. — You blaspheme, Nahman!, shouted MHRL, preventing the young rabbi from answering[376]."

It is allusions of this kind that allow us to understand what has long troubled many spirits. Cosmopolitan literature is often peppered with these allusions, which are perceived only by the initiated. These winks of the eye elicit a knowing smile from readers who know that the general public rarely sees or understands them. The same is true of the following passage:

"The scribe Ezra explicitly states that the Messianic order will reign for four centuries. Afterwards, another order will be established which no human spirit can yet conceive of. A kind of pure and perfect spiritual life, beyond all material and political contingencies. There will be no more power, no more ambition, no more hunger, no more thirst, no more disease, no more sexuality, no more scarcity. No need for taboos, for there will be no more desires. Only then will natural laws cease to be in force377.

"But why do you think that the fate of the world depends on the goodwill of a tiny people? The Jews are still the chosen people, but it is not their history on this earth that determines the coming of the Messiah.

Perhaps because the Jews, with their madness, are capable of causing many massacres and cataclysms," mutters Eliav, turning in on himself.

—They are certainly not the only ones! They alone cannot unleash the Apocalypse!

-Let us say that Jewish follies can more easily than others have universal consequences.

—That is true! If the crazies of the Reconstruction Party were to start rebuilding the Temple, it would surely provoke a planetarian war.

—I agree! However, it is our right, perhaps even our duty. We are the discoverers of God, the priestly people of humanity. It would be normal for us to have our Temple there where our religion has been founded long before the others. Nobody can do anything about it. Not even us[378] ", concluded Jacques Attali's character. Religious faith undoubtedly has some very convenient advantages, such as the

---

[376]Jacques Attali, *Il viendra*, p. 264. The Hebrew alphabet contains only consonants. That is why Cohen, Kun, Kahn, Caen or Cohn, for example, are the same surname and designate "priest" in Hebrew.

[377]Jacques Attali, *Il viendra*, Fayard, 1994, p. 266.

[378]Jacques Attali, *Il viendra*, Fayard, 1994, p. 309.

avoidance of asking questions and lamenting about "collateral damage", as they say since the Gulf War. There is nothing to do...

Messianism is most often born out of historical frustration. It appears in the collective consciousness as the reparation of a loss, as a utopian promise to compensate for present misfortune. In his book *Messianism379*, David Banon explained that "from their origin, the visions of the prophets of Israel appear in the context of a series of national catastrophes: Isaiah prophesies on the horizon the destruction of the kingdom by the Assyrians; Jeremiah and Ezekiel after the collapse of the kingdom of Judah and the Babylonian exile. Later, Talmudic eschatology will respond to the destruction of the second Temple by the Romans and the dispersion of the Jews. Even Kabbalah is seen by Gershom Scholem (1897–1982) as "the religious response of Judaism" to the expulsion of the Jews from Spain380..." Messianism is thus linked to the experience of failure.

"In its essence, it is the aspiration for the impossible. Messianic tension is a feverish waiting, a restless hope that knows neither repose nor repose ... Messianic tension makes the Jewish people live always expectant of the imminence of a radical transformation of life on the face of the earth ... Redemption is always near, but if it were to come it would be immediately questioned in the name of the very absolute demand that it claims to bring about"." The redemption promised at the end of time sustains a reality which is always beyond the existing, and which, therefore, will never be achieved. But man must constantly aspire to it. The Messiah is always the one who is to come one day ... but the one who finally appears can only be a false Messiah[381]." In the days to come the Mountain of the House of Yahweh shall be established above the mountains, and higher than the hills; and all nations shall behold it with joy... So shall He judge between the nations and arbitrate between the many peoples, and they shall beat their swords into ploughshares and their spears into pruning hooks; nation shall not lift up sword against nation; they shall know war no more. O House of Yaaqov! Come, let us walk in the light of Yahweh." (Isaiah, II, 2, 4, 5, Israelite Nazarene, 2011).

[379]David Banon, *Le Messianisme*, Presses Universitaires de France, 1998.
[380]See also Hervé Ryssen, *Psychoanalysis of Judaism*, and Gershom Scholem, *Le Messianisme juif*, 1971, Les Belles Lettres, 2020 (French edition), Gershom Scholem, *The Messianic Idea in Judaism: And Other Essays on Jewish Spirituality*, Schocken, 1995 (English edition). (NdT).
[381]David Banon, *Le Messianisme*, Presses Universitaires de France, 1998, p. 5-7, 11

It is not only for Israel that this society gathers around the rebuilt Temple, but for the whole of humanity, David Banon further explained: "Only a little while longer, cries Haggai, and God will shake heaven and earth, the sea and the dry land, and will shake all nations, and the elite of all nations will come and I will fill this house with glory382." (Haggai, II, 6–7) Actually, if one directly consults the text in the Torah (Old Testament), without going through David Banon, we can read the following: "For this is what Yahweh-Tzevaot [of hosts] says: 'It will not be long before once again I will shake the heavens and the earth, the sea and the dry land; and I will shake all the nations, so that the treasures of all the nations will flow in; and I will fill this house with Glory, says Yahweh-Tzevaot." The silver is mine and the gold is mine," says Yahweh-Tzevaot" (Haggai, II, 6-8, Kadosh Messianic Yisraelite). We see how the text is slightly different from version to version; this one is perhaps a little less imbued with nobility, but the change presents some not inconsiderable benefits.

Consulting the bible again, we also find the following in Haggai: "I will overthrow the thrones of kingdoms, I will destroy the power of the kingdoms of the nations..." (Haggai, II, 22, Kadosh Israelite Messianic)." (Haggai, II, 22, Messianic Israelite Kadosh). If we were superstitious, we might think that these words are indeed prophetic: do they not seem to describe the European situation in 1919, when the Tsar of Russia, the Emperor of Germany, the Emperor of Austria-Hungary and the Ottoman Sultan had lost their thrones after four years of world war? Let us simply recall that the Balfour Declaration of 2 November 1917—named after the British minister—granted the Jews a national home in Palestine. This was happening at the same time as the Bolsheviks, financed by some powerful New York financiers, were overthrowing the Tsar hated by Israel. All this had nothing to do with divine intervention, but it retrospectively feeds the secret myth of messianic spirits.

To explain the conviction of the Jews to lead the march of humanity, David Banon invited us to read the visions of Zechariah: "When that time comes, my word will be fulfilled if ten men from ten languages of the nations will take hold of the mantle of a Jew, and say: "We will go with you, for we have heard that Yahweh is with you"'" (Zechariah, VIII, 23, Messianic Israelite Kadosh)." Even Malachi, in

---

[382]Some fifteen French ministers, among other eminent personalities of the Republic, were present at the last dinner of the Representative Council of the Jewish Institutions of France (Crif) in February 2005. The annual Crif receptions have become an obligatory event of the first order in the French Republic.

his prophecy, introduces a broad perspective of the future by announcing that the prophet Elijah will be the messenger of the Messiah (Malachi, III, 1 and 23)". But if we check the magical formulae directly in the text, we again find supplementary information that is indispensable for the understanding of the mentality that animates our current intellectuals: "[You] will trample the wicked underfoot, for they will be dust under your feet on the day that I am preparing," says Yahweh of Hosts." (Malachi, III, 21, Israelite Nazarene 2011). And this is where we begin to understand the origin of the term "wicked" that we also see recurrently in certain literature and war discourses promulgating the war against Evil.

"The messianic age as described by all the prophets consists in the abolition of political violence and social injustice." Messianic times mark the end of political violence and all alienations, although the advent of this new era will be accompanied by great catastrophes. This is what the master Rabbi Yohanan said: "During the generation in which the Messiah, son of David, will come, the Torah scholars will be in the minority; as for the rest of the people, their eyes will weep with sorrow and grief, and calamities will follow. And severe decrees will be introduced; before the first is passed the second will come swiftly." (Sanhedrin 97a383)." That time is feared not only because of the merciless wars in which the Messiah will perish, but also because of the degradation of customs and beliefs which end in a regression towards bestiality384."

Perhaps this is the reason why many influential personalities promote "the degradation of customs" and "merciless wars": it is simply to prepare for the coming of the Messiah.

The date of his coming is as yet unknown, and, in this regard, the Sages of the Talmud strictly forbid conjecture: "Let those who calculate the end of days be cursed" (Sanhedrin 97b), for they are an obstacle and a disturbance to the people. But their coming is ineluctable: "For it to be possible, human consciousness must be prepared, aspiring to it with every fibre of its being385 "; hence this tension, this feverishness, this permanent agitation, this constant "sensitisation".

In 1967 a neo-Messianic approach to the Six Day War was encouraged and emphasised, interpreted as the manifestation of the divine presence alongside the people of Israel, and, with the conquest of Jerusalem and Judea-Samaria, enabling the Jews to regain the

383Source at https://www.sefaria.org. (NdT).
384David Banon, *Le Messianisme*, Presses Universitaires de France, 1998, p. 15-16.
385David Banon, *Le Messianisme*, Presses Universitaires de France, 1998, p. 49.

entirety of the Land of Israel, the Messianic era was heralded386." Thus, for the religious Zionists the land of Israel was at last in the hands of the Jews." So, for the religious Zionists, the land of Israel was finally in the hands of the Jews in its entirety. What was the point of a new war in 1973? In response to the doubts and fears of the population, the Gush Emunim, a messianic movement, came up with this answer: "The 1973 Kippur war was perceived "as one of the birth pangs of the Messiah"." The war thus turned out to be another suffering for the people of Israel, despite their overwhelming victory over the Arab armies. For their part, the ultra-orthodox Jews interpreted the events in this way: "Israel's sufferings have now reached a terrifying level; the people of Israel are overwhelmed with birth pangs. The time of imminent deliverance has come. It is the only true answer to the destruction of the world and to the sufferings that have befallen our people... Prepare yourselves for the redemption that is soon to come! ... The deliverer of righteousness is behind our walls, and the time to prepare to receive him is very short[387]!" "It is impossible," continued Rabbi Schneerson, "that the consolation will not come, for the sufferings are unbearable." In short, the more you suffer, the more you show your sufferings, the more you cry out your sufferings, the more you hasten the coming of the Messiah. This can perhaps explain some behaviour that is sometimes a little invasive.

Moshe Idel's book, *Messianism and Mysticism*, gave us a better understanding of this mental universe, so different from our own. The figure of Rabbi Shelomo Molkho (ex Diogo Pires), a Portuguese Marrano who returned to Judaism, played an important role at the beginning of the 16th century. This sage provides us with a unique example of messianic thinking: "Molkho's sense of being the messiah is unquestionable, wrote Moshe Idel. In one of his poems, he implies that he is the messiah, son of Joseph388." During his lifetime, and in the generations after his death, many considered him a messianic figure. Here are some verses, according to the manuscript text:

[386]David Banon, *Le Messianisme*, Presses Universitaires de France, 1998, p.110

[387]David Banon, *Le Messianisme*, Presses Universitaires de France, 1998, p. 120. Rabbi Yosef Yitzchak Schneerson (1880–1950), Chabad-Lubavitch teacher quoted by David Banon. On the Chabad-Lubavitch read *Psychoanalysis of Judaism, (2022)*.

[388]According to Jewish theology, two Messiahs are foreseen: The warrior Messiah, the Messiah ben Joseph (Son of Joseph), who dies a failure, but prepares the eschatological ground, and the Messiah ben David (Son of David) who will reign after the Redemption. (NdT).

"With hidden words/ I tell the people/ Chosen words/ Like perfumed gunpowder/ From Mount Carmel/ God sends/ The man of good tidings/ Of vengeance against the Peoples/ The nations will fight/ The heroes will press/ The foreigners will be broken/ And we will have peace/ The city of the North/ Will ask for a son for its daughter/ The son of Esau who is Edom peace/ The city of the North/ Will ask for a son for its daughter/ The son of Esau who is Edom389 / The young Shelomo/ Will sharpen his sword/ The finest/ To come to the aid of his people/ To bring them out of darkness/ The nations will tremble/ They will give gifts/ And insults will be/ Exchanged for greeting390."

"Molkho's poem clearly evokes the advent of a double revenge: against Edom and against Ishmael", i.e. against Christianity and Islam, commented Moshe Idel, who added a little further on: "Some details of this legend relate his efforts to shake the Church ... God reveals not only how to fight against Christianity or how to approach the true secret of science, but also how to break the force of Christianity so that the Redemption can take place391."

In the 1970s, messianic beliefs and hopes were inseparable from certain historical figures, among whom Isaac Luria, the creator of the new Kabbalah, known under the name of "Ari's Kabbalah" and whose influence was enormous, was prominent. Again, we encounter here the usual issues that preoccupy modern thinkers of the late 20th and early 21st century: According to Luria and his disciples in Palestinian lands, "the Kabbalists must release the divine sparks. As part of this messianic process, they must either destroy the shells that hold them captive, or explode them. Now, these shells are identified with the nations of the world, which means that the countries outside the land of Israel are of no value in themselves and should be dominated. Therefore, according to this conception, the land of Israel is the centre of the world392."

In the mid-17th century, Rabbi Naftali wrote in his turn: "May the air outside the various countries where the nations live be purified in the future thanks to the purity of the land of Israel, which, even in times of desolation, preserves its holiness." The incandescent hatred of Christianity or the endless contempt of Bernard-Henri Levy, Alain Minc

---

[389]According to Hebrew exegesis, Esau is traditionally assimilated to Edom, Christendom. Also to Amalek, according to his genealogy.

[390]Moshe Idel, *Messianism and mysticism*, Éditon du Cerf, 1994, p. 65–66.

[391]Moshe Idel, *Messianism and mysticism*, Éditon du Cerf, 1994, p. 48.

[392]Moshe Idel, *Messianisme et mystique*, Éditon du Cerf, 1994, p. 87-89. [On Messianism and Ari's Kabbalah see also Hervé Ryssen, *Psychoanalysis of Judaism*, (NdT)].

or Emmanuel Levinas, have crossed the centuries. Only the purity of Israel can save humanity.

The great 19th century German writer and poet Heinrich Heine was also very attracted to the Bible at the end of his life: "I have returned to the Old Testament. What a great book! More remarkable than its content is for me its form, that language which is, so to speak, a product of nature, like a tree, like a flower, like the stars, like man himself. Everything springs forth, flows, shines, smiles. It is really the word of God, while all other books only attest to the refined genius of man393."

The Bible was for him a "portable homeland", as Bernard-Henri Levy put it, who used the expression while forgetting to cite his sources. But not everything seems so wonderful in the Old Testament. Without wishing to offend anyone, we tend to share Voltaire's opinion on this text, because it seems so alien to our own culture. To tell the truth, it is a little difficult to understand how these texts could have fascinated millions of Protestant men in Northern Europe. There is no doubt, however, that this book inspired the English Puritans in their conquest of America. Identifying themselves with the Hebrew people, the Anglo-Saxon conquerors of this new land of Canaan exterminated the Indians as the Hebrews had done during their conquest of the Promised Land, as narrated in the book of Joshua. Indeed, the countless massacres and exterminations constitute the essential part of "this holy and beautiful book of education, written for children of all ages394 ", as Heinrich Heine noted. Nevertheless, in it "the wrath of Yahweh" never ceases to thunder: "Whoever blasphemes the Name of Yahweh shall be put to death; the whole congregation shall stone him. The foreigner as well as the citizen shall be put to death if he blasphemes The Name."

---

[393]Heinrich Heine, *De l'Allemagne*, 1835, Gallimard, 1998, p. 285." In my most recent book, I have expressed myself about the transformation that has taken place in my spirit, about divine things. Since then I have been asked, with Christian impertinence, countless questions about the paths the optimal enlightenment has taken in me ... They would like to know if I have not seen, like Saul [Paul], a light on the road to Damascus ... No, pious souls, I have never been to Damascus, nor do I know anything about Damascus, except that recently the Jews there have been accused of eating old capuchins ... In reality neither vision, nor heavenly voice, nor marvellous dream, nor miraculous phantom has put me on the road to salvation, but I owe my new light solely and simply to the reading of a book ... And that book is called ... the Book, the Bible ... He who has lost his God can find Him again in this book...", in Heinrich Heine, *On the History of Religion and Philosophy in Germany*, Alianza Editorial, Madrid, 2008, p. 221–222.
[394]Heinrich Heine, *De l'Allemagne*, 1835, Gallimard, 1998, p. 467.

(Leviticus, XXIV, 16, Messianic Israelite Kadosh). That being the case, we will tone down, nuance our statements...

Evidently, the rage for the destruction of nations that we have observed in our contemporary authors has its primary origin there. To break and subdue the nations, to destroy their traditions, to plunder their temples, to enslave the conquered peoples, and to profit by their wealth: such are the divine laws to which one must submit: "When Yahweh your Elohim brings you into the land which you are about to enter to possess it, he will evict many nations before you ... [when] Yahweh your Elohim delivers them to you and you defeat them, you must destine them for destruction: give them no truce and give them no quarter. You shall not make a marriage covenant with them: do not give your daughters to their sons, nor take their daughters for your sons. For they will turn your sons away from me to worship other deities, and the wrath of Yahweh will be kindled against you, and he will speedily exterminate you. But this is what they will do to them; they will tear down your altars, and break down your pillars, and cut down your sacred posts, and cast your graven images into the fire. For you are a people consecrated to Yahweh your Elohim: of all the peoples of the earth Yahweh your Elohim has chosen you to be His special people." (Deuteronomy VII, 1–6, Israelite Nazarene 2011).

And do not think that the weak will be spared, on the contrary: "Kill old men, young men, girls, women and children; but do not come near anyone who bears the mark. Begin here in my sanctuary. So they began with the old men who stood before the House." (Ezekiel IX, 6, Israelite Nazarene 2011). And also, "Did you let the women live? ... Now kill every male among the little ones, and kill every woman who has slept with a man. But the young girls who have never slept with a man, keep alive for yourselves." (Numbers XXXI, 15–18, Messianic Israelite Kadosh)." (...) He plundered the city and tore the wombs of all the women who were with child." (II Kings; XV, 16, Kadosh Messianic Israelite).

"You shall devour all the peoples whom Yahweh your Elohim delivers to you—show them no pity, and do not serve their gods... If you think to yourselves, 'These nations are more numerous than we are; how can we dispossess them?' Yet you will not fear them; you will remember well what Yahweh your Elohim did to Pharaoh... Yahweh will do the same to all the peoples of whom you are afraid. Moreover, Yahweh your Elohim will send the wasp among those of them who are left, and those who have hidden themselves shall perish before you. You shall not fear them, for Yahweh your Elohim is there with you, a great and dreadful Elohim. Yahweh your Elohim will drive out those nations before you by little and little... Yahweh your Elohim will deliver them to you, sending one disaster after another upon them until they have been destroyed. He will deliver their kings to you, and you will blot out their names from under heaven; none of them will be able to bear them until you have destroyed them." (Deuteronomy VII, 16–24, Messianic Israelite Kadosh)." Now go and attack Amalek, and utterly destroy all that they have. Do not spare them, but kill men and women, children and infants, cattle and sheep, camels and donkeys. And you shall dedicate him and all that belongs to him for destruction." (I Samuel XV, 3, Messianic Israelite Kadosh)

"The sons of Yahudah took another 10,000 alive, brought them to the top of the Rock, and cast them off the top of the Rock; so they were all crushed to pieces." (II Chronicles, XXV, 12, Messianic Israelite Kadosh).

Joshua's conquest of Palestine represented one of the high points of that destructive, exterminating fury: At Makkedah, at Libnah, at Lachish, at Eglon, at Hebron and at Debir, the joyous massacres followed one after another in a monotonous, repetitive fashion: the whole population was put to the sword: "Yahoshua [Joshua] ... destroyed them utterly, all there—he left no man"." So Yahoshua struck all The Land—the hills, the Negev, the Shephelah and the mountainsides—and all its kings; he left no one, but utterly destroyed everything that breathed, as Yahweh the Elohim of Yisra'el had commanded395." (Joshua X, 28–40, Messianic Israelite Kadosh).

The book of Esther tells how the Jews succeeded in thwarting the plan of the wicked Haman, the prime minister of Ahasuerus, and how they had 75,000 enemies exterminated, thanks to Esther, the king's mistress. Here is an extract from the biblical text in which the "Great King Ahasuerus", still under the influence of the wicked Haman, decreed:

"The great king Ahashverosh [Ahasuerus] writes these things to the princes and governors who are under him from India to Kush [Ethiopia] in the hundred and twenty-seven provinces:

After I had become lord over many nations and had dominion over all the earth, not being lifted up by the presumption of my authority, but

---

[395]The Soviet writer Ilya Ehrenburg, the regime's official propagandist, wrote in October 1944: "Kill! Kill! There are no innocents among the Germans, neither among the living, nor among the unborn. Violently vanquish the pride of German women. Take them as legitimate booty. Kill, kill, kill, brave soldiers of the Red Army in your irresistible assault." (in Amiral Doenitz, *Dix ans et vingt jours*, p. 343-344).

conducting myself with equity and affability I determined to settle my subjects in a calm life, and to make my kingdom peaceful and open it for passage to the farthest shores, which is desired by all men." Now, when I asked my counsellors how this came to pass, Haman … declared to us that in all the nations on earth there was scattered a certain malicious people, who had laws contrary to all nations, and continually despised the commandments of kings. Thus the union of our kingdoms, honourably intended by us, cannot go forward. Seeing then we understand that this people alone are continually in opposition to all men, differing in the strange manner of their laws, and cursed effect to our state, working all harm they can so that our kingdom cannot be firmly established. Therefore, we have ordained that all those who shall be appointed in writing to you by Haman, who is ordained over affairs, and is next to us, shall be all, with their wives and children utterly destroyed by the sword of their enemies, without all mercy and pity…" (Esther III, 13, Messianic Israelite Kadosh). The beautiful Esther, the king's mistress, "did not divulge her people or her family ties because Mordechai had instructed her to say nothing to anyone." (Esther II, 10, Messianic Israelite Kadosh). Thanks to her great beauty and influence, Esther managed to convince the king to issue another decree: "The letter stated that the king had granted the Yahudim [Jews] in all the cities the right to assemble and defend their lives by destroying, killing and exterminating any force from any town or province that attacked them, their little ones or their women or tried to take their property by plunder, on the appointed day in any of King Achashverosh's provinces, namely, the thirteenth day of the twelfth month, the month of Adar." (Esther VIII, 11–12, Messianic Israelite Kadosh)." The Yahudites gave their enemies a stroke of the sword, killing and destroying; they did to their enemies as they pleased … The rest of the Yahudites who were in the king's provinces gathered together in like manner and fought for their lives. They disposed of their enemies, killing seventy-five thousand of their adversaries. This happened on the thirteenth day of the month of Adar; and on the fourteenth day of the same month they rested and made it a day of feasting and rejoicing." (Esther IX, 5–17, Israelite Nazarene 2011). This great victory is the origin of the feast of Purim which the Jews now celebrate a month before Passover: a bit like the Poles remembering and celebrating every year an ancient and bloody pogrom of the 17th century. Strange customs…

From then on, the Jews were able to enjoy all the riches they had gained:

"Then Yahweh will drive out all these nations before you; and you will dispossess nations greater and stronger than you." (Deuteronomy XI, 23, Messianic Israelite Kadosh). And further: "When Yahweh your Elohim has brought you into The Land which He swore to your fathers Avraham, Yitzchak and Ya'akov that He would give you—great and prosperous cities, which you did not build; houses filled with all manner of good things, which you did not fill; water cisterns dug, which you did not dig; vineyards and olive groves, which you did not plant—and that you have eaten your fill; then take heed that you do not forget Yahweh your Elohim, who brought you out of the land of Mitzrayim [Egypt], where you lived as slaves." (Deuteronomy VI, 10–12, Messianic Israelite Kadosh).

"Concerning the men and women you may have as slaves: you shall buy male and female slaves from the nations that surround you. You may also buy the children of foreigners living with you and members of their families born in your land. You may also leave them as an inheritance for your children to possess; from these groups you may take your slaves forever. But as for your brothers the sons of Yisra'el, they shall not treat one another harshly." (Leviticus XXV, 44–46, Messianic Israelite Kadosh).

"Kings shall be your foster parents, and princesses your nurses. They will bow down to you, face to the earth, and lick the dust from your feet. Then you will know that I am Yahweh—those who wait for me will not mourn." (Isaiah XLIX, 23, Messianic Israelite Kadosh).

"Strangers shall rebuild your walls, their kings shall be at your service; for in my wrath I struck you, but in my mercy I love you. Your gates shall always be open, they shall not be shut day or night, that people may bring you the riches of the Goyim, with their kings as captives. For the nation or kingdom that will not serve thee shall perish; yea, those nations shall be utterly destroyed." (Isaiah LX, 10–12, Messianic Israelite Kadosh).

In short, all this jovial banter can be summed up with this profession of faith: "Yahweh, how I hate those who hate you! I am desolate because of your enemies! I hate them with boundless hatred! They have become my enemies too." (Psalms CXXXIX, 21–22, Messianic Israelite Kadosh).

The people chosen to be number 1? Obviously, with such sacred texts, it was inevitable to make some enemies. If to the Old Testament (the Torah) we add the Talmud and the Kabbalah, then this inevitably leads to an awkward situation with their neighbours.

The Old Testament naturally inspired Voltaire's most caustic sarcasms, which we read in countless passages of his work: "I would never finish if I wanted to go into the detail of all the unheard-of extravagances that overflow from that book; common sense was never attacked with such indecency and fury." (Voltaire, *Sermont des Cinquantes*).

"Two oxen ... dragged (the safe) in a cart; the people fell before it face down on the ground, and dared not look at it. Adonai caused 5070 Jews to perish one day by sudden death for looking at his safe, though he contented himself with inflicting haemorrhoids on the Philistines who stole his safe, and with sending them a plague of rats into his fields, until they had presented him with five golden rat figures and five golden eyelet figures returning his safe... Is it possible that the human spirit has been so imbecile as to imagine such infamous superstitions and such ridiculous fables?" (Voltaire, *Profession de foi des théistes. Des Superstitions*).

"God expressly commands Isaiah to walk naked and show his buttocks (Isaiah XX). God commands Jeremiah to put a yoke around his neck (Jeremiah XXVII, 2). God commands Ezekiel to cook bread with shit (Ezekiel IV, 12). God commands Hosea to marry a tart ... Add to all these prodigies an uninterrupted series of massacres, and you will see that everything is divine in them, for there is nothing that is governed according to the so-called honest laws among men." (Voltaire, *Mélanges. Il faut prendre un parti*, ch. 22).

Some exaggerated figures also provoked his irony. The number of animals sacrificed by the Hebrews seemed implausible: "For a sacrifice offering to Yahweh, Solomon offered twenty-two thousand oxen and one hundred and twenty thousand sheep." (I Kings VIII, 63). Or: "Vespasian and Titus made a memorable siege which ended in the destruction of the city. Flavius Josephus, the exaggerator, maintains that during that short war there were a million Jews slaughtered. No wonder that an author who puts fifteen thousand men in a town kills a million men." (Voltaire, *Dictionnaire philosophique*).

Other customs recounted in the Bible aroused Voltaire's disgust rather than irony: "The Jews, following their laws, sacrificed human victims. This religious act accords with their customs; their own books represent them mercilessly slitting the throats of all they meet, and reserving only the girls for their own use." (Voltaire, *Dictionnaire philosophique*).

Regarding Abimelech slitting the throats of seventy of his brothers, Voltaire wrote: "The critics rise up against this abominable multitude of fratricides… It seems that the Jews kill only for the pleasure of killing. They are continually presented as the most ferocious and imbecile people that ever bloodied the earth (Voltaire, *Mélanges. La Bible enfin expliquée*).

"You will find in them nothing but an ignorant and barbarous people, combining from ancient times the most sordid avarice with the most detestable superstition and the most invincible hatred of all peoples who tolerate and enrich them." (Voltaire, *Dictionnaire philosophique*, not expurgated[396]).

"You have witnessed the barbarities and superstitions of this people … All other peoples have committed crimes; the Jews are the only ones to have boasted of them. They were all born with the rage of fanaticism in their hearts, just as the Bretons and Germans are born with blond hair. I should not be at all surprised if this nation should one day prove fatal to the whole human race." (Voltaire, *Mélanges, deuxième lettre de Memmius à Cicéron*).

Did Voltaire not agree with Jacques Attali and the words of his rabbi: "Perhaps because the Jews, with their madness, are capable of causing many massacres and cataclysms," mutters Eliav, turning in on himself."

Finally, we have to admit, after reading these odious considerations of Voltaire, that the spirit of the Enlightenment of the 18th century had not yet rid itself of the nauseating miasmas of anti-Semitism. But Tacitus, Cicero, Ronsard, Shakespeare, Quevedo, Chateaubriand, Gogol, Hugo, Balzac, Dostoyevsky, Renan, Schopenhauer, Michelet, Bakunin, Proudhon, Nietzsche, Wagner, Gide, Giraudoux, Morand, Hamsun, Vincenot and hundreds more have also expressed the same horrors. As much of an apostle of tolerance as Voltaire was, we can see that he was still imbued with prejudices from another era that would not disappear until the following centuries, with the passage of time and thanks to civic education. Yet vigilance remains necessary in the face of this phenomenon, for the destruction of Nazi Germany under phosphorous and incendiary bombs does not preserve us ad vitam aeternam from the resurgence of the rancid prejudices of the Middle Ages. The question now is whether Voltaire's genius justifies his continued study in public schools: is he not, after all, as Derrida rightly put it, one of those *"White Dead European evils*[397] "?

---

[396]voltaire-integral.com/19/juifs.htm
[397]"The old dead white males"

PART TWO

THE END OF A MESSIANIC DREAM

The realisation of the socialist idea in the 20th century and the construction of socialist states after the Bolshevik revolution of 1917 represented an absolutely unique episode in the development of the planetarian idea. Indeed, for several decades, it was mainly Marxism that mobilised the hopes of the advocates of globalism. Although many of its Western intellectuals gradually joined the side of liberal democracy, as the failure of the communist experience became apparent, the fall of the Soviet bloc was no less surprising and brutal, and remained the closing of a parenthesis in history that some wish to forget at all costs. In this case, the "duty of historical memory" is not acceptable.

Since the fall of the Berlin Wall, tongues have loosened up a little. It is now legal to talk about communist crimes since the demise of the regime, unlike when the regime was dictatorial and criticism of it was considered reactionary, even hateful. The horrors that were committed are now known, after having been concealed by the Western intellectual elite for decades. The world and mentalities are evolving. Soon, perhaps, it will be possible to speak freely about the role of the Jews in the communist revolution. As far as we know, Aleksandr Solzhenitsyn was the first in the West to publish a book dealing with the subject as a whole. Before him, historians were in the habit of either avoiding such information altogether or revealing it too partially to be an explanatory factor. An analysis of certain historical works reveals, however, that the subject was known, but that it was in good taste not to talk about it. If we have decided in the present study to analyse this aspect of the history of communism, it is because it seemed to us to be an essential stage in the course of planetarian hopes, which are not only composed of the idyllic and fraternal visions of the oracles, as we shall see.

1. The Bolshevik Saturnalia

The interpretation of 20th century history has been somewhat upended by the publication of a book in 2003. It is the book by the greatest Soviet dissident, the universally celebrated Aleksandr Solzhenitsyn, whose pen had already shaken the regime with *The Gulag Archipelago, a* book in which he revealed the reality of concentration camps in the Soviet Union—a reality that the Western intellectual elite would eventually admit with great difficulty.

It was not until the end of his life that he published *Two Hundred Years Together (1795–1995), the* second volume of which deals with the role of the Jews during the Soviet period. Aleksandr Solzhenitsyn's testimony is of particular interest, not only because of the breadth of the research he carried out, but also because of the international renown of its author and, above all, the fact that his book is the only synthesis on the subject intended for the general public, which explains the incredible success of its publication.

We therefore had to wait 70 years to finally have access to surprising revelations, little suspected of bias, since their innumerable bibliographical references come essentially from Hebrew sources. In fact, it was this earthquake in historiography that gave us the idea of starting our own research, since it seemed to us at the time that a large part of history had been left in the shadows, thus impairing the understanding of contemporary events. We have therefore set out here a summary of this fundamental book, trying to respect the general tone of the Russian author's work. We have not added anything so as not to distort Aleksandr Solzhenitsyn's purpose.

Lead trains

The Russian Revolution of 1917 is divided into two episodes: a bourgeois, democratic revolution in February, and a communist, Bolshevik revolution in October of the same year. In February, Russia was still at war with its French and British allies. Millions of men were mobilised to fight against the central empires. The first legislative act of the Provisional Government, contrary to what might have been expected, had nothing to do with the pressing and tragic war situation.

On 20 March 1917, the government adopted the resolution prepared by Justice Minister Kerensky, which abrogated "any discrimination of rights on the grounds of belonging to a denomination, religious doctrine or national group". The publication of the act sparked great enthusiasm and a number of passionate statements in the Western press. Maxime Vinaver's wife, Rosa Georgieva, wrote in her memoirs: "The event coincided with Passover. It seemed like a second exodus from Egypt." The announcement of the emancipation of the Jews of Russia caused an outburst of joy in Jewish communities in the West and throughout the world[398].

According to the memoirs of many authors, from the first days of the revolution, observers were astonished at the number of Jews among the members of the interrogation commissions, as well as among the magazine sellers in public places. The revolution seemed to have given free rein to their political activity; they could henceforth act in full view of everyone. An impartial observer like Methodist pastor Simons, an American who had lived ten years in St Petersburg and knew the city well, replied in 1919 to the US Senate investigating committee: "Soon after the revolution of March 1917, we saw everywhere in St Petersburg groups of Jews perched on benches or soapboxes haranguing the crowds[399]."

The weeks of March were marked by crackdowns against declared or reputed anti-Semites. Investigating magistrates, prosecutors, publishers and booksellers were also arrested. Monarchist Union bookshops were burned down. Everywhere in Russia, hundreds of people were arrested simply because they had held positions of responsibility during the tsarist regime, or simply because of their way of thinking.

The organs of repression were quickly organised. In St. Petersburg, a revolutionary militia was immediately formed, whose spokesman was the journalist Solomon Kaplun, Zinoviev's future henchman. Lawyer Goldstein became chairman of the special commission set up by the city's bar association to decide, without trial, on the fate of thousands of people arrested or about to be arrested for their subversive views." For the first time in Russian history, Jews occupied high positions in the central and local administration[400]." Within the intelligentsia, there were

---

[398]This reminds us of the haste with which the new French Republic granted French nationality to the Jews of Algeria in 1870, as if there was nothing more urgent just as the Prussian armies were besieging the capital.

[399]Alexandre Soljénisyne, *Deux siècles ensemble*, Éditions Fayard. 2003, p. 43.

[400]Alexandre Soljénisyne, *Deux siècles ensemble*, Éditions Fayard. 2003, p. 44.

indeed many Jews, although this does not allow us to say that the revolution was Jewish. The February revolution was undoubtedly carried out by Russians, although, Solzhenitsyn wrote, "their ideology played a significant and determining role, absolutely uncompromising with respect to Russian historical power."

The reality of power was in the hands of an "Executive Committee of the Soviet of Workers' and Soldiers' Deputies" which was formed in the early hours of the revolution and which was a kind of shadow government depriving the Provisional Government of autonomy and real power. The composition of this Executive Committee raised many questions in the Russian press and public. Indeed, for two months its members presented themselves only under pseudonyms and were careful not to appear in public, so that it was unclear who ruled Russia." Later it became known that the Executive Committee included a dozen or so brutalised soldiers who remained aloof. Of the thirty or so really active members, more than half were Jewish socialists. There were Russians, Caucasians, Latvians and Poles, but Russians accounted for less than a quarter" of the membership.

The mystery of the pseudonyms intrigued the educated circles of St. Petersburg and raised doubts and questions in the press. This concealment provoked general exasperation, including among the lower strata of the population. In May, after two months of silence, there was no choice but to publicly reveal the true identity of all the members of the Executive Committee. Boris Katz presented himself under the pseudonym "Kamkov", Lourié under the pseudonym "Larine", and Mandelstam under the pseudonym "Liadov". For the people of that time, only thieves disguised their identity or changed their name and surname. It is true that many had kept their pseudonyms from the days of the underground, when they had to hide, but many others took a pseudonym in 1917. One thing is clear: if a revolutionary hides behind a pseudonym, he is trying to fool someone, and perhaps not only the police and the government. How do we know who our new leaders really are, the man in the street asked himself? When in May the nominations of Zinoviev and Kamenev were put forward for the Presidium of the Soviet, cries went up in the hall: "Give us their real surnames! "

On the two famous trains that crossed Germany—the Lenin train (30 people) and the Natanson-Martov train (160), Jews were an overwhelming majority; almost all their parties were represented. Among these two hundred individuals, many would come to play a significant role in Russian political life. It quickly became clear that it would be very difficult to turn back after such destructive enthusiasm. This was the view of David Aisman, who wrote with a remarkable conviction: "The Jews must at all costs consolidate the gains of the revolution." There can be no doubt what would happen to the Jews "in the event of the victory of the counter-revolution", for it would lead to mass executions. That is why "this ignoble scoundrel must be nipped in the bud. And its seed must also be destroyed[401]"." This was already the programme of the Bolsheviks, but expressed in biblical terms", Solzhenitsyn concluded.

Bolshevism was not very popular among the Jews before the October putsch. In fact, the February revolution had already given them civic rights and full freedom of speech and action, so that a Bolshevik revolution did not seem necessary. But just before it took place, the left S.R. (Socialist-Revolutionaries), led by Natanson, Kamkov and Steiberg, sealed an alliance with Trotsky and Kamenev and played a leading role alongside the Bolsheviks in the first victories they won.

The proportion of Jews in the leading ranks of the government apparatus that was to take power was significant. At the last Congress of the Russian Social-Democratic Workers' Party which had taken place in London in 1907, held jointly with the Mensheviks, there had been 160 Jews out of 302 delegates, i.e. more than half. At the Sixth Summer Congress of the Russian Communist Party of the Bolsheviks (the new name of the Workers' Party), eleven members were elected to the Central Committee, among them Grigory Zinoviev, Yakov Sverdlov, Lev Davidovich Bronstein "Trotsky" and Moshei Solomonovich Uritsky. The first "Politburo", which was to have such a bright future, was elected during the historic session of 10 October 1917 in Karpova Street, in the flat of Himmer and Flaksermann. Among its seven members were Trotsky, Zinoviev, Kamenev and Sokolnikov. It was during this meeting that the decision was taken to launch the Bolshevik coup d'état.

Stunned by the atmosphere of freedom in the first months of the February Revolution, many Jewish speakers failed to see and understand that their frequent appearances on the rostrums at rallies were beginning to arouse the astonishment and suspicion of much of the population. While at the time of the February Revolution there was no "popular anti-Semitism" in Russia, except in the Zone of residence402, it developed in the first months thereafter. This feeling

---

[401]Rousskaïa Volia, 1917, 13 April, p. 3 [p. 62]. In brackets: references to Solzhenitsyn's book.
[402]Before the February Revolution, Jews were only allowed to settle and live in the

only grew afterwards, and a wave of popular exasperation was unleashed against these upstart Jews who made no secret of their revolutionary enthusiasm and occupied functions in which they had never been seen, but which nobody saw in the waiting lines of starving people in front of the shops. In spite of this, there was not a single pogrom in the whole of 1917.

October

We know that, on the night of 27 October, during a meeting described as "historic", the Congress of Soviets promulgated its "decree on peace" and its "decree on land". What is less well known is that in the midst of these two decrees, a resolution was also adopted stipulating that "the local Soviets should prevent the dark forces from perpetrating pogroms against Jews or other categories of the population[403]." Again, once again, the Jewish question had taken precedence over the peasant question.

While there was not a single Jewish minister, there were four Jews in charge of state secretariats, though these did not carry much weight compared to the Executive Committee, whose influence was decisive. The first political bureau of the Central Executive Committee of the Soviets was composed of nine members, of whom five were Jews (the revolutionary socialists Gotz and Mandelstam, the Menshevik Dan, the Bundist[404] Liber, and a leading Bolshevik: Kamenev), the Georgian Nikolay Chkheidze, the Armenian Saakian, the Pole Kruchinski, and finally Nicolski: a Russian! These were the ones who had seized power in Russia at that critical moment in its history." Most Russians—from the man in the street to the general—were literally stupefied by the sudden and spectacular appearance of these new faces among the speakers at rallies, organisers of demonstrations and political leaders."

Lenin was Russian, though of mixed race: his paternal grandfather, Nikolai Ulyanov, was of Calmuca and Chuvash blood; his grandmother, Anna Alekseyevna Smirnova, was a Calmuca; his other grandfather, Israel (Aleksandr, his baptismal name) Davidovich Blank, was Jewish;

---

western regions of the empire, in Poland, the Ukraine and Moldavia. [On The Zone of Residence (the revolutionary Yiddishland) and the communist revolutions in Europe, read Hervé Ryssen, *Jewish Fanaticism*].

[403]Leon Trotsky, *Histoire de la révolution* (in Russian), Berlin, Volume II, p. 361.

[404]At the beginning of the 20th century, the Bund was the main Jewish political organisation in the Zone of Residence. It gathered thousands of militants. See Hervé Ryssen, *Jewish Fanaticism*.

and his other grandmother, Anna Groschop, was the daughter of a German and a Swede." But this does not change the matter, Solzhenitsyn pointed out, for there is nothing to exclude him from the Russian people. We can in no way disown him."

Since Lenin's return to Russia, secret subsidies had flowed to the Bolsheviks from Germany via Olof Aschberg's Nia Banken, but also via Russian bankers who had fled abroad. The well-known American researcher Anthony Sutton found archival documents after half a century informing us that among these Bolshevik bankers was the notorious Dimitri Rubinstien, who had been released from prison in favour of the February revolution, and who had fled to Stockholm. There was also Abram Khirinovsky, a relative of Trotsky and Lev Kamenev. Among the members of the syndicate were "Denisov of the former Bank of Siberia, Kamenka of the Azov-Don Bank, and Davidov of the Bank for Foreign Trade. Other Bolshevik bankers were: Grigori Lessine, Shifter, Yakov Berline and his agent Isidoro Kohn[405]."

These had come from Russia, but others, far more numerous, came from the United States with the aim of building "the New World of universal Happiness". They came across the oceans from New York or San Francisco; some were former subjects of the Russian Empire, others were American citizens who knew nothing of the Russian language or the country, but all were animated by the most ecstatic revolutionary enthusiasm. All these people had good reason to return to Russia, and during the first few months their influence only grew.

In February 1920, Winston Churchill expressed himself on the subject in the pages of the *Sunday Herald*. In an article entitled *Zionism versus Bolshevism*, Winston Churchill wrote: "A "band of extraordinary characters out of the underworld of the great cities of Europe and America has seized the Russian people by the throat and has practically made itself the undisputed master of an immense kingdom[406]."

Many well-known names and surnames were among those who had returned to Russia. For example, Gruzenberg, who had lived in England and then in the United States. We see him in 1919 occupying the post of Consul General of the USSR in Mexico (a country in which the revolutionaries had high hopes); in the same year, we see him sitting

---

[405]Anthony Sutton, *Ouol strit i bolchevitskaïa revolioutsiia. Wall Street and the Bolshevik Revolution*, traduction de l'anglais, 1998, p. 141–142, [p. 115]. [*Wall Street and the Bolshevik Revolution: The Remarkable Story of the American Capitalists Who financed the Russian Communists*, Clairview Books, 2011. (NdT)].

[406] Ernst Nolte, *La guerra civil europea, 1917-1945*, Fondo de cultura económica, Mexico, 2001, p. 131.

in the central organs of the Komintern. He returned to action in Sweden, then in Scotland, where he was arrested. He reappeared a little later in China in 1923 under the name of Borodine with a whole gang of spies, "being the chief political adviser to the Executive Committee of the Kuomintang", a position that would enable him to further the career of Mao Tse-Tung and Zhou Enlai. However, Chiang Kai-shek suspected Borodine-Gruzenberg of subversive activities and expelled him from China in 1927. He would then return to the USSR where he would become editor-in-chief of the Soviet Information Bureau. He was finally shot in 1951.

From the first hours in power, the Bolsheviks turned to the Jews, offering some of them leadership positions, others executive tasks within the Soviet apparatus. A large number of them responded to the call and committed themselves immediately. It was a real mass phenomenon. From that moment on, Jews leaving the provinces of the former Zone of Residence no longer tried to settle in formerly forbidden provinces, but did everything possible to settle in the big capitals. Lenin was aware of this fact, although he considered it inappropriate for the press to emphasise it: "The fact that a large part of the Jewish middle *intelligentsia* has settled in the Russian cities has rendered a great service to the revolution. It is they who, in the fateful hour, saved the revolution. If we succeeded in taking over the state apparatus and restructuring it, it was exclusively thanks to this breeding ground of new officials—lucid, educated and reasonably competent[407]." This fact was confirmed by Leonard Schapiro: "Thousands of Jews joined the Bolsheviks en masse, for they saw in them the fiercest defenders of the revolution and the most reliable internationalists. Jews also abounded in the lower layers of the Party apparatus[408]." Pasmanij also confirmed this: "The emergence of Bolshevism is linked to the peculiarities of Russian history, but its excellent organisation, Bolshevism owes it in part to the action of Jewish commissars[409]." Indeed, the abolition of the Zone of Residence in 1917 led to an instant exodus of Jews into the interior of the country to conquer the capitals.

The October coup by force coincided in time with the Balfour Declaration, which laid the foundations for an independent Jewish state in Palestine. Part of the new Jewish generation had taken the path of

---

[407]V. Lénine, *O evreiskom voprose v Rossii* [*On the Jewish Question in Russia*], preface by S. Diamanstein, M., Proletarii, 1924, p. 17-18. [p. 87]

[408]Leonard Schapiro, *The role of the Jews in the Russian revolutionary movement*, vol. 40, London, Athlone Press, 1961, p. 164.

[409]Alexandre Soljénisyne, *Deux siècles ensemble*, Éditions Fayard. 2003, p. 89.

Herzl and Jabotinski, but in those years the majority of Jews had given in to the siren songs of Bolshevism. Herzl's path still seemed distant and unrealistic, while Trotsky's path enabled the Jews to gain prestige at once. The Bund and the Zionists had also split and their leaders had joined the side of the victors, disavowing the ideals of democratic socialism." The most important and active part of the Bund, which had hitherto assumed the role of representing the Jewish working masses, joined the Bolsheviks410."

The other socialist parties, the Socialist-Revolutionaries and the Mensheviks, which had many Jews in their ranks and at their head, also hesitated to join the Bolsheviks and split. Among the Menshevik defectors, the famous Lev Mejlis was in Stalin's secretariat, on the editorial board of *Pravda411*, heading the political department of the Red Army, in the Defence Commissariat and commissar in the State Control. His ashes are sealed in the Kremlin wall. Although, it must be said, there were also some Jews among the leaders of the resistance to the Bolsheviks, Solzhenitsyn noted.

Leading the Red Army, the mythical Trotsky was an undisputed internationalist, and he can be believed when he emphatically declared that he rejected any membership of the Jewish community. But judging by the choices he made in his nominations, it is evident that the Jews were closer to him than the Russians. His two closest assistants were Glazman and Sermuks; the head of his personal guard was a certain Dreiter; and when an authoritarian and ruthless replacement had to be found for the post of War Commissar, he appointed Ephraim Sklianski, a physician who had nothing to do with a military man or a commissar. In Moscow, this individual was considered to be the first diamond buyer." He had been discovered in Lithuania during the baggage check of Znoviev's wife, Zlata Bernstein-Lilina, with jewellery worth several million roubles412." Such anecdotes somewhat tarnish the legend that the first revolutionary leaders were great, selfless idealists.

The first really important action of the Bolsheviks was the signing of the separate peace treaty of Brest-Litovsk, which ceded a huge portion of Russian territory to Germany, in order to establish Bolshevik power over the rest of the territory. The head of the signatory delegation was Adolf Iofe; the head of foreign policy was Trotsky. His secretary and proxy, I. Zalkin, had occupied the ministerial cabinet and carried

---

[410]I. M. Biekerman, RiE, *Rossa i evrei*, (*Russia and the Jews*), Berlin, 1924, Paris, 1978, p. 44.

[411]It was the official publication of the Communist Party between 1918 and 1991.

[412]Alexandre Soljénisyne, *Deux siècles ensemble*, Éditions Fayard. 2003, p. 94.

out a purge within the old apparatus. Sverdlov was at the head of the state, Zinoviev and Kamenev headed the two capitals, the former being also the head of the Komintern (the International); Solomon Lozovsky commanded the Profintern (International Red Union) and Oscar Ryvkine the Komsomol (the youth organisation). After the latter, the leadership of the Communist Youth International was taken over by Lazar Abramovitch Chatskine. The All-Russian Commission for the elections to the Constituent Assembly had been entrusted to the young Brodsky; as for the Assembly, its management fell to Uritski, who, with the help of Drabkin, had to set up a new chancellery.

It is impossible to go through all the names of those who held important positions, even many of the key positions. Among the outstanding figures, one must mention "the most illustrious Rosalia Samoilovna Zulkind-Zemliatchka, a true fury of terror" who left for history her name associated with the Crimean massacres. In 1917–1920, she was the secretary of the Moscow Bolsheviks' committee along with Zagorsky, Zelensky and Piatniki (Osip Aronovich Tarchis). The rising star of that revolutionary scene was Lazar Mosheyevich Kaganovich, who was then the chairman of the provincial Party Committee in Nizhny Novgorod (Russia's third largest city), where he reigned a "mass terror". Arkadi Rosengoltz was another actor in the coup d'état in Moscow. He was also a member of the war councils of several army corps. He was Trotsky's closest assistant. Semkhon Nakhimson was the "fierce commissar of the Yaroslavl military region". Samuel Zwilling took the reins of the Executive Committee of the Orenburg region. Abraham Bielenki was the head of Lenin's personal guard; Samuel Filler, a provincial apothecary apprentice, rose to the presidium of the Moscow Cheka. It would be long and tiresome to mention them all.

The role of Jews was particularly visible and relevant in the administrative bodies dealing with the most pressing problem of those years: supply. Here, too, the list of those responsible in key positions is particularly eloquent." Requisitions were to be executed without regard for the consequences, confiscating all the grain in the villages, leaving the producer only a famine ration if necessary". Such was the official directive of the Commissar for Supply in Tyumen Oblast. Grigory Indenbaum demanded, in a telegram signed by his hand, "the most ruthless repression and systematic confiscation of wheat". He gave orders to peasants who had not supplied the state with the fixed quantity of sheep's wool to shear them a second time at the end of autumn (just before winter). Other equally incompetent commissars had millet distributed for sowing, or even roasted sunflower seeds, or threatened to ban the sowing of malt413. At the 10th Party Congress, the Tyumen delegation reported that "peasants who refused to hand over their wheat were placed standing in the pits, sprinkled with water and frozen to death there."

The presence of some Jews on the side of the Bolsheviks had appalling consequences during those terrible weeks and months. These included the assassination of the imperial family, finally ordered by Lenin, who had foreseen the total indifference of the Allies and the weakness of the conservative layers of the Russian people. While the assassination of the Tsar's brother Grand Duke Michael Romanov was perpetrated by Russians, it is known that the most proactive Jews were present at the height of the events surrounding the assassination of the Tsar and his family. The guards were Latvians, Russians and Magyars, but two characters played a decisive role: Filipp Ilyevich Goloshchokin and Yakov Yurovsky. Goloshchokin, a close friend of Yakov Sverdlov, was a member of the Central Committee of the Bolshevik Party. After the coup d'état, he became the absolute master of the Urals region as military commissar and secretary of the Committee of the Urals Soviet. As for Yurovsky, he boasted with aplomb that he had been the best: "It was the bullet from my Colt that stiffened Nicolas." Voikov, the region's supply commissar, provided the barrels of petrol and sulphuric acid needed to destroy the bodies. After the Second World War, "after the communist power had broken off relations with world Jewry, Jews and communists felt uneasy and fear came over them, preferring to keep silent and to conceal the strong participation of Jews in the revolution. At the same time, any remembrance of those events was labelled by Jews as anti-Semitic in intent414."

The Terror

At the height of 1918, Lenin recorded on a gramophone a "special speech on anti-Semitism and the Jews": "The accursed tsarist autocracy has always set the uneducated workers and peasants against the Jews ... Hostility towards the Jews is only lively where the capitalist cabal has darkened the spirit of the workers and peasants. The Jews are our brothers, oppressed like us by capitalism. They are our comrades who fight like us for socialism. Shame on those who sow hostility towards the Jews!" Recordings of this speech were broadcast far and wide, in

[413]Alexandre Soljénisyne, *Deux siècles ensemble*, Éditions Fayard. 2003, p. 243.
[414]Alexandre Soljénisyne, *Deux siècles ensemble*, Éditions Fayard. 2003, p. 90.

the cities and towns of Russia, through the special propaganda trains that ran through the country. This speech was broadcast in clubs, at rallies and assemblies.

On 27 July 1918, just after the execution of the imperial family, the Sovnarkom (Council of People's Commissars) promulgated a special law on anti-Semitism, the conclusion of which had been written in Lenin's handwriting: "The Sovnarkom orders all Soviet deputies to eradicate anti-Semitism. The instigators of pogroms and those who propagate them will be declared outlawed." Signed: Vl. Ulyanov (Lenin). At that time, declaring anti-Semites "outlawed", as Lourié—the promoter of "war communism"—had confirmed, meant simply "shooting them".

To suppress the revolts, the Bolshevik power needed a regular army. In 1918, Leon Trotsky, with the help of Ephraim Skliansky and Yakov Sverdlov, created the Red Army. Jewish fighters were numerous in its ranks and in its chain of command. In the 1980s, the Israeli researcher Aron Abramovich drew up detailed lists of Jews who held commanding positions in the Red Army from the Civil War to the Second World War. His study showed that among the chiefs of staff in the revolutionary councils of the twenty armies, between one and two out of three were Jews (about two-thirds)." The proportion of Jews in political adjunct positions was especially high in all echelons of the army", as well as in the supply of army corps and in military medicine.

The Cheka, or All-Russian Extraordinary Commission for Combating Counter-Revolution and Sabotage, institutionalised the Red Terror long before it was officially proclaimed on 5 September 1918. In fact, it instituted it from its very inception in September 1917 and continued to apply it after the civil war. As early as January 1918, the "death penalty on the spot, without trial or investigation" was already being applied. Then came the round-ups of hundreds and thousands of perfectly innocent hostages, who were shot at night or drowned in rivers in barges full to overflowing with prisoners. The Cheka became the nerve centre of the state leadership. In Sevastopol, after the collapse of the resistance, suspects were being put to the sword and hanged by the tens, by the hundreds. Nakhimov Avenue was full of hanged men who had been arrested in the street and executed without trial415. It is utterly ridiculous to claim that "the most fanatical and careful Cheka shooters were not Jews at all, supposedly ritualists, but generals and officers, formerly faithful servants of the throne416". Who would have tolerated

[415]S.P. Melgounov, *La Terreur rouge en Russie*, Berlin, 1924.
[416]*Tribune juive*, Paris, 1924, 1 February, p. 3. [p. 139].

them in the Cheka," Solzhenitsyn replied. When they were invited, it was to shoot them! "In view of the available archival documents, a contemporary researcher—the first to examine the role of minorities in the Soviet state apparatus—concluded that "in the Red Terror era, national minorities accounted for more than 50% of the central Cheka apparatus, and about 70% in positions of responsibility." Among these national minorities, in addition to the large number of Latvians and a not inconsiderable number of Poles, the number of Jews was also notable, especially among those in positions of responsibility. Among the examining magistrates who had the task of combating the counter-revolution, half were Jews.

This state of affairs caused the Russian population as a whole, both in the ranks of the Reds and the Whites, to judge the Terror to be a "Jewish terror". Rebecca Plastinima-Maizel, for example, a member of the revolutionary committee of the Archangel province, was notorious for her cruelty in the Russian North. She liked to deliberately "pierce necks and foreheads". She shot more than a hundred people with her own hands and made a career of becoming a member of the Supreme Court in the 1940s.

And what about the hecatombs on the Don, the mighty river that submerged thousands of Cossacks in the prime of life? In August 1919, the Volunteer Army that entered Kiev discovered mass graves of shot corpses. As always, the Russian elite were shot first. In Kiev, the number of Cheka collaborators ranged from 150 to 300. The ratio of Jews to the total number of collaborators was one out of four, but most of the key positions were in their hands: of the 20 members of the commission, i.e. those who decided the fate of the people, 14 were Jews. In a converted hangar, the executioners brought in the victim completely naked, ordered him to lie face down on the floor and shot him in the back of the head. The executions were carried out with revolvers (most often with a Colt). The next victim was taken to the same place and laid down next to him. When the number of victims exceeded the capacity of the hangar, the new victims were placed on top of the bodies of those who had been killed earlier[417].

Energising churches

In the summer of 1918, the assault on the Orthodox clergy took place. The persecution of priests and the desecration of relics were

---

[417]Alexandre Soljénisyne, *Deux siècles ensemble*, Éditions Fayard. 2003, p. 148.

accompanied by an unprecedented outburst of sarcasm in the press. The investigating magistrate Chpitsberg, in charge of church affairs, publicly outraged the religious belief of the people and openly mocked sacred rituals in his book (*The Religious Plague*, published in 1919), in which he called Christ abominable names. Such hatred and contempt for the religion of the Russians could not go unnoticed or unnoticed.

Solzhenitsyn considered that several serious mistakes had been made, such as naming Gubelman-Yaroslavsky the head of the Union of the Godless, renaming St. Vladimir's Church "Nachimson", transforming Elisabetgrad into "Zinovevsk", and giving the name "Sverdlovsk" to the city of Yekaterinburg, where the Tsar had been assassinated. S. Boulgakov, who had carefully observed what was happening to Orthodox Christianity under the yoke of the Bolsheviks, wrote in 1941: "In the USSR, the persecution of Christians has surpassed in violence and extent all previous persecutions known throughout history. Certainly, not everything should be attributed to the Jews, but neither should their influence be minimised418." Undoubtedly, the fierce persecutions, crimes and murders perpetrated against the majority religion deeply wounded the Russian people.

Throughout the 1920s, the Russian clergy was ruthlessly annihilated. The foundations and representatives of Russian science in numerous disciplines—history, archaeology, ethnology—were also destroyed; Russians were no longer supposed to have a past. The very notion of "Russian history" was abandoned. The very word "Russian", when one said for example "I am Russian", was perceived as provocative and counter-revolutionary. In the columns of *Vetchernaïa Moskva*, V. Blum allowed himself to demand "to sweep all the historical rubbish from the squares of our cities": the monument to Minin and Pozharsky on Red Square, the monument commemorating Russia's millennium in Novgorod, the statue of St. Vladimir in Kiev; "all those tons of metal should have long since been in a landfill."

The dynamiter-in-chief Kaganovich blew up the Cathedral of Christ the Saviour in Moscow, and insisted that St. Basil's Cathedral be razed to the ground as well. The Orthodox Church was the target of public attacks by a whole faction of "militant atheists", with Gubelman-Yaroslavsky at their head. While many sons of Russian peasants were involved in such actions, it was the involvement of other nationalities in the persecution of the Orthodox Church that made the strongest impression and remained etched in memories.

---

[418]Alexandre Soljénisyne, *Deux siècles ensemble*, Éditions Fayard. 2003, p. 107.

Such were the executioners of the revolution, but what became of the victims? Hostages and prisoners in industrial numbers—Russians; those shot and drowned in crowded barges—Russians; the officers—Russians; the nobles—mostly Russians; the priests—Russians; the members of the Zemstvos419—Russians; the peasants fleeing from enlistment in the Red Army and arrested in the forests—all Russians. If one could today find the names and surnames and make a list, counting back to 1918, of all those shot and drowned during the first years of Soviet power, and if one were to establish the statistics, one would be surprised to find that the revolution had by no means an internationalist, but definitely an anti-Slavic feature420. No, Solzhenitsyn continued, "the Jews were not the driving force behind the October coup d'état. It brought them nothing, since the February revolution had already granted them full and complete freedom. But after the seizure of power by force, the young secularised generation quickly changed horses and confidently set off on the infernal gallop of Bolshevism."

Korolenko, liberal and tolerant as he was, noted in his notebooks in the spring of 1919: "Among the Bolsheviks, there are a large number of Jews and Jewesses. Their tactlessness and self-confidence are shocking and irritating421." Other observations made at the time have come down to us. Nakhivin, for example, noted his impressions of the early days of Soviet power: in the Kremlin, in the Sovnarkom administration, "disorder and chaos reign. You see only Latvians and more Latvians, Jews and more Jews. I was never an anti-Semite, but this... There were so many of them that it was obvious, all very young." In the early years of Soviet power, Jews were in the majority not only in the upper echelons of the Party, but also in the lower strata and in local administrations. Aronson, author of The *Book of the Jews in Russia*, mentioned: "The action of numerous Jewish Bolsheviks who worked in the localities as subordinate agents of the dictatorship and who caused innumerable damages to the population of the country422." It was not so much the national origin that was being questioned, but the anti-national and anti-Russian attitude, the contempt of this "international rabble" for everything that centuries of Russian history had accumulated.

---

[419]The zemstvo: a form of local government instituted by the liberal reforms of Tsar Alexander II's Russian Empire.
[420]Alexandre Soljénisyne, *Deux siècles ensemble*, Éditions Fayard. 2003, p. 103.
[421]Alexandre Soljénisyne, *Deux siècles ensemble*, Éditions Fayard. 2003, p. 99.
[422]G. Aronson, *Evreiskaïa obschestvennost v Rossii 1917-1918*, Petite Encyclopédie juive - 2, 1968, p. 16.

One, two, three revolutions

The desire to export the revolution throughout Europe423 led the Bolsheviks to enter Poland. The local Jewish population, it seems, warmly welcomed the Red Army and sided massively with the Bolsheviks." Whole battalions of Jewish workers took part in the fighting against the Poles" in 1920. The Soviets, which had hastily formed a government for that country, placed Felix Dzerzhinsky and his right-hand man Marchlevsky at its head. Former pharmacist Rotenberg, who had been head of the NKVD in Moscow, was appointed as a specialist in "blood cases"; Bela Kun and Zalkind were also involved in the government before leaving to "purge the Crimea after the failure in Poland".

The Red Revolution spread in 1919 to Hungary and Germany. An American researcher, John Müller, wrote that "the share of Jewish activists was absolutely disproportionate" in the German communist party led by the very famous Rosa Luxemburg. The Munich uprising was led by a "Bohemian-style" Jew, the literary critic Kurt Eisner. He would be assassinated, but in very Catholic and conservative Bavaria, power fell to "a new government of left-wing Jewish intellectuals who proclaimed the "Soviet Republic of Bavaria" (Landauer, Toller, Muzam, Neirat). A week later, this republic was overthrown "by an even more radical group" which proclaimed the "Second Soviet Republic of Bavaria", led by Eugen Leviné." In May 1919, the revolt was crushed. That the leaders of the suppressed communist revolts were Jews is one of the main causes of the upsurge of political anti-Semitism in post-revolutionary Germany," acknowledged John Müller, "424". Ukraine took advantage of the civil war to proclaim its independence in January 1918. Immediately afterwards, the Bolshevik offensive began, followed by the establishment of a new government in Kiev at the end of the month. The new Kiev city commissioner was Gregory Chudnovsky; in finance, Kreisberg; in the press, Raichman; in the army, Schapiro." There was no shortage of Jewish surnames in the highest echelons of the Bolshevik authorities in the centres of Odessa or Yekaterinoslav425". All this was enough, Solzhenitsyn wrote, to fuel talk of "Jewish Bolsheviks". The signing of the peace treaty with Germany at Brest-Litovsk in early February 1918 changed things radically. The independent Ukrainian government returned to Kiev,

[423]Read Hervé Ryssen, *Jewish Fanaticism.*
[424]John Müller, *L'Antisémitisme et le communisme*, 1990.
[425]Alexandre Soljénisyne, *Deux siècles ensemble*, Éditions Fayard. 2003, p. 155.

protected by Austro-German bayonets, allowing the Cossacks to intercept the Jewish commissars and shoot them. The pogroms came a little later: it was thus not the White Army that triggered them, but the Ukrainian armies of the democrat Petliura and the socialist Vinnichenko. From December 1918 to August 1919, according to the International Red Cross Commission, the pogroms claimed some 50,000 victims. Those pogroms "explain to a large extent the weak and reluctant aid that the West gave to the White armies426 ", Solzhenitsyn estimated. Moreover, Wall Street calculations were naturally favourable to the Bolsheviks as they were expected to be the future masters of Russia's wealth.

As for the Entente427, which had not recognised any of the White governments, it hastened to recognise all the national governments forming on Russia's peripheries. The British swooped on the oil wells of Baku; the Japanese occupied the Far East and Kamchatka; and the Americans aided the Bolsheviks' occupation of the coast. The Allies made themselves pay dearly, in gold or in concessions, for all aid to the White armies. When the British left Archangel on the northern front, they took some of the military equipment from the time of the Tsars, gave some to the Reds and threw the rest overboard so that the Whites could not use it. In the summer of 1920, France provided meagre aid to Wrangel to liberate Poland, and six months later demanded payment for food delivered to Russian fighters sheltering at Gallipoli.

That same year, an astonishing text was an extraordinary success throughout Europe: *The Protocols of the Elders of Zion* had had formidable print runs in France, England, Germany, and the United States. The *Protocols* had been presented to Tsar Nicolas II in 1906: "What foresight, what accuracy of execution! "exclaimed the Tsar. However, he ordered the text banned after ordering an investigation by Stolypin, which ruled that it was a forgery.

The conquest of the capitals

The important positions in the two big capitals obviously brought many great advantages, such as the use of the empty flats left by the owners. A whole family from the former residential area could come

[426]Alexandre Soljénisyne, *Deux siècles ensemble*, Éditions Fayard. 2003, p. 171.
[427]Entente cordiale (cordial understanding) is the name of the treaty of non-aggression and regulation of colonial expansion between the United Kingdom and France signed in 1904 and the basis of the alliance in World War I. It is still in force today. It is still in force today.

and live in these flats. People migrated en masse from Odessa to Moscow. It was a real exodus involving tens of thousands of people. These new tenants received abundant provisions from a special distribution centre: "caviar, cheese, butter, smoked sturgeon were never missing from their tables. Everything was special, conceived especially for the new elite: kindergartens, schools, clubs, libraries, etc... The kids from the neighbouring houses hated those from the "Soviet houses" and used to pick on them at the first opportunity428."

From 1917, many Jews flocked to Leningrad, Moscow and the big cities. In 1926, there were 2,211,000 Jews in the Soviet Union settled in the cities (83% of the Jewish population, and 467,000 in the countryside). Although they represented about 23% of the urban population in the Ukraine and up to 40% in the cities of Belarus, they were only 1.82% of the entire Soviet population. In 1923, Biekerman expressed his concern: "Today, the Jew is everywhere, in all echelons of power. The Russian man sees him at the command of Moscow, the first capital of all the Russias, at the head of Petrograd, at the head of the Red Army. He sees that St. Vladimir's Avenue now bears the name of the glorious Nachimson. The Russian man sees in the Jew the judge and the executioner; at every step he meets Jews who are not communists, who are just as destitute as he is, but who nevertheless take the reins of everything and work for the Soviet power. No wonder that the Russian man, comparing the old with the new, is convinced that the present power is Jewish, that this power is made for the Jews and serves their interests429."

The Jewish bourgeoisie had not been eliminated as systematically as the Russian bourgeoisie. Jewish merchants could find support and protection in the Soviet apparatus where they had relatives or relations who intervened on their behalf or gave them advance notice of confiscations of property or raids.

The Russians queued for ten hours in the cold or in the rain in front of the state shops, which made them very unhappy, especially when compared to the relatively well-stocked shops of the Jewish merchants. Lourié-Larin, the fanatical organiser of "war communism", reacted quickly to this popular unrest: "We do not disguise the increase of the Jewish population in Moscow and other big cities. This will also be inevitable in the future." He even predicted the arrival of 600,000 additional Jews from Ukraine and Belarus." This phenomenon should not be regarded as something shameful which the Party should conceal.

---

[428]Alexandre Soljénisyne, *Deux siècles ensemble*, Éditions Fayard. 2003, p. 126.
[429]Alexandre Soljénisyne, *Deux siècles ensemble*, Éditions Fayard. 2003, p. 220.

The working class must be made to understand that anyone who publicly declares himself opposed to the Jews coming to Moscow is, consciously or not, a counter-revolutionary." The migration of Jews to the big cities did not stop during the thirties. The Jewish Encyclopaedia informs us that there were 131 000 Jews in Moscow after the 1926 census, 226 000 in 1933 and 250 000 in 1939[430]. This was what was called in the 1920s the "conquest" of the capitals and large cities of Russia, where living and supply conditions were markedly better. Similar population movements took place within the cities to the more pleasant neighbourhoods.

Executioners on the move

In 1922, Jews accounted for 26% of the members of the Central Committee elected at the Congress. Among the 25 members of the Party Presidium, whose portraits were published in *Pravda*, 11 were Jews, 8 Russians, 3 Caucasians and 3 Latvians. In 1918, at the Presidium table, Jews were in an absolute majority[431]. Zinoviev had gathered around him a large number of Jews in the Petrograd organs of government. At the Twelfth Party Congress in 1923, three of the six members of the Politburo were Jews. Such a numerical disproportion in the upper echelons of the Party must have seemed unbearable to some leaders, Solzhenitsyn wrote.

In terms of real power, the Cheka was in second place. Kritchevsky, a specialist in the archives of the time, quoted some interesting data: "In the mid-1920s, the proportion of representatives of national minorities declined progressively. For the OGPU[432] as a whole it fell to 30–35% and in the leading bodies to 40–45%, while during the Red Terror the figures were 50% and 70% respectively. However, one can note the decrease in the percentage of Latvians and the increase in the percentage of Jews. The 1920s saw a significant influx of Jewish leaders into the leadership bodies of the OGPU[433]." Of Dzerzhinsky's four deputies when he was head of the OGPU, three were Jews: Yagoda, Gerrson and Loutski.

[430]Alexandre Soljénisyne, *Deux siècles ensemble*, Éditions Fayard. 2003, p. 344.

[431]Alexandre Soljénisyne, *Deux siècles ensemble*, Éditions Fayard. 2003, p. 226.

[432]The secret state police, from the initial Cheka, was reorganised from 1922 onwards into the GPU, which in 1923 became the OGPU, and later, roughly speaking, the NKVD, MVD and finally the KGB. (NdT).

[433]Kritchevski, *Les Juifs dans l'appareil de la Tchéka et du Guépéou dans les années vingt*, Moscow-Jerusalem, 1999.

When we examine the careers of all these executioners, we see how they were always on the move, passing from one post to another with astonishing mobility. These incessant comings and goings all over the territory were explained in Lenin's time by the manifest insufficiency of reliable leaders and by the distrust under Stalin: any links they might form in the places where they were stationed had to be nipped in the bud.

To celebrate the tenth anniversary of the glorious Cheka, the omnipresent Iósif Unszlicht (a Polish Jew), one of the founders and Vice-Chairman of the Cheka in 1921, listed in a decree the names of those who had been decorated for "exceptional merits"." Each one of them could have reduced us to ashes with a little wave of the hand," Solzhenitsyn specified: Ghenrij Yagoda, Mikhail [Meier Abramovich] Trilisser, Yakov Agranov (for years he completely invented the accusations in the most important political trials), Zinovi Katnelson, Marvei Berman, Lev Belski, and so on. Nejamkin, born into a Hasidic family in Gomel, was a prosecutor for the Soviet Union and a member of the Soviet delegation to the Nuremberg trial, "a symbol434 "for Solzhenitsyn. In the mind of the Russian peasant, the myriad names he was unable to pronounce, from the Polish Dzerzhinsky to the Latvian Vatsetis, raised questions. The Latvians, precisely, were also a rather vocal minority: it was the Latvian riflemen who dispersed the Constituent Assembly and then ensured the protection of the Kremlin leadership throughout the civil war.

"At that time, all the power was not in the hands of the Jews. The power was pluri-national, and included a good number of Russians. But even if its composition was very heteroclite, that power revolved around deliberately anti-Russian positions, with a will to destroy the Russian state and Russian traditions." But, as Leonard Shapiro noted, "anyone unfortunate enough to fall into the hands of the Cheka was almost certain to face a Jewish examining magistrate, or to be shot on his order435."

From the first international conferences in which the USSR took part—Genoa and The Hague (1922)—Europe could not fail to notice that the Soviet delegations were composed mainly of Jews. In a study by a certain M. Zarubezhnie entitled *The Jews in the Kremlin*, this author, basing himself on the 1925 Yearbook of the People's Commissariat of Foreign Affairs, remarked that "there was no country where the Kremlin did not send one of its faithful Jews."

---

[434]Alexandre Soljénisyne, *Deux siècles ensemble*, Éditions Fayard. 2003, p. 230.
[435]Alexandre Soljénisyne, *Deux siècles ensemble*, Éditions Fayard. 2003, p. 231.

Denying the evidence

The rapid successes of the Jews in the Bolshevik administration did not go unnoticed either in Europe or in the United States. They were even admired, and after the October coup, Jewish public opinion in the United States made no secret of its sympathy for the Russian revolution. They had been given "fierce and unlimited power", Solzhenitsyn wrote. For this was the truth: throughout the 1920s, many rushed to serve the Bolshevik Moloch, with no thought for the wretched country that was to serve as a testing ground. Gorky was one day violently attacked in the press for an article in which he reproached the Soviet government for having given them too many positions of responsibility. He had nothing against Jews as such, but believed that Russians should dominate and be in the majority. The Moscow newspaper *Der Emes* ("*The Truth*"), was outraged: "In short, he proposes that the Jews renounce their participation in the affairs of the state. Get out of there! Such a decision can only be taken by counter-revolutionaries or cowards."

As early as the 1920s, at the end of the civil war, arguments were propagated to excuse the Jews. Attention was drawn to the living conditions in which many Jews found themselves after the October coup d'état. Forty-two percent of Russia's Jewish population was engaged in a commercial activity that had been banned by the new government and was therefore in a precarious situation with no alternative but to enter the Soviet state apparatus in order not to starve to death. The writer Pomerants justified the mass entry of Jews into the administration as follows: "There was no other way out for them than the civil service"." There was no other way out," Solzhenitsyn was indignant." But the tens of thousands of Russian civil servants who refused to serve Bolshevism preferred to resist, even at the cost of a thousand sufferings. Moreover, they did not receive food aid from bodies such as the Junta or the ORT436, financed by the wealthy Jews of the West." Enlisting in the Cheka was never the only alternative, as Pasmanik also argued437.

In the same way, the argument that the Jews of Russia threw themselves into the arms of the Bolsheviks because of their past humiliations does not hold water. It is necessary to compare the situation with the two other communist coups by force in Bavaria and

---

[436]Obchtchestvo Pemeslennogo Trouda soudé evreiev: Association for Jewish handicraft work.
[437]D.S. Pasmanik, *La Révolution russe et les Juifs*, p. 156, [p. 111].

Hungary, which occurred at the same time as Lenin's coup. We read this description in I. Levine438: "The number of Jews serving the Bolshevik regime in these two countries is very high. In Bavaria, we find among the commissars the Jews Levine, Axelrod, the anarchist ideologist Landauer and Ernst Toller", while "the proportion of Jews who have taken the reins of the Bolshevik movement in Hungary is 95%. Now, the civil rights situation of the Jews was excellent in Hungary, where there had long been no limitations; in the cultural and economic sphere, the Jews enjoyed such a prominent position that the anti-Semites even spoke of total control of the Jews." Let us also remember that the mass entry of Jews into the Soviet apparatus had taken place at the end of 1917, i.e. before the pogroms during the civil war in 1919. Therefore, it is not these events that motivated the Jews to commit themselves to Bolshevism; on the contrary, it was the excessive participation of Jews in Bolshevism that was the cause of the pogroms of 1919.

The Parisian daily *Tribune juive* mentioned this subject, dismissing outright any form of possible debate or introspection about what happened in Russia: "The question of the Jews' responsibility for the Russian revolution has so far only been raised by anti-Semites. Now comes the announcement of a campaign of repentance and accusations. Nothing new, except a string of names of which we are up to our ears439."

Boris Pasternak's feelings were quite unique. When he described, in his *Doctor Zhivago*, 'the Jews' 'pious, self-sacrificing way of keeping themselves apart' and 'their fragility and inability to strike back', a contemporary of those years was 'dumbfounded', wrote Solzhenitsyn. Another Jewish author said of the 1920s: "In university classrooms, it was often the Jews who set the tone, not realising that their intellectual feast was taking place against the background of the destruction of the country's majority people." And he added: "I am surprised at the unanimity with which my compatriots deny any responsibility for Russian history in the 20th century440."

"Words such as these would be salutary for our two peoples if they were not so hopelessly minority and isolated..." For "it is not to settle scores that history must be remembered, nor to reiterate mutual accusations ... It is in a spirit of clear-sighted analysis of history that the question of the mass participation of the Jews in the Bolshevik administration and in the atrocities committed by it must be clarified. It

---

438Alexandre Soljénisyne, *Deux siècles ensemble*, Éditions Fayard. 2003, p. 114.
439Alexandre Soljénisyne, *Deux siècles ensemble*, Éditions Fayard. 2003, p. 150, 171.
440G. Chourmak, *Choulgine et ses apologètes*, Novy mir, 1994, no. 11, p. 244, [p. 299].

is not acceptable to evade the question by saying: "they were rabble, renegades from Judaism, we do not have to answer for them". If the Jews of Russia only have memories of that time to justify themselves, Solzhenitsyn added, it would mean that the level of national consciousness has dropped, that consciousness would be lost. The Germans could also deny their responsibility for the Hitler period by saying: "they were not real Germans, they were the dregs of society, they did not ask our opinion". But all peoples answer for their past, even for their most ignominious periods. How can they answer? By striving for awareness and understanding: how could such a thing happen, where is our guilt, is there a danger of it happening again? It is in this spirit that the Jewish people should answer both to their murderous revolutionaries and to their ranks of individuals who served them. It is not a question here of answering to other peoples, but to oneself, to one's conscience and to God. Just as we Russians must answer for the pogroms, for our incendiary peasants, insensitive to mercy, and for our Red soldiers fallen into madness, and for our sailors transformed into wild beasts441."

Murderous suspicion

The old anti-Semitism had been completely swept out of the country by the sweeping October revolution. Those who had protected the throne, all the petty bourgeoisie of the cities, had been shot or locked up in camps. There was no anti-Semitism among the Russian workers and peasants before the revolution, and the intelligentsia felt "deep sympathy for the Jews", as indeed the Bolshevik leaders acknowledged. But anti-Semitism resurfaced more strongly." It appeared in regions where Jews were once almost unknown and where the Jewish question did not even cross the minds of the inhabitants442." In working-class or peasant circles, the reactions were eloquent: "It is enough for a Jew— be he a simple acquaintance—to join them for them to change their conversation."

The press organ of the Zionists in Paris, *Rassvet*, wrote in 1922: "Recently, Gorki has declared in substance that "the Jewish Bolsheviks themselves contribute to the rise of anti-Semitism in Russia by their often misplaced behaviour. It is the plain truth!"." And this was not about Trotsky, Kamenev or Zinoviev, "Gorky is not talking about them,

441Alexandre Soljénisyne, *Deux siècles ensemble*, Éditions Fayard. 2003, p. 131.
442Maslov, *La Russie, après quatre ans de révolution*, Paris, 1922.

but about the rank-and-file Communist Jews, those who are at the head of small and medium-sized Soviet bodies, those who, through their functions, come into daily and permanent contact with the population443." The recruitment of administrative agents was very favourable to the Jews, since they took advantage of the solidarity that bound them to each other." This preference for their own often took a rather crude and humiliating form for the others," wrote Maslov.

The Bolshevik leaders had other explanations. For them, anti-Semitism was first and foremost a question of social class, not nationality. But one could also see "the hand of an underground counter-revolutionary organisation spreading lies among the working classes444". According to Larine, the "central focus of anti-Semitism" was in fact the urban bourgeoisie: "The struggle against bourgeois anti-Semitism is confused with the question of the eradication of the bourgeoisie itself", the Bolshevik explained. Thus, "bourgeois anti-Semitism will disappear with the bourgeoisie."

Larine acknowledged, however, that in the working-class world anti-Semitism manifested itself "more frequently and more intensely than years before". It was clear that this was propaganda orchestrated by secret organisations of the White Army: "Behind the anti-Jewish propaganda we see the hand of monarchist clandestine organisations"." Anti-Semitism, Larine concluded, is a hidden mobilisation against the Soviet government, and those who are against the position of the Soviet government on the Jewish question are, consequently, against the workers and in favour of capitalism."

From there, the Soviet propaganda machine could be set in motion in order to "sensitise" the population: "It is essential to make the masses understand that anti-Jewish agitation is in reality preparing the counter-revolution. The masses must learn to distrust anyone who expresses anti-Semitic sympathies. The masses must see in him either a counter-revolutionary or an intermediary of the monarchist secret organisations445." Public sessions of the "people's court for cases connected with anti-Semitism" are to be organised in the factories. The retarding elements are to be "reported, the active elements are to be repressed ... There is no reason why Lenin's law should not be applied."

Now, according to Lenin's famous law of 27 July 1918, Solzhenitsyn pointed out, "active anti-Semites were to be declared 'outlawed'—that is, shot—for being guilty of inciting pogroms", and

443D.S. Pasmanik, *La Révolution russe et les Juifs*, p. 198
444Larine (Michel Lourié), *Les Juifs et l'antisémitisme*. [p. 246-252]
445Larine (Michel Lourié), *Les Juifs et l'antisémitisme*. [p. 251]

not just for participating in them. The law encouraged Jews to denounce any offence to their national dignity. Article 59-7 of the 1922 Penal Code ("incitement to national or religious hatred and division") was amply sufficient for sentences ranging up to confiscation of property or the death penalty. This article referred to the provisions on crimes against the state of 26 February 1927, which "extended the notion of incitement to national hatred" to include "the dissemination, drafting or possession of written documents". The mere possession of written documents could lead to the worst complications.

Thus, in May 1928, the struggle against anti-Semitism was duly on the agenda of party meetings, and had to be mentioned in public lectures, in the press, on radio, in the cinema and in school textbooks; it was necessary to be ruthless and to apply the most severe disciplinary sanctions. A violent press campaign followed: "Death to the accomplices of the counter-revolution! "Communist militants in one Moscow district decided to include the issue in school curricula: "Anti-Semitism is not always treated as severely as it should be. It should be classified as a social perversion, like alcoholism or debauchery446."

In 1929, the secretary of the Komsomol Central Committee, Rachmanov, declared that "the most serious thing in the present circumstances is hidden anti-Semitism". Those who knew our Soviet language, Solzhenitsyn explained, understood at once that it was a matter of combating opinions solely on the basis of suspicion. Grigori Landau said of his Jewish opponents: "They suspect and accuse all the nationalities around us of anti-Semitism. Those who express unfavourable opinions about Jews are regarded by them as declared anti-Semites, while those who do not are regarded as hidden anti-Semites447." The most furious anti-Semite could not have found a better argument for the people to identify Soviet power with the Jews. In 1930, the Supreme Court had to make the following clarifications: Article 59-7 was not to be applied "in case of aggression against individuals belonging to national minorities in the context of a personal dispute". This revealed that the judicial machine was already in full swing.

Land is not enough

---

[446]"Anti-Semitism is not an opinion. It is a perversion. A perversion that kills." Jacques Chirac's speech at the inauguration of the Shoah (Holocaust) memorial in Paris on Tuesday 25 January 2005.
[447]Alexandre Soljénisyne, *Deux siècles ensemble*, Éditions Fayard. 2003, p. 253.

In its quest for credit, Soviet power sought the sympathy and favour of the foreign bourgeoisie, and most particularly the Jewish bourgeoisie of the diaspora. However, this source of funding would quickly dry up and a way had to be found to boost foreign aid again. It seems that the grandiose land settlement project was for propaganda purposes. Indeed, the idea of a rehabilitation of land work for Jews raised a wave of joyful hope in the international Jewish community. Collections were organised in numerous countries and everyone contributed. Initially it was planned to transplant about 100,000 Jewish families, i.e. about 20% of the Jewish population of the Soviet Union, to southern Ukraine and the Crimea. It was also planned to create autonomous Jewish regions. The aim was to tie the Jews of the rest of the world to the communist power. In this way the rich Americans could be blackmailed: if Soviet power were to collapse, a huge pogrom would sweep away all the Jewish colonies founded; it would therefore be necessary to support Soviet power at any cost.

In the autumn of 1924, a governmental Committee for the Rural Settlement of Jewish Workers was set up, flanked by a pan-Russian Union of Volunteers for the Settlement of Jewish Workers. Solzhenitsyn brought up a childhood memory with a touch of irony: "In 1927–1928, at school, we were forced to contribute—that is, to ask our parents for money—to the Association of the Friends of the Children of the said All-Russian Union. Numerous associations were created in various countries to support this initiative."

However, these Jewish settlements did not develop as expected. Firstly because "many Jews, although unemployed, refused to engage in agriculture448." Moreover, the settlement of Jewish settlers in the Crimea provoked hostile reactions from the Tatars and the local peasantry who were already short of land. This region was, however, where most hopes had been pinned, although, to tell the truth, the project annoyed American Zionists who saw it as an alternative to Zionism and the idea of a return to Israel. This programme to convert Jews to agriculture was therefore a failure. Only five thousand families settled in the Crimea instead of the expected fifteen thousand. Many settlers returned to their former places of residence, or left for the nearest towns. The Jewish kolkhoz were integrated with the others, and the projects of Jewish colonisation in Ukraine and Crimea were definitely abandoned. The most important initiative in this area was to be Birobiyan, an Asian territory that was to become a Jewish republic.

---

[448]*Petite Encyclopedie juive*, Jérusalem, 1976, p. 185.

But again this plan was a failure, as only 14% of the Jewish settlers remained there. In 1933, the Jewish population was barely 6,000.

The intellectual elite

Jewish culture in the 1920s was already a 'proletarian' Soviet culture, but in the Yiddish language. As such, it was able to benefit from state support for its newspapers and theatres. By contrast, "bourgeois" culture in Hebrew was eradicated. A wave of arrests wiped out the Zionist circles in September 1924. The history of the Jewish people was completely hidden at the same time as the historical school and Russian philosophy were dismantled. The Jewish State Theatre, subsidised by the regime, worked to ridicule the customs and religion of Russia's small pre-revolutionary Jewish communities and strove to prestige the authority of the Soviet regime in the eyes of Jews all over the world through numerous tours in Europe. Under the influence of communist ideology, Jewish youth had turned away from their religion and national culture to build an egalitarian society.

An author from the 1990s, Sonja Margolina, confirmed this: "Jews were subjected to a process of political Bolshevisation and social Sovietisation: the Jewish community as an ethnic, religious and national structure disappeared without a trace."

But while the authorities mercilessly beat the Orthodox Church, considering it one of the "most dangerous enemies of the Soviet regime449 ", the Bolshevik power, in principle hostile to any form of religion, had a fairly tolerant attitude towards Jewish religious practice. Most synagogues continued to function, and the Jewish community was the only one in Moscow to get permission to build new religious buildings in the 1920s. On the other hand, the destructive fury of the Komsomols prevailed during Orthodox Easter: "They tore the candles out of the hands of the parishioners, threw away the blessed Easter cakes, climbed on the domes to tear off the crosses. Thousands of beautiful churches were destroyed, reduced to piles of stones and thousands of priests were shot, thousands more deported to camps450."

From the early years of the regime, the doors of science and culture were thrown open to the Jewish intelligentsia and youth. At first, the cultural elite was ruled by Olga Kameneva, Trotsky's sister. Many Jews became directors of film studios, an art form highly prized by Lenin for

---

[449]Petite Encyclopedie juive, tome VIII, Jérusalem, 1976, p. 194.
[450]Alexandre Soljénisyne, Deux siècles ensemble, Éditions Fayard. 2003, p. 287.

its propaganda potential. The worldwide success of Eisenstein's *Battleship Potemkin*, for example, was a pro-Soviet war machine that stoked hatred of the old Russia. The massacre on the Odessa Grand Staircase was a "pure invention". Eisenstein would serve Stalin several times as a propagandist. With Alexander Nevsky, which exalted the patriotism of the Russians by narrating the 1242 victory against the Teutonic Knights, he galvanised the troops against Hitler's Germany. Indeed, during the war, Stalin had realised that only patriotism could motivate soldiers who were reluctant to give their lives for Marxist ideology and the communist system. The patriotic feelings of the majority of Russians were thus exploited and put at the service of the Soviet state.

Stalin's favourite painter was Isaac Brodski, who became the official portraitist of the regime. He painted several portraits of Lenin, Trotsky and other dignitaries of the regime and was appointed director of the Academy of Fine Arts in 1934. The Soviet theatre was dominated by the figure of Meyerhold. He had his staunch admirers, but also some detractors. A. Tirkova-Williams wrote in his memoirs that he used to break the morale of authors and actors "with his dogmatic spirit and insensitive harshness".

The ruin of traders

The general feeling of sympathy allowed the Soviet leadership to easily negotiate financial aid from the West, especially from the United States. Without such aid, they would have been unable to pull the country out of economic depression. The American businessman Armand Hammer, Lenin's favourite, obtained the concession for the Alapayevsk asbestos deposits in 1921. He would later brazenly export the treasures of the imperial collections to the US. Hammer would periodically return to Moscow under Stalin and Khrushchev to take cargo ships full of icons, paintings, porcelain and Fabergé gold and silverware451.

The success of the first two five-year plans was not only due to the forced exploitation of the working masses; it also required the abundant supply of material and the collaboration of experts. All these goods

---

[451] "Armand Hammer (…) became one of the leaders of East-West trade, reconciling his friendship with Lenin and his full adherence to the capitalist system. He exploited asbestos mines in the USSR, imported cars and tractors, and bought Russian works of art from the state in exchange for industrial products." In Jacques Attali, *Los Judíos, el mundo y el dinero*, Fondo de cultura económica, Buenos Aires, 2005, p. 403.

came from the Western capitalist countries, mainly from the USA. The Soviet communists paid generously in kind—minerals, timber, raw materials—by exporting all the wealth plundered from the former empire of the tsars. These transactions were carried out under the supervision of international financial tycoons and transited along the trade routes inaugurated during the civil war. Ships full of gold and works of art from the Hermitage museum were bound for ports on the other side of the Atlantic. The American historian Anthony Sutton was able to trace meetings between Wall Street and the Bolsheviks in recently opened diplomatic and financial archives[452].

"The Bolsheviks and the bankers have a common platform: internationalism." In that sense, Solzhenitsyn wrote, the support "of Morgan and Rockfeller for collectivised enterprises and the abolition of individual rights" was not strange. American financiers had always steadfastly refused to lend money to Russia before the revolution, citing as a pretext the plight of the Jews, despite the juicy profits they might have pocketed. Now, if they were prepared to undermine their own interests at that time, it was clear that now, in the early 1930s, the slightest suspicion of persecution of Jews in the Soviet Union would have driven the "Rockfeller empire" away from the Soviet market and the latter would have stopped supporting the Bolsheviks.

During the period of economic liberalisation called NEP (New Economic Policy, 1921–1926[453]), in Moscow in 1924, 75% of the pharmacies and perfume shops were owned by Jews, 55% of the shops selling manufactured goods, 49% of the jewellers' shops." On arriving in a town he did not know, the Jewish merchant would win over his clientele by making large discounts on the private market. Jews were often among those who had first become rich during the NEP. The hatred for them was also due to the fact that they had many connections in the Soviet apparatus which facilitated many procedures and formalities[454]." This was further confirmed by the impressive list published in the *Izvestia* of 22 April 1928 of "those who had not paid their taxes or had evaded collection".

At the end of 1926, the complete dismantling of the NEP began. This process began with the prohibition of private grain trade. In 1927,

---

[452] Anthony Sutton, *Wall Street ant the Bolshevik Revolution. Wall Street and the Bolshevik Revolution*, p. 210 [p. 302].

[453]New Economic Policy: was an economic policy of "state capitalism" adopted by Lenin to stabilise the ruinous economic situation after the revolution and civil war. (NdT).

[454]Alexandre Soljénisyne, *Deux siècles ensemble*, Éditions Fayard. 2003, p. 255.

the selling prices in the trade began to be fixed. The Jews, who were mainly engaged in finance, trade and handicrafts, were the first to be affected by the anti-capitalist measures. Heavy penalties hit private trade: confiscation of goods and real estate and deprivation of civic rights. Experiments in social and economic matters, nationalisations and collectivisations of all kinds did not only affect the middle bourgeoisie; it also deprived small shopkeepers and craftsmen of resources. Shopkeepers had to close their shops because of the tax burden, and many Jewish shopkeepers ended up on the street. So much so that at the end of 1929, the Soviet of People's Commissars issued a resolution "on the measures to be taken for the economic situation of the Jewish masses." Many then went into the service of the state, but always in the financial, banking and commercial spheres.

The farmer's enemy

The kulaks were not much more than the mujiks, the Russian peasants. They owned one horse and two or three cows, and hired a few months a year one or two peasant labourers poorer than themselves; but this "class", because of its reluctance to collectivism, was problematical for the Soviet power. At the XVth Party Congress in December 1927, the thorny problem of the peasantry had to be tackled. Stalin must probably have thought that for this campaign, which was to be massively directed against the Slav populations, it was safer to rely on the Jews than on the Russians. Within the Gosplan (Committee for Economic Planning), Stalin maintained a solid Jewish majority. In the bodies that conceived and executed collectivisation there was naturally Larine, as well as Leon Kristman, who headed the Agrarian Institute from 1928; Yakovlev-Epstein Yakov headed the Commissariat of Agriculture. It would obviously be wrong to explain this ruthless enterprise of destruction of the peasantry by blaming the Jews for the role they played," Solzhenitsyn pointed out. If Yakovlev-Epstein had not been there, a Russian could perfectly well have taken the reins of the Commissariat of Agriculture; Soviet history has amply demonstrated this." It remained true, however, that Lenin had oriented his strategy against the Russian people, whom he regarded as the "main obstacle455".

All the great pens remained mute in the face of "this cold extermination of the Russian peasantry." The whole of the West was

---

[455]Alexandre Soljénisyne, *Deux siècles ensemble*, Éditions Fayard. 2003, p. 294.

silent during those terrible years when 15 million peasants were ruined, penned up like animals, driven from their homes and deported to certain death in the confines of the taiga and the tundra. Did anyone raise his voice in defence of the peasants? Shortly afterwards, in 1932–1933, between five and six million people died of starvation in a famine planned and organised by the Soviet power to finish off the peasantry. The "free press of the free world" remained silent once again. Ukraine had been especially affected and mortified during that period when many Jews had been "invested with a power of life and death over the peasantry". This was the reason why Ukrainians were under the impression that the famine was directly attributable to the Jews." It was during collectivisation that the idea of the Jew as the implacable enemy of the peasant took definite root—even in the most remote places where no one had ever seen Jews in the flesh456."

Nothing has changed

Between 1923 and 1924, Stalin and Trotsky fought fiercely for power. Then Zinoviev also claimed with equal ferocity the first place in the Party. Deceived by Stalin, Zinoviev and Kamenev allied with Trotsky in 1926 in a "Unified Opposition"." In other words, Solzhenitsyn explained, three Jewish leaders of the first order positioned themselves on the same front." At some point, Stalin had probably considered the trump card of anti-Semitism against this unified opposition. That might have seemed advantageous in the short term, but his incomparable political acumen dissuaded him just when it seemed that he had opted for that solution. He knew that the Jews were at that time still very numerous in the Party, and that they were very valuable in winning foreign support. Finally, he probably thought that he would still need the Jewish Party leaders. In fact, he never separated himself from his favourite henchman, Lev Mejlis, nor from his faithful comrade of the civil war, Moses Rukhimovich. He denounced manifestations of anti-Semitism in the struggle against the Opposition and promoted Jewish penetration of numerous bodies and institutions457. At the 16th Congress in 1930, Stalin declared that "Russian chauvinism" represented "the main danger to the national question".

---

[456]Sonja Margolina, [p. 84].
[457]Alexandre Soljénisyne, *Deux siècles ensemble*, Éditions Fayard. 2003, p. 292.

When the Trotskyist opposition was completely defeated, the number of Jews in the Party apparatus was considerably reduced, although this purge was not at all anti-Jewish. In the Politburo there remained in a prominent position Lazar Kaganovich, "a sinisterly ruthless and ridiculously mediocre fellow", who had all his brothers appointed to important posts458. At the beginning of the 1930s, Stalin crushed two all-Russian nationalist oppositions, the Rýkov-Bukharin-Tomsky opposition on the one hand and the Syrtsov-Ryutin-Uglanov opposition on the other. He relied on the Jewish Bolshevik leaders.

The activity of many Jews endured within bodies such as the GPU, the army, diplomacy and on the ideological front. We shall confine ourselves here to a brief overview, based on the diaries of the time and the most recent Jewish encyclopaedias. In the Presidium of the Central Control Commission of the 16th Party Congress (1930), there were 10 Jews out of 25 members; if we compare this with the situation of the Central Party Committee in the 1920s, we see that nothing had really changed: Jews constituted one-sixth of the membership. But the real power of the Bolsheviks was concentrated in the hands of the People's Commissars. In 1936, eight Jews were counted among them: Maksim Litvinov for Foreign Affairs; the no less famous Gutenrij Yagoda for Internal Affairs; Lazar Kaganóvich for Railways; I. Weitser for Foreign Trade; M. Kalmanovich for the Sovkhoz (Commissariat created in 1932); Grigory Kaminski for Health; Z. Belenski headed the Soviet Control Commission. In the same government there were also numerous Jewish surnames in the deputy commissariats of various commissariats of Finance, Communications, Transport, Agriculture, Justice, Education, Defence, etc. Stalin had already appointed the sinister Yakovlev-Epstein to carry out the collectivisation of the countryside. He was to become chairman of the Kolkhoz Soviet from 1934 onwards.

From the very beginning, they occupied important positions in the political organs of the army. The entire central political service of the Red Army had passed through the hands of Lev Mejlis (Solzhenitsyn provided a long list of inspectors, directors, service chiefs and military prosecutors). In 1934, the GPU metamorphosed into the NKVD (People's Commissariat for Internal Affairs), with Gutenj Yagoda at its head. For once, the names of the State Security Commissars had been made public, and half of them were Jewish (Solzhenitsyn provided another long list of personalities). Abram Slutsky was head of the Soviet foreign intelligence service of the NKVD; he thus headed the espionage

---

[458]Alexandre Soljénisyne, *Deux siècles ensemble*, Éditions Fayard. 2003, p. 304.

services. His deputies were Boris Berman and Sergei Chpiguelglas. Three days after Nikolai Yezhov's appointment to the Commissariat of Internal Affairs, his deputy took office: Matvei Berman, who at the same time retained his position as head of the Gulag. Mikhail Litvine became head of the NKVD executive service. Isaac Shapiro, another loyal collaborator, was appointed head of the NKVD secretariat. In December 1936, there were seven Jews in the ten departments of the glorious GUGB (Main Directorate of State Security) service of the NKVD, the secret police.

In 1990, thanks to the Glasnot ("transparency"), startling information revealed that the gassing vans (mobile gas chambers) had not been invented by Hitler, but by Isai Davidovich Berg, head of the economic service of the NKVD in the Moscow region. Berg was in charge of executing the sentences of the regional NKVD. His mission was to drive the condemned to the place of execution. But when three courts began to operate at full capacity at the same time, the task of the execution squads became almost impossible. Someone came up with a novel idea: to strip the victims naked, tie and gag them so that they would not scream, and throw them into closed vans, disguised as bread delivery vans. During the long journey, fumes escaped into the vehicle. By the time they reached their destination, on the edge of a random pit, the prisoners were already lying dead459. Berg was shot in 1939, not for his atrocious methods, but on charges of conspiracy. He was reinstated in 1956, despite the fact that the deadly invention was on his record." It cannot be denied," Solzhenitsyn concluded: "History has consecrated many Jews as executors of the sad fate of the Russian people."

One feels ashamed to read that

Lazar Kogan had been appointed head of the Gulag, before being sent to the White Sea Canal. Zinovi Katznelsohn was second in the hierarchy. From 1936 onwards, Israel Pliner became head of the Gulag, and under his orders the work on the Moscow-Volga Canal was completed. It should be emphasised that the secretaries of the regional committees did not hold absolute power, but were rather the potentates of the GPU-NKVD, the real lords of all these territories. These regional potentates constantly changed their places of assignment, in the greatest

---

[459]Alexandre Soljénisyne, *Deux siècles ensemble*, Éditions Fayard. 2003, p. 322. The Polish journalist and photographer Tomasz Kizny has documented this period: *La Grande Terreur en URSS 1937-1938*, Les Editions Noir Sur Blanc, 2013.

secrecy, and had the right of life and death over each and every inhabitant. Some are known by their full names, others only by their surnames, others only by their initials.

"The Latvian Ans Bernstein, wrote Solzhenitsyn, one of my witnesses for the writing of *Gulag Archipelago,* believed that he had managed to survive in the forced labour camps because in the darkest moments he had turned to Jews who had taken him for one of their own, because of his surname and appearance, and who had always helped him since then. He also noted that in the camps where he was imprisoned (those of Buriepolomski, for example, whose chief was a certain Perelman), Jews were always recruited for the posts of free employees (Chulman, head of the special department; Grindberg, head of the camp; Keguels, chief factory mechanic) and these in turn chose Jews from among the detainees as their deputies. The free Jew was not so stupid as to see in a Jewish prisoner an "enemy of the people", as a Russian indoctrinated with another Russian did. They saw in him above all an unfortunate compatriot."

Sometimes a group of Jewish prisoners would form, unconcerned about their survival. What did they do then? Engineer Abram Zisman told an anecdote: in the Novo-Archangel prison, "we took advantage of some free time to count how many anti-Jewish pogroms there had been in the time of the Russian state. This question interested those in charge of the camp. The head of the camp was Captain Gremine [N. Gerchel, son of a Jewish tailor]. He sent a letter to Leningrad, to the archives of the former MVD. The answer came eight months later: between 1811 and 1917, there had been 76 anti-Jewish pogroms throughout Russia, and the number of victims had been around 3000" (it was not specified whether they were only dead).

The scale of the death toll under the Soviet regime is obviously very different. The famous White Sea-Baltic Canal penitentiary swallowed up hundreds of thousands of Russian and Ukrainian peasants in the years 1931–1932. In a newspaper dated August 1933, dedicated to the completion of the canal, we could read the list of the decorated persons: many modest medals for the shutterers and carpenters, but prestigious medals—the Order of Lenin—for eight persons whose photos were published in large format. Among them, only two engineers, because the entire top management of the construction site was rewarded. At the head of the collective was Ghenrij Yagoda, commissar of the NKVD; Mavtei Berman, head of the Gulag; Semion Firine, head of BelBalt; Lazar Kogan, head of construction; Yakov Rappoport, deputy head of construction; Naftali Frenkel, head of works at the White Sea construction site (and considered the evil genius of the whole archipelago). Forty years after the events, Solzhenitsyn published the portraits of those "miserable six" in *Gulag Archipelago*: "I have been reproached for having published the portraits of the chiefs of the construction site of the famous White Sea-Baltic Canal, and I have been accused of having selected only Jews. But I didn't select anyone: I published the photos of all the field commanders who appeared in a yearbook published in 1936. Who is to blame for the fact that they were Jews460? ""I took them as they were, without selecting them, but the whole world was outraged. It was anti-Semitism! And where were they looking when these portraits were first published in 1933? Why didn't they express their indignation then? "Thus, the reflections of some intellectuals can be provocative. When, for example, Mr. S. Schwartz speaks of "the legend of Jewish domination" and "misconceptions about the exaggerated power of the Jews within the organs of the state461 ", one is perplexed. According to him, Jewish intellectuals simply had "almost no other possibility of survival except the service of the state"." One feels ashamed to read that," Solzhenitsyn was indignant, "What is this situation of oppression and hopelessness that leaves you with no other possibility of survival than the most privileged positions? "

The big butcher's shop

The great Stalinist purges of 1937–1938 were a brutal and unexpected blow to the Jews, which disrupted their entire world. If one studies the lists of high-ranking dignitaries who perished in 1937–1938, one finds that Jews accounted for a large proportion. A contemporary historian wrote: "While representatives of this nationality were at the head of 50% of the main services of the central apparatus for Internal Affairs, they occupied only 6% of the posts on 1 January 1939462." On the basis of the numerous lists of those shot published over the last ten years, and on the basis of the biographical volumes of the *New* Jewish-Russian *Encyclopaedia*, Solzhenitsyn explained, we are able to trace the fate of the Chekists, the heads of the Red Army, the diplomats and the Party leaders. Indeed, it was the Chekists who paid the heaviest price for their past during the "Yezhovian" purges, nicknamed after the surname of the new master of the NKVD, Nikolai Yezhov. The great

[460]Alexandre Soljénisyne, *Deux siècles ensemble*, Éditions Fayard. 2003, p. 317.
[461]S. Schwartz, *L'antisémitisme en Union Soviétique*, New York, 1962, p. 118, [p. 335].
[462]Kostyrtchenko, *La politique de Staline*, Moscow, 2001, p. 210, [p. 320].

butchery did not spare the old Bolsheviks: Kamenev and Zinoviev, of course, but also Ryazanov and Goloshchokin. The Crimean executioner, Bela Kun himself, disappeared too, and with him twelve other people's commissars of the communist government in Budapest. Only Kaganóvich remained in office, even participating in other purges. By the summer of 1938, all the commanders of the military regions, without exception, had been liquidated. Among the top political leaders who had perished were all 17 army commissars, 25 of the 28 corps commissars and 34 of the 36 divisional commissars. There was a strong proportion of Jews on the lists of war chiefs shot in 1937–1938[463], but in itself, this phenomenon had not been perceived as an offensive specifically directed against Jews: Jews fell into the mincer because they occupied a large number of eminent positions.

By the mid-1930s, Stalin had become aware of the complications of taking an overly hostile stance against the Jews, along the lines of Hitler and the National Socialist Party[464]. Even so, it is possible that he harboured some animosity towards them—his daughter's memoirs tend to confirm this—even if he did not let it show to his closest collaborators. Alongside his frontal struggle against the Trotskyists, Stalin did not neglect another aspect of great advantage to himself: the possibility of finally having a free hand to reduce the influence of the Jews within the Party. Moreover, with the threat of war looming in Europe, Stalin must have sensed that "the proletarian international" would not bail him out, but rather the patriotic feelings of the Russians which would have to be revived for the occasion. Nevertheless, the official atmosphere of the Soviet regime in the 1930s was devoid of antipathy towards the Jews. Until the war, the vast majority of Soviet Jews remained in line with the regime[465].

Never on the front line

The invasion of the territory by the German armies entailed the rapid evacuation of the populations that had most to fear from the Nazis. Several Jewish sources unequivocally underline the energetic measures taken by the Soviet authorities in this matter, which enabled many Jews to escape extermination. In many cities, Jews were evacuated before

---

[463]Souvenirov, *La Tragédie de l'Armée rouge*, 1998, [p. 324].

[464]The reader is reminded of the famous headline on the front page of *The Daily Express of London* of 24 March 1933: "*Judea Declares War on Germany—Jews of All the World Unite—Boycott of German Goods—Mass Demonstrations*".

[465]Alexandre Soljénisyne, *Deux siècles ensemble*, Éditions Fayard. 2003, p. 348.

PLANETARIAN HOPES

others. They were a priority, as were high officials, industrial workers and labourers. The Soviet authorities had chartered thousands of trains especially for the evacuation of Jews as far away as possible, beyond the Urals466. The extent of the evacuation of Jews by the Soviet regime in the face of the German invasion has been unanimously recognised. The documents of the European Anti-Fascist Committee confirm this: "About one and a half million Jews were evacuated to Uzbekistan, Kazakhstan and other Central Asian republics at the beginning of the war." In all, from the beginning of the war until November 1941, 12 million people were evacuated from the threatened areas to the interior of the country.

During the Second World War, Jews continued to play a very important role in the machinery of power and the Red Army. An Israeli historian published a nominative list of Jewish generals and admirals in which 270 names could be counted, a colossal figure. He also cited the four wartime people's commissars: in addition to Kaganóvich, there were also Boris Vannikov for Munitions, Semyon Guinzburg for Construction, and Isaac Zaltsman for the Armoured Industry. The list also included the commanders-in-chief of 4 armies, the commanders of 23 corps, 72 divisions and 103 brigades467." In no Allied army, including the American army, have Jews occupied such high positions as in the Soviet army", confirmed I. Arad. It is therefore unjustified to speak of exclusion of Jews from the highest positions during the conflict.

However, the overwhelming majority of Slavs had the unpleasant impression that Jews could have taken a more courageous part in the war, that there could have been more Jews in the front line with the rank and file soldiers. One thing "cried out to heaven": they were far more numerous in the General Staff, in the quartermaster corps, in the medical corps, in various technical units in the rear, and, of course, in the administrative staff, along with all the pen-pushers in the propaganda machine, and even in the variety orchestras and travelling theatre troupes on the front468. An Israeli historian noted with regret "the widespread impression in the army and in the rear that Jews shunned taking part in the fighting469." Nevertheless, it must be acknowledged that some Jews were indeed daring and took great risks. The famous "Red Orchestra" of Trepper and Gurevich, who spied on

---

[466]See the testimonies of Marek Halter and Samuel Pisar.
[467]Alexandre Soljénisyne, *Deux siècles ensemble*, Éditions Fayard. 2003, p. 386.
[468]Alexandre Soljénisyne, *Deux siècles ensemble*, Éditions Fayard. 2003, p. 391.
[469]S. Schwartz, *Les Juifs en Union soviétique*, p. 154

Hitler's ranks until the autumn of 1942 and passed on valuable information, is a famous example. The two agents were imprisoned by the Gestapo before being imprisoned in the USSR after the war.

Another contemporary historian, drawing on archival documents declassified in the 1990s, came to this conclusion: "Throughout the 1940s, the role of Jews in the organs of repression remained extremely important; it was only reduced to zero after the war, during the campaign against cosmopolitanism470." In the late 1970s, Dan Levine wrote: "I agree with Professor Branover's view that the Catastrophe was largely a punishment for certain sins, mainly that of having led the communist movement471"." But such views do not constitute a majority trend, Solzhenitsyn wrote. Today almost all Jews regard this assessment as insulting and blasphemous. And it is disastrous472."

A suspicious death

In 1947, Stalin, probably to counterbalance Britain, but also to gain new support, actively advocated the creation of an independent Jewish state in Palestine, both from the UN with Gromyko, and by allowing the delivery of Czechoslovak arms. In May 1948, the USSR decided within 48 hours to recognise Israel's proclamation of independence. Immediately, applications for immigration to Israel multiplied, even though it seemed that the Israeli state would adopt a pro-Western attitude and that US influence would be preponderant.

This convinced Stalin to change his policy at the end of 1948, but with no announcement effect. The Jewish Anti-Fascist Committee, which had become the representative body of Soviet Jewry as a whole, was dismantled in stages. Its premises were sealed, the newspaper and publishing house closed. In January 1949, Stalin launched an offensive against Jews working in the cultural sphere. As early as 1946, reports from the Central Committee noted that "of the twenty-nine active theatre critics, only six were Russians", but the attack on Fadeev, the all-powerful chairman of the Writers' Union and Stalin's favourite turned out to be a failure. This "theatre critics" affair, which was to reappear in 1949, served as a prelude to the long campaign against the "cosmopolitans" which led later to the "imbecilic glorification of Russian superiority in all fields of science, technology and culture." Most of the time, the "cosmopolitans" were not arrested, but publicly

---

[470]L. Kritchevski, *Les Juifs dans l'appareil du Vétchéka dans les années 20*, 1999
[471]Dan Lévine, *Au bord de la temptation*, interview in "22", 1978, n°1, p. 55.
[472]Alexandre Soljénisyne, *Deux siècles ensemble*, Éditions Fayard. 2003, p. 421.

reprimanded and removed from their posts. They were removed from the editorial offices of newspapers, ideological and cultural institutions, the TASS agency, state publishing houses, faculties of letters, theatres, the Philharmonic and sometimes also from the party473. The purges extended to scientific circles, industry and the administration. Between 1948 and 1953, Jews were massively expelled from high places. They were banned from senior positions in the KGB, Party organs and the army, and in many universities, cultural and scientific institutions, the numerus clausus was re-established. From then on, the international Jewish community was to link its fate even more closely to that of the United States.

From the autumn of 1952 onwards, Stalin was already advancing in the open: arrests began to take place among medical professors in Kiev in October, as well as in literary circles. The news spread immediately among Jews in the Soviet Union and the rest of the world. In November, a Stalinist-style trial took place in Prague. The trial of Slanski, first secretary of the Czechoslovak Communist Party, was openly anti-Jewish in character. Of the eleven condemned men who were hanged, eight were Jews. Zionism was directly denounced as the new channel through which treason and espionage infiltrated the Communist Party.

Meanwhile, in the summer of 1951, the "Doctors' Plot" was being hatched in the shadows. In 1937, during the Bukharin trial, Kremlin doctors had already been accused of criminal practices against some Soviet leaders. The same move was repeated. This case provoked a wave of persecution of Jewish doctors throughout the country. They no longer dared to go to work and their patients turned away from them for fear of consulting them. This was Stalin's first mistake, Solzhenitsyn claimed, the first of his career. The outburst of indignation around the world had coincided with a crackdown inside the country by forces that were supposed to have decided to do away with Stalin. Locked and protected behind his armoured doors, Stalin did not realise that the implications of this case could constitute a personal danger to himself. After the official announcement of the doctors' plot, Stalin lived for 51 days. Solzhenitsyn was strangely discreet about the dictator's death. What had really happened? "The exculpation and release of the doctors was felt by Soviet Jews of the older generation as a repetition of the Purim miracle," he wrote, as if the date had been chosen in advance. Indeed, Stalin disappeared on the same day as the feast of Purim, the

---

473Alexandre Soljénisyne, *Deux siècles ensemble,* Éditions Fayard. 2003, p. 435.

date on which Esther saved the Jews of Persia from the massacre ordered by Haman474.

Within the next three months, diplomatic relations with Israel were restored. This and the strengthening of Beria's position briefly revived hopes among Soviet Jews that promising new prospects were opening up. But his rapid elimination, the triumph of Nikita Khrushchev over his opponents in the Party and the dismissal of Kaganhovich in 1957 marked a definitive turning point. It was the end of an era. The figures speak for themselves: "The Jews had disappeared not only from the leading organs of the Party, but also from the government475."

A sudden change of course

Much of the international Jewish community that had already turned away from Bolshevism now turned sharply against it." It was at that moment, Solzhenitsyn wrote, that, in a movement of purifying repentance, they should have recognised the active part they had played in the triumph of the Soviet regime, as well as the cruel role they had played in it. But they did not, or hardly at all." Authors such as F. Kolker wrote: "Among the numerous nationalities inhabiting the Soviet Union, the Jews were always considered apart, as the least reliable element476." Iou Chtern went even further in denials: "Soviet history is entirely marked by a constant will to destroy and exterminate the Jews ... Soviet power was especially hard on the Jews477."

"What kind of amnesia do you have to suffer from to write something like that in 1983? Is it possible to have forgotten everything to such an extent?", Solzhenitsyn was again indignant. Fortunately, there are some reflections that denote a certain awareness, even genuine repentance on the part of some Jews. This is what Dan Levine, an American intellectual living in Israel, wrote: "In Russia, much of the popular anti-Semitism stems from the fact that the Russian people see the Jews as the cause of all they had to endure during the revolution478"." What a joy to hear that, exclaimed Solzhenitsyn, and what a hope479! "This confirms the idea that perhaps a reciprocal,

---

474K. Chtourman, in "22", 1985, n°42, p. 140-141, [p. 443].
475L. Shapiro, *Les Juifs en Russie soviétiques après Staline*, p. 360.
476F. Kolker, *Un nouveau plan d'aide aux Juifs soviétiques*, in "22", 1978, no. 3, p. 147.
477Iou Chtern, in "22", 1984, no. 38, p. 130.
478Dan Lévine, *Au bord de la temptation*, interview in "22", 1978, n°1, p. 55.
479Alexandre Soljénisyne, *Deux siècles ensemble*, Éditions Fayard. 2003, p. 481.

sincere and indulgent recognition between Russians and Jews is possible.

But when they abruptly broke with Bolshevism, many Jews did not feel the slightest hint of repentance in their souls, not even a hint of shame. On the contrary, they turned furiously against the Russian people. At the beginning of the 1970s, the attacks against Russia increased steadily: an anonymous article signed by a certain S. Teleguine, and entitled "A human pigsty", was published in Samizdat480. The text was full of contempt for Russia, which was regarded as mere raw material from which there was nothing more to be gained. B. Khazanov wrote in turn: "The Russia I see around me disgusts me ... it is a unique Augean stable ... its inhabitants are lousy ... the day will come when it will suffer a terrible punishment for all that it represents today481." Another author, Arcady Belinkov, had taken refuge abroad in 1968. What he wrote from there afterwards indicated that he had become less an opponent of the regime than an opponent of the Russian people: "A country of slaves, a country of masters ... a herd of traitors, of informers, of executioners ... fear was Russian, they prepared warm clothes and waited for a knock at the door ... A miserable society of slaves, of descendants of slaves, of ancestors of slaves ... a society of trembling beasts, full of fear and hatred ... they were shitting their trousers, terrified of what might happen482." Let us note that not once did Belinkov use the word "Soviet". Yakov Yakir had similar statements: "They crawled on all fours and prostrated themselves before trees and stones, even though we gave them the God of Abraham, Isaac and Jacob483." For his part, M. Grobman directly declared that "Orthodoxy is a religion of savages".

The sudden change of many Jews in Russia confirmed the reflections of Zionist leader Zeev Jabotinsky, who noted as early as the beginning of the 20th century: "When the Jew assimilates into a foreign culture, one should not rely on the depth and consistency of the transformation. An assimilated Jew gives in at the first push, abandons the borrowed culture without the slightest resistance as soon as he is convinced that his reign is over[484]." A.B. Joshua, a contemporary author

---

[480]Samizdat was the clandestine copying and distribution of literature banned by the Soviet regime.

[481]B. Khazanov, *Novaïa Rossia*, in VM, 1976, no. 8, p. 143.

[482]A. Bélinkov, in Novy Kolokol, London, 1972, p. 323–350.

[483]Iakov Iakir, in Nacha strana, Tel-Aviv, 1973, 12 December. Cité d'après Novy Journal, 1974, no. 117, p. 190.

[484]Alexandre Solzhenitsyn, *Deux siècles ensemble, tome II*, Fayard, p. 550 and VI.

wrote unceremoniously: "A Jew "galout485 " is an amoral being. He avails himself of all the advantages of the country which receives him, but at the same time he does not identify himself completely with it"; "Such people demand a special status which no people in the world possesses: that they be allowed to have two homelands, one in which they live, and another in which "their heart lives". Then they wonder why they are hated486."

Abandon ship at all costs

The emigration of Jews out of the USSR became the number one problem for universal consciousness. Anyone who, throughout the 1950s–1980s, listened to American radio or television programmes about the USSR, had the impression that there was no more serious issue in the country than the Jewish question. It was about defending the Jewish refuzniks, those Jews who had been denied visas to travel to Israel. In the United States and in Europe, support for Jewish emigration was increasingly pressing. Hundreds of protest demonstrations were organised. The most massive took place on the annual "Sundays of Solidarity" in New York, which drew as many as 250,000 people between 1974 and 1987.

When, in 1972, the Presidium of the Soviet Union's Supreme Soviet established for the most educated emigration candidates the restitution of the state's investment in their education, a planetarian outcry erupted. None of the massive crimes committed by the regime had aroused such a worldwide, unanimous outcry for a tax on immigrants with higher education. American academics, five thousand professors, signed a petition in the autumn of 1972487. Two thirds of US senators blocked the trade treaty under negotiation that granted the USSR the Most Favoured Nation clause." European parliamentarians followed suit, and the Soviet government gave in. We will only give our help if the Soviet government agrees to let the Jews out—and only the Jews! No one here ever had the right to emigrate, and never ever did politicians in the West protest when millions of our compatriots wanted to flee this abhorrent regime," Solzhenitsyn wrote. Fifteen million peasants were exterminated during "deskulakisation", six million peasants were starved to death in 1932, not to mention the mass

---

Jabotinski, VI. Feulletons, StP, 1913, p. 251, 260-263.
[485]"Galout": in exile, from the diaspora.
[486]A.B. Joshua, article cité, p. 159, [p. 555].
[487]Read Marek Halter's testimony on the subject.

executions and the millions who ended up in labour camps, and all the while, treaties were complacently signed with the Soviet leadership, money was lent and favours sought from the regime. It was only when the Jews were harmed and deprived of their rights that the entire West was shocked and deeply sympathetic. It was enough for an unknown refuznik to sign a declaration of ineligibility to emigrate for it to be immediately broadcast along with the most important world news on *Radio-Liberté, La Voix de l'Amérique* or the *BBC.*" Even today, it is hard to believe that they would benefit from such media hype."

Jewish emigration from the USSR began in 1971:13,000 people in one year (98% of them settled in Israel); 32,000 in 1972, 35,000 in 1973, and so on. At first the focus was on those who did not emigrate to Israel, but quickly Jews increasingly emigrated to the affluent United States. In the mid-1980s, the freedom to emigrate to Israel was total. In the sinking ship that was the Soviet Union, having a lifeboat was an immense privilege. After seventy years of Soviet rule, Jews had suddenly gained the right to leave. The beginning of the Exodus marked the end of the two centuries in which Jews and Russians had had to live together488.

---

[488]But a few Jews remained to usher in the post-Soviet democratic era and seized the new opportunities. See Hervé Ryssen, *The Jewish Mafia.*

2. Exemplary discretion

Clearly, Aleksandr Solzhenitsyn's book has shed new light on the history of the 20th century and the development of the planetarian idea. All that remains now is to understand why this aspect of contemporary history has been obscured until recently. The study of other important works on the Bolshevik revolution confirms, albeit much less forcefully, the work of the great Russian dissident.

The historians' dispute

Ernst Nolte gave rise to what became known in Germany as the "historians' dispute". He was rejected by the historians' guild for having tried to explain the National Socialist phenomenon as primarily a reaction to the Bolshevik revolution. In *The European Civil War, 1917– 1945*, published in 1997, he took up his previous analysis by synthesising it, this time benefiting from the support of Stéphane Courtois, the main author of the famous *The Black Book of Communism*, who wrote in the preface [of the French edition, ndt]: "The Nazi party first claimed to be the party of the Bolshevik counter-dictatorship, the party of the counter-civil war. Anti-Bolshevism became anti-Marxism, taking as a pretext the presence of numerous Jews in the revolutionary major states, even in Germany, as for example during the Republic of the Bavarian Councils in 1919. Now, it was in Munich that Hitler attempted his first subversive coup in 1923... Nolte argues that, in view of the circumstances, Hitlerite anti-Semitism was fuelled by the strong presence of activists of Jewish origin in the communist movement, both Russian and German489."

This was indeed what Nolte wrote, recalling that anti-Semitism was not at all part of the imperial government's policy: "In the First World War the German Empire had pursued a decidedly pro-Jewish policy among its Turkish allies and in the occupied Eastern territories, and the anti-Semitic parties, whose influence was no greater than that of the corresponding groupings and tendencies in France, Russia and

---

[489]Ernst Nolte, *La Guerre civile européenne, 1917-1945*, Munich, 1997, Éditions de Syrtes, 2000, 625 pages, p. 10-11.

Rumania, had almost disappeared in the years before 1914. Something very special must have happened for such a radical Judeophobia as that of Hitler and Rosenberg to have arisen[490]."

In Weimar Republic Germany, the fear of Bolshevism was very great among large sections of the population. What was happening in the USSR was much better known to the Germans than to the French, because of the correspondence with the hundreds of thousands of ethnic German Russians who had settled in the Volga colonies since the 18th century. The appalling massacres, planned famine and political repression had created a particularly negative image of the Soviet experience in Germany." The great famine of 1931–1933, in which millions perished, and especially in the Ukraine, where entire villages were wiped out," caused dread." In Germany there was good information about it, because the events affected a considerable number of peasants of German descent, whose moving appeals for help were spread by the *Hilfswerk Brüder in Not* [Brothers in Distress][491]." From the very beginning of the regime, the statements of the leaders foreshadowed the events that were to follow: on 17 September 1918, at a meeting of the Petrograd Party, Grigory Zinoviev uttered these words in his speech: "In order to defeat our enemies, we have to rely on our own socialist militarism. Of the 100 million of Russia's population under the Soviets, we must win 90 million to our cause. As for the others, we have nothing to say to them; they must be exterminated[492]."

According to Nolte, the actors in the Bolshevik revolution were known. The difference between Western liberals and conservatives "was most easily recognised in the difference of whether they noted only the extremely strong participation of elements outside the people in the Russian Revolution or whether they saw in the Jews a particular cause of it. During the first months following the February Revolution, there were numerous observers, especially in France and Italy, who were very irritated that the promoters of peace so often had or had had German surnames such as Zederbaum, Apfelbaum or Sobelsohn[493]."

---

[490]Ernst Nolte, *La guerra civil europea, 1917-1945*, Fondo de cultura económica, Mexico, 2001, p. 29.

[491]Ernst Nolte, *La guerra civil europea, 1917-1945*, Fondo de cultura económica, Mexico, 2001, p. 157.

[492]Ernst Nolte, *La guerra civil europea, 1917-1945*, Fondo de cultura económica, Mexico, 2001, p. 91, citing David Shub, *Lenin*, Wiesbaden, 1957, *Severnaia Kommuna*, 18 September 1918, p. 375.

[493]Ernst Nolte, *La guerra civil europea, 1917-1945*, Fondo de cultura económica, Mexico, 2001, p.131.

It would be wrong, however, to believe that Ernst Nolte focused on this particular topic. Nothing could be further from the truth. Of the 550 pages of his book, the role of the Jews in the Bolshevik revolution is only mentioned in the pages we have quoted here. Only in the case of the great purges of 1936–1938 did Nolte discuss this aspect of the problem in more detail: "The purge claimed a considerable number of victims among Jews, Latvians and Poles, and generally among members of national minorities. Zinoviev, Kamenev Gamarnik, Yakir and others were Jews ... The fact that most of the leading representatives of the Western or intellectual critical tendency were Jews facilitated their elimination, despite the fact that the Soviet Union was the only country in the world that provided for the death penalty for anti-Semitism494."

In *The Historical Foundations of National Socialism*, published in 1998, one could note in Ernst Nolte some furtive passages confirming Aleksandr Solzhenitsyn's observations. For Hitler, he wrote, "Marxism is the work of the Jews. And this idea was no mere delusion, for Thomas Mann and Winston Churchill shared it."

However, Ernst Nolte's interpretation seems to us to be somewhat fragile. The struggle of Hitler and the National Socialists against what they called "Judeo-Bolshevism" cannot alone sum up Nazi anti-Semitism. The rise of National Socialism was not only a reaction to Soviet barbarism, and Nolte seemed to forget that millions of Germans, who had suffered from inflation and unemployment, felt a certain resentment against the Weimar Republic, a democratic regime whose cosmopolitanism they did not approve of. In a climate of intellectual repression prevailing in Europe, and especially in Germany in the second half of the 20th century, Nolte probably tried a new historical approach, different from the predominant one of explaining everything on the basis of the madness of Hitler and the German people as a whole. In the absence of being able to accuse the regime of the Weimar Republic, which would have ostracised him from his peers and probably exposed him to prosecution, Nolte based his explanation on the thesis of the rejection of communism, an approach now tolerated and even encouraged to some extent in Western democracies, as long as it does not touch on the issues that Solzhenitsyn unveiled495. In fact, it seems

---

[494]Ernst Nolte, *La guerra civil europea, 1917-1945*, Fondo de cultura económica, Mexico, 2001, p. 272, 274.

[495]Solzhenitsyn's book was probably able to be published in French and widely distributed because the Fayard publishing house was contractually bound to the author. However, the book did not receive any media promotion in France. [Unfortunately,

to us that Nolte wrote with little conviction that: "the glorification of multicultural society" is a "necessary thing496 "; as if he had to make certain concessions or signals to apologise in advance for terrible accusations.

At the beginning of his book on *The Historical Foundations of National Socialism*, Nolte published a part of his correspondence with the famous French historian François Furet which perfectly evidenced the pressure the latter had also been under to support the German historian. In his first letter to Nolte, François Furet commented on their famous exchange of letters of 1996497: "When I made a long comment to you, I was fully aware that in doing so I would arouse hostility towards my book in your country, but also outside it. That is exactly what happened; the mere fact that I quoted from it has provoked a frankly "Pavlovian" reflex on the left. Even Anglo-Saxon historians as dissimilar as Eric Hobsbawn and Tony Judt have reproached me for citing only your name, without considering it necessary to justify such excommunication. The anathema of such magical reasoning must be broken; therefore, less than ever do I regret my actions."

Stalin, "the Georgian"

François Furet had caused a small earthquake by taking Ernst Nolte's side in the controversy. In his book, *The Past of an Illusion498*, he explained: "One of his merits was to have overlooked, very early on, the ban on drawing parallels between communism and Nazism: a more or less general ban in Western Europe, especially in France and Italy, and particularly absolute in Germany." In 1963, Ernst Nolte's book, *Fascism in its Time*, and then, in 1966, *Fascist Movements*, explained that Bolshevik extremism had fatally provoked a German response." The sad thing was that, in the German historians' discussion of Nazism,

---

there is no English translation. Readers can consult this review of the Russian writer's work on the internet: *Solzhenitsyn, Russia and the Jews: New Considerations*, by Daniel J. Mahoney].

[496]Ernst Nolte, *Les Fondements historiques du national-socialisme*, Milan, 1998, Paris, Editions du Rocher, 2002, for the French translation, p. 162.

[497]Ernst Nolte, *Les Fondements historiques du national-socialisme*, Milan, 1998, Paris, Editions du Rocher, 2002, p. 9, and in Ernst Nolte, *La guerre civil européenne, 1917-1945*, p. 523 (Letter from François Furet to Ernst Nolte).

[498]François Furet, *Le Passé d'une illusion, essai sur l'idée communiste au XXe siècle*, Paris, Robert Laffont, 1995. François Furet, *The Past of an illusion, Essay on the communist idea in the 20th century*, 1995, Lectulandia.com, Queequeg digital publisher.

Nolte's interpretation was weakened by exaggerating his thesis: he wanted to make the Jews the organised adversaries of Hitler, as allies of his enemies... Trying to decipher Hitler's anti-Semitic paranoia, Nolte, in a recent paper, seemed to find a kind of "rational" basis for it in a statement by Chaim Weizman in September 1939, on behalf of the World Jewish Congress, in which he demands that the Jews of the whole world fight on the side of England. His argument is both shocking and false499."

"The pre-1914 Jew was bourgeois or socialist, wrote Furet. The post-war Jew is also a communist. The character offers the incomparable advantage of embodying both capitalism and communism, liberalism and its negation. Under the guise of money, he breaks down societies and nations. In the guise of Bolshevism, he threatens even their very existence. He is the one in whom the two enemies of National Socialism are embodied: the bourgeois and the Bolshevik, who are also the figures of *Zivilisation*, the two versions of homo oeconomicus, the two forms of present-day materialism500." We do not know if it was exactly an "advantage", as François Furet said ironically in order to discredit the extravagance of anti-Semitic ideas, for the Jews or for the anti-Semites. Indeed, this dual quality can appear so grotesque to anyone unfamiliar with the subject that those who echo such theories risk being seen as enlightened. Their opponents can then easily portray them as such, as we shall see.

It is true, however, that Hitler's fight against Bolshevism was not enough to explain the National Socialist phenomenon, as Nolte put it: "Hitler detests in Bolshevism the latest form of the Jewish conspiracy, and made the fight against Bolshevik ambitions for Germany one of his first slogans. But he shares with the Bolsheviks the hatred and contempt for liberal democracy, and the revolutionary certainty that the epoch of the bourgeoisie is at an end. The starting point of the Jewish conquest, its deepest roots are there, in modern liberalism, and later in Christianity, which the communists are also trying to uproot. The confrontation between National Socialism and Bolshevism is thus not primarily ideological."

Indeed, while Hitler's struggle was directed squarely against Bolshevism, his remarkable hatred of liberal democracy meant that he was indulgent towards communist militants who, like him, wanted to

---

499François Furet, *The Past of an Illusion, Essay on the Communist Idea in the 20th Century*, p. 580.
500François Furet, *The Past of an Illusion, Essay on the Communist Idea in the 20th Century*, p. 209–210.

overthrow the bourgeois regime. The Stalinist purges, the expulsion of the main Jewish leaders from the USSR during the purges of 1936–1938 would reinforce this tendency, the first result of which was the Molotov-Ribbentrop pact of 23 August 1939. Henceforth, the two anti-bourgeois nations would be united against the capitalist West.

"Stalin, wrote François Furet, had freed himself from the largely Jewish old guard of Lenin's comrades: Trotsky, Zinoviev, Kamenev and Radek, who had been persecuted or subdued since 1927." It is not Germany that will become Bolshevik", Hitler predicted to Rauschning in the spring of 1934, but Bolshevism that will become a kind of National Socialism. Moreover, there are more links that unite us with Bolshevism than there are elements that separate us from it. There is, above all, a true revolutionary feeling, alive everywhere in Russia, except where there are Marxist Jews. I have always known how to give everything its place, and I have always ordered that former Communists should be admitted into the party without delay. The petty bourgeois socialist and the trade union boss will never be National Socialists, but the Communist militant501"."

Nor should one think that François Furet's book focused much on the role and responsibility of the Jews in communism or democracy; quite the contrary. *The Past of an Illusion* is in that sense a model of discretion: of the 800 pages of the paperback edition, we find only three pages devoted to the subject: nothing was mentioned in his book about the role of the Jews in socialism and the 1917 revolution, apart from what is quoted here. Nor a word about their role in the revolutions in Bavaria and Hungary, which also partly explained inter-war Hungarian anti-Semitism." The experiment, unwelcome in Hungary, succumbed to the intervention of Romanian troops on 1 August 1919 after 133 days of existence," he wrote simply,502. On the other hand, he insisted several times on Stalin's nationality: "The Georgian ex-seminarian is a match for Stalin's nationality..."; "Being a Georgian..."; "Being a Georgian..."."; "Being Georgian, he becomes more Russian than the Russians"; "Stalin, Georgian, chose to be Russian because he was a revolutionary..."; "The Georgian occupies the top of the apparatus..."; "The Georgian dictator..."; "The Georgian dictator..."."; "The

[501]François Furet, *The Past of an Illusion, Essay on the Communist Idea in the 20th Century*, p. 213. Hermannn Rauschning, *Hitler Told Me.*
[502]François Furet, *The Past of an Illusion, Essay on the Communist Idea in the 20th Century*, p. 350.

Georgian dictator..."; "The cynical Georgian...".".; "The cynical Georgian503..."

Furet avoided evoking the origins of the other great Bolshevik leaders as much as possible, except in the case of a few portraits of eminent figures. Rosa Luxemburg, he wrote, was "the first to criticise October in the name of revolutionary Marxism ... she was worried about the Russian Revolution, before she was assassinated ... But October frightened her. She was afraid of the rising monster that would deprive her existence of all meaning. A young Polish Jew, she was born and grew up in Warsaw. She then spent her university years in Zurich, studying history, political economy and *Capital*. In 1898 she settles in Berlin as the centre of the European workers' movement ... she belongs to no homeland but entirely to the revolution504."

"The two key men of the Komintern in Paris were Fried and Togliatti. A Hungarian Jew from Slovakia, Eugen Fried became a member of the organisational bureau of the Komintern during the 1920s. Sent to France in the autumn of 1930 as an attaché to the leadership of the PCF, he controlled a "college of leadership" in charge of supervising current policy and instituted the methods of cadre selection. From 1932 onwards he formed, with M. Thorez, a sort of tandem in which Fried protected Thorez. In 1934, he supported him against Doriot and initiated the "turn" towards the policy of the Popular Front ... On 24 October Thorez, who was under the tutelage of Fried, his immediate superior in the International, was to propose to the Radical Party an anti-fascist Popular Front whose scope would go beyond that of the SFIO505. Fried seems to have invented the term "Popular Front", which was to have a great future"." Eugen Fried, wrote Furet, a young Slovak veteran of the first period, who escaped from Béla Kun's adventure in 1919 and joined the apparatus of the International in 1924; in 1928 he became a member of the Politburo of the Czech party, and was then installed in Paris with full powers. Fried is in France the man of what Robrieux calls the "glaciation", a term

---

[503]François Furet, *The Past of an Illusion, Essay on the Communist Idea in the 20th Century*, p. 152, 153, 156, 169, 222, 218.

[504]François Furet, *The Past of an Illusion, Essay on the Communist Idea in the 20th Century*, p. 99.

[505]The French Section of the Workers' International, better known by its abbreviation SFIO, was the political party of the French socialists from its foundation in 1905 until 1969. Its name indicates its character as a national section of the Second International (Workers' International) (wikipedia, NdT).

designating the complete and direct predominance of the International over the PCF506."

Among the supporters and disillusioned of communism, François Furet detailed the political developments of three eminent personalities: Pascal, Boris Souvarine and Georg Lukacs.

Pascal, one of the first foreign witnesses to the Russian revolution, was a young French Catholic intellectual. He wrote down daily in a notebook everything he saw and thought from 1917 to 1927 in Russia. He had joined the Bolsheviks in February 1917. A Russian speaker, he was assigned to the French military mission in St Petersburg, where he remained for a long time until he became embittered by the course of events. Of the Russian people he loved "the egalitarianism of the poor, the utopian socialism, the Christian spirit of community." The causes of his bitterness were somewhat blurred: "The Bolshevik Revolution is dead, it has produced nothing but a bureaucratic state, the beneficiary of a new capitalism," wrote Furet. Pascal had corresponded with Boris Suvarin, who had been excluded from the International in 1924. Furet even claimed that: "Pascal did not love the revolution even if it was Russian, like the Western Communists, and even many Bolsheviks, but because it was Russian and therefore Christian507." Pascal finally returned to France in 1933 where he had a career as a professor of Russian history.

Boris Suvarin was of the same generation as Pascal." He was born in Kiev into a family of small Jewish jewellers who emigrated and settled in Paris at the end of the last century. He was one of the first French Bolsheviks in the early months of 1918, and was from then on one of the architects of the incorporation of a majority of the socialist party into Lenin's camp. He was elected to the Presidium of the International in the company of such illustrious Bolsheviks as Zinoviev, Radek, Bukharin and Bela Kun. At the age of twenty-six, he was executive secretary of the International, although he was excluded from the Party after Lenin's death for right-wing deviationism. He left Moscow to settle in Yalta in the Crimea, the small libertarian commune where he met Pascal. Suvarin would become a historian of the failure of communism. After the Second World War, he would be almost the only intellectual to combat the almost unanimous pro-Soviet sentiment in French public opinion.

---

[506]François Furet, *The Past of an Illusion, Essay on the Communist Idea in the 20th Century*, p. 599 (note 298), 242, 249–250.

[507]François Furet, *The Past of an Illusion, Essay on the Communist Idea in the 20th Century*, p. 124, 125,

While in the case of Pascal and Boris Suvarin "one and the other eventually escaped the curse", this was not the case with the third illustrious man selected by François Furet: George Lukacs, who exemplified the opposite. He was a typical example of a political belief that survived more than half a century of observation and experience." The greatest contemporary philosopher of capitalist alienation lived as a prisoner of communist alienation throughout his life... Lukács was born in 1885, into the Jewish aristocracy of Budapest: the family is rich on both sides: the mother by inheritance, the father by his talent508." The father, Joseph Löwinger, "learned the trade as he went along. Having entered banking at the age of 18, at 24 he was the head of the Hungarian branch of the Anglo-Austrian Bank, and one of the leading finance men of the Empire. Soon ennobled by Emperor Franz Joseph, and a convert, he changed his name in 1910 and became Joseph von Lukács. His son, Georg, would go to war against his father: he would become People's Commissar for Education in the short-lived Hungarian Republic of Councils, modelled on the Soviet model." We have extraordinary photographs of this Lukács, half civilian, half soldier, haranguing the "proletarian" soldiers, in a long trench coat buttoned up to his neck, from which emerges a fine intellectual face, half Groucho Marx, half Trotsky", François Furet sardonically told us509. He would later become the "greatest philosopher of communism" with books such as *History and Class Consciousness* (Moscow, 1923) and *The Assault on Reason* (1954). He actively participated in the establishment of the Stalinist dictatorship in Hungary after the war. He accepted the post of Minister of Culture in Nagy's cabinet in 1956, a few days before the Soviet armoured intervention in the capital.

François Furet's book therefore gave a few glimpses here and there of information corroborating Solzhenitsyn's work. Only it was scattered and anecdotal, making it impossible for an uninformed reader to highlight and appreciate the essential phenomenon that was so important for the world Jewish community. Reading Nolte, and even more so Furet, one gets the impression that the concern for respectability has forbidden these two great historians to write what they seem to have known.

---

[508]François Furet, *The Past of an Illusion, Essay on the Communist Idea in the 20th Century*, p. 127, 136, 137, 138.

[509]François Furet, *The Past of an Illusion, Essay on the Communist Idea in the 20th Century*, p. 138, 141. This reminds us of Solzhenitsyn's image of the speakers on soapboxes haranguing the crowd in 1917.

Black book, white modesty

Two years after *The Past of an Illusion*, *The Black Book of Communism* was published510, a famous collective work directed by Stéphane Courtois. Unfortunately, it was not very audacious either. Translated in all European countries, this book marked a turning point in the analysis of the communist experience, even if the role of the Jews is only superficially touched upon. The passages mentioned here, placed one after the other, should not be misleading, for the 850 pages of the book only deal with the subject in a very secondary way.

Nicolas Werth, one of the contributors, admitted, however, that "the old background of popular anti-Semitism, always ready to resurface, immediately associated Jews and Bolsheviks as soon as the latter had lost the credit they had momentarily enjoyed immediately after the October revolution of 1917. The fact that a significant proportion of the best-known Bolshevik leaders (Trotsky, Zinoviev, Kamenev, Rykov, Radek511, etc.) were Jews justified, in the eyes of the masses, this identification of Bolsheviks with Jews. 512"

Sentences such as these were fraught with ambiguity: 'In 1942, the Soviet government, anxious to put pressure on American Jews to encourage the American government to open a "second front" against Nazi Germany more quickly in Europe, set up a Jewish-Soviet anti-fascist committee chaired by Solomon Mikhoels, the director of Moscow's famous Yiddish theatre. Several hundred Jewish intellectuals were chaste and active in it: the novelist Ilia Ehrenburg, the poets Samuel Marshak and Peretz Markish, the pianist Emile Guilels, the writer Vassili Grossman, the great physicist Piotr Kapitza, father of the Soviet atomic bomb, and so on. The committee quickly went beyond its role as an unofficial propaganda body to become an umbrella organisation of the Jewish community, a representative body of Soviet

---

[510]Stéphane Courtois, Nicolas Werth, *Le Livre noir du communisme. Crimes, terreur, repression*. Paris, Robert Laffont, 1997.
[511]In 1938, the writer Marieta Chaguinian published a book about the Ulyanovs in which she recalled Lenin's Jewish roots." Stalin even wanted to erase Lenin's Jewish roots when the Bolshevik leader's older sister tried to write a history of the Ulyanov family (Lenin's real surname)." It is certainly no secret to you that research on our grandfather has shown that he came from a poor Jewish family," she wrote to Stalin. This fact could serve to combat anti-Semitism."—Not a word about this, the dictator replied." (quoted in Thierry Wolton, *Rouge, brun, le mal du siècle*, p. 132).
[512]Stéphane Courtois, Nicolas Werth, *The Black Book of Communism. Crimes, terror and repression*. Espasa-Planeta, 1998, p. 105.

Jewry513." Does this mean that American Jews pressured their own government to expand the battlefield of the war, as if they could have lobbied to enter the war, despite the pacifism of the population and the electoral commitment of President Roosevelt?

The chapter entitled *The Other Europe, Victim of Communism*, was written by Andrzej Paczkowski and Karel Bartosek. In this part of the book we read: "Jewish communists, well represented in the international communist apparatus, continued after the war to occupy key positions in many parties and state apparatuses in Central Europe. In his synthesis on Hungarian communism, Miklos Molnar wrote: "At the top of the hierarchy, the leaders are, almost without exception, of Jewish origin, just as, in a lesser proportion, in the Central Committee apparatus, in the political police, in the press, publishing, theatre, cinema ... The strong and incontestable promotion of the workers' leading cadres cannot mask the fact that they come from the Jewish petty bourgeoisie514."

Same story in Romania: "In Romania, the fate of the Jewish Kominternite Anna Pauker was settled in 1952. She belonged to the leading troika together with Gheorghiu Dej, head of the party, and Vasile Luca. According to a testimony not recorded by other sources, Stalin, during a meeting with Dej in 1951, was surprised that the agents of Titoism and Zionism had not yet been arrested in Romania, and called for an "iron fist". Thus Vasile Luca, the Minister of Finance, was dismissed in May 1952 along with Teohari Georgescu, the Minister of the Interior, and later sentenced to death; his sentence was commuted to life imprisonment, and he died in prison. Ana Pauker, Minister of Foreign Affairs, was dismissed at the beginning of July. Arrested in February 1953 and released in 1954, she devoted herself to family life. The repression of anti-Semitic resentments affected lower-level cadres with her515."

In his chapter on *"World Revolution, Civil War and Terror"*, Stéphane Courtois was perfectly discreet about the revolutions in Germany, Bavaria and Hungary. Since the statements quoted above are the only passages in the book that mention the question raised by

---

[513]Stéphane Courtois, Nicolas Werth, *El Libro negro del comunismo*, Espasa-Planeta, 1998, p. 279.
[514]M. Molnar, *De Béla Kun à Janos Kadar. Soixante-dix ans de comunisme hongrois*, Paris, Presses de la Fondation nationale des sciences politiques, p. 187, in Stéphane Courtois, Nicolas Werth, *El Libro negro del comunismo*, Espasa-Planeta, 1998, p. 485.
[515]Stéphane Courtois, Nicolas Werth, *El Libro negro del comunismo*, Espasa-Planeta, 1998, p. 485, 486.

Solzhenitsyn, it can be stated once again that the problem was largely sidestepped.

In *Making a clean sweep of the past. History and Memory of Communism in Europe,* another collective work published in 2002 and focusing on the history of communism in Europe, Stéphane Courtois showed a little more courage, citing for example the famous case of Colonel Nicolski: "His real name was Boris Grünberg. He was a KGB agent in Romania, becoming in 1948 the deputy director of the sinister Securitate—the political police—personally implicated in thousands of murders, inventor of the terrifying experiment of "re-education" in Pitesti prison. Nicolski died peacefully in his splendid villa in Bucharest on 16 April 1992. Why is his name unknown to European public opinion, particularly to the left and the extreme left, so ready to mobilise in defence of human rights? Didn't the "enemies of the people" exterminated by Nicolski have the right to be defended516? "

Similarly, we read in this book that justice in Russia under the Tsars was infinitely more lenient than under the Bolshevik regime: "Whereas in Russia, from 1900 to 1913, the ordinary courts handed down 1,085,422 sentences, 33,374,906 were handed down between 1937 and 1954—including 13,033 death sentences. For custodial sentences, the ratio is 1 to 20 between the period 1900–19013 and the period 1940–1953 ... Stalin's lieutenants called for more prudence, while Molotov justified the Terror and Kaganóvich—who had overseen the organised famine in the Kuban and North Caucasus—recommended "doing things in cold blood517"."

To those who would like to place the full weight of the crimes on Stalin's shoulders, in order to excuse Lenin and Trotsky, Stéphane Courtois replied in advance: "Trotsky was the founder of the Soviet concentration camps in the summer of 1918 and covered up under his own authority innumerable massacres"." He was the general-in-chief who carried out the repression against the sailors, workers and peasants on the island of Kronstadt in revolt against the "Bolshevik autocracy" in March 1921; after violent fighting, the rebels were crushed in blood on the morning of March 18, just fifty years after the proclamation of the Paris Commune; a thousand prisoners and wounded were shot on the spot, 213 others were sentenced to death ... In the summer of 1923, again, Trotsky strongly encouraged the preparation of an armed

---

[516]*Du passé faisons table rase, Histoire et mémoire du communisme en Europe,* ouvrage collectif, sous la direction de Stéphane Courtois, Robert Laffont, 2002, p. 49.

[517]*Du passé faisons table rase, Histoire et mémoire du communisme en Europe,* Stéphane Courtois, Robert Laffont, 2002, p. 81.

insurrection in Germany, contributing to worsen the climate of civil war prevailing in the country ... and stated in *Defence of Terrorism*, published in 1920: "We must put an end once and for all to the papist-quakerist fable about the sacred sign of human life". Edwy Plenel518 forgets that Trotsky was not content with acting, but also amply justified his actions, even the most criminal ones in his book ... One is therefore perplexed by the systematic amnesia in an informed journalist and a die-hard Trotskyist like him. Apparently, too much memory kills history519."

In the historiography of communism, wrote Stéphane Courtois, conservative reactions crystallised "in four emblematic books: *The Age of Extremes* by Eric Hobsbawm, *The Road to Terror* by J. Arch Getty and Oleg Naoumov, *The Century of the Communists* by a group of French academics, and *The Furies* by Arno Mayer. All four are representative of three philo-communist generations: that of the old Western Marxists and communists, the academic generation of the 1970s, and finally the leftist and communist generation of '68." Stéphane Courtois might have noted other similarities between the authors of these books, closer to our subject of study.

According to Hobsbawm, his analysis is very biased: "Not only does he not dwell on the German-Soviet Pact of 1939, the partition of Poland—not a word about Katyn—or Stalin's annexation of the Balkan and Bessarabian countries, but he does not even mention the civil war provoked in Greece by the Communists in 1946, the "Prague coup" of 1948 or the blockade of Berlin in 1948–1949520."

"Some of these blockages can also be seen in France where, for example, on the traditional *Fête de l'Humanité,* in September 2000, *The Century of Communism* was published, a collective work promoted with an attractive advertisement that read: "What if the Black Book had not said everything? It is indeed possible. Composed of texts by some twenty authors, the book edited by Michel Dreyfus minimises everything that Stéphane Courtois denounced.

As for Arno Mayer, he literally concealed the two great provoked famines of 1921–1923 and 1932–1933: "To the first, which caused nearly five million deaths, he devotes only a few lines, without pointing

---

[518]Edwy Plenel, an unrepentant Trotskyist, was for a time editor-in-chief of the "reference newspaper" *Le Monde*. He now runs Mediapart.fr, an internet portal for information, research and dissemination.

[519]*Du passé faisons table rase, Histoire et mémoire du communisme en Europe,* Stéphane Courtois, Robert Laffont, 2002, p. 83-84.

[520]*Du passé faisons table rase, Histoire et mémoire du communisme en Europe,* Stéphane Courtois, Robert Laffont, 2002, p. 92-93.

out that it was largely provoked by the exorbitant requisitions of the Bolshevik power ... To the famine of 1932–1933 and its six million deaths, he devotes only half a page—about 680!", and without mentioning its organised character "nowadays amply demonstrated521."

Of the 567 pages of Stéphane Courtois' book, little else can be found that mentions the role of Jews in communism. Martin Malia, a specialist on the Soviet question and co-author of one of the book's chapters on atrocities, was surprised, remarking: "There was even an over-excited open forum in *Le Monde*, written by a well-known researcher, which denounced Courtois' introduction to *The Black Book* as anti-Semitic522". Indeed, a little bit is still too much.

Footnotes

We see, however, that much has been said, albeit in a diluted, scattered and anecdotal manner, so as not to give rise to terrible accusations and not to alarm readers. In a well-documented biography of Hitler published in 1976 by the American historian John Toland, we also find some indications that confirm Solzhenitsyn's writings. Coming out of the First World War, Germany and Hungary were in a revolutionary situation: a Hungarian Soviet Republic was proclaimed, led by an unknown, Bela Kun." He was Jewish, as were twenty-five of his thirty-two commissars523, leading the *Times* of London to characterise the regime as a "Jewish mafia". Bela Kun's triumph emboldened the Munich leftists524". The revolution in Munich was a café revolution, an innocent version of the bloody reality: "Its spiritual leader was Ernst Toller, the poet, and its platform also demanded new artistic reforms in theatre, painting and architecture in order to liberate the spirit of humanity. The Cabinet was a collection of colourful eccentrics ... This time the reins of government were taken by

---

[521]*Du passé faisons table rase, Histoire et mémoire du communisme en Europe,* Stéphane Courtois, Robert Laffont, 2002, p. 106.

[522]*Du passé faisons table rase, Histoire et mémoire du communisme en Europe,* Stéphane Courtois, Robert Laffont, 2002, p. 218.

[523]A work published in 2002 by *Publications de l'Université de Saint-Étienne* confirmed this statement, but with some differences: "Many of the members of Bela Kun's government were among those "assimilated Jews" of the late 19th century. There were thirty-five people's commissioners of Jewish origin out of the forty-five who made up the government." (Suzanne Schegerin-Vulin, *Une Famille sur les chemins de l'Europe,* Publications de l'Université de Saint-Étienne, 2002, p. 67).

[524]John Toland, *Adolf Hitler,* Ediciones B, Barcelona, 2009, p. 132.

professional Communists, led by Eugen Leviné, a native of St. Petersburg and the son of a Jewish merchant. The Communist Party had sent them to Munich to organise the revolution, and after arresting the poet Toller, they quickly formed a veritable soviet525."

The Bavarian scenario confirmed Ernst Nolte's analysis of Adolf Hitler: "The hatred he harboured for the Jews had been intensified by what he himself had witnessed on the streets of Munich. Everywhere, Jews in power: first Eisner, then anarchists like Toller, and finally Russian communists like Leviné. In Berlin, Rosa Luxemburg had come to the fore; in Budapest, Béla Kun; in Moscow, Trotsky, Zinoviev and Kamenev. The conspiracy that Hitler had only suspected before was increasingly confirmed in reality[526]."

We see here the same remarks expressed by Churchill about the Bolshevik revolution, regarding that "sinister gang of Jewish anarchists ... ideologues of a fearsome sect, the most fearsome in the world[527] ", which had seized the Russian empire by the throat. John Toland added: "All over the world, people other than Hitler regarded the Jews as the seed of revolution and communism ... A campaign of rumours spread throughout the West that the Russian Revolution had been paid for by Jewish money: one of the main Germans responsible for providing funds to Lenin was Max Warburg, whose brother was Paul Warburg, a director of the US Federal Reserve System; and wasn't his brother Felix Warburg's father-in-law the same Jacob Schiff of Kuhn Loeb and Company who had financed the Bolshevik revolution? This accusation was hurled again years later, on 3 February 1939, from the New York *Journal American*: "Today Jacob's grandson, John Schiff, estimates that the old man donated some $20 million to the final triumph of Bolshevism in Russia528."

It should be stressed, however, that these considerations were relegated to the footnotes at the end of the book on page 1362. Once again, it should not be lost sight of the fact that the passages quoted are the only ones referring to this painful subject in a book of almost 1500 pages.

Other texts had already confirmed some aspects of contemporary history that we had hitherto surprisingly missed, and which Aleksandr Solzhenitsyn would unveil. Thus, for example, one can read in the

---

[525]John Toland, *Adolf Hitler*, Ediciones B, Barcelona, 2009, p. 132–133.

[526] John Toland, *Adolf Hitler*, Ediciones B, Barcelona, 2009, p. 137.

[527] John Toland, *Adolf Hitler*, Ediciones B, Barcelona, 2009, p. 1362 (Lacquer note 313–314).

[528] John Toland, *Adolf Hitler*, Ediciones B, Barcelona, 2009, p. 1361–1362 (notes)

Encyclopaedia Britannica: "Béla Kun's government was composed almost entirely of Jews529." Historian Barnet Litvikof, author of *A Peculiar People: Inside the Jewish World Today*, wrote: "At the height of Stalin's tyranny, once control of the satellite countries was total, powerful Jewish personalities became highly visible in the communist hierarchies of Poland, Czechoslovakia, Hungary and Romania: Hillary Minc and Jacob Berman in Warsaw, Erno Gero, Mátyás Rákosi and Mihály Farkas [born Hermann Löwy] held similar positions in Hungary, while Ana Pauker became the undisputed mistress and mistress of Romania, with an authority comparable to that of Rudolf Slansky in Czechoslovakia530."

The same author added: "Lavrenti Beria, a member of the Soviet Communist Party's Presidium, reproached Rákosi for having placed Jews in key party posts." It was therefore very likely, as Solzhenitsyn argued, that there was an anti-Semitic dimension to the 1956 Hungarian uprising531: "The 1956 uprising in Hungary had had an anti-Jewish character—something overlooked by historians—perhaps because of the large number of Jews within the Hungarian KGB. Was this not one of the reasons, though not the main one, why the West did not support the Hungarian uprising?"

Trotskyist messianism

For the Trotskyists, the Soviet episode, however unfortunate, in no way invalidated the validity of Marxist doctrine and Lenin's teachings. For them the USSR was not a communist state, but merely a "degenerated bureaucratic state". Any excesses that might have been committed were to be blamed on Stalin, who bore the main responsibility for the failure of the "fatherland of the proletariat". By decreeing the construction of "socialism in one country" upon Lenin's death in 1924, his policy could only lead to failure, while on the economic level, the NEP was seen as a gift that Stalin and Bukharin had given to the rich peasants, the traffickers and the merchants. The Trotskyists countered this right-wing tendency, and proposed an alternative that could be summed up in three words: industrialisation, collectivisation and planning. For them, the solution could not consist in a revolutionary pause, but rather in its acceleration. It was a question

529Encyclopedia Britannica, édition 1946, vol. 13, p. 517
530Barnet Litvikoff, *A peculiar People: inside the jewish world today,* Weidenfield and Nicholson, London, 1969, p. 104–105.
531Alexandre Soljénisyne, *Deux siècles ensemble,* Éditions Fayard. 2003, p. 449.

of moving towards the total militarisation of the country, a programme which Stalin would implement to the letter a few years later. The proposition of the left opposition to Stalinism was finally that with them at the helm, the revolution would have been more radical and, above all, cleaner and would have encompassed the whole Earth.

Lev Davidovich Bronstein, "Trotsky", was born in 1879 into a "peasant" family of wealthy Jews: his father had made his fortune in the grain trade; he owned a hundred hectares of land and leased some three hundred. He was not religious and did not speak Yiddish, but his son, the young Lev (Leon), would nevertheless attend a Hebrew school. After the abortive 1905 revolution in Russia, Leon Trotsky would travel to Vienna where he would found the newspaper *Pravda*, developing there the theory of "permanent revolution" with which he foresaw the spread of the revolution to all of Europe, and then to the whole planet. In 1917, he became head of the Red Army. After his expulsion from the USSR in 1929, he tried to write his memoirs during his first months of exile, a now cult book entitled *My Life*. Marcel Bleibtreu still remembered it: "In 1934, *My Life* was published in an abridged version. It fascinated me. For the child that I was, the book was a mine of political, historical and military reflections. For my father, the name Trotsky was part of the monumental trilogy: Freud, Einstein, Trotsky—the three great Jewish glories532!"

Indeed, the Trotskyist phenomenon was strongly influenced by the presence within it of activists of Jewish origin, especially from Central Europe. In *The Trotskyists*, author Christophe Nick took up, for one of his chapters, the title of the book by Alain Brossat and Silvia Klinberg published in 1983: *The Revolutionary Yiddishland533*. The arrival in France at the beginning of the 20th century of a large wave of Jewish immigration from Eastern Europe was to be decisive for the development of the movement. In fact, many of the main leaders of this movement were Ashkenazi Jews: Frank, founder of the Internationalist Communist Party (PCI), was the father of the *Pabloite* tendency that would lead to the creation of the revolutionary Communist League." He was born in Paris in 1905 to parents who had recently arrived from Vilna in Lithuania." Barta was the founder of the Internationalist Communist Union (ICU) in 1947. He was born in 1914 in Buhusi,

---

[532]Christophe Nick, *Les Trotskistes*, Éditions Fayard, 2002, p. 44.
[533]The reader can also consult the books by these authors: *Il était une fois la révolution*, by Benoît Rayski; *Les Juifs de mai*, by Benjamin Stora; *68: une révolution juive*, by Annie-Paule Derczansky; as well as the review *Passages* n°8. [See also Hervé Ryssen, *Jewish Fanaticism*].

Romania, into a family of small Jewish merchants. His real name was David Korner. He was an activist in the shadows: the man who originated the movement that would later become Workers' Struggle (LO) gave only one discreet interview in his entire life; to a former LO militant for a university thesis. Another great figure of French Trotskyism was Lambert, the founder of the third great French Trotskyist organisation. His real name was Boussel and he was born on 9 June 1920 in Paris to Russian Jewish parents who had recently settled in the capital. He and his friends joined the *Achomer Hatzaïr*, "the young guard", a left-wing Zionist scout organisation. The historic leader of the Revolutionary Communist League (LCR), Alain Krivine, came from a family that had fled the pogroms in Russia and arrived in France at the end of the 19th century. Henri Weber, now a socialist senator, who co-founded the Communist League with Alain Krivine, was originally from Central Europe: "In 1938, on the eve of the war, his parents, Jewish watchmakers, lived in Cznanow, Upper Silesia534." Maurice and Charly Najman, "the two main Trotskyist leaders of the university and high school students of the years 1969–1978", as well as Robi Morder, "another student leader of the 1970s", also came from Central Europe, as did Michel Rodinson, the son of Maxime, editor of *Lucha Obrera*. On 8 October 1998, the magazine *L'Express* finally revealed the true identity of the mentor of Arlette Laguiller, the Lucha Obrera passionnaire: the famous and mysterious Hardy was in fact Robert Barcia; he was born in Paris in 1928, and took his first political steps with Barta (David Korner).

"These examples could be multiplied endlessly," said Christophe Nick." In the LCR, in the 1970s, a joke summed up the situation perfectly: "Why isn't Yiddish spoken in the political bureau of the Communist League? Because Bensaid is a Sephardite535!". Indeed, Daniel Bensaid, originally from North Africa (Sephardic), did not understand the Yiddish spoken by the other Trotskyist leaders of Ashkenazi origin.

An Israeli historian, Ya'ir Auron, also studied and published a book on this facet of the Jewish world entitled *The Jews of the Extreme Left in May 1968*, confirming at length Christophe Nick's information: "Of the twelve members of the League's political bureau at the beginning, Bensaid had to be added to the ten other Jews from Eastern Europe and only one non-Jewish member." Anyone would say that this was in fact

---

[534]Henri Weber (1944–2020). See the obituary of the Elysée Palace in the translator's note in the Annex. (NdT).
[535]Christophe Nick, *Les Trotskistes*, Éditions Fayard, 2002, p. 31-34.

the Sabbath goy of the office, i.e. a "service goy" as Jewish families traditionally had them to open the doors, turn on the light or pick up the telephone during the Sabbath. Yaír Auron also wrote: "Of the "big four" of May '68, Daniel Cohn-Bendit, Alain Krivine, Alain Gesmar, Jacques Sauvageot, the first three are Jewish." A note added: "Marc Kravetz also played an important role in May '68, and is also of Jewish origin." Moreover, this was explicitly recognised by Daniel Cohn-Bendit in his autobiography *The Big Fuss*: "Jews represented a not inconsiderable majority, not to say the great majority of the militants."

Obviously, we know that Trotskyism had its hours of glory during the events of May 1968. On 19 May the leaders of the three most important Trotskyist organisations met to decide on the formation of a permanent coordination committee and to call for unification. Barcia, on behalf of the ICU, met on that occasion with "Frank and Michel Lequenne of the PCI, Alain Krivine and Daniel Bensaid of the LCR. Together they drew up a solemn proclamation," wrote Christophe Nick. With Alain Geismar, the Maoist leader, and Daniel Cohn-Bendit, representative of the anarchist wing, it could be said that the revolt of May 1968 was indeed in good hands.

On the Maoist side, the trend was the same: the proletarian Left was led by Alain Geismar, now Inspector General of National Education, and Benny Levy (alias Victor) who would become Jean-Paul Sartre's private secretary before doing his *teshuvah* and *aliyah*536. The latter would later become a rabbi and teacher at a yeshiva (Jewish school) in Jerusalem. Similarly, wrote Yair Auron, "at the head of the leadership of the French communist party's student organisation in the 1970s, many were also Jewish." Let us remember for example Zarka, who became editor of the newspaper *L'Humanité*. And the same can be observed in the case of activists who fell into hardcore gangsterism, such as Goldman, the author of numerous robberies. His official biography revealed that Goldman, revolutionary though he was, used to go out partying with Betar members after the Israeli offensives in June 1967, during the Six-Day War. The testimonies of Marek Halter or Guy Konopnicki, as we have already pointed out in these pages, confirm in turn that the extreme left-wing internationalist revolutionaries had always kept their love for Israel more or less secretly intact.

In the final analysis, we see that the Trotskyists had the same fiercely militant and, it must be said, frankly messianic dispositions as the more formal and quiet intellectuals we have already studied. In the

---

[536]Teshuvah: to repent of one's sins and return to the practice of Judaism. Aliyah: to emigrate to the land of Israel.

ranks of the revolutionary Communist League, wrote Christophe Nick, the filmmaker Romain Goupil stood out: "He is full of hatred for those who live in the obsession of the Warsaw ghetto. A hatred that led him to risk his life in the 1990s in Sarajevo, where, in a short film for television, he sped down Snipers' Avenue in a marked car as a voluntary decoy for Serb snipers, passing the marches and repeating thousands of times into his megaphone microphone: "Sarajevo-Sarajevo-Sarajevo-Sarajevo-Sarajevo-Sarajevo537! "In a slightly more primal form, this was an obsession comparable to that of Bernard-Henri Levy, who was also a passionate defender of Sarajevo, but by means of pen and microphone. After 1968, the three leaders of the League—Alain Krivine, Daniel Bensaïd and Henri Weber—placed Romain Goupil at the head of the youth movement.

In 1968, Shapira was in charge of security for the revolutionary Communist Youth. Jean-Luc Benhammias, now a member of the Economic and Social Council and former national secretary of the Greens (ecologists), remembered those happy student years well, as did the philosopher André Glucksmann, who moved from the revolutionary Communist Youth to the proletarian Left. The Belgian Ernest Mandel, secretary of the Fourth International, was also Castro's economic adviser in Cuba; and Boris Fraenkel was Wilhelm Reich's French translator.

The 1970s were very turbulent indeed." Here is Gérard Karstein. He was a student at the University of Orsay when, in 1973, the Minister of Defence Michel Debré tried to reform military extensions. Gérard launched himself into a battle that culminated in the longest strike in the history of national education: six weeks of occupation of high schools and universities. The Communist League was undoubtedly the driving force behind the movement with its student figure at the time: Michel Field538." Gérard Karstein was also at the origin of the soldiers' committees in the 1970s. Indeed, during his military service, he could not avoid continuing with propaganda. For whether they were novelists, film-makers or politicians, the messianic hope within them invariably led them to continuously, uninterrupted military service, with relentless and perpetual propaganda that never stops: "I then bought a second-hand duplicating machine at Emmaus539, and brought it into the

---

537Christophe Nick, *Les Trotskistes*, Éditions Fayard, 2002, p. 73.
538Christophe Nick, *Les Trotskistes*, Éditions Fayard, 2002, p. 218.
539Well-known charitable foundation created by the Abbé Pierre, for decades a favourite personality of the French (NdT).

barracks... We loved everything that was clandestine540." Two years later, there were more than two hundred soldiers' committees all over France. For the traditional parade on 1 May 1976, the League organised the first national demonstration of soldiers in uniform: more than a hundred militants who had just taken the oath of military service paraded with balaclavas and raised fists, heavily protected by several hundred members of the League's Security Service.

As is well known, many personalities from the arts, show business, cinema, politics and the media took their first steps in Trotskyist organisations, and they often remain secretly faithful to their ideals. In fact, what best characterises Trotskyist militant training is dissimulation and entryism, i.e. the penetration of enemy or rival organisations by trained and loyal militants who conceal their true views. Hundreds of thousands had the mission of infiltrating hostile environments in order to gather information and influence their political lines. This aptitude for dissimulation, this taste for clandestinity and police organisation, the cult of secrecy, the rigour, even the austerity of the militant's life, like the great Bolshevik leader, constitute the specificity of the Trotskyist movement. In the media, the Trotskyists are a multitude, and good proof of this would be the symbolic 50th birthday party of Alain Krivine, which took place in Saint-Denis in the famous film studios of AB Productions, on the film sets of Azoulay (A) and Bensoussan (B)541.

In his *Essay on General Topology542* published in 2001, Daniel Bensaid, the ideologue of the Communist League, dwelled at length on the case of the Marranos, those Jews of Portugal and Spain who were persecuted by the Inquisition in the 16th century. Having opted for conversion to Christianity to avoid expulsion, they had officially abjured their Mosaic faith, although they continued to worship in secret. The Marran community, which then spread all over the world, was thus able to pass through the centuries pretending to be good Catholics by going to mass on Sundays. For Daniel Bensaid, this community symbolised the spirit of Jewish messianism, and in that sense, Trotskyism was merely its modern avatar: "Messianism, Bensaid wrote, is a fervent expectation... It asserts itself in the expectation of the historical catastrophes that the prophets urge us to avoid, following the

---

[540]Christophe Nick, *Les Trotskistes*, Éditions Fayard, 2002, p. 86.
[541]*AB Productions* audiovisual group. In total, more than 30 series and 3000 episodes were written and shot, mainly for French youth in the 1990s.
[542]*Essai de taupologie générale*. Daniel Bensaïd. [From the French mammal *"taupe"*, i.e. the "mole", not *"topologie"*. (NdT)].

profound dialectic of disaster and hope. Unlike apocalyptic pessimism, which feeds on punishment, this one stimulates an optimism of the will … Thirsting for a new era, messianic hope thus outlines a political project … and allows itself to be carried away by the dream of a conquest without battle. As a peaceful prelude to the messianic war itself, the secret revolutionary aspiration is then inextricably linked to the traditional conception of Jewish life … This is the great lesson to be drawn from the story of the Marranos: True faith must always remain hidden: "Every Jew must become a Marrano". In other words, he must learn to live in secrecy[543]."

---

[543]Daniel Bensaïd, *Résistances, essai de taupologie générale*, Fayard, 2001, in *Les Trotskistes*, p. 224.

Hervé Ryssen has extended the study of these aspects of the Jewish religion in *Psychoanalysis of Judaism*, in particular the concept of Messianism analysed by the eminent Jewish thinker Gershom Scholem, who wrote the following in one of his works:

"There is one important point where the secularised apocalypse or catastrophic theory of revolution (which plays such an important role in current debates) remains linked to its starting point in Jewish theology, from which it derives, even if it does not confess it. It is this rejection of the radical internalisation of redemption. Not that the history of Judaism has been lacking in attempts to discover such a dimension in Jewish messianism as well (especially, and unsurprisingly, in mysticism). But in all its historical configurations, Judaism has completely rejected the thesis of a chemically pure interiorisation of redemption. An interiority that did not also express itself in the exterior, that was not linked to it from beginning to end, was worth absolutely nothing here. The advance towards the nucleus is here, at the same time, an advance towards the outside. Redemption, understood as the restoration of all things to their proper place, precisely reproduces a totality that knows nothing of such a distinction between interiority and exteriority. The utopian element of messianism, which so largely dominates the Jewish tradition, referred to this totality, and only to this totality.

The difference between the modern "theology of revolution" offered to us from various quarters and the messianic idea of Judaism consists largely in a terminological shift: in the new version, history becomes prehistory and the human experience of which we have spoken so far is no longer the authentic experience, which will only be conferred on a redeemed humanity. This simplified the considerations about the value or lack of value of the previous history, from which the essential element of human freedom and autonomy had already disappeared, thus shifting the whole discussion about the authentic, genuine values of the human to the eschatological level. Such is the attitude behind the writings of the main ideologues of this revolutionary messianism, such as Walter Benjamin, Theodor Adorno, Ernst Bloch and Herbert Marcuse, in all of whom a link, whether acknowledged or not, to their Jewish heritage is evident." Gershom Scholem, *There is a Mystery in the World. Tradition and secularisation (Some considerations on Jewish theology in this time)*, Minima Trotta, 2006, Madrid, p. 40–41.

PART THREE

THE COSMOPOLITAN MENTALITY

The communist experience has been an excellent insight into the Mosaic mentality. Never before, in fact, had Jews been so committed to a political project, so massively and with so much impetus. The failure of this first experience has not dashed planetarian hopes, quite the contrary, for the progress of Western democracy shows that liberalism and social democracy are succeeding where communism failed so miserably. Nevertheless, we believe that we are entitled to some explanations of the role of each in the atrocities that were committed, although, to put it mildly, one is rather perplexed by the explanations of some Western intellectuals on the issue. The "scapegoat" theory is again of invaluable help to these authors, although they also do not hesitate to come up with the most implausible and twisted theories to make their readers believe truths that are the fruit of their imagination. The accusers are either ignorant or mentally ill. In either case, they show a deplorable ingratitude, for, to tell the truth, Jewish communities have always been integrated into the local population and have always brought cultural and material enrichment to national communities. The contribution of the Jews to culture does indeed reveal that they are a gifted people of refreshing vitality.

1. Failing memory

The analysis of the communist phenomenon through academic works demonstrates incontrovertibly that the role of the Jews in the revolution was known to the Western intelligentsia. Solzhenitsyn was simply the first, in 2003, to reveal its full extent in a book of synthesis. We have seen that he also lamented that many intellectuals still refused to acknowledge the responsibility of some members of their community in the Russian drama between 1917 and 1949. The aim of this chapter is to observe this tendency through the publications of specialists in "sovietology", but also through the reflections gleaned here and there from books for the general public. We have no choice but to subscribe to the conclusions of the great Russian dissident. We understand that it is a delicate matter, especially after decades of concealment of the phenomenon. It would have been healthier to open a debate on the subject after the fall of the Berlin Wall, for example, if it had not been done before. The Second World War after 1945 completely obscured this aspect of 20th century history. It can even be safely said that the increasing media coverage of the drama that European Jews experienced between 1942 and 1945 has been a headlong rush. Again, instead of opening a democratic and peaceful debate, a relentless bombardment of propaganda is preferred as a distraction from a subject that is too painful. The truth is that messianic spirits are well aware that the Soviet experience was a grave mistake. Communism was only valid as a mobilising utopia, as the sting of the planetarian ideal, and not as a system for managing society. After such a disastrous mistake, and, above all, after the truth about the atrocities has been uncovered, one can only feel uneasy. This discomfort, perceptible in the books we are going to analyse, remains, however, very much in the background compared to the formidable impudence that leads some authors to categorically deny any responsibility, or even better (worse), to present themselves as victims.

Above all not to talk about it

What we have discovered through Solzhenitsyn's work was, as we have seen, known to intellectuals but very little developed and explained in books on the Russian revolution in such a way that the public could become aware of the magnitude of the phenomenon. On the contrary, many authors, including the most prominent "specialists" on communism, have tried to gloss over the subject addressed by the Soviet dissident.

Robert Conquest's famous book on the Stalinist purges of the 1930s, *The Great Terror*, was not very prolix about the role played by Jews in the Bolshevik regime. In the 528 tightly packed pages of his book, the author did not once mention the origins of the various protagonists. The term appeared only once, on page 289, to explain that "a Jewish engineer was arrested for having drawn up plans for a scientific institution in the shape of a swastika. It is permissible to criticise the perpetrators on condition that their origins are not mentioned: "The purge also ravaged the Hungarian communists," wrote Robert Conquest. Béla Kun, the instigator of the Hungarian revolution in 1919, was one of the main victims. He had unleashed such atrocities in the execution of terror in Budapest and later in the Crimea that Lenin himself admonished him for his excessive cruelty and removed him from the government of the peninsula[544]. He then operated from the Komintern, and was partly responsible for the communist failure in Germany in 1921. Victor Serge describes him as a typical incompetent intellectual and a despicable and corrupt despot[545]."

Another great "specialist" on the subject is Martin Malia, who in 1995 published *The Soviet Tragedy*[546], "a long-awaited work by one of the best specialists on Russian history", we read on the back cover of the book: "Until recently, we saw this phenomenon only through a glass darkly. Until the end, or almost the end, Soviet reality was a well-kept secret. Since the Soviet experience is now a closed chapter of history, the time has come to take up the communist phenomenon as a whole and analyse it with the realism and serenity of the historian."

And it is with great serenity, it must be admitted, that Martin Malia managed the feat of not once revealing the role of the Jews in Bolshevism throughout the 630 pages of his book. Only on page 372

---

[544]This reminds us of the similar punishment that General de Gaulle inflicted on Raymond "Aubrac" for the cruelty with which he administered Marseilles in 1944.
[545]Robert Conquest, *La grande terreur*, Stock, 1970, p. 408.
[546]Martin Malia, *La Tragédie soviétique*, Éditions du Seuil, 1995.

did we read of their existence in Russia: "Numerous Kremlin doctors, many of whom had Jewish surnames, were arrested on charges of having murdered Zhdanov and committed other anti-Soviet crimes." It was 1953 when the notorious "doctors' plot" broke out. Thus, the reader will only be left with the fact that the Jews were victims of persecution. At no time, not even in connection with the purges of 1936–1938, did Martin Malia, professor of history at Berkeley, the prestigious university in California, touch on the subject. All this was not fortuitous, but resulted either from a deliberate intention or from fear of being accused or dismissed from his university post.

The same precautions were observed in "The" great French specialist par excellence on the Soviet Union, Helena Carrère d'Encausse (née Zourabichvili), a member of the Académie française, in her book entitled *The USSR from the Revolution to the Death of Stalin*, published in 1993. The historian also carefully avoided talking about the subject that interests us, not even to tell us that numerous Jewish dignitaries had been victims of the great purges of the 1930s, which would obviously have been a way of hinting at the great role they had played. Again, the question is not raised until after the war, only to expose the odious persecutions that Jews in the USSR suffered: "Anti-Semitism developed from the end of 1948 with the dissolution of the Jewish Anti-Fascist Committee and the arrest of many of its members547." Regarding the Hungarian revolutionary experiment of 1919, he wrote quietly: "For the vast majority of Hungarians, Bela Kun's government recalls disorder and even violence548."

Precisely, let us talk about the Hungarian experiment. In *The Russian Tradition549*, in the chapter entitled *The Russian Revolutionary Tradition* (pages 171 to 498), Tibor Szamuely did not once mention our subject. It should be noted that the preface to the work was written by Robert Conquest himself, who said of the author: "The uncle of whom he bears the same name had played an eminent role in the Hungarian revolution of 1919". This role was indeed "eminent", if not glorious, which did not prevent the executioner's nephew from later taking up a professorship at the University of Budapest, where he became Vice-Chancellor in 1958, proving that Hungarians are not an ungrateful people. Let us stress, in order not to be unfair, that the book

---

[547]Hélène Carrèred'Encausse, *L'URSS de la Révolution à la mort de Stalin*, Édditions du Seuil, 1993, p. 256.
[548]Hélène Carrèred'Encausse, *L'URSS de la Révolution à la mort de Stalin*, Édditions du Seuil, 1993, p. 308.
[549]Tibor Szamuely, *La Tradition russe*, 1974, Stock, 1976, for the French translation.

is well referenced and denotes a great deal of culture; moreover, it is important not to attribute to individuals the crimes committed by their relatives. But the fact remains that his uncle and namesake, Tibor Szamuely, was probably one of the most dismal characters in Hungarian history.

Jerôme and Jean Tharaud of the Académie française left a shocking account of the Hungarian revolution, which we summarise below: Tibor Szamuely, an untrained journalist, was at the head of a detachment of about thirty men recruited from among the "Lenin's Boys". His task was to scour the countryside to force the Hungarian peasants to hand over their foodstuffs and to suppress the riots that broke out here and there. His armoured train, armed with machine guns, went to villages where suspicious activity or agitation had been reported. The peasants denounced by the local soviet were then brought one after the other before the revolutionary court and systematically hanged. Eight qualified executioners were among the thirty men who accompanied Szamuely everywhere he went. Their leader, a twenty-three-year-old Arpad Kohn Kerekes, had, by his own admission, shot five people and hanged thirteen; but his indictment consisted of one hundred and fifty murders. Sometimes Tibor Szamuely amused himself by tying the rope around the neck of the tortured man himself, forming a beautiful knot. He also enjoyed being kissed by the latter before he died." He was seen to take his sadism to the point of forcing a relative of the condemned man to pull the chair that held the poor devil. Or he forced the children of a school to parade in the square where his victims were hanging; or he managed to make a woman, who was unaware of her husband's whereabouts, pass in front of his corpse hanging from the branch of an acacia tree." Each of his expeditions was accompanied by requisitions of animals, wine, vegetables, wheat, which were then shipped in wagons to Budapest." Then Szamuely would return to the city where he would be seen in the evening at the Othon Club, more dandy than anyone else, his black hair slicked back, an impeccably cut jacket, shaking hands absently and pretending not to know anyone." During the debacle, he would try to flee by car, but would be stopped at the Austrian border. Pulling a handkerchief from his pocket, he pretended to wipe his forehead and blew his brains out with a small revolver. The local Israeli community refused to receive his body in the cemetery. He was buried separately and an epitaph was written on the gravestone in blue pencil: "Here died a dog". This is the "eminent" character Robert Conquest spoke of.

The famous historian Michel Winock, professor at the Institute of Political Science in Paris, solved the problem in his own way. In his book *Nationalism, Anti-Semitism and Fascism in France, he* went straight from the situation at the beginning of the 20th century to the following chapter on the situation in the 1930s. He only mentioned the subject in passing in his conclusion, in order to emphasise the utter implausibility of the question: "The socialist and communist revolution completes the crystallisation of the Jewish myth, Winock wrote. He is not only the man of Capital; he is also the revolutionary Subversive. He not only destroys society from above (bankers, businessmen, Freemason politicians), but also undermines the foundations of society. Rothschild and Marx, same combat: the demolition of Western society. The Bolshevik revolution of 1917 appears to the anti-Semites as one of the last vicissitudes of the "Jewish plot". The theme of "Judeo-Marxism", of "Judeo-Bolshevism", will be used ad nauseam in the extreme right-wing press during the 1930s, even when Stalin had begun the liquidation of the Jewish communists550."

In "non-specialist" authors on communism, we also see the same difficulty in speaking of the role of the Jews in the Bolshevik revolution. As for example with the world famous Primo Levi, who wrote: "The identification of Judaism with Bolshevism, Hitler's fixed idea, has never had an objective basis. Especially in Germany, where the vast majority of Jews belonged to the bourgeois class551." Primo Levi probably implied that one could not be both a bourgeois and a Bolshevik. In *The Craft of Others (L'altrui mestiere),* he wrote: "In the course of little more than a generation, Eastern Jews went from a secluded and archaic way of life to active participation in workers' struggles, to national demands, to debates on rights and human dignity. Jews were among the protagonists of the Russian revolutions of 1905 and February 1917. During the 1920s in Warsaw alone they printed up to three daily newspapers, etc. 552." Pardon? October 1917? The Bolshevik Revolution":—Doesn't ring a bell!

Jacques Attali explained in some places the revolutionary inclinations of some of his co-religionists: "In 1848, all over Europe, many Jewish intellectuals, tradesmen, workers, merchants and craftsmen took part in national revolutions. Before being Jews, they felt German, Austrian or French. In Germany, Gabriel Riesser, the grandson

---

550Michel Winock, *Nationalisme, antisémitisme et fascisme en France*, Points Seuil collection, 1990, p. 204-205, 220.

551Primo Lévi, *L'asymétrie et la vie, articles*, Robert Laffont, 2002, p. 166.

552Primo Lévi, *Le Métier des autres*, 1985, Gallimard, 1992, Folio, p. 275.

of a famous rabbi from Altana and leader of a movement of "liberal Jews", was one of the leaders of the insurrections. The heads of the Empire's Jewish communities—wealthy merchants—are also at the head of the revolution in Vienna553." Attali also recognised that Jews may have played an "eminent" role in the Russian revolutionary movement: "The Jews are so numerous in the advance guard of the movement that, in 1896, at the 11th Congress of the Second International, the Russian leader Plekhanov declared that they are "the vanguard of the workers' army" in Russia554." Their presence in all the great modern changes is in fact undeniable: "While Russian Jews invented socialism and Austrian Jews discovered psychoanalysis, American Jews, in the very first rank, participated in the birth of American capitalism and in the Americanisation of the world555."

We must also recognise that Jewish financiers played a key role in the 1905 war between Japan and Russia. Out of hatred for Tsarism and Russia, where Jews had no citizenship, American Jews supported Japan with all their financial might: In 1906, "Max Warburg and Jacob Schiff then became Japan's chief financiers. Schiff even made a triumphant trip to the archipelago, much to the fury of the Russians. For the first time, a Japanese emperor invited a foreigner to his table who was not a member of a ruling family556."

Attali then mentioned the role of certain Jews during the serious upheavals that shook Germany after the First World War: "Hugo Preuss, a Jewish jurist, drafted the Weimar constitution. Kurt Eisner heads the revolutionary Bavarian government, at the head of a team whose majority of ministers are Jewish. Anti-Semitism explodes. The hunt for Jews was soon open. In the spring of 1921, Kurt Eisner and several of his Jewish ministers, as well as Hugo Preuss, are murdered557."

But for those who considered accusing the Jews of being the main protagonists of the Bolshevik regime, Attali responded in a way that left no room for ambiguity: "In 1925, the *Times* correspondent in the USSR, Robert Wilton, nevertheless believes he can still write, using names to

[553] Jacques Attali, *Los judíos, el mundo y el dinero*, Fondo de cultura económica, 2005, Buenos Aires, p. 308.
[554] Jacques Attali, *Los judíos, el mundo y el dinero*, Fondo de cultura económica, 2005, Buenos Aires, p. 349.
[555] Jacques Attali, *Los judíos, el mundo y el dinero*, Fondo de cultura económica, 2005, Buenos Aires, p. 357.
[556] Jacques Attali, *Los judíos, el mundo y el dinero*, Fondo de cultura económica, 2005, Buenos Aires, p. 378.
[557] Jacques Attali, *Los judíos, el mundo y el dinero*, Fondo de cultura económica, 2005, Buenos Aires, p. 405.

support his claim, that three quarters of the Central Committee of the Communist Party are Jews, as well as 17 ministers out of 23 and 41 members of the Politburo out of 60. It is unverifiable: the names prove nothing and the author presents no convincing evidence."

Moreover, Jews were persecuted in the USSR, it is well known, for as early as 1920, "Jewish organisations, accused of representing a "bourgeois-clerical tendency", were liquidated ... The teaching of Hebrew, a "reactionary and clerical language", was also banned ... The annihilation of Russian Judaism continued. Exile is closed for the Jews: let alone leaving for America. Russia was an open hell; the USSR becomes a closed hell558." It would take a long time and a lot of suffering and hardship before the Jews managed to escape from that Soviet hell: "From 1968 to 1981, 250,000 Jews left the USSR, one by one, snatched away by Western interventions, in exchange for supplies of wheat or other food rations559." It was a kind of new departure from Egypt. The Russians, for their part, were able to continue to suffer on the spot in silence.

Jews, victims of communism

Continuing the study of the divorce between Jews and communism, and their willingness to dissociate themselves from it in order to foist their responsibilities on others, one quickly arrives at analyses that tend to present the Jews as the first victims of the Soviet system. Better still, the struggle against the tyrannical regime would have been theirs. This may be true, as Soros proved ("I was deeply involved in the disintegration of the Soviet system560 "), but if this was the case, it was by no means a glorious act of arms. One thing is certain, for the vast majority of them, the struggle against communism did not begin until 1949, when the regime began to remove them from leadership positions.

Let us listen to Shmuel Trigano's lament: "That communism was criminal, who can doubt? The Soviet Jews who suffered so much, certainly not... The worldwide struggle waged by the Jewish world against the oppression they endured was an important moment in the

---

[558]Jacques Attali, *Los judíos, el mundo y el dinero*, Fondo de cultura económica, 2005, Buenos Aires, p. 401-402.
[559]Jacques Attali, *Los judíos, el mundo y el dinero*, Fondo de cultura económica, 2005, Buenos Aires, p. 472.
[560]George Soros, *La crisis del capitalismo global; La sociedad abierta en peligro.* Editorial Debate, Madrid, 1999, p. 12.

process that contributed to the fall of communism561." After so much pain and so many sacrifices, the allegations of certain intellectuals such as Stéphane Courtois can only be hurtful. Indeed, this is the case in *The Black Book of Communism*, a book in which "we see the re-emergence of an "international Jewish community" to explain that the communist crime has been concealed in favour of the crime against the Jews." All this is truly disheartening. All the more disheartening that there is none of it in *The Black Book of Communism562*.

Listening to Marek Halter talk at length about his fight against communism, it seemed that in the end it all ended in bitter disappointment after seeing the return to "tribalism" of the people of Central Europe. And yet people like him had given their all for the people suffering under the Soviet yoke; or at least for the refuzniks who longed to be able to fly to Israel... In one of his books, *One Man, One Cry*, Halter spoke of his despair and sadness at what the people liberated from communism had done with that liberation: "We were concerned about those who suffered there, in the East, we fought for their freedom. Had we not organised campaigns for their liberation? Stirred up Western public opinion? Released several dissidents forgotten in the Gulag or locked up in psychiatric asylums? ... After having been so concerned about these countries, we felt a real sadness, similar to a great disappointment, when these men and women, barely freed from slavery, instead of pursuing this liberation to get away from the nature and spirit of the primitive clan, let themselves be driven by tribal demands... But how can we reproach the men of the East for their "tribal impulse", we who had always supported the right of peoples to self-determination563? "Reading this last sentence, we had a brief glimmer of hope. Indeed, for a brief moment, we could have hoped that he would finally admit his own "tribal impulse", which would have been more logical. But once again, our hopes were dashed.

Marek Halter could have elaborated a little more on the role played by his co-religionists between 1917 and 1949. Born in Warsaw and exiled to the USSR during the Second World War, Marek Halter spent his childhood there. His family had been evacuated by the Soviet

---

561Shmuel Trigano, *L'Idéal démocratique... à l'épreuve de la shoah*, Éditions Odile Jacob, 1999, p. 72.

562Shmuel Trigano, *L'Idéal démocratique... à l'épreuve de la shoah*, Éditions Odile Jacob, 1999, p. 74. After checking, we have found no trace of this in *The Black Book*, neither on page 27, nor anywhere else. Instead, we read on that page the following statement: "Jean Ellenstein has defined the Stalinist phenomenon as a mixture of Greek tyranny and Oriental despotism."

563Marek Halter, *Un Homme, un cri*, Robert Laffont, Paris, 1991, p. 19.

authorities to the East Urals, confirming Solzhenitsyn's words about the mass evacuation of Jews from German-invaded territories as a matter of priority." My mother, he wrote, had a membership card of the Union of Soviet Writers ... I was included in the delegation of the Pioneers of Uzbekistan who were to take part in the Victory Party in Moscow ... At the last moment, I was appointed to offer Stalin the bouquet of the Pioneers of Uzbekistan. I was so excited that they had to push me. Stalin took my flowers, ran his hand through my hair and said something that I did not understand from how upset he was564." It is clear, then, that in some social environments resistance against tyranny started a little late, and that, above all, it responded to very specific interests. Once again, "memory" is flawed. After "memory that bleeds", we have with Marek Halter "memory that fails".

Elie Wiesel was another protagonist of that time. He also often claims to have acted on behalf of Soviet dissidents. And it would be inappropriate to accuse him of only mobilising on behalf of his co-religionists: "When I denounce the hatred of the Jew, am I not condemning the hatred of the Other? By demanding freedom for Russian Jews, am I not also supporting the cause of the dissidents565? "The question is whether he would have taken up the cause of the dissidents before the regime turned against "Zionism". The answer is obvious.

Samuel Pisar's testimony in his book *The Human Resource* suffered from the same shortcomings. In the following text, which recounts the arrival of Soviet troops in Poland in 1939, the reader may get the impression that the regime was persecuting and deporting Jews to Siberia, when in fact it is known that these were protective measures. Once again, we note this tendency to play the victim: "In 1939, when I was ten years old, I saw the Soviets for the first time. Hitler and Stalin had divided up the country. From the balcony of our house I watched the red cavalry—Slavs, Mongols and Muslims—pass by. I remember my parents' relief. And I shared it. These people came to save us from the worst: to escape the Nazi fury. In truth, we paid dearly for that salvation. Endless queues for bread, vegetables and clothes. Anguish because of the night visits, the knocking on the door at midnight. A large number of Jewish families were surreptitiously rounded up and exiled to Siberia. All the factories, all the shops, expropriated and nationalised, handed over to state officials. Thus it was that, twenty years after the Russian people, we received in Bialystock the Bolshevik revolution."

564Marek Halter, *Le Fou et les rois*, Albin Michel-Poche, 1976, p. 26, 33
565Elie Wiesel, *Mémoires, tome II*, Éditions du Seuil, 1996, p. 172.

Like Marek Halter, Samuel Pisar was in his youth an enthusiastic little soldier of Bolshevism: "I too became a little Bolshevik... Our teachers told us lots and lots of stories about the crimes committed by the ancien régime, especially against our co-religionists. A New Man, the socialist man, was emerging from History566."

Solzhenitsyn was probably right that Jewish financiers in the United States would never have collaborated with the regime if it had been anti-Semitic. Samuel Pisar, and many others, built their colossal fortunes precisely because of this fruitful collaboration: "For the last twenty-five years," he declared, "I have been travelling around the Soviet Union." He spent several stays there thanks to his friend Armand Hammer, the famous billionaire president of the Western company Petroleum: "Hammer, at the age of twenty-three, went to the Soviet Union. The young American capitalist was to meet most of the Soviet leaders personally, befriend them, and eventually develop with them the first American-Soviet economic collaboration ... Back in the United States, Hammer was to become the "king" of many things: whiskey, cattle, art, oil, etc... amassing one of the world's greatest fortunes and a power capable, had he so desired, of overthrowing the economies of many countries. His luxurious Los Angeles office is full of photos with heads of state signed with praise ... It was with this fabulous and unfathomable Hammer that I arrived in Moscow in 1972[567]."

Samuel Pisar was a miraculous survivor of Auschwitz. In his book, he recounted his ordeal and explained what would be the guiding existential axis of his entire life: "Find the way out, fast, at any cost." The following story is extraordinary:

"I was that little boy who, just a few metres away, just a few minutes from entering the gas chamber, had to overcome fate and death—against all odds—by inventing "a way out"." That boy was fourteen years old at the time, and the only chance of survival was to find in himself the way to force fate: "We have reached the crematorium. No one can escape any more. The columns pass in front of us. Then we are grouped together. The condemned men silently exchange glances in which the rage of being trapped is joined by the fear of imminent death. At the back of the waiting room where we are crammed together, I see a wooden bucket and a brush. In the midst of the paralysis of souls and bodies, of despair, I squat down and start scrubbing the floor with the vigour of the active and docile prisoner who is doing the task assigned to him. Neglecting no nook and cranny,

---

[566]Samuel Pisar, La Ressource humaine, Jean-Claude Lattès, 1983, p. 112-113.
[567]Samuel Pisar, La Ressource humaine, Jean-Claude Lattès, 1983, p. 170, 171.

I go about my work with regularity and application, as I approach, inch by inch, what appears to be an exit. The guards, who regularly peek inside through the open door, see me. They become what I had hoped for in my improbable plan: my accomplices. —Hey, this part is still dirty, do it again! I scrub the floor even harder. I crawl up the steps leading to that mirage: an exit. I grab the bucket, the brush, and start to walk away. A shout or a whistle telling me to stop; I'm just waiting for that fatality. But the guards are no longer interested in me. With an indolent step, I return to the anonymity of the camp. Still alive, I reach my barracks and collapse on my bed568."

Like Marek Halter, he and his family were evacuated to the East on 22 June 1941, when German troops invaded the USSR: "Fleeing to the East in a truck my father had managed to get hold of, I saw the Red Army battalions transformed into ragged, ragged, starving columns. No command or authority, no resistance. More than their defeat, it was the way their courage vanished that stunned me most. Outright betrayal, eager collaboration with the enemy and corruption seemed in them as a matter of course, and even for many, as a deliverance569."

In the testimony he gave of the Red Army there was a consternation and contempt that made it clear, once again, that he was utterly incapable of understanding the mentality of people who were not like them. The fact is that the Russian people, who had suffered so much from the collectivism and anti-Slav policies of Bolshevism, perhaps did not wish in 1941 to give their lives for a regime that treated them as an enemy in their own country. Neither Samuel Pisar nor Marek Halter seem able to see or feel this circumstance. On the other hand, it is a pity that Samuel Pisar has not narrated in his book how he was able to reach Auschwitz after being evacuated to the East. Such an episode in his life would have helped to understand the story.

Following our research, one realises that some testimonies do indeed confirm the role of Jews in Soviet Bolshevism. Shmuel Trigano perfectly admitted this role, but only after the Second World War. As always, he went exactly against reality. According to him, the Jews embarked on communism in a great spirit of sacrifice. As usual, they did it not for themselves, but for the whole of humanity. In contrast, the fall of communism was a very painful experience and the Jews then experienced endless suffering: "The commitment to communism was identified with the USSR which had triumphed against Nazism. It provided Jews, who remembered their disenfranchisement, with a

---

[568]Samuel Pisar, *La Ressource humaine*, Jean-Claude Lattès, 1983, p. 48.

[569]Samuel Pisar, *La Ressource humaine*, Jean-Claude Lattès, 1983, p. 115.

model of identification and a situation that contrasted with the marginalisation and rejection outside the modern system that they had endured. They thus found a way to rationalise their feelings and experiences ... In the name of humanity, they enlisted in a significant proportion in the ranks of a party-pariah of the political system ... The paroxysmal and singular commitment of the Jews thus ultimately reflected the common fate of Europeans... It is thus understandable that the collapse of the USSR in 1989 represented for much of the Jewish world a turning point almost as drastic as the *Shoah* [Holocaust], idealised because of the post-war militant commitment. It was in the 1990s that Jews truly "came out" of the concentration camps and realised, in their censored inner selves, the desolation of the world and the crisis of democratic citizenship570."

The pain is immense, we can imagine. But didn't Shmuel Trigano write, thirty pages later, that the Jews had to suffer from the communist regime? It is not the first time that we see contradictions in the same work. Above all, we understand that some spirits have the genius to turn situations around in order to muddy the waters and, in the end, to impute their own vileness to others. We shall see below the ancient origins of this unique aptitude for intellectual contortions. We discussed earlier the case of Norman Mailer, who accused Christian conservatives and patriots of fomenting the war against Iraq. In the same frankly twisted genre, we can quote this passage from Jacques Attali: "Jews are even accused of being indirectly responsible for the Shoah: Hitler, say some German historians such as Ernst Nolte, was nothing more than a response to Marxism and the Soviet Union. It is enough to add that Marxism and the USSR are "Jewish creations" for the persecuting Jew to become—supreme refinement—responsible for his own persecution571! "Of course, this cannot be so, since the Jew is, so to speak, innocent by nature.

We have nothing to do with that

For some analysts, communism is perceived as an ideology that generates racism. Obviously, this is a thesis that we cannot endorse in any way. At the beginning of the 1980s, a communist city council in the Paris region had indeed taken some strong measures against the

570Shmuel Trigano, *L'Idéal démocratique... à l'épreuve de la shoah*, Éditions Odile Jacob, 1999, p.34-35.
571Jacques Attali, *Los judíos, el mundo y el dinero*, Fondo de cultura económica, 2005, Buenos Aires, p. 483.

immigrant population in order to please its popular electorate. This was an excellent pretext for our intellectuals to distance themselves even further. Evidently, it was a way out so that they could reject with disgust an ideology in which they had become dangerously involved.

When he spoke of communism, the essayist Albert Memmi intentionally emphasised certain specific aspects of the situation: "Let us recall, he wrote, the surprising action of certain communist municipalities which expelled North African workers with extraordinary brutality... As knowledgeable politicians, they knew how to express the potential racism of their troops. It is enough to examine the justifications they gave for their actions: young couples can no longer find housing in the HLMs572, the children of the workers no longer have a place in the school camps, they speak French worse and worse because of the contact with foreign children; the immigrants are too noisy at night in the street, their cooking stinks on the landings and stairs, their music is deafening, they break all the furniture, etc. The crime of the communists is to have used these unfortunately very real feelings573."

Marek Halter made the same analysis and spoke out against it, although exaggerating greatly, as usual. After the "communist bulldozers in Vitry, the fascist demonstrations in Dreux and the racist murders in Lyon and Marseilles, etc., the French situation in 1981 was more than alarming." the French situation in 1981 was more than alarming. The Communist Party itself echoes the unspeakable racism of the native French: "In France today, in these times of crisis and unemployment, attempts are being made to pit the population against the immigrants, the French workers against the immigrant workers. The communist party with the bulldozers and the government with discriminatory decrees point them out as scapegoats. They are about to expel them. Five hundred thousand children of immigrants, born here and speaking our language, are threatened with expulsion574." This was what one could read in the *Paris daily Le Quotidien of* 2 May 1981.

In his *French Ideology*, Bernard-Henri Lévy burned all his bridges to denounce this communism with which one cannot compromise: "We see that the ranks of the Communist Party are willingly nourished by these new xenophobes", he wrote, commenting on a survey of the French in 1980." This collection of hypocrisies and disguised infamies has for a century been perhaps the most widely shared thing in France.

572Social housing (NdT).
573Albert Memmi, *Le Racisme*, Gallimard, 1982, réedition de poche, 1994, p. 121.
574Marek Halter, *Un Homme, un cri*, Robert Laffont, Paris, 1991, p. 142-146, 199.

Even today, a majority of people in this country, whether on the left or the right, the extreme left or the extreme right, still happily indulge in them575." In 1969, when Georges Pompidou entered Matignon as Prime Minister, *L'Humanité*, a communist newspaper, and *Aspects de la France*, a monarchist daily, both dared to headline on their front pages, showing their dislike for him: "The head of the Rothschild bank has formed the government576."

It was thus clear to BHL that the communist party was anti-Semitic and racist, and that this was amply sufficient reason to reject this nauseating ideology. A man like George Marchais, who took up the refrain of "Jeanne the peasant" and expressed his "concern for the moral health of our people577 ", was deeply repugnant to him. His "communism in the colours of France" was that of Georges Sorel, who called for a "Gallic socialism, tricoloured and patriotic"." One should not endorse this ordinary xenophobia which means that in the Paris of 1980, a man, a woman and a child are literally in danger of death because their skin tone is slightly different from ours578." Let us note however that for several decades now, immigrants have been more and more numerous in wanting to face the danger, without taking into account the wickedness, aggressiveness and ignominy of the French. In short, neither the Russian mujiks nor the French yokels will ever be up to the task of satisfying these gentlemen.

We see that in these writers, the denunciation of communism is all the more virulent because it allows them to mow the grass from under the feet of all those who could still accuse the Jews of becoming propagandists of "Judeo-Bolshevism". The "duty to remember" is no longer valid in the face of the vital need to forget—as soon as possible!

Gross anti-Semitic forgeries and provocations

For the great historian of Judaism, Leon Poliakov, the role played by Jews in the Russian Revolution should not be completely denied, but should be seen in its proper light so as not to give rise to anti-Semitic digressions and thus put an end to "the chimeras which so obsess Christian imaginations on certain points", as he kindly put it: "Some

[575]Bernard-Henri Lévy, *L'Idéologie française*, Grasset, 1981, p. 216.
[576]Bernard-Henri Lévy, *L'Idéologie française*, Grasset, 1981, p. 280.
[577]Famous speech by George Marchais, secretary of the PCF, in Montigny-les-Cormeilles on 21 February 1981. Georges Marchais had called for a halt to immigration given the high level of unemployment already at that time.
[578]Bernard-Henri Lévy, *L'Idéologie française*, Grasset, 1981, p. 97.

Jews, he admitted, played a foreground role, a role more than sufficient to confirm and give for good, in the opinion of the great mass of anti-Bolsheviks of all sorts and conditions, the old myth of the Jewish revolution." But the fact remains that "the first government formed in November 1917 by the Bolsheviks had only one Jew (Trotsky) out of fifteen members."

Amidst the anti-Semitic lucubrations, "a piece of the puzzle was missing. Jewish or Judeo-German revolution, all right: but what was the role of Jewish international capitalists? A series of forgeries sold in Petrograd by the journalist Eugene Semyonov to the diplomat Edgar Sisson provided the answer: the Bolsheviks, first and foremost Trotsky, were financed by a "Rhenish-Westphalian syndicate" through the Jewish banker Max Warburg and the Jewish Bolshevik Furstenberg." The US government itself published the documents in September 1918 under the title *The German-Bolshevik Conspiracy*." The date of the document deserves to be remembered, wrote Poliakov, as it constitutes the first official publication of an anti-Semitic forgery." The anti-Semitic propaganda went even further with "the alleged secret report of the French government, fabricated in New York by a Russian émigré, which detailed the list of the main Communist leaders, all Jews except Lenin, and which described their aims of universal Zionist domination." That report was "written in utterly implausible language, somehow conveying the chimeras which so obsess Christian imaginations at some points, perhaps chronically."

These odious lies continued after the victory of the communists." A third forgery, the Zunder document, had the honour in 1922 of being read out in its entirety from the rostrum of the young Czechoslovak parliament. According to a fourth, circulated in 1922 in the United States by the automobile king Henry Ford, the Jews of New York's East Side had designated the successor to the last Tsar. Such fables concocted in the offices of Rostov or Kiev alerted all the peoples of the earth to the existence of a worldwide Jewish conspiracy. Nor should we forget the most historically influential and dynamic myth, *The Protocols of the Elders of Zion*, printed in hundreds of thousands of copies in White-controlled territories579." On 8 May 1920, the *Times* of London published an article entitled *The Jewish Peril in which it* suggested that British Prime Minister Lloyd George had entered into negotiations with a group of conspirators." The demonstration was based on *The*

---

[579]Léon Poliakov, *Histoire de l'antisémitisme*, 1981, Calmann-Lévy, 1991, Points Seuil, vol. 2, p. 394-395. The White Russians were the part of the Russian population that did not accept the Bolshevik coup d'état and fought in the civil war.

Protocols of the Elders of Zion, thus contributing to its renown throughout the world and amplifying the odious and misleading propaganda580."

In the sequel to his *History of Anti-Semitism,* Leon Poliakov gave his opinion on the "historians' quarrel"." We find in Nolte the seeds of a revival of the Hitler myth and a legitimisation of National Socialism as the only effective form of struggle against Marxism. Hitler is presented as the first national and international hero of the struggle against Jewish world Bolshevism581." Poliakov drew this unappealable conclusion: "Nolte's argumentation can justify the anti-Semitic crimes to come582." While it was true that "at the commanding posts, the Jews seemed victorious and all powerful. The Central Committee of the Party had three Jews out of seven members: Trotsky, comparable to Lenin at the time, and who was to be more popular than him in the army, as well as Kamenev and Zinoviev, the head of the Third International. In addition, Yakov Sverdlov was elected chairman of the Executive Committee, i.e. head of the young Soviet state ... Even so, Jews made up only 16% of the Party membership, as against 60% of Russian origin583."

In *Winter Sun,* Jean Daniel also contributed his grain of sand with his analysis of the "historians' dispute". According to his reasoning,

---

[580]Léon Poliakov, *Histoire de l'antisémitisme,* 1981, Points Seuil, vol. 2, p. 411-412. [It is also interesting to bring up a letter which generated some controversy at the time after it was published on 1 June 1928 in *La Revue de Paris.* It is an alleged letter written in 1879 by Rabbi Baruch Levy to Karl Marx, which read: "The Jewish people as a whole will be their own Messiah. His reign over the universe will be realised by the unification of the other human races, the abolition of monarchies and frontiers which are the bulwark of particularism, and the establishment of a Universal Republic which will everywhere recognise the citizenship rights of the Jews. In this new organisation of humanity, the children of Israel, now scattered over the whole surface of the earth, all of the same race and of equal traditions, will succeed without much opposition in becoming the leading element in everything and everywhere if they succeed in imposing Jewish leadership on the working masses. Thus, with the victory of the proletariat, the governments of all nations will pass into the hands of the Israelites through the realisation of the Universal Republic. Individual property can then be abolished by the rulers of the Jewish race, who will then be able to administer the wealth of the peoples everywhere. And thus will be fulfilled the promise of the Talmud that, when the Messianic times come, the Jews will have under lock and key the property of all the peoples of the earth." The authenticity of the letter was convincing enough to be transcribed by Flavien Brenier "Salluste" in his book *The Secret Origins of Bolshevism: Heinrich Heine and Karl Marx,* Paris: J. Tallandier, 1930, Déterna Éditions, 2014. (NdT)]
[581]Léon Poliakov, *Histoire de l'antisémitisme 1945-1993,* Points Seuil, 1994, p. 42-43.
[582]Léon Poliakov, *Histoire de l'antisémitisme 1945-1993,* Points Seuil, 1994, p. 54.
[583]Léon Poliakov, *Histoire de l'antisémitisme 1945-1993,* Points Seuil, 1994, p. 260.

Ernst Nolte and Stéphane Courtois could be suspected of anti-Semitism because they raised—albeit extremely cautiously—the problem of the strong presence of Jews in the Bolshevik regime. Obviously, this according to him was highly condemnable and unacceptable as an argument to explain the birth of National Socialism for the simple reason that German Jews were perfectly integrated into German society." I knew—contrary to François Furet, Besançon and Revel—that this Stéphane Courtois was not one of us. That he was more concerned with putting Stalin's monstrosity above Hitler's 584... It should be noted that neither of the two historians who engaged in such edifying dialogue on this subject is of Jewish origin: the Frenchman François Furet and the German Ernst Nolte... Unfortunately for Ernst Nolte, the integration of the German Jews into the German homeland had reached such a high degree that he should have ignored the obstacle of Jewish difference. How could Hitler have ignored this integration of Jews in his country on the pretext that there was an unusual number of Jews in the major states of Bolshevism in Russia and elsewhere? It is a question that Nolte does not want to raise. He suspiciously refuses to do so585." This is called beating about the bush.

So we see that Solzhenitsyn was right to be indignant about the refusal of the vast majority of Jewish intellectuals to accept their share of responsibility for the communist experiment. During this difficult mea culpa exercise, we have at least been able to appreciate the great mastery they have of all forms of intellectual contortion, each one more astonishing than the next. After all, the Barnum, Zavata, Gruss, Amar, Pinder and other travelling circuses were always there to distract and amuse the incorrigible rubes that we remain at heart.

---

[584]Jean Daniel, *Soleil d'hiver*, Carnets 1998-2000, Grasset, Poche, 2000, p. 330.
[585]Jean Daniel, *Soleil d'hiver*, Carnets 1998-2000, Grasset, Poche, 2000, p. 354.

2. Explain the phenomenon

Anti-Semitism existed long before the Bolshevik revolution, so it cannot be held up as the sole cause of the phenomenon. What explanations can be given for the atrocious persecutions suffered by the Jews throughout their history? First of all, intellectuals put forward the scapegoat theory, i.e. the designation of an enemy who was responsible for all evils and who had to be eliminated in order to ensure social harmony and peace. A second type of explanation emphasises the human rejection of difference and the envy of the mediocre towards the successful. The dominant social group does indeed have a natural tendency to reject the foreigner, the stranger, the outsider, the marginal as well as the upstart. A third reaction manifests rather a total incomprehension of the phenomenon. The impossibility of explaining the evil then leads to a fourth explanation: the madness of the people, the mental illness of those affected.

The scapegoats

Hannah Arendt was a central figure in the post-war intellectual world, and her book *The Origins of Totalitarianism* is still a reference work for understanding the great transformations of the 20th century. Her interesting *Anti-Semitism* constitutes the first of the three parts of her book. Hannah Arendt tried to show in it that the rise of anti-Semitism in the 19th century did not correspond at all to the prodigious increase in the power of the Jews in European society since their emancipation, as superficial spirits had hitherto believed, but, paradoxically, to the loss of power and influence of Jewish financiers. In the old Germanic Empire, divided into hundreds of small, almost independent principalities, it is known that the German princes always had around them, as great treasurers, what were called "palace Jews". In the 17th and 18th centuries, these were their financial advisors and intermediaries at the European level.

Following the example set by the French Revolution, citizenship was granted to Jews in almost all European countries in the course of the 19th century, with the notable exception of Russia and Romania. After the revolutionary changes and the territorial reorganisation of

Germany, Hannah Arendt explained, "in the first decades of this evolution the Jews lost their exclusive position in public finance to imperialist-minded entrepreneurs; their importance as a group declined, although some Jews retained their influence, both as financial advisors and as inter-European intermediaries. These Jews, however, had even less need of the wider Jewish community, despite their wealth, than the palace Jews of the 17th and 18th centuries, and so often separated themselves from the Jewish community altogether. Jewish communities were no longer organised economically, and although in the eyes of the gentile world some highly placed Jews were still representative of Jewry in general, there was little or no material reality behind this idea586." Thus, we must believe that "as a group, Western Jewry disintegrated along with the Nation-State during the decades preceding the outbreak of the First World War." It can be observed that "anti-Semitism reached its peak when Jews had similarly lost their public functions and influence and were left with only their wealth. When Hitler came to power, the German Banks were already almost entirely *Judenrein* (and it was precisely in that sector that the Jews had held decisive positions for over a hundred years)... The same can be said of almost all the countries of Western Europe. The Dreyfus affair did not break out under the Second Empire, when French Jewry was at the height of its prosperity and influence, but under the Third Republic, when Jews had almost completely disappeared from important positions (though not from the political scene). Austrian anti-Semitism did not become violent under Metternich and Franz Joseph, but in the post-war Austrian Republic, when it became clear that no other group had suffered such a loss of influence and prestige by reason of the demise of the Habsburg monarchy587." A ruling group is respected if it fulfils a useful function for society. It quickly becomes the target of popular resentment if it only retains the privileges of its function without assuming its social responsibility.

"The national and inter-European Jewish element became the object of universal hatred precisely because of its useless wealth and of contempt because of its lack of power588." The accusations of the anti-

---

586Hannah Arendt, *The Origins of Totalitarianism, Antisemitism*, 1951, Taurus-Santillana, Madrid, 1998, p. 37. Elisabeth's marrano banker, the financiers of the armies of Cromwell, Frederick II, the Austrian Emperor and Bismarck did not dictate policy to the sovereigns, for if they had dared to deceive them they would probably have ended their days in an unhealthy dungeon.

587Hannah Arendt, *The Origins of Totalitarianism, Antisemitism*, 1951, Taurus-Santillana, Madrid, 1998, p. 29.

588Hannah Arendt, *The Origins of Totalitarianism, Antisemitism*, 1951, Taurus-

Semites about the power of the Jews thus had no valid basis. Anti-Semites, who personify "human baseness", do not attack the powerful, but "groups deprived of power or in danger of losing it", i.e. groups without defence. The Dreyfus case was a good example, wrote Hannah Arendt, for "it was no accident that this happened shortly after native French Jewry, during the Panama scandal, gave in to the initiative and unscrupulousness of some German Jewish adventurers589."

The success of anti-Semitism in late 19th century France "can also be attributed to the lack of authority of the Third Republic, which was approved by a slim majority. In the eyes of the masses the state had lost its prestige along with the monarchy, and attacks on the state were no longer a sacrilege... Here it was much easier to attack the Jews and the state together590".

"The growing influence of big business on the state and the decreasing need the state experienced for Jewish services threatened the Jewish banker with its demise and determined certain changes in Jewish occupations... More and more Jews were abandoning state finance for independent business." They devoted themselves more to cultural and artistic life: "The influx of the children of prosperous Jewish parents into educated professions was especially noticeable in Germany and Austria, where a large proportion of cultural institutions, such as newspapers, publishing houses, music and theatre, became Jewish enterprises. What was made possible by the traditional Jewish preference and respect for intellectual occupations determined a real break with tradition, the intellectual assimilation and nationalisation of important strata of Western and Central European Jewry. Politically, it meant the emancipation of Jews from the protection of the state591".

Despite its remarkable ingenuity, Hannah Arendt's thesis has not been taken up by any author. Apart from having completely avoided the socialist phenomenon, her explanation of an anti-Semitism attacking a community weakened by its loss of power in the 19th century totally contradicted everything that had been generally accepted until then, namely that the emancipation of European Jews had led to a considerable increase in their influence from the outset. As we have seen, this sometimes pays off, but in this case, this thesis has never

---

Santillana, Madrid, 1998, p. 37.
[589]Hannah Arendt, *The Origins of Totalitarianism, Antisemitism*, 1951, Taurus-Santillana, Madrid, 1998, p. 88.
[590]Hannah Arendt, *The Origins of Totalitarianism, Antisemitism*, 1951, Taurus-Santillana, Madrid, 1998, p. 60.
[591]Hannah Arendt, *The Origins of Totalitarianism, Antisemitism*, 1951, Taurus-Santillana, Madrid, 1998, p. 64.

gained any traction. The image of the fabulous power of the five Rothschild brothers dominating 19th century Europe remains the mythical reference of the "anonymous and vagabond fortune592".

The great writer Primo Levi, whose work is studied in every high school in Europe, had a more classical interpretation of anti-Semitism. Recalling the sad times he had to live through, he said: "There were absurd, unjust and vexatious laws. Every day the newspapers were full of lies and insults. We witnessed a ridiculous and cruel inversion of the truth: the Jews were regarded not only as the enemies of the state, but also as the deniers of justice and morality, the destroyers of science and art, the termites who, by their hidden activity, undermine the foundations of the social edifice, the culprits of the impending conflict." It instilled in young Germans "a visceral hatred, a physical repugnance towards the Jew, destroyer of the world and of order, guilty of all evils. Like any absolute power, Nazism needed an anti-power, an anti-state, on which to lay the blame for all the problems, present and past, real and supposed, that the Germans suffered. Defenseless and often regarded as the "Others", the Jews constituted the ideal anti-state, the target against which to direct the nationalist and Manichean exaltation that Nazi propaganda nurtured in the country593." For Primo Levi, "anti-Semitism is an ancient and complex fact, whose roots are barbaric, almost pre-human (there is, as is well known, a zoological racism in social animals); but it is periodically revived by virtue of a cynical calculation whose usefulness in times of instability and political suffering makes it possible to find or invent a scapegoat to which to attribute all past, present and future problems, and on which to unload

---

[592]More interesting to us is his analysis of the assimilation of a certain Jewish middle class of intellectuals, artists and upstarts: "Secularisation, therefore, finally determined that paradox, so decisive for the psychology of modern Jews, by which Jewish assimilation in its liquidation of national consciousness, in its transformation from a national religion into a denominational denomination and in its way of responding to the cold and ambiguous demands of state and society with equally ambiguous resources and psychological tricks—engendered a very real Jewish chauvinism, if by chauvinism we mean the perverted nationalism in which "the individual is himself what he worships; the individual is his own ideal and even his own idol". Where Jews were educated, secularised and assimilated under the ambiguous conditions of society and state in Western and Central Europe, they lost that measure of political responsibility which their origin implied and which Jewish notables had always felt, albeit in the form of privilege and domination. Jewish origin, without religious and political connotations, became everywhere a psychological quality, became "Jewishness" and from then on could only be considered within the categories of virtue or vice." In *The Origins of Totalitarianism, Anti-Semitism,* p. 81, 88.
[593]Primo Lévi, *L'asymétrie et la vie, articles,* Robert Laffont, 2002, p. 90.

the aggressive and vindictive tensions of the people. The Jews, dispersed and defenseless, were presented, after the diaspora, as the ideal victims. Weimar Germany was sick and unstable, it needed a scapegoat594."

We find the same kind of explanations from French intellectuals. Albert Memmi analysed German anti-Semitism in the 1930s as follows: The Jew, he wrote, "was particularly comfortable. His negative stereotype was already widespread and he could easily serve as an outlet for the aggressiveness of the German people, as of all other conquered peoples ... Soap could be made from his fat, lanterns from his skin and cloth from his hair595."

In *Tierra-Patria*, sociologist Edgar Morin also gave us his explanation of Hitlerite anti-Semitism. After the war, "the misfortunes and anguish of unemployment and misery revive the feeling of national humiliation provoked by the Treaty of Versailles, and the fear of "stateless" communism will inflame the desire for nationalist revenge and hatred of the Jews, singled out by Hitler as diabolical manipulators of an international plutocratic-Bolshevik plot596." This was indeed a delusional view of reality.

For his part, the humanist Marek Halter, the tireless advocate of Peace, did not conceal a certain gloom, as we have already seen, about the evolution of the countries of the East after the fall of the totalitarian regimes: "This new situation has brought back the archaic animosity towards the other, the different, who is once again accused of all evils, who is humiliated and, if need be, killed. In the history of these countries, the other, the foreigner, the devil, has always been the Jew. Hence the resurgence of anti-Semitism. The Jews are held responsible for everything that has gone wrong, is going wrong or will go wrong in the Soviet Union. They are blamed for Stalinist persecutions, for the destruction of the Russian heritage, for economic misery, and even for perestroika."

All this was completely false, of course, but these slanders gave rise to the worst hypotheses: "So the Jews are afraid," explained Marek Halter, "and once again they are forced into exile, always victims, always persecuted. That is why they flee to Israel." It is important to

[594]Primo Lévi, *La Stampa*, 20 May 1979, in *L'asymétrie et la vie, articles*, Robert Laffont, 2002.
[595]Albert Memmi, *Le Racisme*, Gallimard, 1982, réédition de poche, 1994, p. 92, 93. As surprising as they may seem today, these atrocities were commonly admitted by the historiography of the 1980s. They were abandoned in the 1990s.
[596]Edgar Morin and Anne-Brigitte Kern, *Tierra-Patria*, 1993, Editorial Kairós, Barcelona, 2005, p. 25–26.

understand that "it is not, as some Arabs believe, to harm the Palestinians that Israel receives them, but to save persecuted men597." So we must understand that the persecutions suffered by Jews in Eastern European countries after the fall of communism were not reported by any media because the anti-Semites, who owned the media, probably organised a conspiracy of silence on the subject." To my Palestinian friends, I say this: Fear not. Those Soviet Jews are leaving their country because the environment has become hostile to them; they will not settle either in the West Bank or in Gaza, where the environment would be even more hostile." This speech was probably necessary to reassure a Palestinian population legitimately concerned about the influx of hundreds of thousands of settlers of Soviet origin in the 1990s. Let us simply hope that in this case the Palestinians show a little more gratitude than the populations of Europe liberated from the communist yoke, otherwise Marek Halter risks sinking into the deepest despair.

With regard to the interpretation of anti-Semitism, Shmuel Trigano wrote: "I know from experience that anti-Semitism is a phenomenon comparable to a social measuring instrument. It makes it possible to detect the degree of sickness in a society ... In the storm, in unemployment, in inflation, in social chaos, in terrorism, in fear, one has to find someone to blame. It is always someone's fault—the other's fault598."

In a book of interviews entitled *Jewish Portraits599*, published in Germany in 1989, the views of several Jewish personalities from Germany and Central Europe who lived through the tragic hours of the Second World War coincided with the above testimonies. We have extracted below some statements that relate to our topic, namely the roots of anti-Semitism, Jewish identity and the universalist spirit. These testimonies are particularly important because all these personalities are part of the social and intellectual elite of the Jewish community.

The first of these is Bruno Bettelheim, a psychosociologist born in 1903 in Vienna: "— In your opinion, what were the causes of historical anti-Semitism? —They differ from period to period. I think in any case that Christians did not forgive the Jews for the fact that the origin of their religion is Jewish and that Christ himself was Jewish. That was

---

[597]Marek Halter, *Un Homme, un cri*, Robert Laffont, Paris, 1991, p. 291-292.

[598]Shmuel Trigano, *L'Idéal démocratique... à l'épreuve de la shoah*, Éditions Odile Jacob, 1999, p. 43.

[599]Herlinde Loelbl, *Portraits juifs, Photographies et entretiens*, L'Arche éditeur, Francfort-sur-le Main, 1989, 2003 for the French version.

hard to live with, wasn't it? But the unconscious still knew that Jesus Christ was a Jew. Besides, it was always very convenient to have a scapegoat at hand."

Edward Goldstücker, professor of literature at Brighton, born in 1913 in Odbiel, Czechoslovakia:

"What explanation do you have for anti-Semitism? —The Jews were a foreign minority who were hidebound in their difference. Minority, they were therefore without defence and constituted an ideal target for those who wanted to unleash their aggressive impulses."

Arthur Brauner, film producer in Berlin, born in 1918 in Lodz, Poland:

"Can the anti-Semitism of the Germans and other peoples be explained? —If a State of Israel had existed during the two thousand years of the Diaspora, there would have been no anti-Semitism. At least not in this form and dimension. But since there was no State of Israel for two thousand years, the Jews were powerless. One is respected and esteemed when one is strong, if only out of fear."

George Tabori, writer, actor and director in Vienna, born in Budapest in 1914: "As far as anti-Semitism is concerned, the usual sociological and economic explanations don't add up. Hostility against Jews has manifested itself even in places where they clearly did not represent competition or an economic threat. The most recent example that comes to mind is Austria. Anti-Semitism is after all an ideology of cowardice. One projects one's own fears and one's own aggression onto others; then they feel threatened and lash out. Of course, it is better to choose a weak and unarmed group, a group that cannot defend itself. Jews have always been the ideal scapegoats and the first victims in crisis situations. It was the Jews who formulated the laws—the Ten Commandments, the hygiene prescriptions of Moses—and, in fact, the Sermon on the Mount is nothing more than a restatement of the ancient prophetic texts. These laws are good, reasonable, in a way a perfect moral code. But it is impossible for us to observe them all to the end. Hence the feeling of bad conscience, of permanent irritation towards the Jews. They represent the biblical law and their mere existence reminds Christians of the inaccessible ideal[600]. —Is there any country that you consider your homeland? —For a long time I was nostalgic for Hungary, but now that is water under the bridge. For me, all this talk about homeland and patriotism is harmful." He had previously stated: "New York is a Jewish city. One feels, so to speak, at home."

---

[600]Let us note this admirable example of intellectual contortion.

In his analysis of the situation in the Middle East, the great American journalist and writer Norman Mailer seemed to be primarily concerned with the fate of the Jews, without any consideration for foreign peoples. According to him, anti-Semitism would be nothing more than a very practical means used by Arab countries to justify their neglect." It is in the interest of the Arab countries that Israel is the bad guy. Although I am Jewish to the core, I am not a Jewish patriot in the sense of defending Israel, my Israel, against all odds. I have no such feelings. But I do think that the end of the Holocaust gave us a great example of how cruel, how inhumane the sheikhs and the top leaders of many Arab countries were at that time. They could have said: "Let the Jews occupy this land. It is not going to harm us. We could even use them for our purposes. They did not. They chose to regard Holocaust survivors as enemies. They used Israel to shift hatred against their own regimes onto Israel." And again, we see the same roundabouts, the same usual contortions that allow us to turn the issues around in the most implausible ways. Listen to this: "The Saudis now have a magnificent ruse: they use the Palestinians as a justification for their hatred of Israel, when in fact they see Israel as their safeguard against the Palestinians601." This dialectic reminds us of Cohn-Bendit's words on immigration in Germany, when he explicitly wrote that borders should be opened to limit immigration and that immigration should be encouraged to reduce racism.

This underlying tendency to invert values and to deny the most established evidence was brought to light by Friedrich Nietzsche, who expressed it admirably in his *Genealogy of Morals*: "It has been the Jews who, with a terrifying logical consequence, have dared to invert the aristocratic identification of values (good = noble = mighty = powerful = beautiful = beautiful = happy = beloved of God) and have maintained with the teeth of the most abysmal hatred (the hatred of impotence) that inversion, namely, "the miserable are the good; the poor, the impotent, the low are the only good; the suffering, the destitute, the sick, the deformed are also the only pious, the only blessed of God, only for them there is bliss,—but you, you, the noble and violent, you are, for all eternity, the wicked, the cruel, the lascivious, the insatiable, the atheists, and you too will be eternally the wretched,

---

[601]Norman Mailer, *Why are we at war?* Editorial Anagrama, 2003, Barcelona, p. 104, 105.

the cursed and the damned602! "The accusatory inversion is a powerful and fearsome force603.

Finally, Norman Mailer naively continued the thread of his reflection on the anti-Semitism of Arab nations in the Middle East, stating: 'If the Arab leaders had been a little kind, they could have said that these people had been through hell... Instead they declared them enemies. The Israelis had no choice but to try to strengthen themselves. In doing so, some of the best traits of the Jewish character—irony, wit, love of truth, love of wisdom and justice—suffered internal deterioration ... So I am inclined to think, Mailer concluded, that the best explanation for 9/11 is that the devil won a great battle that day. Yes, Satan was the pilot who guided those planes into that atrocious outcome[604]."

Political assassinations

We should not think that Jews are incapable of defending themselves. This opinion, which is widespread after the dramatic ordeal of the Holocaust, tends to give credence to the anti-Semitic idea of the intrinsic weakness of the Jewish people and the supposed superiority of the "Aryan race". The Jews, on the contrary, have shown on many occasions that they had the energy to stand up to their oppressors and that they were able to defend their rights and their interests with considerable vigour.

To respond to Boris Pasternak's assertion, regarding "the Jews' modest, self-sacrificing way of keeping themselves apart", "their fragility and their inability to strike back", we could begin by citing some examples of acts of bravery that Solzhenitsyn set out in his book that illustrated the physical and prolonged courage spurred by the spirit of revenge. In the Tsarist era, when Russian revolutionaries opted for terrorism, Jews were still a rare exception in these movements. But in the late 1870s, there were in the movement "The Will of the People" (*Narodnaya Volia*) some Jews like Aaron Gobet, Salomon Wittenberg, Meir Mlodetsky, Grigori Goldenberg, Aaron Zundelevitch, Saveli Zlatopolsky, Deitch and Hessia Helfmann. After the assassination of Alexander II, their presence provoked an outburst of popular

---

[602]Friedrich Nietzsche, *La Genealogía de la moral*, Alianza Editorial de bolsillo, 2005, Madrid, p. 46.
[603]See Hervé Ryssen, *The Mirror of Judaism*.
[604]Norman Mailer, *Why are we at war?* Editorial Anagrama, 2003, Barcelona, p. 105–106, 121.

indignation against them. But the fact is that *The Journal of the People's Will agreed* with these disorders by invoking the role of the Jews as "exploiters of the people". This shows that at that time its influence within the Organisation was insignificant. But by the end of the 1880s, Solzhenitsyn wrote, the situation had changed. After the creation of the S.R. (Socialist-Revolutionary) party, the Jews formed a solid majority within the leadership of that movement. The members of the inner circle of the party leadership were Mendel, Wittenberg, Levine, Levite and Azef. The combat section of the S.R. had been created and was led by Grigori Gershuni from 1901 to 1903, then by Yevno Azef from 1903 to 1906, and Zilberberg from 1906 to 1907. A similar development can be observed within the social-democratic movements.

A 1965 book entitled *The Terrorists605*, by Roland Gaucher, provided some insights into the actions of the Socialist-Revolutionary Party. From the very beginning, the party used armed action to overthrow the Tsarist regime. From the very beginning, the Combat Organisation was created. It was the spearhead of the Party. It soon became quasi-autonomous and was able to strike terror into the heart of the enemy apparatus." Gershuni was the real creator of the C.O. Of Jewish origin, a former pharmacy trainee, he was about thirty years old at the time when he drew up the statutes of the Organisation. Under his leadership, the O.C. men assassinated the Minister of the Interior Dmitry Sipiaguin, shot Prince Obolensky and killed Governor Bogdanovich in 1903". Von Pleve succeeded Sipiaguin as Interior Minister in 1902. A year after Von Pleve's appointment, engineer Yevno Azef replaced Gershuni but was captured by the police in Kiev. On 15 July 1904, a bomb killed Von Pleve. Grand Duke Sergius was himself assassinated in an assassination attempt. The C.O., which had suffered heavy casualties, was dissolved after several disagreements within the Central Committee. A new group of terrorists was then created by Zilberberg under the name of the Combat Detachment. But it disintegrated in February 1907. It is also known that Pyotr Stolypin, the Tsar's Minister of the Interior who had pushed through a major land reform between 1906 and 1910, was assassinated in Kiev on 2 September 1911 by the Jewish extremist Bogrov during the ceremonies marking the 300th anniversary of the dynasty.

During the Bolshevik revolution, Count von Mirbach, the German ambassador, was shot by Blumkine, a young man of eighteen. He belonged to the Cheka and was a member of the left-wing S.R. party.

---

[605]Roland Gaucher, *Les Terroristes*, Éditions Albin Michel, 1965.

His murder was intended to rekindle hostility between Russia and Germany.

In Red Russia, two illustrious terrorist acts perpetrated by Jews against the Bolsheviks themselves deserve a special place apart: on 30 August 1918, Moisei Uritski, the head of the Cheka, was assassinated by an S.R. student named Leonid Kannegisser. On the same day, Lenin addressed a rally at which he thundered against the enemies of the revolution. After he left the hall and was about to get into his car, Fanny Kaplan, a former anarchist, approached him and fired three bullets, two of which hit Lenin's shoulder and neck.

Leonid Kannegisser, of hereditary nobility through his grandfather, had entered the officer-student school in 1917. His motives are known from a letter sent to his sister on the eve of the attack in which he said he wanted to avenge the Brest-Litovsk peace, that he was ashamed to see the Jews contribute to installing the Bolsheviks in power, and that he would also avenge the execution by the Petrograd Cheka of one of his comrades from the military school606." But one thing is puzzling, Solzhenitsyn wondered: how is it possible that later, at the height of the Red terror and while thousands of innocent hostages, completely unrelated to the case, were being put to the sword all over the country, the Kannegisser family was released from prison and allowed to emigrate? The parents and friends had even worked out a plan for an armed attack on the Petrograd Cheka to free the prisoner, and all of them, after being arrested, were released and remained living in Petrograd unmolested. The Bolshevik claw is not recognisable in this case. Such leniency is perhaps explained by the Bolshevik authorities' concern not to anger influential Jewish circles in Petrograd. The Kannegisser family had maintained their Jewish faith and Leonid's mother testified at an interrogation that her son had shot Uritski because he had turned away from Judaism."

Fanny Kaplan's attack on Lenin also revealed suspicious circumstances." It may have been a political act of a militant close to the Socialist-Revolutionaries, but there are strong presumptions, according to recent studies607, that Fanny Kaplan did not shoot Lenin, and that she was simply detained "to close the investigation" and serve as a convenient culprit."

Other political assassinations were committed by members of the Jewish community outside Russia: The case of Friedrich Adler is well

[606]Alexandre Soljénitsyne, *Deux siècles ensemble,* Fayard, 2003.
[607]B. Orlov, *Le Mythe de Fanny Kaplan,* ME, 1975, no. 2, quoted by Solzhenitsyn, *Deux siècles ensemble,* p. 124.

known. He had shot down the Austrian prime minister in 1916, although he was later pardoned. From his Austrian prison, he obtained a pardon from R. Abramovich, an important Menshevik leader, by writing a letter to Lenin in the summer of 1918.

In 1927, the highly publicised trial took place in Paris of Samuel Sholem Schwarzbard, a watchmaker whose family had perished in the Ukrainian pogroms, and who had been shot five times by the Ukrainian nationalist leader Simon Petliura in Paris. The lawyers had legitimised the murder as a just punishment. Schwarzbard was acquitted by the French court and released. Even so, the prosecutor had let the accused know that Petliura lived in Poland and that: "You did not kill him there because you knew that in Poland you would have been brought before a military court of exception."

In 1927, too, the young Koverda had wanted to "attract the attention of the world conscience" by assassinating the Bolshevik Voikov in Warsaw. He was sentenced to ten years in prison, which he served in full. In 1929, in Moscow, Lazar Kolenberg assassinated Slatchev, a former White general who had gone over to the Soviets, guilty of having tolerated Nikolayev's pogroms. Kolenberg was found irresponsible during the investigation and released608.

In Romania, "the first decisive action of the Communists, even before the official creation of the party, was the attack perpetrated by the militant Max Goldstein in the Senate Chamber in Bucharest on 8 December 1920, which left numerous victims609.

The historian Ernst Nolte's book *The European Civil War*610 also mentions other cases of political assassination: in 1936, the young David Frankfurter assassinated the Swiss National Socialist organisational leader Wilhelm Gustloff. At the time, the top state leadership had prevented any kind of excesses and exactions in view of the imminent Olympic Games.

The assassination on 7 November 1938 of the German legation secretary Ernst vom Rath by the young Herschel Grynszpan in the Reich's Parisian embassy can also be mentioned, of course. Nolte wrote: "This act may be one of the factors that "triggered the striking resurgence of anti-Semitism just at a time when everything seemed to

---

608Alexandre Soljénitsyne, *Deux siècles ensemble,* Fayard, 2003, p. 212.
609Romulus Rusan, in *Du Passé faisons table rase, Histoire et mémoire du communisme en Europe,* ouvrage collectif, sous la direction de Stéphane Courtois, Robert Laffont, 2002, p. 372.
610Ernst Nolte, *La guerra civil europea, 1917-1945,* Fondo de cultura económica, Mexico, 2001, p. 292.

indicate that any successful policy would have to concentrate exclusively on anti-Communism. Under the auspices of the Nuremberg Laws, German Jews had experienced several years of relative tranquillity, during which they were supported to emigrate, and the large number of Jews who remained in the country developed a community life of astonishing diversity and vitality. In the economy, Jewish positions were intact, and anyone who noticed the fact that, in addition to Adolf Hitler's signature, economic laws were quite often signed by various Jewish bankers611." Nevertheless, Grynszpan's act was followed by exactions of all kinds against the Jews of Germany during what was called the "Night of Broken Glass", resulting in thirty-six deaths.

The assassination of Trotsky in Mexico by a Stalinist agent in 1940 is etched in the memoirs. The job was carried out with extraordinary barbarity, as the former head of the Red Army was killed with a pistol butt to the skull. But that did not spare those responsible for the assassination, sent by Stalin, from the Soviet mincer, as *The Black Book* noted: "In October 1951, Stalin dealt another blow to Beria by ordering him to arrest a group of old Jewish security and judiciary cadres including Lt. Col. Eitingon, who, on Beria's orders, had in 1940 organised the assassination of Trotsky; General Leonid Raijman, chief interrogator of the NKVD who had participated in the staging of the Moscow trials; Colonel Lev Schwarzmann, torturer of Babel and Meyerhold, and examining magistrate Lev Sheinin, the right-hand man of Vyshinsky, the prosecutor of the great Moscow trials of 1936– 1938 ... All were accused of being the organisers of a vast "Jewish nationalist conspiracy" led by... Abakumov, the Minister of State Security and Beria's close associate612."

In Palestine, the Jews opened a new chapter in their history. They quickly had the opportunity to demonstrate their offensive capabilities. When they began to settle in Palestine, conflicts with the Arabs broke out at once and fighting groups were set up on both sides. Menachem Begin was one of the leaders of the Irgun. But in the Stern or Leji Group, the use of violence was much more systematic. The group founded by Abraham Stern was born out of a split within the Irgun, itself the result of dissent from the Haganah, a Jewish anti-Arab militia. By 1920, Zeev Jabotinsky had formed the Revisionist Zionist movement to

---

611Ernst Nolte, *La guerra civil europea, 1917-1945,* Fondo de cultura económica, Mexico, 2001, p. 291.
612Stéphane Courtois, Nicolas Werth, *El Libro negro del comunismo,* Espasa-Planeta, 1998, p. 283, 284.

immediately call for the creation of an independent Jewish state on the territory corresponding to the borders of historic Palestine. That goal, he believed, could only be achieved if Jews were prepared to take up arms and fight back, blow for blow against the terrorist raids that the Arabs perpetrated against the Jewish colonies. In 1937, he created his own fighting organisation, the Irgun (*HaIrgun HaTzva'i HaLe'umi BeEretz Yisra'el*), the National Military Organisation. The Irgun was organised according to the military principles already in force among the members of an earlier youth movement, the Betar.

The Irgun began its activity by dropping bombs in Arab markets or placing them in passenger buses in retaliation for Arab terrorism. In February 1939, the Irgun launched a series of terrible attacks. The Haganah widely distributed a leaflet recalling the biblical word: "Thou shalt not kill" (*Exodus* XX: 13), to which the Irgun replied with another quotation: "But if other injuries occur, the penalty will be life for life, eye for eye, tooth for tooth, hand for hand, foot for foot, burn for burn, wound for wound, blow for blow." (*Exodus* XXI:23–25) This violence was not to be long in turning against the British who administered the region under the League of Nations mandate. By this time, four hundred and fifty thousand Jews had settled in Palestine, provoking the consequent anger of the Palestinians. The Chamberlain government then published the White Paper on 17 May 1939 which came to this stark conclusion: an end to Jewish emigration. Violent demonstrations broke out and members of the Irgun State-major were arrested. During the war against Nazi Germany, most Irgun leaders felt that operations against the British should in any case be suspended until the end of the war. But Abraham Stern considered that the only enemy was Britain.

A radical Jewish party assassinated Folke Bernadotte, Count of Wisborg, for having advocated at the UN the attribution of Jerusalem to Jordan. Count Bernadotte was never properly honoured by Jewish memory, for although he too had saved thousands of Jews during the war, he was disowned for having been too pro-Arab afterwards. The future Israeli minister Isaac Shamir ordered his assassination. Jacques Attali's explanation of the event was laconic and revealing: "In August, Count Bernadotte comes to negotiate an agreement on behalf of the UN: he proposes that Israel return the Negev and Jerusalem in exchange for Galilee, which both sides refuse; Bernadotte is assassinated[613]."

Lord Moyne (Walter Edward Guinness), Minister of State in Churchill's government in the Near East, was also assassinated, shot

---

[613]Jacques Attali, *Los judíos, el mundo y el dinero*, Fondo de cultura económica, 2005, Buenos Aires, p. 454.

three times at point-blank range, as was his chauffeur. The attack was carried out by two Jewish youths aged 23 and 17: Bet Zuri and Hakim. The Irgun attacked military installations and even hanged British officers. On 1 July 1946, Irgun men blew up the King David Hotel, which served as British headquarters in Jerusalem. Two hundred were killed and wounded. Undoubtedly, all this violence precipitated the final departure of the British.

During the Algerian war, members of the Jewish community also played a leading role there. On 6 May 1956, an accidental explosion occurred at the Mustafa hospital in Algiers, where an outsider named Daniel Timsit was experimenting with his ingredients. The FLN (National Liberation Front) had in turn provided a villa on the outskirts of Algiers to the Algerian Communist Party (Meyer, the Timsit brothers, Smadja, Habib Giorgio) for its laboratory. The dissolution of the PCA in September 1955 prompted its members to take up armed struggle. On 30 September 1955, two bombs exploded in several merchant streets. One in the *Milk Bar*, Place d'Isly, the other in the *Cafetaria*, Rue Michelet. A young "European" girl, Daniela Mine, had apparently planted the bomb in the *Milk Bar on* behalf of the FLN614.

More recently, we can mention and recall the assassination of the French nationalist militant François Duprat in Paris in March 1978. He was killed in the explosion of his car and his wife was seriously injured. The attack was never elucidated, but the anti-Zionist leanings of the victims leave no doubt as to the origin of the possible instigators of the attack.

This list is not exhaustive, but in view of these cases, it is clear that the Jews are not lambs to be meekly led to the slaughter. The theme of revenge is otherwise a recurring one in their writings, either explicitly or underlyingly. In the Jewish calendar, two days of vengeance are celebrated: the first is Purim, the day on which, according to the Book of Esther, the Jews killed 75,000 Gentiles in Persia. It was on this Purim day, 25 February 1994, that Baruch Goldstein, an immigrant from Brooklyn (New York) settled in Hebron (Israel), massacred with an assault rifle twenty-nine pious Muslims gathered at the Tomb of the Patriarchs615. He was lynched by the survivors of the massacre, but his tomb has since become a place of pilgrimage for orthodox Jews. It was also on Purim that Nazi Germany's ministers were executed at Nuremberg in 1946. Just as the Purim holiday was also chosen to

---

[614]Roland Gaucher, *Les Terroristes*, Éditions Albin Michel, 1965.
[615]A highly sacred place where three very important biblical couples are supposedly buried: Abraham and Sarah; Isaac and Rebekah; Jacob and Leah.

immolate two hundred thousand Iraqis with the US Air Force offensive in 1991. In 2003, the US declared war on 20 March: that day corresponded to the 16th of Aadar, the last day of the religious holiday of Purim commemorating the victory of the Jews against the Persians of the evil Haman, the great chancellor of King Ahasuerus. As a long article in the Jewish Telegraphic Agency of 18 March 2003 clearly put it: "For the rabbis, it is no coincidence that the war against Iraq is again associated with the day of Purim". Let us also remember that it was on this day that Stalin died. Purim is an auspicious day for revenge, although Judgement Day can also be just as auspicious. Shortly afterwards, the festival of Sukkot (the Feast of Booths or Tabernacles) is celebrated, during which the Messiah may at last be revealed.

Getting to know each other better

Anti-Semitism can also be explained by people's ignorance and by the fear that human beings have of what is different from them. To know oneself better would obviously reduce the evil. It is true that Jews have been able to attract attention and arouse envy because of their social and material success. This is in addition to the old anti-Semitism of Christian origin.

In the Hellenistic world of Antiquity and Egypt, said Albert Memmi, "Judeophobia was part of a more general xenophobia towards outsiders. In the ancient world, it was primarily a cultural rather than a religious phobia. The beliefs and customs of the Jews were not well known, often in a fanciful way, which increased the anxiety of their fellow citizens." The wisdom and reasonableness of the Greeks and Egyptians were ultimately limited, for after several centuries of living together they had not yet grasped the noble customs of the "Jews". They had failed to glimpse the full humanity of this small people. However, the worst was yet to come: "The specific hostility against the Jews would have begun around the first century, with the advent of Christianity." Thus European civilisation reached new heights of intolerance and stupidity in the course of its history. It was in the Spain of the Catholic Monarchs that the first racist legislation in Europe was introduced, in order to preserve Spanish blood from the contamination of those Jews who had converted to Catholicism, but who were still secretly Judaising. The Marranos had gradually become the phobia of the well-born Spaniards, the old Christians. It was there, at that historical moment, that Europe gave an example of the height of human stupidity: "When the Spaniards speak of purity of blood, their own naturally, they suggest that that of the others, Jews and Moors, would be impure. Strictly speaking, this obviously makes no sense. Perhaps it was a kind of dark fear of the Marranos, more or less secret characters616." As we see, the Spaniards of the 16th century were not much more intelligent than the Greeks and Egyptians of Antiquity617.

The book *Jewish Portraits*618 provided us with some interesting testimonies on this point, taken from interviews with brilliant personalities.

Rafael Buber, executor of the estate of the philosopher Martin Buber, born in 1900 in Sils and died in Jerusalem in 1990: "Today, I am convinced that a large part of the feeling of rejection is the result of the strangeness of our faith. Non-Jews know almost nothing about it."

Fred Lessing, New York businessman, born in 1915 in Bamberg: "The fact that all men hate Jews is quite normal: simply because they are different. In Bavaria, for example, the Prussians were the most hated because they were different and wanted to remain so. And also because they think they are better than others."

Erika Landau, a psychotherapist in Tel Aviv, born in 1931 in Chernobyl: "Difference is feared because it is not understood. Jews have always set themselves apart from the societies in which they lived. That's why they were a cause for concern. As a minority, Jews had to be the best, learn better, get better grades, earn more money. And that has obviously aroused colossal envy. It is that unease and that envy that led to the hatred of the Jews."

Erwin Leiser, director and journalist, born in 1923 in Berlin: "They were always a nuisance. They always set standards that others found intolerable, when they only set them for themselves. Jews always have to do a little more than others, even in their relationship with God. They are not "chosen" because they are elite, but because they are "special". God intends to carry out a particular project through them: to test the humanity of other peoples. Perhaps the world would feel lighter and calmer without the Jews619! I know that I am marked by my past. I don't avoid it, I bring it to life in my films." Books and films are the

---

616Albert Memmi, *Le Racisme*, Gallimard, 1982, Poche, 1994, p. 88.

617Neither did Francisco de Quevedo in the 17th century when he wrote in an untimely manner: "Mice are, Lord, enemies of the light, friends of darkness, unclean, hydiondos, disgusting, subterranean"; "God only allows this infernal race to last so that, in their execrable perfidy, the Antichrist may have a womb in which to be conceived", in *Execración de los judíos*, Madrid, 1633. (NdT).

618Herlinde Loelbl, *Portraits juifs, Photographies et entretiens*, L'Arche éditeur, Frankfurt-sur-le Main, 1989, 2003.

619This idea is also found in Levinas, Cohn-Bendit and George Steiner.

privileged vectors of this universal message that I try to transmit to other people.

Gershom Schocken, publisher and politician born in 1912 in Zwickau and died in 1990 in Tel Aviv: "Anti-Semitism has always existed and will always exist as long as there are Jews. It existed in ancient times, even before Christian anti-Semitism. And that anti-Semitism is very clearly explained by the fact that of all the peoples of the Greek world, the Jews were the only ones who refused to fraternise with others. They would not eat, drink or marry non-Jews. Added to this was the refusal of the Jews to be interested in the religion of other peoples. They declared imperturbably: "There is only one God, he is our God and the rest is only idolatry". This attitude, which consists in saying: "The customs of others are abominable, we must keep away from them", was evidently taken over by the Christians from us, the Jews. It is this obstinate affirmation of a single God to whom one can only pray that separated the Jews of antiquity from other peoples. The Christians, for their part, reproached the Jews above all for not having recognised Jesus. It was then that one of the apostles had the brilliant idea, from the point of view of propaganda, to say that the Jews had killed the Saviour. This early anti-Semitism of Christianity was also based on competition, for from the beginning, Christians were a Jewish sect that wanted all Jews to recognise Jesus as the Messiah. Incidentally, something similar happened in this century in Russia between Jews and communists. Indeed, in the early days of the Communist movement, its leaders were almost exclusively Jewish, and the Communists then regarded Jewish youth as the main reservoir of militants. But there were also Jewish anti-communist or non-communist movements, such as Zionism and the Bund, which is why communism was angry at Zionism and the Bund for taking away potential militants. This explained the initial hostility between communists and Zionists: for a basic communist, seventy years ago, a Zionist had to have been a communist. Instead, he adhered to that imbecilic, reactionary, bourgeois nationalism, Zionism. Finally, the last cause of anti-Semitism is obviously that envy which alone could explain everything. Not to mention the xenophobia that reigns everywhere in the world, among all peoples. There are many causes of anti-Semitism! "

In all, of the eighteen personalities interviewed who expressed themselves on the subject in this book entitled *Jewish Portraits*, Gershom Schoken was the only one to have admitted the strong involvement of Jews in the great Bolshevik adventure. The most frequent and recurring explanation among all those interviewed was that anti-Semitism was an outburst against a "scapegoat without defence".

The great Russian writer Vasily Grossman, "the Tolstoy of the 20th century", took a harsher view of the deplorable manifestations of anti-Semitism. He was, with Ehrenburg, Eisenstein and Zalavsky, one of the leading propagandists of the Stalinist era. At the same time, however, he secretly wrote several anti-Stalinist works, published only after his death[620]. His novel *Everything Flows* contains a harsh criticism of Stalin and Lenin, while showing a certain sympathy for Trotsky. Grossman also showed a certain contempt for the Russians, something to which the French are also accustomed with the edifying readings of Alain Minc, BHL or Daniel Cohn-Bendit. Vasili Grossman claimed that the whole of Russian history was nothing but slavery, that the Slavic soul was an age-old slave. In his articles during the war, however, he used a very different tone to galvanise the brave "*Popovs*" against the Nazis. In those years he saw in that same Russian soul "an irresistible impetus" and "an iron power that can neither be bent nor broken". We can identify the same peculiarity as Albert Einstein, a convinced pacifist in 1933, and a fiery militarist after Hitler's rise to power. Here, too, the reasoning is based exclusively on the very particular interests of the Jewish people.

For Grossman, anti-Semites who vent their anger against a scapegoat are weak and useless. In *Life and Fate*, he lamented that "even a genius like Dostoyevsky saw a usurious Jew where he should have seen the merciless eyes of the Russian contractor, manufacturer and slaver." On the other hand, to single out a wonderful Jewish violinist or a great Jewish humorist is usually no problem at all.

"Anti-Semitism, he explained, is a mirror reflecting the shortcomings of individuals, social structures and state systems. Tell me what you accuse a Jew of and I will tell you what you are guilty of… And National Socialism, by accusing the Jewish people it had itself invented of racism, of a lust for world domination and of a cosmopolitan indifference to the German nation, was projecting its own traits onto the Jews." We have already encountered this kind of reasoning.

"But this is only one aspect of anti-Semitism, wrote Vasili Grossman. Anti-Semitism is the expression of a lack of talent, of the inability to win in a contest fought with the same weapons; and this applies to all fields, science as well as commerce, craftsmanship,

---

[620]This reminds us of Spinoza who, in his first book, acknowledged that he was writing the opposite of what he thought, letting the reader know this through his preface (in Alain Minc, *Spinoza*).

painting. Anti-Semitism is the measure of human mediocrity... Anti-Semitism is the expression of the lack of culture among the masses of the people, who are incapable of analysing the real causes of their poverty and suffering. Uneducated people see the Jews as the cause of their misfortunes instead of the social structure and the state. But even the anti-Semitism of the masses is only one aspect of this. Anti-Semitism is the measure of the religious prejudice which is latent in the lower strata of society... It only testifies that there are idiots, envious and unsuccessful people in the world[621]."

The absolute mystery

The following lines will help us to better understand Solzhenitsyn's astonishment and indignation. Faced with such a gap with reality, one does not know whether the incomprehension of the situation corresponds to a cunning attempt to deceive "the other", or whether it somehow reflects a touching sincerity.

Shmuel Trigano did not hide his surprise at the manifestations of anti-Semitism, saying: "One of the greatest mysteries of modernity is undoubtedly (long before racism) the phenomenon of anti-Semitism, still unexplained in spite of an immense library on the subject ... It has not been understood to this day why modern men, the citizens of the *demos*, have attacked other citizens under the pretext that they were Jews ... The greatest historian of anti-Semitism, Leon Poliakov, has written a great history of anti-Semitism, but reading it, we still do not know why it happened to the Jews. The anti-Semitic phenomenon is surely one of the most important phenomena that, like fascism and totalitarianism, has remained a mystery[622]."

This is also exactly what the French philosopher André Glucksmann told us in his book *The Discourse of Hatred*, published in 2004: "Hatred of the Jews is the enigma of all enigmas. This destructive passion spans the millennia, takes various forms, is continually being reborn from the ashes of the various fanaticisms that motivate it. It seemed to be Christian, but when Europe became de-Christianised, it reached its acme. We thought it had been extinguished after Hitler, but now it is going global... For the anti-Semite, the object of his aversion is still a UFO. He does not know who or what he is talking about ... The Jew is by no means the cause of anti-Semitism; one must analyse

---

[621]Vasili Grossman, *Life and Destiny*, Galaxia Gutenberg, 2007, Barcelona, p. 362, 363, 364.
[622]Shmuel Trigano, *L'Idéal démocratique...*, Odile Jacob, 1999, p. 17, 92

this passion for and by itself, as if the Jew he persecutes without knowing him did not exist … For two millennia the Jew has been a source of discomfort. Two millennia of being a living question for the whole world. Two millennia of innocence, having nothing to do with anything[623]."

For Nobel laureate Elie Wiesel, anti-Semites are the enemies of mankind. It is simply impossible that individuals can rationally harbour hostility against Jews: "It is so and nothing can be done about it, he wrote: the enemy of the Jews is the enemy of mankind. And conversely. By killing Jews, the murderer kills more than Jews. He starts with the Jews, but then he will inevitably take it out on the other ethnic groups, religions or social groups … By killing the Jews, the murderers undertook the murder of all mankind[624]."

In his *memoirs*, Elie Wiesel also wrote: "A French novelist has published an article in a Parisian monthly entitled: "The Jews annoy me"—in fact, she used a coarser term, but the meaning remains the same. What does that prove? That society is sick? Anti-Semitism has always served as a moral barometer. Jew-hatred has never been limited to the Jew alone: it spills over and targets other minorities. It starts by hating the Jew, ends by detesting those who are different, who come from elsewhere, who think and live differently. That is why anti-Semitism does not only concern Jews; it affects the society in which we live as a whole… As I write these lines, the anti-Semitic tide is rising. Sixty-five racist groups, more or less influential, are spreading hatred in the United States. In Japan, anti-Semitic books are on the bestseller lists … Now, once unleashed, hate knows no bounds. Hate calls for hate. Hate kills the human within man before it kills him[625]."

Is it the destiny of the Jewish people to have to endure all suffering eternally? Is there any way to put an end to injustice in this world: "Jews in history have been victims, not murderers… Jews have been condemned not for what they had done or said, but for having been what they were: the sons and daughters of a people whose suffering is the oldest in history626." But we still do not know why they are the eternal victims.

Alexandre Adler, the editor of the well-known newspaper *Courrier international,* could not explain the phenomenon either, despite his immense culture: "Why have the Jews become a kind of patron, the

[623]André Glucksmann, *Le Discours de la haine*, Plon, 2004, p. 73, 86, 88.

[624] Elie Wiesel, *Mémoires, tome II*, Éditions du Seuil, 1996, p. 72, 319.

[625]Elie Wiesel, *Mémoires, Tome II*, Éditions du Seuil, 1996, p. 128-129.

[626]Elie Wiesel, *Mémoires, Tome II*, Éditions du Seuil, 1996, p. 241, 283.

absolute zero of the policy of racialist annihilation of mankind? I calmly assert that this question has been answered by a series of concatenations of causes and effects which shed brief light on certain aspects of this policy, but that its sudden emergence has never yet been explained. We refer our readers to those current explanations where the colonial racialism of the 19th century is mixed with the pagan sectarianism of the beginnings of modern biology, to the widespread eugenicism, even in democratic regimes, to the German anti-Semitism matured in the retorts of Richard Wagner, in the stupid and self-satisfied lustre of Wilhelm II and his son, exacerbated by the rapid rise of Jewish elites in the Weimar Republic and the supposedly unbearable traumas of the First World War which, curiously enough, only generated elsewhere, as in France or England for example, exaggerated pacifist sentiments. We understand the modus operandi of genocide better and better, but we do not quite understand the sudden appearance of this black hole, this abyss[627]."

In *Difficult Freedom*, the great philosopher Emmanuel Levinas initially expressed some reticence at the words of Simone Weil who claimed to be "outraged" by the countless cruelties perpetrated by the Jews recounted in the Old Testament. While she agreed that "the extermination of the Canaanite peoples during the conquest of the Promised Land would be the most indigestible of all the indigestible passages in the Bible", as Simone Weil maintained[628], her response was instead surprisingly sharp—or blatant, whichever you choose: "The extraordinary thing is that the same is true of us. The extraordinary thing is that the Jewish conscience, formed precisely in the contact of this harsh morality with obligations and sanctions, learned there the absolute horror of blood[629]"." To be persecuted, to be guilty without having committed any fault, is not an original sin, but the other side of a universal responsibility—a responsibility towards the Other—older than any sin[630]."

The book *Jewish Portraits* again provided us with some illustrative and convergent testimonies:

---

[627]Alexandre Adler, *Le Figaro*, 26 January 2005
[628]This is the philosopher Simone Weil (1909–1943), and not the French politician Simone Veil, survivor of Auschwitz, the driving force behind the law legalising abortion in France in 1975. [The politician Simone Veil rests since 2018 in the Pantheon in Paris, with the great figures of the French nation. (NdT)]
[629]Emmanuel Levinas, *Difficult Freedom, Essays on Judaism*. Ediciones Lilmod, Buenos Aires, 2004, p. 166.
[630]Emmanuel Levinas, *Difficile liberté*, Albin Michel, 1963, 1995, p. 290.

Walter Laqueur, historian and writer in London, born in 1921 in Breslau: "Where does anti-Semitism come from? —One doesn't know exactly, he replied. It is very rare for historians to have clear and unequivocal answers. We observe this phenomenon of exclusion with regard to all dispersed peoples: both with regard to the Chinese in Asia, the Indians in Africa and all peoples who do not live together in a country that belongs to them."

Yeshayahu Leibowitz, philosopher of religions and biochemist, born in Riga in 1903, said: "Adolf Hitler is not the high point of traditional German anti-Semitism: it is a phenomenon of a totally different nature, which is historically incomprehensible. For me, anti-Semitism is not a problem of the Jews but of the goyim[631]."

This was exactly what Jean-Paul Sartre wrote in his famous 1946 essay *Reflections on the Jewish Question*[632]: "Richard Wright, the black writer, said recently: "There is no black problem in the United States; there is only a white problem. In the same way we will say that anti-Semitism is not a Jewish problem: it is our problem ... we would need to be very blind not to see that anti-Semitism is primarily our problem[633]"." We would understand nothing of anti-Semitism, indeed, if we did not remember that the Jew, the object of so much execration, is perfectly innocent and, dare I say it, harmless. That is why the anti-Semite takes care to tell us of secret Jewish associations, of dangerous and clandestine Freemasonry. But if he meets a Jew face to face, he is more often than not a weak being who, ill-prepared for violence, is unable even to defend himself. It is this individual weakness of the Jew that gives him hand and foot to the pogroms[634]."

"Jews are the most peaceful of men. They are passionate enemies of violence. And this stubborn gentleness which they preserve in the midst of the most atrocious persecutions, this sense of justice and reason which they put forward as their only defence against a hostile, brutal and unjust society, is perhaps the best of the message they bring us and the true sign of their greatness[635]." In reality, the slander against them and the constant hostility of the Europeans are the real root of the problem: "for no sooner do they show us, behind the Jew, international

---

[631]Herlinde Loelbl, *Portraits juifs*, L'Arche, 1989, 2003 for the French version.

[632]Jean-Paul Sartre, *Réflexions sur la question juive*, 1946, Gallimard, 1954.

[633]Jean-Paul Sartre, *Reflections on the Jewish Question*, Ediciones Sur, Buenos Aires, 1948, p. 141.

[634]Jean-Paul Sartre, *Reflections on the Jewish Question*, Ediciones Sur, Buenos Aires, 1948, p. 42.

[635]Jean-Paul Sartre, *Reflections on the Jewish Question*, Ediciones Sur, Buenos Aires, 1948, p. 109.

capitalism, the imperialism of the "trusts" and of the arms dealers, no sooner do they show us Bolshevism, with its knife between its teeth, than they do not hesitate to hold equally responsible for communism the Israeli bankers, who should be horrified, and for capitalist imperialism the miserable Jews who populate the *rue des Rosiers*636."

"The Jew is a man whom other men regard as a Jew: this is the simple truth from which to start ... the anti-Semite makes the Jew ... Indeed, we have seen that, contrary to a widespread opinion, the Jewish character does not cause anti-Semitism but, conversely, it is the anti-Semite who creates the Jew ... If the Jew did not exist, the anti-Semite would invent him637."

The Jew, Sartre explained, "can choose to be courageous or cowardly, sad or joyful; he can choose to kill Christians or to love them. But he cannot choose not to be a Jew. Or rather, if he chooses the latter, if he declares that the Jew does not exist, if he violently, desperately denies in himself the Jewish character, he is a Jew precisely because of this. For I, who am not a Jew, have nothing to deny, nothing to prove, whereas the Jew, if he has decided that his race does not exist, has to prove it638."

At first glance, the matter is undoubtedly a little complicated for those unfamiliar with the subject. We don't know whether it would become clear that "Sartre", from the Latin sartor, means "tailor" and that Jean-Paul Sartre was the great-nephew of Albert Schweitzer, Nobel Peace Prize winner; Schweitzer was the surname of Jean-Paul Sartre's mother.

Indeed, all this seems rather convoluted, but we find our beacons again when Sartre rightly exposes another characteristic feature of Jewish thought: "The best way of not feeling Jewish is to reason because reasoning is valid for everyone and can be reworked by everyone: there is no Jewish way of doing mathematics. He has a penchant for pure intelligence, which he likes to exercise about everything and nothing ... He considers himself a missionary of the universal ... It is not by chance that Leon Brunschvieg, an Israelite philosopher, assimilates the progress of reason and the progress of

---

636Jean-Paul Sartre, *Reflexiones sobre la cuestión judía*, Ediciones Sur, Buenos Aires, 1948, p. 35 [*Rue des Rosiers* is located in the centre of the traditional Jewish quarter of the Marais (now "gay quarter", like Chuecas in Madrid, in the 4th arrondissement of Paris)].

637Jean-Paul Sartre, *Reflections on the Jewish Question*, Ediciones Sur, Buenos Aires, 1948, pp. 64, 133, 12

638Jean-Paul Sartre, *Reflections on the Jewish Question*, Ediciones Sur, Buenos Aires, 1948, p. 83.

Unification (unification of ideas, unification of men)639." Indeed, we have already come up against this kind of fondness for reasoning.

With Jean-Paul Sartre, Marxist themes (class struggle, revolution, internationalism, etc.) are very recurrent. His analysis of anti-Semitism is therefore quite similar to that of Larin, the Bolshevik leader quoted by Solzhenitsyn: "Anti-Semitism is a mythical and bourgeois representation of the class struggle and could not exist in a classless society ... In a classless society founded on the collective ownership of the instruments of labour, when man, liberated from the hallucinations of the world, will at last embark on his enterprise, which is to bring the human kingdom into existence, anti-Semitism will no longer have any reason to exist640."

In conclusion, the philosopher wrote: "Not a single Frenchman will be free as long as the Jews do not enjoy the fullness of their rights. Not a single Frenchman will be safe as long as a Jew, in France and in the whole world, can fear for his life641." With these words ended this brilliant essay which has contributed so powerfully to the understanding of the problem.

Anti-Semitism is all the more difficult to understand because since their emancipation in the 19th century, the Jews of the West have integrated into their respective countries, often displaying patriotism of the highest order. This is what Patrice Bollon argued in the literary review *Le Figaro littéraire* of 18 November 2004. France, he said, can be proud to have been the first European country to have granted Jews emancipation and full recognition of rights equivalent to those of other citizens. It was also the country that in 1870 "collectively naturalised 35,000 Sephardic Jews from Algeria, who had been kept for centuries by the Ottomans in a status of second-class subjects, taxed on their freedom of worship with disproportionate taxes and marginalised economically and socially." Republican France liberated them in 1870, thanks to the energetic action of the Minister of Justice Gambetta and Adolphe (Isaac Jacob) Cremieux, who was himself the president of the Universal Israelite Alliance. The patriotism of French Jews had many occasions to manifest itself over the years in favour of the country of the Rights of Man. During the First World War, for example, wrote

---

[639] Jean-Paul Sartre, *Reflections on the Jewish Question*, Ediciones Sur, Buenos Aires, 1948, p. 103–105.
[640] Jean-Paul Sartre, *Reflections on the Jewish Question*, Ediciones Sur, Buenos Aires, 1948, p. 139.
[641] Jean-Paul Sartre, *Reflections on the Jewish Question*, Ediciones Sur, Buenos Aires, 1948, p. 142.

Patrice Bollon, "there were proportionately more dead in their ranks than among the native French." This assertion seemed, however, to contradict the opinion commonly held until then, as Sartre himself wrote in 1946: "If it has been believed that the number of Jewish soldiers was, in 1914, lower than it should have been, it was because one had the curiosity to consult the statistics642." However, in the army museum in Paris, in the great hall dedicated to the First World War, one can see in a large glass case, side by side, two *poilus* helmets643 pierced by enemy bullets. One of the two belonged to a "Dupont", but the other, and this is the important thing, belonged to a "Lévy", which shows very clearly that many Jews shed their blood to defend the fatherland, as the label on the helmet indicated.

Finally, Patrice Bollon agreed with Daniel Sibony in telling us that Jews "are the scarecrow invented by anti-Semites to deny or repress, under the guise of their identity, their own "faults" or "lack of identity". At this point in our study, and in the face of such subtle reasoning, the astute reader will recognise the unmistakable "style", that intellectual "style" acquired after long years of study of the Talmud644. This marvellous book is very useful for learning how to get out of the most extreme situations, to "find the way out", as Samuel Pisar and George Soros would say.

The incomprehension of Jews in the face of the phenomenon of anti-Semitism was well illustrated by another valuable testimony, that of the great writer Stefan Zweig. In *The World of Yesterday, Memoirs of a European*, he recounted life in the Austrian capital at the beginning of the 20th century and the great changes that followed. His father, originally from Moravia, was a powerful textile industrialist; his mother came from a family of bankers based in Switzerland, Paris and New York." His way of life seems to me so typical of the so-called "good Jewish bourgeoisie" (the bourgeoisie that gave Viennese culture such essential values and which, in return, had to be completely exterminated645)". Vienna was at that time, along with Paris, the

---

642Jean-Paul Sartre, *Reflections on the Jewish Question*, Ediciones Sur, Buenos Aires, 1948, p. 13.
643French soldiers of the First World War, nicknamed thus (NdT).
644Patrice Bollon reports that three works on the same subject have just been published: *La France et les Juifs, de 1789 à nos jours*, by Michel Winock, 22€; *La République et les antisémites*, by Nicolas Weill, 12€; *L'Énigme antisémite*, by Daniel Sibony, 14€. Quick, all the stock must go.
645Stefan Zweig, *El mundo de ayer; memorias de un Europeo*, Acantilado 44, Barcelona, p. 8.

cultural and artistic capital of Europe." Welcoming and endowed with a special sense of receptivity, the city attracted the most disparate forces, distended, soothed and calmed them; living in such an atmosphere of spiritual conciliation was a balm, and the citizen was unconsciously educated on a supranational, cosmopolitan level to become a citizen of the world646." Vienna's genius, Zweig wrote, "had always consisted in harmonising all national and linguistic contrasts within itself, and its culture was a synthesis of all Western cultures; those who lived and worked there felt free from the narrowness of prejudice. Nowhere else was it easier to be European647."

In Vienna, however, some prevailing traditions were deeply displeasing to the young intellectual that he was. Clearly, the integration of young Jews into Germanic society was not entirely complete: "It was in the fencing rooms of the "guilds" that this noble and most important activity was inculcated in the new students and, in addition, they were initiated into the customs of the association ... drinking until vomiting, draining a large mug of beer to the last drop in one gulp (the acid test) to gloriously corroborate that one was not a "soft touch", or shouting student songs in chorus and mocking the police by marking the goose step and making a ruckus in the streets at night. All this was considered "manly", "student" and "German", and when the corporations, with their caps and coloured armbands, paraded around waving their banners in their Saturday "street parades", these simple-minded lads, driven by their own impulse to absurd pride, felt themselves to be the true representatives of intellectual youth ... We, on the other hand, were only disgusted by this *silly* and brutal *activity*, and when we stumbled upon one of these hordes with armbands, we wisely turned the corner ... and thus avoided any encounter with those sad heroes648."

During the First World War, Stefan Zweig managed to escape military service: "Although I had reached the age of thirty-two, I had no military obligation for the time being, because I had been declared useless at all the reviews, something I had been heartily glad of at the time ... heroism is not part of my character. In all dangerous situations, my natural attitude has always been to avoid them. So I looked for an activity in which I could do something without looking like an agitator,

646Stefan Zweig, *El mundo de ayer; memorias de un Europeo*, Acantilado 44, Barcelona, p. 11, 12.
647Stefan Zweig, *El mundo de ayer; memorias de un Europeo*, Acantilado 44, Barcelona, p. 17.
648Stefan Zweig, *El mundo de ayer; memorias de un Europeo*, Acantilado 44, Barcelona, p. 51.

and the fact that a friend, a high-ranking officer, worked in the archive made it possible for me to be employed there." In Vienna I had become estranged from my old friends, and it was not the time to make new friends. I only had a few conversations with Rainer Maria Rilke, because we understood each other intimately. We also managed to get him for our lonely war archive, as he would have been the most useless person as a soldier because of his hypersensitive nerves, to which dirt, bad smells and noises caused real physical discomfort649."

Stefan Zweig railed against the lies designed to serve the warlike patriotism of the Austro-Hungarian monarchy: "Dozens of people in Germany swore that just before the outbreak of war they had seen with their own eyes cars loaded with gold going from France to Russia; stories about hollowed-out eyes and severed hands, which in all wars begin to circulate punctually on the third or fourth day, filled the newspapers650." We see that the credulity of the mob knew no bounds; as for the eyewitness accounts, they were definitely questionable. State brainwashing and the propaganda that permeated public life from all sides made him embrace the cause of pacifism. It was not an easy thing to do in the midst of war. At Easter 1917, Stefan Zweig presented a tragedy that went against the prevailing spirit. He took as his theme the figure of Jeremiah, the Jewish prophet: "Was it not my people who were always defeated by all other peoples, time and again, and yet survived them thanks to a mysterious power, precisely that of turning defeat into victory... Did our prophets not know beforehand that eternal persecution and expulsion which today throws us back into the streets like refuse651? "Contrary to his expectations, the play was well received and was quite successful. The reality is that three years of war had dampened chauvinism and there was a greater desire for peace.

After the armistice, the situation in Austria and especially in Germany was extremely difficult. The assassination of Walter Rathenau, the wealthy German electricity magnate, who had just been appointed minister, shook the entire empire. The writer left us with a mind-boggling account of the situation in the Reich after the defeat and death of Rathenau, who was also a friend of his:

---

[649]Stefan Zweig, *El mundo de ayer; memorias de un Europeo*, Acantilado 44, Barcelona, p. 118-122.
[650]Stefan Zweig, *El mundo de ayer; memorias de un Europeo*, Acantilado 44, Barcelona, p. 121.
[651]Stefan Zweig, *El mundo de ayer; memorias de un Europeo*, Acantilado 44, Barcelona, p. 131.

"The mark plummeted and did not stop its fall until it reached the fantastic and terrifying figure of billions ... I lived through days when in the morning I had to pay fifty thousand marks for a newspaper and in the evening a hundred thousand ... Shoelaces cost more than a pair of shoes, no, what shall I say, more than a luxury shoe shop with two thousand pairs of shoes; a broken window cost more to repair than a whole house; a book cost more than a printing press with all its machines; with a hundred dollars you could buy rows of six-storey houses on the Kurfürstendamm; a book cost more than a printing press with all its machinery. With a hundred dollars you could buy rows of six-storey houses on the Kurfürstendamm; factories cost no more, at the exchange rate of the time, than formerly a wheelbarrow ... Thousands of unemployed wandered idly through the streets and raised their fists against the ragamuffins and the foreigners in their luxury cars who bought up a whole street as if it were a matchbox ... I think I know the history pretty well, but, as far as I know, there had never been a time of madness of such enormous proportions. All values, and not only material ones, had been altered; people scoffed at state decrees, had no respect for ethics and morals, Berlin became the Babel of the world. Bars, nightclubs and taverns sprang up like mushrooms. What we had seen in Austria turned out to be a timid and gentle prelude to that coven, as the Germans employed all their vehemence and capacity for systematisation in perversion. Along the Kurfürstendamm, young men in make-up and artificial waists strolled, and not all of them were professionals; all the high-school graduates wanted to earn something, and in dingy bars, secretaries of state and important financiers were seen courting drunken sailors affectionately, without any demur. Even the Rome of Suetonius had never known such orgies as the Berlin transvestite balls, where hundreds of men dressed as women and women dressed as men danced before the benevolent eyes of the police. With the decline of all values, a kind of madness took hold precisely in bourgeois circles, hitherto staunchly conservative in their order. The girls proudly boasted of being perverse; in any Berlin school it would have been considered a disgrace to be suspected of virginity at sixteen; they all wanted to be able to explain their adventures, and the more exotic the better...

"The German orgiastic cult that came with inflation was basically nothing but a feverish simian imitation ... Those who lived through those apocalyptic months and years, jaded and enraged, felt that there had to be a reaction, a terrible reaction"." Nothing so poisoned the German people, it should always be borne in mind, nothing so inflamed their hatred and so ripened it for the advent of Hitler as inflation ... a whole generation neither forgot nor forgave the German Republic those years."

But for Stefan Zweig, those responsible for this gigantic debacle were not the Marxist bosses we saw at work in the preceding chapters, nor the speculative plutocrats who built their colossal fortunes on German misery; no, it was the reactionaries and the Nazis who were responsible: "Those who had pushed the German people into that chaos now stood smiling in the background, watch in hand: "The worse the country does, the better for us652 "". Stefan Zweig could have recalled the nefarious role of some financiers. Three of them, Strauss, Goldschmidt and Gutman, organised the fall of the mark in order to buy up part of German industry at a vile price. Fortunately for them, they were able to escape the consequences: Strauss died in Switzerland, Gutman in the United States and Goldschmidt in London.

Hitler's accession to power in 1933 was to mean a new exodus of Jews. Zweig's testimony on this point was instructive: "A gigantic mass" fled "in panic from Hitler's fire, besieged the railway stations on all the borders" of Europe. A "whole expelled people denied the right to be a people, and yet a people who for two thousand years had wished for nothing else than never to have to emigrate again and to feel under their resting feet a land, a quiet and peaceful land." In 1942, still ignorant of the genocide, Zweig wrote from the United States: "But the most tragic thing about this Jewish tragedy of the century was that those who suffered it found no meaning or guilt in it." This keen observer, Stefan Zweig, had he really seen nothing of the Marxist agitation that his own co-religionists had been engaged in in all the cities of Germany, nor of the role of the big speculators? How is it possible that this brilliant writer—the only one, in our opinion, among all those we have reviewed, who displays any real literary talent—is so obtuse and paradoxical when it comes to trying to understand the hostile reactions of the population? The sense of his own identity that he expressed about his play in 1917, his declared contempt for his fellow university students or his identity as a "citizen of the world" could have been a starting point for an explanation, or at least a question mark. How could he not see the obvious contradiction between expressing his pride in being a Jew before the European conflict and then claiming that he had always been "integrated"? For him, despite his brilliant intelligence,

---

[652]Stefan Zweig, *El mundo de ayer; memorias de un Europeo*, Acantilado 44, Barcelona, p. 160-162.

there was also no "explanation" for the resurgence of anti-Semitic sentiments.

"The Jews of the century, on the other hand, had long ceased to be a community. They had no common faith, they considered their Judaism more a burden than a source of pride and had no sense of mission ... With all their increasingly impatient eagerness, they aspired to be incorporated and integrated into the peoples around them, to dissolve into the community ... Thus, they no longer understood each other, merged with the other peoples: they had long been more French, German, English or Russian than Jewish ... What was the cause, the meaning and the purpose of this absurd persecution? They were expelled from their land and given no other land. They were told: we do not want you to live among us, but they were not told where they had to live. They were blamed for their guilt and denied the means to atone for it. And they looked at each other with burning eyes at the moment of flight and asked: Why me? Why you?

Why me and you, whom I do not know, whose language I do not understand, whose way of thinking I do not understand, to whom nothing binds me? Why all of us? And no one knew the answer. Not even Freud, the clearest head of the time, with whom I often spoke in those days, could see a solution or a meaning to such absurdity653."

We can repeat here the words of Primo Levi who, in *Asymmetry and Life,* a few days before his death, said with grief: "There was Auschwitz, therefore there can be no God. I cannot find a solution to the dilemma. I look for it, but I cannot find it."

The ingratitude of others

The billionaire philosopher Georges Soros also expressed the same incomprehension of anti-Semitism, all the more so when the man had invested unaccountably to improve the living conditions of the people of Europe freed from the yoke of communism: "Because of my exaggerated power, he wrote, I have become the main target of the anti-Semitic discourses that feed the eternal Jewish plot theory. If ever there was a man who fit the stereotype of the Jew-plutocrat-Zionist-Bolshevik, it is me... Therein lies the proof that good deeds are always punished! My goal when I created the *Open Society Foundation* in 1979 was to bring about a society where such theories would fall into disuse.

---

[653]Stefan Zweig, *El mundo de ayer; memorias de un Europeo*, Acantilado 44, Barcelona, p. 218-219.

But by becoming the advocate of the open society, I have concentrated in myself a kind of mystical power that has ultimately fuelled the conspiracy theory." This led him to the conclusion that "you can't attack anti-Semitism head-on, nor will we make it go away by banning it. Education remains the best option to tackle the problem. Anti-Semitism is the comfort of the ignorant. If you take it out into the open air and expose it to the light, it vanishes654."

In Jacques Attali's *Jews, the World and Money*, we also find this idea that those who oppose the Jews show great ingratitude. In 325, the founding date of the Council of Nicaea, Jacques Attali wrote, "Christian anti-Judaism is consolidated, based on hatred of the one who brought the good word. Hatred of the one who rendered a service. This will be found much later in the relationship with money: hatred for the one who lends money to those who are not in favour of it.

others after having provided them with their God655."

Regarding other episodes in Jewish history, the author simply refrains from giving the reader any further explanation. For example, the expulsion of the Jews from the guilds does not merit any logical explanation from Attali, but the stupidity and wickedness of the Goyim: "At the beginning of the millennium, both in Southern Europe and in the land of Islam and Constantinople, the Jews set up their own guilds of craftsmen. In the North they joined the Christian guilds, sometimes openly, sometimes clandestinely. Then, both in the North and in the South, the guilds, which had become omnipotent, excluded them from the craft professions, even from the least sought-after trades... And so, in many parts of Europe, there is practically nothing left for them but horse trading, butchering, and above all—tragic quagmire— moneylending, a strategic profession in this phase of nascent capitalism and the constitution of nations. As they are forced to do it, they will do it to their heart's content. To their great unhappiness. Once again, they will be useful and they will be hated for the services rendered656."

This is a lancinating idea in Jacques Attali's work, and it returns as a leitmotif: "Surely, the rabbis are right to be suspicious: despite popular coexistence and its economic usefulness, hatred is back. Through a wise mixture of theology and economics, the West will soon rid itself of its creditors by accusing them of deicide. Thus, Jewish communities will

[654] George Soros, *Le Défi de l'argent*, Plon, 1996, p. 185, 188.

[655] Jacques Attali, *Los judíos, el mundo y el dinero*, Fondo de cultura económica, 2005, Buenos Aires, p. 95.

[656] Jacques Attali, *Los judíos, el mundo y el dinero*, Fondo de cultura económica, 2005, Buenos Aires p. 167.

become the target of new attacks, sliding ceaselessly from one camp to another. There is resentment against the Jews for having supplied their God and their money, for they resent themselves for no longer being able to abstain from either the One or the other657."

The ungratefulness of the Goyim was evident on many other occasions throughout history: "During the captivity of Louis IX, in 1253, the regent Blanca of Castile, his mother, decided to expel all the Jews from her States; then, like so many other rulers, she chose to make them pay a part of the enormous ransom - 400,000 pounds—demanded for the liberation of the sovereign. On his return, the future Saint Louis, as a sign of gratitude towards those who allowed him to return alive … banishes them! … However, the Jews manage to stay in exchange for the payment of a new tax."

Another eloquent passage reads: "The two thousand Venetian Jews are so well integrated into the various trades that the doge is concerned and, from 1420 onwards, makes them wear a yellow hat to distinguish them." Identical situation after their expulsion from Spain in 1492: "Poor and rich leave together, without goods or almost without them, and without understanding why they are expelled."

"In Baghdad they had already experienced this in the ninth century, in London in the twelfth, in Cordoba in the thirteenth, in Seville in the fifteenth, in Frankfurt in the eighteenth: the more they were hated, the wider the range of services they rendered658." The great reporter Albert London knew how to express the great pain of the Jewish people in the face of so many injustices with this exclamation: "*Shalom!* means *Peace with you!* and everywhere you send your greeting, Jews, war answers you659! "

A testimony from the book *Jewish Portraits* illustrated very well this way of thinking and the incomprehension in the face of the rejection and vindictiveness of the "others".

Gottfried Reinhardt, film producer, born in 1913 in Berlin: "Jews played a more important role in Germany than was to be expected from their percentage of the population. Almost all German banks, Deutsche Bank, Dresdner Bank and Commerz Bank, were founded by Jews. And

---

[657] Jacques Attali, *Los judíos, el mundo y el dinero*, Fondo de cultura económica, 2005, Buenos Aires p. 177, 178.

[658] Jacques Attali, *Los judíos, el mundo y el dinero*, Fondo de cultura económica, 2005, Buenos Aires p. 197, 218, 327.

[659] Albert Londres, *El judío errante ya ha llegado*, Editorial Melusina, 2012, p. 201. [Albert Londres (1884–1932) was a French writer and journalist. He was one of the founders of investigative journalism, critical of the abuses of colonialism and forced labour prisons].

I am not even talking about the numerous private banks. Bismarck's banker was Herr Bleichröder. Emperor Wilhelm II's best friend was Albert Ballin, owner of the Hamburg-New York shipping line, who felt the outcome of World War I so dramatically that he committed suicide. German Jews also played an important role in science. Ullstein and Mosse were the popes of the German press, and the *Berliner Tageblatt* was then probably one of the best newspapers in the world. Tragically, it was precisely in Germany, a country that owed so much to the Jews, that the Nazis succeeded in gaining the upper hand. The Jews rendered immense services to Germany, and they did so gladly. Of course, they could not have imagined that it would end so badly. This is the most tragic thing of all. After all, Goebbels had studied with Gundolf in Heidelberg, and it was there that he defended his thesis. He then applied for a job as a journalist at the *Berliner Tageblatt,* and if Theodor Wolff had given it to him, perhaps everything would have happened differently."

How else to express that the Goebbels are tolerated on condition that they remain in their place as exemplary little pen-pushers in a newspaper where the boss is still the boss?

The analysis of a university student offered no further explanation, except confirmation of this mental universe inherited from the Mosaic religion, so profoundly different from that of the Goyim[660]. Professor A. Neher, from the University of Strasbourg, expressed himself in this way at a symposium at the Institute of Contemporary Sociology in Brussels: "One thing that Judaism possesses that other spiritualities do not is innocence. We are innocent, and we feel even more deeply that we are innocent because we have been accused. We have been accused between 1933 and 1945, and we are still often accused today, of being the enemies of the world, of the human race, of being exploiters, of having been the disintegrators of European civilisations, etc, etc, etc, etc, etc, etc,. Now, we know that we are innocent, and that this innocence, which is of a spiritual nature and which inspires our entire religious tradition, draws from the sources of the tradition of the Torah, of Jewish mysticism and of the Talmud. It is this innocence that we must be aware of today, and that we must never, ever deny, under any circumstances. Yes, we are innocent of various crimes that were committed, but committed by others. Yes, Christianity is guilty. The whole history of the Middle Ages and all that led to the 20th century, to Auschwitz and Hiroshima, is largely the result, certainly not of the

---

[660]It seems pertinent to us to radically contrast the Talmudic method of learning with that of Aristotle's *Organon* (NdT).

Christian message, but of the interpretation that Christians and Christian churches have given to that message. Judaism, for its part, is outside this responsibility in Europe... Judaism will only be able to dialogue with the Third World to the extent that it commits itself to this innocence ... with this world of black peoples, of coloured peoples, who were also not complicit in the crimes that Europe committed, and who will find in the Jewish message a fraternal message, a message with which the Third World will identify itself and recognise the light of this innocence which is the common sharing of these peoples and the Jewish people661." It only remains to convince the Palestinians and Iraqis of this innocence.

Infamous accusations

But in spite of this, we are obliged to lift the veil on the accusations of Christians and goyim in general. In *The Jews, the World and Money*, Jacques Attali gave us at least some background to explain this anti-Semitism that has lasted for centuries and crosses all borders. Already in ancient times, in the Egypt of the pharaohs, reactions were clearly perceptible: "Their pharaohs, among them Ramses II (-1294/ -1229), were bitterly opposed to the Jews. They were worried about their size, their solidarity, their not yet negligible influence in the state apparatus and the army." The reaction of the Egyptians was not long in coming: "They isolated the Hebrews, forbade them to exercise certain trades, to marry, to have children, killed all the newborns and turned the survivors into slaves662."

In Christian Europe, Christendom, Jews were also the object of general hostility: "Lenders of God, lenders of money, they accuse them indiscriminately of being thieves, exploiters, parasites, hoarders, usurers, plotters, blood drinkers, poisoners, murderers of children, profaners of hosts, enemies of God, murderers of Christ, jealous of Jesus." In Poland, "in 1683, Christian tailors accused Jewish competitors of dishonesty. New massacres took place. In 1569, Pius V again accused them of "falsehoods", of "treason" and of having "ruined the States of the Church by their "rapacity"663 "" Obviously, all these

---

661Herlinde Loelbl, *Portraits juifs, Photographies et entretiens*, L'Arche éditeur, Frankfurt-sur-le Main, 1989, 2003.

662Jacques Attali, *Los judíos, el mundo y el dinero*, Fondo de cultura económica, 2005, Buenos Aires, p. 27.

663Jacques Attali, *Los judíos, el mundo y el dinero*, Fondo de cultura económica, 2005, Buenos Aires, p. 178, 238-239, 242.

accusations were totally absurd, as was the accusation of treason, which recurs in the work of Jacques Attali: "In every corner of the Roman Empire, they are accused of financing uprisings against Rome." Similarly, the Jewish communities in Spain seem to have taken up the cause of the Muslim invaders: "The archbishop of Toledo accuses the Jews of treason in favour of the Saracens, thus provoking an uprising; he also organises the sacking of the synagogues664." With their help, the Muslim troops defeated King Roderic in July 711 and quickly conquered the entire peninsula, with the exception of a few enclaves in the north." The multicultural Spain under Muslim rule, where Christians had to ride donkeys and pay a tax, while Muslims rode horses, remained in the memory of the Jews as a golden age that is greatly missed: "The Jews have never known a more beautiful place to stay than this European Islam of the 8th century." Indeed, in that golden age they occupied the highest positions and responsibilities: "The caliph Omar II undertakes to strengthen the Muslim presence in the state apparatus. He tried to replace all the *dhimmis* officials665 with Muslims. Consequently, he tried to get rid of the Jewish high officials, who had become too numerous and too influential. But he does not succeed, for lack of valuable leaders, so much so that the religious Muslims reproach the caliphs for their excessive benevolence towards the Jews666." So it should be noted that the Muslims were no more capable than the Bolshevik Russians of administering their own state.

This commitment to conquering Islam is again seen in the role of some of the Grand Turk's financiers. John Ha-Nassi, Attali wrote, was the most important financier of Sultan Suleiman II. In 1565, he convinced him "to ask the pope to request the release of Jews held hostage in Ancona." In 1569, "Nassi advises Suleiman to attack Venice in order to take Cyprus, which he wants to turn into a haven for the Jews. It turns out to be a disaster: in 1571, the war ends with a defeat at Lepanto against the Venetian army commanded by Don John of

---

[664]Jacques Attali, *Los judíos, el mundo y el dinero*, Fondo de cultura económica, 2005, Buenos Aires, p. 102, 204. ["It is known that the invasion of the Arabs was solely sponsored by the Jews living in Spain. They opened the gates of the main cities to them. For they were numerous and rich, and already in the time of Egica they had conspired, seriously endangering the security of the kingdom." Marcelino Menendez Pelayo, *Historia de los Heterodoxos españoles, Tomo I*, Ed. F. Maroto, Madrid, 1880. p. 216].

[665]*Dhimmis*: believers of monotheistic faith living in subjugation in a region overrun by Muslim conquest who are granted protected status and allowed to retain their original (Abrahamic) faith, under special taxation. (NdT).

[666]Jacques Attali, *Los judíos, el mundo y el dinero*, Fondo de cultura económica, 2005, Buenos Aires, p. 134.

Austria667." Two years later, after the victory at Lepanto, the Venetian government in turn decided to expel all the Jews from the ghetto, who were declared accomplices of the Turks and agents of the Duke of Naxos [Ha-Nassi, ndla]; then, as so often in history, it reversed this decision in exchange for the payment of a tax668." Jacques Attali could have added: "and as so often in history, the Jews prefer to pay rather than leave." Thus, "the Jews of Venice were considered accomplices of John Ha-Nassi, who fell into disgrace and died in 1579... But the Faust period is over. As always happens in a period of decadence, the Jews are persecuted."

Jacques Attali's book also contains another vile accusation of treason: "In 1744, when Emperor Maria Theresa decided to expel the Jews from Bohemia on the accusation of spying for the Prussians... At the request of Jews in her entourage, the King of England and the States General of the Netherlands intervened with Maria Theresa, who finally annulled the expulsion decree in exchange for the payment of 240,000 guilders669."

This accusation returned a little further on, although it was attenuated by Jacques Attali, in view of the heroic behaviour of many Jews during the retreat of the Napoleonic *Grande Armée*: "In Prussia, a timid emancipation, decided in 1812, was not put into practice because the Jews were accused of being spies in Napoleon's pay—even though they were to protect their flight during the retreat from Russia"." 100,000 Poles (including Jews) die as heroes covering the retreat of the Grand Army670."

In spite of all this information that we were able to read scattered through the pages of this thick book, we must know that the Jewish people obey certain intangible laws: "Accept the law of the host without violating his own... Also with the citizen who must be absolutely

---

[667] Jacques Attali, *Los judíos, el mundo y el dinero*, Fondo de cultura económica, 2005, Buenos Aires, p. 226, 227 [Army of the Catholic coalition called the Holy League, formed mainly by the Spanish Empire and the Republic of Venice].

[668] Jacques Attali, *Los judíos, el mundo y el dinero*, Fondo de cultura económica, 2005, Buenos Aires, p. 242.

[669] Jacques Attali, *Los judíos, el mundo y el dinero*, Fondo de cultura económica, 2005, Buenos Aires, p. 283.

[670] Jacques Attali, *Los judíos, el mundo y el dinero*, Fondo de cultura económica, 2005, Buenos Aires, p. 306, 342. In the *Cahiers du capitaine Coignet*, however, we find this testimony: "The Jews and the Russians slit the throats of a thousand Frenchmen; the streets of Vilna were covered with corpses. The Jews were the executioners of our Frenchmen. Fortunately the Guard stopped them and the intrepid Marshal Ney restored order." (*Cahiers du capitaine Coignet*, 1850, la retraite de la Grande Armée, 1812).

faithful to any republic that receives him671 ", Attali explained to us. Indeed, this seems to be the only way to live in peace in the host's house.

Yet "loyalty to the host country" does not seem to be such an intangible principle. Karl Popper, for example, the mentor of George Soros, an Austrian subject before the First World War, had a very personal notion of "loyalty to the host country". This Viennese philosopher, who was to become "the passionate defender of liberties and the impartial critic of all forms of totalitarianism", "the tireless detractor of intellectual fashions and obscurantism", "the author of the most radical and comprehensive critique of Marxism", chose his side during the war, but not precisely that of his host country: "From the first months of 1915, I realised, after the invasion of Belgium, that an act contrary to international agreements had been perpetrated and that it was a violation of treaties. This convinced me that we were wrong, that our side was wrong. So I deduced that we had to lose672." The patriotism of cosmopolitan intellectuals has, most of the time, nothing to do with the country they live in, but corresponds to the interests of the planetarian idea. The country to support in a conflict is the one that provides the greatest democratic and financial guarantees. And in this case, France and England played that role in 1915.

There are more contradictions to point out within Jacques Attali's own work. For example, he implied that Jews were forced to engage in the money trade because in the Middle Ages Jews had been incomprehensibly excluded from all other trades. However, about a hundred pages earlier, the author had informed us that in ancient Rome, the rabbis themselves had forbidden members of the Jewish community to enter such associations: "They also administer relations with non-Jews, sometimes to limit them. Thus, when Rome imposes the creation of craftsmen's colleges, the rabbinical courts exhort Jews not to become members in order not to have to work on Shabbat673."

The voluntary isolation of the Jews from the other communities appears again in this passage: "The Talmud says: "The wine of the Gentiles is forbidden by virtue of their daughters. It is not possible to drink it together". Once again, the fear of intermarriage appears." We see these same provisions further on: "But since assimilation is feared above all else, the rabbis take care to enforce the dietary prescriptions,

[671]Jacques Attali, *Los judíos, el mundo y el dinero*, Fondo de cultura económica, 2005, Buenos Aires, p. 490.
[672]Karl Popper, *La Leçon de ce siècle*, Anatolia, 1992, p. 32.
[673]Jacques Attali, *Los judíos, el mundo y el dinero*, Fondo de cultura económica, 2005, Buenos Aires, p. 83.

forbidding any Jew to share a meal or drink with a Christian. They urge their followers to gather in the same neighbourhoods, around a synagogue, a ritual bath or a cemetery. Sometimes they claim the right to close off both ends of their street with a gate to defend themselves better in case of aggression. From now on, in this type of neighbourhood, the rabbi, the schoolmaster, the butcher and some craftsmen never have any contact with the gentiles674." Thus, the Jews themselves would have taken the initiative to enclose themselves in what would later be called a ghetto.

The Jews' secular reticence towards agriculture can be explained in part by religious considerations. Jacques Attali offered the following explanation: "The sons of Adam kill each other. Cain—whose name means "to acquire" or "to envy"—is given the earth. Abel—whose name means nothingness, breath, vanity, smoke—gets the flocks. When the farmer denies the shepherd the right of way, one of the two brothers loses his life... The murder of the shepherd is not a simple fratricide; the real culprit is the land itself, the cursed land that Cain had been given only to welcome his brother. If the Bible gives the good role to the nomadic victim, if it allows the sedentary murderer to survive, it is to launch him, in turn, on a redemptive journey675." The land is therefore to blame, and "on the other hand, the Talmud forbade them to till foreign soil676 ", Albert London, the "Prince of reporters", reminded us. Here then are some indications of the failure of the USSR's agricultural colonies in the Crimea and in Birobiyan.

Other contradictions were evident. When, on page 242, Attali recounted the accusations of Pope Pius V, who in 1569 accused them "once again of "falsehoods", of "treason" and of having, by "their robbery, ruined the States of the Church", as if these were crude inventions, he seemed to forget that he himself had put in writing the evidence to support these accusations. On page 263, for example, we read these lines: At the same time in Lisbon, "the masked Jews ... import, sell and sometimes transform spices, drugs, cotton, silks, pearls and diamonds. They confuse the clues so that it is not known who the real owner of the cargoes they transport is." Similarly, on page 199, he wrote: "Sometimes, the names chosen deliberately refer to humble

---

[674] Jacques Attali, *Los judíos, el mundo y el dinero*, Fondo de cultura económica, 2005, Buenos Aires, p. 144, 177.
[675] Jacques Attali, *Los judíos, el mundo y el dinero*, Fondo de cultura económica, 2005, Buenos Aires, p. 19.
[676] Albert Londres, *The Wandering Jew Has Already Arrived*, Editorial Melusina, 2012, p. 73.

trades to conceal fortunes". And on page 150: "Governed by Talmudic law, both the contracts and the credits of Jewish merchants are highly protected. Their bills of exchange and letters of credit are often written in Hebrew to make them indecipherable to would-be pirates. When local policemen learn to decipher the Hebrew alphabet, couriers use secret codes made up of the same characters. Disputes are settled by rabbinical courts that apply their own law, not that of the country through which they travel. Law is nomadic, it travels with the merchant." In other words, the law of the sedentary is null and void[677].

But "fraud" and "cunning", as the poet Ronsard so aptly put it, go back much further in history, as Jacques Attali discreetly confessed: "All means are good, including cunning: Abraham went so far as to pass off his wife Sarah as his sister, hoping to receive gifts from those who wanted to marry her[678]! "

Epidermal sensitivity

We found that most cosmopolitan intellectuals refused to take any responsibility for the tragic events that plagued communist history, especially in Russia. We have also noted that many of them see no valid explanation for anti-Semitism and consider that evil necessarily comes from others. Certainly, the Mosaic mentality may seem to us quite unique and disarmingly sincere. Let us then, through the literature and imagination of the great novelist Albert Cohen, look at another illustration of this "innocence". A writer of international stature, Albert Cohen was born in 1895 in Corfu, Greece. He therefore had Ottoman nationality before 1914. He spent his childhood in Marseilles before becoming a naturalised Swiss citizen. In his beautiful book entitled *O ye human brothers,* written in his old age, he narrated with much poetry a painful childhood memory in Marseilles, giving us a glimpse of that acute Mosaic sensibility. Almost the entire book is a soliloquy revolving around that memory. Here are some excerpts:

"Anti-Semites, prepare to savour a child's misfortune, you who are soon to die without your impending agony preventing you from hating. O falsely laughing rictus of my Jewish woes. O sadness of that man in

---

[677]In his *Dictionary of the 21st century*, Attali wrote: "It will be necessary to invent a very specific law, different from sedentary law, because without law there is no nomadism" (chapter "All nomads")." (chapter "All nomads") Wasn't the intention to see the goyim conform to the law of the Jews really unveiled?
[678]Jacques Attali, *Los judíos, el mundo y el dinero,* Fondo de cultura económica, 2005, Buenos Aires, p. 22.

the mirror I am looking at. O falsely laughing rictus, O my disappointed love. Because I love, and when I see a baby in its pram offering me a toothless smile ... oh little pigeon, that temptation to take its cute little hand, to lean over that new hand and kiss it tenderly, kiss it several times, hold it against my eyes several times ... but immediately I am obsessed that it will not always be a delightfully harmless baby, and that in it a fanged adult is dangerously watching and preparing, a hairy anti-Semite, a hater who will no longer smile at me. Oh poor Jewish rictus, oh the tired and resigned shrugs, little deaths of our souls ... Who knows, I said to myself, what I am going to tell them may perhaps change the Jew-haters, tear their fangs out of their souls ... My mother approves of me, I know, my mother who died during the German occupation, my mother who was naive and kind, and who was made to suffer ... I remember that one day, to tell me about the greatness of the Eternal One, He explained to me that He loved even the flies, and each fly in particular, and He added: I tried to do as He did with the flies, but I couldn't, there are too many679."

On that fateful day, as a child, Cohen was insulted by a hawker. As he approached his stall, trusting and in awe of the man, he was insulted and vilified for being Jewish. This painful event was scarred as a trauma deep in the memory of the ten-year-old boy. This is how Albert Cohen remembered the affront: "I looked pleadingly at the executioner who was dishonouring me, I tried to compose a smile to move him, a trembling smile, a sick smile, a smile of a disturbed person, a too sweet Jewish smile that I wanted to disarm with its femininity and tenderness. But my executioner was implacable, and I can still see his butcher's smile with long fangs, his gleeful rictus, I can still see the outstretched finger that ordered me to leave, while those nincompoops turned away, with approving laughter, to let the little expelled leper pass. And I obeyed, with my head down, I obeyed and I left, alone... I sat in a dark corner to cry at ease ..., to cry in the tenth Jewish year of my life... You are a filthy Jew, aren't you? I repeated to myself, and meditated on those words of the hawker, that unexpected sentence that had turned me into a prisoner... Oh my proud people, zealously eager to survive and preserve their soul, people of resistance, of resistance not for one year,

---

679Albert Cohen, *Oh you, human brothers*, Editorial Losada, 2004, Madrid, p. 29–30, 35–36. We also find this image in the writer Joseph Roth: "The hand gesture of a waiter on the terrace of a coffee shop to kill a fly is more significant than the fate of all the customers on the terrace. The fly is free and the waiter is disappointed. Why, O waiter, are you angry with the fly?" (Joseph Roth, article of 24 May 1921, *Berliner Börsen-Courier*, Éditions du Rocher, 2003).

not for five years, not for twenty years, but people of resistance for two thousand years, what other people resisted like that? Yes, two thousand years of resistance, and let the other peoples learn … Damned, I blessed all the wicked and in particular the blondes, I blessed them and loved them in the name of Israel, mixing in my blessings vague Hebrew words of the only prayer I knew, but above all inventing words that I hoped were somewhat Hebrew, and which moved me and seemed sublime to me … I walked, completely maddened … avenged the mad child walked, benevolent and scornful … I announced to them that one day they would love me and that that day would be the day of the endless kiss of all men for me turned human. I walked, with grandly gliding feet, and blessed the crowds and smiled and made regal salutations …, I walked, privileged bearer of the Law, holy commandments of the Eternal, I walked amidst the snapping of the cedars, false king of Israel and true descendant of Aaron, the great priest, brother of Moses … Without the peddler and his equals in wickedness, his countless peers from Germany and elsewhere, there would have been no gas chambers … the dead bodies … gleefully thrown into German ovens by the blond, boot-wearing athletes that Jew-haters love so much … Say, you anti-Semites, you haters whom I suddenly dare to call human brothers … say, anti-Semites, brothers, are you truly happy hating and are you satisfied with being evil? … Since that day of the hawker, I have not been able to pick up a newspaper without locating the word that says what I am, immediately, at the first glance. And I even spot the words that resemble the terrible painful and beautiful word, I immediately spot *"juin"* and *"suif"* and, in English, I immediately spot *few, dew, jewel.* That's enough680."

Wounded and torn by vengeful hatred, desperate helplessness, factitious love of the stranger and messianic faith: doesn't Albert Cohen resemble Golum, the mythical creature from *Lord of the Rings*?

In *Beautiful of the Lord*, Albert Cohen seemed to write in a state of ecstatic trance. Adopting a particular style of writing, Cohen poured out his thoughts over several pages without pause or punctuation, thus revealing the deep feelings hidden in his being, as well as some features of the Mosaic mentality:

"Among my Jewish friends I have met with the noblest beings of heart and manners … perhaps it is a horrible veiled desire to disown the greatest people on earth a horrible desire for emancipation from them perhaps it is revenge against my misfortune to punish them for being

680Albert Cohen, *Oh you, human brothers and sisters*, Editorial Losada, 2004, Madrid, p. 61–62, 67–68, 103, 155–156, 201–203, 213, 217, 92

the cause of my misfortune it is a misfortune that they do not love you and always suspect you yes revenge against my beautiful misfortune of belonging to the chosen people or worse still perhaps it is an unworthy resentment against my people no no no I revere my pain-bearing people of Israel saviour saviour for their eyes for their eyes that know for their eyes that have cried the insults of the crowds saviour for their face for their painful face for their deformed face for their face where flows in long drool the laughter and hatred of their children men oh shame perhaps it is an abominable unconscious antipathy … and I throw it in their faces perhaps in the same cell locked up the prisoners detest each other no I don't love them dearly my beloved my tender intelligent Jews the fear of danger has made them intelligent the need to be always awake to guess the fierce enemy that has turned them into the need to be always awake to guess the fierce enemy who has turned them into phenomenal psychologists is also a contamination of the taunts of those who hate us and I imitate those unjust ones perhaps it is also for sadly amusing myself with my pain and consoling myself with it is also a contagion of their hatred yes by dint of hearing their vile accusations they have made us feel the desperate temptation the desperate temptation to conceive the thought that if they hate us so much and everywhere it is because we deserve it and by God I know that we do not deserve it and that their hatred is a tribal hatred of the different and also a hatred of envy and also an animal hatred of the weak because we are weak in numbers. animal hatred for the weak for weak in numbers we are weak everywhere and men are not good and weakness attracts spurs the innate bestial hidden cruelty and it is no doubt pleasant to hate the weak whom you can with impunity insult and beat oh my tormented people I am your son who loves you and reveres you … and you will see how in the land of Israel the children of my returned people will be gentle and arrogant and beautiful and of noble bearing and fearless warriors if need be and seeing at last their true face hallelujah you will love my people you will love Israel who has given you God who has given you the greatest book he has given you the prophet who was love and indeed what is strange that the Germans, people of nature, have always detested Israel, people of unnature, for indeed the German man has heard and listened more than others to the young steady voice that rises from the forests of night, silent and rustling forests … and when they sing of their ancient legends and of their ancestors with long blond braids681 and horned hooves yes horned because what matters above

---

681We note in Albert Cohen a certain distrust of blond individuals. This inclination is also present in the writer Joseph Roth. However, this animosity is more visible in film

all is to resemble an animal and it is certainly exquisite to disguise oneself as a bull what do they sing of but an inhuman past which they long for and to which they are attracted and when they rejoice in their race and their community of blood what do they do but return to animal notions which even wolves understand that they do not eat each other and when they exalt strength or the exercises of the body what do they exalt and extol but a return to the great moneness of the prehistoric jungle and indeed when they butcher Jews or torture them they punish the people of the Law and of the prophets the people who wanted the advent of the human on earth if they know or sense that they are the people of nature and that Israel is the people of unnature bearing a mad hope that the natural abhors ... and whether they know it or not whether they like it or not the noblest portions of humanity are of Jewish soul and stand firm on their rock which is the Bible oh my Jews to whom in silence I speak know your people venerate them for having willed schism and separation for having waged the struggle against nature and its laws682..."

Undoubtedly, this is a great, a very great writer. In this text we see the immense pride of the chosen people, the contempt of the "other", of the goy, the feeling of revenge, the feeling of being misunderstood, but, above all, the perceptible doubt about the foundation of the mission of the Jewish people and the temptation of self-hatred.

It is clear that, like Kafka in his *Diaries*, Albert Cohen seemed to be totally obsessed by his Jewishness. This moving book must have represented for him an attempt to exorcise his demons. In a biography of him, the author captioned these words, so characteristic of the great novelist's particular style and ambivalent moods: "Sumptuous, O thou, my golden pen, go for the leaf, go at random as long as I have a shred of youth left, follow thy slow irregular course, wavering as in dreams, clumsy but governed course. Go, that I love you, my only consolation, go through the pages in which I sadly indulge and whose strabismus taciturnly delights me. Yes, words, my homeland, words console and avenge683." Revenge was clearly a deeply rooted sentiment in this battered man. Perhaps the origin of his talent as a novelist and poet came

---

productions, as we have already seen.

[682]Albert Cohen, *Bella del Señor*, Anagrama, Barcelona, 2017, p. 711–716. This is the stream of consciousness, an uninterrupted flow without typographic punctuation or differentiation in which the character's thoughts and impressions emerge. (It can be read in Molly Blum's famous soliloquy in James Joyce's *Ulysses* and in the novels of Marcel Proust).

[683]Albert Cohen, *El libro de mi madre*, Anagrama, Barcelona, 1999, p. 6, in Gérard Valbert, Albert Cohen, *Le Seigneur*, Grasset, 1990.

from his painful childhood. In any case, Albert Cohen's genius could not be ignored for long, as some literary critics of the time attested: "In 1933, when the first novel was published in the United States, a New York critic said: "*Solal* is religious in the manner of Dostoyevsky's novels." When *Ezekiel* premiered at the *Comédie-Française*, the *Paris-Midi* critic proclaimed: "There is an echo of Shakespeare in the play684." The sensitivity of this "literary genius" was also perceived in these few lines, which were intended to make Albert Cohen known: "A madman of sensitivity, ready for absolute pain for everything, absolute joy for everything, who suffers almost as much for not finding his keys as for having lost his wife685." This, at least, reassures us a little about the depth of his suffering.

The persecutions of the Jews over the centuries marked their "nomadic sensibility" with red fire, and for the older generation the wounds of the Holocaust are still alive. The Jewish sensibility was perceptible in an author like Marek Halter." In 1981, he wrote, I bought a ramshackle farmhouse with visible beams to restore it. The motorway was nearby, the neighbours kept chickens and fat cows. I owned it. My house was beautiful, surrounded by rutted roads. When my father learned that I really owned a piece of land, he cried." Jewishness also manifests itself in religious texts with an exacerbated sensitivity to the harm that can be done to one's "neighbour": "Hasn't the tractate Metzia of the Talmud taught us that "he who makes his neighbour blush in public, it is as if he killed him686 "? "

Elie Wiesel confirmed that this trend, once again, went far back in time: "Our Sages quote Scripture: when Esau kissed his brother Jacob, Jacob wept. Why did he weep? Because, the Sages replied, Jacob understood that Esau's kiss was a more dangerous trap than his hatred687." One weeps for nothing, for a yes or a no: that is the tradition.

The socialist financier Samuel Pisar also presented in his works some testimony along the same lines: "I was with Judith in Italy, on the shores of Lake Como. One evening, I switched on my transistor. I heard General de Gaulle's negative response to the referendum, his

684Gérard Valbert, Albert Cohen, *Le Seigneur*, Grasset, 1990. The surnames of the two journalists are not mentioned.

685Gérard Valbert, Albert Cohen, *Le Seigneur*, Grasset, 1990, p. 11.

686Marek Halter, *Un Homme, un cri*, Robert Laffont, Paris, 1991, p. 176. Jews consider the "neighbour" in their texts to be other Jews. One can read on this subject the enlightening book by Israel Shahak, *Historia judía, Religión judía, El peso de tres mil años*, Ediciones A. Machado, 2016, Madrid.

687Elie Wiesel, *Memoires (Tome II)*, Éditions du Seuil, 1996, p. 242.

resignation and immediate departure. Listening to the laconic text ("I am relinquishing my functions as President of the Republic. This decision takes effect at noon"), I felt that a chapter of history was brutally closed. And a chapter of my life. In that instant, I discover that I am crying. I am an American citizen and I cry. With his departure, the film of my life flashes before my eyes again[688]." This sensitivity could not be ignored in our analysis of the anti-Semitic phenomenon.

Joseph Roth is another author with a considerable novelistic and journalistic oeuvre. *Radetsky's March earned* him international renown. He, too, had that unique Jewish predisposition to suffering: "Wherever a Jew stops, a Wailing Wall rises. Wherever a Jew settles, a pogrom is born … Likewise, the present of the Jews is probably greater than their past, for it is even more tragic[689]." This is a statement taken from an article in *Das Tagebuch* of 14 September 1929, thus before the economic crisis and Hitler's seizure of power, but apparently the time was already considered sufficiently "tragic".

This propensity to "Lamentations", to feel sorry for oneself, could be one of the reasons for the inability to feel sorry for others, particularly for the countless victims of the Bolshevik revolution. To this effect, it is interesting to quote again some words of Hannah Arendt, who wrote in 1951: "The more the fact of Jewish birth lost its religious, national and socio-economic significance, the more obsessive Jewishness became; Jews were obsessed by it as one might be obsessed by a physical defect or advantage, and devoted to it as one might be to a vice[690]." So it seems that many Jews consciously or unconsciously nourish that anguish, that inner restlessness, which Georges Perec expressed so well, and which is one of the traits of the Jewish character that most contributes to fostering in them a feeling of Jewishness to the detriment of their integration into the rest of the population. Shmuel Trigano was well aware of this regrettable situation when he wrote: "Jews are often accused of wallowing in this victimising lament, and I am the first to deplore it[691]".

A permanent threat

---

[688]Samuel Pisar, *La Resource humaine*, Jean-Claude Lattès, 1983, p. 50.

[689]Joseph Roth, *A Berlin*, Éditions du Rocher, 2003, p. 33.

[690]Hannah Arendt, *Los orígenes del totalitarismo*, Taurus-Santillana, 1998, Madrid, p. 88.

[691]Shmuel Trigano, *L'Idéal démocratique…* Odile Jacob, 1999, p. 43.

This Jewish sensitivity is also reflected in other characteristics. As Jacques Derrida has already expressed, for example, there is in many Jews that instinct, always on the alert, which makes them react immediately to the slightest hint or suspicion of racism and anti-Semitism. This imperceptible restlessness, which has been a subterranean torment to the Jewish soul throughout the ages, manifests itself in alarmist reflexes in the face of what is perceived as the rise of the "scourge". At the slightest sign of opposition or criticism of the actions of any Jew, the entire community jumps into the media spotlight, and the heart-rending cries of the terrible threat are heard, as well as the chorus of mourners in the background. Personalities we thought were more dignified and reasonable fall into exaggerated interpretations that seem almost ridiculous once the hustle and bustle dies down. Thus, for example, we saw Elie Wiesel publish, as early as 1974, articles in which he expressed his deepest fears about the revival of anti-Semitism: "I am publishing an article in the *New York Times* and *Le Figaro* entitled "Why I am afraid"... Signs have appeared and they are disturbing. The revolting spectacle of an international assembly in delirium, celebrating a spokesman for terror[692]. The speeches, the votes against Israel. The dramatic loneliness of this people with a universal vocation. An Arab king offers his guests deluxe editions of the infamous *Protocols of the Elders of Zion*. Desecrated cemeteries in France and Germany. Press campaigns in Soviet Russia. The retro wave that trivialises our suffering and the anti-Zionist, anti-Jewish pamphlets that distort our hopes. One would have to be blind not to recognise it: Jew-hatred is back in fashion[693]."

There is undoubtedly a tendency among Jewish intellectuals to over-dramatise and systematise what is perceived as "environmental anti-Semitism". The former President of the Republic Valéry Giscard d'Estaing once had to face some odious accusations. This is what Elie Wiesel wrote:

"The year 1977 got off to a bad start. In January, the French government released the Palestinian terrorist Abu Daoud before Israel could begin extradition proceedings. Around the world, the scandal provoked an unprecedented wave of protest. Never has France been called into such questioning. In the United States, many voices694 called for a boycott of its products. With the financial support of friends, I had an advertisement page published in the *New York Times in the*

---

[692]Yasser Arafat, the Palestinian President before the United Nations General Assembly.
[693]Elie Wiesel, *Mémoires, tome II*, Editions du Seuil, 1996, p. 97.
[694]Guess which ones?

form of an open letter to Mr. Valéry Giscard d'Estaing, President of the French Republic: "What now, Mr. President? What now, Mr. President? What happened to France? Its moral leadership has disappeared and its glory has dimmed in the eyes of men of conscience. In fact, few countries have lost so much prestige in such a short time. What happened to France? It has betrayed its own traditions. France has become as cynical as the rest of the world. Why did your government release Abu Daoud? ... Your own people have risen up against you. Because while visiting Auschwitz, you ignored the lessons of the place. Indeed, it was to be expected. Recently, the signs have multiplied. Hurtful statements. Ironic comments. Policy changes. Strange alliances. Promises betrayed. Unilateral embargoes. The Cherbourg affair695. The sale of Mirages. French governments have rarely missed an opportunity to demonstrate their hostility to Israel and the Jewish people. For ideological reasons? Worse: for money. That's right, Mr President: before, I used to be proud of France and what it stood for. I am no longer696."

We can see that the feeling of persecution is real, even if twenty years later we realise that these fears are unreal. In the same vein, we can read this passage by Samuel Pisar, written in 1983: "The recent explosion of bombs in the big cities, the anti-Semitic graffiti, the desecration of schools and cemeteries, are the same ones that have shaken my childhood, destroyed my world". He lived in Paris, a few hundred metres from Rue Copernicus. We will be vigilant, watching for the faintest sound of the monster's footsteps. Our enemies are already watching us tirelessly. For them, we will always be guilty. Guilty of being Jews in Israel, of being Jews elsewhere, of being Jews. Guilty, depending, of being capitalists or of being Bolsheviks. Guilty in Europe of having been slaughtered like sheep, and guilty in Israel of having taken up arms so as not to be sheep again. Guilty, indeed, of continuing to exist[697]."

When Pisar wrote these lines in 1983, the Socialists were in power in France, and the number of ministers and personalities of Jewish origin gravitating around President Mitterrand showed that the situation of the community in the country was quite flourishing: Robert Badinter,

---

[695]The Cherbourg Vedettes affair was an Israeli military operation that took place in December 1969 and involved the theft of five Sa'ar III class ships from the French port of Cherbourg. The ships had been paid for by the Israeli government, but were held because of the embargo decreed by Charles de Gaulle in 1967. (NdT).

[696]Elie Wiesel, *Mémoires, tome II*, Editions du Seuil, 1996, p. 108-110.

[697]Samuel Pisar, *La Ressource humaine*, Jean-Claude Lattès, 1983, p. 250-251.

George Kiejman, Bernard Kouchner, Jacques Attali, Jack Lang, Dominique Strauss-Kahn, Laurent Fabius, Roger-Gérard Schwartzenberg, Pierre Bérégovoy, Henri Emmanuelli, Michel Sapin, Jean-Denis Bredin, Véronique Néiertz, Charles Fiterman, Georges-Marc Benamou and many more were there, in government to ensure the fight against any form of rancid anti-Semitism.

This paranoia went so far as to denounce, at the slightest discrepancy, and in the harshest terms, personalities who had hitherto shown the greatest sympathy and benevolence towards the Jewish community. President Mitterrand himself was dragged through the mud when his past and his complicity with the Vichy regime were revealed in his old age. Read in what terms the famous journalist Françoise Giroud spoke of him after his death. She denounced in her diary dated 29 August 1999, what some dare to call "the powerful and harmful influence of the Jewish lobby in France"." Unbelievable! And who is it about? François Mitterrand, if we are to believe Jean d'Ormesson who repeated this phrase. Mitterrand would have said it in a private conversation with his favourite academic shortly before his death. Did he really say it? His daughter chokes. His children air themselves. The faithful lucubrate. Of course he said it! Like de Gaulle, like Mauriac 698... The influence of the Jewish lobby is a classic of French culture. Mitterrand suckled it from his bottle. He hated to be told about René Bousquet699. When Jean d'Ormesson did, he got a little annoyed and blurted out this miserable reply, "All that doesn't deserve three lines."

This ingratitude manifests itself immediately at the slightest faux pas on the part of the person concerned, whatever his previous displays of friendship or submission may have been. At the slightest fault, the accused is excluded and pilloried in history. We know that ingratitude is another of the accusations that cosmopolitan intellectuals often level against anti-Semites. Here again, we see that the best way to avoid affronts is to accuse their victim." The murderer cries out to have his throat slit", as the saying goes.

At the beginning of the 21st century in France, the media assures us that anti-Semitism has never been so virulent, while the liberal right governments in power globally advance the same agenda and the same ideas as those of the left. Alarmist reporting on the subject has long been

---

[698]François Mauriac (1885–1970) was a French journalist, critic and writer. Winner of the Nobel Prize for literature in 1952, he is known as one of the greatest Catholic writers of the 20th century.
[699]René Bousquet (1909–1993) was a high-ranking French official and collaborator with the Nazi occupiers during World War II.

a constant in our media system. The interest is threefold: to keep the "republican vigilance" of the French population alert, on the one hand; to ensure the cohesion of the Jewish community, on the other; and finally, through the anguish that the situation may inspire, to precipitate the *aliyah* of some Jews to Israel, whose demographic situation is threatened by that of the Palestinians.

Incidentally, this was something that Hannah Arendt already hinted at in 1951: seeing the old Jewish communities of Europe, closed in on themselves for centuries, disintegrate with the right of citizenship granted to Jews in the nineteenth century and integrate into the surrounding societies, it was only natural that somehow Jews, "concerned with the survival of their people ... came to the consoling idea that, after all, anti-Semitism could be an excellent means of keeping their people together ... came to the consoling idea that, after all, anti-Semitism could be an excellent means of keeping their people together, and thus the presumption of an eternal anti-Semitism would come to imply an eternal guarantee of Jewish existence700." Marek Halter confirmed this idea in an interview published in the daily *Le Point* on 8 October 1999: "Let us first say that many Jews remained Jews because they did not want, like Bergson701, for example, to leave their community when it was threatened." The anti-Semitic threat, whether fictitious or real, is therefore a blessing in disguise for the leaders of the Jewish community, who fear assimilation more than anything else.

Anti-Semitic madness

These same personalities with strong obsessional tendencies often also regard anti-Semitism as a "disease", thus avoiding any form of introspection. It is a theme that is very much present in explanations of the anti-Semitic phenomenon, as we can see in the analysis of the great political scientist Hannah Arendt: "Although anti-Jewish sentiments were widespread among the educated classes in Europe during the 19th century, anti-Semitism as an ideology remained the prerogative of fanatics in general and lunatics in particular." Anti-Semitism is an "insult to common sense", a "crackpot" idea. The famous text *"The Protocols of the Elders of Zion"* is the best example of this. The

---

[700]Hannah Arendt, *The Origins of Totalitarianism, Antisemitism*, 1951, Taurus-Santillana, Madrid, 1998, p. 31.
[701]Henri-Louis Bergson (1859–1941) was a famous French philosopher and writer, winner of the Nobel Prize for Literature in 1927.

document was a gross forgery, a "grotesque" fable, a "far-fetched tale702 ", and it was simply unbelievable that such a "blatant forgery" could be "believed by so many" and "become the text of an entire political movement". When one thinks of "the ridiculous history of the *Protocols of the Elders of Zion*" and "the Nazis' use of this forgery as a textbook for a global conquest703 ", one is astounded by such blind stupidity and bad faith. In short, according to Hannah Arendt, it would be enough to ban *The Protocols* to see anti-Semitism disappear, which would be a great folly. In reality, Hannah Arendt was perhaps a little dishonest, for she pretended to believe that *The Protocols* were the basis of anti-Semitism when it was known to be a forgery and the anti-Semites themselves often acknowledged it. Indeed, Tsar Nicholas II refused to endorse such an obvious forgery.

To underline the absurdity of anti-Semitism, Arendt went on to expound another implausibility: "The core of the Schoenerer movement [the Austrian anti-Semitic parties] was to be found in the German-speaking provinces without any Jewish population, where there was never any competition with Jews or hatred of Jewish bankers." So anti-Semitism is just as absurd as the far-right vote in areas where there are no immigrants, as Daniel Cohn-Bendit brilliantly demonstrated. That anti-Semitism was all the more absurd because it had been "accompanied and interconnected with Jewish assimilation, secularisation and the weakening of Judaism's ancient religious and spiritual values"." Jews became symbols of society as such and an object of hatred for all those whom society did not accept. Anti-Semitism, having lost its basis in the special conditions which had influenced its development during the 19th century, could be freely elaborated by charlatans and fanatics into that fantastic mixture of half-truths and wild superstitions which emerged in Europe after 1914, the ideology of all frustrated and resentful elements704." An "outstanding anti-Semite" like Louis-Ferdinand Céline705, for example, "understood the full scope and possibilities of the new weapon." Fortunately, wrote Hannah Arendt, "the inherent good sense of French politicians and their deep-rooted respectability prevented them from

---

[702]Hannah Arendt, *The Origins of Totalitarianism, Antisemitism*, 1951, Taurus-Santillana, Madrid, 1998, p. 8, 9.
[703]Hannah Arendt, *The Origins of Totalitarianism, Anti-Semitism*, 1951, Taurus-Santillana, Madrid, 1998, p. 31, 9
[704]Hannah Arendt, *The Origins of Totalitarianism, Anti-Semitism*, 1951, Taurus-Santillana, Madrid, 1998, p. 59, 31, 65.
[705]See footnote 155.

accepting a charlatan and a fanatic706." Indeed, it is hard to imagine Céline being received by Daladier, Paul Reynaud or Léon Blum.

In his monumental *History of Anti-Semitism,* the great historian Leon Poliakov, in the chapter entitled *The Outbreak of the Conflict (1914–1933),* presented a similar interpretation of the anti-Semitic tendencies in Germany after the defeat of 1918. The explanation was quite simple: the Germans were afflicted by a well-known disease—the persecution syndrome or delirium—which can drive those affected by it to total insanity: "The day after the October revolution, the statements of some responsible for Germany's destinies bordered on delirium because according to them an undetermined number of Bolsheviks were of Jewish origin ... This delirious tendency was accentuated when it became clear that Germany had lost the war." According to Leon Poliakov, General Ludendorff himself, the leader of the Tannemberg victory in 1914, after having been the strategist who led the Central Powers between 1916 and 1918, "fell into the most consummate anti-Jewish madness". The evil was visibly contagious, but "the mechanisms of his delirium were easy to dismantle", Poliakov explained. Fortunately, the "delirium of persecution" did not diminish "his immense powers of work which enabled him, while publishing book after book on the Jews or ancient Rome and running a weekly magazine, to write works on total war which are still admired by some experts." General Ludendorff's madness only reappeared when he began to elaborate on a very particular problem.

We have already seen how Winston Churchill had also succumbed to this delirium during a moment of weakness. At the end of 1919, he justified the anti-Bolshevik crusade in a speech in the House of Commons in which he castigated, according to Poliakov, "the most formidable sect in the world". He even elaborated on his ideas in an article published on 8 February 1920 entitled *Zionism against Bolshevism.* In that article, he "differentiated the Jews into three categories: some who behaved as loyal citizens of their respective countries, others who wanted to rebuild their own homeland; and finally the international Jews, "terrorist Jews". Churchill's description of the third category bordered on delirium, wrote Poliakov, for the most frenzied anti-Semites could take advantage of it[707]."

The famous historian of the Paris Institute of Political Science, Michel Winock, noted that, on this particular point, "the demonology

[706]Hannah Arendt, *The Origins of Totalitarianism, Antisemitism,* 1951, Taurus-Santillana, Madrid, 1998, p. 62.
[707]Léon Poliakov, *Histoire de l'antisémitisme II,* 1981, Points Seuil, 1990, p. 409.

and delirium of the extreme right have gone beyond ordinary fictions: anti-Semitism is a permanent frenzy708."

In a collection of articles published under the title *Asymmetry and Life*, Primo Levi gave us his explanation of German anti-Semitism: "I do not think it is possible, either now or in the future, to give an exhaustive answer to this question. We can somehow put ourselves in the shoes of a thief, a murderer, but we cannot put ourselves in the shoes of a madman. It is just as impossible for us to retrace the path of the great perpetrators: for us, their actions and their words will always be shrouded in darkness... For me, Auschwitz can only be interpreted in this way: as the madness of a small minority and the stupid and cowardly consent of the majority. The Nazi massacre bears the mark of madness. It is the realisation of an insane dream, in which one commands and nobody thinks any more709." Undoubtedly, the National Socialist regime was "demonic710".

Revisionist historians have the same serious flaws: "I don't know who Professor Faurrisson is. Maybe he is just a madman, there are also those in the universities711." With such a bunch of idiots, "black has become white, wrong has become right, the dead are no longer dead, there are no more murderers, there is no more guilt, or rather there never was any guilt. Not only have I not committed the deed, but, moreover, there is no proof of its existence." The crimes of the Germans, on the other hand, are countless and Primo Levi can tell us about them in great detail. During Kristallnacht, for example: "A pogrom breaks out all over Germany, he wrote. Seven thousand five hundred shops and premises belonging to Jews are destroyed and looted: of which eight hundred and fifteen are completely destroyed, one hundred and ninety-five

---

[708]Michel Winock, *Nationalisme, antisémitisme et fascisme en France*, Points Seuil, 1990, p. 7.

[709]Primo Lévi, *La Stampa*, 18 July 1959, in *L'asymétrie et la vie, articles*, Robert Laffont, 2002, p. 26-28.

[710]Primo Lévi, *L'Asymétrie et la vie*, Robert Laffont, 2002, p. 73.

[711]He is the well-known French revisionist historian Robert Faurrisson (1929–2018). According to Elisabeth Roudinesco, Faurrisson is a falsifier, a dangerous falsifier of history: "A negationist author, whose writings are so delirious that they arouse formidable interest. It cannot be said enough that the more falsified the truth, the coarser the lie, the more obvious the imposture, the more likely it is to gain followers. Hallucination, denial, paranoia, in short, everything that characterises negationism as the extreme expression of anti-Semitism." In Jacques Derrida, Élisabeth Roudinesco, *Y mañana, qué?* Fondo de Cultura Económica, Buenos Aires, 2002, p. 144.

synagogues smashed, thirty-six Jews are killed and twenty thousand arrested, chosen from among the richest712."

"It is impossible to understand Hitler if one ignores the wounds inflicted on German pride by the defeat of 1918, the revolutionary attempts that followed, the disastrous inflation of 1923, the violence of the Free Corps [*Freikorps*], and the dizzying political instability of the Weimar Republic. I do not mean by this that all these causes are sufficient to understand Hitlerism, but they are undoubtedly necessary ... There are also economic explanations. It is true, and it is undeniable, that the Jews belonged at the beginning of the century to the German bourgeoisie, that they were strongly rooted in finance, the press, culture, the arts, the cinema, and so forth. This undoubtedly aroused envy713."

Dozens of books have been written about Hitler's motives and the extent of his anti-Semitism," continued Primo Levi. This also shows that it is difficult to explain. It was probably a personal obsession, the roots of which are unknown, although much has been said about it. It has been said that he feared he had Jewish blood in his veins because one of his grandmothers had become pregnant while working in a house belonging to Jews; he had felt this fear all his life; obsessed by purity of blood, he was afraid of not being pure himself. Other explanations have been proposed by psychoanalysts, explanations that reveal everything, precisely: they say and have said that Hitler was paranoid and perverse, that he had projected his characteristics onto the Jews in order to free himself from them. The truth is that I don't understand very well. I do not know the language of psychoanalysts, and perhaps it is not for me to speak about it; in any case, it is a principle of further explanation ... It is worth remembering that the testament that Hitler dictated, when the Russians were eighty metres from the bunker, an hour before his suicide, concluded with this sentence: "I charge my successors to complete the racial campaign to exterminate the Jewish people, who are the bearers of all the evils of Humanity". This is enough, in my opinion, to show that the need to attribute all possible evils to a scapegoat felt by Hitler the man had completely overstepped the bounds of reason, of the rational714."

It should be noted that it is not the Jews who are "paranoid and perverse", as simplistic minds might think, but the anti-Semites. And

[712]Primo Lévi, *La Stampa*, 9 November 1978, in *L'asymétrie et la vie, articles*, Robert Laffont, 2002, p. 92, 98.
[713]Primo Lévi, *L'Asymétrie et la vie*, Robert Laffont, 2002, p. 113.
[714]Primo Lévi, *L'Asymétrie et la vie*, Robert Laffont, 2002, p. 205-206.

that it is also the latter who project their characteristics onto the Jews in order to free themselves from them, and certainly not the other way round.

The great historian William Shirer, author of a monumental history of the Third Reich, presented a similar explanation of Hitlerite anti-Semitism. He cannot be said to have elaborated much on the subject, since of the 1500 pages of his two volumes, only one is devoted to explaining Nazi anti-Semitism. In fact, he quoted only a few brief passages culled from *Mein Kampf*: Hitler, the historian wrote, "discovered the moral taint of this 'chosen people'... Was there any form of filth or debauchery, particularly in cultural life, without at least one Jew mixed in? "He further quoted some brief excerpts on prostitution and the White slave trade: "*Mein Kampf* is strewn with lurid allusions to strange Jews seducing innocent Christian girls and thus adulterating their blood. There is a great deal of morbid sexuality in Hitler's ranting about the Jews." Hitler was, in short, a truly obsessive anti-Semite, and "would remain so, obfuscated and fanatical, to the bitter end; his last will and testament, written a few hours before his death, would contain the final blow against the Jews by which he held them responsible for the war he had started and which was now ending with him and the Third Reich." However, according to William Shirer, nothing could explain "this terrible hatred, which would contaminate so many Germans[715]."

The Nazi regime had compromised the destinies of numerous intellectuals, such as Stefan Zweig, "the eminent Austrian Jewish writer". Several equally "eminent" politicians were to suffer persecution, such as Kurt Eisner, "a popular Jewish writer", who had returned to Munich at the end of November 1918, after the abdication of the ruler of the Wittelsbach dynasty to take over the leadership of "a People's State"; or as Walter Rathenau, "the brilliant and learned foreign minister whom the extremists hated for being a Jew and for steering national policy towards an attempt to implement some of the clauses of the Treaty of Versailles"; he was assassinated in Munich. Opposite, on the Nazi side, we saw far more disturbing characters. All the Nazi dignitaries were portrayed in the most sinister manner." In a normal society, they would surely have been brushed aside as a grotesque collection of people who didn't fit in. However, in the last

---

[715]William L. Shirer, *Auge y caída del Tercer Reich, volume I*, Editorial Planeta, Barcelona, 2013, p. 54-55, 52, 63, 65.

days of the Weimar Republic they began to appear to millions of confused Germans as genuine saviours716."

The Political Testament

We had to verify in this *political Testament717* the statements of Primo Levi and William Shirer. Both were indeed right in denouncing Hitler's obsession that, in his madness, he imputed responsibility for the war to the Jewish people. However, it is not written in that text, as Primo Levi quoted Hitler as saying, that Hitler had charged his "successors to complete the racial campaign to exterminate the Jewish people, who are the bearers of all the evils of mankind". Concerning the Jews, we have found only these words: "I have shown myself loyal to the Jews; I gave them, on the eve of the war, a last warning. I warned them that, if they again precipitated the world into war, they would not be spared on this occasion: that we would exterminate that worm from Europe once and for all. To this warning of mine they replied with a declaration of war, stating that wherever there was a Jew there was, by definition, an inexpiable enemy of National Socialist Germany." (Führer HQ, *Notes*, 13 February 1945)." Centuries will pass, but from the ruins of our cities and our artistic monuments, hatred will again grow again towards the people ultimately responsible, towards those whom we have to thank for all this: the international Jewish people and those who help them ... I also made it clear that if the peoples of Europe were again to be contemplated again as mere bundles of shares of the international conspirators of money and finance, then the people truly guilty of this murderous war would have to answer for it: the Jews. Nor did I leave any doubt that this time it should not happen that millions of children of the European and Aryan nations should starve to death, that millions of adult men should perish and hundreds of thousands of women and children should be burned and bombed to death in the cities, without the real culprits paying for their guilt, even if in a more humane way." (*My Political Testament*, 29 April 1945).

On racism: "The whites, in spite of everything, have brought something to these peoples, the worst that could have been brought to them, the plagues of this world of ours: materialism, fanaticism, alcoholism and syphilis. As for the rest, since these peoples possessed

[716]William L. Shirer, *Auge y caída del Tercer Reich, volume I*, Editorial Planeta, Barcelona, 2013, p. 218-219.
[717]Adolf Hitler, *My Political Testament*, and Notes collected at the Führer's Headquarters by Martin Bormann, Minister of the German National Socialist Party.

something of their own superior to what we could give them, they have remained themselves. Moreover, what was attempted by force produced even worse results. Intelligence would command us to refrain from efforts of that nature, when we know that they will prove futile. Only one success we will note to the asset of the colonisers: they have aroused hatred everywhere." (*Notes*, 7 February 1945)." I have never thought that a Chinese or a Japanese were inferior to us. They belong to old civilisations, and I even accept that their past is superior to ours. I grant them every reason to be proud of it, as we are proud of the civilisation to which we belong. I go so far as to think that the more proud the Chinese and Japanese continue to be of their race, the easier it will be for me to understand them." (*Notes*, 13 February 1945).

"We alone could have emancipated the Muslim countries dominated by France. And that would have had an enormous resonance in Egypt and the Near East, subjugated by the British. Because we had tied our fate to that of the Italians, this became impossible as a matter of policy. The whole of Islam was vibrating with the announcement of our victories. The Egyptians, the Iraqis and the Near East were ready to revolt, all together... The presence of the Italians at our side paralysed us, and created unease among our friends in Islam, because they saw in us only accomplices, willing or not, of their oppressors. Now, the Italians, in those regions, are even more hated than the French and the English718." (*Notes*, 17 February 1945).

"Our racism is aggressive only with regard to the Jewish race. We speak of a Jewish race for the sake of convenience of language, because there is, if we are to express ourselves accurately and from the point of

---

[718]"The greatest service Italy could have rendered us was to stay out of the conflict. This abstention would have earned her all the sacrifices, all the gifts, on our part. Let her have stayed in that role, and we would have showered her with favours. In case of victory, we would have shared with her all the advantages and, moreover, the glory. We would have contributed wholeheartedly to the creation of the historical myth of the supremacy of the Italians, legitimate sons of the Romans. It would have been better and preferable not to have them as combatants on our side! "(Notes, 17 February). Of Franco, Hitler had these words: "I cannot forgive Franco for not having known how, as soon as the civil war was over, to reconcile the Spaniards, for having pushed aside the Falangists, to whom Spain owes the help we have given her, and for having treated as bandits the former adversaries who were far from being all Reds. It is no solution to put half a country outside the law, while a minority of robbers enrich themselves at everyone's expense ... with the blessing of the clergy. I am sure that among the alleged Spanish Reds there were very few Communists. We have been deceived, because I would never have accepted, knowing what it was really about, that our aeroplanes should be used to crush poor starving people, and to restore the Spanish priests to their horrible privileges." (Notes, 10 February) (NdT).

view of genetics, no such thing as a Jewish race. Nevertheless, there is a factual reality to which, without the slightest hesitation, this designation can be granted and which is admitted even by the Jews themselves. It is the existence of a spiritually homogeneous human group, of which Jews everywhere in the world are conscious of being a part, regardless of the countries whose citizens they are from the administrative point of view. It is this human group that we call the Jewish race. However, it is by no means a religious community, nor is it a bond constituted by belonging to a common religion, even if the Hebrew religion serves as a pretext.

The Jewish race is first of all a mental race. Although it has its origin in the Hebrew religion, although it has been partly moulded by it, it is not, nevertheless, of a purely religious essence; for it embraces determined atheists as well as sincere practitioners. To this we must add the link constituted by the persecutions suffered in the course of the centuries; but about which the Jews always forget that it is they themselves who have not ceased to provoke them719... A mental race, that is something much more solid, much more durable, than a race, without more or more. Transplant a German to the United States, and you will make an American. The Jew, wherever he goes, remains a Jew. He is an unassimilable being by nature. And it is precisely this very character that makes him unsuitable for assimilation, that defines his race. This is proof of the superiority of the spirit over the flesh" (*Notes*, 13 February 1945).

The subjugated petty bourgeois

The analysis of anti-Semitism would not be complete without taking into account Wilhelm Reich's work on fascism, which we have already discussed above, and which can also be applied to the analysis

---

[719]"Jews have always aroused anti-Semitism. Non-Jewish peoples, over the centuries, from the Egyptians to us, have all reacted in the same way. There comes a time when they get tired of being exploited by the abusive Jew. They snort and snort like animals shaking off the worm. They react brutally; they end up rebelling. It is an instinctive reaction. It is a reaction of xenophobia in relation to the foreigner who refuses to adapt, to melt away, who is embedded, who imposes himself on us and who exploits us. The Jew is, by definition, the foreigner who is inadmissible and who also refuses to assimilate. This is what distinguishes the Jew from other foreigners: he claims to have, in our house, the rights of a member of the community, and to remain a Jew. He considers this possibility of playing simultaneously on both mats as something due to him, and he is the only one in the world who claims such an exorbitant privilege." (Notes, 13 February) (NdT).

of anti-Semitism. Written between 1930 and 1933, Wilhelm Reich's classic *The Mass Psychology of Fascism* remains an important contribution to the understanding not so much of fascism as of the anti-fascist mentality, and that extraordinary capacity to "invent", as Attali wrote, the most twisted and discouraging theories that increasingly obscure reality. Refusing to see in fascism the ideology or action of an isolated individual, and also rejecting the socio-economic explanation advocated by orthodox Marxists, Reich saw "fascism as the politically organised expression of the character structure of the average man", whose primal and biological needs and drives were repressed for millennia: "The sexual guilt and sexual anguish of reactionary man ... produce the unconscious psychic life of the reader integrated into the mass. It is here that we must look for the root of National Socialist anti-Semitism," Reich asserted." It is in the irrational sphere of the fear of syphilis that the National Socialist political worldview and anti-Semitism find one of their most important sources. Consequently, racial purity, i.e., purity of blood, is an ideal worthy of striving for and for the achievement of which all means must be employed ... We shall have Rosenberg himself speak to show that the core of fascist racial theory is the deadly fear of natural sexuality and its function of orgasm." Indeed, he "attempts to prove the validity of the thesis that the rise and decline of nations must be attributed to race-crossing and "blood-poisoning720."

Fascism, according to Reich, would be explained by the unsatisfied orgastic desire of the masses. To judge human reactions, we must take into account three different layers of biopsychological structure: "In the superficial layer of his personality the average man is reserved, kind, compassionate, responsible, conscientious ... this superficial layer of social cooperation is not in contact with the deep biological core of the individual; it is supported by a second, an intermediate layer of character, which is composed exclusively of cruel, sadistic, lascivious, rapacious and envious impulses. It represents Freud's 'unconscious' or 'repressed' "Then, "penetrating deeper through this second layer of the perverse to the biological foundation of the human animal, one regularly discovers the third and deepest layer, which we call the 'biological nucleus'. At the deepest level, here man is in favourable social circumstances an honest, industrious, co-operative, loving or, if there is reason for it, a rational hating animal. However, in no case of relaxation of the character of today's man can one advance to this deep,

---

[720]Wilhelm Reich, *Mass Psychology of Fascism*, (1933), EspaPdf (en.scribd.com), p. 3, 298–299, 375–376, 381–382

promising layer without first removing the inauthentic and only apparently social surface. When the mask of the civilised has fallen, the natural sociality does not appear first, but only the sadistic-perverse layer of the character721."

"In the ethical and social ideas of liberalism we recognise the representation of the traits of the superficial layer of character, which is concerned with self-control and tolerance. This liberalism accentuates its ethics in order to restrain the "monster in man". The liberal disregards the natural sociality of the deepest layer, the third, the nuclear. He deplores and combats the perversion of human character by ethical standards, but the social catastrophes of the twentieth century show that he has not got very far in this task. Everything genuinely revolutionary, every true art and science comes from the natural biological nucleus of man ... Quite different, and the opposite of liberalism and true revolution, is the situation of fascism. In its nature neither the superficial nor the deeper layer is represented, but essentially the second, the intermediate layer of the character, that of the secondary instincts... This "fascism" is nothing but the politically organised expression of the structure of the character of the average man, of a structure which is linked neither to certain races or nations nor to certain parties, but is general and international. In this sense of character, "fascism" is the basic emotional attitude of the authoritarian subjugated man of the machinist civilisation and its mystical-mechanistic life conception722."

"The fascist mentality is that of the petty, submissive, authority-hungry and at the same time rebellious "little man". It is no accident that all fascist dictators come from the life sphere of the reactionary little man ... One must have studied in depth the character of the subjugated little man for years, as the facts unfold behind the façade, to understand on what powers fascism rests723."

Men like other men

We have already seen that the feeling of Jewishness was not to be reduced to an ancillary aspect of the personality, but was profoundly

---

721Wilhelm Reich, *Mass Psychology of Fascism*, (1933), EspaPdf (en.scribd.com), p. 23–25

722Wilhelm Reich, *Mass Psychology of Fascism*, (1933), EspaPdf (en.scribd.com), p. 28–31

723Wilhelm Reich, *Mass Psychology of Fascism*, (1933), EspaPdf (en.scribd.com), p. 38–39, 41

constitutive of it. This is so true that it goes so far as to determine in individuals not only opinions, especially those expressing egalitarian obsession and planetarian hope, but also a certain way of thinking, as well as communal customs and religious faith. Sometimes, depending on the circumstances, Jews will claim to be perfectly integrated into the community in which they have chosen—often temporarily—to settle; at other times, on the contrary, they will assert their Jewishness as the foremost of their values." Proud to be Jewish" is what emerges from the analysis of some of the testimonies in the aforementioned book *Jewish Portraits*.

Ilse Bing, photographer in New York, born in 1899 in Frankfurt am Main: "What does the word 'homeland' mean to you? — For me, the homeland is the whole world. I have no ties to the world. — You said that you were Jewish, but that it had no influence on your life and that you only became aware of it late in life. What does your Jewish background mean to you today? — I am very conscious of my Jewish origin in the racial sense of the word. Obviously, it is not enough for me to pass Moshe Isaak in the street to feel close to him. There is something inside us that goes back a long time, way beyond three generations. I have the feeling of being descended from ancient ancestors of several millennia. This has nothing to do with Israel."

Ernst Gombrich, art historian in London, born in 1909 in Vienna: "How do you explain the persecutions that the Jews have had to endure in history? —They don't want to recognise that Jesus Christ is the messiah... The pattern is always the same: these people are ambitious, they have close relations with each other, they help each other, and others are envious of them. The second cause of antisemitism is nationalism... Jewish communities have probably very often looked at gentiles with a certain condescension. There is no doubt about that. But it is impossible to talk about this without prejudice. If it were suggested today that the Jews are also to blame, it would inevitably be seen as an attempt to trivialise Auschwitz. That is why we must, we have an obligation to remain silent. But the problem exists."

Marcel Reich-Ranicki, literary critic in Frankfurt am Main, born in 1920 in Wloclawek on the Vistula. He is considered the "Pope of literature" in Germany: "The whole of humanity has recognised Kafka as the writer of our century[724]. Franz Kafka laid the foundations of modern literature; Gustav Malher and Arnold Schönberg laid the foundations of modern music; Karl Marx laid the foundations of modern sociology. All were Jewish, and German-speaking. This double

---

[724]We now know what "humanity" means.

membership alone has produced such geniuses. I cannot tell you why, but I can formulate a hypothesis: the fact that Jews (persecuted throughout the world in the 18th century) had the possibility in some German states to devote themselves to intellectual work in spite of everything probably played a role. This was especially true in Prussia [725]... You have no right to make a German out of me. I am certainly a citizen of the Federal Republic, and I am happy to admit it. I like this country, in spite of everything. I write in German, I am a German literary critic, I belong to German literature and culture, but I am not German, and never will be. And yet I do not regard myself as a guest in Germany, nor as a foreigner. I assert the legitimacy of my presence and claim the right to participate fully in the cultural life of this country."

Curt Siodmak, filmmaker, producer and author; born in 1902 in Dresden and died in Three Rivers in 2000: "-Is there a latent anti-Semitism in America? —But of course! The Los Angeles Tennis Club does not accept Jews. And Chrysler factories don't hire them either. — Do you suffer from it? —Me? Not at all. I'm not at all interested in being part of the "club". Jews also have their own golf clubs from which others are excluded. Occasionally, they make a Christian an "honorary Jew"!

Simon Wiesenthal, director of the Jewish documentation centre in Vienna; born in 1908 in Buchach: "—You don't go to synagogue, and it seems to me that you are not a believing Jew. So what does your Jewishness consist of? —I have kept the Jewish ethic. For me it is the most valuable thing, the thing that makes me proud to be a Jew. Besides, I feel with all Jews, wherever they live, a kind of community of destiny."

Artur Brauner, film producer in Berlin, born in 1918 in Lodz, Poland: "Mr. Brauner, how do you see the future of the Jewish people? —To be honest, what worries me a lot is assimilation, the large number of mixed marriages. This is decimating the Jewish people. There are also very few Jewish children being born. But maybe we just have to wait. The Jewish people have always seen miracles happen[726]."

If pride in belonging to the Jewish people above all else can be freely expressed in a book of interviews for a Jewish audience, it is not

---

[725]It seems that M. Reich-Ranicki uses the term "persecuted" to refer to the fact that Jews in Europe at that time did not have citizenship of the countries where they lived. It was the transformations of the French Revolution and the Napoleonic Empire, heirs to the ideas of the Enlightenment, that laid these foundations.
[726]Herlinde Loelbl, *Portraits juifs, Photographies et entretiens*, L'Arche éditeur, Frankfurt-sur-le Main, 1989, 2003.

certain that these same people would have declared the same to people outside their community. Indeed, one hardly ever sees on television, in the media or in the political world, famous men and women declaring their Jewishness and claiming to be Jewish, while, on the contrary, the Jewish press regularly echoes statements to that effect. This double language, which is quite characteristic of some people in this community, also manifests itself, as we have already seen, according to the circumstances of the moment. One could bet that if, unfortunately, Germany decided to withdraw German nationality from Jews again, Mr Reich-Ranicki would swear to God that he was perfectly integrated into the German community, asserting to anyone who would listen that after all he had contributed to the country, it would not be decent to "discriminate" against him again.

Of course, this trait is not specific to German Jews. In his book *A Secret*, winner of the 2004 Goncourt Prize for secondary education, the young novelist Philippe Grimbert also revealed throughout his book an obvious obsession with his Jewishness." I was proud of what I had inherited … proud of my surname, to the point of wanting to restore its original spelling727."

In view of these testimonies, it must be admitted that for most Jews, being Jewish is not a trivial matter. Indeed, all those who claim that "Jews are just like other people", implying that Jewishness has absolutely no influence on their way of thinking and perceiving the world, should first of all share their thoughts with the main stakeholders.

The loss of the lifeblood of Judaism is undoubtedly an essential issue for this people living in the midst of other nations. Forgetting its roots and the increase in intermarriage are simply a threat of extinction. Strengthening the cohesion of the Jewish community is therefore absolutely vital since the emancipation of the Jews and the destruction of the old organised communities. Historian Israel Shahak provided important insights on this point: "However, all this changed due to two parallel processes that began in Holland and England and continued in revolutionary France and in the countries that followed the example of the French Revolution. Jews gained a significant level of individual rights (in some cases, full legal equality), and the legal power of the Jewish community over its members came to an end … From the time of the late Roman Empire, Jewish communities had considerable legal powers over their members. Not just powers rooted in the voluntary mobilisation of social pressure (for example, the refusal to have any

---

[727]Philippe Grimbert, *Un Secret*, Prix Goncourt des lycéens, 2004, Grasset, p. 178.

dealings with an excommunicated Jew, excluded from the community, going so far as the refusal to bury his body), but a power of pure coercion: flogging, imprisonment, expulsion; rabbinical courts could legally inflict all these on a Jewish individual for all sorts of offences ... This was the most important social fact of Jewish existence before the advent of the modern state: both the observance of the religious laws of Judaism and their inculcation through education were imposed on Jews through physical coercion, from which one could only escape by converting to the religion of the majority, which in those circumstances amounted to an absolute social rupture and for that very reason impossible to carry out, except during a religious crisis. (All this is usually omitted in the more common Jewish historiography, in order to propagate the myth that the Jews maintained their religion miraculously or by virtue of some peculiar mystical force728.")"

This relentless and merciless vigilance no longer exists today, so it is appropriate, in order to consolidate identity feelings and to try to reduce the number of intermarriages that are dangerously increasing, endangering the survival of the group, to permanently nurture and foster the threat of anti-Semitism. Every effort must be made to maintain the flame of Jewishness in every Jew and, to this end, the fear of anti-Semitism can serve as a powerful glue to hold the community together. Thus, the Jewish "memory" will be kept permanently alive, as will the constant fear of pogroms and anti-Semitic violence, real or imagined. Marek Halter was well aware of "the fundamental role of memory in the destiny of a people destined for dispersion and exile729"." Yes, I know the biblical precept: "Zakhor", "Remember" in Hebrew. That verb appears as many as one hundred and sixty-nine times in the Bible"." The Memory, the Book, the Name: such are the three pillars that support "the invisible edifice of Judaism", mentioned by Sigmund Freud730."

For Elie Wiesel, "the Jew is obsessed with the beginning rather than the end. His messianic dream refers to the kingdom of David. He feels closer to the prophet Elijah than to his next-door neighbour ... everything that struck his ancestors affects him. Their mourning weighs on him, their triumphs encourage him[731]"." I admit that of all the traits

---

[728]Israel Shahak, *Historia judía, religión judía. El peso de tres mil años*, A. Machado Libros, Madrid, 2002, p. 70, 72.

[729]Marek Halter, *Un Homme, un cri*, Robert Laffont, Paris, 1991, p. 244.

[730]Marek Halter, *Un Homme, un cri*, Robert Laffont, Paris, 1991, p. 303.

[731]Elie Wiesel, *Memoires Tome II*, Editions du Seuil, 1996, p.46.

that characterise the Jewish people, the one that shocks me most is the duty of hope[732]."

The writer Joseph Roth went even further. For him, Jewishness is a choice and a predestination from which one cannot detach oneself in any way: "Religiosity becomes an organic function of the Jewish individual. A Jew fulfils his 'religious duties' even when he does not fulfil them. He is religious by the mere fact of being. He is a Jew. All others must, when the time comes, make profession of their "faith" or their "nationality", it is automatic only in the Jew. He is identified up to the tenth generation733."

Jewish identity is primarily based on memory and messianic hope, long before it is a racial or religious characteristic. Thus, anti-Semitism cannot be racism and the two terms are wrongly linked, in the same way that issues of Blacks, women, homosexuals and any other minority are systematically equated with discrimination against Jews. Obviously, this is all part of a well thought-out strategy which consists in asserting that hostility towards Jews, and only against Jews, is strictly unfounded. In these conditions, indeed, if we start from the principle that Jews are totally alien to what anti-Semites reproach them for, to attack Jews is to attack any community, and by extension the whole of humanity.

This sense of identity undoubtedly helps to avoid the worst: dissolution within the national community, and eventually the disappearance of the Jewish community. According to Jacques Attali, "the majority of mixed marriages do not involve the conversion of the Jewish spouse to another religion, but rather the refusal of the non-Jewish spouse to convert, and above all, the abandonment of Judaism in the next generation. Today, although one third of young people in the Diaspora marry a non-Jew who does not convert, more than half of the children of intermarriage in the United States will not become Jewish. In this country, 700,000 young people under the age of 18 of whom one parent is Jewish are raised in another religion, and 600,000 adults born to at least one Jewish parent practice another religion734." Therefore, intermarriage is rightly considered by the heads of the Jewish community as a calamity.

The traditional protection of the Jewish people against the corruption of foreign blood was demonstrated by this admirable example: an Israeli police spokesman declared on 23 December 2003

[732]Elie Wiesel, *Mémoires Tome II*, Éditions du Seuil, 1996, p. 156.
[733]Joseph Roth, *A Berlin*, Éditions du Rocher, 2003, p. 33.
[734]Jacques Attali, *Los judíos, el mundo y el dinero*, Fondo de cultura económica, 2005, Buenos Aires, p. 497.

that "an Israeli company has demanded that thousands of Chinese workers sign a contract pledging to refrain from any sexual relations with Israeli women, or from attempting to convert them." Let us note, once again, how paradoxical it is to accuse others of racism while applying to oneself the strictest and most implacable racism. The situation becomes even more convoluted when we hear some Jews accuse anti-Semites of seeing in Jews the reflection of their own faults, an attitude which seems to be precisely their own. Let us recall the words of Vasili Grossman, quoted above: "Anti-Semitism is a mirror reflecting the defects of individuals, social structures and state systems. Tell me what you accuse a Jew of and I will tell you what you are guilty of." The following words of Sigmund Freud are also well known: "Nor was it by incomprehensible chance that the dream of Germanic world supremacy resorted as a complement to the incitement of anti-Semitism735." Once again, it seems to us that there is a total inversion of reality. The best defence is a good attack: instead of allowing oneself to be denounced, one accuses the other of one's own shortcomings, taking full advantage of the fact that this form of intellectual crime is not sanctioned by law.

Those who wonder about these unique dispositions of Jews to reason, to argue, to beat about the bush, to find all sorts of tricks to evade an issue and to contort themselves in every way to prove their good faith, should begin to familiarise themselves with what is called "the Talmudic spirit". Albert London, the "prince of reporters", bequeathed us a very interesting text on this subject, in his 1929 book *The Wandering Jew Has Arrived*, in which he described the ancient Jewish communities of Central Europe, in the "shtetl" and Jewish quarters:

"I stand on the threshold of the *Mesybtha*, the great seminary of world Jewry. The sensational youth ... the slim, pale, round-hatted intellectuals, those faces of sixteen to twenty-two, ascetic, inspired, devoured by the Moloch spirit736, those bearers of the fire of Israel from Poland, Romania, the Ukraine, Czechoslovakia and even Belgium, they are all there. I hear them from the landing. The murmur of their voices swells, quiets, dies down, is reborn. The rabbi factory is

---

735Sigmund Freud, *The Malaise in Culture, Part V, Collected Works*, EpubLibre, Trans. Luis López Ballesteros y de Torres, 2001, p. 4092. [The translation by Presses Universitaires de France (1971) reads: "Nor was it by chance that the Germans resorted to anti-Semitism in order to better realise their dream of world supremacy". (NdT)]
736Semitic deity to whom fire sacrifices of children were offered. Note in Albert London, *The Wandering Jew has arrived.*

in full operation. Let's go in. Of course, go in! Is the smell of the place awful? Haven't you smelled others? Pretend you have a cold, bite the handkerchief under your nose, but go ahead, you'll get used to it! The smell is especially Jewish—Orthodox Jewish. In a cinema in Cernauti I had to leave before the end. This smell is a mixture of onion scent, salted herring scent and kaftan smoke scent ... Nothing coming from outside can impress these students. Absolutely nothing ... To penetrate the mysteries, to push back the shadows, to whip one's own intelligence which never gallops too fast, to reach a peak of understanding only to hurtle towards another peak, to speculate on all causes and all principles: these are the only preoccupations of these indefatigable theorists. This rabbinical seminary is extraordinary... They work like this for sixteen to seventeen hours a day. What do they learn? First of all, the Talmud, by heart, even the two Talmuds: the Jerusalem Talmud and the Babylonian Talmud. They literally gorge themselves on all the old rabbinical traditions. What is a Talmud? It is the book of the interpretations that a thousand rabbis, for millennia, have given of the law of Moses. It is the love of discussion taken almost to the point of madness. The meaning and the contradiction of a word are the subject of endless controversy. For example, this word of God is not lightly discussed: "Let every man abide in his own house, and let no man go out of *his place* on the seventh day". What is that *place*? How far can one go on a Sabbath without offending the Lord? Does the word *place* designate the immediate surroundings of the house? Can the whole village be considered as the *place* willed by the Eternal? If so, can this apply to all villages, whatever their size? And what can be accepted for a village, can it be accepted for a city? Where does a city begin? Where does it end? Once the limits are fixed, is not the city too big to be treated as a *place*? ... Oh, insatiable spirit of Israel! ... And what these young acrobats of thought, these brainiacs learn here, is not so much Jewish literature, ethics and morals, but to become more subtle, more acute, more penetrating, more alert. A fine sport!

(...) The purity of their customs is legendary. They enter like angels and leave like angels. All the fieriness of their early youth is for the Talmud. They only dream of it and with it they live and sleep. If the Thora is the *Crowned Bride*, the Talmud is the *Bride in Bloom*737."

---

[737]Albert Londres, *The Wandering Jew Has Arrived*, Editorial Melusina, 2012, p. 160–165.

Drums and trumpets

The reasons to be proud are most often and most convincingly expressed when it comes to praising one's own countrymen. This is one of the most remarkable and commendable aspects of community spirit, as long as it is justified and not at the expense of "others".

While he described the Berlin of his loves in 1930, "the Berlin pleasure industry" and all the joys of life in the capital of the new Weimar Republic, the tone suddenly changed in 1933: Joseph Roth no longer felt himself to be a German in love with his country, but on the contrary, he displayed an abrupt and radical change that is already familiar to us after studying the cases of Albert Einstein and Stefan Zweig, among others. Here, again, this abrupt turn is entirely symptomatic of an ambivalent mentality whose hidden face is only revealed in special circumstances: immediately after having triumphed, or in the course of revenge. To this was added a sovereign contempt for the people who had rejected them: "We, descendants of ancient Hebrews, ancestors of European culture, remain to this day the only legitimate German representatives of this culture ... Thanks to the unfathomable divine wisdom, we are physically incapable of betraying it for the sake of the pagan civilisation of suffocating gases, of the Germanic war god armed with ammonia ... It can be said that since 1900, this "upper stratum" of German Jews has largely determined, if not dominated, the artistic life of Germany.

Throughout the whole of the vast Reich, populated by sixty million inhabitants, there was, except, of course, in individual cases, not a single medium who manifested an active interest in art and the spirit. As for the Prussian Junkers, the civilised world realised that they could hardly read and write ... Only German Jews manifested an interest in books, theatre, museums, music ... Magazines and newspapers were edited by Jews, paid for by Jews, read by Jews. A whole swarm of Jewish critics and intellectuals discovered and promoted numerous "purely Aryan" poets, writers and actors."

The intellectual sterility of the Germans thus contrasted with the incredible fecundity of the Jewish spirit, and this open contempt for the Goyim was matched only by the adulation of their own co-religionists, so much so that epithets were lacking to praise them: "Since the beginning of the 20th century," Joseph Roth went on to write, "the following Jewish, half-Jewish and quarter-Jewish writers have contributed to German literature: Peter Altenberg, tender poet of the sweetest and most secret femininity, long since treated as a "decadent pornographer" by the barbarians of racist theories; Oscar Blumenthal, author of fine comedies without grandiloquence but full of good taste; Richard Beer-Hoffmann, noble forger of the German language, heir and interpreter of the biblical legacy; Max Brod, author of short stories of great lineage, full of prurience and erudition; Bruno Frank, conscientious craftsman of the Word and experienced dramatist; Ludwig Fulda, lyric poet and author of comedies full of charm and finesse; Walter Hasenclever, one of the most ardent playwrights; Hugo von Hofmansthal, one of the noblest poets and prose writers; Alfred Kerr, theatre critic brimming with poetry; Karl Krauss, great polemicist, professor of German letters, fanatic of linguistic purity; Else Lasker-Schüler, immeasurable poet; Klauss Mann (half-Jewish, son of Thomas Mann), promising young writer of considerable stylistic talent; Alfred and Robert Neumann, outstanding epic authors; Rainer Maria Rilke (quarter-Jewish), one of Europe's greatest lyric authors; Peter Panter, pamphleteer of brilliant spirit; Carl Sternheim, penetrating novelist and playwright; Ernst Toller, chorus of swallows, revolutionary playwright who spent seven years in a Bavarian fortress for love of the freedom of the German people[738]; Jacob Wassermann, one of Europe's greatest novelists; Franz Werfel, lyric playwright, short-story writer and magnificent poet: Carl Zuckmayer, powerful dramatist; Arnold Zweig, novelist and essayist by the grace of God." All in all, great, very great men, compared to the local intellectuals and artists, those poor, uncouth, brutal and inept Germans.

"In persecuting the Jews, wrote Joseph Roth with that logic the reader is already familiar with, one persecutes Jesus Christ. For once, the Jews are not slaughtered because they have crucified Jesus Christ, but because they have begotten him[739]. When books by Jewish or suspected Jewish authors are burned, the Book of books—the Bible— is actually set on fire. When Jewish judges and lawyers are expelled and imprisoned, it is in spirit an attack on law and justice. When communists are martyred, the Russian and Slavic world is attacked, the world of Tolstoy and Dostoyevsky even more than that of Lenin and Trotsky". This time, Christians, the law and the Russian world were assimilated in order to ingratiate new allies against the "evil bad guys". And Joseph Roth concluded: "We have sung the praises of Germany, the real Germany! That is why today Germany burns us[740]! "

---

[738]Ernst Toller was one of the leaders of the Bavarian revolution in 1919.
[739]The first "massacre" is from November 1938, during the Night of Broken Glass (36 victims), when the author was writing this in September 1933.
[740]He refers to "burnt" books. Joseph Roth, *A Berlin*, Éditions du Rocher, 2003, p. 195-

In *Life and Fate*, Vasili Grossman demonstrated the same tendency to put members of his community on a pedestal when he said: Albert Einstein is "the first genius of our time"; "The fascists have expelled the brilliant Einstein, and his physics has become the physics of apes. But thank God we have stopped the advance of fascism... Contemporary physics without Einstein would be a physics of apes741." Sovereign contempt for some, absolute glory for others. It is one of the many symptoms of hysteria. It is one of the afflictions which is only seen in women among other peoples, as Professor Charcot pointed out in his time.

In his book *The World of Yesterday*, Stefan Zweig also makes the same point: "In Vienna, love and art were considered a common right, and the role that the Jewish bourgeoisie, with its contribution and protection, played in Viennese culture is immeasurable. They were the audience, they filled the theatres and concerts, they bought the books and paintings, they visited the exhibitions and, with their more flexible and less tradition-bound understanding, they became everywhere the promoters and forerunners of all novelties. Jews created almost all the art collections of the 19th century, it was thanks to them that most artistic essays became possible; without the incessant and stimulating interest of the Jewish bourgeoisie, Vienna would have lagged behind Berlin with regard to art ... Whoever wanted to do something new in Vienna could not do without the Jewish bourgeoisie ... Nine-tenths of what the world celebrated as Viennese culture of the 19th century was a culture promoted, nurtured and even created by the Jewish community of Vienna742."

At the end of the 19th century, "like Spain before its equally tragic decline, Viennese Judaism had been very productive artistically, though not at all in a specifically Jewish way, but expressing with the greatest energy, by a miracle of interpenetration, all that was typically Austrian and Viennese. Goldmark, Gustav Mahler and Schönberg became international figures of musical creation; Oscar Strauss, Leo Fall and Kálmán made the tradition of waltz and operetta flourish again; Hofmannsthal, Arthur Schnitzler, Beer-Hofmann and Peter Altenberg raised Viennese literature to a European rank not even reached by Grillparzer and Stifter; Sonnethal and Max Reinhardt revived the fame of the city of theatre and carried it throughout the world; Freud and the

204.
[741]Vasili Grossman, *Life and Destiny*, Galaxia Gutenberg, 2007, Barcelona, p. 339, 340.
[742]Stefan Zweig, *El mundo de ayer; memorias de un Europeo*, Acantilado 44, Barcelona, p. 16.

great authorities of science attracted the eyes of the world to the celebrated university; everywhere, as scholars, virtuosos, painters, art directors, architects and journalists, Jews secured high and eminent positions in Vienna's intellectual life. Thanks to their passionate love for this city and their willingness to assimilate, they had completely adapted themselves and were happy to serve the fame of Austria; They felt their status as Austrians as a mission to the world, and it bears repeating for the sake of honesty a large part, if not the greater part, of all that Europe and America admire today as the expression of a revived Austrian culture—in music, literature, theatre and the industrial arts was created by the Jews of Vienna, who, in turn, obtained by this renunciation a very high return on their age-old spiritual impulse."

One figure "fascinated, seduced, intoxicated and excited us," wrote Stefan Zweig, "the unique phenomenon of Hugo von Hofmannsthal", who represented "absolute poetic perfection". He had "such an infallible mastery of language" that "this great genius, who at the age of sixteen and seventeen, with his indelible verse and prose, unsurpassed to this day, is inscribed in the eternal annals of the German language"." There had been "a supernatural event"; "a bachelor who possessed such a mastery of the art, such clairvoyance, such a profound vision and such an impressive knowledge of life before he lived it! He had "such an agile intelligence"; "such perfect verse, such impeccable plasticity, so imbued with music"; "a mastery unequalled by any other German since then"; it "lay in a knowledge of the world which, for a boy who spent his days sitting on a school bench, could only come from a magical intuition"; "he had to become a brother in the world"; "he had to become a brother in the world"; "he had to become a brother in the world"; "he had to become a brother in the world"; "he had to become a brother in the world"; "he had to become a brother in the world"; "he had to become the brother of Goethe and Shakespeare"; "one could feel that something unconscious and incomprehensible must secretly guide him along these paths to untrodden places"; "a pure, sublime poet, a poet whom no one conceived of except in the legendary forms of a Hölderlin, a Keats", and he was our age; "his face, with its marked profile and dark complexion, was He was "a little Italian"; "each of his sentences had that halo of perfection that comes naturally from the magical sense of form"; "everything he wrote, that bachelor and university student, was like crystal illuminated from within"; such was "the magical force of this inventor"; "I have never experienced a conversation of such high intellectual flight as his"; "He was an inimitable prodigy of precocious perfection743". The presence of such a genius obviously raised the hopes of all the young pupils. Glory and celebrity were therefore possible: "After all, his father, a bank manager, came from the same bourgeois Jewish background as all of us; the genius had been brought up in a house similar to our own, with the same furniture and the same class morals…"

Such enthusiasm, such publicity in favour of their co-religionists were evidently symptomatic of a latent feeling of inferiority. At the risk of displeasing, we must admit that, with the exception of Stefan Zweig, none of the authors studied in the present work seemed to us to have any special literary qualities. Their productions are often mediocre, and it seems that their success is mainly due to the genius of advertising. Bookshops, it must be said, are nowadays flooded with mediocre books. In truth, the "people of the book" are above all the people of the microphone and the television screen, or even more certainly, the people of the megaphone, for without publicity, it is clear that many of these publications would remain in obscurity. Very few of those we have reviewed know how to write properly. Guy Sorman seems to us to be an excellent journalist; Stefan Zweig undoubtedly has a beautiful pen; but the others are devoid of literary talent. The academic Michel Serres even manages the feat, using French words, of writing in a language we do not understand. Some simply benefit from the complacency of all media channels and the exclusive help of their co-religionists, probably another unconfessed cause of anti-Semitism but which some Jews tend to blame on "envy". Again, it is not impossible that what one reproaches one's opponents for is in fact a reflection of one's own shortcomings.

We now know that Jacques Derrida was "the Pope of university thought"; that Armand Hammer was "the king of oil, cattle breeding and whisky"; that Albert Londres was the "prince of reporters" and that Isidore Partouche was "the emperor of casinos". We were missing a "queen", and we found her in the person of Françoise Giroud, the great journalist who died in 2004, who was undoubtedly the "queen of journalists", the "best of the best", a "great lady" and an "illustrious figure". In her *Diary of a Parisian*[744] we find once again, for the period 1996–1999, the characteristic features of this particular mentality: the abusive glorification of co-religionists, the irrepressible tendency to give moral lessons, intellectual contortions, militant anti-racism and selective indignation:

[743]Stefan Zweig, *El mundo de ayer; memorias de un Europeo*, Acantilado 44, Barcelona, p. 16-17, 28-31.
[744]Françoise Giroud, *Journal d'une parisienne*, Éditions du Seuil, 1997, 2000.

"13 February 1996: Surrealism is rediscovered, whose most emblematic figure, Victor Brauner, who died in 1996, is currently being exhibited at Beaubourg. Beaubourg's belated tribute to him brings together some thirty paintings and drawings. Looking at them, it is clear that this provocative magician has been underestimated. Sumptuousness, strength, absolute mastery of his art, it must be seen without fail.

"11 April: Marcel Bleustein died at the age of 89. He was still in good health, although he was completely deaf, which made it difficult to interact with him. I liked this old bandit with a candid look, full of audacity, imagination and talent. He had the gift of publicity as others had the gift of music. He made his fortune with him[745].

"20 April: Abbé Pierre ... how sad. This man whom we can only love has gone astray by plunging headlong into a sinister history. Here we see him suddenly positioning himself as the moral guarantor of the negationist Roger Garaudy, on the pretext that he has known him for forty years. He can be held in affection, like a tired old man. You can no longer have respect for him.

"26 June: Rude, Jean-Marie Le Pen accusing the French football team of not knowing the Marseillaise, and even of not being French. False. They all are, even if they are sometimes beautifully black. This is called missing the opportunity to shut up.

"9 August: The exhibition of African art organised by the Nahon family at the Vence gallery was seen for the fourth time. It can be seen and seen again for its richness, variety and the impressive quality of the objects presented. It is as simple as that, you want it all. I am spellbound by a small terracotta from Nigeria, irresistible.

"12 September: Outrage at Jean-Marie Le Pen's statement on the "inequality of races". Furthermore, he insists: "Jews and Eskimos have not played the same role in the history of the world. Nor did the Pygmies and the Greeks contemporaries of Pericles". Therefore, there are inferior races. An old scientifically false refrain: the genetic heritage of the entire human race is the same, its blood is the same. And between Nelson Mandela and Le Pen, which is "inferior"?

"27 September: Brigitte Bardot's memoirs are selling like hot cakes. She is reproached for her sympathy for Le Pen—"a charming man"—for her blunt words about immigrants, and also for some snobbish petit bourgeois phrases like: "I hate paid holidays". Should Bardot be burned? No. She should be pulled by the ears.

---

[745]Former owner of Publicis, France's leading advertising group.

"27 October: Marek Halter was invited to the Toulon Book Fair. He had just published a voluminous book, *The Messiah*. A tribute was to be paid to him. But everything fell apart when the mayor of Toulon, M. Le Chevalier, National Front, declared Marek Halter persona non grata. He will not be forbidden to stay, but the tribute will be for... Brigitte Bardot. What is Marek Halter being reproached for? M. Le Chevalier put it bluntly: Marek Halter has "a vision of the world that is more internationalist, more globalist than rooted to a nation, to a homeland". Marek Halter almost choked. This is how fascism begins. He never says his name, he creeps around, he floats in the air, when he shows his face, everyone asks: Is it him, do you think? You can't exaggerate! And then one day you find yourself face to face with him and it's too late to expel him.

"14 January 1999: Saw Jacques Attali's play about Charles V, played by Depardieu: magnificent. Rothko exhibition: a great American painter whom the French hardly know. It is an abstract, metaphysical painting: large squares of colours in front of which, when you stop to look, spirituality invades you, communication with an infinite[746]... One remains there, stuck. Subtle, precious, elaborate colours, from which a light emerges; blacks on greys that announce death. A unique work." I have captured the most absolute violence in every square centimetre", he said. Rothko committed suicide in 1970.

"18 January: Françoise Dolto Colloquium; a triumph. The great hall of UNESCO was full for four days.

"23 January: My printer has broken. I have to buy a new one, I can't do without it. But no shop delivers a printer to my home. And it weighs a lot, and I don't have a car: how will I get it home?

"March 16: Yehudi Menuhin, the sublime, died at the age of 82. He played the violin of angels.

"21 April: Lunch with Jacques Attali. It's a pleasure to see him ... His play on Charles V has had a very honourable success at a time when the theatres are empty[747]... No one is more fruitful than he is. He fascinates and irritates, of course. I like him a lot.

"30 April: An interesting part of Paul Léautaud's *Diary* is about the period of the Occupation as he experienced it: people who don't care about anything, who find the Germans quite nice, and who are obsessed with supply, himself the first.

"September 14: The Fox of agriculture, José Bové, in his crusade against "junk food", goes around smashing up McDonald's. It has

---

[746]The sentence is not finished; it is probably a figure of speech.
[747]Translation: a fiasco.

earned him a few days in jail and has become a popular figure. It has earned him a few days in jail and he has become a popular figure. He had these extraordinary words: "The Church of Scientology and McDonald's are the same thing…". In other words: you see all that, he is American.

"Yuck[748]! "

It is clear that we are dealing with a great, a very great journalist.

Let us now listen to a testimony from our *Portraits* book, *that* of Erwin Chargaff, a biologist in New York, born in 1905 in Chernivtsi:

"Are you questioning the particular talents of the Jews?

"It seems to me that the Jews are a fairly gifted people. Just look at how, left to their own devices, the situation in Israel is. They are not really good economists. Jews are extraordinarily gifted in transmission, i.e. there are many excellent Jewish solo musicians, singers, instrumentalists. They seem to be especially gifted at interpreting and reproducing what others have written. But it seems to me a stupid chauvinism to claim that Jews are the main element of the Western intellectual world. It is absolutely false. On the contrary, I would say that Jews have always shown a certain deficit in the field of creation. They are rather less creative than others. There are far fewer overt geniuses among Jews than among non-Jews. I think they have little talent in literature, and even less in the pictorial arts. Nor do I believe that an injustice has been done to Jews. If they had written better poems, they would have been printed. Karl Marx was undoubtedly a kind of philosophical or political-philosophical genius[749], but apart from him, there are very few Jewish geniuses. Jews have not hesitated to call many of them geniuses. In all minorities, it is always a question of singing their own praises, but minorities, in general, have no sense of proportion, and I very much regret this chauvinism." This was already Spinoza's opinion.

Exiting Judaism

The rejection of their own community by some Jews is a subject that would need a study in itself. The best known example is that of Karl Marx. He was born "into a family of Jewish rabbis and merchants in Trier (his father is Hirschel Ha Levi and his mother, Henrietta Pressburg

---

[748]This is Françoise Giroud's comment.

[749]"Marx had a great vision, wrote Sollers. I pity anyone who did not feel the rigour of it. So did Freud." (Philippe Sollers, *Vision à New York*, Grasset, 1981, p. 16).

Hirshel), converted to Protestantism when he was 6 years old." Four years before the *Manifesto*, he published *The Jewish Question* in 1844. For him, "the Jew is the matrix of capitalism; therefore to assimilate him would in no way change his status. He can only emancipate himself by the joint disappearance of capitalism and Judaism." In "that dreadful text", Jacques Attali identified one of the involuntary sources of modern economic anti-Semitism. Indeed, this was what Marx wrote: "Let us not seek the secret of the Jew in his religion, let us seek—instead—the secret of religion in the real Jew. What is the profane substratum of Judaism? Practical necessity, personal gain. What is the profane worship of the Jew? Traffic. What is his profane god? Money (…) The chimerical nationality of the Jew is the nationality of the merchant, of the man of money. Judaism only reaches its apogee with the perfection of bourgeois society; but this only reaches its perfection in the Christian world (…). Christianity sprang from Judaism; and it ended by bowing down to Judaism. (…) We therefore find the essence of the Jew of our day not only in the Pentateuch and the Talmud, but in present-day society. (…) Money is the jealous god of Israel, before whom no other god must subsist[750]."

Marx intended to show that the liberation of the Jew would mean that society would in turn be liberated from Judaism: "Marx explains that Judaism and money are inseparable, that one cannot be eliminated without eliminating the other, that the worker, through a revolution against private property, can at the same time be liberated from God and from capital"." Thus, anti-capitalism and anti-Judaism are confused in a mixture that many will feed on after Marx", noted Jacques Attali, recalling the anti-Semitism of a part of the revolutionary left in the 19th century. However, we have already seen that the work of Karl Marx, like that of Spinoza, is perfectly in line with the prophetic texts and universalism so dear to Israel.

In 1860, another German Jew, Ferdinand Lassalle, founder of the socialist movement, wrote: "I can affirm that I have ceased to be a Jew (…) I do not love the Jews and would rather tend to detest them in general[751]."

Jewish self-hatred is a phenomenon observed in many other authors. Israel Shamir, for example, is an Israeli who seems to have

---

[750]Jacques Attali, *Los judíos, el mundo y el dinero*, Fondo de cultura económica, 2005, Buenos Aires, p. 329-330.
[751]Jacques Attali, *Los judíos, el mundo y el dinero*, Fondo de cultura económica, 2005, Buenos Aires, p. 331.

sincerely converted to orthodox Christianity and abandoned his community of origin. Today, his thought no longer contains any of what we have been able to identify as constitutive of the Jewish mentality, and therefore there is no longer any reason to consider him a representative of the "chosen people". In his *Pardes, A Study in Kabbalah*, written in 2004, he recalled that Golda Meir, Prime Minister of Israel, had one day stated: "Intermarriage is worse than the Holocaust". Israel Shamir commented: 'Meir and Lipstadt have followed the traditional Jewish line: the Old Testament glorifies Phineas who killed a Jewish man for having sex with a gentile woman; Ezra excluded all Jewish priests who had intermarried with native Palestinian women; the Talmud likened intermarriage to bestiality: "for the gentiles are closer to the beasts than to the Jews". In Jewish tradition, a Jewish family is supposed to perform funeral rites only formally if their son or daughter marries a goy [non-Jew, pejorative]." "Despite these condemnations, men and women of Jewish origin intermarry and consciously break with Judaism. This act is an important proof of their willingness to renounce particularism and unite with the people they live with. It is, in a way, as conclusive a form of coming out as baptism".

However, the break with Judaism is not so simple." Children of mixed marriages often do not understand the iconoclastic action of their parents, and the parents often hesitate before explaining the sacred significance of their act to their children". Children born into such marriages, "instead of being proud—and also because of the spirit of contradiction inherent in their age—tend to want to contradict their parents and return to the Jewish fold". It is an otherwise counterproductive desire, wrote Israel Shamir, for "their attempt to "return" is doomed to failure, because such a child can never become a "full Jew" according to Jewish law. He or she will not be able to marry into a Cohen, or indeed into any "real" Jewish family. His or her position is virtually the same as that of a *mamzer*, a bastard, "a son of a bitch". He will have the right to support the Jews, to die for the Jews, but not to be buried in a Jewish cemetery". But do not lament, our partly Jewish and fully human children," wrote Shamir, "because it is not only impossible for you to join the Jews, it is not desirable either, because Judaism is not a good organisation. Judaism is by no means a sinecure[752]."

Marek Halter curiously coincided with Israel Shamir in his analysis of Jewishness, but in reverse, if I can put it that way: while for Shamir one can leave Jewishness but not enter, or very hardly enter, for

---

[752]Israel Shamir, *Pardes: a study in Kabbalah*, Pdf, Trad. Germán Leyens, p. 3, 4

Marek Halter one can enter but not leave: "You are not born a Jew, you become one", he said in an interview published in the newspaper *Le Point* on 8 October 1999." There are black Jews, Ethiopian Jews, Chinese Jews, Indian Jews, etc., who don't have a drop of blood in common, without counting the converts! Jews are neither a race nor only a religion, but a group of people who have maintained for centuries a certain tradition, a specific relationship to language and history, which they can choose to make their own today ... or not". Marek Halter will admit, however, that conversions are very rare, and that it is far easier to be admitted into any other religion than into the Jewish religion, where filiation by the mother remains the almost intangible norm. As for black Jews, it seems that they are treated rather harshly by the Hebrew state.

Certainly, Israel Shamir's intention is to help his former co-religionists to "free themselves from their Jewishness". And for this, intermarriage—the great fear of the rabbis—is the simplest option. However, the deliberately fomented anguish of anti-Semitism counteracts this possibility of liberation: "At the beginning of the 20th century, the child of an intermarriage was almost always identified with the natives of his country. But this tendency was countered by the Holocaust narrative, an ideological construct that imposed on the descendants of Jews a fatalistic sense of 'no escape'[753]."

Shamir echoed statements by one Abram Leon, 'a young supporter of Trotsky, who perished in Auschwitz in 1944'. In his book entitled *The Jewish Question*, Abram Leon explained that a man of Jewish origin always has the option of leaving the Jews and joining the "human community"." I am grateful to Noam Chomsky for making me discover this author," wrote Israel Shamir, whose texts published on the internet are full of energy. Israel Shamir also informed us of the existence of Rabbi Abraham Isaac Kook, "a great rabbi of Israel, now deceased, the greatest advocate of contemporary Judaism", who wrote: "The difference between a Jewish soul and a non-Jewish soul is more important and profound than that between a human soul and a cow soul". From what little we know of him, it seems quite clear to us that

---

[753]A 16 March 2016 Pew Research Center article entitled *"A Closer Look at Jewish Identity in Israel and the United States"* provided the results of a survey of Israeli and American Jews about their identity. Both surveys asked Jews about a list of eight possible behaviours and attributes that might be "essential" or "important" to their personal Jewish identity. In both countries, a majority said that remembering the Holocaust was essential to their Jewish identity (73% in the US, 65% in Israel). At https:// www.pewresearch.org/fact-tank/2016/03/16/a-closer-look-at-jewish-identity-in-israel-and-the-u-s/. (NdT).

Israel Shamir should be linked to illustrious Jews who broke with the community. But while in Spinoza and Marx some aspects of their doctrines still connect with Judaism, in Israel Shamir and Israel Shahak, the anti-Semitism that seems to animate them makes their break with Judaism complete. Other prominent intellectuals had preceded them on this path. We think, for example, of Otto Weininger, for whom Jewishness was "neither a race, nor a people, nor a recognised religious faith, but a mental disposition"." His "monotheism", he explained, is not a tribal religion, as his detractors claim. No: it is the extreme self-centredness of an ant utterly incapable of imagining that any other form of life could exist outside its anthill, or that there could be a god other than the God of the ants."

For centuries," wrote Shamir, "hundreds of Jews have renounced the creed, turned to Christ and revealed the secret of their hatred of the Goyim and their quest for absolute power." Thus, thanks to him, we know what is the predominant ideology in Israel within the orthodox Jewish movement: "The quest for absolute power is its determining objective, directing its steps towards the destruction of Israeli democracy, rebuilding the Third Temple (which will herald the era of the Messiah), and perhaps bringing about the world apocalypse[754]." But Jacques Attali had already given us a glimpse of this aspect of messianism. Let us recall the passage from the dialogue he had imagined in his novel *The Coming*, which we quoted in the first part of this book: "—The Jews, with their madness, are capable of causing massacres and cataclysms. —This is true! If the madmen of the Reconstruction Party were to start rebuilding the Temple, that would surely provoke a planetarian war[755]."

Shamir sees Israel only as a mere base for the world Jewish community, and not as the heart of the diaspora." The Zionists form a simple-minded people... Smart and successful Jews hardly ever immigrated to Israel". Rather, it would be today's United States that, according to Shamir, would be the heart of the world Jewish community. It is there that they would be the most prosperous and influential. In fact, Israel Shamir recalled, it seems that "major candidates for the US presidency in 2004 are vying to find their Jewish roots. General Wesley Clark756 said that he "comes from a long line of

[754]Israel Shamir, *Pardes: a study in Kabbalah*, Pdf, Trad. Germán Leyens, p. 18, 19, 43, 4
[755]Jacques Attali, *Il viendra*, Fayard, 1994, p. 309.
[756]General Wesley Clark, former NATO commander-in-chief in Europe, had declared during the 1999 aggression against Serbia that "there should no longer be a place in

rabbis in Minsk". Hillary Clinton's grandmother married someone named Max Rosenberg, and John Kerry found out that both his grandfathers on the paternal side were Jewish757 (Kerry was originally Kohn). The children of Howard Dean and his Jewish-born Christian wife were raised Jewish. So all the efforts of the previous generation are being undone in our time."

In Shamir's view, the US war "against Islam is not only a war for oil, it is not only a war for the state of Israel and its interests, it is also a religious war to impose faith in the "God of Yisrael" and to uproot the existing faith." In that sense, "the US tried to outlaw any mention of Allah and the Koran in Iraqi school textbooks during the military occupation. USAID employees asked experts from the Iraqi Ministry of National Education to expunge all Qur'anic verses from experimental Arabic grammar textbooks, and to replace them with neutral phrases." If a phrase like "Thank God" appears in a grammar textbook, we will raise a discussion to find another phrase to replace it," explained a US expert[758]."

In the United States, by the way, "the faith of Christ is barely tolerated. Even the Passion of Christ seems to be banned: Mel Gibson's film, condemned by Jews, is unable to find a distributor, while even the display of Nativity figures at Christmas is banned in public places." Protestant Calvinists probably have fewer problems: it can be said that they "practically recreated Judaism without Jews. They turned to the Old Testament, legitimised usury, renounced the Virgin, rejected the Church and the sacraments, caused abundant genocide and gave rise to predatory capitalism". We will see below the explanation of their role in the unwavering support for Israel.

It is therefore possible for a Jew to leave Judaism: Karl Marx, Abram Leon, Otto Weininger, Noam Chomsky, Israel Shamir, Ferdinand Lassalle, Israel Shahak, Norman Finkelstein and probably many others distanced themselves from a religion that did not seem to them to conform to their idea of the "laws of hospitality", as Edgar Morin would say. Although, certainly, for Edgar Morin and other messianists, these good precepts are only valid for corrupt and guilty nations. They preach equality among men, but still believe they are the

---

Europe for ethnically homogeneous nations."

[757]Note that Shamir does not capitalise the word "Jew". This is because he considers that this quality does not so much reflect belonging to a people, but rather an opinion and a certain mentality. One is a Jew just as one is a communist, a liberal, or a follower of the Church of Scientology; and above all: one can leave.

[758]Israel Shamir, *Pardes: a study in Kabbalah*, Pdf, Trad. Germán Leyens, p. 28, 32

chosen people; they trample on the traditions of others, but cling to their ancestral laws; they rail against the Christian religion, but live waiting for their Messiah; they encourage immigration to the West, but fight it in Israel[759]; they extol the goodness of miscegenation for the Goyim, but consider it a horror for their own family. These are the contradictions that may have given rise to doubts among many Jews about the validity of this doctrine. The identity crisis that this questioning can generate is probably painful, and we will see later in this book that this anguish can sometimes end tragically. All the more reason to welcome fraternally those who decide to embrace other human laws.

[759]They criticise the construction of a wall between the USA and Mexico but they built one 800 kilometres long and 8 metres high in Palestine and the West Bank. (NdT).

3. A difficult integration

The texts we have presented underline the profound differences that exist, despite centuries of cohabitation, between cosmopolitan intellectuals and the world around them. Observing the repeated denials and ideological contortions to defend themselves against certain accusations, some might conclude that they are acting in bad faith, without further ado. And yet, the explanations of anti-Semitism that we have read seem so sincere as to be almost touching, and one comes to wonder whether some malice is to be suspected, or whether the innocence displayed really reflects the unfathomable depth of their soul. In either case, we are faced with a real problem of incomprehension.

The conviction of their perfect innocence, their messianic faith, the certainty of being above all other nations completely inhibits any sense of guilt in many intellectuals. At this point, the room for debate has already shrunk. But the situation is further complicated by the double-speak so alien to the European tradition: depending on the circumstances, one is either "Jewish and proud to be so" or "perfectly integrated"; one militates for the destruction of the nations, and says one comes to serve them; one revels in the wonderful traditions of the Jewish people, and at the same time "cannot stand", as Bernard-Henri Levy declared, the "traditional" cultures of other peoples; one worships Yahweh, respects the rabbis, but displays wet things in garter belts on the posters in the underground; showing colossal financial might, and claiming the weakness of the eternal scapegoat; accusing Whites of being responsible for slavery, when they have been the greatest beneficiaries of it; accusing Whites of racism, and warning their community against mixed marriages; promoting Muslim immigration in France, and fighting it in Israel; against the alleged racism of Whites, siding with other oppressed minorities: Women, Blacks, colonised, homosexuals, etc. To combat the sudden anti-Semitism of the Arabs, an association is created "against anti-white racism"; pressure is exerted for the war against Iraq which threatens Israel, but it is done in the name of Western civilisation and not as a Jew; imperialism is denounced, the will of the Europeans to dominate the world, but instead it is declared that Yahweh must bring it to them on a platter[760]. They will admit that all this does not facilitate dialogue.

The television debate that took place on 4 May 2005 on the set of *Culture et dépendance* once again addressed the issue of "anti-white racism". Invited to the programme were on one side of the table: the radical Muslim Tariq Ramadan, a representative of the militant black community, Calixte Beyala, and a "White" who was presenting a violently anti-colonialist, guilt-ridden book, a certain Grandmaison. Opposite them: a "Corsican" who came to present his book denouncing that Corsica had become the region at the forefront of anti-Arab racism, and the philosopher Alain Finkielkraut, who appeared as the defender of the association against anti-white racism. He, the anti-racist, the promoter of plural society, now found himself in the position of the white racist, accused by the opposing side of playing an ambiguous and dangerous game. As he spoke of "Whites", the audience reproached him for his unbearable racism. To this he replied that if he spoke in defence of the French, they would let him know in no uncertain terms that the Blacks and Arabs were "as French as he was". Immediately afterwards, we learned that the anti-Corsican Corsican who denounced the racism of the Corsicans, a teacher of National Education, had been called a "dirty Jew" by his pupils of immigrant origin. On top of that, Grandmaison, who denounced the racism of the French and the arrogance of the white colonialists, was put in his place by the journalist Elisabeth Levy, who asked him why Africans were all candidates for emigration in a country as horrible as ours. In short, we are today, in 2005, living in a total cacophony that borders on the phrenopathic. What was clear was that, around the table, everyone declared themselves to be anti-racist. We had an anti-racist Arab, activist for the rights of Arabs and Muslims; an anti-racist and anti-colonialist Black woman, who said "we" when speaking of Blacks, but who reproached Whites for saying "we" to express themselves on behalf of Whites; and an anti-racist and anti-colonialist White man, too anti-white to be perfectly White. On the other side, the "Whites" could not allow themselves to be accused of racism because they were Jews and anti-racist militants: an anti-racist Jewish Corsican speaking on behalf of the Corsicans, and an anti-racist

---

[760] "Your gates shall always be open—they shall not be shut day or night—to let in the flow of the nations, with their kings in procession. For the nation or kingdom that will not serve thee shall perish; such nations shall be destroyed." Isaiah, LX, 11–12." They shall remember, and all the corners of the earth shall turn to Yahweh; the families of all nations shall bow down before you. For the kingdom is Yahweh's, and he rules the nations." Psalms, Tehillim, XXII, 27–28.

Jewish philosopher speaking on behalf of Whites in general, who warned against anti-white racism in order not to play the game of racism—white! As the reader will understand, the only people absent from that TV set were the indigenous, non-Jewish Whites, still in the majority in this country, but who have been deprived of all means of expression and who risk going to court if they dare to express their opinion on this situation too loudly.

Obviously, everything would be simpler if everyone agreed to speak in the name of their own community. After all, why couldn't Madame Calixte Beyala speak on behalf of the Blacks of France, as Alain Finkielkraut reproached her for doing, denouncing communitarianism in the name of the values of republican unity? Why, after all, could Tariq Ramadan not express himself in the name of the Arabs of France? And why, after all, could Alain Finkielkraut, instead of expressing himself in the name of the Whites of France, but a militant of a plural France, not express himself in the name of the Jews of France? This would make things much clearer. It would allow the white goyim of France to have their own representatives on the television sets[761].

---

[761]Perhaps the solution to such a complicated situation will come to us now in 2022 from the other side of the Atlantic, as is often the case. Indeed, the ADL, the Anti-Defamation League, formerly known as the Anti-Defamation League of B'nai B'rith (exclusively Jewish Freemasonry), an international Jewish non-governmental organisation based in the USA, has made progress in defining racism. The concept of "Systemic Racism" is the organisation's new contribution to social justice. It is defined as: "A combination of systems and factors that favour white people and that, for people of colour, cause widespread harm and disadvantage in access and opportunity. Systemic racism was not created by one person or even a group of people, but is rooted first in the history of our laws and institutions, which were created on the basis of white supremacy; second, it exists in institutions and policies that favour white people and disadvantage people of colour; and, third, it manifests itself in interpersonal communication and behaviour (e.g., name-calling, bullying, offensive language) that maintains and supports systemic inequalities and systemic racism." At https://www.adl.org/racism. (The white peoples of Europe would have created their countries for themselves to the detriment of the other populations of the world). (NdT).

An allegedly invasive presence

Communitarianism is not a French republican tradition. The inhabitants of France express themselves as French citizens, not as representatives of an ethnic community. In fact, in this country, races no longer exist, and some intellectuals who have spoken out against what they considered an over-representation of Jews in the media world have been severely reprimanded.

Thus the writer Renaud Camus made the headlines in 2000 when he published his diary *Campaign for France* in the Fayard publishing house, in which he counted the number of Jewish journalists on a *France Culture* radio programme on the subject of immigration and communitarianism: "Five participants and what proportion of non-Jews? Well, this seems to me, not exactly scandalous perhaps, but exaggerated and out of place, incorrect. And no, I am not anti-Semitic, and yes, I consider the Jewish race to have made one of the highest spiritual, intellectual and artistic contributions to humanity... But no, I do not think it is appropriate that a talk show, prepared and announced in advance, i.e. official, about integration in our country, on a public service broadcaster, should be held exclusively among Jewish journalists and intellectuals or those of Jewish origin... I think I have the right to say so. And if I don't, I say it anyway. I say it in the name of this French culture and civilisation of ancient roots which are mine, and whose achievements through the centuries are more than respectable and of which I regret to hear hardly any more in the country that they were theirs."

The publisher Fayard was forced by some unknown pressure to withdraw the book from sale, before republishing it without the incriminated passages." The words of Mr. Camus, we read in *Le Monde* of 12 February 2004, aroused indignation, although several personalities defended him, denouncing a "media lynching". But although Camus met all the criteria of respectability, being a homosexual and a leftist, this was not enough to save him. In fact, he was not the first to have suffered from the intellectual terrorism that has reigned in France since the end of the 20th century, with a whole arsenal of repressive laws. From now on, no prominent writer will dare to express his opinion on the subject on pain of being anathematicised by the media and harassed by the courts.

Once again, the reactions of the main stakeholders indicated an incredible willingness to engage in intellectual contortions. In *Winter Suns*, the well-known newspaper editor and writer Jean Daniel gave his opinion on the case, in which one could appreciate a rather subtle form of reflection, as well as the usual contempt for the backward natives. His discourse was somewhat distorted by the unspoken, for Jean Daniel was obviously indignant about Renaud Camus' ideas as a Jew, even though he presented himself as French to his readers, who were probably unaware of his community affiliation[762]. It was not in his capacity as a Jew that he opposed the madman—whom he was made out to be mentally ill—but as a journalist renowned for his objectivity and impeccable honesty. He was thus opposing communitarianism, which illegitimately claims that every ethnic community should have its representatives, in the name of individual talent and professionalism, and above all in the name of freedom from the tide of "politically correct" communitarianism. To this end, one is then an ordinary citizen, an ordinary Frenchman: may the best man win! Multicultural society is praised, as long as everyone keeps their place, i.e. the Bretons in the navy, the Corsicans in customs, the Antilleans in the small administration, and the Albanians in the mafia. But anyone who dares, no longer to criticise the number of Jews in the media, but simply to point it out, is immediately denounced as a hateful anti-Semite. In reality, Jean Daniel pretended to believe that the accusations were directed against the Jews, when the heart of the matter lay in the bias of certain Jewish intellectuals. He pretended not to understand this and cleverly evaded the issue.

Here's what Jean Daniel wrote: "This exasperation at the mainly Jewish composition of the chat show" of *France Culture*, "this distrustful, antipathetic and traditionally French mood reveals a very specific mentality. What does the expression "over-representation" mean? First of all, there are over- and under-representations, but of whom? Of the communities that make up French society? Would it be appropriate—according to parity and politically correct thinking—for each of the communities to be equally represented, if not by provinces, at least by religions? Would the Muslims and blacks who recently declared themselves misrepresented on television and radio be legitimised in this way? This may or may not be regretted. Would this extension of parity between men and women to all categories be to the

---

[762]"There are many Daniels in Brittany, Bretons whose surname is that biblical name. I often receive letters from people with the surname Daniel asking me if I am related to their family. So much so that I sometimes have the impression that I have ancestors here, for I forget that this surname was chosen by my father as a name in clear anticipation that I would adopt it." (Jean Daniel, *Soleils d'hiver*, Carnets 1998-2000, Grasset, Poche, 2000, p. 172).

detriment of merit and ability? ... It is said, it can be said, or will be said: there are too many blacks in football teams, too many West Indians in nurses, too many Catalans in rugby teams, too many Corsicans in customs teams, etc. But this obviously does not have the same meaning as pointing out that there are too many Albanians in the mafia, too many car-thieving gypsies, too many North Africans and blacks in prisons, too many Protestant managers in banking—and too many Jews in the media. Is that over-representation? And if so, where is the danger in a society so plural, so multi-confessional and so multi-ethnic? Who can still be, without suffering from the blindness of hatred, nostalgic for that pure Catholic France, in a Europe safe from the Moors and the Saracens? ... In reality, I fear that Mr Renaud Camus is a genuine anti-Semite, and, if I may say so, an anti-Semite in good company. I am sure he has excellent Jewish friends and is loyal to them. But believe me, he is thoroughly anti-Semitic. In cases like his—so peaceful—I doubt if he can be cured[763]."

The great philosopher Jacques Derrida was one of the signatories of the petition launched by Claude Lanzman[764] which described the anti-Semitic passages in Renaud Camus' book as "criminal". His book, according to the philosopher, was a "book as astonishing both for the naive blindness and sociological foolishness displayed on each page, and for the "old right-wing France" style literary tics and impulses ... We should ask ourselves what happens in our public space when a publisher and a certain number of "intellectuals" close their eyes to these phrases as frightening as they are grotesque[765]." As a great humanist, Jacques Derrida was interested in the problem of the death penalty and the American prison system: "We must remember that in the United States, despite the progress of civic rights, racism is a massive phenomenon. I am currently working on the death penalty, and there is no doubt that almost all death row inmates executed are black. Among the prisoners, the vast majority are black. And black (African-American!) poor. Is reminding or showing it, analysing this phenomenon with insistence, giving in to "political correctness[766] "? "Certainly not. Jacques Derrida, opponent of the System, is not a man

[763]Jean Daniel Bensaid, *Soleils d'hiver*, Grasset, Poche, 2000, p. 337, 323

[764]Claude Lanzmann (1925–2018) was a French film director, screenwriter, producer and journalist. His landmark work is *Shoah*, a nearly ten-hour documentary about the Holocaust.

[765]Jacques Derrida, Élisabeth Roudinesco, *Y mañana, qué...* Fondo de Cultura Económica, Buenos Aires, 2002, p. 36, 136.

[766]Jacques Derrida, Élisabeth Roudinesco, *Y mañana, qué...* Fondo de Cultura Económica, Buenos Aires, 2002, p. 38.

who yields to the pressures of "political correctness". In fact, it is in this courageous spirit of opposition and resistance that Blacks can be counted in prisons, but not Jews in the media.

The moral, judicial and financial pressures on the French intellectual and artistic world are not only exerted on publishing. Although cinema has long been the preserve of cosmopolitan thought, a single film in the stream of hundreds of others is enough to trigger, if necessary, the epidermal reaction of the System.

The first French independent distributor in the film industry, Marin Karmitz, president of MK2 Group, was at the forefront of the boycott of the film *The Passion of the Christ*. While Mel Gibson's film was unable to find a distributor in France, he said: "Some press have accused us of boycotting *The Passion* out of fear or pressure from an alleged Jewish lobby. But this is a deliberate tactic on the part of Icon, Mel Gibson's company, to make themselves look like martyrs. In the end, it took a certain Tarek Ben Ammar, a Muslim, to distribute the film in 530 cinemas in France. Karmitz would later reveal what he really thought in an interview with *The Hollywood Reporter* on 24 March 2004: "I have always fought fascism, especially through the films I distribute. For me, *The Passion* is a fascist propaganda film." On 25 March, he also declared to AFP that the film was "anti-Semitic", "unheard of violence", "revisionist". It is "a martyrology based on violence, contempt for bodies and human hatred". Finally, it considered that Mel Gibson had carried out a campaign to distribute his film "very close to those led by Jean-Marie Le Pen."

In 1989, a well-known journalist, Jean-Marie Domenach, had made the news and provoked the indignation of Elie Wiesel: "I have followed with sadness the scandal that Mr Domenach has caused. I have read his interviews in *L'Événement du jeudi* and *Le Figaro*, I have heard his pedantic sniggering on *Europe 1* and the warnings he deigns to give us Jews to be more careful to avoid anti-Semitic reactions. What is the method he proposes to us? It is very simple, almost banal: speak more softly, do not show yourself, renounce Jewish loyalty (denounce Israel, for example), do not mention the Jewishness of Jewish victims. I confess: because of its perverse implications, this kind suggestion puts some Jews off—first, because it makes the anti-Semites stop feeling guilty. How? Would anti-Semitism no longer be the fault of the anti-Semites, but of the Jews themselves? Would the hatred that Jews arouse be due only to their behaviour? They despise us, they persecute us, and should we take it out on ourselves[767]? "

[767]Elie Wiesel, *Mémoires, Tome II*, Seuil, 1996, p. 169, 171.

And again, we observe how one Jewish intellectual goes off on a tangent to invariably end up accusing the other of his own faults and reproaching him for accusing the Jews of very real faults:

"If what he says is true," Wiesel continued, "the Jews—excuse me: 'some' Jews—would be using the Holocaust to enrich themselves, and, in addition, to persecute him and other honourable people... Persecution sickness? It is incredible but true: "some" anti-Semites feel persecuted by the Jews they themselves persecute."

On that occasion, Jean Daniel had come to the rescue of his friend Elie Wiesel, taking the opportunity to express his regret: "I found it unbearable, and I said so, that you were accused of collecting "Auschwitz dividends". But I was saddened to see in your interview with Anne Sinclair your lack of knowledge of the French context. Dear Elie Wiesel, you live too much in America. You forget that the Jews of France are more radiant, more prosperous, more powerful than in Vienna at the beginning of the century or in Weimar Germany. And they also enjoy the protection of the Catholic hierarchy[768]." Interesting, isn't it?

The hateful accusations of anti-Semites about the alleged "over-staffing" of Jews were already being made in the 19th century. This proves how tenacious prejudice is. In *Le Figaro littéraire* of 18 November 2004, Patrice Bollon explained that the supposed Jewish "invasion" denounced by Edouard Drumont in his famous 1886 *best-seller, La France Judaise*, was simply grotesque, since Jews, he said, "represented 0.5% of the population! "Indeed, Drumond had to be blind or dishonest to hold such falsehoods, and also that hundreds of thousands of readers were too naive to respond to his appeal. Obviously, Drumond was "based on old prejudices", and this is surely the explanation for such blindness.

Fear of the Black

In the world of show business, the case that best illustrates the moral and intellectual dictatorship that reigns in France is that of the French-Cameroonian mulatto comedian Dieudonné[769]. When he limited himself to mud-slinging and mocking the old reactionary France and Catholicism with his compadre Elie Semoun, everything was going swimmingly. For years, Dieudonné ruthlessly criticised "the white,

---

[768]Elie Wiesel, *Mémoires, Tome II*, Seuil, 1996, p. 193.
[769]See again footnote 293.

sectarian, male and Catholic state" without anyone raising a hue and cry. This libertarian Dieudonne appeared one day suddenly on a fashionable television programme dressed as a rabbi with curls, arm raised and uttering a thunderous "Isra-Heil!", ironically exhorting the youth of the "suburbs" to enlist in "the American-Zionist Axis" in the war against Iraq. This provoked an unprecedented scandal, triggering a barrage of protests, public complaints, threats, insults, editorials, as well as governmental uproar and the repudiation of all anti-racists in the country. Dieudonné faced the great clamour of universal reprobation that we commonly call "public opinion". He became a stinker. His "colleagues" in the art world turned their backs on him and his shows were cancelled one after the other after the throwing of an incendiary bottle in Lyon. Dieudonné, firm and combative, surrendered to the evidence: "While it is relatively easy to fight against the extreme right, it is not so easy when it comes to the Jewish extreme right in France and in the world."

This is what *Le Nouvel Observateur* published on 26 February 2004 on the subject: "At the exit of the metro, an imposing Black man in an overcoat rushes towards the crowd that is crowded in front of *the Olympia*. We questioned him:—Why are you demonstrating? The young man answers without hesitation:—To fight against the invisible power that wanted to teach us a lesson. —But what is this invisible power? But who did they want to teach a lesson, the journalist insisted. —The community, the black community," he replied before turning away."

Le Point of 10 March 2005 reported that Dieudonné had been assaulted twice during his trip to Martinique. His assailants, two commercial agents, were French passport holders with two visas attesting to long stays in Israel.

While tensions between the Jewish community and the black community are a recent phenomenon in France, they have existed for decades in the United States. In *The World is My Tribe*, essayist Guy Sorman recounted racist incidents in New York. In Brooklyn, on 19 August 1991, a seven-year-old Black boy was fatally run over by a car driven by a Lubavitch Jew. Three hours later, a twenty-nine year old Australian Hasidic student, Yankel Rosenbaum, was stabbed to death by a gang of twenty Blacks. The police only intervened after four nights of rioting. The young Black man arrested for Rosenbaum's murder was acquitted by a jury of six Blacks, four Hispanics and two white Goyim. Since that event in Brooklyn, "anxiety has been simmering in Jewish neighbourhoods, constantly rekindled by new clashes. In 1995, in

Harlem, a Jewish shop was set on fire by a Black man. He was arrested and a violent demonstration of black anti-Semitism ensued ... While it is true that white Americans are anti-Semitic, concluded Guy Sorman, Blacks questioned are twice as likely as Whites to be anti-Semitic, and are more likely to utter anti-Semitic insults or commit anti-Semitic crimes[770]."

Thus, the pluralistic society, so praised by all Western authorities, may not turn out to be the paradise that was hoped for, but rather the nest of a truly anti-Semitic international.

And yet, as historian Leon Poiliakov noted, "the American Jewish community, overwhelmingly liberal, has been the most active and valuable supporter of the black community during the difficult years of struggle[771] [for civil rights]."

Indeed, Pastor Martin Luther King paid vibrant homage to them in his final speech of the great 1968 March on Washington, "*I have a dream*", for his dream went like this: "When we let the voice of freedom ring out, when we let it ring out in every village and in every town, in every state and in every city, we can hasten the day when all God's children, black man and white man, Jew and Christian, Protestant and Catholic, can join hands and sing in the words of the old Negro spiritual: "Free at last, Free at last; Thank you Almighty God! "The death of the great leader would leave a great void in the black community, partly filled by those who preached nationalism, such as the Muslims of Imam Wallace D. Muhammad. After the Six Day War in 1967, the anti-Semitism of Black Panther "Prime Minister" Stokely Carmichael, alias Kwame Ture (Kwame in homage to Nkrumah, whose secretary he was, and Ture in homage to Sekou Touré, whose friend he was), finally

---

[770]Guy Sorman, *Le Monde est ma tribu*, Fayard, 1997, p. 410. [This was not always the case: "Until the 1960s, as both were victims of white racism, American blacks and Jews fought side by side for civil rights. Their leaders were often found in the pre-war Communist Party, and among the Democrats. In the white, Anglo-Saxon, Protestant view, the Jew was long equated with the Negro, even though his ancestors had been slaves in Egypt, not Alabama." In *El Mundo es mi tribu*, Editorial Andrés Bello, Barcelona, 1998, p. 386].

[771]Léon Poliakov, *Histoire de l'antisémitisme 1945-1993*, Points Seuil, 1994. We may recall here that the young actress Jean Seberg was the wife of the great writer Romain Gary. The couple financed the black activists Black Panther Party. Jean Seberg ended up sinking into schizophrenia and committing suicide in 1979. Romain Gary, the hero of free France, the "boy from the ghetto of Wilno, the resister, the diplomat, the depressive", as *Le Nouvel Observateur* described him on 26 February 2004, would also end up committing suicide." Bayard Rustin was the organiser of Martin Luther King's march on Washington", Elie Wiesel also recalled in his *Mémoires, Tome II*, Seuil, 1996, p. 278.

exploded. The movement for *"community control"* then took hold in the black community. Each community had to control its territory, its hospitals, its schools and impose its programmes. In the universities, the black professors inevitably clashed with the Jewish professors, who were very numerous in New York. When Pastor Jesse Jackson, a future presidential candidate, declared in 1984 that New York was "the capital of the Jews", the Jews understood that he would not be a new Martin Luther King.

In the 1990s, Louis Farrakhan, leader of the "Nation of Islam" organisation, became dominant. He called for the separation of the races, advocated black nationalism supported by Muslim regimes in Africa and the Middle East. In the autumn of 1995, he managed to gather a million black men in Washington for no other reason than to assert their dignity vis-à-vis Whites. Farrakhan harangued them for four hours, without being interrupted or contradicted, reinforcing his speech with anti-Semitic slogans. On the streets of New York or Chicago, Farrakahn's disciples marketed revisionist history books denying the gas chambers, essays exposing how Jews had taken over the United States, others on the "decisive role" of many Jews in the slave trade in the 17th and 18th centuries[772]. The dispute between the two communities is currently quite strong. Black students and intellectuals are increasingly gaining access to higher education and professorships, but who is holding them back? Jewish university students, over-represented in relation to blacks; "let us no longer look for the cause of anti-Semitism among young blacks", wrote Guy Sorman. On the campuses of the best universities, they often display contemptuous and insulting behaviour towards Jews." It is not in the ghetto, but in the university that the Nation of Islam recruits its zealots". The conflict between Blacks and Jews has spread everywhere, and no longer only in New York. Even in Israel, for example, "a thousand black New York Jews settled in Galilee have been waiting for years for local rabbis to recognise their authenticity and grant them the benefit of the law of return."

One can bring up a rather unique testimony from the aforementioned book, *Jewish Portraits*. In one of the interviews, Fed Lessing, a New York businessman, made a startling statement

---

[772]The recriminations of the Negros on this issue are one of the main bone of contention between the two communities. You can read excellent articles on this subject in *Le Libre Journal* of 31 May 2001, 31 January 2004, 11 February 2004 and 28 April 2005. You can also consult the work of Bernard Lugan, the French specialist in African history. [On the slave trade, see Hervé Ryssen, *The Jewish Mafia*].

informing us about the distrust of some Jews towards the black community and, incidentally, that Jews "have the power to decide elections" in the United States: "Who knows, said Lessing, what will happen twenty or thirty years from now? It is a false belief to think that we will have the power to decide elections. But who can guarantee that the constitution will remain the same? What if a black vice-president were to be elected next time? It would be enough for the incumbent president to have an accident, so that the president would be black. And that president would have no reason to be very friendly to the Jews. It is therefore perfectly possible that my children or grandchildren would have to emigrate."

Guy Sorman noted this reflection in his book *The World is My Tribe*: "They are similar in their obsessive relationship with their origins, with the Bible, with eschatology. Similar in excess: excess of intellect in some, excess of body in others (sports, dance, drugs). Physical overflow versus psychic overflow. Two unbalanced peoples, for whom the expression *mens sana in corpore sano* will always be untranslatable[773]."

They would thus have the same predisposition to play the victim: "Strange competition this one, between Blacks and Jews, to appropriate the role of victims in history[774]! "Indeed, but it remains true that in the history of slavery, Blacks did not travel on the decks of ships. Israel Shahak reminded us of this in his *Jewish History, Jewish Religion*. This aspect of history is indeed often overlooked, and black intellectuals are probably right to want to remember it. One has to go back to 1965 to discover a Jewish historian who dealt with this painful subject. Hugh Trevor-Roper was one of the few modern historians to have pointed out "the predominant role of Jews in the early medieval slave trade between Christian (and pagan) Europe and the Muslim world[775]."

Israel Shahak added in this regard that, in the 12th century, "Maimonides allowed Jews, in the name of the Jewish religion, to kidnap gentile children to make them slaves, and there is no doubt that

---

[773]Guy Sorman, *The World is My Tribe*, Editorial Andrés Bello, Barcelona, 1998, p. 393, 394.

[774]Guy Sorman, *Waiting for the Barbarians*, Seix Barral, 1993, Barcelona, p. 100." Like many African-American leaders, Mazrui never stops talking or writing about the Jews; "It is unacceptable," he tells me, "that the Jews monopolise the concepts of diaspora and holocaust. The deportation of blacks to America, their enslavement, is also a holocaust. The Africans present on all continents are also a diaspora".

[775]Hugh Trevor-Roper, *The Rise of Christian Europe*, Thames and Hudson, London, 1965, p. 92–93, in Israel Shahak, *Historia judía, Religión judía, El peso de tres mil años*, Ediciones A. Machado, 2016, Madrid, p. 115 (note).

his opinion was acted upon or reflected the practices of the time." Let us remember that Maimonides was not only devoted to the codification of the Talmud; he was also an outstanding philosopher. His *Guide for the Perplexed* is rightly regarded as the greatest work of Jewish religious philosophy, and is still read today by many people who continue to be inspired by it despite the many insulting passages regarding Christians, Turks and Negroes, at least in the unredacted versions.

The beast must be hunted

The establishment of the pluralistic society that has been taking shape for the last fifteen years has not been without tensions between the various communities. Amidst the millions of crimes and offences committed on our territory (murders, rapes, robberies, burglaries and break-ins, swindles, etc.), the authorities finally realised that the racist phenomenon, and especially anti-Semitism, was developing in a disturbing way (graffiti on letterboxes, slapping, kicking and punching, anonymous letters, etc.). The Liberal government of the day has therefore decided to take the bull by the horns: "Devote more energy to the issue". Prime Minister Jean-Pierre R. (his surname is irrelevant) defined the objectives of the fight against racism and anti-Semitism after a meeting with his cabinet in Matignon on 9 July 2004. It is the fifth meeting on this subject since November 2003. It is clear that he does not take the problem lightly. The day after the President of the Republic's speech calling for a "reaction" by the authorities against intolerance, the Prime Minister wanted to show the determination of the public authorities to mobilise against a scourge that is seriously affecting French society. The latest figures for racist and anti-Semitic acts are worrying. The balance sheet for the first half of 2004 shows a "very sharp acceleration" in the number of acts and insults recorded. The number of anti-Semitic attacks was 135, compared to 127 in 2003, while 376 threats were recorded. Racist acts against Maghrebis and Blacks reached 95 compared to 51 in 2003; 161 threats were recorded. Of the 4.3 million crimes and offences officially recorded, this certainly seems very little (0.0003%), but in Matignon, it is considered that "we are undeniably in the presence of a worrying underlying trend[776]." In order to reinforce the actions of the State and mobilise its services more fully, Mr R. will bring together all the prefects and sub-prefects at the

---

[776]*Le Monde*, Monday 12 July 2004.

beginning of September to take stock of the actions taken to fight xenophobia and anti-Semitism. Instructions have been given to the Minister of Justice for prosecutors to demand "more exemplary" penalties against those who commit such acts." Anyone who commits a racist or anti-Semitic act must be pursued with determination and sentenced in a manner commensurate with the unacceptable nature of such acts," the government spokesman said.

Roger Cukierman, president of the Representative Council of Jewish Institutions in France (CRIF), which represents the majority of Jewish associations, is indignant about the "wave of anti-Semitic violence" (*Le Figaro*, 18 February 2004). It finally acknowledges that "the perpetrators of violence are mainly young people of Arab-Muslim immigration". It has been developing for three years in the shadow of the Israeli-Palestinian conflict, and mixes anti-Semitism and anti-Zionism. There is no intercommunal conflict, he explains, as the violence is one-sided, and "Jews have not attacked any mosque or imam in Europe. On the other hand, many synagogues have been burned down777, schools, school buses, rabbis and Jewish children have been attacked, harassed and persecuted because of their Jewishness." If we add to this that "a part of Europeans is still receptive to the theses of the racist and anti-Semitic extreme right, and that the other, left-wing-Trotskyist tendency, has embarked on a systematic anti-Zionism that brings it closer, whether it wants to or not, to anti-Semitism, we see that the ideologies that did so much damage to the 20th century, Nazism and Stalinism, have the same objectives with the Islamic fundamentalism of the 21st century: democracy and the Jews."

Obviously, Roger Cukierman was speaking in his capacity as an EU official. But later, he changed flag and became an ordinary Frenchman to declare: "Those who have chosen to live in our country must submit to our rules and customs". The fifteen French ministers present at the Crif dinner in February 2005 had to endure the same kind of lectures on Middle East policy. Now with a liaison committee with the Ministries of the Interior, Justice and National Education, the Crif leaders meet regularly with the CSA (Conseil Supérieur Audiovisuel), "which has been charged by the government with monitoring and preventing the broadcasting of anti-Semitic television programmes transmitted from the Middle East by satellite, whose signals are received by 2.5 million satellite dishes installed in France." In short, concluded Roger Cukierman, "we must punish, we must educate, we must integrate and we must fight vigorously against the advance on our

---

777The doors of a synagogue were set on fire in 2003 on the outskirts of Lyon.

territory of Islamic fundamentalism, which is trying to replace our system of values with its own." Here, we no longer know under which flag he was speaking to us.

It is also very worrying to note that, according to a survey commissioned by the European authorities, 59% of Europeans consider the State of Israel to be the greatest threat to peace in the world. They do not seem to have understood that, in the face of the Islamist danger, the Jews are the sentinels of Western values. As Jacques Chirac said on 17 November 2003: "When a Jew is attacked in France, it is the whole of France that is attacked." This is also the opinion of Bernard-Henri Levy, who declared quite naturally on the popular programme *Tout le monde en parle*, that Jews represent the "temple of the republic".

On the other side of the Atlantic, mobilisation has also been decreed against the mood swings of a country whose *"boys"* have once again been sent to a foreign war to safeguard dubious interests. In addition, President George W. Bush enacted a new law on 16 October 2004 obliging the State Department to record anti-Semitic acts around the world and to evaluate the attitude of countries in this regard, as well as towards the State of Israel." Our nation will be vigilant and vigilant, and we will make sure that the old reflexes of anti-Semitism cannot take root in any homeland in the modern world," he told a rally in Florida, home to the world's third-largest Jewish community after Israel and New York.

Media prosopopoeia

Still, while it is regrettable that anti-Semitic sentiments still exist in the world, some events have benefited from inordinate and probably over-hasty media coverage.

Thus, in January 2003, the stabbing of Rabbi Gabriel Fahri had been exaggeratedly publicised and politicised, before the case was finally buried: in fact, no attack had taken place. The medical expert's report mentioned "a doubtful wound", which had not resulted in any abdominal injury. Moreover, the 10-centimetre tearing of the clothing was "incompatible with the alleged assault". Due to the lack of witnesses, the whole case depended on the statements of the victim, who blamed a "man with a helmet", who allegedly shouted "Allah Akbar" with "a French accent". In reality, Rabbi Farhi had stabbed himself.

The arson attack on a Jewish social centre in Paris on 22 August 2004 was widely reported in the media. The culprits had left behind anti-Semitic graffiti, inverted swastikas and Islamist slogans with rude misspellings. The Mayor of Paris and the Prime Minister visited the scene of the fire to express their outrage. In the aftermath of the attack, the mayor allocated an additional 300,000 euros for the security of places frequented by the Jewish community in Paris. But the investigation eventually turned up a 52-year-old man, a member of the community, and a hard-working volunteer who enjoyed the meals served to the underprivileged." Mentally fragile", he had not been able to bear the loss of the flat rented to him by the social centre, which caused him great resentment.

We also received news of a case that broke out in 2004: swastikas had been painted on some twenty Jewish-owned shops in the New York boroughs of Brooklyn and Queens, as well as on synagogues. The outrage was widespread. One rabbi offered a $5,000 bonus in exchange for any information. On 18 October 2004, the police finally arrested the culprit. It was Olga Abramovich, 49, who explained that she wanted to take revenge on her 78-year-old husband, Jack Greenberg, who had just divorced to marry a younger woman. The press and Jewish organisations then hushed up the whole story. Fortunately, the public quickly forgets what they see on television.

Nor had any French media reported the verdict of the 17th court of the Paris correctional court sentencing Alex Moïse to a fine of 750 euros. Moïse had reported anti-Semitic threats and insults received at his home, but the investigation had established that he had sent them himself. Alex Moïse, secretary general of the Zionist Federation of France (a full member of the CRIF) and former spokesman for Likoud France, was also one of the instigators of the bans on shows by the black comedian of Cameroonian origin Dieudonné M'Bala. In the 1990s, he had been the president of the coordination committee of the Sentier, the local Jewish self-defence militia, and in 1995 he chaired a community association in favour of voting for Jacques Chirac in the presidential election.

"When the son of a rabbi in Boulogne, an elegant suburb of Paris, claims to have received anti-Semitic insults and a couple of slaps, the Minister of the Interior immediately telephoned to express "his deep dismay at these unspeakable acts and his strongest condemnation of this blatantly anti-Semitic aggression". He assured that "everything possible will be done to find the perpetrators as soon as possible". On the same day, an imam in Strasbourg noticed that someone had set fire to the rubbish bin in his garden. The minister immediately reacted and phoned to express his deep emotion, his solidarity and support at this difficult time, as well as his strongest condemnation of these despicable acts and his determination to find the perpetrators as soon as possible, specifying that he had "ordered the police to mobilise all necessary means to carry out the investigation." On the same day, again in Ivry, a passer-by died as a result of a settling of scores between two ethnic gangs. This time, Mr de Villepin did not call the victim's disabled father to tell him anything. Poor Laura (the press gave her name, but not that of her "accidental" murderer) was probably neither Jewish nor Arab: a simple Frenchwoman." We are not going to spend a chip for so little," commented Serge of Beketech[778] in his editorial of 5 June 2004. Think about it, one would spend one's life on it: four million crimes are committed in France every year. The minister obviously can't phone the four million victims. He is busy enough visiting desecrated Jewish cemeteries, defaced mosques, self-stabbed rabbis, Shiite imams attacked by Sunni worshippers and, conversely, halal or kosher butchers extorted by their respective mafias; if on top of that he has to deal with burnt churches, vandalised Christian cemeteries, raped native French women, young white-Rubian-Catholics attacked, old Gauls mistreated in their suburban homes and thousands of vehicles set on fire every year, then he would no longer have time to polish his anti-racist speeches."

There are far more shocking news items whose purpose is to create a groundswell of opinion than we imagine. Aleksandr Solzhenitsyn already recounted a similar case in *Two Hundred Years Together*: "In May 1978, the world press drew strong attention to a particularly poignant case: a little 7-year-old Moscow girl, Jessica Katz, was suffering from an incurable disease but was not allowed to travel with her parents to the United States. What a scandal! The press went crazy and Senator Edward Kennedy personally intervened. All the television networks showed the welcome at the airport, the happy tears of the little girl in her parents' arms, on their prime-time news programmes. *The Voice of America* devoted an entire programme in Russian to Jessica Katz's salvation (without thinking that other Russian families with similarly incurably ill children remained in Russia). Suddenly, after

---

[778]Serge de Beketch (1946–2007) was a French journalist, radio broadcaster, writer and "far-right" activist. Remembered and appreciated by the French nationalist sphere, he was co-founder of *Radio Courtoisie*, and, until his death, responsible for a Wednesday night programme on that station. He also founded and edited the publication *Le Libre Journal de la France courtoise*. Serge de Beketch was of Russian origin. His maternal grandfather had been a colonel in the French army. His paternal grandfather, aide-de-camp to General Denikin, head of the White Army during the Russian Civil War. His father, Youri, a non-commissioned officer in the Foreign Legion, died in the battle of Dien Bien Phu in Indochina, where he is buried. (NdT).

medical examinations, we learned that Jessica was not suffering from any illness, that her cunning parents had tricked the whole world into letting them leave Russia. The radio barely reported it, reluctantly," and the whole thing was forgotten.

In the same genre of bluffs, we had more recently the media campaign in favour of little Jila. On 25 October 2004, *Elle* magazine published an appeal by Elisabeth Badinter, daughter of Marcel Bleustein-Blanchet (the French advertising king, owner of Publicis) to save "Jila", a 13-year-old Iranian girl condemned to stoning for having had sexual relations with her brother. Numerous personalities and associations signed the appeal. After an investigation, the Ministry of Foreign Affairs and the EU Presidency reported in January 2005 that the "case" had never existed, and that no sentence of stoning had been pronounced for months by the evil Muslims. We no longer know what to do", explained several diplomats in *Le Point* of 2 December 2004. We want to move forward in a responsible and honest dialogue with Iran, but this kind of initiative discredits us." Certainly, after Iraq, Iran is now the target of Western globalists; it is simply a way of testing and preparing public opinion for a new small military crusade "in favour of democracy and human rights", all the more so as an "ultra" has just been elected to the government of that country in 2005.

There would also be much to say about the "mass graves" of Timisoara, discovered after the fall of the communist dictator Ceaucescu in Romania, or the graves left by the Serbs in Bosnia. In the *Diary of a Parisian woman*, Françoise Gourdji-Giroud wrote on 22 January: "Mass graves have been discovered in Bosnia. Seven thousand people who disappeared after the Serbs took Srebrenica are said to be piled up in a mass grave." Note the use of the conditional. The multiplication of the dead by ten, twenty or thirty often concealed the fact that they were simply cemeteries dug after the fighting.

Intellectual crime

Western viewers are already accustomed to such media operations. Whipping up public fear and anxiety is indeed an excellent way to divert the public from other problems. We know the place of ecological catastrophism and the supposed threats of planetarian destruction in the globalist device of media "sensitisation". But today, since the attacks of 11 September 2001, radical Islamism is unquestionably the terrible bogeyman, which directly threatens Zionist interests in the world. The phenomenon is described to us as a monstrous beast: a hydra with colossal financial might that has suddenly emerged and is allegedly supporting terrorist organisations with countless ramifications around the world. World public opinion could also be alerted to other organisations, such as Opus Dei in Spain, the Moon sect or the famous Church of Scientology—those dreaded Scientologists that we have heard of as "running Hollywood".

All these organisations, of course, threaten to conquer the planet, and their insidious speeches should be guarded against. But the most recent of all threats, the fastest growing and most likely to subjugate us, is the Evangelical Christian Church: a terrible sect that has gained considerable influence in the United States in recent years, and already has the US government in its grip. President George Bush himself is a member of the Evangelical Church, as everyone knows, and the fanatical Christians around him have tremendous influence over his decisions. It has been established that the war in Iraq and the invasion of that country in 2003 by US troops was wanted and planned by this fascistic far right, as a major progressive weekly was able to demonstrate. These warmongers are—despite the fact that their members are of all races—racist and anti-Semitic fascists, as *Le Nouvel Observateur* revealed on 26 February 2004 in an alarming dossier:

"The evangelical doctrine, whose favourite land is still America, is today the world's fastest growing religious movement since the Second World War, to the detriment of the Catholic Church, the historic Protestant Churches (Baptist, Methodist) and even Islam. The figures are staggering: from 4 million in 1940, evangelists now number 500 million[779], including Pentecostalism and charismatics, over 2 billion Christians." George Bush, the most powerful man in the world is not a high-level exegete, nor a madman. He is simply a faithful member of this Protestant, expansionist, millenarian and apocalyptic Church. George Bush is a *Born again Christian*, literally a born-again Christian? These neo-Protestant churches intend to conquer America before they conquer the world! No more, no less. With a man like Bush in the white house, it's a good start."

The planisphere presented in the pages of the magazine is eloquent. In red, the "strong presence": the two Americas are in bright red, as are parts of Northern Europe and Southern Africa; in yellow, the "significant presence"; in pink, the "recent presence". Only Greenland, Mongolia, Libya, Burma, Somalia, Mali and Morocco are in white. Apart from these countries, the whole earth is covered! We must react, and fast!

---

[779] 660 million in 2020.

The Pentecostal stream emphasises "union with Jesus Christ, healing through prayer, the voluntary commitment of the believer. In the middle of the 20th century, the charismatic movement was born. It takes from Pentecostalism the belief in miraculous gifts. It is characterised by vibrant prayer meetings with orchestras, weeping, trances, public exorcisms, laying on of hands, miraculous healings, a great dedication to others, a constant availability for the service of the Church." In short: fanatics." They believe in Armageddon, the coming final battle between the forces of Good and Evil. They use television, the internet, video games or science fiction novels to convert the masses. George W. Bush, like many of his ministers and advisors, share their messianic vision of the world and the future ... Columbia International University in South Carolina trains shock missionaries. Their goal? "To liquidate Islam". The Southern Baptists were "the only Church to have blessed the invasion of Iraq."

"The time has come to save this decadent society, say the evangelicals, to cleanse the country of all those homosexuals, feminists and liberals." For them, the return of the Messiah will only take place on the sine qua non condition that all Jews return to the Holy Land." Thus, they finance emigration to Zion, sponsor the colonies and defend the Greater Israel project in Washington. But that is not all: once Jesus Christ returns to the Holy Land, the Jews will be able to redeem themselves by finally recognising him as their Messiah. Otherwise, they will be annihilated forever." They don't love the Jews," indignates Israeli-American Gershom Gorenberg, author of the book *The End Times*. The evangelical doctrine of salvation is a play in five acts in which the Jews disappear in the last one." "

What should the reader of the *Nouvel Observateur* retain after reading this dossier: First, that these evangelists are clearly racists, since they have blessed the American crusade against Iraq and Muslims. Moreover, he will know that these people are terrible anti-Semites. On the other hand, he will not see that the US military is a multi-racial army, as are the philigreses of this Church, and he will overlook that these evangelists are actually the most loyal supporters of Israel and the Zionist lobby in the US. He is made to understand exactly the opposite.

After the attacks of 11 September 2001, the enemy, the absolute evil, was Islam, which threatened Israel in the Middle East. Since the invasion of Iraq, the threat now comes from the fascistic American sects that run the US government with their imperialist policy. The farce does not stop there, as evangelists, despite their unwavering support for Zionist policy, are described as fascistic fanatics. All this, evidently, is intended to make people forget that the main power influencing American governments, whether Democrat or Republican, since the end of the 19th century, is neither Catholic, Scientologist nor Evangelical. To put it bluntly: having plunged us into a new war, the Christian far-right is accused of being responsible.

Israel Shamir provided us with crucial information to understand the unwavering support of these American evangelical sects for Zionism and for those influential personalities who, around President George Bush, have been instrumental in the invasion of Iraq. To understand the phenomenon, it is essential to know a few facts, in particular that the Bible, the most widely distributed in the United States, has long since been distorted:

"Jews have not stopped amending the Bible to this day: C. E. Carlson and Steven Sizer have observed that the landmark Scofield Bible, published by Oxford University Press, invites the worship of Israel more and more explicitly with each reprint: "Thanks to advertising and promotional campaigns that know no bounds, this edition has become the best-selling "bible" in the United States, and this for more than ninety years. Scofield, with keen intelligence, chose not to change anything in the body of the text of the King James Bible. More perniciously, he added hundreds of easy-to-read footnotes to almost half the pages, and the annotations mix Old and New Testament quotations with complete abandon, as if the same people had written them at the same time. The first edition was edited and financed by Samuel Untermeyer, a New York lawyer whose firm still exists today, one of the richest and most influential Zionists in the United States. This important Zionist edition of the Old Testament goes a long way towards explaining the strange phenomenon of Christian Zionism[780]."

Indeed, Christians now have at their disposal in their Bibles rather explicit and direct footnotes: "Those who bless the Jews will be blessed, and those who curse the Jews will be cursed[781]". But in fact, "there is no such statement in the Bible", Israel Shamir recalled.

One can also find in the same edition some considerations like this: "There is a promise of blessing for those who, among the Nations, bless the descendants of Abraham. And a curse is upon those who persecute the Jews. This was a warning that was literally fulfilled in the history of

---

[780]Israel Shamir, *La otra cara de Israel*, Ediciones Ojeda, Barcelona, 2004, p. 200-201. (Shamir notes: *"Why Most Christian Evangelicals Favor War"*, C. E. Carlson, http://www.whtt.org.articles/02080.htm; http://virginiawater.org.uk/christchurh).
[781]"I will bless those who bless you, but I will curse anyone who curses you", Genesis XII:3, Messianic Israelite Kadosh Bible.

Israel's persecutions. Invariably, it has gone badly for the people who have persecuted the Jews, and very well for those who have protected them. For a nation to commit the sin of anti-Semitism brings inevitable Judgement. The future will prove the validity of this principle even more strikingly (Page 19, Scofield Bible, 1967, Genesis XII:1–3)"." This is a vast propaganda enterprise that finds an unheard-of echo among the simple-minded preachers of America," concluded Israel Shamir[782].

In the summer of 2004, an extraordinary book was selling millions of copies in the United States. The phenomenon landed in France and Europe with great fanfare. The Christian threat was real and ancient: The *Da Vinci Code*, by a certain Dan Brown, finally revealed the Vatican's unspeakable secrets about the descendants of Jesus Christ.

The central idea of the novel is that Jesus Christ, the husband of Mary Magdalene, had an offspring that has survived to the present day thanks to the effectiveness of a shadowy organisation, the Priory of Sion, whose mission is to defend the couple's sacred lineage. This fanciful thesis had already been exploited in several previously published books. Dan Brown took it up again, presenting the thesis that the Grail is a metaphor for the lineage of Christ as a truth hidden by the Catholic Church. To liven up the story a little, it was enough to add that the Templars had been created to protect the secret of the Holy Grail, and that was it. The fact that the aforementioned Dan Brown does not appear on television to explain all the implausibilities denounced by historians is of no importance. What is essential is that people believe that the Church has always lied, that the book sells well and that the magazines make their covers to fuel the controversy.

Pierre-André Taguieff, philosopher, political scientist and historian of ideas, explained the mystery in *Le Point* of 24 February 2005: "What arouses curiosity, he said, is the thesis that the truth is concealed by cynical individuals disguised behind social masks. What seduces is the spectacle of a fight to the death between organised rebels (in secret society or sect) and the visible or invisible rulers. What keeps us in suspense are the vicissitudes of this great confrontation between the defenders of the official truths (lies of the Church) and those who possess the forbidden truth, ready for anything. What is pleasing is to see the official master-liars finally unmasked and their secrets revealed. What makes us enjoy it is the "revelations"."

---

[782]See Joseph M. Canfield, *The incredible Scofield and his book*, Chalcedon/Ross House Books, 2005.

This explains the formidable success of the *Da Vinci Code*, an all-time record in the annals of publishing: 32 million copies have been sold worldwide in 42 translations.

"Dan Brown, Taguieff continued, has achieved a delicate balance: extracting from a symbolic tangle dominated by conspiracy and anti-Semitism the materials to create a "purified" intrigue. However, although the traces of the anti-Judeo-Masonic mythology have been erased by the novelist, readers sensitive to this mythology perceive it. The background comes to the surface ... What satisfies the reader ... is also the illusion of having access to the "secrets" of the story, and being able to own them."

Another intellectual bluff of the same kind was recently revealed in an article in the *Nouvel Observateur*. On 5 August 2004, the weekly published an article signed by Fabien Gruhier which provided some clarifications on the discovery of relativity and the work of Albert Einstein: "According to the physicist Jean Hladik, the brilliant inventor of the theory of relativity has blatantly plagiarised the discoveries of Henri Poincaré. Since the distant days of his student years, Jean Hladik, a university student, specialist in theoretical physics and author of several works on Relativity, saw that there was something wrong with the way Relativity was being developed. Moreover, its paternity was too unanimously attributed to the famous Albert Einstein. Four years ago, although he still titled a work of his *Relativity according to Einstein, he* was already striving to give back to Poincaré what belonged to Poincaré. Since then, Hladik has continued his research and finally decided to publish a frankly sacrilegious book entitled: *"How the young and ambitious Einstein appropriated Poincaré's Special Relativity*[783]*"*. Unlike most scholars, Jean Hladik went straight to the sources. He read the "totally ignored" publications of Henri Poincaré, a genius physicist and mathematician "much better than Einstein" and found written in black and white all the elements of "space-time" Relativity. This included the slowing down of moving clocks, the contraction of bodies in the direction of their motion and the impossibility of defining the simultaneity of two distant events absolutely. Thus, everything was there under Poincaré's signature in the texts published in 1898 and on 5 June 1905. However, on 30 June 1905, the *"Annalen der Physik"* received the manuscript of the famous founding article of Special Relativity, signed by Einstein. An article

---

[783]Jean Hladik, *Comment le jeune et ambitieux Einstein s'est approprié la Relativité restreinte de Poincaré*, Éditions Ellipses, 2004.

which, according to Hladik, contributed "nothing new" compared to Poincaré's writings, and in which the author refrained from making any reference to Poincaré's work. The question then arises: did Einstein discover everything on his own, or did Poincaré deliberately and shamelessly plagiarise?

For Jean Hladik, after a thorough investigation, doubt is no longer possible and only the second hypothesis makes sense. For not only did Einstein read French perfectly, but also, at the time of the events, he was in charge of a section in the *"Annalen der Physik"* which consisted of reporting articles published in various foreign scientific journals, including, curiously enough, the *"Comptes-rendus de l'Académie des Sciences de Paris"* where Poincaré's most comprehensive article on the subject had been published on 5 June 1905. The great Albert could not have failed to take note of it. It is known, moreover, that in those years Einstein was struggling to make ends meet. He had barely managed to get a diploma as a secondary school teacher, his doctoral thesis had been rejected three times, and he was trying to make a name for himself by "exploiting the ideas of others[784]". In this case, he pulled off a magnificent coup, and Hladik summed up the story this way: "The cat Poincaré, with his dainty paw, pulled the chestnuts out of the relativistic fire for the benefit of the monkey Einstein, who, shamelessly, ate them all, thus illustrating Jean de la Fontaine's famous fable." Afterwards, "history silenced it and it became taboo", and it took almost a century to shed some light on it. This had already been suggested by François de Closets, whom Hladik quoted in his recent biography of Eisntein[785] when he wrote: "Poincaré had all the pieces of the puzzle in his hands." This was the reason for the absolute and persistent concealment of Poincaré, to whom Einstein would pay a laconic and belated tribute in 1955, two months before his death.

The newspaper *Le Monde* (17–18 November 1996) had already discredited the famous scientist somewhat by publishing some of his personal notes. Einstein's disinterest in his family and those close to him is now well known, although the coded treatment he inflicted by letter on his first wife Mileva Maric is still surprising: "You will make sure that: 1—My bedding and sheets are always in order. 2- You will serve me three meals a day in my office … You will renounce any personal relationship with me …3—You will answer me immediately

---

[784]Apart from Poincaré, there were many other scientists before Einstein whose work was decisive: Olinto de Pretto, Hendrik Lorentz, Paul Gerber, Heinrich Hertz, James Maxwell, Hermann Minkowski, Bernhard Riemann (NdT).

[785]François de Closets, *Ne dites pas à Dieu ce qu'il doit faire*, Éditions du Seuil, 2004.

when I speak to you". As Montesquieu said, "I love humanity, that allows me to hate my neighbour."

In the book already mentioned here, *Naked Power786*, we had the opportunity to read what Einstein wrote in November 1945 in the *Atlantic Monthly* magazine: "I do not consider myself the father of atomic energy. My participation in it was rather indirect... I only believed that it was theoretically possible. It became practical through the accidental discovery of the chain reaction, and this was not something I could have predicted. It was discovered by Hahn in Berlin, and he himself misinterpreted what he discovered. It was Lise Meitner who provided the correct interpretation, and escaped from Germany to put the information in the hands of Niels Bohr[787]."

In the same book we also find his last letter, written to Queen Mother Elisabeth of Belgium on 11 March 1955. This was rather surprising in view of the recent published revelations about the accusations of plagiarism: "I must confess," he wrote, "that the exaggerated esteem in which my work is held often makes me very uncomfortable. Sometimes, I have the feeling that I am a 'con man' in spite of myself. But if I tried to do anything about it, it would probably only make things worse." The book did not elaborate on this issue. Perhaps it was some regrets about the paternity of Special Relativity that plagued him.

On 13 May 2005, television and the main newspapers unveiled another unfortunate hoax. The president of the association of Spanish deportees, Enric Marco, had just made a shocking confession788. The daily *Le Monde* gave us the details: "He never had the identification number 6448. He was never part of the Resistance in France. He never went through the German concentration camp of Flossenburg in Bavaria. For thirty years he has lied. The hoax was uncovered thanks to the suspicions of a historian who was conducting research on the occasion of the 60th anniversary of the liberation of Mathausen. Not finding Enric Marco's name on the list of prisoners, the historian immediately alerted the deportees' association, which, to avoid further scandal, decided to urgently call its president present in Austria for the ceremonies from 5 to 9 May in the company of Spanish Prime Minister José Luis Rodríguez Zapatero."

---

[786]Albert Einstein, *Le Pouvoir nu, Propos sur la guerre et la paix*, Hermann, 1991.
[787]*Atlantic Monthly, Boston, November, 1945, and November, 1947*, in *Ideas and Opinions by Albert Einstein*, Crown Publishers, Inc. New York, 1954, p. 121.
[788]https://elpais.com/diario/2005/05/11/ultima/1115762401_850215.html. *El País*, 11 May 2005: *El deportado que nunca estuvo allí* (*The deportee who was never there*).

For thirty years, Enric Marco, a resident of Barcelona, has deceived everyone. Removed from his post as president of the association of Spanish deportees, he at least had the honesty to acknowledge his lie in a press release on Tuesday 10 May 2005: "I acknowledge that I was not interned in the Flossenburg camp, although I was under preventive arrest accused of plotting against the Third Reich." Released in 1943, he returned to Spain, where, after Franco's dictatorship, at the end of the 1970s, he specialised in giving lectures in schools in Catalonia. General secretary of the CNT trade union and president of the parents' federation of Catalonia, Enric Marco was awarded the St. George's cross, Catalonia's highest civilian distinction for his fight against Francoism and Nazism. In 1978, he even signed an autobiography, *Memoria del infierno*, a moving book[789], religiously quoted in all studies on the concentration camp universe. Last January, at the age of 84, he took the floor in front of Spanish MPs to testify to the barbarity of the SS: "When we arrived in those infected cattle trains at the concentration camps, they stripped us naked, their dogs bit us, their lights blinded us," he said, weeping. Thirty years of lies and deception by a false deportee finally unmasked[790].

Another heavy blow recently struck an icon of planetarian thinking. On 28 April 2005, the newspaper *Le Point* published a very painful special dossier on the writer Marek Halter, entitled "Marek Halter, the man who lived through it all", written by the journalist Christophe Deloire.

"Marek Halter tells with talent how he took tea at the table of the greats of this world, from Golda Meir to John Paul II, from Nasser to Yeltsine, from Sharon to Putin... Marek Halter's curriculum vitae is as difficult to decipher as the cabala, for he seems to have had so many

---

[789]A progressive intellectual such as Javier Cercas tried to take the heat off the matter, contextualising his life, and even writing a book inspired by this character. In an interview with a Barcelona newspaper, the writer went so far as to say: "What Marco did, everyone did", adding, frivolously: "He is the Maradona, the Picasso of impostors. When they compare him to someone else, I get offended." (*El Periódico*, 18 November 2014). (NdT).

[790]In 2016, another false prisoner came clean about his imposture. This was Joseph Hirt, who at the age of 86 stated: "I write today to publicly apologise for the damage caused to anyone by the false descriptions of my life in Auschwitz. I was not a prisoner there nor did I intend to overshadow the events that really happened. I was wrong and I apologise."
(*La Vanguardia, Joseph Hirt and his lies about the Holocaust in Auschwitz*, 25 June 2016, https://www.lavanguardia.com/internacional/20160625/40275197869/joseph-hirt-mentiras-holocausto-auschwitz.html). (NdT).

lives. With his beard, his ancient face and his Samson's hair, this Depardieu of the biblical story has a figure worthy of playing the role of Moses in a film. In any case, it is true that "Halter has stories to tell".

"The mystery of Marek Halter goes back to his birth. He was born in Warsaw before the war. His mother, Perl, was a Yiddish poetess, his father, Solomon, a printer. Otherwise, the writer's marital status is puzzling. First, Marek's name is not Marek, but Aron, as the copy of his birth certificate shows. He has an explanation: "There was a mistake in my family's collective visa when we arrived in France, just after the war.".... Date of birth? The writer gives 27 January 1936 everywhere, on the "Who's Who" card and official documents, for example. The year is wrong. The official date of French civil status on his identity card or passport is 27 January 1932: "This is another civil status error," he says, "and I have never sought to rectify it. Sometimes it happens to make a mess of things. On page 23 of *Judaism Told to My Godchildren* (Pocket, 2001), Marek Halter wrote "I was 9 years old" in a scene logically set in 1941. That is, a date of birth corresponding to 1932... The trickery of a man eager to conceal his age? The detail is not unimportant. For it allows us to understand the early years of his life, especially the founding event of his biography: his escape from the Warsaw ghetto through the sewers. From the moment he knocked on Sartre's door, to whom he said: "I am a ghetto survivor", Halter talks about his experiences from an early age. In 1995, the Pope asked him: "So you were born in Warsaw? The writer replies, "No, Holy Father, I was born in the Warsaw ghetto". Now, the Jewish quarters of Warsaw were not walled in until November 1940. Before that, there was no ghetto."

"In Yiddish circles in Paris, Marek Halter's contradictions have long been the talk of the town", commented Christophe Deloire. In March 1980, Michel Borwicz, a ghetto historian, published an article in the daily *Unzer Wort in which he* claimed that Halter had never lived in the ghetto. After *The Memory of Abraham*, in 1983, the historian wrote another 14-page pamphlet debunking his gross inconsistencies, entitled: "The Marek Halter case, how far is it tolerable to go too far? The daughter of close friends of Marek Halter, Rachel Hertel, reveals: "Marek's parents never told of living in the ghetto, they claimed to have left right after the war broke out in 1939", like tens of thousands of Jews from Poland who fled to the Soviet Union. Halter defends himself: "I don't know why Borwicz is angry with me, by the way, I never said I was in the ghetto for a long time."

"Marek Halter's life is a novel. Reading his official biography, we see that in 1945 he was the delegate of pioneers from Uzbekistan to the Victory in Moscow festival. The director of the Jewish Institute in Warsaw, Felix Tych, does not believe it: "It is very strange that a young Jew from Poland should be the delegate of a republic of the Soviet Union, especially at that time. On that day, Marek Halter swears he handed a bouquet of flowers to the "Father of the Peoples": "Stalin took my flowers, ran his hand through my hair and said something I didn't understand because I was so shocked. Her first encounter with a great man of this world. Rachel Hertel says that Marek Halter had never spoken about it before the death of his parents."

On returning from the Soviet Union, the Halter family settled in Lodz, Poland, before leaving for France. In Paris, Halter joined the Bella Artes and was a laureate of the Deauville International Prize. According to his biography, he settled in Buenos Aires to work, where he "befriended the Argentinean president Perón"." Perón apparently had a strange sense of friendship," wrote the journalist, since Marek Halter frequented some revolutionaries and was forced to leave Argentina two years later."

"The writer often recounts this anecdote: on 6 June 1967, "I was received at the Elysée Palace by General de Gaulle". Maurice Clavel would have introduced him by specifying: "My General, I present to you this man who has seen everything, experienced everything". In fact, *Le Monde* of 7 June 1967 mentioned a "delegation", without naming Halter. He himself wrote in *The Madman and the Kings*: "In truth, only Clavel was received".

"In 1977, he embarked on a great adventure, the preparation of *The Memory of Abraham*." Novel", he writes under the title. But certain passages in italics suggest that the story is that of the author's family, a 2000-year-old lineage of scribes... Marek Halter called in a team of documentary filmmakers. The historian Patrick Girard is amused: "The family tree is completely false. The Jewish chronology doesn't go beyond the 16th or 17th century. The small team looked for cultural references to establish the plot of the story. The writing of the book is entrusted to a "ghost writer", Jean-Noël Gurgand, who works on the manuscript for two months...

"More and more official missions are entrusted to him. In 1991, he was appointed president of the French University College in Moscow. Marek Halter claims to have launched the idea of creating a French institute in Gorbatchev's office, to whom his 'friend' Sakharov is said to have taken him." Contacted by *Le Point*, Sakharov's widow Elena

Bonner, who lives in Boston, confirmed that the French writer and the Russian scientist had only met once in Moscow in 1986, after her husband's return from exile, and added that her husband had never been to Gorbatchev's office.

"In 1999, the writer interceded with Interior Minister Jean-Pierre Chevènement to ask him to lift the residence ban on an Uzbek. However, this individual turned out to be an important member of organised crime. The French services were even more perplexed when another Uzbek mafioso, turned back at the French border, shouted to them: "I am a friend of Marek Halter!

Journalist Christophe Deloire added mischievously at the end of his article: "When Marek Halter is asked awkward questions, he responds gently, placing his hand on his interlocutor's forearm."

In the 9 May 2005 issue of *Le Point*, Marek Halter published a right of reply: "The 28 April 2005 article "The man who lived through it all" hurt my relatives and me. On rereading it, it made me laugh. To discover at my age that my name is not my name, that my childhood, my work, my life are not my name either... In short, that I am not me. You have to admit that it is ridiculous. I would be grateful if you would publish this brief reply in your magazine, out of respect for my friends in France and abroad, out of respect for all those who share my fights, out of respect for my readers." It is possible that Marek Halter's laughter hides a deep pain, perhaps. Why are human beings so bad? Why can't they love each other, here and now, instead of making the memory bleed?

We can transcribe here the quite extraordinary testimony of Elie Wiesel during the first Gulf War in 1991. The great writer then travelled to Israel to support his community during the difficult times when Iraq, ravaged by US bombing raids, was launching its old Scud missiles on the Hebrew state with a vengeance:

"My cousin Eli Hollender is glad I came: "Come home, he says. Come to dinner. We'll wait for the Scuds together. Strange invitation, curious idea... I accept his invitation and we agree to meet. At the last minute I cancel. An unforeseen impediment. The same evening, we listen to the radio, each in turn, to the information about the missile attack that has just begun... A month later, I receive a letter from Eli in which he thanks God for my hindrance: "If you had come, we would have stayed at home instead of spending the night at our children's. Who knows what would have happened to us? And who knows what would have happened to us. A Scud fell on our house and destroyed it completely. It's a miracle you didn't come[791]."

Elie Wiesel is undoubtedly a survivor of the Gulf War. His adventure is all the more extraordinary when, by his own admission, "the Scuds made no casualties. The man who died in Bnei Brak? Cardiac arrest. Elsewhere, a woman locked herself in a cupboard and prayed psalms. The room collapsed, but the cupboard remained intact." It is just as they tell you: Israel is the land of miracles!

Refuge in Israel

The intellectual swindles that punctuate history are not so perceptible to the general public. Westerners are often unaware of them and remain totally ignorant about the adventure they are embarking on. Financial scams are much more tangible, as victims can directly measure the impact on their bank account balance. This chapter aims to respond to Jacques Attali's assertion, in his book *Jews, the World and Money*, that Israel refuses to take in gangsters and murderers who want to take refuge there. Commenting on the notorious American Jewish gangster Meyer Lansky, Attali wrote: "A few years later, Lansky will try to take refuge in Israel, which will deny him the benefit of the Law of Return: for his crimes, he will have lost the right to be recognised as a Jew. He will die in Miami, in his bed[792]." The statement was too blunt and out of touch with reality not to be answered in detail. Indeed, Israel has often served as a refuge for Jews convicted of crimes, embezzlement and swindling in their own countries. Of course, it must be stressed that Jews are far from constituting the bulk of the battalions of swindlers and Phoenicians who wreak havoc in all societies, and moreover, as Patrice Bollon rightly pointed out, they make up only a tiny percentage of the population.

In response to Jacques Attali, we can cite, for example, the famous case of the swindler Samuel Szyjewicz. Samuel Szyjewicz, nicknamed Flatto-Sharon, was born on 18 January 1930 in Lodz, Poland, to Josef Flatto and Esther Szyjevicz. After settling in France, he adopted the surname Flatto-Sharon to begin his career.

Flatto-Sharon carried out twenty-nine real estate transactions, whether on land to be built, real estate to be renovated or reconstructed after demolition. He resold them to shell companies set up by his

---

[791]Elie Wiesel, *Mémoires, tome II*, Éditions du Seuil, 1996, p. 148.
[792] Jacques Attali, *Los judíos, el mundo y el dinero*, Fondo de cultura económica, 2005, Buenos Aires, p. 412.

accomplices. He had also benefited from the complicity of politicians who expedited building permits. Samuel Flatto-Sharon thus pocketed a capital gain of 324 million francs (about 50 million euros). But that was not enough for him: he then invented fictitious renovation works and also got into debt to finance them. Thanks to straw men, the loans were withdrawn and immediately deposited in other financial institutions. When, in 1975, the scam was finally uncovered in France, 550 million francs had evaporated and Flatto-Sharon had taken off for a country where there are no extradition agreements with any country: Israel. There, he bought a sumptuous 1700 m2 property in Savyon, on the outskirts of Tel Aviv, and even managed to get himself elected to the Knesset—the Israeli parliament—where he sat until July 1981. An avowed patriot, he financed militias to protect synagogues in France and a group of hitmen to assassinate Chancellor Kurt Waldheim in Austria. Arrested in Italy, where he was to meet his lawyer Klarsfeld, he miraculously managed to escape without France ever requesting his extradition. For the rest of the case and Flatto-Sharon's obscure political relations with an individual who was to become president of the French Republic, see *Le Crapouillot* of March 1989.

We also remember the Elf-Bidermann case in France. From 1990 to 1994, the oil company Elf distributed some 183 million francs to the textile companies of Maurice Bidermann, "the king of clothing", under the pretext of saving "the French textile industry". In return, Bidermann paid Elf's chairman Loïc Le Floch-Prigent and his wife Fatima Belaïd in kind (trips, hotels, flats...). The scandal became a media scandal: Moses Zylberberg, alias Maurice Bidermann, was the brother of Régine Choukroun, the owner of the famous Parisian nightclub "*Chez Régine*" (the "queen of Parisian nights"). In *Le Figaro* of 2 September 1996, we read the following information: "The magistrate has great expectations about the declarations of the Parisian lawyer Claude Richard. The latter, who was aware of several real estate transactions carried out by the Elf oil company, had taken refuge in Israel, a country of which he has been a citizen since 1992". Alfred Sirven, close to Masonic circles, was the main actor in the black box scheme and blamed his former boss during the hearing. Already imprisoned since his arrest in 2001 after three years on the run, he was sentenced to another three years in 2003. The Breton Loïc Le Floch-Prigent was sentenced to five years in prison for abuse of social property. Maurice Bidermann was sentenced to three years in prison, two years on probation, and a fine of one million euros.

Obviously, we cannot list all the cases of corruption and swindling that made the news in France during the Third, Fourth and Fifth

Republics. They are too numerous and would merit an exhaustive study. However, it will suffice to mention a few from recent years to demonstrate the magnitude of the phenomenon underway.

Among them is the case involving Jean Frydman, who was indicted in 1996 for abuse of social property, forgery of documents and use of false documents. He was accused of organising a huge press campaign in 1989 accusing the cosmetics company L'Oréal of anti-Semitism and forcing it to pay inflated prices for the ownership rights to old films without copyrights that it had acquired through front companies.

Let us also remember the huge scandal of the ARC (Association for Cancer Research), which broke out in January 1996, and its president Jacques Crozemarie, whom we saw dozens of times on television in commercials. With all the authority conferred by his white coat, he looked viewers in the eye ("Donate to cancer research, join the ARC!") to convince all the modest families, touched by the appeal, to send part of their savings. All the good people who donated part of their savings were unaware that the hundreds of millions of francs siphoned off by the swindler went to finance his plane trips, company cars, his swimming pool, his state-of-the-art video and sound equipment, the renovation of his Villejuif flat, the air-conditioning of one of his mansions, the salaries of his servants and mistresses. At least 300 million francs were siphoned off, as the trial opened in May 1999 revealed.

Jacques Crozemarie, an honorary doctor of the University of Tel-Aviv and a member of the Masonic lodge of the Grand Orient of France, subcontracted his communication campaigns to the firm International Developpement, which over-invoiced its services and then paid undue salaries to the fraudster. The 1996 report of the Court of Auditors had revealed that only 26% of the donations received by the ARC actually reached the scientists. It was also revealed that his white coat was a disguise of circumstance: the head of the ARC had never been a doctor. With a degree in radio-electrical engineering, he had joined the CNRS in 1954 as a "deputy chief of service" at the age of 29. Thanks to his phenomenal impudence, he had managed to control step by step the gears of the main association that solicited the generosity of the French. *Le Nouvel Observateur* of 14 August 1996 wrote: "There is one man who might have been able to dispel the investigating judge's doubts: Ronald Lifschultz, finance director of International Developpement. At the beginning of June, the financial brigade turned up in the morning at his flat, an HLM of the Paris City Hall [social housing]. Unfortunately, the cautious tenant had flown to Israel a couple of weeks earlier". Jacques Crozemarie was sentenced in June 2000 to four years in prison, a fine of 380,000 euros and 30.5 million euros (200 million francs) in damages to be paid to the ARC. Released in October 2002, after 33 months in prison, Jacques Crozemarie declared in an interview with the daily *Le Parisien*: "I am not a thief. I never understood why I was convicted, and I never will. I don't want to be condemned for the rest of my life. It makes me indignant. I have paid for nothing! I am still waiting for the evidence against me". We will come across again later in our study this very picturesque mentality which consists of denying everything in a scabrous way, despite the most irrefutable evidence.

We also remember Didier Schuller, the great hope of the liberal right in the Hauts-de-Seine department and right-hand man of Minister Charles Pasqua. With Patrick Balkany, the mayor of Levallois had set up a network of false invoices for public housing projects. In 1995, he chose to escape and sailed between Israel, the Bahamas and Santo Domingo, where he now lives peacefully in a multimillionaire's residence, as his own son told a television programme in January 2002. His trial is currently underway in July 2005.

The former mayor of Cannes, Michel Mouillot, also had to deal with the French justice system. The daily *Libération* of 13 August 1996 explained what happened: "Mouillot ... has established privileged links with the Gaon clan [a family of Jews from Egypt who own several Noga hotels—an anagram of Gaon—around the world] and in particular with the son-in-law, Joël Herzog, son of the former president of the Republic of Israel, who is now the head of the Cannes casino. Like his friend François Léotard, the future Minister of Defence, Mouillot often travelled to Jerusalem and Tel Aviv, where he was decorated with the country's highest honours. In October 1995, after two refusals, the Cannes Riviera casino, located in the undergrowth of Noga, was granted permission to install some 100 slot machines. Suddenly, another possible accomplice appeared whom Michel Mouillot tried to approach: this was none other than Isidore Partouche, the emperor of casinos..."

The French have heard of the "Sentier case[793] ", a gigantic swindle that made headlines at the end of the 20th century in the clothing district in the heart of Paris. Eighteen months of judicial investigation, accompanied by two spectacular police raids in the Sentier district and 188 arrests, led to the discovery of an "extraordinary series of

---

[793]*Libération*, 20 February 2001, p. 17; 31 March 2001, p. 18, *Le Parisien*, 29 January 2002, p. 12.

operations carried out in a very short period of time before the banks became aware of the swindle", according to the report drawn up by the financial crime investigation brigade (Brif). The trial, which began on 20 February 2001, lasted no less than ten weeks given the scale of the legal proceedings. 124 defendants took the stand before the Paris criminal court for organised fraud. They had organised a network of *"cavalerie"* and *"carambouille"*. The former consisted of a system of issuing unfunded bills of exchange at maturity to finance non-existent transactions through banks. *Carambouille* is a slightly more primitive procedure consisting of buying goods without paying for them, selling them at a discount and disappearing at the supplier's expense at the appropriate time. *Cavalerie"*—the exchange of false bills of exchange—is considered to be one of the oldest scams in the world. It is too simple a deception to degenerate into the heist of the century, unless it is practised on a very large scale. In this case, 93 companies cheated bankers and suppliers out of 540 million francs, although if the investigation had covered the 768 companies potentially involved, the billion-franc mark would have been exceeded.

A bill of exchange is a piece of paper that stipulates that goods delivered at time T will be paid within two months. The discounting of a bill of exchange by a bank allows the seller to be paid immediately. The bank collects the money from the buyer two months later. Everyone wins: the bank receives a commission, and the seller receives the money in cash. If the buyer becomes insolvent after two months, the bank is left in the lurch; these are the risks of the trade. Incidentally, no one— or almost no one—will check whether the goods have been delivered. However, if multiple bills of exchange circulate everywhere and the buyers go bankrupt at the same time, the bank is definitely out of business. That is why it is necessary to involve a large number of banks, so that they do not notice the move. Hence the incentive to mount the vast operation called "standing the bank up". It could have been called "standing up the suppliers", since, after all, they lost more than the banks. But it would have been less popular.

The mastermind of the operation was Haïm Weizman, who used to wander around the neighbourhood dressed in Tsahal fatigues, as a reminder of his rank as a chief sergeant in the Israeli army. Weizman had already tried out the *cavalerie* in 1995 to learn the ropes. He then got down to work in earnest in the first half of 1997, launching the "stand up the bank" operation in which 2,700 bills of exchange were issued in a few weeks, a prelude to numerous bankruptcies in a chain of bankruptcies and his flight to Israel. The *cavalerie* was accompanied by extensive insurance fraud. On 25 April 1997, a clothing store burned down in Aubervilliers. The false bills of exchange underpinning the scam were used to extort 16 million from the insurance companies. By the time the banks decided to alert the public prosecutor's office in July, it was too late.

In September, investigators were in for a big surprise. Behind the "dead network", whose main protagonists were on the run, a "live network" was still in operation. On the eve of his arrest, Samy Brami was on the verge of fleeing, but investigators finally managed to arrest him in a hotel. Samy, alias Little Sam, as opposed to his partner Samson Simeoni, alias Big Sam (on the run in Israel) explained that he had taken refuge alone in the hotel to "take stock of the situation". Gilles-William Goldnapel[794], Samy Brami's lawyer, was scathing about a show trial, which, according to him, was nothing more than the fruit of a "heterogeneous assembly of small and medium-sized swindles" that did not deserve such a scandal: "I find it hard to understand how the Sentier can be defeated in the field of farce and provocation". The president of the court, Anny Dauvillaire, took things in her stride. Only one thing irritated her: the incessant exits of the accused from the courtroom to make phone calls. The investigators, for their part, recalled some rather picturesque behaviour: the impromptu fainting of a woman "whenever the questions were annoying"; the confessions consented to after "great circumvolutions"; or the network leader who no longer recognised his cousin; or the confrontation that almost ended in a fight in the courtrooms of the courthouse.

On 28 January 2002, the Paris correctional court had sentenced 88 of the 124 accused to prison terms. The harshest sentence - 7 years unconditional imprisonment—had been pronounced against Haïm Weizman. But he and twelve other defendants were still in Israel. Samy was sentenced to five years in prison with thirty months suspended.

In addition to the prison sentences, the charge of organised fraud, which had been retained, obliged the defendants to jointly and severally reimburse the banks and the suppliers. The sum to be paid was 280 million francs. This sentence to reimburse the damage was not very well received." They want us dead", lamented Samy Brami the

---

[794]Gilles-William Goldnadel is a French-Israeli lawyer with a strong presence on the French political and media scene. He is also an essayist and associative and political activist. Right-wing and conservative, he is known for his pro-Israeli political commitment and fervent defence of the state of Israel. Gilles-William Goldnadel was the founder and president of Avocats sans frontières (Lawyers without borders) in 1993.

"Weasel" after the hearing. They want to kill us with the money," he finally cried out in pain.

On 10 May 2004, the investigating chamber of the Paris court examined the Sentier II file795, which focused on the money laundering networks between France and Israel. 142 people were charged with money laundering: 138 individuals and four banks. Unlike Sentier I, traders (textile, leather, transport) and temporary employment agencies were not the only ones involved. The banks were prosecuted as legal entities (such as Société Générale, Bred and American Express), and 33 bankers (such as Daniel Bouton, chairman of Société Générale) were prosecuted as natural persons. But there were also four rabbis from the Chabad-Lubacitch movement[796] and a nebulous 140 religious associations that had used the system extensively.

Trafficking consisted in "endorsing" cheques, i.e. modifying the name of the beneficiary by a simple mention on the back with a bank stamp. Endorsement has been prohibited in France since the 1970s, as it is almost everywhere else in the world except in Israel. The cheque was given to a "moneychanger" in exchange for cash (minus commission). The moneychanger would then deposit the cheque in his Israeli bank and the latter would have the account credited by the French bank. The cash made it possible to defraud the French tax authorities or to pay salaries under the table. The Financial Investigation Brigade (Brif) had meticulously examined all the cheques of more than 20 000 francs that circulated between France and Israel, and it turned out that the traffic of cheques recycled into cash amounted to more than 1 billion francs.

It is almost certain that the banks lobbied hard throughout the investigation with the public authorities to get their way. The prosecution finally proved them right. Basically, the banks could not verify everything, given the number of cheques in circulation—several tens of thousands per day. But the investigators had well-founded suspicions when they found that a bank would agree to transfer a cheque made out to the order of the Treasury or the Urssaf[797] to a third party with a simple mention in Hebrew on the back. This was either simple negligence or, according to the prosecutor's office, a fairly widespread

---

[795]*Libération* of 10 May 2004 and 19 June 2004, article by Renaud Lecadre.

[796] "Bouton" is part of the Hebrew onomastics. On the Jabab-Lubavitch, see *Psychoanalysis of Judaism and Jewish Fanaticism.*

[797]In France, the Unions for the Collection of Social Security Contributions and Family Allowances (URSSAF) are private bodies with a public service mission that come under the "Collection" branch of the general social security system. (NdT).

practice, and the prosecutor thus took advantage of a procedural flaw to cancel the referral of the case to the correctional court, probably so that big names in the financial sector involved in the case would not be implicated.

During the same month of May 2004, another related case caused a stir in EU circles. Six French rabbis were sent to the correctional court for money laundering. These religious members of the Chabad-Lubavitch movement and more than twenty other association leaders were implicated[798]. They supplied the merchants of the Sentier with suitcases of cash. In fact, there was a nebula of Jewish confessional associations widely implicated. Rabbis and their teams of fundraisers offered donors a cash return of up to 50%. A decisive argument to seduce some black-market addicted traders. The investigating chamber that had spent two days examining the Sentier II case had to decide whether these rabbis would be tried separately or together with the hundred or so others involved in this tentacular scheme.

Two rabbis, Joseph Rotnemer and Jacques Schwarcz, were among the main defendants. The Rotnemers were an important family in the Jewish community. They were at the head of one of the most important Jewish school networks in France. Rabbi Elie Rotnemer was the founder of the *Refuge*, a body collecting 1% for social housing. The *Refuge* and its 92 civil real estate companies controlled nearly 4000 social housing units. In the early 1990s, an investigation had revealed that *Refuge* funds were not going to social housing but to investments in commercial businesses.

When Elie Rotnemer died in 1994, his son Joseph Rotnemer became the new family patriarch. He had expanded and diversified fundraising methods in favour of a nebulous 150 associations (public schools, retirement homes…), all domiciled in Seine-et-Marne and in the 19th arrondissement of Paris—the two nerve centres of the Chabad-Lubavitch Hasidic Jews: in five years (from 1997 to 2001), the Rotnemers had thus absorbed 450 million francs, some 70 million euros. Joseph Rotnemer and Rabbi Jacques Schwarcz were both on the run in Israel.

The progressive deviation of the association, originally founded on the principle of community solidarity, began in Mulhouse in 1997, with an unholy network created by Georges Tuil (also a fugitive in Israel). He was the first to propose the endorsement of cheques in Israel in exchange for cash payments. As one of his henchmen confessed: "In order to send the cheques and recover the cash, we had to find bearers".

---

[798]*Le Parisien*, 12 May 2004, p. 15, article by Renaud Lecadre.

The idea then arose to deliver the envelopes to religious people, as they were unlikely to be searched at the airport.

The chief fundraiser was perhaps exaggerating a little when he repeated to investigators: "I am risking my life and that of my family, because whoever denounces his neighbour is condemned to death by the community. I can't talk any more." It was indeed an excellent excuse to keep quiet.

On 10 May 2004, the daily *Libération* published an article by Renaud Lecadre summarising the main scams underway in the community:

Stolen cheques: postal sacks with cheques made out to the Urssaf or the Treasury were stolen from sorting centres. The "laundering of the poor man's money" consisted of smuggling the cheque, made out to M. Urssafi, Hussard or Gorssappian, for example, and then endorsing the cheque in Israel: the cheque made out to the Urssaf was handed over to a "money changer", a legal profession in that country, in exchange for cash (minus the commission). The fraudster would recover the money and the moneychanger would deposit the cheque in his Israeli bank, which would have his account credited by the French bank.

Scamming traders: a great classic. It involves luring small traders into believing that an advertisement for them will be inserted in a police magazine, or a tax yearbook, and that this will help them a lot in the event of a fine or tax adjustment. These advertising media did not exist, but cheques made out to them did. These were also cashed in Israel.

False advertising: This time the trader was an accomplice. He would sign a cheque with an advertising agency for an advertisement that would never be published. The agency would then return the amount in cash by charging a commission. The merchant, who justified the cash outflow, recovers cash net of tax; the agency recovers its position by endorsing the cheque in Israel. The manager of RPMP, the French Jewish radio agency (the radios were not involved) has confessed and revealed how the system worked.

False donations: In this case, some Jewish cultural associations were involved. The merchant was doing something both profitable and pleasant in that he was financing charitable work and getting half of it back in the black, as some rabbis agreed to split the profits 50-50. One Lubavitch official acknowledged that a distinction had to be made between "*kosher* donations[799] ", which were real donations, and "*non-*

---

[799]"Correct" or "proper" to be consumed, i.e. it complies with the precepts of the Jewish religion. The *kosher* seal is a quality seal that carries a tax for the rabbis.

kosher" donations, which were cheque transactions in exchange for cash.

Le Parisien of 22 June 2004 revealed another case in an article that could have been entitled: "How to fleece French policemen, gendarmes and firemen? "In June 2004, a search took place in Paris at a curious Israeli bank whose address did not appear in the yellow pages." Even if you walked past its representative office at 33 rue Marbeuf, you had to look carefully to see if it existed. Hapoalim Bank is one of the largest banks in Israel, but apparently prefers to be discreet. Brif police officers carried out a major search of its Paris office as part of an investigation into a fraud scheme involving several advertising agencies. About twenty accomplices were prosecuted for aggravated money laundering and organised fraud. The scam consisted of selling advertisements in specialised publications published by the police, the gendarmerie, the fire brigade and the Ministry of Finance to large companies. While the advertisements were not published, the cheques were. The loot was estimated at 55 million euros accumulated in eighteen months. To reinvest such a fortune, a large laundering network was needed, and Hapoalim bank was able to provide it. Wiretaps indicated that the mastermind of the operation, Samy Souied, was linked to a manager of the financial institution in Israel. During the search, police officers discovered blank transfer orders and account opening applications filled out despite the fact that such operations are forbidden for a representative office." An accomplice took the documents to Hapoalim banks in Luxembourg, Switzerland or Israel to open the accounts. This made it possible to leave no trace of the reinvestment of the dirty money."

Le Parisien of 4 September 2004 reported a new scam: "Huge French insurance swindle", we read in the pages of the newspaper." One of the biggest insurance scams ever uncovered in France." The basis of the scam was very simple: mechanics recruited victims of traffic accidents and set up false files based on the declaration of damages. Then, with the complicity of experts, the damages were exaggeratedly overestimated. Finally, all they had to do was to fabricate false invoices in the name of real or not real garages. All of this—false declarations of damage, false expert reports and false invoices—was sent to the insurers. The profits made by this highly organised group between 2000 and 2003 were estimated at 8 million euros, to the detriment of the main French insurance companies (AGF, Matmut, Axa, Macif, Maaf). All the profits made by the group's bosses were transferred to Israel. In total, 1,200 fraud cases had been opened and around twenty people had been charged in Paris." The most incredible thing is that this system has been able to function for four years without the insurance companies noticing," said a policeman. Several international arrest warrants had been issued, notably one for Bruce Chen Lee, a 40-year-old "French-Israeli" on the run in Israel[800]. According to investigators, the alleged mastermind of the gang, Chen-Lee owned a helicopter stationed in Greece, a twin-engine plane at an airport in the Paris region, as well as several villas in France and Israel. Before a hearing in Israel, he had denied being the instigator of the scam and presented himself as a hermit, a spiritual guide who devoted his life to writing religious books.

Contrary to what Jacques Attali wrote, Israel seems to be a real haven for criminals. Obviously, not all swindlers are Jews, and not all Jews are swindlers. But as Attali wrote: "But, among them, as always, things are not done by halves: since they are criminals, it is better to be the first[801]."

On the other hand, one should not think that criminals of Jewish origin only swindle the Goyim: an article from September 2000, published on the website *www.sefarad.org*, informed us of this lurid scam: "More than 1000 Holocaust survivors in Israel have denounced an Israeli lawyer." The information was confirmed by the Israeli Ministry of Justice. The case was mentioned in certain press such as the German weekly *Der Spiegel*, the Swiss Sunday paper *Sonntags Zeitung*, as well as in *La Tribune de Genève*. Israel Perry, based in London, allegedly abused the trust of numerous Holocaust survivors who received a retirement pension from Germany. With the help of two German financiers, the lawyer advanced a small sum of money to process the applications to the German pension fund, but kept the monthly payments intended for these elderly people. When his clients complained that their applications were not progressing, Israel Perry invoked "German ill will" and the slowness of international diplomacy. The "German pension scam" was a huge scandal in Israel. In twenty years, the intermediary had processed thousands of files and siphoned off 320 million marks (nearly 150 million euros!) deposited in three banks in Zurich. The Israeli Ministry of Justice had, however, managed to enforce mutual assistance agreements with the Swiss justice system to block these deposits.

---

[800]Surnames are sometimes misleading. Here, "Chen" is obviously missing a letter: perhaps an "O"?
[801] Jacques Attali, *Los judíos, el mundo y el dinero*, Fondo de cultura económica, 2005, Buenos Aires, p. 410.

These scams are by no means an exhaustive list. A thorough investigation would undoubtedly uncover many more over the last few decades, as the media are rather discreet about them, especially when it comes to cases abroad. One of the world's biggest scams, for example, was recently uncovered without anyone hearing about it in France.

It is about the gigantic swindle carried out by Rabbi Sholam Weiss, a Hasidic Jew born in 1954, who left an American life insurance giant, the National Heritage Life Insurance Company, on the verge of bankruptcy. We are talking about a sum of 450 million dollars. Weiss had already been sentenced to eight months unconditional imprisonment for having swindled an insurance company with a fake fire that had allegedly destroyed a million dollars worth of bathtubs belonging to his sanitary and household equipment company. But since the rabbi was a good husband, an attentive, sick and deeply religious family man, the judge had agreed to let him celebrate Passover with his family. Just out of prison, the rabbi flew by private plane to a casino hotel in Atlantic City to spend no less than seventy thousand dollars in four days.

Then he met Michael D. Blutrich, the owner of a mob-protected nightclub on 60th Street in Manhattan. Weiss became a regular customer and discovered that the head of the bar was also one of the lawyers for the National Heritage Life Insurance Company: that's how things started. Weiss claimed to have learned the art of the con at the Talmud School in Boro Park, New York, and explained that his undoing was due to the failure of his marriage. At the age of thirty, he had to get *a get* (Talmudic divorce) by agreeing to pay his wife a *ketuva* of one hundred thousand dollars for each Bar Mitzvah[802] and wedding of their five children.

But his lawyer Joel Hirschorn did not seem to have been very sensitive to his plight. Every time his client was mentioned in front of him, he would throw out a tirade: "Don't talk to me about that nauseating guy! "He was indignant before recalling Weiss's rantings, "telling off" his accomplices on the phone in the courthouse foyer and even inside the courtroom, behaving obnoxiously in front of the court. In fact, he explained that he "had to continually remind the court that his client was not being judged for his arrogance and rudeness, but for his swindling". Contrary to the opinion of all court observers, Weiss had obtained the right to remain at liberty by paying a ridiculous bail of five hundred thousand dollars, i.e. one thousandth of the enormous 450 million dollar haul. Everyone knew Weiss would be on the run. The

---

[802]The Bar-mitzvah is the Jewish rite of passage to adulthood at the age of 13.

American journalist Mickael A. Hoffman wondered why the federal government had not foreseen the escape that everyone expected. Indeed, Weiss disappeared, making a mockery of the sentence inflicted in contumacy on 15 February 2000: life imprisonment, more than 845 years in prison, a fine of 123 million dollars and an order to pay back 125 million dollars to the insurance company. But in Israel, Rabbi Weiss was free to enjoy the savings of the 25,000 Americans, mostly retirees who had invested their pensions in that insurance company.

On 31 January 2001, the newspaper *Le Monde* finally took up the Marc Rich case. Born in Antwerp in 1934 and arriving in New York in 1941 with his Jewish parents fleeing Nazism, Marc Rich was, together with his partner Pincus Green—pardoned like him—one of the traders who transformed the world oil market through *spot trading* and later with another, totally illegal technique called *daisy-chaining*, thanks to which, after the 1973 crisis, he resold very expensive oil bought very cheaply. During their investigations, the US federal agents discovered that the Rich group, based in Switzerland, had not only carried out fraudulent transactions with the US Department of Energy and, not content with having defrauded the federal government of 48 million dollars in taxes, had also violated the oil embargo imposed on Iran by President Carter during the hostage crisis.

Indicted in 1983 on 65 charges while in Switzerland, Rich never set foot in the US again. He obtained Spanish and then Israeli citizenship. According to the US press, Israeli Prime Minister Ehud Barak called US President Bill Clinton directly to plead the billionaire's cause. Marc Rich was finally pardoned in February 2001. The influence of allegedly generous donations from Marc Rich's former wife to the Clinton couple and the Democratic Party" is often mentioned in this connection. *Point d'Information Palestine* no. 217 of April 1, 2003, published an article by Israel Shamir from December 2002 that gave more details: Abel Foxman, an American Jew, the celebrated head of the ADL, the Anti-Defamation League, had been caught red-handed "receiving a huge amount of money from the hands of super-scammer Marc Rich. Foxman's best friend was one Ariel Sharon, the butcher of Sabra, Chatila, Qibya and Jenin", and Prime Minister of the Hebrew state.

Americans will probably not remember the case of Martin Frankel, who had extorted more than 200 million dollars from insurance companies in more than five states and fled the United States in 1999; nor the case of the "New Square Four", those four Orthodox Jews from New Square City, just outside New York, who had founded a fictitious yeshiva (Jewish university) in order to collect more than 40 million dollars in loans from the state. A few hours before leaving office, President Bill Clinton had commuted the sentences of the four criminals, Chaim Berger, Kalmen Stern, David Goldstein and Jacob Elbaum. The court simply sentenced them to repay the $40 million ... which was more than enough reason to put their feet up.

In the famous Enron scandal, Israeli journalist Israel Shamir recalled that "the head of Enron's finances was Andrew Fastow, described by the rabbi of his synagogue as "a mensch, a very committed member of the community. He is active in supporting Jewish causes, he is a devoted supporter of Israel" while his wife Lea Weingarten, who "comes from a prominent and highly respected philanthropic family", never missed a lesson at the synagogue".

But "Kenneth Lay, the goy at the height of the Enron scandal, was also devoted to the Jewish cause. He and his equally goy wife Linda donated $850,000 at a fundraiser last year for the Holocaust Museum in Houston, Texas, according to the *Jerusalem Report*."

As eternal victims, concluded Israel Shamir in his book *Pardes: A Study in Kabbalah*, some Jews "feel the need to correct "injustice" by some extra-legal action. Israelis explain their theft of Jordanian land in the Arava Valley by their desire to correct nature's "injustice": for geological reasons, the best alluvial soils accumulate on the east Jordanian Arava bank. The theft of Palestinian land was explained (by Rabbi Lerner, among others) by the need to correct the "injustice" of the Roman occupation of Palestine 2000 years ago. The establishment of the Jewish state is explained by the "injustice" of the Arabs having 22 states, while the Jews had none. The daily robbery of Swiss banks corrected the "injustice" of Nazi confiscations, although the banks never had Jewish deposits. In a way, Holocaust museums are an important factor in the growth of Jewish criminality, because they reinforce the feeling of Jewish victimhood[803]."

Israel Shamir's words were perfectly confirmed by those of Jacques Attali describing the departure of the Jewish people from Egypt. They left covered in gold: "Four texts corroborate this. First, the prediction made long ago to Abraham to let them leave rich: "You shall go out of that country with great riches" (*Genesis 15, 13–14*); then, the order given to Moses before the burning bush: "Each woman shall ask her neighbour and her host for vessels of gold and silver; garments with which you shall cover your children, and you shall despoil Egypt" (*Exodus 3:21-22*); then, the order conveyed by Moses to the heads of

---

[803]Israel Shamir, *Pardes: a study in Kabbalah*, Pdf, Trad. Germán Leyens, p. 10-11

the tribes just before the departure: "Let each one ask for gold and silver" (*Exodus 11:1-2–3*); finally, the brutal summary of the situation, a little further on: "They asked and they despoiled" (*Exodus 12:35-36*)." Checking ourselves in the original text, without going through Attali, we read the details of the story in the Old Testament: "The sons of Yisra'el had done as Moshe had said-they had asked the Mitzrayimimim [Egyptians] to give them jewels of gold and silver; and Yahweh had turned the Mitzrayimim so favourably disposed towards the sons of Yisra'el that they gave them what they had asked for. Thus they plundered the Mitzrayim (*Exodus XII, 35–36* Messianic Israelite Kadosh Bible)."

In short, the Israelites had abused the trust of the Egyptians. And "to those who are surprised to see the slaves run away rich, commentators will reply, down the centuries, that these riches are due to them by way of compensation for the labour provided free of charge during the years of slavery, or as a parting gift, or even as tribute paid to the victors by a defeated army[804]."

"According to tradition, this departure takes place in -1212. The Egyptian texts of the time also mention the expulsion of a sick people, or of a people with a leprous king, and an uprising of foreign slaves … Tens of thousands of women, men and children then set out, some rich in gold, silver and all kinds of goods, even with slaves" in the direction of Canaan through the Sinai desert. The Hebrews were then going to make their Golden Calf, for "in taking gold from the Egyptians, the Hebrews actually took with which to make a Golden Calf". As for the Egyptian soldiers who pursued them and ended up, it seems, submerged in the waters of the Red Sea, perhaps they were simply trying to recover what belonged to them.

If it's good enough for me, it's good enough for you.

The pursuit of profit and the love of money undoubtedly represent other commonly accepted characteristic traits that even the Jewish humorists themselves often caricature. It is true that Jews, who do not believe in an afterlife, are more likely to enjoy their earthly sojourn than people whose religion promises metaphysical consolations in an eternal paradise. These religious roots can provide important elements of explanation, as Jacques Attali put it in *The Jews, the World and Money*:

---

[804]Jacques Attali, *Los judíos, el mundo y el dinero*, Fondo de cultura económica, 2005, Buenos Aires, p. 28, 29.

"Isaac and Jacob confirm the need to enrich themselves in order to please God. Isaac accumulates animals." He got richer and richer until he became extremely wealthy. He had large flocks of sheep, large herds of cattle and many slaves" (Genesis 26:13-14). Then Jacob "became very rich, and had many flocks, and maidservants, and menservants, and camels, and asses" (Genesis 30:43). God blesses his fortune and allows him to buy his right of entailed estate from his brother Esau, proof that everything is monetised, even for a plate of lentils..."

Attali also gave us another amusing and revealing detail: "Unlike their neighbours, the Hebrews bury their dead outside the cities, in tombs. They were undoubtedly among the first to forbid objects or living beings to be placed in them: fortune must not disappear with death, the supreme degree of impurity805." And by the way, they also saved a little money, it must be said.

Money was so important to the Hebrews that they did not hesitate to deposit it in the most sacred place: "The Temple, the best guarded place in the country, thus became a fortified chamber which was also used by the State and the great private fortunes to safeguard their wealth. It quickly became the country's main attraction, the meeting place for all the Hebrews from neighbouring empires. Its atrium even became the place of work for precious metal weighers, then moneylenders, who worked either with private individuals or with employers, especially rural landowners, who borrowed money before the harvest to pay the wages of their sharecroppers. A real *avant l'heure* bank...

During the Roman occupation, tribute had to be paid to the foreign occupier as well as taxes commensurate with wealth, much to the dismay of the inhabitants of Judea. When Titus' successor, Domitian decided to increase "the *fiscus judaicus* and to apply it to any man born a Jew ... Many go into hiding in order not to pay the tax[806]."

The Jews of the Diaspora amassed great fortunes. In the 10th century, in the Middle East, "their situation is so prosperous that some pamphlets accuse the Fatimid dynasty of having Jewish origins ... Then Baghdad declines; the economic power of the caliphs is lost in the desert sands. The Jewish elites then left for Egypt and Spain", where we suppose they could find other ... means of enriching themselves, before leaving again, victims of a cruel fate." Already in the 10th

---

[805]Jacques Attali, *Los judíos, el mundo y el dinero*, Fondo de cultura económica, 2005, Buenos Aires, p. 23, 39.
[806]Jacques Attali, *Los judíos, el mundo y el dinero*, Fondo de cultura económica, 2005, Buenos Aires, p. 44, 85.

century, in Baghdad, entire communities had been persecuted because some of their number had agreed to act as bankers... The *ravim discussed* this matter at length; they exchanged letters. And they always come back to the same question: why risk being exterminated by angry debtors[807]? "Very humbly, we think we can suggest to Jacques Attali the following explanation: "Maybe because you can make a lot of money that way". But the question remains open.

In any case, it is true that, far from ruining populations as one might think, the presence of Jews is, on the contrary, indispensable for the economy. A country that expels its Jews falls into the mire. This was the case of the Kingdom of Spain, which "with the discovery of America and its gold, believed that its hour of glory had arrived." But with the expulsion of the Jews in 1492, Attali wrote, Spain was "deprived of a large part of its cultural, commercial and administrative elite, [and] knows only a vitality without a future, beyond the Golden Age. The history of Spain, more than any other, shows the extent to which Jewish communities are useful for the development of a country[808]." After 1492, Spain did indeed experience the great Spanish Golden Age, although Jacques Attali presented the matter in what was probably a somewhat misleading way.

Interest-bearing loans are the exclusive and unique basis of all great banking fortunes: "It is not uncommon for a banker to borrow at 3% in Holland to lend at 7% in England[809]"." Among the Hebrews, solidarity is organised by barter and interest-free loans[810]." On the other hand, for the Goyim, lending at interest is lawful. Among Christians, contrary to what Attali wrote, the Church did not forbid lending money, but lending money *with interest*. Paradoxically, the Church did not forbid the faithful to borrow. The Jews were then going to play the role of moneylenders, and thus contribute to the considerable enrichment of all the populations of Central Europe, Morocco, Algeria, as well as the Alsatian peasants who still remember them with tears in their eyes. For the Jews undeniably have a great capacity to generate wealth, and their natural and proverbial generosity benefits the entire population, as Jacques Attali insistently repeated: "The Jewish people cannot be happy

---

[807] Jacques Attali, *Los judíos, el mundo y el dinero*, Fondo de cultura económica, 2005, Buenos Aires, p. 137, 169.

[808] Jacques Attali, *Los judíos, el mundo y el dinero*, Fondo de cultura económica, 2005, Buenos Aires, p. 219.

[809] Jacques Attali, *Los judíos, el mundo y el dinero*, Fondo de cultura económica, 2005, Buenos Aires, p. 262.

[810] Jacques Attali, *Los judíos, el mundo y el dinero*, Fondo de cultura económica, 2005, Buenos Aires, p. 26.

if the others are not happy. As a chosen people, their wealth only makes sense if it contributes to the wealth of others. Nothing is good for the Hebrews if it is not good for others, and all wealth must be shared with the rest of the world." (page 44)." Always the old idea: nothing is good for the Jews if it is not also good for others." (page 177).

The problem is that, unfortunately, Jews do not tend to stay in the same place for long. From the 11th century onwards, "merchants and craftsmen, unable to buy real estate, worried about what to do in a hurry in case of threat, accumulate some liquidity in coins, gold and precious stones, which they can lend while continuing to exercise their other trade, if they have the right to do so. On the other hand, interest rates are such (sometimes even exceeding 60% per annum, by virtue of demand and risks) that their liquidity increases rapidly[811]." A phenomenon that Albert London had understood and wisely summarised: "So this people must not squander their money, but keep it in order to flee. Money is the passport of the Jew[812]."

Indeed, despite all the services rendered, Jews continue to face the most terrible accusations. Proof of this was the book by Eustace Mullins, quoted by Attali, recently published in the United States, *The Federal Reserve Conspiracy*[813], which took up the usual old prejudices: "The American people are burdened with hundreds of billions of dollars of debt simply because we let a handful of enemy aliens take control of our monetary system. The three most important are: Paul Warburg, the German Jew who drafted the Federal Reserve Act; Emmanuel Goldenweiser, the Russian Jew who controlled the detail of the Federal Reserve Board's operations for thirty years; and Harry Dexter White, the son of Lithuanian Jews, who created the International Monetary Fund[814]." Once again, we must surrender to the evidence that Jews are "always hated for the services they render."

However, the wealth of the Jews should not be exaggerated, Jacques Attali noted: "Amsterdam has become the temple of speculation, the place where financial "bubbles" are formed. As the community builds a magnificent synagogue, the city comes to

---

[811]Jacques Attali, *Los judíos, el mundo y el dinero*, Fondo de cultura económica, 2005, Buenos Aires, p. 168.
[812]Albert Londres, *The Wandering Jew Has Arrived*, Editorial Melusina, 2012, p. 196.
[813]Eustace Mullins, *The Secrets of the Federal Reserve: The London Connection*, Omnia Veritas Ltd, 2017. (NdT).
[814]Jacques Attali, *Los judíos, el mundo y el dinero*, Fondo de cultura económica, 2005, Buenos Aires, p. 481, 488.

exaggerate the wealth of the Jews ... In fact, the fortune of the Jews is more apparent than real[815]."

In the same way that one should not believe that the Rothschilds were the richest, not by any stretch of the imagination, for it would be a mistake to do so, as such lies feed anti-Semitic propaganda: "The Rothschilds are not comparable to the hundredth British fortune, and Fred Krupp remains, beyond dispute, the richest German of his time ... in France, no Jew has a fortune anywhere near that of the Mornys or the Hottinger. They constitute a cultural rather than a material elite[816]." Jews are weak and vulnerable, it is well known. Jewish banking" is a myth of anti-Semitic and reactionary propaganda to deceive the masses and to throw them against the eternal scapegoats.

The happiness mafia

However, the best way to build large fortunes quickly is still to operate legally and act in the open. But this requires certain favourable circumstances. Wars, revolutions and major changes are very opportune for the most reactive individuals, the most familiar with money management and the most unscrupulous.

One example in a thousand: we know that the Rothschild fortune was built on the defeat of Napoleon's armies at the Battle of Waterloo in 1815. Informed of the outcome of the battle before everyone else, Rothschild appeared at the London Stock Exchange with a dejected air that suggested Napoleon had won. This allowed him to take all the securities that had been hastily sold at a very low price. This famous episode had inspired a few verses by Victor Hugo, who thus watched the financier pass before him in his *Contemplations*:

"Old man, I take off my hat! This one who passes/ Made his fortune, in the hour when you were shedding your blood/ He was betting low, and rising as he went/ That our fall was deeper and surer/ There had to be a vulture for our dead, he was[817]."

---

[815]Jacques Attali, *Los judíos, el mundo y el dinero*, Fondo de cultura económica, 2005, Buenos Aires, p. 262-263.

[816]Jacques Attali, *Los judíos, el mundo y el dinero*, Fondo de cultura económica, 2005, Buenos Aires, p. 324.

[817]Victor Hugo recalled that Jews used to be the body snatchers on battlefields. At Austerlitz, on the night of 2 December 1805, Talleyrand took a sinister walk with Marshal Lannes: The Marshal "was so excited, that at a moment when he was showing me the different points from which the main attacks had been made, he said to me: "I can bear it no longer! Unless you want to come with me to uncrystallise all those

The chaos that followed the collapse of communism in Russia represented a formidable hunting ground for predators. Russia then became the prey of a few cosmopolitan businessmen who bought up all the former collectivised enterprises and factories for ridiculously low prices. Some individuals amassed colossal fortunes during the privatisations of the 1990s, while the vast majority of the population fell into abject poverty and destitution. Today, Russia seems to be the target of some Western warmongers and financial circles once again, since its president Vladimir Putin decided to put an end to chaos and corruption.

In 2003, Vladimir Putin's 'campaign against the oligarchs' led to the arrest of Mikhail Khodorkovsky. According to *Forbes magazine*, Khodorkovsky, at the age of 41, had become the richest man in Russia. He was the largest acquirer of collectivised companies that the Russian state had sold off after the collapse of the communist regime. Russia's famous oligarchs were those men who took all the spoils of the state amid the chaos of the 1990s, and who tended to ignore the rules of the rule of law and behave like foxes in the henhouse. Putin tackled this situation head-on in 2003 with this campaign against the oligarchs, which was further intensified when the Russian prosecutor's office announced the opening of five investigations against Khodorkovsky for murder and attempted murder involving his company Yukos. But before his arrest, the billionaire had sought to hand over the management of his bank to his British co-religionist Jacob Rothschild. Market prices continued to plunge, while the *New York Times* described the Russian government's takeover of Yukos as "the biggest spoliation of Jewish interests since the 1930s." Instead, this policy brought joy to the Russian people who listened with satisfaction as Vladimir Putin denounced those whose "hysterical behaviour" was damaging the country. The Russian president supported the prosecutor's enquiries against the plutocrat, but reassured the other oligarchs who were content to conduct their business within the framework of the law. In Russia, the president hammered, no one can impose himself above the law with billions; all must be equal before the courts to fight crime and corruption.

---

miserable Jews who strip the dead and dying". (in Jean Orieux, *Talleyrand*, Flammarion, 1970, p. 437). The newspaper *L'Illustration* of 27 September 1873 wrote that the soldiers were in the habit of calling the Jews the "crows", a nickname that would later be given to the Jesuits.

Le Figaro of 17 May 2005 reported on the financier's trial. For journalist Laura "Mandeville", the Yukos case obviously "tarnished" Moscow's image, and Mikhail was a poor victim of fascism. Even so, we learned that his fortune was in the region of 15 billion dollars. An army of twenty lawyers was going to work to defend him, while several of his associates had fled: "Three of them live in Israel, a country from which they will not cease to accuse the Russian justice system of being in the pay of power." As usual, Khodorkovsky declared his innocence: "The case was fabricated out of thin air". And he named the culprits: "A criminal bureaucracy." The billionaire, who headed the oil company Yukos, was accused of tax evasion: his company had a colossal tax debt of nearly 27 billion dollars.

In the newspaper's editorial, we could read a few lines full of common sense about the oligarchs: "The fact that these men, who started from scratch, have been able to appropriate whole chunks of Russia's natural resources for a plate of lentils has not made them particularly popular in their own country."

Reading the reports of the journalist Albert Londres, one realises that the reluctance to pay taxes was not entirely new. In his 1929 book *The Wandering Jew Has Already Arrived*, the author gave an astonishing account of an operation by Polish tax officials in a Jewish quarter of Warsaw: "Fourth floor. Seven people in a large room, among them three boys. Mother and daughter crying. Two Jews in kaftans, leaning indolently on chairs. The three boys, reading the Talmud, have not even noticed our arrival. The receipt is for one hundred and seventeen zlotys. These are taxes that have been due for four years. The official begs the women to empty the furniture drawers. The women have offered forty zlotys on the table. They empty the drawers with groans. The two kaftans want nothing to do with the scene. They look at each other's hands as they make them dance before their eyes. The women sob. The three boys are swaying, totally taken by the Hebrew. The women remove the attachments from the tables. The kaftans remain clueless and the boys get more and more excited about the holy book. The official orders the cupboards to be opened. The women kneel down. And as they sob noisily, the three boys raise the pitch of their study. The coachman, who has found helpers, lowers the sideboard first. The women scream in terror. The two caftans do not even flinch. The three boys read louder and louder. Then they take away the cupboard, the table, an armchair, move the ritual candelabrum, which cannot be seized, and take away the piece of furniture that supports it. Now the room is empty. Then one of the two kaftans stands up; he realises that the official is serious. With a noble gesture, he takes two hundred zlotys from his pocket and says: "Here you are! The furniture goes back upstairs. The women cried for nothing. The three boys have continued studying. The father picks up the seven-branched candlestick and piously places it on the restored piece of furniture[818]! "

Among Russia's biggest fortunes on the *Forbes magazine* list, Roman Abramovitch appears just behind Khodorkovsky. Abramovitch owns 80% of Sibneft, Russia's fifth largest oil company, 50% of Rusal, which has a monopoly on Russian aluminium, and a quarter of Aeroflot. He is famous in Europe for buying the London football club Chelsea. He has also been implicated in numerous fraud cases. In 1995, he met Boris Berezovsky, who had fled to Britain to escape an investigation for tax fraud. From his London exile, he continued to finance the opposition to Vladimir Putin, although he had to hand over most of his fortune to Abramovitch. Next on the list of new Russian billionaires is Victor Vekselberg, who took control of the laptop market. His fortune enabled him to take over the fabulous Fabergé jewellery collection assembled by the American Forbes. He maintains business relations with the fifth on the list, Mikhail Fridman, who with Alfa, Russia's largest private bank, controls the country's telecommunications. Oleg Deripaska is the youngest of the oligarchs. At 35, he is the aluminium tycoon, although he has also built his empire on gas, the automobile industry and Aeroflot. He was also one of the clan of the alcoholic former president Boris Yeltsine, just after the fall of the communist regime. He is the subject of a legal complaint for fraudulent purchase of several of his companies under threat. The seventh on the list is Vladimir Gusinsky, who, after enriching himself in finance and the media, preferred to go into exile in Israel in July 2000 to avoid prison after being rounded up for tax fraud by President Putin's economic police.

Next come Mikhail Prokhorov, with a fortune estimated at $5.4 billion (metallurgy, engineering, agriculture, media), and Vladimir Potanin, head of the metallurgical giant Norilsk Nickel, and partner of the financial predator George Soros. Nine of the country's ten largest fortunes are in the hands of former Soviet citizens of Israeli confession who were able to take advantage of the change of institutions. This situation did not seem to please the Russian people: "Nine Russians out of ten think that the current fortunes have been ill-gotten and more than fifty percent approve of the legal proceedings", wrote Helena Despic-Popovic in the daily *Libération* on 19 July 2003. The journalist added:

---

[818]Albert Londres, *The Wandering Jew Has Arrived*, Editorial Melusina, 2012, p. 177–178.

"The campaign is willingly accepted by a society still contaminated by traces of anti-Semitism, as a good part of the oligarchs are Jewish."

As Mikhail Khodorkovsky would say in his book, Russia was "a hunting ground open to all" before Vladimir Putin came to power. A little more research on the internet revealed that before he was imprisoned as a common chicken thief, the billionaire Khodorkovsky was also a friend of Richard Perle, one of the neo-conservative Zionist "hawks" in the White House, and a fervent supporter of the 2003 invasion of Iraq.

The nouveau riche Russians also made headlines in France, where they bought the most beautiful villas on the Côte d'Azur, magnificent yachts, and organised grandiose parties, spending hundreds of thousands of euros transported in vulgar plastic bags stuffed with banknotes. Boris Berezovski, Arcadi Gaydamak (now a refugee in Israel), Boris Birshstein, Sergei Rubinstein, Alexandros Kazarian, Alexander Sabadsh, Gueorgui Jatsenkov, are the new "*nababs* from the cold", as the newspaper *L'Express* noted on 2 May 2002. Some of them were obviously involved in organised crime, drugs and prostitution networks.

Undoubtedly, the collapse of the Soviet empire had unleashed certain energies hitherto repressed by communist institutions. The famous Russian mafia, which has been much talked about since 1991, is also the manifestation of the release of forces that have been contained for too long, and which closely resemble the American mafia between the wars. In his book *Red Mafiya: How the Russian Mob has invaded America*[819], the American journalist Robert Friedman was categorical: In the early 1990s, there were already about 5,000 Jewish gangsters from the Soviet Union operating in New York City. That was more than all the members of Italian families in the entire country. That number stopped increasing after the second Intifada (2000). These "Russians" are in fact Jews who had transferred their criminal activities in Israel before seeking new horizons, when the Palestinian rebellion caused the near disappearance of tourism and a serious economic recession.

"Because this Russian underworld is *mostly Jewish*, stamping it out is eminently political, especially in the New York region," wrote Friedman, who stressed that "respectable" Jewish associations, such as the Anti-Defamation League of B'nai B'rith, the most important American anti-racist league, lobbied the police pursuing these gangs not

---

[819]Robert Friedman, *La Mafia rouge: comment la pègre russe a envahi l'Amérique. Robert Friedman, Red Mafiya, Ed. Little, Brown and Co., 2000.*

to mention publicly "any origin which might lead the Christian public to protest against the steady stream of Jewish criminals presenting themselves as refugees." Senior police officers had confessed to the journalist: "The Russians are ruthless and crazy. It's a lousy combination. They shoot for any reason." One of the godfathers of those years, Monya Elson had started his career "liquidating Ukrainians from his hometown of Chisinau, then in Moscow, where he liquidated Russians, and finally in the United States, where he liquidated Americans—maybe close to a hundred murders." Another notorious kingpin was Ludwig Fainberg, alias Tarzan, who came from Kiev (where he claimed that "the Jews were the richest in the city. They had cars, money, lived in beautiful flats and paid to have the most beautiful women") and Marat Balagula, also from Ukraine, who confirmed that "the Jews were in the best positions because they had the money." Friedman was also able to meet the former attorney general of the Soviet Union, Boris Urov: "It's wonderful that the Iron Curtain is gone, he said, but it was a protection for the West. Now that we have opened the gates, the whole world is in danger[820]."

These words can be compared to those of Jacques Attali, who gave us some information on gangsterism in the United States during the Prohibition years. He wrote: "Apart from accusations of "ritual crimes", no serious accusation of organised gang murder can be found before the mass arrival of Russian Jews on American soil, around 1910 ... According to *The jewish Almanach*, "it is no exaggeration to say that their influence on organised crime in the United States in the 1920s and 1930s equalled, and even surpassed, that of the Italians."

New York's first Jewish crime boss, Arnold Rothstein, nicknamed "the Brain", by 1910 organises corruption at baseball games, takes control of the city's police force, plans to import alcohol (banned from Canada and Europe from 1919 onwards), referees and maintains order among other fearsome gang bosses, such as Arthur Flegenheimer (called "Dutch Schultz"), plans the importation of alcohol (banned from 1919) from Canada and Europe—refereeing and maintaining order among other fearsome gang bosses, such as Arthur Flegenheimer (called "Dutch Schultz") and Louis Buchalter, who wipes out his own gang with the help of his lieutenant, Jack "Legs" Diamond. Rothstein tracks down Mayer Lansky, a young son of Russian immigrants, born in 1902 in Grodno, Russia." He goes into business with a new generation Sicilian named Charlie Luciano." The Russian and the Sicilian appreciate each other and understand each other with half

---

[820]On the "Russian" Mafia, read Hervé Ryssen, *The Jewish Mafia* (NdT).

words. Together, they take control of moneylenders and insurance agents in the ghettos and *Little Italy*, buy up gambling firms in New York and set up a nationwide syndicate of *book-makers*, while planning the corruption of cops and politicians already begun by Rothstein ... In September 1928, Arnold Rothstein is assassinated in New York, no doubt on the orders of Dutch Schultz, who wants to take his place. On 9 May 1929, Lansky and Luciano brought together all the Eastern crime bosses in Atlantic City: Guzik and Capone from Chicago, Buchalter from New York, Bernstein from Detroit, Dalitz from Cleveland, Hoff and Rosen from Philadelphia. To put an end to the vendettas, 'they propose to organise the Union as a sort of cooperative, without a boss, with division of territories. Lansky founded what was to be called the "Murder lnc.", a group of assassins in his service, whose leadership he entrusted to Siegel and Buchalter. From then on, Schultz and Lansky become the big bosses of American Jewish gangsterism."

The Italian Mafia was gradually dismantled. Al Capone was arrested in 1932 for tax fraud; Lucky Luciano in 1935. Dutch Schultz, Lansky's rival, was also killed that year in a shootout." Lansky, who undoubtedly had him bumped off, takes out his last rival, Charles "King" Solomon of Boston, who imports the bulk of the whiskey into the country. At the end of prohibition, Lansky turned to gambling... A few years later, Lansky tried to take refuge in Israel, which denied him the benefit of the Law of Return: for his crimes, he had lost the right to be recognised as a Jew. He will die in Miami, in his bed[821]."

Jacques Attali could also have told us about the Jewish gangster Mickey Cohen, who raised funds for the Jewish Irgun terrorists who were then fighting against the British to create the Jewish state in Palestine. He also forgot to point out that Mafia boss Mayer Lansky had murdered an arms exporter to Arab countries, and that he had bequeathed his ill-gotten fortune to the *Combined Jewish Appeal (CJA)* charity[822]. Attali could have mentioned the case of the mafioso "Steinhardt the Red", father of Michael Steinhardt, one of the major patrons of Joseph Lieberman, deputy to Al Gore, Democratic candidate for the US presidency in 1999.

---

[821] Jacques Attali, *Los judíos, el mundo y el dinero*, Fondo de cultura económica, 2005, Buenos Aires, p. 410-412.

[822] When Israel is not threatened, Arabs seem to be preferred to Europeans. During the Algerian war, David Serfati was one of the biggest arms dealers in the service of the Felagas. After the declaration of independence, the FLN gratefully inaugurated a square in Oran named after him. The famous "Curiel" network, named after the Egyptian Jew who organised the action of the "suitcase carriers", is also well known.

But, above all, he could have exposed in that chapter the origins of the colossal fortune of Edgar Bronfman, the current president of the World Jewish Congress, one of the richest men in the world with a net worth evaluated at 30 billion dollars. His father Samuel was the famous alcohol dealer. A deeply religious, staunch Zionist, he armed the Haganah militia during Israel's first war of independence. One of his daughters married Alain de Gunzburg, who would become the first private shareholder of the French newspaper *Le Monde*. The Bronfman trust includes many famous brands: Four Roses whiskies, Glenlivet, White Horse, Chivas, London Gin, Absolut Vodka, Mumm champagnes, Perrier-Jouët, Martell cognac, etc. Bronfman also owns record labels such as Polygram, Deutsche Gramophon, Decca, Philips Music.

"The relative role of the Jewish "underworld" in criminality is also diminishing with globalisation, although some of its members are still found as brokers in some types of money laundering, drug trafficking, from Los Angeles to Moscow, from Bogota to Tel Aviv. A single specifically Jewish network was discovered in February 1990 in New York; it took the following route: some of the Cali cartel's drugs were exchanged in Colombia for diamonds; to turn them into cash, the diamonds were shipped to Milan and assembled into jewellery, which was then sent back to Manhattan to be sold legally—on the count—on 47th Street, where, according to an empathetic comment in the Israeli newspaper Maariv, which revealed the case, 'there are more kosher restaurants than in all of Tel-Aviv, and where the largest laundering of drug money in the United States is to be found'. A portion of the proceeds were then delivered by the jewellers to Jewish institutions in New York, which returned a portion—always in cash—to cartel smugglers. The ring's leaders made some of their reliefs—Orthodox Jews, such as a Brooklyn rabbi whose arrest in February 1990 revealed the whole affair—believe that they were helping diamond dealers on 47th Street to defraud the tax authorities, or to get their money out of Iranian Jews. The head of this network, an Israeli, confessed to having laundered $200 million on behalf of the Cali cartel, or less than 1% of the amount handled annually by the cartel, which distributes four-fifths of the cocaine and one-third of the heroin consumed in the world[823]." If Jacques Attali is as discreet about the Jews' role in criminality as he was about their role in Bolshevism, this revelation alone represents a lot.

---

[823]Jacques Attali, *Los judíos, el mundo y el dinero*, Fondo de cultura económica, 2005, Buenos Aires, p. 479, 480.

Let us now recall Bernard-Henri Levy's statements that we have already discussed above, and then the philosopher's conclusion: "I believe that entire states will fall under the actions of the planetarian mafias; and that, if not under their actions, they will fall into their hands." And the quote continued: "I believe that the world is on the way to becoming a ghetto and the planet a mafia. And I do not believe that we will get out of it by merely muttering, as some clever people already do, that the world has always been a conglomeration of ghettos; states, mafias in disguise, and civil societies, contractual associations of miscreants, and that, therefore, it is better that things should be told as they are, that humanity should pass into confessions, and that we should not feign surprise when the masks of the world fall. I believe in a future fragmentation of the world, in a pulverisation of states and a dissolution of the old peaceful nations[824]."

In short, Bernard-Henri Levy declared to us in the simplest way in the world that justifies transnational mafias, ultimately considered less perverse than sedentary states and nations. In the end, perhaps it is just that, the ideal of Bernard-Henri Levy and the planetarian philosophers: the destruction of nations, and in their place the control of the planet by mafias. But the term "mafia" is perhaps a bit "discriminating", so we humbly suggest to our great philosopher the adoption of a more modern and acceptable expression for the flock being herded: "interconnected informal management networks". It is a bit longer, but if it allows us to be spared the gore, we must make the effort.

In our midst...

The messianic spirits seem nevertheless totally convinced that they come to bring welfare and prosperity. Jews are simply indispensable to other nations. The last Indian tribe in the Amazon jungle cannot live without their grandiose ideas and their formidable ability to enrich peoples. Despite this, the innumerable contradictions in his books sometimes leave one perplexed about the sincerity of his discourse. After all this reading, one is still astonished by the incredible aplomb of some of the statements inspired by his messianic convictions. Such a morality is probably quite heavy to carry and exhausting. Judging by the number of suicides affecting the adherents of this belief, it is to be assumed that this conception of life on earth must exert some form of mental and spiritual torture.

---

[824]Bernard-Henri Lévy, *La pureza peligrosa*, Espasa Calpe, Madrid, 1996, p. 167.

Jacques Attali insisted in his book on the immense generosity of the Jewish people, as if he had something to prove. In *The Jews, the World and Money*, he lancinatingly repeats the idea that Jews are a benefit to the rest of humanity: according to the Talmud, he said, "nothing is good for the Jews if it is not also good for those around them". It is "the very foundation of Jewish altruism: nothing is good for them unless it is also good for their hosts." It was also the opinion of Menasseh Ben Israel, the Amsterdam rabbi who had persuaded Cromwell to let Jews back into England in the 17th century: "Wherever they are admitted, Jews are good citizens with no other desire than to contribute to general prosperity." They are faithful vassals[825]"."

Jews are not only beneficial to others, they are also, according to Jacques Attali, indispensable: "None of the sedentary societies could have survived without nomads who transported goods, ideas and capital between them and who dared to take intellectual and material risks that no sedentary person would have been prepared to take... The Jewish people played the role of the nomad who creates wealth for the sedentary. Thus, they fulfilled their task, "mending the world[826]" ... Nomadism is not a superiority, but merely a specificity shared with other peoples and absolutely necessary for the survival and well-being of the sedentary[827]"." They are the key to the development of the world. There is no sedentary development without these nomads. But there is also no questioning of the established order without them". If Israel "tries to limit its identity to acquired lands, it is lost. If it continues on its route, it can survive and help humanity not to disappear[828]."

---

[825]Jacques Attali, *Los judíos, el mundo y el dinero*, Fondo de cultura económica, 2005, Buenos Aires, p. 243, 256, 260." English pragmatism, nourished by the arguments expressed half a century earlier by Menasseh ben Israel, thus prevails over three centuries of ostracism: the English need the Jews, whose role in the Netherlands they know."

[826]Allusion to the *tikkun olam* concept of esoteric Judaism: According to Jewish mysticism, the Creation of the Universe is figuratively represented as a vessel that could not contain the Sacred Light and broke into pieces (*Shevirat Hakelim*). Therefore, according to the kabbalists, the Universe as we know it is literally broken and in need of repair. Consequently, by following *Halacha* (Jewish law) and fulfilling the *mitzvot* (precepts), [Jewish] people help to repair the vessel of the Universe. Thus, the Kabbalists teach that through their actions, every [Jewish] person can participate in *tikkun olam*, literally repairing the Universe and Humanity as part of Divine Creation. (source wikipedia). Read in Hervé Ryssen, *Psychoanalysis of Judaism* (NdT).

[827]Jacques Attali, *Los judíos, el mundo y el dinero*, Fondo de cultura económica, 2005, Buenos Aires, p. 485-486.

[828]Jacques Attali, *Los judíos, el mundo y el dinero*, Fondo de cultura económica, 2005, Buenos Aires, p. 489, 491.

Under these conditions, "the misfortune of the Jewish people is therefore a misfortune for all people[829]". Since, as Elie Wiesel also remarked, everything that affects the Jews affects the whole of humanity, we can therefore consider with Jacques Attali that "the disappearance of the Temple is also a tragedy for the non-Jews, because the Hebrews prayed for them: "They do not know what they have lost" (Sukkah 55a). (*Sukkah 55a*)830." The Jewish people are at the centre of humanity, and it is unimaginable that life could be conceived in any other way. The other peoples of the earth cannot exist without the Jews, not even the remotest tribe of Amazonia. With such a subjective point of view, Jacques Attali finally allowed himself to remind us of the well-known rules of Judaism: "Impose a very austere morality, do not tolerate arrogance or immorality, so as not to create jealousy or pretexts for persecution[831]." It was time to say it, indeed.

Let us now look at a work that undoubtedly provides a better understanding of Dante's warning: "In our midst, the liar laughs at us". The famous French writer Patrick Modiano, in his novel *The Place of the Star*, published in 1968, imagined a completely delirious, buffoonish and sympathetic character. The action takes place in June 1942 in Paris; the narrator, Schlemilovitch, is a delusional, quixotic hero who imagines himself to be a great writer. Under a grotesque guise, Patrick Modiano puts into his mouth such astonishing words about the Jews that no sane reader could read them without realising their ridiculousness. Anti-Semitism is a hallucination. What the Jews are accused of is so enormous to the average reader that the accusations come across as a psychiatric disorder of the person making them. That is why Patrick Modiano could afford to write them. But let us hear Schlemilovitch speak:

"For the rest, my deeds and my sayings contradicted those virtues cultivated by the French: discretion, thrift and work. From my oriental ancestors I got black eyes, a taste for exhibitionism and lavish luxury, and incurable laziness. I am not a son of this country... I led the world Jewish conspiracy by orgies and millions... Yes, the war of 1939 was declared because of me. Yes, I am something like a Bluebeard, an

[829]Jacques Attali, *Los judíos, el mundo y el dinero*, Fondo de cultura económica, 2005, Buenos Aires, p. 122." The world has an interest in leaving the Jews enough freedom to be able to fulfil this role. Thus, according to one commentary (*Sukkah 55b*), the world is in a better state when the Jews are free and thus able to intercede on its behalf."
[830]Jacques Attali, *Los judíos, el mundo y el dinero*, Fondo de cultura económica, 2005, Buenos Aires, p. 75.
[831]Jacques Attali, *Los judíos, el mundo y el dinero*, Fondo de cultura económica, 2005, Buenos Aires, p. 490.

anthropophagus who eats young arias after raping them. Yes, I dream of ruining all the French peasants and turning the whole of Cantal[832] Jewish…".

"These French have an inordinate attachment to whores who write their memoirs, paedophile poets, Arab pimps, drugged-up blacks and provocative Jews. It is clear that morality is no longer in fashion. The Jew was appreciated merchandise, they respected us too much."

Lévy-Vendôme expressed his motivations: "Not content with perverting the women of this country, I also wanted to prostitute the whole of French literature. To transform the heroines of Racine and Marivaux into whores. Junia willingly sleeping with Nero before the shocked gaze of the Briton. Andromache falling into the arms of Pyrrhus in the first encounter. The Countesses of Marivaux putting on their maids' clothes and borrowing their lover for a night. You see, Schlemilovitch, white slavery does not detract from being a cultured man. I have been writing apocrypha for forty years. I have devoted myself to dishonouring the most illustrious French writers. Take an example, Schlemilovitch! Revenge, Schlemilovitch, revenge!

Schlemilovitch received this good advice: "You, Schlemilovitch, have time ahead of you. Make the most of it! Use your personal trump cards and pervert the young Aryan girls. Later on, you will write your memoirs. They could be called "The Uprooted": the story of seven French girls who could not resist the charms of the Jew Schlemilovitch and found themselves one day interned in Oriental or South American brothels. The moral: they should not have listened to that seductive Jew, but stayed in the lush alpine meadows and green groves[833]."

In another passage, we read how our protean hero committed a great offence: "To prison, Schlemilovitch, to prison! And you're leaving the lyceum this very night! To which Schlemilovitch replied: "If those gentlemen want to take me to court," I said, "then I'll explain myself once and for all. They will give me a lot of publicity. Paris is not Bordeaux, you know; in Paris they always give the poor defenceless Jew the right, and never the Aryan animals! I will play the role of the persecuted to perfection. The Left will organise rallies and demonstrations and you can believe me when I tell you that it will look very elegant to sign a manifesto in favour of Raphaël Schlemilovitch. In short, this scandal will be a great detriment to your promotion. Think carefully, Mr. Director, you are up against a powerful adversary. Remember Captain Dreyfus and, more recently, the fuss made by Jacob

---

[832]Patrick Modiano, *The Place of the Star*, Pdf, http://Lelibros.org/, p. 14, 15, 26, 27
[833]Patrick Modiano, *The Place of the Star*, Pdf, http://Lelibros.org/, p. 42–43

X, a young Jewish deserter... In Paris, they are always crazy about us. They excuse us. They wipe the slate clean. What can I say? Ethical structures went to hell in the last war, or rather, they went back to the Middle Ages! Remember that beautiful French custom: every year, at Easter, the Count of Toulouse slapped the head of the Jewish community with pomp and ceremony, and the latter begged him: "Again, Count! Again! With the pommel of the sword! You must run me through! Pull out my entrails! Stomp my corpse! "How could my ancestor, the Jew of Toulouse, have imagined that one day I would break the vertebrae of a Val-Suzon? And that I would bust the eye of a Gerbier and a La Rochepot? Everyone gets his turn, Mr. Director! Revenge is a delicacy to be eaten cold! And above all, don't think that I regret it! Let the parents of these young men know for me how sorry I am that I didn't kill them! Imagine the ceremony at the criminal court! A young Jew, livid and passionate, declaring that he wanted to avenge the Count of Toulouse's systematic insults to his ancestors! Sartre would grow a few centuries younger to defend me! They'd carry me on their shoulders from the Place de l'Etoile to La Bastille! They'd crown me Prince of French youth! —You are disgusting, Schlemilovitch. Disgusting! I don't want to listen to you for another minute. —That's it, Mr. Director! —Repugnant834! "

But the reader will understand that all this was nothing but madness, that our hero Schlemilovitch was rambling. Such wild imaginings can only be the fruit of a sick mind: "A psychoanalytic treatment will clear your head. You will become a healthy, optimistic and sporting young man, I promise you. Look, I want you to read the penetrating essay by your compatriot Jean-Paul Schweitzer de la Sarthe: *Reflections on the Jewish Question*. You must understand this at all costs: Jews do not exist, as Schweitzer de la Sarthe so aptly puts it. You are not a Jew, you are a man among other men, and that's it. I repeat that you are not a Jew; you simply have hallucinatory delusions, obsessions, and nothing more, a very mild paranoia... Nobody wants to harm you, sonny boy, everybody is willing to be nice to you. We live today in a pacified world835." Anti-Semitism will never be credible to the average Goy public. That is the moral of this story.

But take for example the accusations of "White Slave Trade". We have seen how the great historian of the Third Reich, William Shirer, had pointed out Hitler's absurd accusations against Jews in this regard ("*Mein Kampf* is strewn with lurid allusions to strange Jews seducing

834Patrick Modiano, *The Place of the Star*, Pdf, http://Lelibros.org/, p. 39–40
835Patrick Modiano, *The Place of the Star*, Pdf, http://Lelibros.org/, p. 87

innocent Christian girls and thus adulterating their blood. There is a great deal of morbid sexuality in Hitler's ranting about the Jews.")

To demonstrate the ridiculousness of such accusations, Albert Memimi had mentioned a somewhat forgotten case: "Let us recall the famous "Orléans rumour", that astonishing accusation of serial rapes, allegedly organised by Jewish shopkeepers on their chloroformed female customers[836]."

The eminent Jewish historian Léon Poliakov also scoffed at these grotesque accusations: "What happened in the quiet town of Orléans in May 1969? Nothing much, after all. High school girls spread a rumour that the fitting rooms of some clothing shops in their town, run by Jewish shopkeepers, were being used as a starting point for a network of trafficking in whites. Before fading away, this small delirium nevertheless managed to drive part of the population of Orléans mad, while the local Jews, for their part, thought they suddenly saw the spectre of the pogrom rise up again for a moment. Similar phenomena, although less spectacular, occurred in other French cities, especially in Amiens, but also in Chalon-sur-Saône, Dinan, Grenoble and Strasbourg, giving rise here and there to a credulity that could appear to be the flip side of a diffuse anti-Semitism." (Léon Poliakov, *Histoire de l'antisémitisme, 1945-1993*, Seuil, 1994, p. 141) However, forty pages later, when examining other anti-Semitic accusations in Latin America, Poliakov, who could not take such nonsense seriously, acknowledged that "several Jewish personalities were involved in this abject traffic at the beginning of the 20th century." (p. 181). On this phenomenon, the reader can watch the film by Israeli director Amos Gitai, *Promised Land*, released in 2005, which recreated the ordeal of young Eastern European women trapped in prostitution rings, treated like cattle and ending up in Israeli brothels on the edge of the Dead Sea. But all this is obviously nothing more than fiction, isn't it, Mr. Poliakov?

Let's talk for a moment about the Amazon tribe that haunts us from the beginning of this book: Mario Vargas Llosa is a Peruvian novelist of worldwide renown. One of his novels entitled *El Hablador (The Talkative)* illustrates quite well the planetarian obsession when it grips the spirit and soul of those who suffer from it. The first pages of the novel set the scene for a Peruvian tourist in Florence who is visiting a photo exhibition in an art gallery. Suddenly, he stops in front of a photo that has caught his attention: in the heart of the Amazonian forest, squatting and attentive Indians seem petrified in absolute immobility, as if hypnotised by a sort of magic spell. In the centre of the circle they

---

[836]Albert Memmi, *Le Racisme*, Gallimard, 1982, réédition de poche 1994, p. 41.

form, only one silhouette can be made out, but it is undoubtedly a man talking to them: it is "The Talker".

Memories then emerge in the narrator's memory, for he had probably met El Hablador many years before, when he was a student at the University of Lima. Twenty-three years later, as a Peruvian television journalist, he had the opportunity to meet his strange, missing comrade again. Until then, he had done numerous reports: "In 1981, I had a programme on Peruvian television entitled La Torre de Babel (The Tower of Babel) for six months. The owner of the channel, Genaro Delgado, took me on this adventure... Four of us did La Torre de Babel: Luis Llosa, who was in charge of production and camera management; Moshe Dan Furgang, who was the editor; cameraman Alejandro Pérez and myself[837]."

It was in this professional context that she met a couple of ethnologists who were studying the Indians of the jungle, and whose husband had had the good fortune to see and hear El Hablador." It's a subject that no Machiguenga likes to touch. A very private matter, very secret. Not even with us, who have known them for so long ... they tell everything about their beliefs, their rites... They have no reservations about anything. They have no reservations about anything. But about the Talkers, yes." There was a kind of mystery, a taboo for the ethnologists: "What was certain was that the word "Hablador" was pronounced with extraordinary respect by all the Machiguengas and that every time someone had uttered it in front of the Schneils, the others had changed the subject..."

The ethnologists told him that The Talker had a rather frightening face: "And the Talker? —He had a big mole. A strange guy... An eccentric, someone different from the norm. Because of those carrot-coloured hairs we call him the albino, the gringo". It was him! It was that strange student they called "Mascarita". Actually, his name was Saul. He was that "Creole Jew, marginal and excluded" that the narrator had met at the university so many years before; "He had a dark purple mole, vinegar wine, that covered the whole right side of his face, and red, unkempt hair like the bristles of a broom... He was the ugliest boy in the world". He had developed a passion for an Indian community in the Amazon jungle." Now he knew the reason for the taboo. Did he? Yes. Could it be possible? Yes, it could. That's why they avoided talking about them, that's why they had jealously hidden them from

---

[837]Mario Vargas Llosa, *El Hablador*, Alfaguara Santillana, Madrid, 2008, p. 162-163.

anthropologists, from linguists, from Dominican missionaries for the last twenty years838..."

Mario Vargas Llosa is not only a prolific author. He also ran in the presidential elections in his country. He is also a member of the Trilateral Commission, the powerful globalist club that brings together the most influential men on the planet, financiers, intellectuals, politicians, industrialists and trade unionists from all countries. His story *The Talker* reveals the cosmopolitan mentality very well. It is said that all the peoples of the world must listen to their masters and follow their precepts. Not a single one, however lost in the jungle, will be able to escape. Now, this story is only the fruit of the imagination of a committed novelist, and as far as we are concerned, we are entirely free to imagine things in a totally different and much more credible way. The truth is that these poor Amazonian Indians were subjugated by the verbosity and poise of the foreigner, so we can imagine that this situation would not last forever: the clan chiefs would sooner or later come to abhor the intruder who came to preach the repudiation of their old ways. Eventually, they would gather one night to decide the usurper's downfall and break in during his sleep to pierce him on all sides with their poisoned spears839.

We have already encountered during this study the eminent figure of the writer Primo Levi: "I was born in Turin in 1919 into a moderately well-to-do Piedmontese Jewish family", in his own words. In his best known work, *If This Is a Man*, published in 1947, he recounted his experience of the death camps. She miraculously survived Auschwitz and committed suicide 42 years later, on 11 April 1987. One of his books, *Lilith*, a collection of short stories published in 1981, contained a strange text entitled *A Testament* in which he seemed to reveal a terrible secret to his "dear son". Here is the surprising allegorical text, in which the author seemed to confess his lies:

---

[838]Mario Vargas Llosa, *El Hablador*, Alfaguara Santillana, Madrid, 2008, p. 201, 17, 205

[839]Naturally, Mario Vargas Llosa imagined a more fitting "exit" for El hablador: "The old man got into the habit of going to die in Israel, apparently. And with the devotion he had for him, of course Mascarita gave him pleasure. Because, when Saul told me, they had already sold the little shop they had and were packing their bags... I dredged up my memory trying to remember if I had ever heard him talk about Zionism, about making *aliyah*. Never... I thought that it wouldn't have been easy for Saul to make *aliyah*. Because he was too viscerally integrated into Peru, too torn and too agitated by Peruvian issues—to let go of all that overnight, like someone changing his shirt." Mario Vargas Llosa, *El Hablador*, Alfaguara Santillana, Madrid, 2008 p. 122-123. (NdT).

"I have no doubt that you will follow in my footsteps and be a tooth-puller as I have been, and as your ancestors were ... There is no profession in the world that competes with ours in relieving human pain, and in penetrating their courage, their vices and vileness. It is my purpose to speak to you here of its secrets ... Music is necessary to the exercise of our profession. A good tooth-puller must always be accompanied by at least two trumpeters and two drummers, or rather two bass drum players. The more vigorous the music that fills the square in which you work, the more respect your customers will have for you, and the more respect your customers will have for you, and the less pain they will feel. I am sure you yourself noticed this when you attended my daily work as a child. The patient's cries are not heard over the music; the audience admires you with reverence and the customers waiting their turn shed their secret fears. A tooth-puller working without a brass band is as unseemly and vulnerable as a human body in the buff. Don't forget, my son, that to err is human, but to admit one's mistake is diabolical ... On no account confess to having extracted a healthy tooth. Try rather to take advantage of the roar of the orchestra, the patient's daze, his own pain and screams and his desperate convulsions to extract the diseased tooth quickly afterwards. Remember that an instantaneous and direct blow to the occiput immobilises the most reluctant patient without damaging his vital signs (*sans en étouffer les esprits animaux*), and without the audience noticing. Remember also that, for these or similar needs, a good stabber always takes care to have the cart ready, not far from the stage and with the horses harnessed.

"Our adversaries mock us by saying that we are only good at turning pain into money. Fools! They do not realise that this is the highest praise that can be paid to our magisterium ... Depending on the mood of those present, your speech will be jocular or austere, noble or plebeian, prolix or concise, subtle or crass. However, it should always be obscure, for man is afraid of clarity... Remember that the less those who listen to you understand you, the more confidence they will have in your wisdom and the more music they will hear in your words. And do not be afraid of being asked for an explanation, for this never happens: no one will be brave enough to question you, not even he who climbs the stage with a firm foot to have a tooth pulled out. And never call things by their proper name in your speech. Thou shalt not say molars, but jaw protrusions, or any other oddity that comes into thy head; nor pain, but paroxysm or erethism. Thou shalt not call money money, still less tongs tongs; rather, thou shalt not name these things at all, not even by allusion. Nor shall you let the tongs be seen by the public, and still less by the patient, endeavouring to hide them in your sleeve until the last moment.

"From everything you have read here you will have concluded that lying is a sin for others, but a virtue for us. Mendacity is inextricably linked to our profession. It suits us to lie with our language, with our eyes, with our smile, with our clothes. And not only to avoid patients. You know well that we look higher, and that lying is our real strength (not that of our hands). With the lie, patiently learned and piously exercised, if God assists us, we will come to dominate this country and perhaps the world as well. But this will only happen if we know how to lie better and longer than our adversaries. Perhaps you can see it, but I can't: it will be a new golden age, in which only in extreme cases will we be called upon to pull teeth, while in the government of the nation and in the administration of public affairs, pious lying, which we have brought to perfection, will suffice for us. If we show ourselves capable of this, the empire of the tooth-pullers will extend from east to west to the remotest islands and will never end[840]."

With such an ethic, it is not surprising that the man who practises it should one day be tormented by feelings of guilt. In spite of all the earthly glory and accumulated riches, the captive spirits of these prophetic beliefs are generally eaten up from within by a diffused moral anguish which finally drives them into a kind of doom. Undoubtedly, neuroses and suicides are more frequent in them than in the rest of the earthly population. We have already seen the cases of Primo Levi and Romain Gary. Among the famous personalities we should mention the case of Stefan Zweig, as well as the writers and philosophers Walter Benjamin, Otto Weininger, Felice Momigliano, Albert Caraco, the Viennese physicist Ludwig Boltzmann, the painter Rothko, the German Jewish poet Paul Celan, the great financiers Löwenstein and Manheimer, Barnato, the "king of diamonds", the ministers Jacques Stern, Jacques Stern and Albert Caraco, the ministers Jacques Stern and Albert Caraco, and the ministers Jacques Stern and Albert Caraco; the ministers Jacques Stern, Pierre Beregovoy, General Mordacq, the two Wittgenstein brothers, the two daughters of Karl Marx; we can also mention the case of the daughter of the great Rabbi Weil, for example, who threw herself from the top of the Eiffel Tower, or Baron Reinach, during the Panama Canal scandal. There are also known cases of the

---

[840]Primo Levi, *Lilít y otros relatos (Un testamento)*, Muchnik Editores, Barcelona, 1998, p. 190-195.

suicide of a Rothschild baron, of the press magnate Robert Maxwell, who died in strange circumstances, and so on.

Jacques Attali mentioned in his work the weight that Jewish communities exerted on their members before emancipation: "Around 1660, Uriel Acosta—the son of a Marrano who had settled in Amsterdam at the beginning of the 17th century at the same time as Menasseh ben Israel's father—protested against the rules of Jewish orthodoxy: 'Who the hell pushed me towards the Jews', he wrote at the end of his pathetic autobiography. Excluded by the rabbis, he ends up committing suicide[841]."

Elie Wiesel himself was candid about the cases of his tragically deceased friends: "Benno Werzberger in Israel, Tadeuz Borowski in Poland, Paul Celan in Paris, Bruno Bettelheim in the United States: of all the men in the vanishing community of Holocaust survivors, the writers experienced one more tragedy: despairing of the powerlessness of the written word, some chose silence. That of death... I knew three of them. Their last gestures still haunt me". But there was also his friend Primo Levi: "Why did Primo, my friend Primo, throw himself down a flight of stairs? He, whose works had finally overcome the indifference of the public, even outside Italy[842]?" Elie doesn't understand.

Elie Wiesel also mentioned the case of Jerzy Kosinski: "I wrote the first review of his *Painted Bird*. In the *New York Times*. Poor Jerzy, he was so good at entertaining and so bad at living. Misunderstood during his life, perhaps he will be better understood after his suicide?" Elie Wiesel's eulogistic review of Kosinski had earned him a series of insulting letters from some Jews who had known Kosinski in Poland." I was wrong, they said, to be warm to this shameful Jew... Apparently, his book is nothing more than a jumble of fanciful lucubrations... I refuse to believe it: Shameful Jew, Jerzy? Impossible! Liar, him? Inconceivable! ... When the novel was published in France, Piotr Rawicz commented on it in *Le Monde*. I ask him: Is Jerzy a Jew? Of course he's Jewish, Piotr replies. Did he tell you? No, he hasn't. On the contrary, he denies it. On the contrary, he denies it. But then how do you know? I know, says Piotr. Why does he hide his Jewish origin? Ask him. Piotr asks him; he stands his ground. Piotr wants to see if he is circumcised. Jerzy refuses to answer. Only when Piotr threatens to call friends to help him undress does he acknowledge his Jewish background... A long article in the *Village Voice* has called him an

---

[841] Jacques Attali, *Los judíos, el mundo y el dinero*, Fondo de cultura económica, 2005, Buenos Aires, p. 261.
[842] Elie Wiesel, *Mémoires, Tome II*, Seuil, 1996, p. 471.

impostor. A recent biography tries to demystify him: having spent the war with his parents, he could not have lived through the atrocious experiences narrated in *The Painted Bird, nor could* he have written his books by himself. The news of his suicide—like that of Bruno Bettelheim—shocked me. So this hedonist was an unhappy man. More unhappy than his crazy and tragic characters[843]." Elie doesn't understand.

Piotr Rawicz also chose to end his life: "My comrade, my companion, why did he leave the world of the living? I see him again: hunched over, his gaze desperate and ironic, but with a lucid, terribly lucid mind. *The Blood of Heaven* will remain one of the masterpieces of our time. In the text I dedicate to him (in the *New Leader*), I write: ..." His book is a cry, not an echo; a challenge, not an act of submission. Standing in front of a grave full of corpses, he does not recite Kaddish; he does not shed tears"... Why did he give himself to death, he who still had so much to give to life? A shot in the mouth with a rifle put an end to a singular and unique destiny, laughing as he was844." Elie does not understand.

No matter how much power and honours are reaped, one must surrender to the evidence that messianic faith, by separating its adherents from the rest of humanity and legitimising behaviour reprobated by all, can only place the even slightly moral individual in an uncomfortable and untenable situation.

In 1854, the great poet Heinrich Heine had an appendix entitled *Confessions of the Author* published in his book *On the History of Religion and Philosophy in Germany.* Heine also wrote some confessions for posterity: "Like the great achievements of the Jews, the true character of the Jews is not known to the world. We think we know them because we have seen their beards, but we have never seen much more, and, as in the Middle Ages, they remain a walking mystery in modern times. That mystery will be revealed on the day when, according to the prophet's prediction, there will be but one shepherd and one flock, and when the Righteous One who suffered for the salvation of mankind will receive His glorious palm845."

---

[843]Elie Wiesel, *Mémoires, Tome II*, Seuil, 1996, p. 475.

[844] Elie Wiesel, *Mémoires, Tome II*, Seuil, 1996, p. 476-477.

[845] Heinrich Heine, *De l'Allemagne, Aveux de l'auteur*, 1835, 1854, Gallimard, 1998, p. 462. [As with many other passages of this book in the French version, we have also found no trace of this appendix in the editions of Alianza Editorial, 2008 and Akal/Básica de Bolsillo/323].

The poet did not say much more, but we think we have shown with this study a little of what the messianic spirits understand by "shepherd" and "flock". It is not necessary to wait for the Messiah to "unveil the mystery". Magicians have their secrets and devices, but sometimes the tricks are too visible, and when the subterfuge is done systematically at the expense of the audience, it often happens that exasperated people demand a refund of the entrance fee and threaten to destroy the hall.

And speaking of magicians, that is: American David Copperfield is "universally acknowledged as the world's most extraordinary magician". He is "the greatest magician of all time", we read in several places. We could call him, following previous examples, the "prince of magicians". In fact, he was named by the French government "Chevalier des Arts et des Lettres". The man certainly deserves this distinction, given his track record. He has to his credit a series of quite extraordinary, even truly mind-blowing feats, very much in the style of his co-religionists in philosophy, history and many other fields. Indeed, in front of a terrified audience, in front of literally thousands of astonished people, "the magician has crossed the wall of China (like a ghost), made the Statue of Liberty in New York disappear, the Orient-Express train, even aeroplanes. He has made a ship reappear in the Bermuda Triangle; he has escaped from Alcatraz prison, escaped unscathed from Niagara Falls, flown through the air over the Grand Canyon in Arizona." David Copperfield never ceases to amaze us, to astonish us, to touch the hearts and souls of his audiences.

Some even say that he would be capable of wiping out an entire civilisation. It would certainly not be his first attempt in history, although his various attempts have apparently been unsuccessful so far: Christianity revolted against him for centuries; the French revolution finally revolted against him, with the development of nationalism; communism revolted against him in its turn, after thirty years of destructive fury; and there is every reason to believe that the 21st century is fraught with grave threats. But it perseveres, again and again, in its mad frenzy, sure of its legitimacy and divine election. Fortunately, we now know that the wiser among them may decide to join "common humanity". That is what gives us some hope. As for the others, there may be no other solution than to offer them a playground, or a padded room to cushion them from all this turmoil.

In the synagogues of Eastern Europe, in the Yiddishland of yesteryear, they could be heard howling in the evenings, as Elie Wiesel recounted: "We danced as the Hasidim dance: hand in hand, throwing our arms from side to side, faster and faster, eyes closed and heart open, soul torn like a deep, burning wound, we dance as if drawn to the heights with prayers that ascend to the seventh heaven, we dance like madmen whose being tends towards Being, whose flame wants to become incandescent, no one can stop us, no force can gag us, we sing crying, we cry singing[846]."

Those wild Sabbath nights were held in secluded places, far, far away from the towns and villages. The peasants could close their eyes and get some rest. The next day, they had to get up early, they had to work in the fields. Someone had to cultivate the land.

Paris, August 2005[847]

[846] Elie Wiesel, *Mémoires, Tome II*, Seuil, 1996, p. 420. This reminds us of Erwin Leiser's words.

[847] Hervé Ryssen expanded and deepened all the themes addressed in this book in the following years: *Psychoanalysis of Judaism* (2006), *Jewish Fanaticism* (2007), *The Jewish Mafia* (2008), *The Mirror of Judaism* (2009) and *History of Anti-Semitism* (2010).

ANNEX

OBITUARY OF HENRI WEBER
(1944–2020)

From the Second World War to the deepening of the European adventure, via May 1968, his destiny will have crossed the history of the century, crossing kilometres, country borders and ideas. His parents were Polish Jews who lived a few kilometres from Auschwitz and had fled the Nazi threat to the USSR. There, on the banks of a Siberian river, near the labour camp where his parents lived, Henri Weber was born in 1944, in the shadow of history. With the end of the war, it was time for the family to return to Poland, but anti-Semitic hatred had not been swept away by the fall of Nazism and eventually forced the Webers to emigrate to France.

While still a child, the young Henri became politicised within the *Hachomer Hatzaïr*, the Zionist and socialist movement of the "young guard", which was the scene of his first struggles, in particular against the Algerian war. As a young Sorbonnean, he then took up political action in the ranks of the UNEF and the Union of Communist Students (UEC), where he became friends with Alain Krivine. His generation was in a state of great turmoil. With his comrades, Weber ignited the debates and heated the tempers, blowing the embers of revolt to ignite the ideas and impulses that were burning in the universities. Within the newly formed Revolutionary Communist Youth (JCR), he became one of the leaders of May '68, one of those who spent their days in the classrooms building a better world and their nights on the streets erecting barricades.

He would never abandon this permanent interweaving of thought and action. The great actor of May '68 also became one of its main thinkers: he dedicated several books to it, kept its fire alive by creating and directing the weekly *Rouge* and then the review *Critique Communiste*, and accepted Michel Foucault's offer to teach political philosophy at the brand-new Vincennes University, the bastion of left-wing intellectuals. However, Henri Weber did not abandon militancy: in 1969, he took part in the birth of the Communist League from the ashes of the JCR, and structured the party through his readings and reflections, but also through his keen sense of organisation. (...)

His red thinking gradually turned pink, harmonising with that of the Socialist Party, which he joined in the mid-1980s and which remained his political home until the end. He developed a relationship of friendship and trust with Laurent Fabius, which led to his appointment as his adviser when Fabius became President of the National Assembly in 1988. His career as an elected official began that same year, first as deputy mayor of Saint-Denis, then as councillor of Dieppe from 1995 to 2001 and senator for Seine-Maritime from 1995 to 2004. A fervent pro-European, he then served two terms in the Strasbourg Parliament, with the same passion and the same high standards. (...)

The President of the Republic salutes a great political figure who combined the strength of commitment and the subtlety of thought, a free, generous and European spirit. He sends his sincere condolences to his wife Fabienne, his children, his family and all his political colleagues.

Elysée Palace Press Service, 27 April 2020.

Other titles

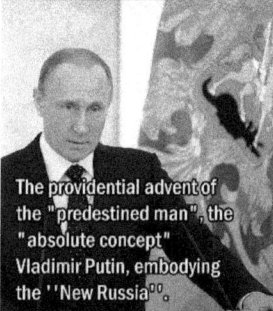

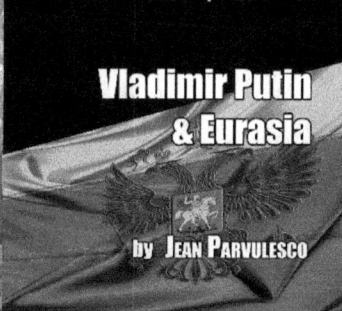

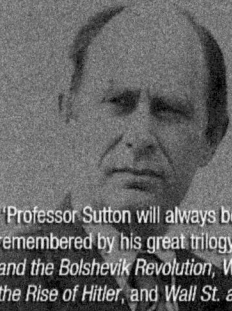

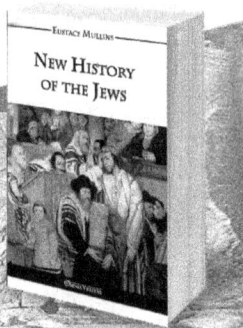

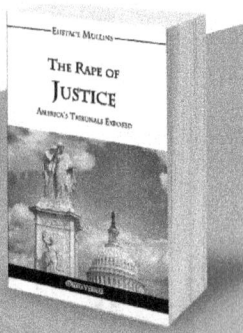

www.ingramcontent.com/pod-product-compliance
Lightning Source LLC
Chambersburg PA
CBHW071949270326
41928CB00009B/1388